Advances in Differential and Difference Equations and Their Applications

Advances in Differential and Difference Equations and Their Applications

Guest Editors

Lingju Kong
Min Wang

MDPI

Basel • Beijing • Wuhan • Barcelona • Belgrade • Novi Sad • Cluj • Manchester

Guest Editors
Lingju Kong
University of Tennessee at Chattanooga
Chattanooga, TN
USA

Min Wang
Kennesaw State University
Marietta, GA
USA

Editorial Office
MDPI AG
Grosspeteranlage 5
4052 Basel, Switzerland

This is a reprint of the Special Issue, published open access by the journal *Mathematics* (ISSN 2227-7390), freely accessible at: https://www.mdpi.com/journal/mathematics/special_issues/8597U1432T.

For citation purposes, cite each article independently as indicated on the article page online and as indicated below:

Lastname, A.A.; Lastname, B.B. Article Title. *Journal Name* **Year**, *Volume Number*, Page Range.

ISBN 978-3-7258-2973-6 (Hbk)
ISBN 978-3-7258-2974-3 (PDF)
https://doi.org/10.3390/books978-3-7258-2974-3

Contents

Lingju Kong and Min Wang
Editorial for the Special Issue "Advances in Differential and Difference Equations and Their Applications"
Reprinted from: *Mathematics* **2024**, *12*, 3880, https://doi.org/10.3390/math12243880 . . . . **1**

Zihao Guan and Ning Pan
Global Existence, Blowup, and Asymptotic Behavior for a Kirchhoff-Type Parabolic Problem Involving the Fractional Laplacian with Logarithmic Term
Reprinted from: *Mathematics* **2024**, *12*, 5, https://doi.org/10.3390/math12010005 . . . . **3**

Yun-Ho Kim and Taek-Jun Jeong
Multiplicity Results of Solutions to the Double Phase Problems of Schrödinger–Kirchhoff Type with Concave–Convex Nonlinearities
Reprinted from: *Mathematics* **2024**, *12*, 60, https://doi.org/10.3390/math12010060 . . . . **31**

Bachir Slimani, John R. Graef and Abdelghani Ouahab
Multivalued Contraction Fixed-Point Theorem in *b*-Metric Spaces
Reprinted from: *Mathematics* **2024**, *12*, 567, https://doi.org/10.3390/math12040567 . . . . **66**

Xincai Zhu and Hanxiao Wu
Existence and Limit Behavior of Constraint Minimizers for a Varying Non-Local Kirchhoff-Type Energy Functional
Reprinted from: *Mathematics* **2024**, *12*, 661, https://doi.org/10.3390/math12050661 . . . . **77**

Sergey Kashchenko
Chains with Connections of Diffusion and Advective Types
Reprinted from: *Mathematics* **2024**, *12*, 790, https://doi.org/10.3390/math12060790 . . . . **91**

Daniel Maroncelli
Periodic Solutions to Nonlinear Second-Order Difference Equations with Two-Dimensional Kernel
Reprinted from: *Mathematics* **2024**, *12*, 849, https://doi.org/10.3390/math12060849 . . . . **119**

Paul W. Eloe, Yulong Li and Jeffrey T. Neugebauer
A Signed Maximum Principle for Boundary Value Problems for Riemann–Liouville Fractional Differential Equations with Analogues of Neumann or Periodic Boundary Conditions
Reprinted from: *Mathematics* **2024**, *12*, 1000, https://doi.org/10.3390/math12071000 . . . . **133**

Yulong Liu
The Blow-Up of the Local Energy Solution to the Wave Equation with a Nontrivial Boundary Condition
Reprinted from: *Mathematics* **2024**, *12*, 1317, https://doi.org/10.3390/math12091317 . . . . **153**

Liancheng Wang and Min Wang
Bifurcation Analysis for an OSN Model with Two Delays
Reprinted from: *Mathematics* **2024**, *12*, 1321, https://doi.org/10.3390/math12091321 . . . . **162**

Alexandru Tudorache and Rodica Luca
Existence of Solutions to a System of Fractional $\mathfrak{q}$-Difference Boundary Value Problems
Reprinted from: *Mathematics* **2024**, *12*, 1335, https://doi.org/10.3390/math12091335 . . . . **179**

Hail S. Alrashdi, Wedad Albalawi, Ali Muhib, Osama Moaaz and Elmetwally M. Elabbasy
Kamenev-Type Criteria for Testing the Asymptotic Behavior of Solutions of Third-Order Quasi-Linear Neutral Differential Equations
Reprinted from: *Mathematics* **2024**, *12*, 1734, https://doi.org/10.3390/math12111734 . . . . **203**

Jeffrey W. Lyons
Differentiation of Solutions of Caputo Boundary Value Problems with Respect to Boundary Data
Reprinted from: *Mathematics* **2024**, *12*, 1790, https://doi.org/10.3390/math12121790 . . . . **219**

Luyao Lv and Xianyi Li
Stability and Bifurcation Analysis in a Discrete Predator–Prey System of Leslie Type with Radio-Dependent Simplified Holling Type IV Functional Response
Reprinted from: *Mathematics* **2024**, *12*, 1803, https://doi.org/10.3390/math12121803 . . . . **228**

Seyyid Ali Saiah, Abdelatif Kainane Mezadek, Mohamed Kainane Mezadek, Abdelhamid Mohammed Djaouti, Ashraf Al-Quran and Ali M. A. Bany Awad
Global Existence of Small Data Solutions to Weakly Coupled Systems of Semi-Linear Fractional σ–Evolution Equations with Mass and Different Nonlinear Memory terms
Reprinted from: *Mathematics* **2024**, *12*, 1942, https://doi.org/10.3390/math12131942 . . . . **244**

Phuc Ngo and Kunquan Lan
Minimum Principles for Sturm–Liouville Inequalities and Applications
Reprinted from: *Mathematics* **2024**, *12*, 2088, https://doi.org/10.3390/math12132088 . . . . **264**

Bo Yang
Radially Symmetric Positive Solutions of the Dirichlet Problem for the p-Laplace Equation
Reprinted from: *Mathematics* **2024**, *12*, 2351, https://doi.org/10.3390/math12152351 . . . . **277**

mathematics

MDPI

Editorial

Editorial for the Special Issue "Advances in Differential and Difference Equations and Their Applications"

Lingju Kong [1,*] and Min Wang [2]

1 Department of Mathematics, University of Tennessee at Chattanooga, Chattanooga, TN 37403, USA
2 Department of Mathematics, Kennesaw State University, Marietta, GA 30060, USA; mwang23@kennesaw.edu
* Correspondence: lingju-kong@utc.edu

This Special Issue of *Mathematics* titled "Advances in Differential and Difference Equations and Their Applications" presents a collection of articles that highlight the significant progress in the study of differential and difference equations. These contributions cover a wide range of topics, from boundary value problems and the asymptotic behavior of solutions to complex mathematical models and the application of fractional and difference equations in various scientific and engineering fields.

Differential equations are a core mathematical tool for modeling dynamic systems in a diverse range of areas, such as physics, biology, economics, and engineering. Likewise, difference equations provide discrete counterparts to continuous models, which are crucial in understanding phenomena occurring in digital systems and various computational models. The papers presented in this issue reflect the latest theoretical advancements and applications in these important research areas.

1. **Radially Symmetric Positive Solutions of the Dirichlet Problem for the p-Laplace Equation**, by Bo Yang, presents new lower estimates for positive solutions of the p-Laplace boundary value problem, offering significant insights into the existence and nonexistence conditions for such solutions (https://doi.org/10.3390/math12152351).
2. **Minimum Principles for Sturm–Liouville Inequalities and Applications**, by Phuc Ngo and Kunquan Lan, introduces a minimum principle for Sturm–Liouville inequalities, providing a framework to understand solution behavior in boundary-value contexts (https://doi.org/10.3390/math12132088).
3. **Global Existence of Small Data Solutions to Weakly Coupled Systems of Semi-Linear Fractional σ-Evolution Equations**, by Seyyid Ali Saiah et al., explores the existence of a long-term solution in fractional evolution equations, analyzing memory terms and initial conditions (https://doi.org/10.3390/math12131942).
4. **Stability and Bifurcation Analysis in a Discrete Predator–Prey System**, by Luyao Lv and Xianyi Li, investigates a Leslie-type predator–prey model, focusing on the influence of functional responses on stability, bifurcation, and dynamics (https://doi.org/10.3390/math12121803).
5. **Differentiation of Solutions of Caputo Boundary Value Problems**, by Jeffrey W. Lyons, generalizes differentiation techniques for fractional boundary value problems, expanding upon classical results (https://doi.org/10.3390/math12121790).
6. **Kamenev-Type Criteria for Testing Asymptotic Behavior of Solutions**, by Hail S. Alrashdi et al., examines third-order quasi-linear neutral differential equations, offering new tools for studying the asymptotic behavior of solutions (https://doi.org/10.3390/math12111734).
7. **Existence of Solutions to a System of Fractional q-Difference Boundary Value Problems**, by Alexandru Tudorache and Rodica Luca, analyzes multi-point boundary conditions in q-difference systems, demonstrating their existence (https://doi.org/10.3390/math12091335).

Citation: Kong, L.; Wang, M. Editorial for the Special Issue "Advances in Differential and Difference Equations and Their Applications". *Mathematics* **2024**, *12*, 3880. https://doi.org/10.3390/math12243880

Received: 28 November 2024
Revised: 6 December 2024
Accepted: 6 December 2024
Published: 10 December 2024

8. **Bifurcation Analysis for an OSN Model with Two Delays**, by Liancheng Wang and Min Wang, delves into the dynamics of online social networks, focusing on delays representing user activity transitions (https://doi.org/10.3390/math12091321).
9. **The Blow-Up of the Local Energy Solution to the Wave Equation**, by Yulong Liu, studies finite-time blow-up and local existence for wave equations with nontrivial boundary conditions (https://doi.org/10.3390/math12091317).
10. **A Signed Maximum Principle for Riemann–Liouville Fractional Differential Equations**, by Paul W. Eloe et al., derives conditions for maximum principles in fractional differential equations with periodic boundary conditions (https://doi.org/10.3390/math12071000).
11. **Periodic Solutions to Nonlinear Second-Order Difference Equations**, by Daniel Maroncelli, offers conditions for periodic solutions in nonlinear difference equations, highlighting their computational and theoretical implications (https://doi.org/10.3390/math12060849).
12. **Chains with Connections of Diffusion and Advective Types**, by Sergey Kashchenko, investigates oscillator chains, emphasizing their stability under diffusive and advective couplings (https://doi.org/10.3390/math12060790).
13. **Existence and Limit Behavior of Constraint Minimizers for a Non-Local Kirchhoff-Type Energy Functional**, by Xincai Zhu and Hanxiao Wu, studies minimization problems in energy functionals, connecting them to Kirchhoff-type equations (https://doi.org/10.3390/math12050661).
14. **Multivalued Contraction Fixed-Point Theorem in b-Metric Spaces**, by Bachir Slimani et al., extends fixed-point theorems in *b*-metric spaces, contributing to fixed-point theory (https://doi.org/10.3390/math12040567).
15. **Multiplicity Results of Solutions to Schrödinger–Kirchhoff-Type Double Phase Problems**, by Yun-Ho Kim and Taek-Jun Jeong, establishes solutions for double phase problems with concave–convex nonlinearities using advanced theorems (https://doi.org/10.3390/math12010060).
16. **Global Existence, Blowup, and Asymptotic Behavior for a Kirchhoff-Type Parabolic Problem**, by Zihao Guan and Ning Pan, investigates pseudo-parabolic equations with fractional Laplacians and logarithmic nonlinearities, analyzing the dynamics of the solution (https://doi.org/10.3390/math12010005).

We extend our gratitude to all of the authors who contributed their original work to this Special Issue, and to the reviewers whose critical evaluations ensured the high quality of this collection. Finally, we thank the Editorial team of *Mathematics* for their professional support and for providing a platform to publish this important body of work.

We hope that this Special Issue serves as a valuable resource for researchers, sparks new ideas, and strengthens the connections within the global mathematical community.

Conflicts of Interest: The authors declare no conflicts of interest.

mathematics

MDPI

Article

Global Existence, Blowup, and Asymptotic Behavior for a Kirchhoff-Type Parabolic Problem Involving the Fractional Laplacian with Logarithmic Term

Zihao Guan † **and Ning Pan** *,†

Department of Mathematics, Northeast Forestry University, Harbin 150040, China; gzh2023108@nefu.edu.cn
* Correspondence: pn@nefu.edu.cn
† These authors contributed equally to this work.

Abstract: In this paper, we studied a class of semilinear pseudo-parabolic equations of the Kirchhoff type involving the fractional Laplacian with logarithmic nonlinearity: $\begin{cases} u_t + M([u]_s^2)(-\Delta)^s u + (-\Delta)^s u_t = |u|^{p-2}u\ln|u|, & \text{in } \Omega \times (0,T), \\ u(x,0) = u_0(x), & \text{in } \Omega, \\ u(x,t) = 0, & \text{on } \partial\Omega \times (0,T), \end{cases}$ where $[u]_s$ is the Gagliardo semi-norm of u, $(-\Delta)^s$ is the fractional Laplacian, $s \in (0,1)$, $2\lambda < p < 2_s^* = 2N/(N-2s)$, $\Omega \in \mathbb{R}^N$ is a bounded domain with $N > 2s$, and u_0 is the initial function. To start with, we combined the potential well theory and Galerkin method to prove the existence of global solutions. Finally, we introduced the concavity method and some special inequalities to discuss the blowup and asymptotic properties of the above problem and obtained the upper and lower bounds on the blowup at the sublevel and initial level.

Keywords: parabolic; Kirchhoff type; logarithmic; Galerkin method; potential wells

MSC: 35R11; 35K92; 47G20

Citation: Guan, Z.; Pan, N. Global Existence, Blowup, and Asymptotic Behavior for a Kirchhoff-Type Parabolic Problem Involving the Fractional Laplacian with Logarithmic Term. *Mathematics* **2024**, *12*, 5. https://doi.org/10.3390/math12010005

Academic Editors: Lingju Kong and Min Wang

Received: 8 October 2023
Revised: 12 December 2023
Accepted: 14 December 2023
Published: 19 December 2023

1. Introduction

We deal with the following fractional Kirchhoff-type semilinear pseudo-parabolic problem involving logarithmic nonlinearity:

$$\begin{cases} u_t + M([u]_s^2)\mathscr{L}_K u + \mathscr{L}_K u_t = f(u), & \text{in } \Omega \times (0,T), \\ u(x,0) = u_0(x), & \text{in } \Omega, \\ u(x,t) = 0, & \text{on } \partial\Omega \times (0,T), \end{cases} \tag{1}$$

where $f(u) = |u|^{p-2}u\ln|u|$ and the Kirchhoff function $M(t) = t^{\lambda-1}$ with $t \in \mathbb{R}_0^+$ and $\lambda \in [1, \frac{2_s^*}{2})$ for $2_s^* = 2N/(N-2s)$. For convenience, we set the functions:

$$\mathscr{T}^{\varphi}(x,y) = |\varphi(x) - \varphi(y)|^2 K(x,y),$$

$$\mathscr{T}^{\varphi,\phi}(x,y) = (\varphi(x) - \varphi(y))(\phi(x) - \phi(y))K(x,y).$$

As a non-local integration operator, $\mathscr{L}_K$ satisfies:

$$\mathscr{L}_K\varphi(x) = 2\lim_{\varepsilon\to 0^+}\int_{\mathbb{R}^N\setminus D_\omega(x)} \mathscr{T}^{\varphi}(x,y)dy,$$

$$[\varphi]_s = \left(\iint_{\mathbb{R}^{2N}} |u(x) - u(y)|^2 K(x-y)dxdy\right)^{1/2},$$

for $\forall\varphi \in C_0^\infty(\mathbb{R}^N)$, where $D_\omega(x)$ refers to a sphere in $\mathbb{R}^N$ with $x \in \mathbb{R}^N$ as the center and $\omega > 0$ as the radius. The function $K : \mathbb{R}^N\backslash\{0\} \to \mathbb{R}^+$ satisfies: $K(x) \geq m|x|^{-(N+2s)}$ for $\forall x \in \mathbb{R}^N\backslash\{0\}$, where m is a positive number and $s \in (0,1)$, so that $K_0 K \in L^1(\mathbb{R}^N)$ when $K_0(x) = \min\{|x|^2, 1\}$. Usually, we set $K(x) = |x|^{-(N+2s)}$ to meet the above conditions. Ergo, it can be inferred that $\mathscr{L}_K u = (-\Delta)^s u$ for $\forall u \in C_0^\infty(\mathbb{R}^N)$. For more-relevant details about the fractional Laplacian and fractional Sobolev space, we can refer to the literature [1,2].

In recent years, research on the problem of parabolic equations with the fractional Laplacian and Kirchhoff term has been a hot topic. In [3], the prototype of the Kirchhoff termcan be traced back to 1883:

$$\chi \frac{\partial^2 u}{Bythedescriptionoft^2} - \left(\frac{P_0}{h} + \frac{E}{2L}\int_0^L |\frac{\partial u(x)}{\partial x}|^2 dx\right)\frac{\partial^2 u}{\partial x^2} = 0,$$

which described the physical phenomenon of elastic string vibration. As a result, more and more scholars are attempting to introduce the Kirchhoff model into the study of parabolic equations, obtaining many interesting results and more-complex changes. In [4], the authors put forward the following Kirchhoff-type problems with a non-local integral operator:

$$-M(\|u\|_Z^2)\mathscr{L}_K u = \lambda f(x,u) + |u|^{2^*-2}u; \tag{2}$$

here, 2_* is equal to 2_s^* in this article. (2) imposes a special constraint on f when proving the existence of non-negative solutions, while considered an auxiliary problem with

$$M_a(t) = \begin{cases} M(t), & \text{if } 0 \leq t \leq t_0, \\ 0, & \text{if } t \geq t_0. \end{cases}$$

Application and research on the Kirchhoff term can be found in [4–12], where we note that, in each of these papers, the authors gave the following restrictions to the Kirchhoff function:

$(M_0) M : \mathbb{R}_0^+ \to \mathbb{R}^+$ is a continuous and non-decreasing function.
$(M_1) M(t) \geq a$, where $a > 0$, for $\forall t \in \mathbb{R}_0^+$.

We let $M(t) = a + b\,t^{\lambda-1}$ $(t \geq 1)$ meet the conditions M_0 and M_1, where $a \geq 0$ and $b > 0$. Specifically, in this article, we set $a = 0$, $b = 1$, and $\lambda \in [1, \frac{2_s^*}{2})$.

In [13], since Sattinger introduced the theory of potential wells in the construction of the global existence of the solution for hyperbolic equations, a growing number of authors have introduced the theory of potential wells in the study of various properties of solutions of parabolic equations; see [5–8,14]. On the other hand, Levine established the concavity method in [15,16]. In [5], Pan and Zhang opened up a way of investigating the nature of Kirchhoff-type parabolic problems containing the fractional p-Laplacian when they investigated the existence of global solutions at sublevel ($\mathscr{H}(u_0) < d$) and critical energy level ($\mathscr{H}(u_0) = d$) for (3), combining, for the first time, the theory of the potential wells and the Galerkin method:

$$u_t + [u]_{s,p}^{(\lambda-1)p}(-\triangle)_p^s u = |u|^{q-2}u, \tag{3}$$

where $p < q < NP/(N-sp)$ with $1 < p < N/s$ and $1 \leq \lambda < N/(N-sp)$. In [9], Yang and Tian took a deeper look at (3) by letting p and q satisfy $2 < p\lambda < q < Np/(N-sp)$ with $1 \leq \lambda < N/(N-sp)$. They obtained the blowup properties and asymptotic behavior of the weak solutions at the sublevel and critical energy level by means of the potential well theory, the concavity method, and some inequality tricks. In [10], Zhang and Xiang investigated the burstiness of non-negative solutions at sublevel ($\mathscr{H}(u_0) < d$), critical ($\mathscr{H}(u_0) = d$), and supercritical ($\mathscr{H}(u_0) > 0$) in $p = 2$, in addition to obtaining the corresponding upper and lower bounds on the blowup at different energy levels. We can also see [11,12,17,18] for more details on the application of these two methods.

In [19], Ding and Zhou made $p = 2$ and replaced the polynomial term at the right of Equation (3) with the logarithmic nonlinear term:

$$u_t + M([u]_s^2)\mathscr{L}_K u = |u|^{q-2}u \ln |u|; \tag{4}$$

at this point, the Kirchhoff term $M(t) = a + bt^{\lambda-1}(a \geq 0, b > 0)$ was taken. In order to analyze the effect of the logarithmic terms on (4), the logarithmic fractional-order Sobolev spaces were introduced, and some inequality tricks were cleverly used to analyze the problem in depth and to obtain the global existence, invariance of the region, blowup, and asymptotic behavior. In [20], the authors also considered (4), with the difference that the Kirchhoff function is an unknown function, and they used differential inequality techniques to overcome these difficulties to obtain upper and lower bounds for the blowup.

For the problem:

$$u_t - \triangle u_t - \triangle u = u^p,$$

the authors studied the initial-boundary-value problem with subcritical level $\mathscr{H}(u_0) < d$ for $\mathscr{P}(u_0) < 0$ and $\mathscr{P}(u_0) > 0$, critical level $\mathscr{H}(u_0) = d$ with $\mathscr{P}(u_0) \geq 0$, and high initial energy $\mathscr{H}(u_0) > d$ and also introduced invariants for three sets $\mathcal{B}$, $\mathcal{G}$, and $\mathcal{G}_0$. Moreover, to learn more about the nature of solutions and the definition of the sets, we can refer to [21]. In [22], Chen and Tian introduced a logarithmic term on the above model to obtain the following semilinear pseudo-parabolic equation:

$$u_t - \triangle u_t - \triangle u = u^p \ln |u|;$$

for the above model, the authors utilized a modified potential well theory and the definition of the logarithmic Sobolev space to obtain quite different results from parabolic equations containing polynomial nonlinear terms. The details with logarithmic Sobolev spaces can be found in [7,8,12,19,23–25].

Inspired by the above work, we added a fractional-order nonlinear dissipative term $(-\Delta)^s u_t$ to (4) and let $M(t) = t^{\lambda-1}$, different from the Kirchhoff function considered in [19]. In the subsequent proofs, we introduce the correlation function $\mathscr{P}_\iota(u)$, as well as the new set of potential wells Ψ_ι and a tighter control of the logarithmic terms. In this article, we considered the problem (1). In Section 2, we give the definition and related properties of the logarithmic fractional Sobolev space. In Section 3, we give the modified potential well theory and some necessary Lemmas. In Section 4, we construct an approximate solution to the problem (1) using the Galerkin method. In Section 5, we focus on proving the existence of global solutions when $\mathscr{H}(u_0) = d$ for $\mathscr{P}(u_0) > 0$ or $0 \leq \mathscr{H}(u_0) \leq d$ for $\mathscr{P}(u_0) = 0$. In Section 6, we prove the finite-time blowup at subcritical ($\mathscr{H}(u_0) < d$) and critical ($\mathscr{H}(u_0) = d$) energy levels and derive the corresponding upper and lower bounds. At the same time, we obtain the asymptotic behaviors of the global solutions. In Section 7, we give an example to illustrate our results. In Section 8, we provide a conclusion of the entire article.

2. Preliminaries

In the following, we first give some necessary definitions about fractional Sobolev spaces and related properties, and we can refer to [26,27] for more details.

Now, we introduce some definitions. We define $L^\gamma(\Omega)$ to be the usual Lebesgue space for $\gamma \geq 1$ with the norm:

$$\|u\|_\gamma = \left(\int_\Omega |u|^\gamma dx\right)^{1/\gamma};$$

in particular, when $\gamma = 2$, we define the inner-product in the following form:

$$(u, v) = \int_\Omega uv dx.$$

In the following, let $0 < s < 1$ and define the fractional critical exponent 2_s^* by

$$2_s^* = \begin{cases} \dfrac{2N}{N-2s}, & \text{if } 2s < N, \\ \infty, & \text{if } 2s \geq N. \end{cases}$$

Put $Q = \mathbb{R}^N \backslash \mathfrak{O}$, where $\mathfrak{O} = \mathfrak{C}(\Omega) \times \mathfrak{C}(\Omega) \subset \mathbb{R}^{2N}$ and $\mathfrak{C}(\Omega) = \mathbb{R}^N \backslash \Omega$. We considered the fractional Sobolev space Ψ satisfying the Lebesgue measurable functions u from $\mathbb{R}^N$ to $\mathbb{R}$, i.e.,

$$\iint_Q \mathcal{T}^u(x,y)dxdy < \infty.$$

The space Ψ is prescribed the norm:

$$\|u\|_\Psi = \left(\|u\|^2_{L^2(\Omega)} + \iint_Q \mathcal{T}^u(x,y)dxdy \right)^{1/2}.$$

We considered the closed linear subspace:

$$\Psi_0 = \{u \in \Psi : u(x) = 0 \ \ a.e. \text{ in } \partial\Omega\},$$

its norm being defined as

$$\|u\|_{\Psi_0} = \left(\iint_Q \mathcal{T}^u(x,y)dxdy \right)^{\frac{1}{2}}. \quad (5)$$

The function space Ψ_0 denotes that

$$\Psi_0 = \overline{C_0^\infty(\Omega)}^{\Psi}.$$

For all $u,\ v \in \Psi_0$, we define

$$(u,v)_{\Psi_0} = \iint_Q \mathcal{T}^{u,v}(x,y)dxdy.$$

From now on, we will only consider the general case where $K(x-y) = |x-y|^{-(N+2s)}$, and more relevant details can be found in [27].

Lemma 1. *(i) There exists $\sigma = \sigma(N,\nu,s) > 0$, where $\nu \in [1, 2_s^*]$, such that, for arbitrary $v \in \Psi_0$,*

$$\|v\|^2_{L^\nu(\Omega)} \leq \sigma \iint_{\Omega\times\Omega} \mathcal{T}^v(x,y)dxdy \leq \frac{\sigma}{\beta} \iint_Q \mathcal{T}^v(x,y)dxdy.$$

(ii) There exists $\tilde{\sigma} = \tilde{\sigma}(N,s,\beta,\Omega) > 0$ such that, for arbitrary $v \in \Psi_0$,

$$\iint_Q \mathcal{T}^v(x,y)dxdy \leq \|v\|^2_\Psi \leq \tilde{\sigma} \iint_Q \mathcal{T}^v(x,y)dxdy.$$

(iii) For any bounded sequence $(v_j)_j$ in Ψ_0, there exists $v \in L^\nu(\mathbb{R}^N)$, with $v = 0$ a.e. in $\partial\Omega$, such that, up to a subsequence, still denoted by $(v_j)_j$,

$$v_j \to v \quad \textit{strongly in } L^\nu(\Omega) \textit{ as } j \to \infty,$$

for any $\nu \in [1, 2_s^*)$.

Definition 1 ([28])**.** *(Maximal existence time) T for which u is a weak solution of Equation* (1) *and satisfies the following two conditions is called the maximal existence time:*

(1) If $u(t)$ exists for $\forall t \in [0, +\infty)$, then$T = +\infty$.

(2) *Let $t_0 \in (0, +\infty)$ and $u(t)$ exist for $0 \le t < t_0$, but be non-existent at t_0, so that $T = t_0$.*

3. The Potential Well

In the following, we will give some notations and Lemmas. First of all, we define

$$\mathscr{H}(u) = \frac{1}{2\lambda}\|u\|_{\Psi_0}^{2\lambda} - \frac{1}{p}\int_\Omega |u|^p \ln|u|dx + \frac{1}{p^2}\|u\|_p^p, \tag{6}$$

and

$$\mathscr{P}(u) = \|u\|_{\Psi_0}^{2\lambda} - \int_\Omega |u|^p \ln|u|dx. \tag{7}$$

A definition of potential well as followsin Equation (1) is defined as follows:

$$\Psi = \{u(x) \in \Psi_0 | \mathscr{P}(u) > 0,\ \mathscr{H}(u) < d\} \cup \{0\};$$

the external set Θ is indicated as

$$\Theta = \{u(x) \in \Psi_0 | \mathscr{P}(u) < 0,\ \mathscr{H}(u) < d\},$$

where

$$d = \inf_{u \in \mathscr{I}} \mathscr{H}(u), \tag{8}$$

denotes the depth of the potential well and the Nehari manifold is indicated as

$$\mathscr{I} = \{u \in \Psi_0 | \mathscr{P}(u) = 0,\ u \neq 0\}.$$

Moreover, the positive set and negative set are represented as

$$\mathscr{I}_+ = \{u \in \Psi_0 | \mathscr{P}(u) > 0\},$$
$$\mathscr{I}_- = \{u \in \Psi_0 | \mathscr{P}(u) < 0\}.$$

Obviously, from (6) and (7), we have

$$\mathscr{H}(u) = \frac{1}{p}\mathscr{P}(u) + (\frac{1}{2\lambda} - \frac{1}{p})\|u\|_{\Psi_0}^{2\lambda} + \frac{1}{p^2}\|u\|_p^p. \tag{9}$$

Moreover, for $\forall \iota \in [0, \infty)$, we set

$$\begin{aligned} \mathscr{P}_\iota(u) &= \iota\|u\|_{\Psi_0}^{2\lambda} - \int_\Omega |u|^p \ln|u|dx, \\ \delta(\iota, \varepsilon) &= (\frac{\iota\varepsilon e}{E_*^{p+\varepsilon}})^{\frac{1}{p+\varepsilon-2\lambda}}, \end{aligned} \tag{10}$$

where $2\lambda < p + \varepsilon < 2_s^*$ and E_* is the optimal embedding constant for embedding Ψ_0 into $L^{p+\varepsilon}$, i.e.,

$$E_* = \sup_{u \in \Psi_0 \setminus \{0\}} \frac{\|u\|_{p+\varepsilon}}{\|u\|_{\Psi_0}}.$$

We impose a new series of potential wells such that

$$\Psi_\iota = \{u(x) \in \Psi_0(\Omega) | \mathscr{P}_\iota(u) > 0,\ \mathscr{H}(u) < d(\iota)\} \cup \{0\},$$

$$\Theta_\iota = \{u(x) \in \Psi_0(\Omega) | \mathscr{P}_\iota(u) < 0,\ \mathscr{H}(u) < d(\iota)\},$$

where

$$d(\iota) = \inf_{u \in \mathscr{I}} \mathscr{H}(u),$$

and

$$\mathscr{I} = \{u \in \Psi_0 | \mathscr{P}_\iota(u) = 0, u \neq 0\}.$$

Specifically, we can substitute (10) for (9):

$$\mathscr{H}(u) = \frac{1}{p}\mathscr{P}_\iota(u) + (\frac{1}{2\lambda} - \frac{\iota}{p})\|u\|_{\Psi_0}^{2\lambda} + \frac{1}{p^2}\|u\|_p^p. \tag{11}$$

Definition 2. *$u = u(t)$ is named a weak solution of the problem (1), if $u(t) \in L^\infty(0, \infty; \Psi_0)$ with $u_t \in L^2(0, \infty; L^2(\Omega))$ and it satisfies the following equation*

$$\int_\Omega u_t v dx + \langle u, v\rangle_{\Psi_0} + (u_t, v)_{\Psi_0} = \int_\Omega |u|^{p-2}u \ln|u| v dx,$$

where

$$\langle u, v\rangle_{\Psi_0} = M([u]_s^2) \iint_Q \mathscr{T}^{u,v}(x,y)dxdy,$$

$$(u_t, v)_{\Psi_0} = \iint_Q \mathscr{T}^{u_t,v}(x,y)dxdy,$$

for any $v \in \Psi_0$.

Lemma 2. *Let ε be a positive number; we can obtain*

$$\ln s \leq \frac{1}{e\varepsilon}s^\varepsilon, \quad \forall s \in [1, +\infty).$$

Proof. Let $g(s) = \ln s - \frac{1}{e\varepsilon}s^\varepsilon$ for all $s \geq 1$. Clearly, g attains its maximum value at $s_* = e^{\frac{1}{\varepsilon}}$; thus, $g(s) \leq g(s_*) = 0$ for all $s \geq 1$. □

Lemma 3. *Let $u \in \Psi_0 \backslash \{0\}$, and consider a function $l: \varpi \mapsto \mathscr{H}(\varpi u)$ for $\forall \varpi > 0$:*

(1) $\lim_{\varpi \to 0^+} l(\varpi) = 0$, $\lim_{\varpi \to +\infty} l(\varpi) = -\infty$.

(2) *Function $l(\varpi)$ is strictly monotonically increasing on $(0, \varpi^*)$, strictly monotonically decreasing on (ϖ^*, ∞) for unique ϖ^*, and $\max l(\varpi) = l(\varpi^*)$.*

(3) *$\mathscr{P}(\varpi u) > 0$ for $\varpi \in (0, \varpi^*)$, $\mathscr{P}(\varpi u) < 0$ for $\varpi \in (\varpi^*, \infty)$, and $\mathscr{P}(\varpi^* u) = 0$.*

Proof. (1) By the description of $\mathscr{H}(u)$ in (6), we have

$$l(\varpi) = \frac{\varpi^{2\lambda}}{2\lambda}\|u\|_{\Psi_0}^{2\lambda} - \frac{\varpi^p}{p}\int_\Omega |u|^p \ln|u| dx - \frac{\varpi^p}{p}\ln\varpi\|u\|_p^p + \frac{\varpi^p}{p^2}\|u\|_p^p.$$

Obviously, (1) holds.

(2) By simple calculations, we have

$$l'(\varpi) = \varpi^{2\lambda-1}\left(\|u\|_{\Psi_0}^{2\lambda} - \varpi^{p-2\lambda}\int_\Omega |u|^p \ln|u| dx - \varpi^{p-2\lambda}\ln k\|u\|_p^p\right).$$

Set $o(\varpi) = \varpi^{1-2\lambda}l'(\varpi)$, then we have

$$o'(\varpi) = -\varpi^{p-2\lambda-1}\left((p-2\lambda)\ln\varpi\|u\|_p^p + (p-2\lambda)\int_\Omega |u|^p \ln|u| dx + \|u\|_p^p\right);$$

therefore, by taking

$$\varpi_1 = exp\left\{\frac{-\|u\|_p^p - (p-2\lambda)\int_\Omega |u|^p \ln|u| dx}{(p-2\lambda)\|u\|_p^p}\right\} > 0,$$

thus $o'(\varpi) > 0$ for $\varpi \in (0, \varpi_1)$, $o'(\varpi) < 0$ for $\varpi \in (\varpi_1, +\infty)$ and $o'(\varpi_1) = 0$. We can notice that $o(0) = \|u\|_{\Psi_0}^{2\lambda} > 0$ and $\lim_{\varpi \to +\infty} o(\varpi) = -\infty$, so $o(\varpi^*) = 0$ for a unique $\varpi^* \in (0, +\infty)$ yields $l'(\varpi^*) = \varpi^{2\lambda-1} o(\varpi^*) = 0$; it is shown that (2) holds.

(3) By the description of $\mathscr{P}(u)$, we can obtain $\varpi l'(\varpi) = I(\varpi u)$; thus, (3) holds.

□

Lemma 4. *If $u \in \Psi_0$ and for $\varepsilon > 0$, it satisfies $2\lambda < p + \varepsilon < 2_s^*$, then:*

(1) If $0 < \|u\|_{\Psi_0} \le \delta(\iota, \varepsilon)$, then $\mathscr{P}_\iota(u) \ge 0$. Pre-eminently, if $0 < \|u\|_{\Psi_0} \le \delta(1, \varepsilon)$, then $\mathscr{P}(u) > 0$.

(2) If $\mathscr{P}_\iota(u) < 0$, then $\|u\|_{\Psi_0} > \delta(\iota, \varepsilon)$. Pre-eminently, if $\mathscr{P}(u) < 0$, then $\|u\|_{\Psi_0} > \delta(1, \varepsilon)$.

(3) If $\mathscr{P}_\iota(u) = 0$, then $\|u\|_{\Psi_0} \ge \delta(\iota, \varepsilon)$ or $\|u\|_{\Psi_0} = 0$ holds. Pre-eminently, $||u||_{\Psi_0} \ge \delta(1, \varepsilon)$ or $\|u\|_{\Psi_0} = 0$ when $\mathscr{P}(u) = 0$.

Proof. (1) $0 < \|u\|_{\Psi_0} \le \delta(\iota, \varepsilon)$, (10) and Lemma 2 gives

$$\int_\Omega |u|^p \ln |u| dx \le \frac{1}{e\varepsilon} \|u\|_{p+\varepsilon}^{p+\varepsilon} \le \frac{E_*^{p+\varepsilon}}{e\varepsilon} \|u\|_{\Psi_0}^{p+\varepsilon} = \frac{E_*^{p+\varepsilon}}{e\varepsilon} \|u\|_{\Psi_0}^{2\lambda} \|u\|_{\Psi_0}^{p+\varepsilon-2\lambda} \le \iota \|u\|_{\Psi_0}^{2\lambda},$$

implying $\mathscr{P}_\iota(u) \ge 0$. Pre-eminently, $\mathscr{P}(u) \ge 0$, where $\iota = 1$.

(2) By Lemma 2 and $\mathscr{P}_\iota(u) < 0$,

$$\iota \|u\|_{\Psi_0}^{2\lambda} < \int_\Omega |u|^p \ln |u| dx \le \frac{1}{e\varepsilon} \|u\|_{p+\varepsilon}^{p+\varepsilon} \le \frac{E_*^{p+\varepsilon}}{e\varepsilon} \|u\|_{\Psi_0}^{p+\varepsilon} = \frac{E_*^{p+\varepsilon}}{e\varepsilon} \|u\|_{\Psi_0}^{2\lambda} \|u\|_{\Psi_0}^{p+\varepsilon-2\lambda};$$

thus, $\|u\|_{\Psi_0} > \delta(\iota, \varepsilon)$. If we put $\iota = 1$, we can conclude that $\|u\|_{\Psi_0} > \delta(1, \varepsilon)$.

(3) $\mathscr{P}_\iota(u) = 0$ when $\|u\|_{\Psi_0} = 0$. In contrast, if $\mathscr{P}_\iota(u) = 0$ and $\|u\|_{\Psi_0} \ne 0$, we can obtain

$$\iota \|u\|_{\Psi_0}^{2\lambda} = \int_\Omega |u|^p \ln |u| dx \le \frac{1}{e\varepsilon} \|u\|_{p+\varepsilon}^{p+\varepsilon} \le \frac{E_*^{p+\varepsilon}}{e\varepsilon} \|u\|_{\Psi_0}^{p+\varepsilon} = \frac{E_*^{p+\varepsilon}}{e\varepsilon} \|u\|_{\Psi_0}^{2\lambda} \|u\|_{\Psi_0}^{p+\varepsilon-2\lambda},$$

i.e., $\|u\|_{\Psi_0} \ge \delta(\iota, \varepsilon)$. If we put $\iota = 1$, (3) is valid.

□

Lemma 5. *For all $\iota > 0$ and for $\varepsilon > 0$ satisfying $2\lambda < p + \varepsilon < 2_s^*$,*

$$d(\iota) = (\frac{1}{2\lambda} - \frac{\iota}{p}) \delta^{2\lambda}(\iota, \varepsilon),$$

and it is description as follows:

$$d(\iota) = inf\{\mathscr{H}(u) | u \in \Psi_0, ||u||_{\Psi_0} \ne 0, \mathscr{P}_\iota(u) = 0\}.$$

Proof. Fix $\iota > 0$. $\mathscr{P}_\iota(u) = 0$ and $||u||_{\Psi_0} \ne 0$ with $u \in \Psi_0$, then

$$\iota \|u\|_{\Psi_0}^{2\lambda} = \int_\Omega |u|^p \ln |u| dx \le \frac{1}{e\varepsilon} \|u\|_{p+\varepsilon}^{p+\varepsilon} \le \frac{E_*^{p+\varepsilon}}{e\varepsilon} \|u\|_{\Psi_0}^{p+\varepsilon} = \frac{E_*^{p+\varepsilon}}{e\varepsilon} \|u\|_{\Psi_0}^{2\lambda} \|u\|_{\Psi_0}^{p+\varepsilon-2\lambda}.$$

Hence,

$$\|u\|_{\Psi_0} \ge (\frac{\iota\varepsilon e}{E_*^{p+\varepsilon}})^{\frac{1}{p+\varepsilon-2\lambda}} = \delta(\iota, \varepsilon).$$

Therefore, by Lemma 4(3),

$$\begin{aligned}\mathscr{H}(u) =&\frac{1}{p}\mathscr{P}_\iota(u) + (\frac{1}{2\lambda} - \frac{\iota}{p})\|u\|_{\Psi_0}^{2\lambda} + \frac{1}{p}\|u\|_p^p \\ \geq& (\frac{1}{2\lambda} - \frac{\iota}{p})\|u\|_{\Psi_0}^{2\lambda} \\ \geq& (\frac{1}{2\lambda} - \frac{\iota}{p})\delta^{2\lambda}(\iota, \varepsilon).\end{aligned}$$

Thus, $d(\iota) = inf\{\mathscr{H}(u)|u \in \Psi_0, ||u||_{\Psi_0} \neq 0, \mathscr{P}_\iota(u) = 0\}$, as claimed. If we let $\iota = 1$, we can deduce that

$$d = d(1) = (\frac{1}{2\lambda} - \frac{\iota}{p})\delta^{2\lambda}(1, \varepsilon). \tag{12}$$

□

Lemma 6. *If $u \in \Psi_0$, $d(\iota)$ follows these properties:*

(1) *$d(\iota) \geq k(\iota)\delta^{2\lambda}(\iota, \varepsilon)$, where $k(\iota) = \frac{1}{2\lambda} - \frac{\iota}{p}, 0 < \iota < \frac{p}{2\lambda}$.*

(2) *There exists a unique $\pi \in (1, +\infty)$, such that $d(\pi) = 0$, and $d(\iota) > 0$, where $\iota \in (1, \pi)$.*

(3) *When $\iota \in (0, 1]$, $d(\iota)$ is monotonically increasing and monotonically decreasing, where $\iota \in (1, \pi)$ with a maximum at $\iota = 1$.*

Proof. (1) Let $u \in \mathscr{I}_\iota$; the definition of $\mathscr{H}(u)$ and Lemma 4(3) give

$$\begin{aligned}\mathscr{H}(u) =& (\frac{1}{2\lambda} - \frac{\iota}{p})||u||_{\Psi_0}^{2\lambda} + \frac{1}{p}\mathscr{P}_\iota(u) + \frac{1}{p^2}||u||_p^p \\ \geq& k(\iota)||u||_{\Psi_0}^{2\lambda} \\ \geq& k(\iota)\delta^{2\lambda}(\iota, \varepsilon).\end{aligned}$$

(2) Set

$$h(\theta) = \iota||u||_{\Psi_0}^{2\lambda} - \theta^{p-2\lambda}\int_\Omega |u|^p \ln|u|dx - \theta^{p-2\lambda}\ln\theta||u||_p^p,$$

then

$$h'(\theta) = -\theta^{p-2\lambda-1}\left[(p-2\lambda)\ln\theta||u||_p^p + (p-2\lambda)\int_\Omega |u|^p \ln|u|dx + ||u||_p^p\right];$$

let $h'(\theta) = 0$; we can obtain

$$\theta^* = exp\left\{\frac{-||u||_p^p - (p-2\lambda)\int_\Omega |u|^p \ln|u|dx}{(p-2\lambda)||u||_p^p}\right\} > 0;$$

thus $h'(\theta) > 0$ on $(0, \theta^*)$, $h'(\theta) < 0$ on $(\theta^*, +\infty)$. We can clearly see that $h(0) = \iota||u||_{\Psi_0}^{2\lambda} > 0$, as well as $\lim_{\theta \to +\infty} h(\theta) = -\infty$ for all $u \in \Psi_0$ satisfy $||u||_{\Psi_0} \neq 0$; by the definition of $\mathscr{P}_\iota(u)$, we have

$$\mathscr{P}_\iota(\theta u) = \theta^{2\lambda}h(\theta);$$

therefore, there exists a unique $\theta_1 \in [0, +\infty)$ such that $\mathscr{P}_\iota(\theta_1 u) = 0$, which implies $\theta_1 u \in \mathscr{I}_\iota$. By the expression $d(\iota)$, one obtains

$$\begin{aligned} d(\iota) &\le \mathscr{H}(\theta u) \\ &= \theta^p \left(\frac{\theta^{2\lambda - p}}{2\lambda} ||u||_{\Psi_0}^{2\lambda} - \frac{1}{p} \int_\Omega |u|^p \ln |u| dx - \frac{1}{p} \ln \theta ||u||_p^p + \frac{1}{p^2} ||u||_p^p \right) \\ &\to -\infty (\theta \to +\infty); \end{aligned}$$

hence,

$$\lim_{\iota \to +\infty} d(\iota) \le 0.$$

In addition, due to $d = d(1) > 0$ by (12) and $d(\iota)$ being continuous about ι, so letting $d'(\iota) = 0$, we have $\iota = \frac{p}{p+\varepsilon}$, which implies that $d(\iota)$ is increasing when $\iota \in (0, \frac{p}{p+\varepsilon}]$ and decreasing when $\iota \in (\frac{p}{p+\varepsilon}, +\infty)$. Since $\frac{p}{p+\varepsilon} < 1$, we have $d(\frac{p}{p+\varepsilon}) > d(1) > 0$, and we have that $d(\iota)$ is decreasing in $[1, +\infty)$, which leads to the existence of a unique $\pi \in [1, +\infty)$ such that $d(\pi) = 0$ and $d(\iota) > 0$ when $\iota \in [1, \pi)$.

(3) For arbitrary $0 < \iota' < \iota'' < 1$ or $1 < \iota'' < \iota' < \pi$ and arbitrary $u \in \mathscr{I}_{\iota''}$, there exist $v \in \mathscr{I}_{\iota'}$ and a constant $\zeta(\iota', \iota'') > 0$ such that $\mathscr{H}(v) < \mathscr{H}(u) - \zeta(\iota', \iota'')$ holds. Clearly, for the above u, we can define the same $\theta_1(\iota)$ that appears in the proof of Lemma 6(2) to be satisfied, such that $\mathscr{P}_\iota(\theta_1(\iota)u) = 0$ and $\theta_1(\iota'') = 1$. Let $\phi(\theta_1) = \mathscr{H}(\theta_1 u)$, then

$$\frac{d}{d\theta_1} \phi(\theta_1) = \frac{1}{\theta_1} [(1 - \iota) \|\theta_1 u\|_{\Psi_0}^{2\lambda} + I_\iota(\theta_1 u)] = \theta_1^{2\lambda - 1} (1 - \iota) \|u\|_{\Psi_0}^{2\lambda}.$$

Taking $v = \theta_1(\iota'')u$, then $v \in \mathscr{I}_{\iota''}$. If $0 < \iota' < \iota'' < 1$, then

$$\begin{aligned} \mathscr{H}(u) - \mathscr{H}(v) = \phi(1) - \phi(\theta_1(\iota')) &= \int_{\theta_1(\iota')}^1 \frac{d}{d\theta_1} (\phi(\theta_1)) d\theta_1 \\ &= \int_{\theta_1(\iota')}^1 (1 - \iota) \theta_1^{2\lambda - 1} \|u\|_{\Psi_0}^{2\lambda} d\theta_1 \\ &> (1 - \iota'') r^{2\lambda - 1}(\iota'', \varepsilon) \theta_1^{2\lambda - 1}(\iota')(1 - \theta_1(\iota')) \\ &:= \zeta(\iota', \iota'') > 0. \end{aligned}$$

If $1 < \iota'' < \iota' < \pi$, then

$$\begin{aligned} \mathscr{H}(u) - \mathscr{H}(v) &= \phi(1) - \phi(\theta_1(\iota')) \\ &> (\iota'' - 1) r^{2\lambda - 1}(\iota'', \varepsilon) \theta_1^{2\lambda - 1}(\iota'')(\theta_1(\iota') - 1) \\ &:= \zeta(\iota', \iota'') > 0. \end{aligned}$$

Thus, (3) holds.

□

Lemma 7. *Let $0 < \mathscr{H}(u) < d$ for $u \in \Psi_0$ and $\iota_1 < 1 < \iota_2$ be two roots of $d(\iota) = \mathscr{H}(u)$. Then, the sign of $\mathscr{P}_\iota(u)$ remains unchanged for $\iota_1 < \iota < \iota_2$.*

Proof. If the sign of $\mathscr{P}_\iota(u)$ changes in (ι_1, ι_2), $\mathscr{H}(u) > 0$ implies $\|u\|_{\Psi_0} \ne 0$, according to $\mathscr{P}_\iota(u)$ being continuous about ι, and we can pick an $\iota_* \in (\iota_1, \iota_2)$ such that $I_{\iota_*}(u) = 0$. Thus, $\mathscr{H}(u) \ge d(\iota_*)$, which forms a contradiction with $\mathscr{H}(u) = d(\iota_1) = d(\iota_2) < d(\iota_*)$. □

Lemma 8. *Let $\iota \in (0, \frac{p}{2\lambda})$ and $u \in \Psi_0$. Assuming $\mathscr{H}(u) \le d(\iota)$, then:*

(1) *If $\mathscr{P}_\iota(u) > 0$, then $\|u\|_{\Psi_0}^{2\lambda} < \frac{d(\iota)}{k(\iota)}$, where $k(\iota) = \frac{1}{2\lambda} - \frac{\iota}{p}$.*

(2) *If $\|u\|_{\Psi_0}^{2\lambda} > \frac{d(\iota)}{k(\iota)}$, then $\mathscr{P}_\iota(u) < 0$.*

(3) *If* $\mathscr{P}_\iota(u) = 0$, *then* $\|u\|_{\Psi_0}^{2\lambda} \leq \frac{d(\iota)}{k(\iota)}$.

Proof. For $0 < \iota < \frac{p}{2\lambda}$:

$$\mathscr{H}(u) = (\frac{1}{2\lambda} - \frac{\iota}{p})\|u\|_{\Psi_0}^{2\lambda} + \frac{1}{p^2}\|u\|_p^p + \frac{1}{p}\mathscr{P}_\iota(u) \leq d(\iota),$$

then $\|u\|_{\Psi_0}^{2\lambda} < \frac{d(\iota)}{k(\iota)}$.

The proofs of (2) and (3) closely resemble the proof of (1). □

Lemma 9. *Assume* $\mathscr{H}(u) \leq d$ *with* $u \in \Psi_0$. *Then,* $\mathscr{P}(u) \geq 0$ *if and only if*

$$\|u\|_{\Psi_0}^{2\lambda} \leq \delta^{2\lambda}(1,\varepsilon). \tag{13}$$

Proof. If (13) holds, from

$$\int_\Omega |u|^p \ln|u| dx \leq \frac{1}{e\varepsilon}\|u\|_{p+\varepsilon}^{p+\varepsilon} \leq \frac{E_*^{p+\varepsilon}}{e\varepsilon}\|u\|_{\Psi_0}^{p+\varepsilon} = \frac{E_*^{p+\varepsilon}}{e\varepsilon}\|u\|_{\Psi_0}^{2\lambda}\|u\|_{\Psi_0}^{p+\varepsilon-2\lambda} = \|u\|_{\Psi_0}^{2\lambda},$$

$\mathscr{P}(u) \geq 0$ is valid.

In contrast, $\mathscr{P}(u) \geq 0$ and

$$\mathscr{H}(u) = \frac{1}{p}\mathscr{P}(u) + \frac{p-2\lambda}{2\lambda p}\|u\|_{\Psi_0}^{2\lambda} + \frac{1}{p^2}\|u\|_p^p \leq d = \frac{p-2\lambda}{2\lambda p}\delta^{2\lambda}(1,\varepsilon),$$

yield

$$\frac{p-2\lambda}{2\lambda p}\|u\|_{\Psi_0}^{2\lambda} \leq \frac{p-2\lambda}{2\lambda p}\delta^{2\lambda}(1,\varepsilon).$$

□

4. Galerkin Method

In the following that, we prove that there is an approximate solution to (1) by the Galerkin method. For the Galerkin solution, we refer to [5,29,30].

Put $\{\omega_j\}_{j=1}^\infty$ as a column of a base function in $L^2(\Omega)$. Firstly, we define $m(t,\kappa) : [0,T] \times \mathbb{R}^N \to \mathbb{R}$ and $\eta_n(t,\kappa) : [0,T] \times \mathbb{R}^N \to \mathbb{R}^N$ by

$$(\eta_n(t,\kappa))_i = \iint_Q |\sum_{j=1}^n \kappa_j(t)\omega_j(x) - \sum_{j=1}^n \kappa_j(t)\omega_j(y)|[\omega_i(x) - \omega_i(y)]K(x-y)dxdy,$$

$$m(t,\kappa) = \left(\iint_Q |\sum_{j=1}^n \kappa_j(t)\omega_j(x) - \sum_{j=1}^n \kappa_j(t)\omega_j(y)|^2 K(x-y)dxdy\right)^{\lambda-1},$$

where $\kappa = (\kappa_1, \kappa_2, \cdots, \kappa_n)$ and $m(t,h)$ and $\eta_n(t,k)$ are continuous about t and k; we consider the ordinary differential equation.

$$\begin{cases} V' + m(t,V)\eta_n(t,V) + \eta_n(t,V') = f_n(V), \\ V(0) = A_n(0), \end{cases}$$

where $A_n(0)_i = \int_\Omega u_n(0)\omega_i dx$, $g_n(V)_i = \int_\Omega \varphi(V)\omega_i dx$.

Multiplying the above equation by V to obtain

$$V'V + m(t,V)\eta_n(t,V)V + \eta_n(t,V')V = f_n(V)V,$$

where

$$m(t,V)\eta_n(t,V)V = \left[\iint_Q |\sum_{j=1}^n V_j(t)\omega_j(x) - \sum_{j=1}^n V_j(t)\omega_j(y)|^2 K(x-y)dxdy\right]^{\lambda-1}$$
$$\cdot \iint_Q |\sum_{j=1}^n V_j(t)\omega_j(x) - \sum_{j=1}^n V_j(t)\omega_j(y)|$$
$$\cdot \left[\sum_{i=1}^n V_i(t)\omega_i(x) - \sum_{i=1}^n V_i(t)\omega_i(y)\right] K(x-y)dxdy > 0,$$

$$\nu_n(t,V')V = \iint_Q |\sum_{j=1}^n V'_j(t)\omega_j(x) - \sum_{j=1}^n V'_j(t)\omega_j(y)|$$
$$\cdot \left[\sum_{i=1}^n V_i(t)\omega_i(x) - \sum_{i=1}^n V_i(t)\omega_i(y)\right] K(x-y)dxdy,$$

thus

$$V'V + \eta_n(t,V')V \le f_n(V)V,$$

i.e.,

$$\frac{1}{2}\frac{\partial}{\partial t}|V(t)|^2 + \frac{1}{2}\frac{\partial}{\partial t}\eta_n(t,V)V \le |f_n(V)||V| \le \frac{1}{2}|f_n(V)|^2|V|^2,$$

and combining this with Gronwall's Lemma yields $|V(t)| \le C_n(T)$ for $t \in [0,T]$.

Let

$$t_0 = 0, \quad |V(t) - V(0)| \le 2C_n(T),$$
$$\mathfrak{H} = \max_{(t,V)\in[0,T]\times\mathbb{R}^N} |f_n(V) - m(t,V)\eta_n(t,V)|,$$

and

$$h = \min\{T, \frac{2C_n(T)}{\mathfrak{H}}\},$$

for which there exists a local solution when $|t - t_0| \le h$. Letting $t_1 = h$ as an initial value, one obtains the existence of the local solution to the ordinary differential equation in $[t_1, t_2]$, $t_2 = t_1 + h, \ldots,$ then we divide $[0,T]$ into $[0,t_1], \ldots, [t_{n-1}, t_n]$, where $t_i = t_{i-1} + h$, $i = 1, \ldots, n-1, t_n = T$; thus, there is a local solution on the interval $[t_{i-1}, t_i]$. So, $b \in C^1[0,T]$ as a solution to the above ordinary differential equation. By the definitions of $m(t,V)$ and $\eta_n(t,V)$, we construct the following approximate solution $u_n(x,t)$ of the problem (1):

$$u_n(x,t) = \sum_{j=1}^n b_{jn}(t)\omega_j(x), \quad n = 1,2,\ldots, \tag{14}$$

satisfying

$$(u_{nt}, \omega_j) + \langle u_n, \omega_j\rangle_{\Psi_0} + (u_{nt}, \omega_j)_{\Psi_0} = (|u_n|^{p-2}u_n \ln|u_n|, \omega_j), \tag{15}$$

where

$$\langle u_n, \omega_j\rangle_{\Psi_0} = \left[\iint_Q \mathscr{T}^{u_n}(x,y)dxdy\right]^{\lambda-1} \cdot \iint_Q \mathscr{T}^{u_n,\omega_j}(x,y)dxdy,$$

and

$$(u_{nt}, \omega_j)_{\Psi_0} = \iint_Q \mathscr{T}^{u_{nt},\omega_j}(x,y)dxdy.$$

$$u_n(0) \in W, \quad u_n(0) = \sum_{j=1}^{n} \xi_{jn}\omega_j(x) \to u_0 \in \Psi_0 \quad \text{as } n \to \infty. \tag{16}$$

Since $V \in C^1[0,T]$, then $u_n \in C^1([0,T];\Psi_0)$. Multiplying (15) by $V'_{jn}(t)$ and adding j from 1 to n, we obtain

$$\begin{aligned}&\int_\Omega |u_{nt}|_2^2 dx + \left[\iint_Q \mathscr{T}^{u_n}(x,y)dxdy\right]^{\lambda-1} \iint_Q \mathscr{T}^{u_n,u_{nt}}(x,y)dxdy + \iint_Q \mathscr{T}^{u_{nt}}(x,y)dxdy \\ &= \int_\Omega |u_n|^{p-2}u_n u_{nt} \ln|u_n|dx,\end{aligned}$$

i.e.,

$$\begin{aligned}&\int_\Omega |u_{nt}|_2^2 dx + \frac{1}{2\lambda}\frac{d}{dt}\left[\iint_Q \mathscr{T}^{u_n}(x,y)dxdy\right]^{\lambda} + \iint_Q \mathscr{T}^{u_{nt}}(x,y)dxdy \\ &= \frac{d}{dt}\left(\frac{1}{p}\int_\Omega |u_n|^p \ln|u_n|dx - \frac{1}{p^2}\|u_n\|_p^p\right),\end{aligned} \tag{17}$$

then integrating (17) about t yields

$$\begin{aligned}&\int_0^t \|u_{nt}\|_2^2 dt + \int_0^t \|u_{nt}\|_{\Psi_0}^2 dt + \frac{1}{2\lambda}\|u_n\|_{\Psi_0}^{2\lambda} - \frac{1}{p}\int_\Omega |u_n|^p \ln|u_n|dx + \frac{1}{p^2}\|u_n\|_p^p \\ &= \frac{1}{2\lambda}\|u_n(0)\|_{\Psi_0}^{2\lambda} - \frac{1}{p}\int_\Omega |u_n(0)|^p \ln|u_n(0)|dx + \frac{1}{p^2}\|u_n(0)\|_p^p;\end{aligned}$$

since $u_n(0) \in W$, we can obtain

$$\int_0^t f_{u_{nt}}(t)dt + \mathscr{H}(u_n(t)) = \mathscr{H}(u_n(0)) < d, \quad 0 \le t \le T, \tag{18}$$

where the description of $f_u(t)$ can be seen in Theorem 4; we will not emphasize this in the sequel.

Next, we show that $u_n(t) \in \Psi$ holds for n large enough. If the conclusion is incorrect, there exists a $t_0 \in (0,T]$ such that $u_n(t_0) \in \partial\Psi$, i.e., $\mathscr{H}(u_n(t_0)) = d$ and $u_n(t_0) \in \Psi_0 \backslash \{0\}$ or $\mathscr{P}(u_n(t_0)) = 0$. Obviously, $\mathscr{H}(u_n(t_0)) = d$ contradicts (18). In fact, $\mathscr{H}(u_n(t_0)) \ge d$ from the description of d in (8) in the even of $u_n(t_0) \in \mathscr{I}$, which denies the truth of (18). So, we have $u_n(t) \in \Psi$ for large enough$n$ and $t \in [0,T]$.

$u_n(t) \in \Psi$; thus, $\mathscr{P}(u_n(t)) > 0$. Furthermore, by (18) and the definition of $\mathscr{H}(u)$ in (9), for large enough n and all $t \in [0,T]$,

$$\int_0^t \|u_{nt}\|_2^2 dt + \int_0^t \|u_{nt}\|_{\Psi_0}^2 dt + \frac{p-2\lambda}{2\lambda p}\|u_n(t)\|_{\Psi_0}^{2\lambda} + \frac{1}{p^2}\|u_n(t)\|_p^p < d,$$

which yields

$$\int_0^t \|u_{nt}(t)\|_2^2 dt < d, \quad \forall t \in [0,T], \tag{19}$$

$$\|u_n(t)\|_{\Psi_0}^{2\lambda} < \frac{2\lambda p d}{p-2\lambda}, \quad \forall t \in [0,T], \tag{20}$$

$$\|u_n(t)\|_p^p < p^2 d, \quad \forall t \in [0,T], \tag{21}$$

for arbitrary $T > 0$. By a straightforward calculation,

$$\int_{\Omega}\left||u_n(t)|^{p-2}u_n(t)\ln|u_n(t)|\right|^{\frac{p}{p-1}}dx$$
$$=\int_{\Omega_1}\left||u_n(t)|^{p-2}u_n(t)\ln|u_n(t)|\right|^{\frac{p}{p-1}}dx+\int_{\Omega_2}\left||u_n(t)|^{p-2}u_n(t)\ln|u_n(t)|\right|^{\frac{p}{p-1}}dx,$$

where

$$\Omega_1=\{x\in\Omega|\ |u(x,t)|\leq 1\},\ \ \Omega_2=\{x\in\Omega|\ |u(x,t)|>1\}.$$

Since

$$\inf_{s\in(0,1)} s^{p-1}lns=s^{p-1}lns\Big|_{s=e^{-\frac{1}{p-1}}}=-\frac{1}{(p-1)e},$$

we deduce that

$$\int_{\Omega_1}\left||u_n(t)|^{p-2}u_n(t)\ln|u_n(t)|\right|^{\frac{p}{p-1}}dx\leq(\frac{1}{(p-1)e})^{\frac{p}{p-1}}|\Omega|:=D_0,\ \ \forall t\in[0,\infty).$$

Taking $\varepsilon=\frac{(2_s^*-p)(p-1)}{p}$ into Lemma 2, by Lemma 1(i) and (20), we have

$$\begin{aligned}\int_{\Omega_2}\left||u_n(t)|^{p-2}u_n(t)\ln|u_n(t)|\right|^{\frac{p}{p-1}}dx&\leq C\int_{\Omega_2}|u_n(t)|^{2_s^*}dx\leq C\|u_n(t)\|^{2_s^*}_{L^{2_s^*}(\Omega)}\\&\leq CC_1\|u_n(t)\|^{2_s^*}_{\Psi_0}\leq CC_1(\frac{2\lambda pd}{p-2\lambda})^{\frac{2_s^*}{2\lambda}},\end{aligned}$$

where $C_1=\frac{C_0}{\beta}$ in Lemma 1(i). Thus, from the above proof, it follows that

$$\int_{\Omega}\left||u_n(t)|^{p-2}u_n(t)\ln|u_n(t)|\right|^{\frac{p}{p-1}}dx\leq D_0+CC_1(\frac{2\lambda pd}{p-2\lambda})^{\frac{2_s^*}{2\lambda}}:=D_1. \tag{22}$$

Next, we prove $u_n(t)\in L^\infty(0,\infty;\Psi_0)$, $u_{nt}\in L^2(0,\infty;L^2(\Omega))$.

Combining (19) and (20) with (22), there exists $u(t)\in L^\infty(0,\infty;\Psi_0)$ with $u_t\in L^2(0,\infty;L^2(\Omega))$, $|u|^{p-2}u\ln|u|\in L^2(0,\infty;L^{\frac{p}{p-1}}(\Omega))$ and a subsequence of $\{u_n\}_{n=1}^\infty$, still denoted by $\{u_n\}_{n=1}^\infty$, such that

$$u_n\overset{*}{\rightharpoonup}u \text{ in } L^\infty(0,\infty;\Psi_0), \tag{23}$$
$$u_{nt}\rightharpoonup u_t \text{ in } L^2(0,\infty;L^2(\Omega)), \tag{24}$$
$$|u_n|^{p-2}u_n\ln|u_n|\overset{*}{\rightharpoonup}|u|^{p-2}u\ln|u| \text{ in } L^\infty(0,\infty;L^{\frac{p}{p-1}}(\Omega)); \tag{25}$$

by (23), (24) and Lemma 1(iii),

$$u_n\to u \text{ in } L^2(0,\infty;L^p(\Omega)), \tag{26}$$

which implies $|u_n|^{p-2}u_n\ln|u_n|\to|u|^{p-2}u\ln|u|$ a.e. in $\Omega\times(0,\infty)$.

By (23)–(25), letting $\omega_j=v\in\Psi_0$ and $n\to\infty$ in (15),

$$(u_t,v)+\langle u,v\rangle_{\Psi_0}+(u_t,v)_{\Psi_0}=(|u|^{p-2}u\ln|u|,v).$$

Indeed, as indicated by (23) and (24), we have $u_n(x,0)\rightharpoonup u(x,0)$ in $L^2(\Omega)$, then for the union with (16), $u(x,0)=u_0(x)\in\Psi_0$.

Finally, we prove the energy level inequality:

$$\int_0^t f_{u_t}(t)dt+\mathscr{H}(u)\leq\mathscr{H}(u_0). \tag{27}$$

By (22), (25), and Hölder's inequality, we obtain

$$
\begin{aligned}
&\left|\int_\Omega |u_n|^p \ln|u_n|dx - \int_\Omega |u|^p \ln|u|dx\right| \\
&= \left|\int_\Omega |u_n|^p \ln|u_n| - uu_n|u_n|^{p-2}\ln|u_n| + uu_n|u_n|^{p-2}\ln|u_n| - |u|^p\ln|u|dx\right| \\
&\le \left|\int_\Omega (u_n - u)u_n|u_n|^{p-2}\ln|u_n|dx\right| + \left|\int_\Omega u(|u_n|^{p-2}u_n\ln|u_n| - |u|^{p-2}n\ln|u|)dx\right| \\
&\le D^{\frac{p-1}{p}}\|u_n - u\|_p + \left|\int_\Omega u(|u_n|^{p-2}u_n\ln|u_n| - |u|^{p-2}n\ln|u|)dx\right| \\
&\to 0 \text{ as } n \to \infty.
\end{aligned} \tag{28}
$$

By (18), (23), (24), (26), and (28), the construction of the approximate solution in (14) and (16), and the definition of $\mathscr{H}(u)$ in (6), we deduce that

$$
\begin{aligned}
&\int_0^t f_{u_t}(t)dt + \frac{1}{2\lambda}\|u\|_{\Psi_0}^{2\lambda} + \frac{1}{p^2}\|u\|_p^p \\
&\le \liminf_{n\to\infty}\int_0^t \|u_{nt}\|_2^2 dt + \liminf_{n\to\infty}\int_0^t \|u_{nt}\|_{\Psi_0}^2 dt + \liminf_{n\to\infty}\|u_n\|_{\Psi_0}^{2\lambda} + \frac{1}{p^2}\liminf_{n\to\infty}\|u_n\|_p^p \\
&\le \liminf_{n\to\infty}\left(\int_0^t \|u_{nt}\|_2^2 dt + \int_0^t \|u_{nt}\|_{\Psi_0}^2 dt + \|u_n\|_{\Psi_0}^{2\lambda} + \frac{1}{p^2}\|u_n\|_p^p\right) \\
&= \liminf_{n\to\infty}\left(E(u_n) + \frac{1}{p}\int_\Omega |u_n|^p\ln|u_n|dx + \int_0^t \|u_{nt}\|_2^2 dt + \int_0^t \|u_{nt}\|_{\Psi_0}^2 dt\right) \\
&= \lim_{n\to\infty}\left(E(u_n(0)) + \frac{1}{p}\int_\Omega |u_n|^p\ln|u_n|dx\right) \\
&= \mathscr{H}(u_0) + \frac{1}{p}\int_\Omega |u|^p\ln|u|dx,
\end{aligned}
$$

which implies that (27) holds.

5. Existence of Global Solutions

In the following, we consider the global existence solutions of the problem (1).

Theorem 1. *Suppose that* $u_0 \in \Psi_0$, $\mathscr{H}(u_0) = d$, $\mathscr{P}(u_0) > 0$ *or* $0 \le \mathscr{H}(u_0) \le d$, $\mathscr{P}(u_0) = 0$. *Then, the problem* (1) *has a global solution* $u(t) \in L^\infty(0,\infty;\Psi_0)$ *such that* $u_t \in L^2(0,\infty;L^2(\Omega))$ *and* $u(t) \in \overline{\Psi}$, *where*

$$
\overline{\Psi} = \Psi \cup \partial\Psi = \{u \in \Psi_0 | \mathscr{P}(u_0) \ge 0,\ \mathscr{H}(u_0) \le d\}.
$$

Proof. Let $\theta_m = 1 - \frac{1}{m}$, $u_{0m}(x) = \theta_m u_0(x)$, $m = 2,3,\ldots$. Consider the initial condition $u(x,0) = u_{0m}(x)$ and the corresponding equation:

$$
\begin{cases}
u_t + M([u]_s^2)\mathscr{L}_k u + \mathscr{L}_k u_t = |u|^{p-2}u\ln|u|, & \text{in } \Omega\times\mathbb{R}^+, \\
u(x,t) = u_{0m}(x), & \text{in } \Omega \\
u(x,t) = 0, & \text{in } \partial\Omega\times\mathbb{R}_0^+.
\end{cases} \tag{29}
$$

If $u_0 = 0$, the problem (1) has a global solution $u(t) \equiv 0$, so we mainly consider $u_0 \in \Psi_0\backslash\{0\}$ in the following proofs. Now, we prove $\mathscr{P}(u_{0m}) > 0$; in fact,

$$
\begin{aligned}
\mathscr{P}(u_{0m}) &= \theta_m^{2\lambda}\|u_0\|_{\Psi_0}^{2\lambda} - \theta_m^p\int_\Omega |u_0|^p\ln|u_0|dx - \theta_m^p\ln\theta_m\int_\Omega |u_0|^p dx \\
&> \theta_m^{2\lambda}\|u_0\|_{\Psi_0}^{2\lambda} - \theta_m^p\int_\Omega |u_0|^p\ln|u_0|dx \\
&= \theta_m^{2\lambda}(\|u_0\|_{\Psi_0}^{2\lambda} - \theta_m^{p-2\lambda}\int_\Omega |u_0|^p\ln|u_0|dx);
\end{aligned} \tag{30}
$$

we note that there are two aspects: (1) $\int_\Omega |u_0|^p \ln|u_0|dx > 0$ and (2) $\int_\Omega |u_0|^p \ln|u_0|dx \le 0$:
(1) If $\int_\Omega |u_0|^p \ln|u_0|dx > 0$, by $\mathscr{P}(u_0) > 0$ or $\mathscr{P}(u_0) = 0$, we have

$$\|u_0\|_{\Psi_0}^{2\lambda} \ge \int_\Omega |u_0|^p \ln|u_0|dx,$$

and from (30), we obtain

$$\mathscr{P}(u_{0m}) > \theta_m^{2\lambda}(\|u_0\|_{\Psi_0}^{2\lambda} - \theta_m^{p-2\lambda}\int_\Omega |u_0|^p \ln|u_0|dx) > 0. \tag{31}$$

(2) If $\int_\Omega |u_0|^p \ln|u_0|dx \le 0$, from (30), we obtain

$$\mathscr{P}(u_{0m}) > \theta_m^{2\lambda}\|u_0\|_{\Psi_0}^{2\lambda} > 0. \tag{32}$$

Thus, we obtain $\mathscr{P}(u_{0m}) > 0$. By the calculation,

$$\begin{aligned}\frac{d}{d\theta_m}\mathscr{H}(\theta_m u) &= \theta_m^{2\lambda-1}\|u\|_{\Psi_0}^{2\lambda} - \theta_m^{p-1}\int_\Omega |u|^p \ln|u|dx - \theta_m^{p-1}\ln\theta_m\|u\|_p^p \\ &= \frac{1}{\theta_m}(\theta_m^{2\lambda}\|u\|_{\Psi_0}^{2\lambda} - \theta_m^{p}\int_\Omega |u|^p \ln|u|dx - \theta_m^{p}\ln\theta_m\|u\|_p^p) \\ &= \frac{1}{\theta_m}\mathscr{P}(\theta_m u).\end{aligned} \tag{33}$$

Therefore, combining (31)–(33), we obtain

$$\frac{d}{d\theta_m}\mathscr{H}(u_{0m}) = \frac{d}{d\theta_m}\mathscr{H}(\theta_m u_0) = \frac{1}{\theta_m}\mathscr{P}(\theta_m u_0) > 0;$$

this means that $\mathscr{H}(u_{0m})$ is strictly monotonically increasing with θ_m. So, we have

$$\mathscr{H}(u_{0m}) = \mathscr{H}(\theta_m u_0) < \mathscr{H}(u_0) \le d.$$

In Section 4, we proved that the problem (29) admits a global solution $u_m(t) \in L^\infty(0,\infty;\Psi_0)$ with $u_{mt} \in L^2(0,\infty;L^2(\Omega))$ and $u_m(t) \in \Psi$ for $0 \le t < \infty$, satisfying

$$(u_{mt}, v) + \langle u_m, v\rangle_{\Psi_0} + (u_{mt}, v)_{\Psi_0} = (|u_m|^{p-2}u_m \ln|u_m|, v), \quad \forall v \in \Psi_0. \tag{34}$$

Combining (18) with (9), we deduce that

$$\int_0^t \|u_{mt}\|_2^2 dt + \int_0^t \|u_{mt}\|_{\Psi_0}^2 dt + \frac{p-2\lambda}{2\lambda p}\|u_m\|_{\Psi_0}^{2\lambda} + \frac{1}{p^2}\|u_m\|_p^p + \frac{1}{p}\mathscr{P}(u_m(t)) < d. \tag{35}$$

Since $\mathscr{P}(u_m(t)) > 0$, from (35), we have

$$\begin{aligned}&\int_0^t \|u_{mt}\|_2^2 dt < d, \\ &\|u_m\|_{\Psi_0}^{2\lambda} < \frac{2\lambda p d}{p-2\lambda}, \\ &\|u_m\|_p^p < p^2 d;\end{aligned}$$

thus, by a similar discussion as in Section 4, there exists u and a subsequence of $\{u_m\}_{m=1}^\infty$, still denoted by $\{u_m\}_{m=1}^\infty$, such that

$$u_m \overset{*}{\rightharpoonup} u \text{ in } L^\infty(0,\infty;\Psi_0),$$

$$u_{mt} \rightharpoonup u_t \text{ in } L^2(0,\infty;L^2(\Omega)),$$

$$|u_m|^{p-2}u_m \ln|u_m| \xrightarrow{*} |u|^{p-2}u\ln|u| \text{ in } L^\infty(0,\infty;L^{\frac{p}{p-1}}(\Omega)).$$

Making $m \to \infty$ in (34),

$$(u_t, v) + \langle u, v\rangle_{\Psi_0} + (u_t, v)_{\Psi_0} = (|u|^{p-2}u\ln|u|, v), \quad \forall v \in \Psi_0, \quad t \geq 0.$$

Making $m \to \infty$ in $u_m(0) = u_{0m}(x)$, we can obtain $u(0) = u_0(x) \in \Psi_0$. Therefore, $u(x,t)$ is a global solution of the problem (1). Moreover,

$$\int_0^t f_{u_t}(t)dt + \mathscr{H}(u) \leq \mathscr{H}(u_0).$$

Then, the subsequent proof is in common with Section 4. □

6. Blowup and Decay of Solutions

In the following, we discuss the blowup and asymptotic stability of the solutions to the problem (1). For this purpose, we provide some preliminary Lemmas.

Lemma 10 ([15]). *Suppose that $0 < T \leq \infty$ and the function $\mathbb{G}(t) \in C^2[0,T)$ with $\mathbb{G}(t) \geq 0$ satisfies*

$$\mathbb{G}(t)\mathbb{G}''(t) - (1+\xi)(\mathbb{G}'(t))^2 \geq 0,$$

for some constants $\xi > 0$. If $\mathbb{G}(0) > 0$ and $\mathbb{G}'(0) > 0$, then

$$T \leq \frac{\mathbb{G}(0)}{\xi\mathbb{G}'(0)} < +\infty,$$

and $\mathbb{G}(t) \to +\infty$ as $t \to T$.

Lemma 11. *Taking $\mathscr{H}(u_0) \leq d$ and the sets $\mathscr{I}_-$ and $\mathscr{I}_+$ as both invariant for $u(t)$, we have:*

(1) *If $u_0 \in \mathscr{I}_-$, then $u(t) \in \mathscr{I}_-$ for $\forall t \in [0,T)$.*
(2) *If $u_0 \in \mathscr{I}_+$, then $u(t) \in \mathscr{I}_+$ for $\forall t \in [0,T)$.*

Proof. (1) We begin by considering $\mathscr{H}(u_0) < d$. Conversely, if $u(t) \notin \mathscr{I}_-$, by the description of the energy inequality in (27),

$$\mathscr{H}(u(t)) \leq \mathscr{H}(u_0) < d; \tag{36}$$

thus, $\mathscr{P}(u(t_0)) = 0$ and $\mathscr{P}(u(t)) < 0$ for $t_0 \in (0,T)$ with $t \in (0,t_0)$ hold. By Lemma 4(2), we have $\|u(t_0)\|_{\Psi_0} > \delta(1,\varepsilon) > 0$, so $u(t_0) \in \mathscr{I}$. We can deduce $\mathscr{H}(u(t_0)) \geq d$ from (8), which contradicts (36).
Next, we consider $\mathscr{H}(u_0) = d$. Conversely, if $u(t) \notin \mathscr{I}_-$, since $\mathscr{P}(u_0) < 0$, there exists t_1 such that $\mathscr{P}(u(t_1)) = 0$ and $\mathscr{P}(u(t)) < 0$ for $t \in [0,t_1)$. From (2) of Lemma 4, we have $\|u\|_{\Psi_0} > \delta(1,\varepsilon) > 0$ for $t \in [0,t_0)$; this means that $u(t_1) \neq 0$, and we can obtain $u(t_1) \in \mathscr{I}$; by the description of d in (8), we can obtain

$$\mathscr{H}(u(t_1)) \geq d. \tag{37}$$

In contrast, from $(u_t,u) + (u_t,u)_{\Psi_0} = -\mathscr{P}(u(t)) > 0$ for $t \in [0,t_1)$ and $u(t)|_{\partial\Omega} = 0$, we can obtain $u_t \neq 0$ and $\int_0^{t_1} f_{u_t}(t)dt > 0$. From the energy inequality, we obtain

$$\mathscr{H}(u(t_1)) \leq \mathscr{H}(u_0) - \int_0^{t_1} f_{u_t}(t)dt < d,$$

which conflicts with (37).

(2) This is similar to the proof of (1) and will not be repeated.

□

Lemma 12. *If $u \in \Psi_0$ and $\mathscr{P}(u) < 0$, then there exists a $k_* \in (0,1)$, such that $\mathscr{P}(k_* u) = 0$.*

Proof. Set

$$\chi(k) = k^{p-2\lambda} \int_\Omega |u|^p \ln |u| dx + k^{p-2\lambda} \ln k \|u\|_p^p,$$

then we have

$$\mathscr{P}(ku) = k^{2\lambda} \|u\|_{\Psi_0}^{2\lambda} - \int_\Omega |ku|^p \ln |ku| dx = k^{2\lambda}(\|u\|_{\Psi_0}^{2\lambda} - \chi(k));$$

since $p > 2\lambda$, $\lim_{k \to 0^+} \chi(k) = 0$ holds and there exists a $k \in (0,1)$, such that $\mathscr{P}(ku) > 0$ and $\mathscr{P}(u) < 0$ when $k = 1$, the final conclusion can be drawn. □

Lemma 13. *Assume $u \in \Psi_0$ with $\mathscr{P}(u) < 0$; thus,*

$$\mathscr{P}(u) < p(\mathscr{H}(u) - d).$$

Proof. Set

$$\Lambda(k) = p\mathscr{H}(ku) - \mathscr{P}(ku).$$

By calculation,

$$\Lambda(k) = \frac{k^{2\lambda}(p - 2\lambda)}{2\lambda} \|u\|_{\Psi_0}^{2\lambda} + \frac{k^p}{p} \|u\|_p^p,$$

in view of Lemma 4(2), we have

$$\begin{aligned}
\Lambda'(k) &= k^{2\lambda-1}(p - 2\lambda)\|u\|_{\Psi_0}^{2\lambda} + k^{p-1}\|u\|_p^p \\
&\geq k^{2\lambda-1}(p - 2\lambda)\|u\|_{\Psi_0}^{2\lambda} \\
&> k^{2\lambda-1}(p - 2\lambda)\delta^{2\lambda}(1,\varepsilon) > 0,
\end{aligned}$$

which implies that Λ is strictly monotonically increasing; thus, $\Lambda(1) > \Lambda(k)$ for $\forall k \in (0,1)$. By Lemma 12, letting $k = k_* \in (0,1)$ and $\mathscr{P}(k_* u) = 0$, then

$$\Lambda(1) = p\mathscr{H}(u) - \mathscr{P}(u) > \Lambda(k_*) = p\mathscr{H}(k_* u) - \mathscr{P}(k_* u) = p\mathscr{H}(k_* u) \geq pd;$$

this completes the proof. □

Lemma 14. *Assume $u \in \Psi_0$ is a (weak) solution of the problem* (1), *then $(u_t, u)_{\Psi_0} \leq \|u\|_{\Psi_0}\|u_t\|_{\Psi_0}$.*

Proof. Let $v = u$ in Definition 2:

$$(u_t, u)_{\Psi_0} = \iint_Q \mathscr{T}^{u_t,u}(x,y)dxdy;$$

from the definition'sequivalent norm on Ψ_0 in (5),

$$\|u\|_{\Psi_0} = \left(\iint_Q \mathscr{T}^u(x,y)dxdy\right)^{\frac{1}{2}},$$

$$\|u_t\|_{\Psi_0} = \left(\iint_Q \mathscr{T}^{u_t}(x,y)dxdy\right)^{\frac{1}{2}}.$$

Set a function:

$$\gamma(k) = k^2 \iint_Q \mathscr{T}^u(x,y)dxdy + 2k \iint_Q \mathscr{T}^{u_t,u}(x,y)dxdy + \iint_Q \mathscr{T}^{u_t}(x,y)dxdy.$$

Then, for any k, we have

$$\gamma(k) = \iint_Q (|u(x) - u(y)|k + |u_t(x) - u_t(y)|)^2 K(x-y)dxdy \geq 0.$$

Hence,

$$\left(\iint_Q \mathscr{T}^{u_t,u}(x,y)dxdy\right)^2 \leq \iint_Q \mathscr{T}^u(x,y)dxdy \iint_Q \mathscr{T}^{u_t}(x,y)dxdy,$$

i.e.,

$$(u_t, u)_{\Psi_0} \leq \|u\|_{\Psi_0}\|u_t\|_{\Psi_0}.$$

□

Lemma 15. *If $u \in \Psi_0$ and ϑ and $\varkappa > 0$ are two constants, thus*

$$\left(\int_0^t f_u(t)dt + \vartheta(t+\varkappa)^2\right)\left(\int_0^t f_{u_t}(t)dt + \vartheta\right) \geq \left(\int_0^t (u,u_t) + (u,u_t)_{\Psi_0}dt + \vartheta(t+\varkappa)\right)^2.$$

Proof. In view of Lemma 14 and the Cauchy inequality,

$$\int_0^t (u,u_t)dt \leq \int_0^t \|u\|_2\|u_t\|_2 dt \leq \left(\int_0^t \|u\|_2^2 dt\right)^{\frac{1}{2}}\left(\int_0^t \|u_t\|_2^2\right)^{\frac{1}{2}}, \tag{38}$$

$$\int_0^t (u,u_t)_{\Psi_0}dt \leq \int_0^t \|u\|_{\Psi_0}\|u_t\|_{\Psi_0}dt \leq \left(\int_0^t \|u\|_{\Psi_0}^2 dt\right)^{\frac{1}{2}}\left(\int_0^t \|u_t\|_{\Psi_0}^2\right)^{\frac{1}{2}}. \tag{39}$$

Let

$$\begin{aligned} \nu_1(t) &= (\int_0^t \|u_t\|_2^2 dt)^{\frac{1}{2}}, \quad \mu_1(t) = (\int_0^t \|u\|_2^2 dt)^{\frac{1}{2}}, \\ \nu_2(t) &= (\int_0^t \|u_t\|_{\Psi_0}^2 dt)^{\frac{1}{2}}, \quad \mu_2(t) = (\int_0^t \|u\|_{\Psi_0}^2 dt)^{\frac{1}{2}}. \end{aligned}$$

Then,

$$\begin{aligned} &(\int_0^t f_u(t)dt + \vartheta(t+\varkappa)^2)(\int_0^t f_{u_t}(t)dt + \vartheta) \\ &= (\mu_1^2(t) + \mu_2^2(t) + \vartheta(t+\varkappa)^2)(\nu_1^2(t) + \nu_2^2(t) + \vartheta) \\ &= \mu_1^2(t)\nu_1^2(t) + \mu_2^2(t)\nu_1^2(t) + \vartheta(t+\varkappa)^2\nu_1^2(t) + \mu_1^2(t)\nu_2^2(t) + \mu_2^2(t)\nu_2^2(t) \\ &\quad + \vartheta(t+\varkappa)^2\nu_2^2(t) + \vartheta\mu_1^2(t) + \vartheta\mu_2^2(t) + \vartheta^2(t+\sigma)^2; \end{aligned} \tag{40}$$

by (38) and (39),

$$\begin{aligned} &(\int_0^t (u,u_t) + (u,u_t)_{\Psi_0}dt + \vartheta(t+\varkappa))^2 \\ &= (\int_0^t (u,u_t)dt)^2 + (\int_0^t (u,u_t)_{\Psi_0}dt)^2 + \vartheta^2(t+\varkappa)^2 + 2\int_0^t (u,u_t)dt\int_0^t (u,u_t)_{\Psi_0}dt \\ &\quad + 2\vartheta(t+\sigma)\int_0^t (u,u_t)dt + 2\vartheta(t+\varkappa)\int_0^t (u,u_t)_{\Psi_0}dt \\ &\leq \mu_1^2(t)\nu_1^2(t) + \mu_2^2(t)\nu_2^2(t) + 2\nu_1(t)\mu_1(t)\nu_2(t)\mu_2(t) + 2\vartheta(t+\varkappa)\nu_1(t)\mu_1(t) \\ &\quad + 2\vartheta(t+\varkappa)\nu_2(t)\mu_2(t) + \vartheta^2(t+\varkappa)^2. \end{aligned} \tag{41}$$

Combining (40) with (41),

$$\begin{aligned}
&(\int_0^t f_u(t)dt + \vartheta(t+\varkappa)^2)(\int_0^t f_{u_t}(t)dt + \vartheta) - (\int_0^t (u,u_t) + (u,u_t)_{\Psi_0}dt + \vartheta(t+\varkappa)^2 \\
&\geq \vartheta(t+\varkappa)^2 v_1^2(t) + \mu_1^2(t)v_2^2(t) + \mu_2^2(t)v_1^2(t) + \vartheta(t+\varkappa)^2 v_2^2(t) + \vartheta\mu_1^2(t) + \vartheta\mu_2^2(t) \\
&- (2v_1(t)\mu_1(t)v_2(t)\mu_2(t) + 2\vartheta(t+\varkappa)v_1(t)\mu_1(t) + 2\vartheta(t+\varkappa)v_2(t)\mu_2(t)) \\
&= (\sqrt{\vartheta}(t+\varkappa)v_1(t) - \sqrt{\vartheta}\mu_2(t))^2 + (\sqrt{\vartheta}(t+\varkappa)v_2(t) - \sqrt{\vartheta}\mu_1(t))^2 \\
&+ (\mu_1(t)v_2(t) - \mu_2(t)v_1(t))^2 \geq 0,
\end{aligned}$$

which ends of proof. □

Corollary 1. *Let $u \in \Psi_0$, then*

$$\left(\int_0^t f_u(t)dt\right)\left(\int_0^t f_{u_t}(t)dt\right) \geq \left(\int_0^t (u,u_t) + (u,u_t)_{\Psi_0}dt\right)^2.$$

Proof. Specifically, we make $\vartheta = 0$ in Lemma 15, then the conclusion holds. □

Theorem 2. *Let $u_0 \in \Psi_0$, satisfying $\mathscr{H}(u_0) < d$ and $\mathscr{P}(u_0) < 0$, then the solution $u(x,t)$ of the problem* (1) *blows up in finite time, i.e., there exists $T > 0$ such that*

$$\lim_{t\to T}\int_0^t f_u(t)dt = +\infty.$$

Proof. By contradiction, if $T = \infty$, we set

$$A(t) = \int_0^t f_u(t)dt + (T-t)f_u(0).$$

By the description of weak solutions and making $v = u$ in Definition 2, we obtain

$$\int_\Omega u_t u dx + M([u]_s^2)\iint_Q \mathscr{T}^u(x,y)dxdy + \iint_Q \mathscr{T}^{u_t,u}(x,y)dxdy = \int_\Omega |u|^{p-1}u\ln|u|dx;$$

we can deduce from the above equation that

$$\frac{d}{dt}f_u(t) = -2(\|u\|_{\Psi_0}^{2\lambda} - \int_\Omega |u|^{p-1}u\ln|u|dx) = -2\mathscr{P}(u). \tag{42}$$

Therefore,

$$A'(t) = f_u(t) - f_u(0) = 2\int_0^t (u,u_t) + (u,u_t)_{\Psi_0}, dt$$

and

$$A''(t) = 2((u,u_t) + (u,u_t)_{\Psi_0}) = -2\mathscr{P}(u).$$

By Lemma 13, Lemma 15, and the description of energy inequality in (27),

$$\begin{aligned}
A''(t) &= -2\mathscr{P}(u) > 2pd - 2p\mathscr{H}(u) \\
A &\geq 2p(d - \mathscr{H}(u_0)) + 2p\int_0^t f_{u_t}(t)dt;
\end{aligned}$$

thus, by Corollary 1,

$$A''(t)A(t) - \frac{p}{2}(A'(t))^2 > 2p(d - \mathscr{H}(u_0))A(t) + 2p\int_0^t f_{u_t}(t)dt \int_0^t f_u(t)dt$$
$$- 2p\left(\int_0^t (u,u_t) + (u,u_t)_{\Psi_0}dt\right)^2$$
$$\geq 2p(d - \mathscr{H}(u_0))A(t) > 0.$$

Therefore, we have

$$(A^{-b}(t))'' = \frac{-b}{A^{b+2}(t)}\left(A(t)A''(t) - (b+1)(A'(t))^2\right) \leq 0, \quad b = \frac{p-2}{2} > 0, \tag{43}$$

Lemma 10 and (43) imply that there exists a $T > 0$ such that

$$\lim_{t\to T} A^{-b}(t) = 0 \quad \text{and} \quad \lim_{t\to T} A(t) = +\infty,$$

which contradicts $T = \infty$. □

Theorem 3. *Under the assumptions of Theorem 2, the blowup upper bound is*

$$\frac{4(p-1)f_u(0)}{p(d - \mathscr{H}(u_0))(p-2)^2}.$$

Proof. Set

$$B(t) = \int_0^t f_u(t)dt + (T-t)f_u(0) + \vartheta(t+\varkappa)^2,$$

where ϑ and $\varkappa > 0$ are two constants.

Obviously, $\mathscr{P}(u) < 0$ from Lemma 36, and (42) implies that $f_u(t)$ is strictly monotonically increasing, so

$$B'(t) = f_u(t) - f_u(0) + 2\vartheta(t+\varkappa) > 0,$$

i.e.,

$$B(t) > B(0) = Tf_u(0) + \vartheta\varkappa^2.$$

From

$$\int_0^t (u_t,u)dt = \frac{1}{2}\int_0^t \frac{d}{dt}\|u\|_2^2 dt = \frac{1}{2}(\|u\|_2^2 - \|u_0\|_2^2),$$

and

$$\int_0^t (u_t,u)_{\Psi_0}dt = \frac{1}{2}\int_0^t \frac{d}{dt}\|u\|_{\Psi_0}^2 dt = \frac{1}{2}(\|u\|_{\Psi_0}^2 - \|u_0\|_{\Psi_0}^2),$$

we have

$$B'(t) = 2\int_0^t (u_t,u)dt + 2\int_0^t (u_t,u)_{\Psi_0}dt + 2\vartheta(t+\varkappa).$$

Combining Lemma 13 with (27),

$$\begin{aligned} B''(t) &= 2(u,u_t) + 2(u,u_t)_{\Psi_0} + 2\vartheta \\ &= -2\mathscr{P}(u) + 2\vartheta \\ &> 2pd - 2p\mathscr{H}(u) + 2\vartheta \\ &\geq -2p\mathscr{H}(u_0) + 2p\int_0^t f_{u_t}(t)dt + 2pd + 2\vartheta. \end{aligned}$$

With the above calculations,

$$
\begin{aligned}
& B''(t)B(t) - \frac{p}{2}(B'(t))^2 \\
& > \left(-2p\mathscr{H}(u_0) + 2p\int_0^t f_{u_t}(t)dt + 2pd + 2\vartheta\right)B(t) \\
& \quad - 2p\left(\int_0^t (u_t, u)dt + \int_0^t (u_t, u)_{\Psi_0}dt + \vartheta(t+\varkappa)\right)^2 \\
& \geq 2pB(t)\left(-\mathscr{H}(u_0) + \int_0^t f_{u_t}(t)dt + d + \frac{\vartheta}{p}\right) \\
& \quad - 2p\left(\int_0^t f_u(t)dt + \vartheta(t+\varkappa)^2\right)\left(\int_0^t f_{u_t}(t)dt + \vartheta\right) \\
& \geq 2pB(t)\left(-\mathscr{H}(u_0) + \int_0^t f_{u_t}(t)dt + d + \frac{\vartheta}{p}\right) - 2pB(t)\left(\int_0^t f_{u_t}(t)dt + \vartheta\right) \\
& = 2pB(t)\left(-\mathscr{H}(u_0) + d - \frac{p-1}{p}\vartheta\right),
\end{aligned}
$$

which is non-negative if we let ϑ be sufficiently small and satisfy

$$0 \leq \vartheta < \frac{p}{p-1}(d - \mathscr{H}(u_0)).$$

By Lemma 10, we can obtain

$$T \leq \frac{F(0)}{(\frac{p}{2}-1)F'(0)} = \frac{f_u(0)}{(p-2)\vartheta\varkappa}T + \frac{\varkappa}{p-2}, \tag{44}$$

taking $\varkappa$ large enough and satisfying

$$\varkappa > \frac{f_u(0)}{(p-2)\vartheta}.$$

By calculating (44), we can obtain

$$T \leq \frac{\vartheta\varkappa^2}{(p-2)\vartheta\varkappa - f_u(0)};$$

let

$$\pi(\chi, \varkappa) = \frac{\vartheta\varkappa^2}{(p-2)\vartheta\varkappa - f_u(0)},$$

then

$$T \leq \inf_{(\chi,\varkappa)\in\mathbb{Z}} \pi(\chi, \varkappa) = \frac{4(p-1)(f_u(0))}{p(d - \mathscr{H}(u_0))(p-2)^2},$$

where $\chi = \vartheta\varkappa$ and

$$\mathbb{Z} = \left\{(\chi, \varkappa) | \chi > \frac{f_u(0)}{p-2}, \varkappa \geq \frac{(p-1)\chi}{p(d - \mathscr{H}(u_0))}\right\}.$$

□

Theorem 4. *Under the assumptions of Theorem 2, the blowup lower bound is*

$$\frac{\varepsilon e(f_u(0))^{1-\xi}}{2(\xi-1)\tilde{C}},$$

where

$$\tilde{C} = (\overline{C})^{\frac{2\lambda}{2\lambda-(1-\theta)(p+\varepsilon)}} (e\varepsilon)^{\frac{(\theta-1)(p+\varepsilon)}{2\lambda-(1-\theta)(p+\varepsilon)}},$$

$$\xi = \frac{\theta\lambda(p+\varepsilon)}{2\lambda-(1-\theta)(p+\varepsilon)}.$$

Here,

$$\overline{C} = \sup_{u\in\Psi_0} \frac{\|u\|_{p+\varepsilon}}{\|u\|_{\Psi_0}^{1-\theta}\|u\|_2^{\theta}},$$

and

$$\theta = \frac{2(2_s^* - p - \varepsilon)}{(2_s^* - 2)(p+\varepsilon)}, \quad \varepsilon \in (0, 2\lambda + 2 - 4\lambda/2_s^* - p).$$

Proof. As shown in [19], as $\theta \in (0,1)$, $\overline{C}$ is well-defined, and $\xi > 1$. Set

$$f_u(t) = \|u\|_2^2 + \|u\|_{\Psi_0}^2,$$

satisfying

$$f_u(T) = \infty. \tag{45}$$

It follows that

$$f_u{}'(t) = 2(u_t, u) + 2(u_t, u)_{\Psi_0} = -2\mathscr{P}(u).$$

We know that $\mathscr{P}(u_0) < 0$, and by Lemma 11, we have $\mathscr{P}(u) < 0$, so that

$$\|u\|_{\Psi_0}^{2\lambda} < \int_\Omega |u|^p \ln|u| dx. \tag{46}$$

Specifically, we chose $\varepsilon \in (0, 2\lambda + 2 - 4\theta/2_s^* - p)$ in Lemma 2, and combining the interpolation inequality with (46),

$$\begin{aligned}
\int_\Omega |u|^p \ln|u| dx &\leq \frac{1}{e\varepsilon}\|u\|_{p+\varepsilon}^{p+\varepsilon} \leq \frac{1}{e\varepsilon}\overline{C}\|u\|_{\Psi_0}^{(1-\theta)(p+\varepsilon)}\|u\|_2^{\theta(p+\varepsilon)} \\
&= \frac{1}{e\varepsilon}\overline{C}(\|u\|_{\Psi_0}^{2\lambda})^{\frac{(1-\theta)(p+\varepsilon)}{2\lambda}}\|u\|_2^{\theta(p+\varepsilon)} \\
&< \frac{1}{e\varepsilon}\overline{C}(\int_\Omega |u|^p ln|u|)^{\frac{(1-\theta)(p+\varepsilon)}{2\lambda}}\|u\|_2^{\theta(p+\varepsilon)} \\
&\leq \overline{C}(e\varepsilon)^{\frac{(\theta-1)(p+\varepsilon)}{2\lambda}-1}(\|u\|_{p+\varepsilon}^{p+\varepsilon})^{\frac{(1-\theta)(p+\varepsilon)}{2\lambda}}\|u\|_2^{\theta(p+\varepsilon)}.
\end{aligned} \tag{47}$$

Since $0 < \varepsilon < 2\lambda + 2 - 4\lambda/2_s^* - p$, $2\lambda < p < p + \varepsilon$ and $\theta = \frac{2(2_s^*-p-\varepsilon)}{(2_s^*-2)(p+\varepsilon)} \in (0,1)$, we can obtain

$$\frac{(1-\theta)(p+\varepsilon)}{2\lambda} < 1.$$

Therefore, (47) yields

$$\|u\|_{p+\varepsilon}^{p+\varepsilon} < \tilde{C}(\|u\|_2^2)^{\xi} \leq \tilde{C}(f_u(t))^{\xi}, \tag{48}$$

where

$$\xi = \frac{\theta\lambda(p+\varepsilon)}{2\lambda-(1-\theta)(p+\varepsilon)},$$

and

$$\tilde{C} = (\overline{C})^{\frac{2\lambda}{2\lambda-(1-\theta)(p+\varepsilon)}} (e\varepsilon)^{\frac{(\theta-1)(p+\varepsilon)}{2\lambda-(1-\theta)(p+\varepsilon)}}.$$

Thus,

$$
\begin{aligned}
{f_u}'(t) &= -2\mathscr{P}(u) = -2\|u\|_{\Psi_0}^{2\lambda} + 2\int_{\Omega} |u|^p \ln|u| dx \\
&\leq 2\int_{\Omega} |u|^p \ln|u| dx \leq \frac{2}{e\varepsilon}\|u\|_{p+\varepsilon}^{p+\varepsilon} \\
&< \frac{2}{e\varepsilon}\tilde{C}(f_u(t))^{\xi}.
\end{aligned}
\tag{49}
$$

Next, we inform that $f_u(t) > 0$ for any $t \in [0, T)$. As a paradox, there exists a $t_1 \geq 0$ such that

$$f_u(t_1) = 0,$$

which is a paradox with respect to (48). Then, we can deduce from (49) that

$$\frac{{f_u}'(t)}{(f_u(t))^{\xi}} < \frac{2}{e\varepsilon}\tilde{C}. \tag{50}$$

Integrating (50) from 0 to t,

$$(f_u(0))^{1-\xi} - (f_u(t))^{1-\xi} < \frac{2}{e\varepsilon}(\xi - 1)\tilde{C}t, \tag{51}$$

from (45) and letting $t \to T$ in (51),

$$T > \frac{\varepsilon e (f_u(0))^{1-\xi}}{2(\xi - 1)\tilde{C}}.$$

□

Theorem 5. *Let $u_0 \in \Psi_0$, satisfying $\mathscr{H}(u_0) = d$ and $\mathscr{P}(u_0) < 0$, then the solution $u(x,t)$ of the problem (1) blows up in finite time, i.e., there exists $T > 0$ such that*

$$\lim_{t \to T} \int_0^t f_u(t) dt = +\infty.$$

Proof. We deduce that $\mathscr{P}(u(t)) < 0$ for $t \geq 0$ from Lemma 11; thus,

$$(u, u_t) + (u, u_t)_{\Psi_0} = -\mathscr{P}(u(t)) > 0,$$

which yields $f_{u_t}(0) > 0$ for $t \geq 0$; there exists a $t_1 > 0$ such that we let t_1 be a new initial time and satisfy

$$\mathscr{H}(u(t_1)) \leq \mathscr{H}(u_0) - \int_0^{t_1} f_{u_t}(t) dt < d.$$

This is similar to Theorem 2. □

Theorem 6. *Put $u_0 \in \Psi_0$, satisfying $\mathscr{H}(u_0) < 0$, and $u(t)$ is a weak solution of the problem (1), then the blowup upper bound is*

$$\frac{f_u(0)}{p(p-2)\mathscr{H}(u_0)}.$$

Proof. By the description of $\mathscr{H}(u)$ in (6) and $\mathscr{P}(u)$ in (7), set

$$
\begin{aligned}
\mu(t) &= -2p\mathscr{H}(u) = -2p\left(\frac{1}{2\lambda}\|u\|_{\Psi_0}^{2\lambda} - \frac{1}{p}\int_{\Omega} |u|^p \ln|u| dx + \frac{1}{p^2}\|u\|_p^p\right) \\
&= 2\int_{\Omega} |u|^p \ln|u| dx - \frac{2}{p}\|u\|_p^p - \frac{p}{\lambda}\|u\|_{\Psi_0}^{2\lambda}.
\end{aligned}
$$

Obviously,

$$\begin{aligned} f_u{}'(t) &= 2(u,u_t) + 2(u,u_t)_{\Psi_0} \\ &= -2\mathscr{P}(u) = 2\int_\Omega |u|^p \ln|u|dx - 2\|u\|_{\Psi_0}^{2\lambda} \geq \mu(t). \end{aligned} \tag{52}$$

By the description of weak solutions and making $v = u_t$ in Definition 2,

$$\int_\Omega u_t^2 dx + M([u]_s^2)\iint_Q \mathscr{T}^{u,u_t}(x,y)dxdy + \iint_Q \mathscr{T}^{u_t}(x,y)dxdy = \int_\Omega |u|^{p-2}uu_t \ln|u|dx,$$

we can deduce from the above equation that

$$f_{u_t}(t) = -\frac{1}{2\lambda}\frac{d}{dt}\|u\|_{\Psi_0}^{2\lambda} + \frac{1}{p}\frac{d}{dt}\int_\Omega |u|^p \ln|u|dx - \frac{1}{p^2}\frac{d}{dt}\|u\|_p^p,$$

i.e.,

$$\frac{d}{dt}\mathscr{H}(u) = -f_{u_t}(t). \tag{53}$$

By (53), we have

$$\mu'(t) = -2p\frac{d}{dt}\mathscr{H}(u) = 2p(f_{u_t}(t)) \geq 0,$$

and $\mu(0) = -2p\mathscr{H}(u_0) > 0$; therefore, $\mu(t) > 0$ for $0 \geq t > T$. By Theorem 4, we have $f_u(t) > 0$ for $t \in [0,T)$, according to Corollary 1,

$$f_u(t)\mu'(t) \geq 2p((u,u_t) + (u,u_t)_{\Psi_0})^2 = \frac{p}{2}(f_u{}'(t))^2. \tag{54}$$

Combining (52) with (54), we can obtain

$$f_u(t)\mu'(t) \geq \frac{p}{2}f_u{}'(t)\mu,$$

i.e.,

$$\frac{\mu'(t)}{\mu} \geq \frac{p}{2}\frac{f_u{}'(t)}{f_u(t)}, \tag{55}$$

and integration of (55) over $(0,t)$ yields

$$\frac{\mu}{(f_u(t))^{p/2}} \geq \frac{\mu(0)}{(f_u(0))^{p/2}},$$

thereby having

$$\frac{f_u{}'(t)}{(f_u(t))^{p/2}} \geq \frac{\mu(0)}{(f_u(0))^{p/2}}. \tag{56}$$

Now, we integrate (56) over $(0,t)$, yielding

$$\frac{1}{(f_u(t))^{(p-2)/2}} \leq \frac{1}{(f_u(0))^{(p-2)/2}} - \frac{p-2}{2}\frac{\mu(0)}{(f_u(0))^{p/2}}t,$$

and letting $t \to T$ in the above inequality,

$$T \leq \frac{f_u(0)}{p(p-2)\mathscr{H}(u_0)}.$$

□

Next, we begin to compute the decay estimates for arbitrary solutions of the problem (1), and before proving this, we give some properties about the vacuum isolating behavior of the solutions.

Lemma 16. *Assume $u_0 \in \Psi_0$, $0 < \overline{q} < d$, and ι_1 and ι_2, with $0 < \iota_1 < \iota_2$ are the two roots of $d(\iota) = \overline{q}$, where $\iota \in (\iota_1, \iota_2)$, then:*

(1) *All solutions u of (1) with $\mathscr{H}(u_0) = \overline{q}$ belong to Ψ_ι, provided $\mathscr{P}(u_0) > 0$.*
(2) *All solutions u of (1) with $\mathscr{H}(u_0) = \overline{q}$ belong to Θ_ι, provided $\mathscr{P}(u_0) < 0$.*

Proof. (1) Taking $u(t)$ as an arbitrary solution to (1) satisfying $\mathscr{H}(u_0) = \overline{q}$, $\mathscr{P}(u_0) > 0$ or $\|u_0\|_{\Psi_0} = 0$, T is the maximum existence time of u. If $\|u_0\|_{\Psi_0} = 0$, then $u_0(x) \in \Psi_\iota$ for all $\iota \in (0, \frac{p}{2\lambda})$. If $\mathscr{P}(u_0) > 0$, from Lemma 5, the energy level inequality in (27), and Lemma 7, we can deduce that $\mathscr{P}_\iota(u_0) > 0$ and $\mathscr{H}(u_0) < d(\iota)$ are valid, which implies $u_0 \in \Psi_\iota$ for all $\iota \in (\iota_1, \iota_2)$.
We prove that $u(x,t) \in \Psi_0$ for all $\iota \in (\iota_1, \iota_2)$ with $t \in (0, T)$. As a paradox, there is $u(t) \in \partial\Psi_{\iota_0}$ for $t_0 \in (0, T)$ and $\iota_0 \in (\iota_1, \iota_2)$. That is, $\mathscr{P}_{\iota_0}(u(t)) = 0$ either $\|u(t_0)\|_{\Psi_0} \neq 0$ or $\mathscr{H}(u(t_0)) = d(\iota_0)$, which together with (27) give

$$\int_0^t f_{u_t}(0)dt + \mathscr{H}(u) \leq \mathscr{H}(u_0) < d(\iota), \quad \iota \in (\iota_1, \iota_2); \tag{57}$$

thus, $\mathscr{H}(u(t_0)) \neq d(\iota_0)$. Meanwhile, $\mathscr{H}(u(t_0)) \geq d(\iota_0)$ when $\mathscr{P}_{\iota_0}(u(t_0)) = 0$ and $\|u(t_0)\|_{\Psi_0} \neq 0$, which contradicts (57).

(2) Similar to the proof of (1), assume that either $\mathscr{P}(u_0) < 0$ or $\|u_0\|_{\Psi_0} = 0$. We prove that $u(x,t) \in \Psi_0$. As a paradox, there is some $t_0 \in (0, T)$, $\iota_0 \in (\iota_1, \iota_2)$, such that $u(t) \in \partial\Psi_{\iota_0}$, that is $\mathscr{P}_{\iota_0}(u(t)) = 0$, and either $\|u(t_0)\|_{\Psi_0} \neq 0$ or $\mathscr{H}(u(t_0)) = d(\iota_0)$. Again, (57) shows that $\mathscr{H}(u(t_0)) \neq d(\iota_0)$. Otherwise, take $t_0 \in (0, T)$ as the initial time satisfying $\mathscr{P}_{\iota_0}(u(t_0)) = 0$, then $\mathscr{P}_{\iota_0}(u(t)) < 0$ for $0 \leq t < t_0$. By Lemma 4(2), we have $\|u(t_0)\|_{\Psi_0} > \delta(\iota_0, \varepsilon)$ for $0 \leq t < t_0$ and $\mathscr{H}(u(t_0)) \neq d(\iota_0)$; this contradicts (57) and proves the claim.
□

Theorem 7. *Let $u_0 \in \Psi_0$, satisfying $\mathscr{H}(u_0) < d$ and $\mathscr{P}(u_0) > 0$; arbitrary global weak solutions u of the problem (1) have the following decay estimate*

$$f_u(t) \leq \mathscr{M}(t) := \begin{cases} (f_u^2(0)) \exp\left\{\frac{-2\lambda_1}{1+\lambda_1}(1-\iota_1)t\right\}, & \lambda = 1, \\ \left[2(1-\iota_1)(\lambda-1)(\frac{\lambda_1}{1+\lambda_1})^\lambda t + (f_u(0))^{1-\lambda}\right]^{\frac{1}{1-\lambda}}, & \lambda > 1, \end{cases}$$

where $\lambda_1 = \inf\limits_{u \in \Psi_0 \setminus \{0\}} \dfrac{\|u\|_{\Psi_0}^2}{\|u\|_2^2}$.

Proof. Take $u(t)$ as a global weak solution of the problem (1). By $0 < \mathscr{H}(u_0) < d$, $\mathscr{P}(u_0) > 0$, and Lemma 16, we deduce that $u(t) \in \Psi_\iota$ for all $\iota \in (\iota_1, \iota_2)$ and $t \in [0, \infty)$, where ι_1 and ι_2 are two roots of $d(\iota) = \mathscr{H}(u_0)$; Lemma 7 indicates that $\mathscr{P}_\iota(u) \geq 0$ for all $\iota \in (\iota_1, \iota_2)$ and $\mathscr{P}_{\iota_1}(u) \geq 0$ for $t \in [0, \infty)$. Thus, (42) gives

$$\frac{d}{dt} f_u(t) + 2(1-\iota_1)\|u\|_{\Psi_0}^{2\lambda} = -2\mathscr{P}_{\iota_1}(u) \leq 0; \tag{58}$$

from (58) we also obtain

$$\frac{d}{dt} f_u(t) \leq -2(1-\iota_1)\|u\|_{\Psi_0}^{2\lambda}. \tag{59}$$

Now, we consider two situations: (1) $\lambda = 1$; (2) $\lambda > 1$:

(1) If $\lambda = 1$,

$$\frac{d}{dt} f_u(t) \leq -2(1-\iota_1) f_u(t) + 2(1-\iota_1)\|u\|_2^2, \tag{60}$$

then divide by $f_u(t)$ on both sides of (60), and by the definition of λ_1,

$$\begin{aligned}\frac{\frac{d}{dt} f_u(t)}{f_u(t)} &\leq -2(1-\iota_1) + 2(1-\iota_1)\frac{\|u\|_2^2}{f_u(t)} \\ &\leq -2(1-\iota_1) + 2(1-\iota_1)\frac{1}{1+\lambda_1} \\ &= -\frac{2\lambda_1}{1+\lambda_1}(1-\iota_1),\end{aligned} \tag{61}$$

i.e.,

$$f_u(t) \leq (f_u(0)) \exp\left\{-\frac{2\lambda_1}{1+\lambda_1}(1-\iota_1)t\right\}.$$

(2) If $\lambda > 1$, by the definition of λ_1, we can obtain

$$f_u(t) \leq (1 + \frac{1}{\lambda_1})\|u\|_{\Psi_0}^2. \tag{62}$$

Thus, (59) and (62) lead to

$$\frac{d}{dt}(f_u(t)) \leq -2(\frac{\lambda_1}{1+\lambda_1})^\lambda (1-\iota_1)(\|u\|_2^2 + \|u\|_{\Psi_0}^2)^\lambda,$$

and a simple calculation yields

$$f_u(t) \leq \left[2(1-\iota_1)(\lambda-1)(\frac{\lambda_1}{1+\lambda_1})^\lambda t + (f_u(0))^{1-\lambda}\right]^{\frac{1}{1-\lambda}}.$$

End of the proof.

□

Theorem 8. *Let $u_0 \in \Psi_0$, satisfying $\mathscr{H}(u_0) = d$ and $\mathscr{P}(u_0) > 0$; any global weak solution u of the problem* (1) *has the following decay estimate:*

$$f_u(t) \leq \mathscr{N}(t) := \begin{cases} f_u(t_1) \exp\left\{\frac{-2\lambda_1}{1+\lambda_1}(1-\iota_1)(t-t_1)\right\}, & \lambda = 1, \\ \left[2(1-\iota_1)(\lambda-1)(\frac{\lambda_1}{1+\lambda_1})^\lambda (t-t_1) + (f_u(t_1))^{1-\lambda}\right]^{\frac{1}{1-\lambda}}, & \lambda > 1, \end{cases}$$

where $\lambda_1 = \inf\limits_{u \in \Psi_0 \setminus \{0\}} \frac{\|u\|_{\Psi_0}^2}{\|u\|_2^2}$.

Proof. Taking $u(t)$ as a global weak solution of the problem (1) with $\mathscr{H}(u_0) = d$, $\mathscr{P}(u_0) > 0$, by the definition of the energy inequality in (27) and Lemma 11, we obtain $\mathscr{H}(u) < d$ and $\mathscr{P}(u) > 0$ for $0 \leq t < \infty$. Immediately afterwards, by $(u_t, u) + (u_t, u)_{\Psi_0} = -\mathscr{P}(u) < 0$ and $f_u(t) > 0$, we have $\int_0^t f_{u_t}(t)dt$ monotonically increasing for all $0 \leq t < \infty$. For any $t_1 > 0$, let

$$\varrho = d - \int_0^t f_{u_t}(t)dt.$$

It follows from (27) that $0 < \mathscr{H}(u) \leq \varrho < d$ and $u(t) \in \Psi_\iota$ hold on $\iota_1 < \iota < \iota_2$ and $0 \leq t < \infty$, where ι_1 and ι_2 are two roots of $d(\iota) = \overline{p}$; thus, $\mathscr{P}_{\iota_1}(u) \geq 0$ on $t \geq t_1$.

The subsequent steps are similar to Theorem 7.

□

7. Example

We take $\lambda = 1$ in the Kirchhoff function $M(t) = t^{\lambda-1}$ of (1), which gives us the problem below:

$$\begin{cases} u_t + (-\Delta)^s u + (-\Delta)^s u_t = |u|^{p-2}u\ln|u|, & \text{in } \Omega \times (0,T), \\ u(x,0) = u_0(x), & \text{in } \Omega, \\ u(x,t) = 0, & \text{on } \partial\Omega \times (0,T). \end{cases}$$

From the main theorem of this article, it can be concluded that the global solution of the problem exists and blows up in finite time.

In particular, let $p = 2$; the above problem becomes

$$\begin{cases} u_t + (-\Delta)^s u + (-\Delta)^s u_t = u\ln|u|, & \text{in } \Omega \times (0,T), \\ u(x,0) = u_0(x), & \text{in } \Omega, \\ u(x,t) = 0, & \text{on } \partial\Omega \times (0,T), \end{cases}$$

which was studied in [31]; the authors considered both blowup and decay solutions; furthermore, they obtained relevant conclusions.

8. Conclusions

In this paper, we studied the suitability of solutions to a class of fractional-order parabolic equations with Kirchhoff terms $M(t)$ involving the fractional-order damping $(-\Delta)^s$ and logarithmic source terms $|u|^{q-2}u\ln|u|$. Firstly, the correlation functions $\mathscr{H}(u)$, $\mathscr{P}(u)$ and some necessary Lemmas were introduced; in addition, we introduced fractional Sobolev spaces for logarithmic terms. Based on these, we combined the Galerkin method and potential wells to prove the global existence of the solutions. Then, using some inequality techniques and an improved concave function method to simultaneously select a new auxiliary function, it was proven that the solution blows up in finite time, and the upper and lower bounds on the blowup time were also obtained. Finally, the invariant set at subcritical energy levels was obtained by combining $\mathscr{H}(u)$, $\mathscr{P}(u)$, and the potential well Ψ. Using the Galerkin method and Gronwall's inequality, the asymptotic behavior of the solution was proven.

Author Contributions: Conceptualization, N.P. and Z.G.; methodology, N.P. and Z.G.; validation, N.P. and Z.G.; writing—original draft preparation, Z.G.; writing—review and editing, N.P.; funding acquisition, N.P. All authors have read and agreed to the published version of the manuscript.

Funding: This research was funded by the National Natural Science Foundation of China, grant number: 12001088, and the Fundamental Research Funds for the Central Universities, grant number: 2572021BC01.

Institutional Review Board Statement: Not applicable.

Informed Consent Statement: Not applicable.

Data Availability Statement: No new data were created nor analyzed in this study. Data sharing is not applicable to this article.

Acknowledgments: We are grateful to the Editor, Associated Editor, and referees for their valuable suggestions and comments, which greatly improved the article.

Conflicts of Interest: The authors declare no conflict of interest.

References

1. Di Nezza, E.; Palatucci, G.; Valdinaci, E. Hitchhiker's guide to the fractional Sobolev spaces. *Bull. Sci. Math.* **2012**, *136*, 521–573. [CrossRef]
2. Molica Bisci, G.; Radulescu, V.; Servadei, R. *Variational Methods for Nonlocal Fractional Problems*; Cambridge University Press: Cambridge, UK, 2016.
3. Kirchhoff, G. *Vorlesungen uber Mathematische Physik: Mechanik*, 3rd ed.; Teubner: Leipzig, Germany, 1883.
4. Fiscella, A.; Valdinoci, E. A critical Kirchhoff type problem involving a nonlocal operator. *Nonlinear Anal.* **2014**, *94*, 156–170. [CrossRef]

5. Pan, N.; Zhang, B.L.; Cao, J. Degenerate Kirchhoff-type diffusion problems involving the fractional p-Laplacian. *Nonlinear Anal. Real World Appl.* **2017**, *37*, 56–70. [CrossRef]
6. Pan, N.; Pucci, P.; Xu, R.; Zhang, B.L. Degenerate Kirchhoff-type wave problems involving the fractional Laplacian with nonlinear damping and source terms. *J. Evol. Equ.* **2019**, *19*, 615–643. [CrossRef]
7. Boudjeriou, T. Global existence and blow-up for the fractional p-Laplacian with logarithmic nonlinearity. *Mediterr. J. Math.* **2020**, *17*, 162. [CrossRef]
8. Zeng, F.; Shi, P.; Jiang, M. Global existence and finite time blow-up for a class of fractional p-Laplacian Kirchhoff type equations with logarithmic nonlinearity. *AIMS Math.* **2021**, *6*, 2559–2578. [CrossRef]
9. Yang, Y.; Tian, X.; Zhang, M. Blowup of solutions to degenerate Kirchhoff-type diffusion problems involving the fractional p-Laplacian. *Electron. J. Differ. Equ.* **2018** ,*155*, 1–22.
10. Xiang, M.; Radulescu, V.; Zhang, B.L. Nonlocal Kirchhoff diffusion problems: Local existence and blow-up of solutions. *Nonlinearity* **2018**, *31*, 3228–3250.
11. Sun, F.; Liu, L.; Wu, Y. Finite time blow-up for a class of parabolic or pseudo-parabolic equations. *Comp. Math. Appl.* **2018**, *75*, 3685–3701. [CrossRef]
12. Xiang, M.; Yang, D.; Zhang, B.L. Degenerate Kirchhoff-type fractional diffusion problem with logarithmic nonlinearity. *Asymptot. Anal.* **2020**, *118*, 313–329. [CrossRef]
13. Sattinger, D.H. On global solution of nonlinear hyperbolic equations. *Arch. Ration. Mech. Anal.* **1968**, *30*, 147–172. [CrossRef]
14. Tsutsumi, M. Existence and nonexistence of global solutions for nonlinear parabolic equations. *Publ. Res. Inst. Math. Sci.* **1972**, *8*, 211–229. [CrossRef]
15. Levine, H.A. Instability and nonexistence of global solutions to nonlinear wave equations of the form $Pu_{tt} = -Au + \mathcal{F}(u)$. *Tran. Am. Math. Soc.* **1974**, *192*, 2076–2091.
16. Levine, H.A. Some additional remarks on the nonexistence of global solutions to nonlinear wave equations. *SIAM J. Math. Anal.* **1974**, *4*, 138–146. [CrossRef]
17. Dong, Z.; Zhou, J. Global existence and finite time blow-up for a class of thin-film equation. *Z. Angew. Math. Phys.* **2017**, *68*, 89. [CrossRef]
18. Feng, M.; Zhou, J. Global existence and blow-up of solutions to a nonlocal parabolic equation with singular potential. *J. Math. Anal. Appl.* **2018**, *464*, 1213–1242. [CrossRef]
19. Ding, H.; Zhou, J. Global existence and blow-Up for a parabolic problem of kirchhoff type with logarithmic nonlinearity. *Appl. Math. Optim.* **2021**, *83*, 1651–1707. [CrossRef]
20. Guo, B.; Ding, H.; Wang, R.; Zhou, J. Blowup for a Kirchhoff-type parabolic equation with logarithmic nonlinearity. *Anal. Appl.* **2022**, *20*, 1089–1101. [CrossRef]
21. Xu, R.; Su, J. Global existence and finite time blow-up for a class of semilinear pseudo-parabolic equations. *J. Funct. Anal.* **2013**, *264*, 2732–2763. [CrossRef]
22. Chen, H.; Tian, S. Initial boundary value problem for a class of semilinear pseudo-parabolic equations with logarithmic nonlinearity. *J. Diff. Equ.* **2015**, *258*, 4424–4442. [CrossRef]
23. Le, C.N.; Le, X.T. Global solution and blow-up for a class of pseudo p-Laplacian evolution equations with logarithmic nonlinearity. *Comp. Math. Appl.* **2017**, *73*, 2076–2091.
24. Truong, L. The Nehari manifold for functional p Laplacian equation with logarithmic nonlinearity on whole space. *Comp. Math. Appl.* **2019**, *78*, 3931–3940. [CrossRef]
25. Ardila, A.; Alex, H. Existence and stability of standing waves for nonlinear fractional Schrodinger equation with logarithmic nonlinearity. *Nonl. Anal.* **2017**, *155*, 52–64. [CrossRef]
26. Fiscella, A.; Servadei, R.; Valdinoci, E. Density properties for fractional Sobolev spaces. *Ann. Acad. Sci. Fenn. Math.* **2015**, *40*, 235–253. [CrossRef]
27. Servadei, R.; Valdinoci, E. Mountain pass solutions for non-local elliptic operators. *J. Math. Anal. Appl.* **2012**, *389*, 887–898. [CrossRef]
28. Kalantarov, V.K.; Ladyzhenskaya, O.A. The occurrence of collapse for quasilinear equations of parabolic and hyperbolic types. *J. Math. Sci.* **1978**, *10*, 53–70. [CrossRef]
29. Cockburn, B.; Shu, C. The local discontinuous Galerkin method for time-dependent convection-diffusion systems. *SIAM J. Numer. Anal.* **1997**, *35*, 2440–2463. [CrossRef]
30. Fu, Y.Q.; Pan, N. Existence of solutions for nonlinear parabolic problems with $p(x)$-growth. *J. Math. Anal. Appl.* **2010**, *362*, 313–326. [CrossRef]
31. Liu, W.J.; Yu, J.; Li, G. Global existence, exponential decay and blow-up of solutions for a class of fractional pseudo-parabolic equations with logarithmic nonlinearity. *Am. Inst. Math. Sci.* **2021**, *14*, 4337–4366. [CrossRef]

Article

Multiplicity Results of Solutions to the Double Phase Problems of Schrödinger–Kirchhoff Type with Concave–Convex Nonlinearities

Yun-Ho Kim *,† and Taek-Jun Jeong †

Department of Mathematics Education, Sangmyung University, Seoul 03016, Republic of Korea; 201811425@sangmyung.kr
* Correspondence: kyh1213@smu.ac.kr
† These authors contributed equally to this work.

Abstract: The present paper is devoted to establishing several existence results for infinitely many solutions to Schrödinger–Kirchhoff-type double phase problems with concave–convex nonlinearities. The first aim is to demonstrate the existence of a sequence of infinitely many large-energy solutions by applying the fountain theorem as the main tool. The second aim is to obtain that our problem admits a sequence of infinitely many small-energy solutions. To obtain these results, we utilize the dual fountain theorem. In addition, we prove the existence of a sequence of infinitely many weak solutions converging to 0 in L^∞-space. To derive this result, we exploit the dual fountain theorem and the modified functional method.

Keywords: Kirchhoff function; double phase problems; Musielak–Orlicz–Sobolev spaces; multiple solutions; variational methods

MSC: 35B38; 35D30; 35J10; 35J20; 35J62

1. Introduction

In this paper, we demonstrate the existence of multiple solutions for the following double phase problem in $\mathbb{R}^N$:

$$-M\left(\int_{\mathbb{R}^N} \frac{1}{p}|\nabla w|^p + \frac{\nu(y)}{q}|\nabla w|^q\,dy\right)\mathrm{div}(|\nabla w|^{p-2}\nabla w + \nu(y)|\nabla w|^{q-2}\nabla w)$$
$$+ \mathfrak{V}(y)(|w|^{p-2}w + \nu(y)|w|^{q-2}w) = \sigma(y)|w|^{r-2}w + \theta g(y,w) \quad \text{in } \mathbb{R}^N, \quad (1)$$

where $N \geq 2$, $1 < p < q < N$, $1 < r < p$, θ is a positive real parameter, $g : \mathbb{R}^N \times \mathbb{R} \to \mathbb{R}$ is a Carathéodory function,

$$\frac{q}{p} \leq 1 + \frac{1}{N}, \quad \nu : \mathbb{R}^N \to [0,\infty) \text{ is Lipschitz continuous},$$

and $\mathfrak{V} : \mathbb{R}^N \to (0,\infty)$ is a potential function satisfying

(V) $\mathfrak{V} \in C(\mathbb{R}^N)$, $\mathrm{ess\,inf}_{y\in\mathbb{R}^N}\mathfrak{V}(y) > 0$, and $\mathrm{meas}\{y \in \mathbb{R}^N : \mathfrak{V}(y) \leq \mathcal{V}_0\} < +\infty$, for all $\mathcal{V}_0 \in \mathbb{R}$.

Furthermore, let us assume that a Kirchhoff function $M : \mathbb{R}_0^+ \to \mathbb{R}^+$ satisfies the following conditions:

(M1) $M \in C(\mathbb{R}^+)$ fulfills $\inf_{\zeta \in \mathbb{R}^+} M(\zeta) \geq \kappa_0 > 0$, where κ_0 is a constant;

(M2) There exists a constant $\vartheta \geq 1$ such that $\vartheta\mathcal{M}(\zeta) = \vartheta \int_0^\zeta M(\tau)d\tau \geq M(\zeta)\zeta$ for $\zeta \geq 0$.

The double phase operator, which is the natural generalization of the p-Laplace operator, has been studied extensively by many researchers. The research interest in differential

Citation: Kim, Y.-H.; Jeong, T.-J. Multiplicity Results of Solutions to the Double Phase Problems of Schrödinger–Kirchhoff Type with Concave–Convex Nonlinearities. *Mathematics* **2024**, *12*, 60. https://doi.org/10.3390/math12010060

Academic Editors: Lingju Kong and Min Wang

Received: 22 November 2023
Revised: 19 December 2023
Accepted: 21 December 2023
Published: 24 December 2023

Copyright: © 2023 by the authors. Licensee MDPI, Basel, Switzerland. This article is an open access article distributed under the terms and conditions of the Creative Commons Attribution (CC BY) license (https:// creativecommons.org/licenses/by/ 4.0/).

equations and variational problems with double phase operators can be regarded as a key factor in diverse fields of mathematical physics, such as strongly anisotropic materials, the Lavrentiev phenomenon, plasma physics, biophysics, chemical reactions, etc.; for more information, see [1,2]. In relation to regularity theory for double phase functionals, there is a series of remarkable papers by Mingione et al. [3–8]. Eigenvalue problems for a class of double phase variational integrals driven by Dirichlet double phase operators have been dealt with [9]. A study on a remarkable existence result of solutions to quasilinear equations involving a general variable exponent elliptic operator was investigated in the recent work by Zhang and Radulescu [10]. Recently, the authors in [11] provided a new class of double phase operators with variable exponents. As its application, they gave the existence and uniqueness results for quasilinear elliptic equations with a convection term. Other existence results for double phase problems can be found in the papers [12,13].

The study of elliptic problems with the non-local Kirchhoff term was initially introduced by Kirchhoff [14] in order to study an extension of the classical d'Alembert's wave equation by taking into account the changes to the lengths of strings during vibration. The variational problems of the Kirchhoff type have had influence in various applications in physics and have been intensively investigated by many researchers in recent years; for examples, see [15–28] and the references therein. A detailed discussion about the physical implications based on the fractional Kirchhoff model was initially suggested by the work of Fiscella and Valdinoci [20]. They derived the existence of non-trivial solutions by taking advantage of the mountain-pass theorem and a truncation argument on a non-local Kirchhoff term. In particular, the conditions imposed on the non-degenerated Kirchhoff function $M : \mathbb{R}_0^+ \to \mathbb{R}_0^+$ were that M is an increasing and continuous function with (M1); also, see [24] and references therein. However, this increasing condition eliminated the case that is not monotone; for example,

$$M(\zeta) = (1+\zeta)^k + (1+\zeta)^{-1} \text{ with } 0 < k < 1$$

for all $\zeta \in \mathbb{R}_0^+$. In this regard, the existence of multiple solutions to a class of Schrödinger–Kirchhoff-type equations involving the fractional p-Laplacian was provided by reference [25] when the Kirchhoff function M is continuous and satisfies (M1) and the condition:

(M3) For $0 < s < 1$, there is $\vartheta \in [1, \frac{N}{N-sp})$ such that $\vartheta \mathcal{M}(\zeta) \geq M(\zeta)\zeta$ for any $\zeta \geq 0$.

We also referred to [15,16,25–29] for recent results.

Recently, the authors of [22] studied the existence result of a positive ground-state solution for an elliptic problem of the Kirchhoff type with critical exponential growth under the following condition:

(M4) There exists $\vartheta > 1$ such that $\frac{M(\zeta)}{\zeta^{\vartheta-1}}$ is non-increasing for $\zeta > 0$.

From this condition and direct computation, we immediately recognize that $\vartheta \mathcal{M}(\zeta) - M(\zeta)\zeta$ is non-decreasing for all $\zeta \geq 0$, and thus, this implies the condition (M2). A typical model for the Kirchhoff function M satisfying (M2) is given by $M(\zeta) = 1 + a\zeta^{\vartheta}$, with $a \geq 0$ for all $\zeta \geq 0$. Hence, the condition (M2) includes this classical example as well as cases that are not monotone. Under this condition, the authors of [18] obtained multiplicity results for certain classes of double phase problems of the Kirchhoff type with nonlinear boundary conditions; also, see [19] for the Dirichlet boundary condition. For these reasons, the nonlinear elliptic equations with a Kirchhoff coefficient satisfying (M2) have been comprehensively investigated by many researchers in recent years [15,17–19,21,25,27,28].

The main aim of the present paper is to provide several multiplicity results of solutions for Schrödinger–Kirchhoff-type problems involving a double phase operator for the combined effect of concave–convex nonlinearities. In this paper, we first discuss that Problem (1) has infinitely many large-energy solutions. Second, we demonstrate the existence of a sequence of infinitely many small-energy solutions. Finally, we provide the existence of a sequence of infinitely many weak solutions converging to 0 in L^∞-space. To derive such results, we exploit the fountain theorem, the dual fountain theorem, and the modified functional method as the main tools. The present paper is motivated by recent work in [30,31]. Moreover, the authors of [30] obtained multiplicity results to the double phase problem as follows:

$$-\text{div}(|\nabla u|^{p-2}\nabla u + \nu(y)|\nabla u|^{q-2}\nabla u) + \mathfrak{V}(y)(|u|^{p-2}u + \nu(y)|u|^{q-2}u)$$
$$= \lambda\sigma(y)|w|^{r-2}w + g(y,u) \text{ in } \mathbb{R}^N,$$

where $\mathfrak{V} : \mathbb{R}^N \to (0,\infty)$ is a potential function satisfying (V) and $g : \mathbb{R}^N \times \mathbb{R} \to \mathbb{R}$ fulfills the Carathéodory condition. In particular, in the work [30], the authors obtained the existence of a sequence of small-energy solutions under specific conditions of the nonlinear term that were different from those in previous studies [23,32–37]. More precisely, in view of [32–35], the conditions of the nonlinear term g near zero as well as at infinity were decisive for proving the hypotheses in the dual-fountain theorem. However, the authors also ensured the hypotheses when the behavior at infinity was not assumed, and the condition near zero—namely, $g(y,\zeta) = o(|\zeta|^{p-2}\zeta)$ as $|\zeta| \to 0$ uniformly for all $y \in \mathbb{R}^N$—was replaced by (G4), which is discussed in Section 2. Although this study is inspired by [30,31], the presence of the non-local Kirchhoff coefficient M required more complicated analyses that had to be performed meticulously. In particular, one of the key ingredients to obtain this multiplicity result in [30,31] is that the potential function $V \in C(\mathbb{R}^N,(0,\infty))$ is coercive: that is, $\lim_{|x|\to\infty} V(x) = +\infty$, which is crucial to guarantee the compactness condition of the Palais–Smale type. However, in order to prove this condition, we employ a weaker condition (V) than the coercivity of the function V. Therefore, in this study, we develop a multiplicity result for double phase problems of the Kirchhoff type under various conditions on the convex term g.

Our multiplicity result of infinitely many small-energy solutions converging to 0 in L^∞-space is motivated by [38–42]. However, in contrast to [38,41,42], we utilize the dual-fountain theorem instead of the global variational formulation in [43]. This multiplicity result yielding small-energy solutions for variational elliptic equations based on the dual fountain theorem does not guarantee the boundedness of the solutions. For this reason, the authors of [39,40] combined the modified functional method with the dual-fountain theorem in order to demonstrate the existence of multiple small-energy solutions converging to zero in L^∞-space. In this direction, our final result is based on recent research [39,40]. However, our approach differs from [40] when validating a condition in the dual fountain theorem, as shown in the Section 4. Furthermore, we have to carry out more complicated analyses than those in [39]: not only because our problem has the Kirchhoff coefficient M but also because the given domain is the whole space $\mathbb{R}^N$.

The outline of this paper is as follows. We present necessary preliminary knowledge of function spaces for the present paper. Next, we provide the variational framework related to problem (1), and then we establish various existence results of infinitely many nontrivial solutions to the Kirchhoff-type double phase equations with concave–convex-type nonlinearities under certain conditions on g.

2. Preliminaries

In this section, we briefly discuss the definitions and the essential properties of Musielak–Orlicz–Sobolev space. For more in-depth examinations of these spaces, we refer to [9,44–46].

The functions $\mathcal{H} : \mathbb{R}^N \times [0,\infty) \to [0,\infty)$ and $\mathcal{H}_{\mathfrak{V}} : \mathbb{R}^N \times [0,\infty) \to [0,\infty)$ are defined as follows:

$$\mathcal{H}(y,\zeta) := \zeta^p + \nu(y)\zeta^q, \quad \mathcal{H}_{\mathfrak{V}}(y,\zeta) := \mathfrak{V}(y)(\zeta^p + \nu(y)\zeta^q) \tag{2}$$

For almost all $y \in \mathbb{R}^N$ and for any $\zeta \in [0,\infty)$ with $1 < p < q$,

$$\frac{q}{p} \le 1 + \frac{1}{N}, \quad \nu : \mathbb{R}^N \to [0,\infty) \text{ is Lipschitz continuous,}$$

and $\mathfrak{V} : \mathbb{R}^N \to \mathbb{R}$ is a function satisfying (V).

We define the Musielak–Orlicz space $L^{\mathcal{H}}(\mathbb{R}^N)$ as

$$L^{\mathcal{H}}(\mathbb{R}^N) := \Big\{ v : \mathbb{R}^N \to \mathbb{R} \text{ is measurable} : \ \varsigma_{\mathcal{H}}(v) < \infty \Big\},$$

induced by the Luxemburg norm

$$\|v\|_{\mathcal{H}} := \inf\Big\{ \lambda > 0 : \ \varsigma_{\mathcal{H}}\Big(y, \Big|\frac{v}{\lambda}\Big|\Big) \le 1 \Big\},$$

where $\varsigma_{\mathcal{H}}$ denotes the $\mathcal{H}$-modular function with

$$\varsigma_{\mathcal{H}}(v) := \int_{\mathbb{R}^N} \mathcal{H}(y, |v|) dy. \tag{3}$$

If we replace $\mathcal{H}$ with $\mathcal{H}_{\mathfrak{V}}$, we obtain the definition of the Musielak–Orlicz space $(L_{\mathcal{H}_{\mathfrak{V}}}(\mathbb{R}^N), \|\cdot\|_{\mathcal{H}_{\mathfrak{V}}})$, i.e.,

$$L_{\mathcal{H}_{\mathfrak{V}}}(\mathbb{R}^N) := \Big\{ v : \mathbb{R}^N \to \mathbb{R} \text{ is measurable} : \ \varsigma^{\mathcal{H}}_{\mathfrak{V}}(v) < \infty \Big\},$$

induced by the Luxemburg norm

$$\|v\|_{\mathcal{H}_{\mathfrak{V}}} := \inf\Big\{ \lambda > 0 : \ \varsigma^{\mathcal{H}}_{\mathcal{V}}\Big(y, \Big|\frac{v}{\lambda}\Big|\Big) \le 1 \Big\},$$

where $\varsigma^{\mathcal{H}}_{\mathfrak{V}}$ denotes the $\mathcal{H}_{\mathfrak{V}}$-modular function as

$$\varsigma^{\mathcal{H}}_{\mathfrak{V}}(v) := \int_{\mathbb{R}^N} \mathcal{H}_{\mathfrak{V}}(y, |v|) dy. \tag{4}$$

According to [45,47], the spaces $L^{\mathcal{H}}(\mathbb{R}^N)$ and $L_{\mathcal{H}_{\mathfrak{V}}}(\mathbb{R}^N)$ are separable and reflexive Banach spaces.

Lemma 1 ([47]). *For $\varsigma^{\mathcal{H}}_{\mathfrak{V}}(v)$ given in* (4) *and $v \in L_{\mathcal{H}_{\mathfrak{V}}}(\mathbb{R}^N)$, we have:*
(i) *for $v \neq 0$, $\|v\|_{\mathcal{H}_{\mathfrak{V}}} = \lambda$ iff $\varsigma^{\mathcal{H}}_{\mathfrak{V}}(\frac{v}{\lambda}) = 1$;*
(ii) *$\|v\|_{\mathcal{H}_{\mathfrak{V}}} < 1 (= 1; > 1)$ iff $\varsigma^{\mathcal{H}}_{\mathfrak{V}}(v) < 1 (= 1; > 1)$;*
(iii) *if $\|v\|_{\mathcal{H}_{\mathfrak{V}}} > 1$, then $\|v\|^p_{\mathcal{H}_{\mathfrak{V}}} \le \varsigma^{\mathcal{H}}_{\mathfrak{V}}(v) \le \|v\|^q_{\mathcal{H}_{\mathfrak{V}}}$;*
(iv) *if $\|v\|_{\mathcal{H}_{\mathfrak{V}}} < 1$, then $\|v\|^q_{\mathcal{H}_{\mathfrak{V}}} \le \varsigma^{\mathcal{H}}_{\mathfrak{V}}(v) \le \|v\|^p_{\mathcal{H}_{\mathfrak{V}}}$.*
Furthermore, analogous results hold for $\varsigma_{\mathcal{H}}(u)$, given in (3), *and $\|\cdot\|_{\mathcal{H}}$.*

The weighted Musielak–Orlicz–Sobolev space $W^{1,\mathcal{H}}_{\mathfrak{V}}(\mathbb{R}^N)$ is defined by

$$W^{1,\mathcal{H}}_{\mathfrak{V}}(\mathbb{R}^N) = \{ v \in L_{\mathcal{H}_{\mathfrak{V}}}(\mathbb{R}^N) : |\nabla v| \in L^{\mathcal{H}}(\mathbb{R}^N) \}.$$

Then, it is provided with the following norm:

$$\|v\| = \|\nabla v\|_{\mathcal{H}} + \|v\|_{\mathcal{H}_{\mathfrak{V}}}.$$

Note that $W^{1,\mathcal{H}}_{\mathfrak{V}}(\mathbb{R}^N)$ is a separable reflexive Banach space [45]. In the following calculations, the notation $E \hookrightarrow F$ indicates that space E is *continuously* embedded into space F, while $E \hookrightarrow\hookrightarrow F$ denotes that E is *compactly* embedded into F.

According to Lemma 1, we obtain the following results:

Lemma 2 ([47]). *The following embeddings hold:*
(i) $L_{\mathcal{H}_{\mathfrak{V}}}(\mathbb{R}^N) \hookrightarrow L^{\mathcal{H}}(\mathbb{R}^N)$;
(ii) $W^{1,\mathcal{H}}_{\mathfrak{V}}(\mathbb{R}^N) \hookrightarrow L^{\tau}(\mathbb{R}^N)$ *for* $\tau \in [p, p^*]$;

(iii) $W^{1,\mathcal{H}}_{\mathfrak{V}}(\mathbb{R}^N) \hookrightarrow\hookrightarrow L^{\tau}(\mathbb{R}^N)$ *for* $\tau \in [p, p^*)$.

Lemma 3 ([47]). *Let*

$$A(v) := \int_{\mathbb{R}^N} \mathcal{H}(y, |\nabla v|)dy + \int_{\mathbb{R}^N} \mathcal{H}_{\mathfrak{V}}(y, |v|)dy.$$

Then, the following properties hold:

(i) $A(v) \leq \|v\|^p + \|v\|^q$ *for all* $v \in W^{1,\mathcal{H}}_{\mathfrak{V}}(\mathbb{R}^N)$;
(ii) *If* $\|v\| \leq 1$, *then* $2^{1-q}\|v\|^q \leq A(v) \leq \|v\|^p$;
(iii) *If* $\|v\| \geq 1$, *then* $2^{-p}\|v\|^p \leq A(v) \leq 2\|v\|^q$.

Let us define the functional $\Phi : \mathfrak{E} := W^{1,\mathcal{H}}_{\mathfrak{V}}(\mathbb{R}^N) \to \mathbb{R}$ by

$$\Phi(w) = \mathcal{M}\left(\int_{\mathbb{R}^N} \mathcal{H}_{p,q}(y, |\nabla w|)\, dy\right) + \int_{\mathbb{R}^N} \mathcal{H}_{\mathfrak{V},p,q}(y, |w|)\, dy,$$

where the functions $\mathcal{H}_{p,q} : \mathbb{R}^N \times [0, \infty) \to [0, \infty)$ and $\mathcal{H}_{\mathfrak{V},p,q} : \mathbb{R}^N \times [0, \infty) \to [0, \infty)$ are defined as

$$\mathcal{H}_{p,q}(y, \zeta) := \frac{1}{p}\zeta^p + \frac{\nu(y)}{q}\zeta^q \quad \text{and} \quad \mathcal{H}_{\mathfrak{V},p,q}(y, \zeta) := \mathfrak{V}(y)\left(\frac{1}{p}\zeta^p + \frac{\nu(y)}{q}\zeta^q\right).$$

Then, it is standard to check that $\Phi \in C^1(\mathfrak{E}, \mathbb{R})$, and its Fréchet derivative $\Phi' : \mathfrak{E} \to \mathfrak{E}^*$ is defined as follows:

$$\begin{aligned}\langle \Phi'(w), v\rangle =& M\left(\int_{\mathbb{R}^N} \mathcal{H}_{p,q}(y, |\nabla w|)\, dy\right) \int_{\mathbb{R}^N} (|\nabla w|^{p-2}\nabla w \cdot \nabla v + \nu(y)|\nabla w|^{q-2}\nabla w \cdot \nabla v)\, dy \\ &+ \int_{\mathbb{R}^N} \mathfrak{V}(y)(|w|^{p-2}wv + \nu(y)|w|^{q-2}wv)\, dy\end{aligned}$$

for all $w, v \in \mathfrak{E}$, where $\mathfrak{E}^*$ denotes the dual space of $\mathfrak{E}$, and $\langle \cdot, \cdot \rangle$ denotes the pairing between $\mathfrak{E}$ and $\mathfrak{E}^*$.

Throughout this paper, the Kirchhoff function M satisfies the conditions (M1)–(M2), and the potential $\mathfrak{V}$ fulfills the condition (V).

Definition 1. *We say that* $w \in \mathfrak{E}$ *is a weak solution for Problem* (1) *if*

$$\begin{aligned}&M\left(\int_{\mathbb{R}^N} \mathcal{H}_{p,q}(y, |\nabla w|)\, dy\right) \int_{\mathbb{R}^N} (|\nabla w|^{p-2}\nabla w \cdot \nabla u + \nu(y)|\nabla w|^{q-2}\nabla w \cdot \nabla u)\, dy \\ &+ \int_{\mathbb{R}^N} \mathfrak{V}(y)(|w|^{p-2}wu + \nu(y)|w|^{q-2}wu)\, dy = \int_{\mathbb{R}^N} \sigma(y)|w|^{r-2}wu\, dy + \theta \int_{\mathbb{R}^N} g(y, w)u\, dy\end{aligned}$$

for any $u \in \mathfrak{E}$.

We assume the following:

(B1) $1 < r < p < q < \ell < p^*$;
(B2) $0 \leq \sigma \in L^{\frac{\gamma_0}{\gamma_0 - r}}(\mathbb{R}^N) \cap L^{\infty}(\mathbb{R}^N)$ with meas $\{y \in \mathbb{R}^N : \sigma(y) \neq 0\} > 0$ for any γ_0 with $p < \gamma_0 < p^*$;
(G1) $g : \mathbb{R}^N \times \mathbb{R} \to \mathbb{R}$ satisfies the Carathéodory condition, and there is an $s \in [p, p^*)$, $0 \leq \rho_1 \in L^{s'}(\mathbb{R}^N) \cap L^{\infty}(\mathbb{R}^N)$ and a positive constant ρ_2 such that

$$|g(y, \zeta)| \leq \rho_1(y) + \rho_2|\zeta|^{\ell-1}$$

for all $\zeta \in \mathbb{R}$ and for almost all $y \in \mathbb{R}^N$;

(G2) There exist $\mu > \vartheta q$ and $\mathfrak{M}_0 > 0$ such that

$$g(y,\zeta)\zeta - \mu G(y,\zeta) \geq 0$$

for all $(y,\zeta) \in \mathbb{R}^N \times \mathbb{R}$ with $|\zeta| \geq \mathfrak{M}_0$ where $G(y,\zeta) = \int_0^\zeta g(y,s)\,ds$;

(G3) There exist $\mu > \vartheta q$, $\varsigma \geq 0$, and $\mathfrak{M}_1 > 0$ such that

$$g(y,\zeta)\zeta - \mu G(y,\zeta) \geq -\varsigma|\zeta|^p$$

for all $(y,\zeta) \in \mathbb{R}^N \times \mathbb{R}$ with $|\zeta| \geq \mathfrak{M}_1$;

(G4) There exist $\mathfrak{M}_2 > 0$, $1 < d < p$, $\tau > 1$ with $p \leq \tau' d \leq p^*$, and a positive function $\xi \in L^\tau(\mathbb{R}^N) \cap L^\infty(\mathbb{R}^N)$ such that

$$\liminf_{|\zeta|\to 0} \frac{g(y,\zeta)}{\xi(y)|\zeta|^{d-2}\zeta} \geq \mathfrak{M}_2$$

uniformly for almost all $y \in \mathbb{R}^N$.

Remark 1. *It is clear that the condition* (G3) *is weaker than* (G2), *which was initially provided by [48]. If we consider the function*

$$g(y,\zeta) = \rho(y)\left(\xi(y)|\zeta|^{d-2}\zeta + |\zeta|^{p-2}\zeta + \frac{2}{p}\sin\zeta\right)$$

with its primitive function

$$G(y,\zeta) = \rho(y)\left(\frac{\xi(y)}{d}|\zeta|^d + \frac{1}{p}|\zeta|^p - \frac{2}{p}\cos\zeta + \frac{2}{p}\right),$$

where $\rho \in C(\mathbb{R}^N,\mathbb{R})$ *with* $0 < \inf_{y\in\mathbb{R}^N}\rho(y) \leq \sup_{y\in\mathbb{R}^N}\rho(y) < \infty$, *and* d, ξ *are given in* (G4), *then it is obvious that this example satisfies the condition* (G3) *but not* (G2). *However, the conditions* (G1) *and* (G4) *are also satisfied.*

Let us define the functional $\Psi_\theta : \mathfrak{E} \to \mathbb{R}$ as

$$\Psi_\theta(w) = \frac{1}{r}\int_{\mathbb{R}^N} \sigma(y)|w|^r\,dy + \theta\int_{\mathbb{R}^N} G(y,w)\,dy.$$

Then, it is easy to show that $\Psi_\theta \in C^1(\mathfrak{E},\mathbb{R})$, and its Fréchet derivative is

$$\langle \Psi'_\theta(w), z\rangle = \int_{\mathbb{R}^N} \sigma(y)|w|^{r-2}wz\,dy + \theta\int_{\mathbb{R}^N} g(y,w)z\,dy$$

for any $w,z \in \mathfrak{E}$ [47]. Next, we define the functional $\mathcal{E}_\theta : \mathfrak{E} \to \mathbb{R}$ by

$$\mathcal{E}_\theta(w) = \Phi(w) - \Psi_\theta(w).$$

Then, it follows that the functional $\mathcal{E}_\theta \in C^1(\mathfrak{E},\mathbb{R})$ and its Fréchet derivative is:

$$\langle \mathcal{E}'_\theta(w), z\rangle = \langle \Phi'(w), z\rangle - \langle \Psi'_\theta(w), z\rangle \quad \text{for any } w,z \in \mathfrak{E}.$$

Before describing the proofs of our results, we present several preliminary assertions.

Lemma 4 ([47]). *Assume that* (B1), (B2), *and* (G1) *hold. Then,* Ψ_θ *and* Ψ'_θ *are sequentially weakly strongly continuous.*

Definition 2. *Suppose that* $\mathfrak{X}$ *is a real Banach space. We say that the functional* $\mathcal{F}$ *satisfies the Cerami condition at level* c *(*$(C)_c$*-condition for short) in* $\mathfrak{X}$ *if any* $(C)_c$*-sequence* $\{w_n\} \subset \mathfrak{X}$, *i.e.,* $\mathcal{F}(w_n) \to c$ *and* $\|\mathcal{F}'(w_n)\|_{\mathfrak{X}^*}(1+\|w_n\|_{\mathfrak{X}}) \to 0$ *as* $n \to \infty$ *has a convergent subsequence in* $\mathfrak{X}$.

The following Lemmas 5 and 6 are the compactness condition for the Palais–Smale type that play a crucial role in obtaining our main results. The basic concepts behind the proofs of these logical consequences follows the analogous arguments in [30]. However, more complicated analyses have to be carried out because of the presence of the non-local Kirchhoff coefficient M.

Remark 2. *The basic concepts of the proofs for the following logical consequences use similar arguments to those in [30,31]. From this point of view, it is important that the potential function* $V \in C(\mathbb{R}^N, (0,\infty))$ *is coercive. As mentioned in the introduction, we show this condition without assuming the coercivity of the function* V.

Lemma 5. *Suppose that* (B1), (B2), (G1), *and* (G2) *hold. Then, the functional* $\mathcal{E}_\theta$ *ensures the* $(C)_c$*-condition for any* $\theta > 0$.

Proof. For $c \in \mathbb{R}$, let $\{w_n\}$ be a $(C)_c$-sequence in $\mathfrak{E}$, i.e.,

$$\mathcal{E}_\theta(w_n) \to c \text{ and } \|\mathcal{E}_\theta'(w_n)\|_{\mathfrak{X}^*}(1+\|w_n\|_{\mathfrak{X}}) \to 0 \text{ as } n \to \infty, \tag{5}$$

which show that

$$c = \mathcal{E}_\theta(w_n) + o(1) \text{ and } \langle \mathcal{E}_\theta(w_n), w_n \rangle = o(1), \tag{6}$$

where $o(1) \to 0$ as $n \to \infty$. Firstly, we verify that the sequence $\{w_n\}$ is bounded in $\mathfrak{E}$. To do this, we claim that

$$\begin{aligned} &\left(\frac{1}{\vartheta q} - \frac{1}{\mu}\right) \int_{\mathbb{R}^N} \mathcal{H}_{\mathfrak{V}}(y, |w_n|)\, dy - C_1 \int_{\{|w_n| \le \mathfrak{M}_0\}} |w_n|^p + \rho_1(y)|w_n| + \rho_2 |w_n|^\ell \, dy \\ &\geq \frac{1}{2}\left(\frac{1}{\vartheta q} - \frac{1}{\mu}\right) \int_{\mathbb{R}^N} \mathcal{H}_{\mathfrak{V}}(y, |w_n|)\, dy - \mathcal{K}_0 \end{aligned} \tag{7}$$

for any positive constant C_1 and for some positive constant $\mathcal{K}_0$, where $\mathcal{H}_{\mathfrak{V}}$, as given in (2). Indeed, without the loss of generality, we suppose that $\mathfrak{M}_0 > 1$. By Young's inequality, we know that

$$\begin{aligned} &\left(\frac{1}{\vartheta q} - \frac{1}{\mu}\right) \int_{\mathbb{R}^N} \mathcal{H}_{\mathfrak{V}}(y, |w_n|)\, dy \\ &- C_1 \int_{\{|w_n| \le \mathfrak{M}_0\}} (|w_n|^p + \rho_1(y)|w_n| + \rho_2 |w_n|^\ell)\, dy \\ &\geq \left(\frac{1}{\vartheta q} - \frac{1}{\mu}\right) \int_{\mathbb{R}^N} \mathcal{H}_{\mathfrak{V}}(y, |w_n|)\, dy \\ &- C_1 \int_{\{|w_n| \le \mathfrak{M}_0\}} \left(|w_n|^p + \rho_1^{s'}(y) + |w_n|^s + \rho_2 |w_n|^\ell\right) dy \\ &\geq \frac{1}{2}\left(\frac{1}{\vartheta q} - \frac{1}{\mu}\right) \left[\int_{\mathbb{R}^N} \mathcal{H}_{\mathfrak{V}}(y, |w_n|)\, dy + \int_{\{|w_n| \le \mathfrak{M}_0\}} \mathcal{H}_{\mathfrak{V}}(y, |w_n|)\, dy\right] \\ &- C_1 \int_{\{|w_n| \le 1\}} \left(|w_n|^p + |w_n|^s + \rho_2 |w_n|^\ell\right) dy \\ &- C_1 \int_{\{1 < |w_n| \le \mathfrak{M}_0\}} \left(|w_n|^p + |w_n|^s + \rho_2 |w_n|^\ell\right) dy - C_1 \|\rho_1\|_{L^{s'}(\mathbb{R}^N)}^{s'} \\ &\geq \frac{1}{2}\left(\frac{1}{\vartheta q} - \frac{1}{\mu}\right) \left[\int_{\mathbb{R}^N} \mathcal{H}_{\mathfrak{V}}(y, |w_n|)\, dy + \int_{\{|w_n| \le \mathfrak{M}_0\}} \mathcal{H}_{\mathfrak{V}}(y, |w_n|)\, dy\right] \\ &- C_1(2+\rho_2) \int_{\{|w_n| \le 1\}} |w_n|^p \, dy - C_1 \|\rho_1\|_{L^{s'}(\mathbb{R}^N)}^{s'} \end{aligned} \tag{8}$$

$$
\begin{aligned}
&- C_1\Big(1+\mathfrak{M}_0{}^{s-p}+\mathfrak{M}_0{}^{\ell-p}\rho_2\Big)\int_{\{1<|w_n|\le\mathfrak{M}_0\}}|w_n|^p\,dy\\
&\ge \frac{1}{2}\Big(\frac{1}{\vartheta q}-\frac{1}{\mu}\Big)\Big[\int_{\mathbb{R}^N}\mathcal{H}_{\mathfrak{V}}(y,|w_n|)\,dy+\int_{\{|w_n|\le\mathfrak{M}_0\}}\mathcal{H}_{\mathfrak{V}}(y,|w_n|)\,dy\Big]\\
&- C_1(2+\rho_2)\int_{\{|w_n|\le 1\}}\mathcal{H}(y,|w_n|)\,dy - C_1\|\rho_1\|_{L^{s'}(\mathbb{R}^N)}^{s'}\\
&- C_1\Big(1+\mathfrak{M}_0{}^{s-p}+\mathfrak{M}_0{}^{\ell-p}\rho_2\Big)\int_{\{1<|w_n|\le\mathfrak{M}_0\}}\mathcal{H}(y,|w_n|)\,dy\\
&\ge \frac{1}{2}\Big(\frac{1}{\vartheta q}-\frac{1}{\mu}\Big)\Big[\int_{\mathbb{R}^N}\mathcal{H}_{\mathfrak{V}}(y,|w_n|)\,dy+\int_{\{|w_n|\le\mathfrak{M}_0\}}\mathcal{H}_{\mathfrak{V}}(y,|w_n|)\,dy\Big]\\
&- \widetilde{C}_0\int_{\{|w_n|\le\mathfrak{M}_0\}}\mathcal{H}(y,|w_n|)\,dy-\widetilde{C}_1,
\end{aligned}
$$

where $\mathcal{H}$, as given in (2), $\widetilde{C}_0 := C_1\Big(1+\mathfrak{M}_0{}^{s-p}+\mathfrak{M}_0{}^{\ell-p}\rho_2\Big)$. and $\widetilde{C}_1 := C_1\|\rho_1\|_{L^{s'}(\mathbb{R}^N)}^{s'}$. We set

$$\mathbb{B}_{r_0}=\{y\in\mathbb{R}^N:|y|<r_0\},\quad \mathcal{A}=\{y\in\mathbb{R}^N\setminus\mathbb{B}_{r_0}:\mathfrak{V}(y)\ge\mathcal{V}_0\}$$

and

$$\mathcal{B}=\{y\in\mathbb{R}^N\setminus\mathbb{B}_{r_0}:\mathfrak{V}(y)<\mathcal{V}_0\}$$

for any $\mathcal{V}_0>0$. Then, it is clear that $\mathcal{A}\cup\mathcal{B}=\mathbb{B}_{r_0}^c$, where $\mathcal{A}$ and $\mathcal{B}$ are disjoint. If $y\in\mathcal{A}$, then for any $\mathcal{V}_0\ge\frac{2\vartheta q\mu\widetilde{C}_0}{\mu-\vartheta q}$, we know that

$$\mathcal{H}_{\mathfrak{V}}(y,|w_n|)\ge\frac{2\vartheta q\mu\widetilde{C}_0}{\mu-\vartheta q}\mathcal{H}(y,|w_n|)\tag{9}$$

for $|y|\ge r_0$. Furthermore, since $\mathfrak{V}\in L^1(\mathbb{B}_{r_0})$, we infer

$$\int_{\{|w_n|\le\mathfrak{M}_0\}\cap\mathbb{B}_{r_0}}\mathcal{H}_{\mathfrak{V}}(y,|w_n|)\,dy<+\infty\quad\text{and}\quad\int_{\{|w_n|\le\mathfrak{M}_0\}\cap\mathbb{B}_{r_0}}\mathcal{H}(y,|w_n|)\,dy<+\infty\tag{10}$$

for some positive constants $\widetilde{C}_2,\widetilde{C}_3$. Using (V), we know $\operatorname{meas}\big(\{y\in\mathbb{R}^N:|w_n(y)|\le\mathfrak{M}_0\}\cap\mathcal{B}\big)$ is finite, and thus,

$$\int_{\{|w_n|\le\mathfrak{M}_0\}\cap\mathcal{B}}\mathcal{H}_{\mathfrak{V}}(y,|w_n|)\,dy<+\infty\quad\text{and}\quad\int_{\{|w_n|\le\mathfrak{M}_0\}\cap\mathcal{B}}\mathcal{H}(y,|w_n|)\,dy<+\infty.\tag{11}$$

This, together with (8)–(11), yields the following:

$$
\begin{aligned}
&\Big(\frac{1}{\vartheta q}-\frac{1}{\mu}\Big)\int_{\mathbb{R}^N}\mathcal{H}_{\mathfrak{V}}(y,|w_n|)\,dy - C_1\int_{\{|w_n|\le\mathfrak{M}_0\}}(|w_n|^p+\rho_1(y)|w_n|+\rho_2|w_n|^\ell)\,dy\\
&\ge\frac{1}{2}\Big(\frac{1}{\vartheta q}-\frac{1}{\mu}\Big)\Big[\int_{\mathbb{R}^N}\mathcal{H}_{\mathfrak{V}}(y,|w_n|)\,dy+\int_{\{|w_n|\le\mathfrak{M}_0\}\cap\mathbb{B}_{r_0}^c}\mathcal{H}_{\mathfrak{V}}(y,|w_n|)\,dy\\
&\qquad+\int_{\{|w_n|\le\mathfrak{M}_0\}\cap\mathbb{B}_{r_0}}\mathcal{H}_{\mathfrak{V}}(y,|w_n|)\,dy\Big]\\
&-\widetilde{C}_0\Big[\int_{\{|w_n|\le\mathfrak{M}_0\}\cap\mathbb{B}_{r_0}^c}\mathcal{H}(y,|w_n|)\,dy+\int_{\{|w_n|\le\mathfrak{M}_0\}\cap\mathbb{B}_{r_0}}\mathcal{H}(y,|w_n|)\,dy\Big]-\widetilde{C}_1\\
&\ge\frac{1}{2}\Big(\frac{1}{\vartheta q}-\frac{1}{\mu}\Big)\Big[\int_{\mathbb{R}^N}\mathcal{H}_{\mathfrak{V}}(y,|w_n|)\,dy+\int_{\{|w_n|\le\mathfrak{M}_0\}\cap\mathcal{A}}\mathcal{H}_{\mathfrak{V}}(y,|w_n|)\,dy\\
&+\int_{\{|w_n|\le\mathfrak{M}_0\}\cap\mathcal{B}}\mathcal{H}_{\mathfrak{V}}(y,|w_n|)\,dy\Big]-\widetilde{C}_0\Big[\int_{\{|w_n|\le\mathfrak{M}_0\}\cap\mathcal{A}}\mathcal{H}(y,|w_n|)\,dy\\
&+\int_{\{|w_n|\le\mathfrak{M}_0\}\cap\mathcal{B}}\mathcal{H}(y,|w_n|)\,dy\Big]-\widetilde{\mathcal{K}}_0
\end{aligned}
$$

$$
\begin{aligned}
&\geq \frac{1}{2}\Big(\frac{1}{\vartheta q}-\frac{1}{\mu}\Big)\int_{\mathbb{R}^N}\mathcal{H}_{\mathfrak{V}}(y,|w_n|)\,dy+\frac{\mu-\vartheta q}{2\vartheta q\mu}\int_{\{|w_n|\leq\mathfrak{M}_0\}\cap\mathcal{A}}\mathcal{H}_{\mathfrak{V}}(y,|w_n|)\,dy\\
&-\widetilde{C}_0\int_{\{|w_n|\leq\mathfrak{M}_0\}\cap\mathcal{A}}\mathcal{H}(y,|w_n|)\,dy-\mathcal{K}_0\\
&\geq \frac{1}{2}\Big(\frac{1}{\vartheta q}-\frac{1}{\mu}\Big)\int_{\mathbb{R}^N}\mathcal{H}_{\mathfrak{V}}(y,|w_n|)\,dy-\mathcal{K}_0
\end{aligned}
$$

where $\widetilde{\mathcal{K}}_0$ and $\mathcal{K}_0$ are suitable constants. From this, the relation (7) is proved. Combining (7) with (B1), (B2), (G1), and (G2), we find the following:

$$
\begin{aligned}
c+1 &\geq \mathcal{E}_\theta(w_n)-\frac{1}{\mu}\langle\mathcal{E}'_\theta(w_n),w_n\rangle\\
&=\mathcal{M}\Big(\int_{\mathbb{R}^N}\mathcal{H}_{p,q}(y,|\nabla w_n|)\,dy\Big)+\int_{\mathbb{R}^N}\mathcal{H}_{\mathfrak{V},p,q}(y,|w_n|)\,dy\\
&-\frac{1}{r}\int_{\mathbb{R}^N}\sigma(y)|w_n|^r\,dy-\theta\int_{\mathbb{R}^N}G(y,w_n)\,dy\\
&-\frac{1}{\mu}M\Big(\int_{\mathbb{R}^N}\mathcal{H}_{p,q}(y,|\nabla w_n|)\,dy\Big)\int_{\mathbb{R}^N}\mathcal{H}(y,|\nabla w_n|)\,dy\\
&-\frac{1}{\mu}\int_{\mathbb{R}^N}\mathcal{H}_{\mathfrak{V}}(y,|w_n|)\,dy+\frac{1}{\mu}\int_{\mathbb{R}^N}\sigma(y)|w_n|^r\,dy+\frac{\theta}{\mu}\int_{\mathbb{R}^N}g(y,w_n)w_n\,dy\\
&\geq\frac{1}{\vartheta}M\Big(\int_{\mathbb{R}^N}\mathcal{H}_{p,q}(y,|\nabla w_n|)\,dy\Big)\int_{\mathbb{R}^N}\mathcal{H}_{p,q}(y,|\nabla w_n|)\,dy\\
&+\int_{\mathbb{R}^N}\mathcal{H}_{\mathfrak{V},p,q}(y,|w_n|)\,dy-\frac{1}{r}\int_{\mathbb{R}^N}\sigma(y)|w_n|^r\,dy-\theta\int_{\mathbb{R}^N}G(y,w_n)\,dy\\
&-\frac{1}{\mu}M\Big(\int_{\mathbb{R}^N}\mathcal{H}_{p,q}(y,|\nabla w_n|)\,dy\Big)\int_{\mathbb{R}^N}\mathcal{H}(y,|\nabla w_n|)\,dy\\
&-\frac{1}{\mu}\int_{\mathbb{R}^N}\mathcal{H}_{\mathfrak{V}}(y,|w_n|)\,dy+\frac{1}{\mu}\int_{\mathbb{R}^N}\sigma(y)|w_n|^r\,dy+\frac{\theta}{\mu}\int_{\mathbb{R}^N}g(y,w_n)w_n\,dy\\
&\geq\Big(\frac{1}{\vartheta q}-\frac{1}{\mu}\Big)M\Big(\int_{\mathbb{R}^N}\mathcal{H}_{p,q}(y,|\nabla w_n|)\,dy\Big)\int_{\mathbb{R}^N}\mathcal{H}(y,|\nabla w_n|)\,dy\\
&+\Big(\frac{1}{q}-\frac{1}{\mu}\Big)\int_{\mathbb{R}^N}\mathcal{H}_{\mathfrak{V}}(y,|w_n|)\,dy-\Big(\frac{1}{r}-\frac{1}{\mu}\Big)\int_{\mathbb{R}^N}\sigma(y)|w_n|^r\,dy\\
&+\frac{\theta}{\mu}\int_{\mathbb{R}^N}g(y,w_n)w_n-\mu G(y,w_n)\,dy\\
&\geq\kappa_0\Big(\frac{1}{\vartheta q}-\frac{1}{\mu}\Big)\int_{\mathbb{R}^N}\mathcal{H}(y,|\nabla w_n|)\,dy+\Big(\frac{1}{q}-\frac{1}{\mu}\Big)\int_{\mathbb{R}^N}\mathcal{H}_{\mathfrak{V}}(y,|w_n|)\,dy\\
&-\Big(\frac{1}{r}-\frac{1}{\mu}\Big)\int_{\mathbb{R}^N}\sigma(y)|w_n|^r\,dy+\frac{\theta}{\mu}\int_{\{|w_n|\leq\mathfrak{M}_0\}}g(y,w_n)w_n-\mu G(y,w_n)\,dy\\
&+\frac{\theta}{\mu}\int_{\{|w_n|\geq\mathfrak{M}_0\}}g(y,w_n)w_n-\mu G(y,w_n)\,dy\\
&\geq\kappa_0\Big(\frac{1}{\vartheta q}-\frac{1}{\mu}\Big)\int_{\mathbb{R}^N}\mathcal{H}(y,|\nabla w_n|)\,dy+\Big(\frac{1}{q}-\frac{1}{\mu}\Big)\int_{\mathbb{R}^N}\mathcal{H}_{\mathfrak{V}}(y,|w_n|)\,dy\\
&-\Big(\frac{1}{r}-\frac{1}{\mu}\Big)\int_{\mathbb{R}^N}\sigma(y)|w_n|^r\,dy\\
&-C_1\int_{\{|w_n|\leq\mathfrak{M}_0\}}|w_n|^p+\rho_1(y)|w_n|+\rho_2|w_n|^\ell\,dy\\
&\geq\kappa_0\Big(\frac{1}{\vartheta q}-\frac{1}{\mu}\Big)\int_{\mathbb{R}^N}\mathcal{H}(y,|\nabla w_n|)\,dy+\frac{1}{2}\Big(\frac{1}{q}-\frac{1}{\mu}\Big)\int_{\mathbb{R}^N}\mathcal{H}_{\mathfrak{V}}(y,|w_n|)\,dy\\
&-\Big(\frac{1}{r}-\frac{1}{\mu}\Big)\int_{\mathbb{R}^N}\sigma(y)|w_n|^r\,dy-\mathcal{K}_0
\end{aligned}
$$

$$
\begin{aligned}
&\geq \frac{\min\{\kappa_0,1\}(\mu-\vartheta q)}{2\vartheta q\mu}\left[\int_{\mathbb{R}^N}\mathcal{H}(y,|\nabla w_n|)\,dy+\int_{\mathbb{R}^N}\mathcal{H}_{\mathfrak{V}}(y,|w_n|)\,dy\right]\\
&\quad-\left(\frac{1}{r}-\frac{1}{\mu}\right)\|\sigma\|_{L^{\frac{\gamma_0}{\gamma_0-r}}(\mathbb{R}^N)}\|w_n\|^r_{L^{\gamma_0}(\mathbb{R}^N)}-\mathcal{K}_0\\
&\geq \frac{\min\{\kappa_0,1\}(\mu-\vartheta q)}{2\vartheta q\mu}\min\left\{\frac{\|w_n\|^p}{2^p},\frac{\|w_n\|^q}{2^{q-1}}\right\}\\
&\quad-\left(\frac{1}{r}-\frac{1}{\mu}\right)\|\sigma\|_{L^{\frac{\gamma_0}{\gamma_0-r}}(\mathbb{R}^N)}\|w_n\|^r_{L^{\gamma_0}(\mathbb{R}^N)}-\mathcal{K}_0\\
&\geq \frac{\min\{\kappa_0,1\}(\mu-\vartheta q)}{2\vartheta q\mu}\min\left\{\frac{\|w_n\|^p}{2^p},\frac{\|w_n\|^q}{2^{q-1}}\right\}\\
&\quad-\left(\frac{1}{r}-\frac{1}{\mu}\right)\|\sigma\|_{L^{\frac{\gamma_0}{\gamma_0-r}}(\mathbb{R}^N)}C_{\gamma_0,imb}\|w_n\|^r-\mathcal{K}_0,
\end{aligned}
$$

where $C_{\gamma_0,imb}$ is an embedding constant of $\mathfrak{E}\hookrightarrow L^{\gamma_0}(\mathbb{R}^N)$. Since $p>r>1$, we assert that the sequence $\{w_n\}$ is bounded in $\mathfrak{E}$, and thus, $\{w_n\}$ has a weakly convergent subsequence in $\mathfrak{E}$. Passing to the limit, if necessary, to a subsequence according to Lemma 2, we have the following:

$$
w_n \rightharpoonup w_0 \text{ in } \mathfrak{E},\quad w_n(y)\to w_0(y) \text{ a.e. in } \mathbb{R}^N \quad\text{and}\quad w_n\to w_0 \text{ in } L^{\tau}(\mathbb{R}^N) \tag{12}
$$

as $n\to\infty$ for any $\tau\in[p,p^*)$. To prove that $\{w_n\}$ converges strongly to w_0 in $\mathfrak{E}$ as $n\to\infty$, we let $\psi\in\mathfrak{E}$ be fixed and let $\tilde{\Phi}_\psi$ denote the linear function on $\mathfrak{E}$ as defined by

$$
\tilde{\Phi}_\psi(v)=\int_{\mathbb{R}^N}|\nabla\psi|^{p-2}\nabla\psi\cdot\nabla v\,dy+\int_{\mathbb{R}^N}\nu(y)|\nabla\psi|^{q-2}\nabla\psi\cdot\nabla v\,dy \tag{13}
$$

for all $v\in\mathfrak{E}$. Obviously, by the Hölder inequality, $\tilde{\Phi}_\psi$ is also continuous, as

$$
\begin{aligned}
|\tilde{\Phi}_\psi(v)| &\leq C_2\left(\||\nabla\psi|^{p-1}\|_{L^{p'}(\mathbb{R}^N)}+\||\nabla\psi|^{q-1}\|_{L^{q'}(\nu,\mathbb{R}^N)}\right)\|v\|\\
&\leq C_2\left(\|\nabla\psi\|^{p-1}_{L^p(\mathbb{R}^N)}+\|\nabla\psi\|^{q-1}_{L^q(\nu,\mathbb{R}^N)}\right)\|v\|
\end{aligned}
$$

for any $v\in\mathfrak{E}$ and a positive constant C_2. Hence, (12) yields

$$
\lim_{n\to\infty}\left[M\left(\int_{\mathbb{R}^N}\mathcal{H}_{p,q}(y,|\nabla w_n|)\,dy\right)-M\left(\int_{\mathbb{R}^N}\mathcal{H}_{p,q}(y,|\nabla w_0|)\,dy\right)\right]\tilde{\Phi}_{w_0}(w_n-w_0)=0, \tag{14}
$$

as the sequence $\left\{M\left(\int_{\mathbb{R}^N}\mathcal{H}_{p,q}(y,|\nabla w_n|)\,dy\right)-M\left(\int_{\mathbb{R}^N}\mathcal{H}_{p,q}(y,|\nabla w_0|)\,dy\right)\right\}$ is bounded in $\mathbb{R}$. Using (G1) and the Hölder inequality, it follows that

$$
\begin{aligned}
&\int_{\mathbb{R}^N}|(g(y,w_n)-g(y,w_0))(w_n-w_0)|\,dy\\
&\leq\int_{\mathbb{R}^N}\left[2\rho_1(y)+\rho_2\left(|w_n|^{\ell-1}+|w_0|^{\ell-1}\right)\right]|w_n-w_0|\,dy\\
&\leq 2\|\rho_1\|_{L^{s'}(\mathbb{R}^N)}\|w_n-w_0\|_{L^s(\mathbb{R}^N)}\\
&\quad+\rho_2\left(\|w_n\|^{\ell-1}_{L^{\ell'}(\mathbb{R}^N)}+\|w_0\|^{\ell-1}_{L^{\ell'}(\mathbb{R}^N)}\right)\|w_n-w_0\|_{L^{\ell}(\mathbb{R}^N)}.
\end{aligned}
$$

Then, (12) implies that

$$
\lim_{n\to\infty}\int_{\mathbb{R}^N}(g(y,w_n)-g(y,w_0))(w_n-w_0)\,dy=0. \tag{15}
$$

Let us denote $\gamma := \frac{\gamma_0}{\gamma_0 - r}$. Then, by Young's inequality, we obtain the following:

$$\begin{aligned}
&\int_{\mathbb{R}^N} \left|\sigma(y)\left(|w_n|^{r-2}w_n - |w_0|^{r-2}w_0\right)\right|^{\gamma_0'} dy \\
&= \int_{\mathbb{R}^N} |\sigma(y)|^{\gamma_0}\left|\left(|w_n|^{r-2}w_n - |w_0|^{r-2}w_0\right)\right|^{\gamma_0'} dy \\
&\leq \int_{\mathbb{R}^N} |\sigma(y)|^{\gamma_0}\left(|w_n|^{r-1} + |w_0|^{r-1}\right)^{\gamma_0'} dy \\
&\leq \int_{\mathbb{R}^N} \left[\frac{(|\sigma(y)|^{\gamma_0})^{\frac{\gamma}{\gamma_0'}}}{\frac{\gamma}{\gamma_0'}} + \frac{\left[(|w_n|^{r-1} + |w_0|^{r-1})^{\gamma_0'}\right]^{\left(\frac{\gamma}{\gamma_0}\right)'}}{\left(\frac{\gamma}{\gamma_0}\right)'}\right] dy \qquad (16) \\
&= \int_{\mathbb{R}^N} \left[\frac{\gamma_0'}{\gamma}|\sigma(y)|^{\gamma} + \frac{r-1}{\gamma_0 - 1}\left(|w_n|^{r-1} + |w_0|^{r-1}\right)^{\frac{\gamma_0}{r-1}}\right] dy \\
&\leq C_3 \int_{\mathbb{R}^N} \frac{\gamma_0'}{\gamma}|\sigma(y)|^{\gamma} + \frac{r-1}{\gamma_0 - 1}(|w_n|^{\gamma_0} + |w_0|^{\gamma_0})\, dy
\end{aligned}$$

for a positive constant C_3. Invoking (12), (16), and the convergence principle, we have

$$\left|\sigma(y)|w_n|^{r-2}w_n - \sigma(y)|w_0|^{r-2}w_0\right|^{\gamma_0'} \leq f_1(y)$$

for almost all $y \in \mathbb{R}^N$ and for some $f_1 \in L^1(\mathbb{R}^N)$, and thus, $\sigma(y)|w_n|^{r-2}w_n \to \sigma(y)|w_0|^{r-2}w_0$ as $n \to \infty$ for almost all $y \in \mathbb{R}^N$. This, together with Lebesgue's dominated convergence theorem, yields the following:

$$\lim_{n\to\infty} \int_{\mathbb{R}^N} \sigma(y)\left(|w_n|^{r-2}w_n - |w_0|^{r-2}w_0\right)(w_n - w_0)\, dy = 0. \qquad (17)$$

Because $w_n \rightharpoonup w_0$ in $\mathfrak{E}$ and $\mathcal{E}_\theta'(w_n) \to 0$ in $\mathfrak{E}^*$, as $n \to \infty$, we obtain the following:

$$\langle \mathcal{E}_\theta'(w_n) - \mathcal{E}_\theta'(w_0), w_n - w_0\rangle \to 0 \text{ as } n \to \infty. \qquad (18)$$

Let us denote $\tilde{\Psi}_\psi$ in $\mathfrak{E}$ with

$$\tilde{\Psi}_\psi(v) := \int_{\mathbb{R}^N} \mathfrak{V}(y)\left(|\psi|^{p-2}\psi + \nu(y)|\psi|^{q-2}\psi\right) v\, dy.$$

Then, we infer

$$\begin{aligned}
&\langle \mathcal{E}_\theta'(w_n) - \mathcal{E}_\theta'(w_0), w_n - w_0\rangle \\
&= M\left(\int_{\mathbb{R}^N} \mathcal{H}_{p,q}(y, |\nabla w_n|)\, dy\right)\tilde{\Phi}_{w_n}(w_n - w_0) \\
&\quad - M\left(\int_{\mathbb{R}^N} \mathcal{H}_{p,q}(y, |\nabla w_0|)\, dy\right)\tilde{\Phi}_{w_0}(w_n - w_0) \\
&\quad + \int_{\mathbb{R}^N} \mathfrak{V}(y)\left(|w_n|^{p-2}w_n + \nu(y)|w_n|^{q-2}w_n\right)(w_n - w_0)\, dy \\
&\quad - \int_{\mathbb{R}^N} \mathfrak{V}(y)\left(|w_0|^{p-2}w_0 + \nu(y)|w_0|^{q-2}w_0\right)(w_n - w_0)\, dy \\
&\quad - \int_{\mathbb{R}^N} \sigma(y)\left(|w_n|^{r-2}w_n - |w_0|^{r-2}w_0\right)(w_n - w_0)\, dy \\
&\quad - \theta\int_{\mathbb{R}^N} \left(g(y, w_n) - g(y, w_0)\right)(w_n - w_0)\, dy \\
&= M\left(\int_{\mathbb{R}^N} \mathcal{H}_{p,q}(y, |\nabla w_n|)\, dy\right)\left[\tilde{\Phi}_{w_n}(w_n - w_0) - \tilde{\Phi}_{w_0}(w_n - w_0)\right]
\end{aligned}$$

$$
\begin{aligned}
&+\Big[M\Big(\int_{\mathbb{R}^N}\mathcal{H}_{p,q}(y,|\nabla w_n|)\,dy\Big)-M\Big(\int_{\mathbb{R}^N}\mathcal{H}_{p,q}(y,|\nabla w_0|)\,dy\Big)\Big]\tilde{\Phi}_{w_0}(w_n-w_0)\\
&+\int_{\mathbb{R}^N}\mathfrak{V}(y)\Big(|w_n|^{p-2}w_n-|w_0|^{p-2}w_0+\nu(y)(|w_n|^{q-2}w_n-|w_0|^{q-2}w_0)\Big)\\
&\qquad\qquad\qquad\qquad\qquad\qquad\qquad\qquad\times(w_n-w_0)\,dy\\
&-\int_{\mathbb{R}^N}\sigma(y)\Big(|w_n|^{r-2}w_n-|w_0|^{r-2}w_0\Big)(w_n-w_0)\,dy\\
&-\theta\int_{\mathbb{R}^N}\Big(g(y,w_n)-g(y,w_0)\Big)(w_n-w_0)\,dy\\
=&\Big[M\Big(\int_{\mathbb{R}^N}\mathcal{H}_{p,q}(y,|\nabla w_n|)\,dy\Big)\big[\tilde{\Phi}_{w_n}(w_n-w_0)-\tilde{\Phi}_{w_0}(w_n-w_0)\big]\\
&\qquad\qquad\qquad\qquad\qquad+\tilde{\Psi}_{w_n}(w_n-w_0)-\tilde{\Psi}_{w_0}(w_n-w_0)\Big]\\
&+\Big[M\Big(\int_{\mathbb{R}^N}\mathcal{H}_{p,q}(y,|\nabla w_n|)\,dy\Big)-M\Big(\int_{\mathbb{R}^N}\mathcal{H}_{p,q}(y,|\nabla w_0|)\,dy\Big)\Big]\tilde{\Phi}_{w_0}(w_n-w_0)\\
&-\int_{\mathbb{R}^N}\sigma(y)\Big(|w_n|^{r-2}w_n-|w_0|^{r-2}w_0\Big)(w_n-w_0)\,dy\\
&-\theta\int_{\mathbb{R}^N}\Big(g(y,w_n)-g(y,w_0)\Big)(w_n-w_0)\,dy.
\end{aligned}
$$

This together with Equations (14), (15), (17), and (18) yields

$$
\begin{aligned}
\lim_{n\to\infty}\Big[M\Big(\int_{\mathbb{R}^N}\mathcal{H}_{p,q}(y,|\nabla w_n|)\,dy\Big)&\big[\tilde{\Phi}_{w_n}(w_n-w_0)-\tilde{\Phi}_{w_0}(w_n-w_0)\big]\\
&+\tilde{\Psi}_{w_n}(w_n-w_0)-\tilde{\Psi}_{w_0}(w_n-w_0)\Big]=0.
\end{aligned}
$$

By convexity, (M1), and (V), we have the following:

$$
M\Big(\int_{\mathbb{R}^N}\mathcal{H}_{p,q}(y,|\nabla w_n|)\,dy\Big)\big[\tilde{\Phi}_{w_n}(w_n-w_0)-\tilde{\Phi}_{w_0}(w_n-w_0)\big]\geq 0 \tag{19}
$$

and

$$
\mathfrak{V}(y)\Big(|w_n|^{p-2}w_n-|w_0|^{p-2}w_0+\nu(y)\Big(|w_n|^{q-2}w_n-|w_0|^{q-2}w_0\Big)\Big)(w_n-w_0)\geq 0. \tag{20}
$$

It follows that

$$
\lim_{n\to\infty}\big[\tilde{\Phi}_{w_n}(w_n-w_0)-\tilde{\Phi}_{w_0}(w_n-w_0)\big]=0 \tag{21}
$$

and

$$
\lim_{n\to\infty}\big[\tilde{\Psi}_{w_n}(w_n-w_0)-\tilde{\Psi}_{w_0}(w_n-w_0)\big]=0. \tag{22}
$$

It should be noted that there are the well-known vector inequalities:

$$
|\xi-\eta|^m\leq\begin{cases}C(m)(|\xi|^{m-2}\xi-|\eta|^{m-2}\eta)\cdot(\xi-\eta) & \text{for } m\geq 2,\\ C(m)\Big[(|\xi|^{m-2}\xi-|\eta|^{m-2}\eta)\cdot(\xi-\eta)\Big]^{\frac{m}{2}} & \\ \qquad\qquad\times(|\xi|^m+|\eta|^m)^{\frac{2-m}{2}} & \text{for } 1<m<2\end{cases} \tag{23}
$$

for all $\xi,\eta\in\mathbb{R}^N$, where $C(m)$ is a positive constant depending only on m [49]. It is now assumed that $2\leq p<q$. Then, according to (23), we know the following:

$$
\int_{\mathbb{R}^N}|\nabla w_n-\nabla w_0|^p\,dy
$$

$$\leq C(p)\int_{\mathbb{R}^N}(|\nabla w_n|^{p-2}\nabla w_n-|\nabla w_0|^{p-2}\nabla w_0)\cdot(\nabla w_n-\nabla w_0)\,dy \tag{24}$$

and

$$\begin{aligned}&\int_{\mathbb{R}^N}\nu(y)|\nabla w_n-\nabla w_0|^q\,dy\\&\leq C(q)\int_{\mathbb{R}^N}\nu(y)(|\nabla w_n|^{q-2}\nabla w_n-|\nabla w_0|^{q-2}\nabla w_0)\cdot(\nabla w_n-\nabla w_0)\,dy.\end{aligned} \tag{25}$$

Then, based on (24), (25), and the definition of $\tilde{\Phi}_\psi$ in (13), it follows that

$$\begin{aligned}&\int_{\mathbb{R}^N}|\nabla w_n-\nabla w_0|^p+\nu(y)|\nabla w_n-\nabla w_0|^q\,dy\\&\leq\max\{C(p),C(q)\}\left(\tilde{\Phi}_{w_n}(w_n-w_0)-\tilde{\Phi}_{w_0}(w_n-w_0)\right).\end{aligned} \tag{26}$$

Similarly, utilizing (V) and (23),

$$\begin{aligned}&\int_{\mathbb{R}^N}\mathfrak{V}(y)|w_n-w_0|^p\,dy\\&\leq\tilde{C}(p)\int_{\mathbb{R}^N}\mathfrak{V}(y)(|w_n|^{p-2}w_n-|w_0|^{p-2}w_0)(w_n-w_0)\,dy\end{aligned} \tag{27}$$

and

$$\begin{aligned}&\int_{\mathbb{R}^N}\mathfrak{V}(y)\nu(y)|w_n-w_0|^q\,dy\\&\leq\tilde{C}(q)\int_{\mathbb{R}^N}\mathfrak{V}(y)\Big(\nu(y)|w_n|^{q-2}w_n-\nu(y)|w_0|^{q-2}w_0\Big)(w_n-w_0)\,dy.\end{aligned} \tag{28}$$

Then, according to (27) and (28), we deduce that

$$\begin{aligned}&\int_{\mathbb{R}^N}\mathfrak{V}(y)\left(|w_n-w_0|^p+\nu(y)|w_n-w_0|^q\right)dy\\&\leq\max\{\tilde{C}(p),\tilde{C}(q)\}\left[\tilde{\Psi}_{w_n}(w_n-w_0)-\tilde{\Psi}_{w_0}(w_n-w_0)\right].\end{aligned} \tag{29}$$

However, we consider the case where $1<p<q<2$. As $\{w_n\}$ is bounded in $\mathfrak{E}$, there exist positive constants of C_4 and C_5 such that $\int_{\mathbb{R}^N}|\nabla w_n|^p\,dy\leq C_4$ and $\int_{\mathbb{R}^N}\nu(y)|\nabla w_n|^q\,dy\leq C_5$ for all $n\in\mathbb{N}$. By (23) and the Hölder inequality, we have

$$\begin{aligned}&\int_{\mathbb{R}^N}|\nabla w_n-\nabla w_0|^p\,dy\\&\leq C(p)\int_{\mathbb{R}^N}\left[(|\nabla w_n|^{p-2}\nabla w_n-|\nabla w_0|^{p-2}\nabla w_0)\cdot(\nabla w_n-\nabla w_0)\right]^{\frac{p}{2}}\\&\qquad\times(|\nabla w_n|^p+|\nabla w_0|^p)^{\frac{2-p}{2}}\,dy\\&\leq C(p)\left(\int_{\mathbb{R}^N}(|\nabla w_n|^{p-2}\nabla w_n-|\nabla w_0|^{p-2}\nabla w_0)\cdot(\nabla w_n-\nabla w_0)\,dy\right)^{\frac{p}{2}}\\&\qquad\times\left(\int_{\mathbb{R}^N}(|\nabla w_n|^p+|\nabla w_0|^p)\,dy\right)^{\frac{2-p}{2}}\\&\leq C(p)(2C_4)^{\frac{2-p}{2}}\left(\int_{\mathbb{R}^N}(|\nabla w_n|^{p-2}\nabla w_n-|\nabla w_0|^{p-2}\nabla w_0)\cdot(\nabla w_n-\nabla w_0)\,dy\right)^{\frac{p}{2}}\end{aligned} \tag{30}$$

and

$$\begin{aligned}&\int_{\mathbb{R}^N}\nu(y)|\nabla w_n-\nabla w_0|^q\,dy\\&\leq C(q)\int_{\mathbb{R}^N}\left[\nu(y)(|\nabla w_n|^{q-2}\nabla w_n-|\nabla w_0|^{q-2}\nabla w_0)\cdot(\nabla w_n-\nabla w_0)\right]^{\frac{q}{2}}\end{aligned}$$

$$\times \left[\nu(y)(|\nabla w_n|^q + |\nabla w_0|^q)\right]^{\frac{2-q}{2}} dy$$

$$\le C(q)\left(\int_{\mathbb{R}^N} \nu(y)(|\nabla w_n|^{q-2}\nabla w_n - |\nabla w_0|^{q-2}\nabla w_0)\cdot(\nabla w_n - \nabla w_0)\, dy\right)^{\frac{q}{2}} \tag{31}$$

$$\times \left(\int_{\mathbb{R}^N} \nu(y)|\nabla w_n|^q + \nu(y)|\nabla w_0|^q\, dy\right)^{\frac{2-q}{2}}$$

$$\le C(q)(2C_5)^{\frac{2-q}{2}}\left(\int_{\mathbb{R}^N} \nu(y)\left(|\nabla w_n|^{q-2}\nabla w_n - |\nabla w_0|^{q-2}\nabla w_0\right)\cdot(\nabla w_n - \nabla w_0)\, dy\right)^{\frac{q}{2}}.$$

Then, according to (30), (31), and the definition of $\tilde{\Phi}_\psi$ in (13), it follows that

$$\int_{\mathbb{R}^N} |\nabla w_n - \nabla w_0|^p + \nu(y)|\nabla w_n - \nabla w_0|^q\, dy$$
$$\le C(\tilde{\Phi}_{w_n}(w_n - w_0) - \tilde{\Phi}_{w_0}(w_n - w_0))^\alpha, \tag{32}$$

where $C := \max\left\{C(p)(2C_4)^{\frac{2-p}{2}}, C(q)(2C_5)^{\frac{2-q}{2}}\right\}$ and α is either $\frac{p}{2}$ or $\frac{q}{2}$. Similarly, from (V) and the boundedness of $\{w_n\}$ in $\mathfrak{E}$, there exist positive constants C_6 and C_7 such that $\int_{\mathbb{R}^N} \mathfrak{V}(y)|w_n|^p\, dy \le C_6$ and $\int_{\mathbb{R}^N} \mathfrak{V}(y)\nu(y)|w_n|^q\, dy \le C_7$ for all $n \in \mathbb{N}$. According to (23) and the Hölder inequality, we have the following:

$$\int_{\mathbb{R}^N} \mathfrak{V}(y)|w_n - w_0|^p\, dy$$

$$\le \tilde{C}(p)\int_{\mathbb{R}^N} \left[\mathfrak{V}(y)\left(|w_n|^{p-2}w_n - |w_0|^{p-2}w_0\right)(w_n - w_0)\right]^{\frac{p}{2}}$$

$$\times \left[\mathfrak{V}(y)(|w_n|^p + |w_0|^p)\right]^{\frac{2-p}{2}} dy$$

$$\le \tilde{C}(p)\left(\int_{\mathbb{R}^N} \mathfrak{V}(y)\left[(|w_n|^{p-2}w_n - |w_0|^{p-2}w_0)(w_n - w_0)\right] dy\right)^{\frac{p}{2}} \tag{33}$$

$$\times \left(\int_{\mathbb{R}^N} \mathfrak{V}(y)|w_n|^p + \mathfrak{V}(y)|w_0|^p\, dy\right)^{\frac{2-p}{2}}$$

$$\le \tilde{C}(p)(2C_6)^{\frac{2-p}{2}}\left(\int_{\mathbb{R}^N} \mathfrak{V}(y)\left[(|w_n|^{p-2}w_n - |w_0|^{p-2}w_0)(w_n - w_0)\right] dy\right)^{\frac{p}{2}}$$

and

$$\int_{\mathbb{R}^N} \mathfrak{V}(y)\nu(y)|w_n - w_0|^q\, dy$$

$$\le \tilde{C}(q)\int_{\mathbb{R}^N} \left[\mathfrak{V}(y)\nu(y)\left(|w_n|^{q-2}w_n - |w_0|^{q-2}w_0\right)(w_n - w_0)\right]^{\frac{q}{2}}$$

$$\times \left[\mathfrak{V}(y)\nu(y)(|w_n|^q + |w_0|^q)\right]^{\frac{2-q}{2}} dy$$

$$\le \tilde{C}(q)\left(\int_{\mathbb{R}^N} \mathfrak{V}(y)\nu(y)\left[(|w_n|^{q-2}w_n - |w_0|^{q-2}w_0)(w_n - w_0)\right] dy\right)^{\frac{q}{2}} \tag{34}$$

$$\times \left(\int_{\mathbb{R}^N} \mathfrak{V}(y)\nu(y)|w_n|^q + \mathfrak{V}(y)\nu(y)|w_0|^q\, dy\right)^{\frac{2-q}{2}}$$

$$\le \tilde{C}(q)(2C_7)^{\frac{2-q}{2}}\left(\int_{\mathbb{R}^N} \mathfrak{V}(y)\nu(y)\left[(|w_n|^{q-2}w_n - |w_0|^{q-2}w_0)(w_n - w_0)\right] dy\right)^{\frac{q}{2}}.$$

Then, based on (33) and (34), we get that

$$\begin{aligned} &\int_{\mathbb{R}^N} \mathfrak{V}(y)(|w_n - w_0|^p + \nu(y)|w_n - w_0|^q)\, dy \\ &\quad \le \tilde{C}(\tilde{\Psi}_{w_n}(w_n - w_0) - \tilde{\Psi}_{w_0}(w_n - w_0))^{\beta}, \end{aligned} \tag{35}$$

where $\tilde{C} := \max\left\{\tilde{C}(p)(2C_6)^{\frac{2-p}{2}}, \tilde{C}(q)(2C_7)^{\frac{2-q}{2}}\right\}$ and β is either $\frac{p}{2}$ or $\frac{q}{2}$. Then, with the foundation of (21) and (22) and according to (26), (29), (32), and (35), we obtain $\|w_n - w_0\| \to 0$ as $n \to \infty$. Hence, $\mathcal{E}_\theta$ satisfies the $(C)_c$-condition. This completes the proof. □

Remark 3. *As mentioned in Remark 1, condition* (G3) *is weaker than* (G2). *However, to obtain the following compactness condition, we need an additional assumption on the nonlinear term g at infinity.*

Lemma 6. *Suppose that* (B1), (B2), (G1), *and* (G3) *hold. In addition,*

(G5) $\lim_{|\zeta|\to\infty} \frac{G(y,\zeta)}{|\zeta|^{\vartheta q}} = \infty$ *uniformly for almost all* $y \in \mathbb{R}^N$

holds. Then, the functional $\mathcal{E}_\theta$ *fulfills the* $(C)_c$*-condition for any* $\theta > 0$.

Proof. For $c \in \mathbb{R}$, let $\{w_n\}$ be a $(C)_c$-sequence in $\mathfrak{E}$ satisfying (5). Based on Lemma 5, it is sufficient to prove that $\{w_n\}$ is bounded in $\mathfrak{E}$. To this end, suppose, to the contrary, that $\|w_n\| > 1$ and $\|w_n\| \to \infty$ as $n \to \infty$, and a sequence $\{\varpi_n\}$ is defined by $\varpi_n = w_n/\|w_n\|$. Then, up to the subsequence denoted by $\{\varpi_n\}$, we obtain $\varpi_n \rightharpoonup \varpi_0$ in $\mathfrak{E}$ as $n \to \infty$, and due to Lemma 2,

$$\varpi_n \to \varpi_0 \text{ a.e. in } \mathbb{R}^N \text{ and } \varpi_n \to \varpi_0 \text{ in } L^t(\mathbb{R}^N) \tag{36}$$

as $n \to \infty$ for any t with $p \le t < p^*$. By Lemma 3 and assumption (B2), we have

$$\begin{aligned} \mathcal{E}_\theta(w_n) &= \mathcal{M}\left(\int_{\mathbb{R}^N} \mathcal{H}_{p,q}(y, |\nabla w_n|)\, dy\right) + \int_{\mathbb{R}^N} \mathcal{H}_{\mathfrak{V},p,q}(y, |w_n|)\, dy \\ &\quad - \frac{1}{r}\int_{\mathbb{R}^N} \sigma(y)|w_n|^r\, dy - \theta \int_{\mathbb{R}^N} G(y, w_n)\, dy \\ &\ge \frac{1}{\vartheta} M\left(\int_{\mathbb{R}^N} \mathcal{H}_{p,q}(y, |\nabla w_n|)\, dy\right) \int_{\mathbb{R}^N} \mathcal{H}_{p,q}(y, |\nabla w_n|)\, dy \\ &\quad + \int_{\mathbb{R}^N} \mathcal{H}_{\mathfrak{V},p,q}(y, |w_n|)\, dy - \frac{1}{r}\int_{\mathbb{R}^N} \sigma(y)|w_n|^r\, dy - \theta \int_{\mathbb{R}^N} G(y, w_n)\, dy \\ &\ge \frac{\kappa_0}{\vartheta q}\int_{\mathbb{R}^N} \mathcal{H}(y, |\nabla w_n|)\, dy + \frac{1}{q}\int_{\mathbb{R}^N} \mathcal{H}_{\mathfrak{V}}(y, |w_n|)\, dy \\ &\quad - \frac{1}{r}\int_{\mathbb{R}^N} \sigma(y)|w_n|^r\, dy - \theta \int_{\mathbb{R}^N} G(y, w_n)\, dy \\ &\ge \frac{\min\{\kappa_0, \vartheta\}}{\vartheta q}\left(\int_{\mathbb{R}^N} \mathcal{H}(y, |\nabla w_n|)\, dy + \int_{\mathbb{R}^N} \mathcal{H}_{\mathfrak{V}}(y, |w_n|)\, dy\right) \\ &\quad - \frac{1}{r}\int_{\mathbb{R}^N} \sigma(y)|w_n|^r\, dy - \theta \int_{\mathbb{R}^N} G(y, w_n)\, dy \\ &\ge \frac{\min\{\kappa_0, \vartheta\}}{\vartheta q 2^p}\|w_n\|^p - \frac{1}{r}\|\sigma\|_{L^{\frac{\gamma_0}{\gamma_0 - r}}(\mathbb{R}^N)} \|w_n\|^r_{L^{\gamma_0}(\mathbb{R}^N)} - \theta \int_{\mathbb{R}^N} G(y, w_n)\, dy \\ &\ge \frac{\min\{\kappa_0, \vartheta\}}{\vartheta q 2^p}\|w_n\|^p - \frac{C_8}{r}\|w_n\|^r - \theta \int_{\mathbb{R}^N} G(y, w_n)\, dy \end{aligned} \tag{37}$$

for a positive constant C_8. Since $\mathcal{E}_\theta(w_n) \to c$ as $n \to \infty$, $\|w_n\| \to \infty$ as $n \to \infty$, and $r < p$, we assert that

$$\int_{\mathbb{R}^N} G(y, w_n)\, dy \geq \frac{1}{\theta}\left(\frac{\min\{\kappa_0, \vartheta\}}{\vartheta q 2^p}\|w_n\|^p - \frac{C_8}{r}\|w_n\|^r - \mathcal{E}_\theta(w_n)\right) \to \infty \quad \text{as} \quad n \to \infty. \tag{38}$$

According to Lemma 3, we have

$$\begin{aligned}
\mathcal{E}_\theta(w_n) &= \mathcal{M}\left(\int_{\mathbb{R}^N} \mathcal{H}_{p,q}(y, |\nabla w_n|)\, dy\right) + \int_{\mathbb{R}^N} \mathcal{H}_{\mathfrak{V},p,q}(y, |w_n|)\, dy \\
&\quad - \frac{1}{r}\int_{\mathbb{R}^N} \sigma(y)|w_n|^r\, dy - \theta\int_{\mathbb{R}^N} G(y, w_n)\, dy \\
&\leq \mathcal{M}\left(\int_{\mathbb{R}^N} \mathcal{H}_{p,q}(y, |\nabla w_n|)\, dy\right) + \int_{\mathbb{R}^N} \mathcal{H}_{\mathfrak{V},p,q}(y, |w_n|)\, dy \\
&\quad - \theta\int_{\mathbb{R}^N} G(y, w_n)\, dy \\
&\leq \mathcal{M}\left(\int_{\mathbb{R}^N} \mathcal{H}_{p,q}(y, |\nabla w_n|)\, dy\right) + \frac{1}{p}\int_{\mathbb{R}^N} \mathcal{H}_{\mathfrak{V}}(y, |w_n|)\, dy \\
&\quad - \theta\int_{\mathbb{R}^N} G(y, w_n)\, dy \\
&\leq \mathcal{M}(1)\left(1 + \left(\int_{\mathbb{R}^N} \mathcal{H}_{p,q}(y, |\nabla w_n|)\, dy\right)^{\vartheta}\right) \\
&\quad + \int_{\mathbb{R}^N} \mathcal{H}_{\mathfrak{V}}(y, |w_n|)\, dy - \int_{\mathbb{R}^N} G(y, w_n)\, dy \\
&\leq C_9 \max\{\mathcal{M}(1), 1\}\left(1 + \int_{\mathbb{R}^N} \mathcal{H}(y, |\nabla w_n|)\, dy + \int_{\mathbb{R}^N} \mathcal{H}_{\mathfrak{V}}(y, |w_n|)\, dy\right)^{\vartheta} \\
&\quad - \theta\int_{\mathbb{R}^N} G(y, w_n)\, dy \\
&\leq C_9 \max\{\mathcal{M}(1), 1\}(1 + 2\|w_n\|^q)^{\vartheta} - \theta\int_{\mathbb{R}^N} G(y, w_n)\, dy \\
&\leq 4^{\vartheta} C_9 \max\{\mathcal{M}(1), 1\}\|w_n\|^{\vartheta q} - \theta\int_{\mathbb{R}^N} G(y, w_n)\, dy
\end{aligned} \tag{39}$$

for a positive constant C_9, where $\mathcal{M}(\tau) \leq \mathcal{M}(1)(1 + \tau^{\vartheta})$ for all $\tau \in \mathbb{R}^+$ because if $0 \leq \tau < 1$, then $\mathcal{M}(\tau) = \int_0^\tau M(s)\, ds \leq \mathcal{M}(1)$, and if $\tau > 1$, then $\mathcal{M}(\tau) \leq \mathcal{M}(1)\tau^{\vartheta}$. Furthermore,

$$4^{\vartheta} C_9 \max\{\mathcal{M}(1), 1\}\|w_n\|^{\vartheta q} \geq \mathcal{E}_\theta(w_n) + \theta\int_{\mathbb{R}^N} G(y, w_n)\, dy. \tag{40}$$

Due to assumption (G5), there exists a $\delta > 1$ such that $G(y, \zeta) > |\zeta|^{\vartheta q}$ for all $x \in \mathbb{R}^N$ and $|\zeta| > \delta$. Taking into account (G1), we obtain $|G(y, \zeta)| \leq \hat{\mathcal{C}}$ for all $(y, \zeta) \in \mathbb{R}^N \times [-\zeta_0, \zeta_0]$ for a constant $\hat{\mathcal{C}} > 0$. Therefore, there is $\mathcal{C}_1 \in \mathbb{R}$ such that $G(y, \zeta) \geq \mathcal{C}_1$ for all $(y, \zeta) \in \mathbb{R}^N \times \mathbb{R}$, and thus,

$$\frac{G(y, w_n) - \mathcal{C}_1}{4^{\vartheta} C_9 \max\{\mathcal{M}(1), 1\}\|w_n\|^{\vartheta q}} \geq 0 \tag{41}$$

for all $y \in \mathbb{R}^N$ and $n \in \mathbb{N}$. Combining (7) with (B1), (B2), (G1), and (G3), we have the following:

$$\begin{aligned}
c + 1 &\geq \mathcal{E}_\theta(w_n) - \frac{1}{\mu}\langle \mathcal{E}'_\theta(w_n), w_n\rangle \\
&= \mathcal{M}\left(\int_{\mathbb{R}^N} \mathcal{H}_{p,q}(y, |\nabla w_n|)\, dy\right) + \int_{\mathbb{R}^N} \mathcal{H}_{\mathfrak{V},p,q}(y, |w_n|)\, dy \\
&\quad - \frac{1}{r}\int_{\mathbb{R}^N} \sigma(y)|w_n|^r\, dy - \theta\int_{\mathbb{R}^N} G(y, w_n)\, dy
\end{aligned}$$

$$
\begin{aligned}
&-\frac{1}{\mu}M(\mathcal{H}_{p,q}(y,|\nabla w_n|))\int_{\mathbb{R}^N}\mathcal{H}(y,|\nabla w_n|)\,dy\\
&-\frac{1}{\mu}\int_{\mathbb{R}^N}\mathcal{H}_{\mathfrak{V}}(y,|w_n|)\,dy+\frac{1}{\mu}\int_{\mathbb{R}^N}\sigma(y)|w_n|^r\,dy\\
&+\frac{\theta}{\mu}\int_{\mathbb{R}^N}g(y,w_n)w_n\,dy\\
&\geq \kappa_0\left(\frac{1}{\vartheta q}-\frac{1}{\mu}\right)\int_{\mathbb{R}^N}\mathcal{H}(y,|\nabla w_n|)\,dy\\
&+\left(\frac{1}{q}-\frac{1}{\mu}\right)\int_{\mathbb{R}^N}\mathcal{H}_{\mathfrak{V}}(y,|w_n|)\,dy-\left(\frac{1}{r}-\frac{1}{\mu}\right)\int_{\mathbb{R}^N}\sigma(y)|w_n|^r\,dy\\
&+\frac{\theta}{\mu}\int_{\{|w_n|\leq\mathfrak{M}_1\}}g(y,w_n)w_n-\mu G(y,w_n)\,dy\\
&+\frac{\theta}{\mu}\int_{\{|w_n|\geq\mathfrak{M}_1\}}g(y,w_n)w_n-\mu G(y,w_n)\,dy\\
&\geq \kappa_0\left(\frac{1}{\vartheta q}-\frac{1}{\mu}\right)\int_{\mathbb{R}^N}\mathcal{H}(y,|\nabla w_n|)\,dy\\
&+\left(\frac{1}{q}-\frac{1}{\mu}\right)\int_{\mathbb{R}^N}\mathcal{H}_{\mathfrak{V}}(y,|w_n|)\,dy-\left(\frac{1}{r}-\frac{1}{\mu}\right)\int_{\mathbb{R}^N}\sigma(y)|w_n|^r\,dy\\
&-C_1\int_{\{|w_n|\leq\mathfrak{M}_1\}}|w_n|^p+\rho_1(y)|w_n|+\rho_2|w_n|^\ell\,dy\\
&-\frac{\theta}{\mu}\int_{\{|w_n|\geq\mathfrak{M}_1\}}\varsigma|w_n|^p\,dy\\
&\geq \kappa_0\left(\frac{1}{\vartheta q}-\frac{1}{\mu}\right)\int_{\mathbb{R}^N}\mathcal{H}(y,|\nabla w_n|)\,dy\\
&+\frac{1}{2}\left(\frac{1}{q}-\frac{1}{\mu}\right)\int_{\mathbb{R}^N}\mathcal{H}_{\mathfrak{V}}(y,|w_n|)\,dy-\left(\frac{1}{r}-\frac{1}{\mu}\right)\int_{\mathbb{R}^N}\sigma(y)|w_n|^r\,dy\\
&-\frac{\theta}{\mu}\int_{\mathbb{R}^N}\varsigma|w_n|^p\,dy-\mathcal{K}_0\\
&\geq\frac{\min\{\kappa_0,1\}}{2}\left(\frac{1}{\vartheta q}-\frac{1}{\mu}\right)\\
&\times\left[\int_{\mathbb{R}^N}\mathcal{H}(y,|\nabla w_n|)\,dy+\int_{\mathbb{R}^N}\mathcal{H}_{\mathfrak{V}}(y,|w_n|)\,dy\right]\\
&-\left(\frac{1}{r}-\frac{1}{\mu}\right)\|\sigma\|_{L^{\frac{\gamma_0}{\gamma_0-r}}(\mathbb{R}^N)}\|w_n\|^r_{L^{\gamma_0}(\mathbb{R}^N)}\\
&-\frac{\theta\varsigma}{\mu}\|w_n\|^p_{L^p(\mathbb{R}^N)}-\mathcal{K}_0\\
&\geq\frac{\min\{\kappa_0,1\}(\mu-\vartheta q)}{2^{p+1}\vartheta q\mu}\|w_n\|^p\\
&-\left(\frac{1}{r}-\frac{1}{\mu}\right)\|\sigma\|_{L^{\frac{\gamma_0}{\gamma_0-r}}(\mathbb{R}^N)}C_{\gamma_0,imb}\|w_n\|^r\\
&-\frac{\theta\varsigma}{\mu}\|w_n\|^p_{L^p(\mathbb{R}^N)}-\mathcal{K}_0.
\end{aligned}
$$

Hence, we know that

$$
\begin{aligned}
&c+\left(\frac{1}{r}-\frac{1}{\mu}\right)\|\sigma\|_{L^{\frac{\gamma_0}{\gamma_0-r}}(\mathbb{R}^N)}C_{\gamma_0,imb}\|w_n\|^r+\frac{\theta\varsigma}{\mu}\|w_n\|^p_{L^p(\mathbb{R}^N)}+\mathcal{K}_0+1\\
&\geq\frac{\min\{\kappa_0,1\}(\mu-\vartheta q)}{2^{p+1}\vartheta q\mu}\|w_n\|^p.
\end{aligned}
$$

Dividing this by $\frac{\min\{\kappa_0,1\}(\mu-\vartheta q)}{2^{p+1}\vartheta q\mu}\|w_n\|^p$ and then taking the limit supremum of this inequality as $n \to \infty$, we find the following:

$$1 \le \frac{2^{p+1}\vartheta q\theta\varsigma}{\min\{\kappa_0,1\}(\mu-\vartheta q)}\limsup_{n\to\infty}\|\varpi_n\|^p_{L^p(\mathbb{R}^N)} = \frac{2^{p+1}\vartheta q\theta\varsigma}{\min\{\kappa_0,1\}(\mu-\vartheta q)}\|\varpi_0\|^p_{L^p(\mathbb{R}^N)}. \tag{42}$$

Hence, based on (42), it follows that $\varpi_0 \neq 0$. Set $A_1 = \{y \in \mathbb{R}^N : \varpi_0(y) \neq 0\}$. By Equation (36), we infer that $|w_n(y)| = |\varpi_n(y)|\|w_n\| \to \infty$ as $n \to \infty$ for all $y \in A_1$. Thus, by using (G5),

$$\lim_{n\to\infty}\frac{G(y,w_n)}{\|w_n\|^{\vartheta q}} = \lim_{n\to\infty}\frac{G(y,w_n)}{|w_n|^{\vartheta q}}|\varpi_n|^{\vartheta q} = +\infty, \text{ for } y \in A_1. \tag{43}$$

Hence, we obtain that $\text{meas}(A_1) = 0$. Indeed, if $\text{meas}(A_1) \neq 0$, according to Equations (38)–(43) and the Fatou lemma, we have the following:

$$\begin{aligned}
\frac{1}{\theta} &= \liminf_{n\to\infty}\frac{\int_{\mathbb{R}^N}G(y,w_n)\,dy}{\theta\int_{\mathbb{R}^N}G(y,w_n)\,dy + \mathcal{E}_\theta(w_n)} \\
&\ge \liminf_{n\to\infty}\int_{\mathbb{R}^N}\frac{G(y,w_n)}{4^\theta C_9\max\{\mathcal{M}(1),1\}\|w_n\|^{\vartheta q}}\,dy \\
&= \liminf_{n\to\infty}\int_{\mathbb{R}^N}\frac{G(y,w_n)}{4^\theta C_9\max\{\mathcal{M}(1),1\}\|w_n\|^{\vartheta q}}\,dy \\
&\quad - \limsup_{n\to\infty}\int_{\mathbb{R}^N}\frac{C_1}{4^\theta C_9\max\{\mathcal{M}(1),1\}\|w_n\|^{\vartheta q}}\,dy \\
&= \liminf_{n\to\infty}\int_{A_1}\frac{G(y,w_n)-C_1}{4^\theta C_9\max\{\mathcal{M}(1),1\}\|w_n\|^{\vartheta q}}\,dy \\
&\ge \int_{A_1}\liminf_{n\to\infty}\frac{G(y,w_n)-C_1}{4^\theta C_9\max\{\mathcal{M}(1),1\}\|w_n\|^{\vartheta q}}\,dy \\
&= \int_{A_1}\liminf_{n\to\infty}\frac{G(y,w_n)}{4^\theta C_9\max\{\mathcal{M}(1),1\}\|w_n\|^{\vartheta q}}\,dy \\
&\quad - \int_{A_1}\limsup_{n\to\infty}\frac{C_1}{4^\theta C_9\max\{\mathcal{M}(1),1\}\|w_n\|^{\vartheta q}}\,dy = \infty,
\end{aligned}$$

which is impossible. Thus, $\varpi_0(y) = 0$ for almost all $y \in \mathbb{R}^N$. Consequently, we yielded a contradiction, and thus, the sequence $\{w_n\}$ is bounded in $\mathfrak{E}$. The proof is completed. □

3. Main Results

In this section, we illustrate two existence results for a sequence of infinitely many solutions to Problem (1). The primary tools for these consequences are the fountain theorem and the dual-fountain theorem in [37]. Let $\mathfrak{X}$ be a real reflexive and separable Banach space; then, it can be known (see [50,51]) that $\{e_k\} \subseteq \mathfrak{X}$ and $\{f_k^*\} \subseteq \mathfrak{X}^*$ exist such that

$$\mathfrak{X} = \overline{\text{span}\{e_k : k = 1,2,\cdots\}}, \quad \mathfrak{X}^* = \overline{\text{span}\{f_k^* : k = 1,2,\cdots\}}$$

and

$$\langle f_i^*, e_j\rangle = \begin{cases} 1 & \text{if } i = j \\ 0 & \text{if } i \neq j. \end{cases}$$

Let us denote $\mathfrak{X}_k = \text{span}\{e_k\}$, $\mathfrak{F}_n = \bigoplus_{k=1}^n \mathfrak{X}_k$, and $\mathfrak{G}_n = \overline{\bigoplus_{k=n}^\infty \mathfrak{X}_k}$.

Lemma 7 (Fountain Theorem [34,37]). *Assume that $(\mathfrak{X}, \|\cdot\|)$ is a Banach space, the functional $\mathcal{F} \in C^1(\mathfrak{X}, \mathbb{R})$ satisfies the $(C)_c$-condition for any $c > 0$, and $\mathcal{F}$ is even. Therefore, if, for each sufficiently large $n \in \mathbb{N}$, there are $\beta_n > \alpha_n > 0$ such that*

(1) $\delta_n := \inf\{\mathcal{F}(\varpi) : \varpi \in \mathfrak{G}_n, \|\varpi\| = \alpha_n\} \to \infty \quad as \quad n \to \infty;$
(2) $\rho_n := \max\{\mathcal{F}(\varpi) : \varpi \in \mathfrak{F}_n, \|\varpi\| = \beta_n\} \le 0.$

Then $\mathcal{F}$ has an unbounded sequence of critical values, i.e., there is a sequence $\{\varpi_k\} \subset \mathfrak{X}$ such that $\mathcal{F}'(\varpi_k) = 0$ and $\mathcal{F}(\varpi_k) \to +\infty$ as $k \to +\infty$.

Lemma 8. *Let us denote*

$$\chi_{\iota,n} = \sup_{\|u\|=1, u \in \mathfrak{G}_n} \|u\|_{L^\iota(\mathbb{R}^N)}$$

and

$$\chi_n = \max\{\chi_{\ell,n}, \chi_{s,n}, \chi_{\gamma_0,n}\}. \tag{44}$$

Then $\chi_n \to 0$ as $n \to \infty$ (see [34]*).*

Lemma 9. *Assume that* (B1), (B2), (G1), *and* (G5) *hold. Then, there are $\beta_n > \alpha_n > 0$ such that*

(1) $\delta_n := \inf\{\mathcal{E}_\lambda(w) : w \in \mathfrak{G}_n, \|w\| = \alpha_n\} \to \infty \quad as \quad n \to \infty;$
(2) $t_n := \max\{\mathcal{E}_\lambda(w) : w \in \mathfrak{F}_n, \|w\| = \beta_n\} \le 0$

for a sufficiently large n .

Proof. The basic concept of the proof is carried out similarly to [52] (see also [32]). For the reader's convenience, we provide the proof. For any $w \in \mathfrak{G}_n$, suppose that $\|w\| > 1$. From assumptions (B1), (B2), (G1), and Lemma 3, as well as the similar argument in (37), it follows that

$$\begin{aligned}
\mathcal{E}_\theta(w) &= \mathcal{M}\left(\int_{\mathbb{R}^N} \mathcal{H}_{p,q}(y, |\nabla w|)\, dy\right) + \int_{\mathbb{R}^N} \mathcal{H}_{\mathfrak{V},p,q}(y, |w|)\, dy \\
&\quad - \frac{1}{r}\int_{\mathbb{R}^N} \sigma(y)|w|^r\, dy - \theta \int_{\mathbb{R}^N} G(y, w)\, dy \\
&\ge \frac{\min\{\kappa_0, \vartheta\}}{\vartheta q}\left(\int_{\mathbb{R}^N} \mathcal{H}(y, |\nabla w|)\, dy + \int_{\mathbb{R}^N} \mathcal{H}_{\mathfrak{V}}(y, |w|)\, dy\right) \\
&\quad - \frac{1}{r}\int_{\mathbb{R}^N} \sigma(y)|w|^r\, dy - \theta \int_{\mathbb{R}^N} G(y, w)\, dy \\
&\ge \frac{\min\{\kappa_0, \vartheta\}}{\vartheta q 2^p}\|w\|^p - \frac{1}{r}\|\sigma\|_{L^{\frac{\gamma_0}{\gamma_0 - r}}(\mathbb{R}^N)} \|w\|^r_{L^{\gamma_0}(\mathbb{R}^N)} \\
&\quad - \theta\|\rho_1\|_{L^{s'}(\mathbb{R}^N)}\|w\|_{L^s(\mathbb{R}^N)} - \frac{\theta\rho_2}{\ell}\|w\|^\ell_{L^\ell(\mathbb{R}^N)} \\
&\ge \frac{\min\{\kappa_0, \vartheta\}}{\vartheta q 2^p}\|w\|^p - \frac{1}{r}\|\sigma\|_{L^{\frac{\gamma_0}{\gamma_0 - r}}(\mathbb{R}^N)} \chi_n^r\|w\|^r \\
&\quad - \theta\|\rho_1\|_{L^{s'}(\mathbb{R}^N)}\chi_n\|w\| - \frac{\theta\rho_2}{\ell}\chi_n^\ell\|w\|^\ell \\
&\ge \left(\frac{\min\{\kappa_0, \vartheta\}}{\vartheta q 2^p} - \frac{\chi_n^\ell\theta\rho_2}{\ell}\|w\|^{\ell-p}\right)\|w\|^p - \frac{1}{r}\|\sigma\|_{L^{\frac{\gamma_0}{\gamma_0 - r}}(\mathbb{R}^N)} \chi_n^r\|w\|^r \\
&\quad - \theta\|\rho_1\|_{L^{s'}(\mathbb{R}^N)}\chi_n\|w\|.
\end{aligned}$$

Since $p < \ell$, we obtain

$$\alpha_n = \left(\frac{\vartheta q 2^{p+1}\chi_n^\ell\theta\rho_2}{\min\{\kappa_0, \vartheta\}\ell}\right)^{\frac{1}{p-\ell}} \to \infty$$

as $n \to \infty$. Hence, if $w \in \mathfrak{G}_n$ and $\|w\| = \alpha_n$, then we find that

$$\mathcal{E}_\theta(w) \geq \frac{\min\{\kappa_0, \vartheta\}}{\vartheta q 2^{p+1}} \alpha_n^p - \frac{1}{r} \|\sigma\|_{L^{\frac{\gamma_0}{\gamma_0 - r}}(\mathbb{R}^N)} \chi_n^r \alpha_n^r - \theta \|\rho_1\|_{L^{s'}(\mathbb{R}^N)} \chi_n \alpha_n \to \infty \quad \text{as} \quad n \to \infty,$$

which implies (1) because $\alpha_n \to \infty$, $\chi_n \to 0$ as $n \to \infty$ and $p > r > 1$.

Next, we show condition (2). To the contrary, suppose there is $n \in \mathbb{N}$ such that condition (2) is not fulfilled. Then, sequence $\{w_k\}$ exists in $\mathfrak{F}_n$ such that

$$\|w_k\| \to \infty \text{ as } k \to \infty \quad \text{and} \quad \mathcal{E}_\lambda(w_k) \geq 0. \tag{45}$$

Let $z_k = w_k / \|w_k\|$. Since $\dim \mathfrak{F}_n < \infty$, there is a $z \in \mathfrak{F}_n \setminus \{0\}$ such that, up to a subsequence still denoted by $\{z_k\}$,

$$\|z_k - z\| \to 0 \quad \text{and} \quad z_k(y) \to z(y)$$

for almost all $y \in \mathbb{R}^N$ as $k \to \infty$. We assert that $z(y) = 0$ for almost all $y \in \mathbb{R}^N$. If $z(y) \neq 0$, then $|w_k(y)| \to \infty$ for all $y \in \mathbb{R}^N$ as $k \to \infty$. Hence, in accordance with (G5), it follows that

$$\lim_{k \to \infty} \frac{G(y, w_k)}{\|w_k\|^{\vartheta q}} = \lim_{k \to \infty} \frac{G(y, w_k)}{|w_k(y)|^{\vartheta q}} |z_k(y)|^{\vartheta q} = \infty \tag{46}$$

for all $y \in \mathcal{B}_1 := \{y \in \mathbb{R}^N : z(y) \neq 0\}$. In the same fashion as in the proof of Lemma 6, we can choose a $\mathcal{C}_2 \in \mathbb{R}$ such that $G(y, \zeta) \geq \mathcal{C}_2$ for all $(y, \zeta) \in \mathbb{R}^N \times \mathbb{R}$, and so

$$\frac{G(y, w_k) - \mathcal{C}_2}{\|w_k\|^{\vartheta q}} \geq 0$$

for all $y \in \mathbb{R}^N$ and $k \in \mathbb{N}$. Using (46) and the Fatou lemma, we have the following:

$$\begin{aligned}
\liminf_{k \to \infty} \int_{\mathbb{R}^N} \frac{G(y, w_k)}{\|w_k\|^{\vartheta q}} dy &\geq \liminf_{k \to \infty} \int_{\mathcal{B}_1} \frac{G(y, w_k)}{\|w_k\|^{\vartheta q}} dy - \limsup_{k \to \infty} \int_{\mathcal{B}_1} \frac{\mathcal{C}_2}{\|w_k\|^{\vartheta q}} dy \\
&= \liminf_{k \to \infty} \int_{\mathcal{B}_1} \frac{G(y, w_k) - \mathcal{C}_2}{\|w_k\|^{\vartheta q}} dy \\
&\geq \int_{\mathcal{B}_1} \liminf_{k \to \infty} \frac{G(y, w_k) - \mathcal{C}_2}{\|w_k\|^{\vartheta q}} dy \\
&= \int_{\mathcal{B}_1} \liminf_{k \to \infty} \frac{G(y, w_k)}{\|w_k\|^{\vartheta q}} dy - \int_{\mathcal{B}_1} \limsup_{k \to \infty} \frac{\mathcal{C}_2}{\|w_k\|^{\vartheta q}} dy.
\end{aligned}$$

Thus, we infer

$$\int_{\mathbb{R}^N} \frac{G(y, w_k)}{\|w_k\|^{\vartheta q}} dy \to \infty \quad \text{as } k \to \infty.$$

We may assume that $\|w_k\| > 1$. Therefore, by (39), we have

$$\begin{aligned}
\mathcal{E}_\theta(w_k) &\leq 4^\vartheta C_9 \max\{\mathcal{M}(1), 1\} \|w_k\|^{\vartheta q} - \theta \int_{\mathbb{R}^N} G(y, w_k)\, dy \\
&\leq \|w_k\|^{\vartheta q} \left(4^\vartheta C_9 \max\{\mathcal{M}(1), 1\} - \theta \int_{\mathbb{R}^N} \frac{G(y, w_k)}{\|w_k\|^{\vartheta q}} dy \right) \to -\infty \quad \text{as } k \to \infty,
\end{aligned}$$

which contradicts (45). This completes the proof. □

With the help of Lemma 7, we are ready to establish the existence of infinitely many large-energy solutions.

Theorem 1. *Assume that* (B1), (B2), (G1), (G2), *and* (G5) *hold. If $g(y,-\zeta) = -g(y,\zeta)$ holds for all $(y,\zeta) \in \mathbb{R}^N \times \mathbb{R}$, then for any $\theta > 0$, Problem* (1) *yields a sequence of non-trivial weak solutions $\{w_k\}$ in $\mathfrak{E}$ such that $\mathcal{E}_\theta(w_k) \to \infty$ as $k \to \infty$.*

Proof. Clearly, $\mathcal{E}_\theta$ is an even functional and the $(C)_c$-condition by Lemma 5 is ensured. From Lemma 9, this assertion can be immediately derived from the fountain theorem. This completes the proof. □

Theorem 2. *Assume that* (B1), (B2), (G1), (G3), *and* (G5) *hold. If g is odd in $\mathfrak{E}$, then for any $\theta > 0$, Problem* (1) *yields a sequence of non-trivial weak solutions $\{w_k\}$ in $\mathfrak{E}$ such that $\mathcal{E}_\theta(w_k) \to \infty$ as $k \to \infty$.*

Proof. If we replace Lemma 5 with Lemma 6, the proof is the same as in Theorem 1. □

Definition 3. *Suppose that $(\mathfrak{X}, \|\cdot\|)$ is a real separable and reflexive Banach space. We say that $\mathcal{F}$ satisfies the $(C)_c^*$-condition (with respect to $\mathfrak{F}_k$) if any sequence $\{w_k\}_{k\in\mathbb{N}} \subset \mathfrak{X}$ for which $w_k \in \mathfrak{F}_k$ for any $k \in \mathbb{N}$*

$$\mathcal{F}(w_k) \to c \quad \text{and} \quad \|(\mathcal{F}|_{\mathfrak{F}_k})'(w_k)\|_{\mathfrak{X}^*}(1 + \|w_k\|) \to 0 \text{ as } k \to \infty,$$

possesses a subsequence converging to a critical point of $\mathcal{F}$.

Lemma 10 (Dual Fountain Theorem [34]). *Assume that $(\mathfrak{X}, \|\cdot\|)$ is a Banach space, and $\mathcal{F} \in C^1(\mathfrak{X}, \mathbb{R})$ is an even functional. If $n_0 > 0$ so that for each $n \geq n_0$ there exists $\beta_n > \alpha_n > 0$ such that the following holds:*

$(\mathcal{A}_1)$ $\inf\{\mathcal{F}(\varpi) : \varpi \in \mathfrak{G}_n, \|\varpi\| = \beta_n\} \geq 0$;
$(\mathcal{A}_2)$ $\delta_n := \max\{\mathcal{F}(\varpi) : \varpi \in \mathfrak{F}_n, \|\varpi\| = \alpha_n\} < 0$;
$(\mathcal{A}_3)$ $\phi_n := \inf\{\mathcal{F}(\varpi) : \varpi \in \mathfrak{G}_n, \|\varpi\| \leq \beta_n\} \to 0$ as $n \to \infty$;
$(\mathcal{A}_4)$ $\mathcal{F}$ fulfills the $(C)_c^*$-condition for every $c \in [\phi_{n_0}, 0)$,

then $\mathcal{F}$ yields a sequence of negative critical values $d_k < 0$ satisfying $d_k \to 0$ as $k \to \infty$.

Next, we check all the conditions of the dual fountain theorem.

Lemma 11. *Assume that* (B1), (B2), (G1), *and* (G2) *hold. Then, the functional $\mathcal{E}_\theta$ satisfies the $(C)_c^*$-condition for any $\theta > 0$.*

Proof. First, we claim that Φ' is a mapping of type (S_+). Let $\{w_k\}$ be any sequence in $\mathfrak{E}$ such that $w_k \rightharpoonup w_0$ in $\mathfrak{E}$ as $k \to \infty$ and

$$\limsup_{k\to\infty} \langle \Phi'(w_k) - \Phi'(w_0), w_k - w_0 \rangle \leq 0.$$

Then, by using the notation in Lemma 5, we know the following:

$$\lim_{k\to\infty} \Big[M\Big(\int_{\mathbb{R}^N} \mathcal{H}_{p,q}(y, |\nabla w_k|)\,dy \Big) [\tilde{\Phi}_{w_k}(w_k - w_0) - \tilde{\Phi}_{w_0}(w_k - w_0)] + \tilde{\Psi}_{w_k}(w_k - w_0) + \tilde{\Psi}_{w_0}(w_k - w_0) \Big] \leq 0.$$

According to (19) and (20), we find the following:

$$\lim_{k\to\infty} \langle \Phi'(w_k) - \Phi'(w_0), w_k - w_0 \rangle = 0.$$

Therefore, using (12), (26), (29), (32), and (35), $w_k \to w_0$ in $\mathfrak{E}$ as $k \to \infty$ as claimed.

Let $c \in \mathbb{R}$, and let the sequence $\{w_k\}$ in $\mathfrak{E}$ be such that $w_k \in \mathfrak{F}_k$ for any $k \in \mathbb{N}$

$$\mathcal{E}_\theta(w_k) \to c \quad \text{and} \quad \|(\mathcal{E}_\theta|_{\mathfrak{F}_k})'(w_k)\|_{\mathfrak{E}^*}(1+\|w_k\|) \to 0 \text{ as } k \to \infty.$$

Therefore, we obtain $c = \mathcal{E}_\theta(w_k) + o_k(1)$ and $\langle \mathcal{E}_\theta'(w_k), w_k \rangle = o_k(1)$, where $o_k(1) \to 0$ as $k \to \infty$. Repeating the argument from Lemma 6 proof, we derive the boundedness of $\{w_k\}$ in $\mathfrak{E}$. Therefore, there is a subsequence, still denoted by $\{w_k\}$, and a function w_0 in $\mathfrak{E}$ such that $w_k \rightharpoonup w_0$ in $\mathfrak{E}$ as $k \to \infty$.

To complete this proof, we will show that $w_k \to w_0$ in $\mathfrak{E}$ as $k \to \infty$, and also, w_0 is a critical point of $\mathcal{E}_\theta$. Though the concept of this proof follows that in [34] (Lemma 3.12), we provide it here for convenience. As $\mathfrak{E} = \overline{\bigcup_{k\in\mathbb{N}} \mathfrak{F}_k}$, we can choose $v_k \in \mathfrak{F}_k, k \in \mathbb{N}$ such that $v_k \to w_0$ as $k \to \infty$. Since $\|(\mathcal{E}_\theta|_{\mathfrak{F}_k})'(w_k)\|_{\mathfrak{E}^*} \to 0$, $\{w_k - v_k\}$ is bounded, and $w_k - v_k \in \mathfrak{F}_k$, we have

$$\langle \mathcal{E}_\theta'(w_k), w_k - v_k \rangle = \langle (\mathcal{E}_\theta|_{\mathfrak{F}_k})'(w_k), w_k - v_k \rangle \to 0 \text{ as } k \to \infty. \tag{47}$$

The analogous argument in Lemma 9 [47] implies that Φ' is continuous, bounded, and strictly monotone. This, together with Lemma 4, indicates that $\{\mathcal{E}_\theta'(w_k)\}$ is bounded because $\{w_k\}$ is bounded. Thus,

$$\langle \mathcal{E}_\theta'(w_k), v_k - w_0 \rangle \to 0 \text{ as } k \to \infty. \tag{48}$$

Using (47) and (48), we find that

$$\langle \mathcal{E}_\theta'(w_k), w_k - w_0 \rangle \to 0 \text{ as } k \to \infty.$$

Therefore,

$$\langle \mathcal{E}_\theta'(w_k) - \mathcal{E}_\theta'(w_0), w_k - w_0 \rangle \to 0 \text{ as } k \to \infty. \tag{49}$$

According to Lemma 4, we know the following:

$$\langle \Psi_\theta'(w_k) - \Psi_\theta'(w_0), w_k - w_0 \rangle \to 0 \text{ as } k \to \infty. \tag{50}$$

Based on (49) and (50), we derive that

$$\langle \Phi'(w_k) - \Phi'(w_0), w_k - w_0 \rangle \to 0 \text{ as } k \to \infty.$$

Since Φ' is a mapping of type (S_+), we conclude that $w_k \to w_0$ as $k \to \infty$. Furthermore, we have $\mathcal{E}_\theta'(w_k) \to \mathcal{E}_\theta'(w_0)$ as $k \to \infty$. Then, we can prove that w_0 is a critical point of $\mathcal{E}_\theta$. Indeed, fix $k_0 \in \mathbb{N}$ and take any $u \in \mathfrak{F}_{k_0}$. For $k \geq k_0$, we find that

$$\begin{aligned}
\langle \mathcal{E}_\theta'(w_0), u \rangle &= \langle \mathcal{E}_\theta'(w_0) - \mathcal{E}_\theta'(w_k), u \rangle + \langle \mathcal{E}_\theta'(w_k), u \rangle \\
&= \langle \mathcal{E}_\theta'(w_0) - \mathcal{E}_\theta'(w_k), u \rangle + \langle (\mathcal{E}_\theta|_{\mathfrak{F}_k})'(w_k), u \rangle;
\end{aligned}$$

thus, passing the limit on the right side of the previous equation, as $k \to \infty$, we obtain

$$\langle \mathcal{E}_\theta'(w_0), u \rangle = 0 \text{ for all } u \in \mathfrak{F}_{k_0}.$$

As k_0 is taken arbitrarily and $\bigcup_{k\in\mathbb{N}} \mathfrak{F}_k$ is dense in $\mathfrak{E}$, we have $\mathcal{E}_\theta'(w_0) = 0$ as required. Then, we conclude that $\mathcal{E}_\theta$ satisfies the $(\mathrm{C})_c^*$-condition for any $c \in \mathbb{R}$ and for any $\theta > 0$. □

Lemma 12. *Assume that* (B1), (B2), (G3), *and* (G5) *hold. Then, the functional $\mathcal{E}_\theta$ satisfies the $(\mathrm{C})_c^*$-condition for any $\theta > 0$.*

Proof. Based on Lemma 6, we obtain that $\{w_n\}$ is a bounded sequence in $\mathfrak{E}$. The proof is the same as for Lemma 11. □

Lemma 13. *Assume that* (B1), (B2), *and* (G1) *hold. Then, there is $n_0 > 0$ so that for each $n \geq n_0$, there exists $\beta_n > 0$ such that*

$$\inf\{\mathcal{E}_\theta(w) : w \in \mathfrak{G}_n, \|w\| = \beta_n\} \geq 0.$$

Proof. Let $\chi_n < 1$ for a sufficiently large n. Based on (G1), Lemma 3, and the definition of χ_n, we find

$$\begin{aligned}
\mathcal{E}_\theta(w) \geq & \frac{\min\{\kappa_0, \vartheta\}}{\vartheta q}\Big(\int_{\mathbb{R}^N} \mathcal{H}(y, |\nabla w|)\, dy + \int_{\mathbb{R}^N} \mathcal{H}_{\mathfrak{V}}(y, |w|)\, dy\Big) \\
& - \frac{1}{r}\int_{\mathbb{R}^N} \sigma(y)|w|^r\, dy - \theta \int_{\mathbb{R}^N} G(y, w)\, dy \\
\geq & \frac{\min\{\kappa_0, \vartheta\}}{\vartheta q 2^p}\|w\|^p - \frac{1}{r}\|\sigma\|_{L^{\frac{\gamma_0}{\gamma_0 - r}}(\mathbb{R}^N)} \chi_n^r \|w\|^r \\
& - \theta\|\rho_1\|_{L^{s'}(\mathbb{R}^N)}\chi_n\|w\| - \frac{\theta\rho_2}{\ell}\chi_n^\ell\|w\|^\ell \\
\geq & \frac{\min\{\kappa_0, \vartheta\}}{\vartheta q 2^p}\|w\|^p - \Big(\frac{1}{r}\|\sigma\|_{L^{\frac{\gamma_0}{\gamma_0 - r}}(\mathbb{R}^N)} + \frac{\theta\rho_2}{\ell}\Big)\chi_n^r\|w\|^\ell \\
& - \theta\|\rho_1\|_{L^{s'}(\mathbb{R}^N)}\chi_n\|w\|
\end{aligned}$$

for a sufficiently large n and $\|w\| \geq 1$. Let us choose

$$\beta_n = \left[\left(\frac{1}{r}\|\sigma\|_{L^{\frac{\gamma_0}{\gamma_0 - r}}(\mathbb{R}^N)} + \frac{\theta\rho_2}{\ell}\right)\frac{\vartheta q 2^{p+1}}{\min\{\kappa_0, \vartheta\}}\chi_n^r\right]^{\frac{1}{p-2\ell}}. \tag{51}$$

Let $w \in \mathfrak{G}_n$ with $\|w\| = \beta_n > 1$ for a sufficiently large k . Then, there is $n_0 \in \mathbb{N}$ such that

$$\begin{aligned}
\mathcal{E}_\theta(w) \geq & \frac{\min\{\kappa_0, \vartheta\}}{\vartheta q 2^p}\|w\|^p \\
& - \left(\frac{1}{r}\|\sigma\|_{L^{\frac{\gamma_0}{\gamma_0 - r}}(\mathbb{R}^N)} + \frac{\theta\rho_2}{\ell}\right)\chi_n^r\|w\|^\ell - \theta\|\rho_1\|_{L^{s'}(\mathbb{R}^N)}\chi_n\|w\| \\
\geq & \frac{\min\{\kappa_0, \vartheta\}}{\vartheta q 2^{p+1}}\beta_n^p \\
& - \theta\|\rho_1\|_{L^{s'}(\mathbb{R}^N)}\left[\left(\frac{1}{r}\|\sigma\|_{L^{\frac{\gamma_0}{\gamma_0 - r}}(\mathbb{R}^N)} + \frac{\theta\rho_2}{\ell}\right)\frac{\vartheta q 2^{p+1}}{\min\{\kappa_0, \vartheta\}}\right]^{\frac{1}{p-2\ell}}\chi_n^{\frac{r+p-2\ell}{p-2\ell}} \\
\geq & 0
\end{aligned}$$

for all $n \in \mathbb{N}$ with $n \geq n_0$, which implies that the conclusion holds since $\lim_{n\to\infty}\beta_n^p = \infty$ and $\chi_n \to 0$ as $n \to \infty$. $\square$

Lemma 14. *Assume that* (B1), (B2), (G1), *and* (G4) *hold. Then for each sufficiently large $n \in \mathbb{N}$, there exists $\alpha_n > 0$ with $0 < \alpha_n < \beta_n$ such that*

(1) $\delta_n := \max\{\mathcal{E}_\theta(w) : w \in \mathfrak{F}_n, \|w\| = \alpha_n\} < 0$;

(2) $\phi_n := \inf\{\mathcal{E}_\theta(w) : w \in \mathfrak{G}_n, \|w\| \leq \beta_n\} \to 0$ *as* $n \to \infty$,

where β_n is given in Lemma 13.

Proof. (1): Since $\mathfrak{F}_n$ is a finite dimensional, $\|\cdot\|_{L^d(\xi, \mathbb{R}^N)}$, $\|\cdot\|_{L^\ell(\mathbb{R}^N)}$, and $\|\cdot\|$ are equivalent on $\mathfrak{F}_n$. Then, $\varrho_{1,n} > 0$ and $\varrho_{2,n} > 0$ exist such that

$$\varrho_{1,n}\|w\| \leq \|w\|_{L^d(\xi, \mathbb{R}^N)} \text{ and } \|w\|_{L^\ell(\mathbb{R}^N)} \leq \varrho_{2,n}\|w\|$$

for any $w \in \mathfrak{F}_n$. Let $w \in \mathfrak{F}_n$ with $\|w\| \le 1$. Based on (G1) and (G4), there are $C_{10}, C_{11} > 0$ such that

$$G(y,\zeta) \ge C_{10}\xi(y)|\zeta|^d - C_{11}|\zeta|^\ell$$

for almost all $(y,\zeta) \in \mathbb{R}^N \times \mathbb{R}$. According to Lemma 3, we obtain

$$\int_{\mathbb{R}^N} \mathcal{H}_{p,q}(y,|\nabla w|)\,dy \le \mathcal{K}$$

for some positive constant $\mathcal{K}$. Then, we have

$$\begin{aligned}
\mathcal{E}_\theta(w) &\le \mathcal{M}\left(\int_{\mathbb{R}^N} \mathcal{H}_{p,q}(y,|\nabla w|)\,dy\right) + \int_{\mathbb{R}^N} \mathcal{H}_{\mathfrak{V},p,q}(y,|w|)\,dy \\
&\quad - \frac{1}{r}\int_{\mathbb{R}^N} \sigma(y)|w|^r\,dy - \theta\int_{\mathbb{R}^N} G(y,w)\,dy \\
&\le \left(\sup_{0\le\tilde{\zeta}\le\mathcal{K}} M(\tilde{\zeta})\right)\int_{\mathbb{R}^N} \mathcal{H}_{p,q}(y,|\nabla w|)\,dy + \int_{\mathbb{R}^N} \mathcal{H}_{\mathfrak{V},p,q}(y,|w|)\,dy \\
&\quad - \theta C_{10}\int_{\mathbb{R}^N} \xi(y)|w|^d\,dy + \theta C_{11}\int_{\mathbb{R}^N} |w|^\ell\,dy \\
&\le C_{12}\|w\|^p - \theta C_{10}\|w\|^d_{L^d(\xi,\mathbb{R}^N)} + \theta C_{11}\|w\|^\ell_{L^\ell(\mathbb{R}^N)} \\
&\le C_{12}\|w\|^p - \theta C_{10}\varrho^d_{1,n}\|w\|^d + \theta C_{11}\varrho^\ell_{2,n}\|w\|^\ell
\end{aligned} \tag{52}$$

for some positive constant C_{12}. Let $f(x) = C_{12}x^p - \theta C_{10}\varrho^d_{1,n}x^d + \theta C_{11}\varrho^\ell_{2,n}x^\ell$. Since $d < p < \ell$, we infer $f(x) < 0$ for all $x \in (0,x_0)$ for sufficiently small $x_0 \in (0,1)$. Hence, we can find $\alpha_n > 0$ such that $\mathcal{E}_\theta(w) < 0$ for all $w \in \mathfrak{F}_n$ with $\|w\| = \alpha_n < x_0$ for a sufficiently large k. If necessary, we can change n_0 to a large value so that $\beta_n > \alpha_n > 0$ and

$$\delta_n := \max\{\mathcal{E}_\theta(w) : w \in \mathfrak{F}_n, \|w\| = \alpha_n\} < 0$$

for all $n \ge n_0$.

(2): Because $\mathfrak{F}_n \cap \mathfrak{G}_n \neq \phi$ and $0 < \alpha_n < \beta_n$, we have $\phi_n \le \delta_n < 0$ for all $n \ge n_0$. For any $w \in \mathfrak{G}_n$ with $\|w\| = 1$ and $0 < t < \beta_n$, we have

$$\begin{aligned}
\mathcal{E}_\theta(tw) &\ge \mathcal{M}\left(\int_{\mathbb{R}^N} \mathcal{H}_{p,q}(y,|\nabla tw|)\,dy\right) + \int_{\mathbb{R}^N} \mathcal{H}_{\mathfrak{V},p,q}(y,|tw|)\,dy \\
&\quad - \frac{1}{r}\int_{\mathbb{R}^N} \sigma(y)|tw|^r\,dy - \theta\int_{\mathbb{R}^N} G(y,tw)\,dy \\
&\ge -\frac{1}{r}\int_{\mathbb{R}^N} \sigma(y)|tw|^r\,dy - \theta\int_{\mathbb{R}^N} G(y,tw)\,dy \\
&\ge -\frac{1}{r}\|\sigma\|_{L^{\frac{\gamma_0}{\gamma_0-r}}(\mathbb{R}^N)}\|tw\|^r_{L^{\gamma_0}(\mathbb{R}^N)} \\
&\quad - \theta\int_{\mathbb{R}^N} \rho_1(y)|tw|dy - \frac{\theta\rho_2}{\ell}\int_{\mathbb{R}^N} |tw|^\ell dy \\
&\ge -\frac{1}{r}\|\sigma\|_{L^{\frac{\gamma_0}{\gamma_0-r}}(\mathbb{R}^N)}\beta_n^r\|w\|^r_{L^{\gamma_0}(\mathbb{R}^N)} \\
&\quad - \beta_n\theta\int_{\mathbb{R}^N} \rho_1(y)|w|dy - \frac{\theta\rho_2}{\ell}\beta_n^\ell\int_{\mathbb{R}^N} |w|^\ell dy \\
&\ge -\frac{1}{r}\|\sigma\|_{L^{\frac{\gamma_0}{\gamma_0-r}}(\mathbb{R}^N)}\beta_n^r\chi_n^r - \theta\|\rho_1\|_{L^{s'}(\mathbb{R}^N)}\beta_n\chi_n - \frac{\theta\rho_2}{\ell}\beta_n^\ell\chi_n^\ell
\end{aligned} \tag{53}$$

for a sufficiently large n, where χ_n and β_n are given in (44) and (51), respectively. Hence, based on the definition of β_n, it follows that

$$
\begin{aligned}
0 > \phi_n &\geq -\frac{\|\sigma\|_{L^{\frac{\gamma_0}{\gamma_0 - r}}(\mathbb{R}^N)}}{r}\beta_n^r\chi_n^r - \theta\|\rho_1\|_{L^{s'}(\mathbb{R}^N)}\beta_n\chi_n - \frac{\theta\rho_2}{\ell}\beta_n^\ell\chi_n^\ell \\
&= -\frac{\|\sigma\|_{L^{\frac{\gamma_0}{\gamma_0 - r}}(\mathbb{R}^N)}}{r}\left[\left(\frac{1}{r}\|\sigma\|_{L^{\frac{\gamma_0}{\gamma_0 - r}}(\mathbb{R}^N)} + \frac{\theta\rho_2}{\ell}\right)q2^{p+1}\right]^{\frac{r}{p-2\ell}}\chi_n^{\frac{(r+p-2\ell)r}{p-2\ell}} \\
&\quad - \|\rho_1\|_{L^{s'}(\mathbb{R}^N)}\left[\left(\frac{1}{r}\|\sigma\|_{L^{\frac{\gamma_0}{\gamma_0 - r}}(\mathbb{R}^N)} + \frac{\theta\rho_2}{\ell}\right)q2^{p+1}\right]^{\frac{1}{p-2\ell}}\chi_n^{\frac{r+p-2\ell}{p-2\ell}} \\
&\quad - \frac{\rho_2}{\ell}\left[\left(\frac{1}{r}\|\sigma\|_{L^{\frac{\gamma_0}{\gamma_0 - r}}(\mathbb{R}^N)} + \frac{\theta\rho_2}{\ell}\right)q2^{p+1}\right]^{\frac{\ell}{p-2\ell}}\chi_n^{\frac{(r+p-2\ell)\ell}{p-2\ell}}.
\end{aligned}
$$

Because $p < p + r < 2\ell$ and $\chi_n \to 0$ as $n \to \infty$, we derive that $\lim_{n\to\infty}\phi_n = 0$. □

With the aid of Lemmas 10 and 11, we are in a position to establish our final consequences.

Theorem 3. *Under the assumptions in Theorem 1, if* (G4) *holds, then Problem* (1) *yields a sequence of non-trivial weak solutions* $\{w_k\}$ *in* $\mathfrak{E}$ *such that* $\mathcal{E}_\theta(w_k) \to 0$ *as* $k \to \infty$ *for any* $\theta > 0$.

Proof. Due to Lemma 11, we note that the functional $\mathcal{E}_\theta$ is even and fulfills the $(C)_c^*$-condition for every $c \in [\phi_{n_0}, 0)$. Based on Lemmas 13 and 14, we ensure that properties $(\mathcal{A}_1)$, $(\mathcal{A}_2)$, and $(\mathcal{A}_3)$ in the dual fountain theorem hold. Therefore, problem (1) possesses a sequence of weak solutions $\{w_k\}$ with a sufficiently large k. The proof is complete. □

Theorem 4. *Under the assumptions in Theorem 2, if* (G4) *holds, then Problem* (1) *yields a sequence of non-trivial weak solutions* $\{w_k\}$ *in* $\mathfrak{E}$ *such that* $\mathcal{E}_\theta(w_k) \to 0$ *as* $k \to \infty$ *for any* $\theta > 0$.

Proof. Similar to Theorem 3, instead of Lemma 11, we apply Lemma 12 to obtain this result. □

Finally, we demonstrate the existence of a sequence of infinitely many weak solutions to (1) that converges to 0 in L^∞-space. To accomplish this, we needed the following additional assumptions regarding g:

(G6) There exists a constant $\zeta_1 > 0$ such that $g(y, \zeta)$ is odd in $\mathbb{R}^N \times (-\zeta_1, \zeta_1)$ and $pG(y, \zeta) - g(y, \zeta)\zeta > 0$ for all $y \in \mathbb{R}^N$ and for $0 < |\zeta| < \zeta_1$;

(G7) $\lim_{|\zeta|\to 0} \frac{g(y,\zeta)}{|\zeta|^{p-2}\zeta} = +\infty$ uniformly for all $y \in \mathbb{R}^N$.

The following assertion follows upon the analogous arguments of Proposition 1 in [40] and Proposition 3.1 in [39].

Proposition 1. *Assume that* (G1) *holds. If* w *is a weak solution of Problem* (1), *then* $w \in L^\infty(\mathbb{R}^N)$, *and there exist positive constants* C, η *independent of* w *such that*

$$
\|w\|_{L^\infty(\mathbb{R}^N)} \leq C\|w\|_{L^\ell(\mathbb{R}^N)}^\eta.
$$

With the help of Lemma 10 and Proposition 1, we are in a position to derive our final major result.

Theorem 5. *Suppose that* (B1), (B2), (G1), (G6), *and* (G7) *hold. In addition, suppose that*

(M5) $\mathcal{M}(t) \leq M(t)t$ *for any* $t \geq 0$.

Then, there exists an interval Γ *such that problem* (1) *has a sequence of non-trivial solutions* $\{w_n\}$ *in* $\mathfrak{E}$ *whose* $\mathcal{E}_\theta(w_n) \to 0$ *and* $\|w_n\|_{L^\infty(\mathbb{R}^N)} \to 0$ *as* $n \to \infty$ *for every* $\theta \in \Gamma$.

Proof. To obtain the desired properties of the energy functional, as in Lemma 10, we modify the nonlinear term g as follows. According to (G6) and (G7), for any $\mathfrak{M}_3 > 0$, there exists $\zeta_2 \in (0, \min\{\zeta_1, 1\})$ such that

$$G(y,\zeta) \geq \mathfrak{M}_3|\zeta|^p \quad \text{for a.e. } y \in \mathbb{R}^N \text{ and all } |\zeta| < \zeta_2. \tag{54}$$

Fix $\zeta_3 \in (0, \zeta_2/2)$, and let $\varphi \in C^1(\mathbb{R}, \mathbb{R})$ be such that φ is even, $\varphi(\zeta) = 1$ for $|\zeta| \leq \zeta_3$, $\varphi(\zeta) = 0$ for $|\zeta| \geq 2\zeta_3$, $|\varphi'(\zeta)| \leq 2/\zeta_3$, and $\varphi'(\zeta)\zeta \leq 0$. We then define the modified function $\widetilde{g} : \mathbb{R}^N \times \mathbb{R} \to \mathbb{R}$ as

$$\widetilde{g}(y,\zeta) := \frac{\partial}{\partial \zeta}\widetilde{G}(y,\zeta),$$

where

$$\widetilde{G}(y,\zeta) := \varphi(\zeta)G(y,\zeta) + (1 - \varphi(\zeta))\xi|\zeta|^p$$

for some fixed $\xi \in \left(0, \min\left\{\frac{1}{p}, \frac{1}{qC_{p,imb}^p}\right\}\right)$ with $C_{p,imb}$ being the embedding constant for the embedding $\mathfrak{E} \hookrightarrow L^p(\mathbb{R}^N)$ by means of Lemma 2. Clearly, $\widetilde{G}$ is even in ζ,

$$\widetilde{g}(y,\zeta) = \varphi'(\zeta)G(y,\zeta) + \varphi(\zeta)g(y,\zeta) - \varphi'(\zeta)\xi|\zeta|^p + (1 - \varphi(\zeta))\xi p|\zeta|^{p-2}\zeta, \tag{55}$$

and

$$p\widetilde{G}(y,\zeta) - \widetilde{g}(y,\zeta)\zeta = \varphi(\zeta)\left[pG(y,\zeta) - g(y,\zeta)\zeta\right] - \varphi'(\zeta)\zeta\left[G(y,\zeta) - \xi|\zeta|^p\right].$$

Thus, the definition of φ and (54) yield the following:

$$p\widetilde{G}(y,\zeta) - \widetilde{g}(y,\zeta)\zeta \geq 0 \quad \text{for a.e. } y \in \mathbb{R}^N \text{ and all } \zeta \in \mathbb{R}, \tag{56}$$

and

$$p\widetilde{G}(y,\zeta) - \widetilde{g}(y,\zeta)\zeta = 0 \quad \text{if and only if } \zeta = 0 \text{ or } |\zeta| \geq 2\zeta_3. \tag{57}$$

By the definition of $\widetilde{G}$ and (G1), we infer

$$\widetilde{G}(y,\zeta) \leq \rho_1(y)|\zeta| + \frac{\rho_2}{\ell}|\zeta|^\ell + \xi|\zeta|^p \tag{58}$$

for a.e. $y \in \mathbb{R}^N$ and all $\zeta \in \mathbb{R}$. Consider the modified energy functional $\widetilde{\mathcal{E}}_\theta : \mathfrak{E} \to \mathbb{R}$ given by

$$\widetilde{\mathcal{E}}_\theta(w) := \Phi(w) - \widetilde{\Psi}_\theta(w),$$

where

$$\widetilde{\Psi}_\theta(w) = \frac{1}{r}\int_{\mathbb{R}^N} \sigma(y)|w|^r\,dy + \theta\int_{\mathbb{R}^N} \widetilde{G}(y,w)\,dy.$$

Subsequently, by a standard argument invoking the embedding $\mathfrak{E} \hookrightarrow L^p(\mathbb{R}^N)$ and the differentiability of Φ, we can show that $\widetilde{\mathcal{E}}_\theta \in C^1(\mathfrak{E}, \mathbb{R})$ is an even functional. Furthermore, we have

$$\widetilde{\mathcal{E}}_\theta(u) = 0 = \langle \widetilde{\mathcal{E}}_\theta'(u), u\rangle \quad \text{if and only if} \quad u = 0. \tag{59}$$

Indeed, let $\widetilde{\mathcal{E}}_\theta(u) = \langle \widetilde{\mathcal{E}}_\theta'(u), u\rangle = 0$. Then, according to (M5), we find that

$$\begin{aligned}
0 &= -p\widetilde{\mathcal{E}}_\theta(u) \\
&= -p\mathcal{M}\left(\int_{\mathbb{R}^N} \mathcal{H}_{p,q}(y, |\nabla u|)\,dy\right) - p\int_{\mathbb{R}^N} \mathcal{H}_{\mathfrak{V},p,q}(y, |u|)\,dy \\
&\quad + \frac{p}{r}\int_{\mathbb{R}^N} \sigma(y)|u|^r\,dy + \theta p\int_{\mathbb{R}^N} \widetilde{G}(y,u)\,dy \\
&\geq -pM\left(\int_{\mathbb{R}^N} \mathcal{H}_{p,q}(y, |\nabla u|)\,dy\right)\int_{\mathbb{R}^N} \mathcal{H}_{p,q}(y, |\nabla u|)\,dy
\end{aligned} \tag{60}$$

$$
\begin{aligned}
&- \int_{\mathbb{R}^N} \mathcal{H}_{\mathfrak{V}}(y, |\nabla u|)\, dy + \int_{\mathbb{R}^N} \sigma(y)|u|^r\, dy + \theta \int_{\mathbb{R}^N} p\widetilde{G}(y, u)\, dy \\
&\geq -M\Big(\int_{\mathbb{R}^N} \mathcal{H}_{p,q}(y, |\nabla u|)\, dy\Big) \int_{\mathbb{R}^N} \mathcal{H}(y, |\nabla u|)\, dy \\
&- \int_{\mathbb{R}^N} \mathcal{H}_{\mathfrak{V}}(y, |\nabla u|)\, dy + \int_{\mathbb{R}^N} \sigma(y)|u|^r\, dy + \theta \int_{\mathbb{R}^N} p\widetilde{G}(y, u)\, dy
\end{aligned}
$$

and

$$
\begin{aligned}
\langle \widetilde{\mathcal{E}}_\theta'(u), u\rangle &= M\Big(\int_{\mathbb{R}^N} \mathcal{H}_{p,q}(y, |\nabla u|)\, dy\Big) \int_{\mathbb{R}^N} \mathcal{H}(y, |\nabla u|)\, dy \\
&+ \int_{\mathbb{R}^N} \mathcal{H}_{\mathfrak{V}}(y, |\nabla u|)\, dy - \int_{\mathbb{R}^N} \sigma(y)|u|^r\, dy - \theta \int_{\mathbb{R}^N} \widetilde{g}(y, u)u\, dy = 0. \qquad (61)
\end{aligned}
$$

Based on Equations (60) and (61), it follows that

$$
\int_{\mathbb{R}^N} \Big(p\widetilde{G}(y, u) - \widetilde{g}(y, u)u\Big)\, dy \leq 0.
$$

Consequently, the relations (56) and (57) imply $u = 0$.

$(\mathcal{A}_1)$: Let $\chi_n < 1$ for a sufficiently large n. Based on Lemmas 1 and 3 as well as the similar argument in (37), it follows that

$$
\begin{aligned}
\widetilde{\mathcal{E}}_\theta(w) &= \Phi(w) - \widetilde{\Psi}_\theta(w) \\
&= \mathcal{M}\Big(\int_{\mathbb{R}^N} \mathcal{H}_{p,q}(y, |\nabla w|)\, dy\Big) + \int_{\mathbb{R}^N} \mathcal{H}_{\mathfrak{V},p,q}(y, |w|)\, dy \\
&\quad - \frac{1}{r}\int_{\mathbb{R}^N} \sigma(y)|w|^r\, dy - \theta \int_{\mathbb{R}^N} \widetilde{G}(y, w)\, dy \\
&\geq \frac{\min\{\kappa_0, \vartheta\}}{\vartheta q}\Big[\int_{\mathbb{R}^N} \mathcal{H}_{p,q}(y, |\nabla w|)\, dy + \mathcal{H}_{\mathfrak{V},p,q}(y, |w|)\, dy\Big] \\
&\quad - \frac{1}{r}\int_{\mathbb{R}^N} \sigma(y)|w|^r\, dy - \theta \int_{\mathbb{R}^N} (G(y, w) + \xi|w|^p)\, dy \\
&\geq \frac{\min\{\kappa_0, \vartheta\}}{\vartheta q 2^p}\|w\|^p - \frac{1}{r}\|\sigma\|_{L^{\frac{\gamma_0}{\gamma_0 - r}}(\mathbb{R}^N)}\|w\|^r_{L^{\gamma_0}(\mathbb{R}^N)} \\
&\quad - \theta \int_{\mathbb{R}^N} G(y, w)\, dy - \theta\xi \int_{\mathbb{R}^N} |w|^p\, dy \\
&\geq \frac{\min\{\kappa_0, \vartheta\}}{\vartheta q 2^p}\|w\|^p - \frac{1}{r}\|\sigma\|_{L^{\frac{\gamma_0}{\gamma_0 - r}}(\mathbb{R}^N)}\|w\|^r_{L^{\gamma_0}(\mathbb{R}^N)} \\
&\quad - \theta \int_{\mathbb{R}^N} \Big(\rho_1(y)|w| + \frac{\rho_2}{\ell}|w|^\ell\Big)\, dy - \theta\xi\chi_n^p\|w\|^p \\
&\geq \frac{\min\{\kappa_0, \vartheta\}}{\vartheta q 2^p}\|w\|^p - \frac{1}{r}\|\sigma\|_{L^{\frac{\gamma_0}{\gamma_0 - r}}(\mathbb{R}^N)}\|w\|^r_{L^{\gamma_0}(\mathbb{R}^N)} \\
&\quad - \theta\|\rho_1\|_{L^{s'}(\mathbb{R}^N)}\|w\|_{L^s(\mathbb{R}^N)} - \frac{\theta\rho_2}{\ell}\|w\|^\ell_{L^\ell(\mathbb{R}^N)} - \theta\xi\chi_n^p\|w\|^p \\
&\geq \frac{\min\{\kappa_0, \vartheta\}}{\vartheta q 2^p}\|w\|^p - \frac{1}{r}\|\sigma\|_{L^{\frac{\gamma_0}{\gamma_0 - r}}(\mathbb{R}^N)}\chi_n^r\|w\|^r \\
&\quad - \theta\|\rho_1\|_{L^{s'}(\mathbb{R}^N)}\chi_n\|w\| - \frac{\theta\rho_2}{\ell}\chi_n^\ell\|w\|^\ell - \theta\xi\chi_n^p\|w\|^p \\
&\geq \frac{\min\{\kappa_0, \vartheta\}}{\vartheta q 2^p}\|w\|^p - \frac{1}{r}\|\sigma\|_{L^{\frac{\gamma_0}{\gamma_0 - r}}(\mathbb{R}^N)}\chi_n^r\|w\|^r \\
&\quad - \theta\|\rho_1\|_{L^{s'}(\mathbb{R}^N)}\chi_n\|w\| - \theta\Big(\frac{\rho_2}{\ell} + \xi\Big)\chi_n^p\|w\|^\ell.
\end{aligned}
$$

for a sufficiently large n and $\|w\| \geq 1$. Let us choose

$$\widetilde{\beta}_n = \left[\theta\left(\frac{\rho_2}{\ell} + \xi\right)\frac{\vartheta q 2^{p+1}\chi_n^p}{\min\{\kappa_0, \vartheta\}}\right]^{\frac{1}{p-2\ell}}$$

and let $w \in \mathfrak{G}_n$ with $\|w\| = \widetilde{\beta}_n > 1$ for a sufficiently large n. Then, there exists $n_0 \in \mathbb{N}$ such that

$$\begin{aligned}
\widetilde{\mathcal{E}}_\theta(w) \geq & \frac{\min\{\kappa_0, \vartheta\}}{\vartheta q 2^p}\|w\|^p - \frac{1}{r}\|\sigma\|_{L^{\frac{\gamma_0}{\gamma_0 - r}}(\mathbb{R}^N)}\chi_n^r\|w\|^r \\
& - \theta\|\rho_1\|_{L^{s'}(\mathbb{R}^N)}\chi_n\|w\| - \theta\left(\frac{\rho_2}{\ell} + \xi\right)\chi_n^p\|w\|^\ell \\
\geq & \frac{\min\{\kappa_0, \vartheta\}}{\vartheta q 2^{p+1}}\widetilde{\beta}_n^p - \frac{1}{r}\|\sigma\|_{L^{\frac{\gamma_0}{\gamma_0 - r}}(\mathbb{R}^N)}\left[\theta\left(\frac{\rho_2}{\ell} + \xi\right)\frac{\vartheta q 2^{p+1}}{\min\{\kappa_0, \vartheta\}}\right]^{\frac{r}{p-2\ell}}\chi_n^{\frac{2r(p-\ell)}{p-2\ell}} \\
& - \theta\|\rho_1\|_{L^{s'}(\mathbb{R}^N)}\left[\theta\left(\frac{\rho_2}{\ell} + \xi\right)\frac{\vartheta q 2^{p+1}}{\min\{\kappa_0, \vartheta\}}\right]^{\frac{1}{p-2\ell}}\chi_n^{\frac{2(p-\ell)}{p-2\ell}} \\
\geq & 0
\end{aligned}$$

for all $n \in \mathbb{N}$ with $n \geq n_0$ by being

$$\lim_{n\to\infty} \frac{\min\{\kappa_0, \vartheta\}}{\vartheta q 2^{p+1}}\widetilde{\beta}_n^p = \infty.$$

Then, we find the following:

$$\inf\{\widetilde{\mathcal{E}}_\theta(w) : w \in \mathfrak{G}_n, \|w\| = \widetilde{\beta}_n\} \geq 0.$$

$(\mathcal{A}_2)$: Observe that $\|\cdot\|_{L^\infty(\mathbb{R}^N)}$, $\|\cdot\|_{L^p(\mathbb{R}^N)}$, and $\|\cdot\|$ are equivalent on $\mathfrak{F}_n$. Then, there are positive constants $\widetilde{\varrho}_{1,n}$ and $\widetilde{\varrho}_{2,n}$ such that

$$\widetilde{\varrho}_{1,n}\|w\|_{L^\infty(\mathbb{R}^N)} \leq \|w\| \leq \widetilde{\varrho}_{2,n}\|w\|_{L^p(\mathbb{R}^N)} \tag{62}$$

for any $w \in \mathfrak{F}_n$. From (G6) and (G7), for any $\mathfrak{M}_3 > 0$, there exists $\zeta_3 \in (0, \zeta_2/2)$ such that

$$G(y, \zeta) \geq \frac{\mathfrak{M}_3\widetilde{\varrho}_{2,n}^p}{p}|\zeta|^p$$

for almost all $y \in \mathbb{R}^N$ and all $|\zeta| \leq \zeta_3$. Choose $\widetilde{\alpha}_n := \min\{\frac{1}{2}, \zeta_3\widetilde{\varrho}_{1,n}\}$ for all $n \in \mathbb{N}$. Then, we know that $\|w\|_{L^\infty(\mathbb{R}^N)} \leq \zeta_3$ for $w \in \mathfrak{F}_n$ with $\|w\| = \widetilde{\alpha}_n$, and so $\widetilde{G}(y, w) = G(y, w)$. From the analogous argument in (52) and based on (62), we derive the following:

$$\begin{aligned}
\widetilde{\mathcal{E}}_\theta(w) &= \mathcal{M}\left(\int_{\mathbb{R}^N}\mathcal{H}_{p,q}(y, |\nabla w|)\,dy\right) + \int_{\mathbb{R}^N}\mathcal{H}_{\mathfrak{V},p,q}(y, |w|)\,dy \\
&\quad - \frac{1}{r}\int_{\mathbb{R}^N}\sigma(y)|w|^r\,dy - \theta\int_{\mathbb{R}^N}\widetilde{G}(y, w)\,dy \\
&\leq \left(\sup_{0\leq\xi\leq\mathcal{K}} M(\xi)\right)\int_{\mathbb{R}^N}\mathcal{H}_{p,q}(y, |\nabla w|)\,dy \\
&\quad + \int_{\mathbb{R}^N}\mathcal{H}_{\mathfrak{V},p,q}(y, |w|)\,dy - \theta\int_{\mathbb{R}^N}\frac{\mathfrak{M}_3\widetilde{\varrho}_{2,n}^p}{p}|w|^p\,dy \\
&\leq C_{12}\|w\|^p - \frac{\theta\mathfrak{M}_3\widetilde{\varrho}_{2,n}^p}{p}\|w\|_{L^p(\mathbb{R}^N)}^p
\end{aligned}$$

$$
\begin{aligned}
&\le C_{12}\|w\|^p - \frac{\theta \mathfrak{M}_3}{p}\|w\|^p \\
&\le \frac{pC_{12} - \theta \mathfrak{M}_3}{p}\widetilde{\alpha}_n^p
\end{aligned}
$$

for any $w \in \mathfrak{F}_n$ with $\|w\| = \widetilde{\alpha}_n$. If we choose a sufficiently large $\mathfrak{M}_3$ such that $1 < \theta\mathfrak{M}_3$, we obtain the following:

$$\widetilde{\delta}_n = \max\{\widetilde{\mathcal{E}}_\theta(w) : w \in \mathfrak{F}_n, \|w\| = \widetilde{\alpha}_n\} < 0.$$

If necessary, we can change n_0 to a larger value so that $\widetilde{\beta}_n > \widetilde{\alpha}_n > 0$ for all $n \ge n_0$.

($\mathcal{A}_3$): Because $\mathfrak{Y}_n \cap \mathfrak{G}_n \neq \phi$ and $0 < \widetilde{\alpha}_n < \widetilde{\beta}_n$, we have $\widetilde{\phi}_n \le \widetilde{\delta}_n < 0$ for all $n \ge n_0$. For any $w \in \mathfrak{G}_n$ with $\|w\| = 1$ and $0 < t < \widetilde{\beta}_n$, we have

$$
\begin{aligned}
\widetilde{\mathcal{E}}_\theta(tw) &= \mathcal{M}\left(\int_{\mathbb{R}^N} \mathcal{H}_{p,q}(y, |\nabla tw|)\,dy\right) + \int_{\mathbb{R}^N} \mathcal{H}_{\mathfrak{V},p,q}(y, |tw|)\,dy \\
&\quad - \frac{1}{r}\int_{\mathbb{R}^N} \sigma(y)|tw|^r\,dy - \theta\int_{\mathbb{R}^N} \widetilde{G}(y, tw)\,dy \\
&\ge -\frac{1}{r}\widetilde{\beta}_n^r \int_{\mathbb{R}^N} \sigma(y)|w|^r\,dy - \theta\int_{\mathbb{R}^N} (G(y, tw) + \xi|tw|^p)\,dy \\
&\ge -\frac{1}{r}\widetilde{\beta}_n^r \|\sigma\|_{L^{\frac{\gamma_0}{\gamma_0 - r}}(\mathbb{R}^N)} \|w\|^r_{L^{\gamma_0}(\mathbb{R}^N)} \\
&\quad - \theta\int_{\mathbb{R}^N} G(y, tw)\,dy - \theta\xi\int_{\mathbb{R}^N} |tw|^p\,dy \\
&\ge -\frac{1}{r}\widetilde{\beta}_n^r \|\sigma\|_{L^{\frac{\gamma_0}{\gamma_0 - r}}(\mathbb{R}^N)} \|w\|^r_{L^{\gamma_0}(\mathbb{R}^N)} \\
&\quad - \theta\int_{\mathbb{R}^N} \rho_1(y)|tw|\,dy - \frac{\theta\rho_2}{\ell}\int_{\mathbb{R}^N} |tw|^\ell\,dy - \theta\xi\int_{\mathbb{R}^N} |tw|^p dy \\
&\ge -\frac{1}{r}\widetilde{\beta}_n^r \|\sigma\|_{L^{\frac{\gamma_0}{\gamma_0 - r}}(\mathbb{R}^N)} \|w\|^r_{L^{\gamma_0}(\mathbb{R}^N)} \\
&\quad - \theta\widetilde{\beta}_n\int_{\mathbb{R}^N} \rho_1(y)|w|\,dy - \frac{\theta\rho_2}{\ell}\widetilde{\beta}_n^\ell\int_{\mathbb{R}^N} |w|^\ell\,dy - \theta\xi\widetilde{\beta}_n^p\int_{\mathbb{R}^N} |w|^p\,dy \\
&\ge -\frac{1}{r}\|\sigma\|_{L^{\frac{\gamma_0}{\gamma_0 - r}}(\mathbb{R}^N)} \widetilde{\beta}_n^r\chi_n^r - \theta\|\rho_1\|_{L^{s'}(\mathbb{R}^N)}\widetilde{\beta}_n\chi_n - \frac{\theta\rho_2}{\ell}\widetilde{\beta}_n^\ell\chi_n^\ell - \theta\xi\widetilde{\beta}_n^p\chi_n^p,
\end{aligned}
$$

where χ_n is given in (44). Hence, we achieve

$$
\begin{aligned}
0 > \widetilde{\phi}_n &\ge -\frac{\|\sigma\|_{L^{\frac{\gamma_0}{\gamma_0 - r}}(\mathbb{R}^N)}}{r}\widetilde{\beta}_n^r\chi_n^r - \theta\|\rho_1\|_{L^{s'}(\mathbb{R}^N)}\widetilde{\beta}_n\chi_n - \frac{\theta\rho_2}{\ell}\widetilde{\beta}_n^\ell\chi_n^\ell - \theta\xi\widetilde{\beta}_n^p\chi_n^p \\
&\ge -\frac{\|\sigma\|_{L^{\frac{\gamma_0}{\gamma_0 - r}}(\mathbb{R}^N)}}{r}\left[\theta\left(\frac{\rho_2}{\ell} + \xi\right)\frac{\vartheta q 2^{p+1}}{\min\{\kappa_0, \vartheta\}}\right]^{\frac{r}{p-2\ell}} \chi_n^{\frac{2r(p-\ell)}{p-2\ell}} \\
&\quad - \theta\|\rho_1\|_{L^{s'}(\mathbb{R}^N)}\left[\theta\left(\frac{\rho_2}{\ell} + \xi\right)\frac{\vartheta q 2^{p+1}}{\min\{\kappa_0, \vartheta\}}\right]^{\frac{1}{p-2\ell}} \chi_n^{\frac{2(p-\ell)}{p-2\ell}} \\
&\quad - \frac{\theta\rho_2}{\ell}\left[\theta\left(\frac{\rho_2}{\ell} + \xi\right)\frac{\vartheta q 2^{p+1}}{\min\{\kappa_0, \vartheta\}}\right]^{\frac{\ell}{p-2\ell}} \chi_n^{\frac{2\ell(p-\ell)}{p-2\ell}} \\
&\quad - \theta\xi\left[\theta\left(\frac{\rho_2}{\ell} + \xi\right)\frac{\vartheta q 2^{p+1}}{\min\{\kappa_0, \vartheta\}}\right]^{\frac{p}{p-2\ell}} \chi_n^{\frac{2p(p-\ell)}{p-2\ell}}.
\end{aligned}
$$

Because $p < \ell$ and $\chi_n \to 0$ as $n \to \infty$, we conclude that $\lim_{n\to\infty}\widetilde{\phi}_n = 0$.

($\mathcal{A}_4$): Before proving that $\widetilde{\mathcal{E}}_\theta$ ensures the $(C)_c^*$-condition, we have to show that $\widetilde{\Psi}'_\theta$ is sequentially weakly strongly continuous on $\mathfrak{E}$ for any $\theta > 0$ and that $\widetilde{\mathcal{E}}_\theta$ is coercive.

Therefore, we first derive that $\widetilde{\mathcal{E}}_\theta$ ensures the $(C)_c$-condition for any $c \in \mathbb{R}$ and for every $\theta \in \Gamma$. Let $\{w_k\}$ be a sequence in $\mathfrak{E}$ such that $w_k \rightharpoonup w$ in $\mathfrak{E}$ as $k \to \infty$. Since $\{w_k\}$ is bounded in $\mathfrak{E}$, Lemma 3 guarantees that there exists a subsequence $\left\{w_{k_j}\right\}$ such that

$$w_{k_j}(y) \to w(y) \text{ a.e. in } \mathbb{R}^N \text{ and } w_{k_j} \to w \text{ in } L^m(\mathbb{R}^N) \text{ as } j \to \infty, \tag{63}$$

where $p \le m < p^*$. By the convergence principle, there exists a subsequence $\{w_{k_j}\}$ and a non-negative function $v \in L^p(\mathbb{R}^N) \cap L^\ell(\mathbb{R}^N) \cap L^{\gamma_0}(\mathbb{R}^N)$ such that $w_{k_j}(y) \to v(y)$ as $j \to \infty$ for almost all $y \in \mathbb{R}^N$, and $|w_{k_j}(y)| \le v(y)$ for all $j \in \mathbb{N}$ and for almost all $y \in \mathbb{R}^N$. For any $u \in \mathfrak{E}$, we have

$$\begin{aligned}
&\left|\langle \widetilde{\Psi}'_\theta\left(w_{k_j}\right) - \widetilde{\Psi}'_\theta(w), u\rangle\right| \\
&= \Bigg| \int_{\mathbb{R}^N} \left(\sigma(y)\left|w_{k_j}\right|^{r-2} w_{k_j} - \sigma(y)|w|^{r-2}w\right) u\, dy \\
&\qquad + \theta \int_{\mathbb{R}^N} \left(\widetilde{g}\left(y, w_{k_j}\right) - \widetilde{g}(y,w)\right) u\, dy \Bigg| \\
&\le \left(\int_{\mathbb{R}^N} \left|\sigma(y)\left|w_{k_j}\right|^{r-2} w_{k_j} - \sigma(y)|w|^{r-2}w\right|^{r'} dy\right) \|u\|_{L^r(\mathbb{R}^N)} \\
&\qquad + \theta \left|\int_{\mathbb{R}^N} \left(\widetilde{g}\left(y, w_{k_j}\right) - \widetilde{g}(y,w)\right) u\, dy\right|.
\end{aligned}$$

By Young's inequality, we infer that

$$\begin{aligned}
&\int_{\mathbb{R}^N} \left|\sigma(y)\left|w_{k_j}\right|^{r-2} w_{k_j} - \sigma(y)|w|^{r-2}w\right|^{r'} dy \\
&\le C_{13} \int_{\mathbb{R}^N} |\sigma(y)|^{\frac{1}{r-1}} |\sigma(y)| \left(\left|w_{k_j}\right|^r + |w|^r\right) dy \\
&\le C_{14} \int_{\mathbb{R}^N} |\sigma(y)| \left(\left|w_{k_j}\right|^r + |w|^r\right) dy \\
&\le C_{15} \int_{\mathbb{R}^N} \left(\frac{2(\gamma_0 - r)}{\gamma_0} |\sigma(y)|^{\frac{\gamma_0}{\gamma_0 - r}} + \frac{r}{\gamma_0}|v|^{\gamma_0} + \frac{r}{\gamma_0}|w|^{\gamma_0}\right) dy
\end{aligned} \tag{64}$$

for some positive constants C_{13}, C_{14}, and C_{15}. By the definition of φ and (G1) and based on (55), we deduce that

$$|\widetilde{g}(y,\zeta)| \le C_{16}\left(\rho_1(y) + \rho_2|\zeta|^{\ell-1} + \xi p|\zeta|^{p-1}\right). \tag{65}$$

Due to (65), we obtain

$$\begin{aligned}
&\left|\int_{\mathbb{R}^N} \left(\widetilde{g}\left(y, w_{k_j}\right) - \widetilde{g}(y,w)\right) u\, dy\right| \\
&\le \int_{\mathbb{R}^N} \left(\left|\widetilde{g}\left(y, w_{k_j}\right)\right| + |\widetilde{g}(y,w)|\right)|u|\, dy \\
&\le C_{17} \int_{\mathbb{R}^N} \left(2\rho_1(y) + \rho_2\left|w_{k_j}\right|^{\ell-1} + \xi p\left|w_{k_j}\right|^{p-1} + \rho_2|w|^{\ell-1} + \xi p|w|^{p-1}\right)|u|\, dy \\
&\le C_{17} \int_{\mathbb{R}^N} \left(2\rho_1(y) + \rho_2\left(|v|^{\ell-1} + |w|^{\ell-1}\right) + \xi p\left(|v|^{p-1} + |w|^{p-1}\right)\right)|u|\, dy
\end{aligned} \tag{66}$$

for some positive constants C_{16} and C_{17}. Invoking (63)–(66) and the convergence principle, we find the following:

$$\left|\sigma(y)\left|w_{k_j}\right|^{r-2} w_{k_j} - \sigma(y)|w|^{r-2}w\right|^{r'} \le f_1(y) \text{ and } \left|\left(\widetilde{g}\left(y, w_{k_j}\right) - \widetilde{g}(y,w)\right)u\right| \le f_2(y)$$

for almost all $y \in \mathbb{R}^N$ and for some $f_1, f_2 \in L^1(\mathbb{R}^N)$, and also, $\sigma(y)\left|w_{k_j}\right|^{r-2} w_{k_j} \to \sigma(y)|w|^{r-2}w$ and $\left|\left(\widetilde{g}\left(y, w_{k_j}\right) - \widetilde{g}(y,w)\right)u\right| \to 0$ as $j \to \infty$ for almost all $y \in \mathbb{R}^N$. This, together with Lebesgue's dominated convergence theorem, yields that

$$\begin{aligned}
&\|\widetilde{\Psi}'_\theta\left(w_{k_j}\right) - \widetilde{\Psi}'_\theta(w)\|_{\mathfrak{E}^*} \\
&= \sup_{\|u\|\le 1}\left|\left\langle \widetilde{\Psi}'_\theta\left(w_{k_j}\right) - \widetilde{\Psi}'_\theta(w), u\right\rangle\right| \\
&= \sup_{\|u\|\le 1}\left|\int_{\mathbb{R}^N}\left(\sigma(y)\left|w_{k_j}\right|^{r-2} w_{k_j} - \sigma(y)|w|^{\gamma-2}w\right)u\,dy\right. \\
&\qquad \left. + \theta\int_{\mathbb{R}^N}\left(\widetilde{g}\left(y, w_{k_j}\right) - \widetilde{g}(y,w)\right)u\,dy\right| \to 0
\end{aligned}$$

as $j \to \infty$. Therefore, we derive that $\widetilde{\Psi}'_\theta\left(w_{k_j}\right) \to \widetilde{\Psi}'_\theta(w)$ in $\mathfrak{E}^*$ as $j \to \infty$. Let $w \in \mathfrak{E}$ with $\|w\| \ge 1$. We set $\Lambda_1 := \{y \in \mathbb{R}^N : |w(y)| \le \zeta_3\}$, $\Lambda_2 := \{y \in \mathbb{R}^N : \zeta_3 \le |w(y)| \le 2\zeta_3\}$, and $\Lambda_3 := \{y \in \mathbb{R}^N : 2\zeta_3 \le |w(y)|\}$, where ζ_3 is given in (57). From the condition of φ, we have

$$\begin{aligned}
\widetilde{\mathcal{E}}_\theta(w) &= \mathcal{M}\left(\int_{\mathbb{R}^N}\mathcal{H}_{p,q}(y,|\nabla w|)\,dy\right) + \int_{\mathbb{R}^N}\mathcal{H}_{\mathfrak{V},p,q}(y,|w|)\,dy \\
&\quad - \frac{1}{r}\int_{\mathbb{R}^N}\sigma(y)|w|^r\,dy - \theta\int_{\mathbb{R}^N}\widetilde{G}(y,w)\,dy \\
&\ge \frac{\min\{\kappa_0,\vartheta\}}{\vartheta q 2^p}\|w\|^p - \frac{1}{r}\|\sigma\|_{L^{\frac{\gamma_0}{\gamma_0-r}}(\mathbb{R}^N)}\|w\|^r_{L^{\gamma_0}(\mathbb{R}^N)} - \theta\int_{\Lambda_1}|G(y,w)|\,dy \\
&\quad - \theta\int_{\Lambda_2}\varphi(w)|G(y,w)| + (1-\varphi(w))\xi|w|^p\,dy - \theta\int_{\Lambda_3}\xi|w|^p\,dy \\
&\ge \frac{\min\{\kappa_0,\vartheta\}}{\vartheta q 2^p}\|w\|^p - \frac{1}{r}\|\sigma\|_{L^{\frac{\gamma_0}{\gamma_0-r}}(\mathbb{R}^N)} C^r_{\gamma_0,imb}\|w\|^r \\
&\quad - \theta\int_{\Lambda_1\cup\Lambda_2}|G(y,w)|\,dy - \theta\int_{\Lambda_2\cup\Lambda_3}\xi|w|^p\,dy \\
&\ge \frac{\min\{\kappa_0,\vartheta\}}{\vartheta q 2^p}\|w\|^p - \frac{1}{r}\|\sigma\|_{L^{\frac{\gamma_0}{\gamma_0-r}}(\mathbb{R}^N)} C^r_{\gamma_0,imb}\|w\|^r \\
&\quad - \theta\int_{\Lambda_1\cup\Lambda_2}\rho_1(y)|w|\,dy - \theta\int_{\Lambda_1\cup\Lambda_2}\frac{\rho_2}{\ell}|w|^\ell\,dy - \theta\int_{\Lambda_2\cup\Lambda_3}\xi|w|^p\,dy \\
&\ge \frac{\min\{\kappa_0,\vartheta\}}{\vartheta q 2^p}\|w\|^p - \frac{1}{r}\|\sigma\|_{L^{\frac{\gamma_0}{\gamma_0-r}}(\mathbb{R}^N)} C^r_{\gamma_0,imb}\|w\|^r \\
&\quad - 2\theta\|\rho_1\|_{L^{s'}(\mathbb{R}^N)}\|w\|_{L^s(\mathbb{R}^N)} - \theta\left(\frac{\rho_2}{\ell} + \xi\right)\int_{\mathbb{R}^N}|w|^p\,dy \\
&\ge \frac{\min\{\kappa_0,\vartheta\}}{\vartheta q 2^p}\|w\|^p - \frac{1}{r}\|\sigma\|_{L^{\frac{\gamma_0}{\gamma_0-r}}(\mathbb{R}^N)} C^r_{\gamma_0,imb}\|w\|^r \\
&\quad - 2C_{s,imb}\theta\|\rho_1\|_{L^{s'}(\mathbb{R}^N)}\|w\| - \theta\left(\frac{\rho_2}{\ell} + \xi\right)\|w\|^p_{L^p(\mathbb{R}^N)} \\
&\ge \left[\frac{\min\{\kappa_0,\vartheta\}}{\vartheta q 2^p} - \theta\left(\frac{\rho_2}{\ell} + \xi\right)C_{p,imb}\right]\|w\|^p \\
&\quad - \frac{1}{r}\|\sigma\|_{L^{\frac{\gamma_0}{\gamma_0-r}}(\mathbb{R}^N)} C^r_{\gamma_0,imb}\|w\|^r - 2C_{s,imb}\theta\|\rho_1\|_{L^{s'}(\mathbb{R}^N)}\|w\|
\end{aligned}$$

where $C_{m,imb}$ is an embedding constant of $\mathfrak{E} \hookrightarrow L^m(\mathbb{R}^N)$ for any m with $p \le m < p^*$. Therefore, we deduce that for any

$$\theta \in \Gamma := \left(0, \frac{\ell\min\{\kappa_0,\vartheta\}}{\vartheta q 2^p(\rho_2 + \ell\xi)C_{p,imb}}\right),$$

the functional $\widetilde{\mathcal{E}}_\theta$ is coercive in $\mathfrak{E}$; that is, $\widetilde{\mathcal{E}}_\theta(w) \to \infty$ as $\|w\| \to \infty$. Based on the analogous argument in Lemma 9 in [47], it follows that Φ' is strictly monotone and coercive. Similar to the proof of Lemma 11, Φ' is a mapping of type (S_+). According to the Browder–Minty theorem, the inverse operator of Φ' exists (see Theorem 26.A in [53]). Since Φ' is of type (S_+), it is clear that it has a continuous inverse. From the compactness of the operator $\widetilde{\Psi}'_\theta$ and the coercivity of $\widetilde{\mathcal{E}}_\theta$, it follows that the functional $\widetilde{\mathcal{E}}_\theta$ satisfies the $(C)_c$-condition for any $c \in \mathbb{R}$ and for every $\theta \in \Gamma$ as required.

Finally, we show that $(\mathcal{A}_4)$ is verified. Let $c \in \mathbb{R}$ and let the sequence $\{w_k\}$ in $\mathfrak{E}$ be such that $w_k \in \mathfrak{F}_k$ for any $k \in \mathbb{N}$,

$$\widetilde{\mathcal{E}}_\theta(w_k) \to c \quad \text{and} \quad \|(\widetilde{\mathcal{E}}_\theta|_{\mathfrak{F}_k})'(w_k)\|_{\mathfrak{E}^*}(1 + \|w_k\|) \to 0 \text{ as } k \to \infty.$$

Then, based on the coercivity of $\widetilde{\mathcal{E}}_\theta$, it follows that $\{w_k\}$ is bounded in $\mathfrak{E}$ for every $\theta \in \Gamma$. Following the concept of the proof of Lemma 11, we deduce that $w_k \to w_0$ in $\mathfrak{E}$ as $k \to \infty$ and also that w_0 is a critical point of $\widetilde{\mathcal{E}}_\theta$. Therefore, we conclude that the functional $\widetilde{\mathcal{E}}_\theta$ satisfies the $(C)^*_c$-condition for any $c \in \mathbb{R}$ and for any $\theta > 0$. This shows the condition $(\mathcal{A}_4)$.

Consequently, all conditions of Proposition 10 hold, and thus, for $\theta \in \Gamma$, we find a sequence of negative critical values d_k for $\widetilde{\mathcal{E}}_\theta$ satisfying $d_k \to 0$ when k goes to ∞. Then, for any $\{w_k\} \in \mathfrak{E}$ with $\widetilde{\mathcal{E}}_\theta(w_k) = d_k$ and $\|\widetilde{\mathcal{E}}'_\theta(w_k)\|_{\mathfrak{E}^*} = 0$, the sequence $\{w_k\}$ is a $(C)_0$-sequence of $\widetilde{\mathcal{E}}_\theta(w)$, and $\{w_k\}$ yields a convergent subsequence. Thus, up to the subsequence denoted by $\{w_k\}$, we have $w_k \to w$ in $\mathfrak{E}$ as $k \to \infty$. Equations (56), (57), and (59) imply that 0 is the only critical point with 0 energy and the subsequence $\{w_k\}$ has to converge to 0 in $\mathfrak{E}$; thus, $\|w_k\|_{L^t(\mathbb{R}^N)} \to 0$ as $n \to \infty$ for any t with $p \le t \le p^*$. By virtue of Proposition 1, any weak solution w of (1) belongs to the space $L^\infty(\mathbb{R}^N)$, and there are positive constants of C, η independent of w such that

$$\|w\|_{L^\infty(\mathbb{R}^N)} \le C\|w\|^\eta_{L^\ell(\mathbb{R}^N)}.$$

Therefore, we know $\|w_k\|_{L^\infty(\mathbb{R}^N)} \to 0$. Hence, by applying (56) and (57) once again, we achieve $\|w_k\|_{L^\infty(\mathbb{R}^N)} \le \zeta_3$ for a sufficiently large k. Thus, $\{w_k\}$ with a sufficiently large k is a sequence of weak solutions to (1). The proof is complete. □

4. Conclusions

In order to use the dual fountain theorem, the authors of [23,36,37,40,47] considered the existence of two sequences $0 < \alpha_n < \beta_n \to 0$ as $n \to \infty$. However, our approach differs from the above papers. In view of the papers [32–35], we adopted the conditions (G5) and

(g) $G(y, \zeta) = o(|\zeta|^q)$ as $\zeta \to 0$ uniformly for all $y \in \mathbb{R}^N$.

These conditions play an important role in proving the assumptions of the dual fountain theorem, and the authors of [30,32–35] established the existence of two sequences $0 < \alpha_n < \beta_n$, which are both sufficiently large. However, when utilizing the analogous argument from [33,34], we cannot ensure property (2) in Lemma 14. More precisely, if we replace β_n in (51) with

$$\hat{\beta}_n = \left[\left(\frac{1}{r}\|\sigma\|_{L^{\frac{\gamma_0}{\gamma_0 - r}}(\mathbb{R}^N)} + \frac{\theta\rho_2}{\ell}\right)\frac{\vartheta q 2^{p+1}}{\min\{\kappa_0, \vartheta\}}\chi_n^r\right]^{\frac{1}{p-\ell}},$$

and $r + p > \ell$, then in Equation (53),

$$\hat{\beta}_n\chi_n = \left[\left(\frac{1}{r}\|\sigma\|_{L^{\frac{\gamma_0}{\gamma_0 - r}}(\mathbb{R}^N)} + \frac{\theta\rho_2}{\ell}\right)\frac{\vartheta q 2^{p+1}}{\min\{\kappa_0, \vartheta\}}\right]^{\frac{1}{p-\ell}}\chi_n^{\frac{r+p-\ell}{p-\ell}} \to \infty \text{ as } n \to \infty.$$

However, the authors of [32,35] overcame this difficulty with a new setting for β_n, as in (51). Although the basic idea for proving Lemmas 13 and 14 is analogous to [32,35], in this paper, we derive these conditions without assuming (G5) and (g). For this reason, our approach is slightly different from those of previous related studies [23,32–37,40,47].

Additionally, a new research direction is the study of Kirchhoff-Schrödinger-type problems with Hardy potentials:

$$-M\left(\int_{\mathbb{R}^N}\frac{1}{p}|\nabla w|^p+\frac{\nu(y)}{q}|\nabla w|^q\,dy\right)\operatorname{div}(|\nabla w|^{p-2}\nabla w+\nu(y)|\nabla w|^{q-2}\nabla w)$$
$$+\mathfrak{V}(y)(|w|^{p-2}w+\nu(y)|w|^{q-2}w)=\lambda\left(\frac{|w|^{p-2}w}{|y|^p}+\nu(y)\frac{|w|^{q-2}w}{|y|^q}\right)+\theta g(y,w)\quad \text{in } \mathbb{R}^N,$$

where $N\geq 2, 1<p<q<N, \lambda\in(-\infty,\lambda^*)$ for some $\lambda^*>0$, θ is a positive real parameter, $g:\mathbb{R}^N\times\mathbb{R}\to\mathbb{R}$ is a Carathéodory function,

$$\frac{q}{p}\leq 1+\frac{1}{N},\qquad \nu:\mathbb{R}^N\to[0,\infty) \text{ is Lipschitz continuous,}$$

and $\mathfrak{V}:\mathbb{R}^N\to(0,\infty)$ is a potential function satisfying (V), and a Kirchhoff function $M:\mathbb{R}_0^+\to\mathbb{R}^+$ satisfies the conditions (M1) and (M2).

Because of the term $\lambda(|w|^{p-2}w|y|^{-p}+\nu(y)|w|^{q-2}w|y|^{-q})$, when $\lambda\neq 0$, the classical variational approach is not applicable to our focus in the present paper. The reason is that the Hardy inequality only guarantees the embeddings of the Musielak–Orlicz–Sobolev space $W_0^{1,\mathcal{H}}(\mathbb{R}^N)\hookrightarrow L^p(\mathbb{R}^N,|y|^{-p})$ and $W_0^{1,\mathcal{H}}(\mathbb{R}^N)\hookrightarrow L^q(\mathbb{R}^N,\nu(y),|y|^{-q})$. However, these embeddings are not compact. Hence, problems with $\lambda\neq 0$ must be handled more carefully due to the lack of compactness.

Also, we indicate some further research for degenerated Kirchhoff coefficients as follows.

$$\begin{cases}-M(\varphi_{\mathcal{H}}(|\nabla u|))\operatorname{div}\big((|\nabla u|^{p-2}+b(y)|\nabla u|^{q-2})\nabla u\big)=g(u) & \text{in } \Omega,\\ u=0 & \text{on } \partial\Omega,\end{cases}$$

where the modular function $\varphi_{\mathcal{H}}$ is defined by $\varphi_{\mathcal{H}}(|\nabla u|):=\int_\Omega|\nabla u|^p+b(y)|\nabla u|^q\,dy$ for all $u\in W_0^{1,\mathcal{H}}(\Omega)$, g is a continuous function with suitable conditions, and the exponents p,q and the weight function $b:\Omega\to[0,+\infty)$ satisfy the following condition:

(K1) $1<p<N, p<q<p^*:=\frac{Np}{N-p}$, and $b\in L^\infty(\Omega;[0,+\infty))$.

Also, $M:[0,+\infty)\to[0,+\infty)$ is the Kirchhoff function satisfying the condition:

(K2) M is continuous and there are constants $0=s_0<s_1<s_2<\cdots<s_R$ such that $M(s_\ell)=0$ for each $\ell\in\{0,1,\ldots,R\}$ and $M(s)>0$ for all $s\in[0,s_R]\setminus\{s_0,s_1,\ldots,s_R\}$.

Regarding this problem, the authors of [54] considered a nonlinear elliptic equation involving a nonlocal term that vanishes at finitely many points, a double phase differential operator that satisfies unbalanced growth, and a nonlinear reaction term. The model is referred as the double phase degenerate Kirchhoff problem, as it involves a nonlocal Kirchhoff term, too. The major contribution of this paper is to establish a multiplicity theorem in which the main method is based on a truncation technique and variational method.

Author Contributions: Conceptualization, Y.-H.K.; Formal analysis, T.-J.J. All authors contributed equally to the writing of this paper. All authors have read and approved of the final manuscript.

Funding: This research received no funding.

Data Availability Statement: Data sharing is not applicable to this article, as no data sets were generated or analyzed during the current study.

Conflicts of Interest: The authors declare that they have no competing interests.

References

1. Zhikov, V.V. Averaging of functionals of the calculus of variations and elasticity theory. *Izv. Ross. Akad. Nauk Ser. Mat.* **1986**, *50*, 675–710. [CrossRef]
2. Zhikov, V.V. On Lavrentiev's phenomenon. *Russ. J. Math. Phys.* **1995**, *3*, 249–269.
3. Baroni, P.; Colombo, M.; Mingione, G. Harnack inequalites for double-phase functionals. *Nonlinear Anal.* **2015**, *121*, 206–222. [CrossRef]
4. Baroni, P.; Colombo, M.; Mingione, G. Non-autonomous functionals, borderline cases and related function classes. *St. Petersburg Math. J.* **2016**, *27*, 347–379. [CrossRef]
5. Baroni, P.; Colombo, M.; Mingione, G. Regularity for general functionals with double phase. *Calc. Var. Partial Differential Equations* **2018**, *57*, 62. [CrossRef]
6. Colombo, M.; Mingione, G. Regularity for double phase variational problems. *Arch. Ration. Mech. Anal.* **2015**, *215*, 443–496. [CrossRef]
7. Colombo, M.; Mingione, G. Bounded minimisers of double phase variational integrals. *Arch. Ration. Mech. Anal.* **2015**, *218*, 219–273. [CrossRef]
8. Colombo, M.; Mingione, G. Calderón-Zygmund estimates and non-uniformly elliptic operators. *J. Funct. Anal.* **2016**, *270*, 1416–1478. [CrossRef]
9. Colasuonno, F.; Squassina, M. Eigenvalues for double phase variational integrals. *Ann. Mat. Pura Appl.* **2016**, *195*, 1917–1959. [CrossRef]
10. Zhang, Q.; Rădulescu, V.D. Double phase anisotropic variational problems and combined effects of reaction and absorption terms. *J. Math. Pures Appl.* **2018**, *118*, 159–203. [CrossRef]
11. Crespo-Blanco, Á.; Gasiński, L.; Harjulehto, P.; Winkert, P. A new class of double phase variable exponent problems: Existence and uniqueness. *J. Differential Equations* **2022**, *323*, 182–228. [CrossRef]
12. Gasiński, L.; Winkert, P. Existence and uniqueness results for double phase problems with convection term. *J. Differential Equations* **2020**, *268*, 4183–4193. [CrossRef]
13. Zeng, S.D.; Bai, Y.R.; Gasiński, L.; Winkert, P. Existence results for double phase implicit obstacle problems involving multivalued operators. *Calc. Var. Partial. Differ. Equ.* **2020**, *59*, 176. [CrossRef]
14. Kirchhoff, G.R. *Vorlesungen über Mathematische Physik, Mechanik*; Teubner: Leipzig, Germany, 1876.
15. Autuori, G.; Fiscella, A.; Pucci, P. Stationary Kirchhoff problems involving a fractional elliptic operator and a critical nonlinearity. *Nonlinear Anal.* **2015**, *125*, 699–714. [CrossRef]
16. Bisci, G.M.; Repovš, D. Higher non-local problems with bounded potential. *J. Math. Anal. Appl.* **2014**, *420*, 167–176. [CrossRef]
17. Dai, G.W.; Hao, R.F. Existence of solutions of a $p(x)$-Kirchhoff-type equation. *J. Math. Anal. Appl.* **2009**, *359*, 275–284. [CrossRef]
18. Fiscella, A.; Marino, G.; Pinamonti, A.; Verzellesi, S. Multiple solutions for nonlinear boundary value problems of Kirchhoff type on a double phase setting. *Rev. Mat. Complut.* **2023**, 1–32. . [CrossRef]
19. Fiscella, A.; Pinamonti, A. Existence and Multiplicity Results for Kirchhoff-Type Problems on a Double-Phase Setting. *Mediterr. J. Math.* **2023**, *20*, 33. [CrossRef]
20. Fiscella, A.; Valdinoci, E. A critical Kirchhoff-type problem involving a non-local operator. *Nonlinear Anal.* **2014**, *94*, 156–170. [CrossRef]
21. Gupta, S.; Dwivedi, G. Kirchhoff type elliptic equations with double criticality in Musielak-Sobolev spaces. *Math. Methods Appl. Sci.* **2023**, *46*, 8463–8477. [CrossRef]
22. Huang, T.; Deng, S. Existence of ground state solutions for Kirchhoff-type problem without the Ambrosetti–Rabinowitz condition. *Appl. Math. Lett.* **2021**, *113*, 106866. [CrossRef]
23. Liu, D.C. On a $p(x)$-Kirchhoff-type equation via fountain theorem and dual-fountain theorem. *Nonlinear Anal.* **2010**, *72*, 302–308. [CrossRef]
24. Pucci, P.; Saldi, S. Critical stationary Kirchhoff equations in $\mathbb{R}^N$ involving non-local operators. *Rev. Mat. Iberoam.* **2016**, *32*, 1–22. [CrossRef]
25. Pucci, P.; Xiang, M.Q.; Zhang, B.L. Multiple solutions for nonhomogeneous Schrödinger–Kirchhoff type equations involving the fractional p-Laplacian in $\mathbb{R}^N$. *Calc. Var. Partial Differential Equations* **2015**, *54*, 2785–2806. [CrossRef]
26. Pucci, P.; Xiang, M.Q.; Zhang, B.L. Existence and multiplicity of entire solutions for fractional p-Kirchhoff equations. *Adv. Nonlinear Anal.* **2016**, *5*, 27–55. [CrossRef]
27. Xiang, M.Q.; Zhang, B.L.; Ferrara, M. Existence of solutions for Kirchhoff-type problem involving the non-local fractional p-Laplacian. *J. Math. Anal. Appl.* **2015**, *424*, 1021–1041. [CrossRef]
28. Xiang, M.Q.; Zhang, B.L.; Guo, X.Y. Infinitely many solutions for a fractional Kirchhoff-type problem via Fountain Theorem. *Nonlinear Anal.* **2015**, *120*, 299–313. [CrossRef]
29. Bisci, G.M.; Rădulescu, V. Mountain pass solutions for non-local equations. *Ann. Acad. Sci. Fenn.* **2014**, *39*, 579–592. [CrossRef]
30. Kim, J.M.; Kim, Y.-H. Multiple solutions to the double phase problems involving concave–convex nonlinearities. *AIMS Math.* **2023**, *8*, 5060–5079. [CrossRef]
31. Kim, Y.-H. Multiple solutions to Kirchhoff-Schrödinger equations involving the $p(\cdot)$-Laplace-type operator. *AIMS Math.* **2023**, *8*, 9461–9482. [CrossRef]

32. Cen, J.; Kim, S.J.; Kim, Y.-H.; Zeng, S. Multiplicity results of solutions to the double phase anisotropic variational problems involving variable exponent. *Adv. Differential Equations* **2023**, *28*, 467–504. [CrossRef]
33. Ge, B.; Lv, D.-J.; Lu, J.-F. Multiple solutions for a class of double phase problem without the Ambrosetti-Rabinowitz conditions. *Nonlinear Anal.* **2019**, *188*, 294–315. [CrossRef]
34. Hurtado, E.J.; Miyagaki, O.H.; Rodrigues, R.S. Existence and multiplicity of solutions for a class of elliptic equations without Ambrosetti-Rabinowitz type conditions. *J. Dynam. Differential Equation* **2018**, *30*, 405–432. [CrossRef]
35. Lee, J.; Kim, J.-M.; Kim, Y.-H.; Scapellato, A. On multiple solutions to a non-local Fractional $p(\cdot)$-Laplacian problem with concave–convex nonlinearities. *Adv. Cont. Discr. Mod.* **2022**, *14*, 1–25.
36. Teng, K. Multiple solutions for a class of fractional Schrödinger equations in $\mathbb{R}^N$. *Nonlinear Anal. Real World Appl.* **2015**, *21*, 76–86. [CrossRef]
37. Willem, M. *Minimax Theorems*; Birkhauser: Basel, Switzerland, 1996.
38. Ho, K.; Winkert, P. Infinitely many solutions to Kirchhoff double phase problems with variable exponents. *Appl. Math. Lett.* **2023**, *145*, 108783. [CrossRef]
39. Joe, W.J.; Kim, S.J.; Kim, Y.-H.; Oh, M.W. Multiplicity of solutions for double phase equations with concave–convex nonlinearities. *J. Appl. Anal. Comput.* **2021**, *11*, 2921–2946. [CrossRef]
40. Lee, J.I.; Kim, Y.-H. Multiplicity of Radially Symmetric Small Energy Solutions for Quasilinear Elliptic Equations Involving Nonhomogeneous Operators. *Mathematics* **2020**, *8*, 128. [CrossRef]
41. Tan, Z.; Fang, F. On superlinear $p(x)$-Laplacian problems without Ambrosetti and Rabinowitz condition. *Nonlinear Anal.* **2012**, *75*, 3902–3915. [CrossRef]
42. Wang, Z.-Q. Nonlinear boundary value problems with concave nonlinearities near the origin. *Nonlinear Differ. Equ. Appl.* **2001**, *8*, 15–33. [CrossRef]
43. Heinz, H.P. Free Ljusternik-Schnirelman theory and the bifurcation diagrams of certain singular nonlinear problems. *J. Differ. Equ.* **1987**, *66*, 263–300. [CrossRef]
44. Diening, L.; Harjulehto, P.; Hästö, P.; Růžička, M. *Lebesgue and Sobolev Spaces with Variable Exponents*; Lecture Notes in Mathematics; Springer: Heidelberg, Germany, 2011; Volume 2017.
45. Harjulehto, P.; Hästö, P. *Orlicz Spaces and Generalized Orlicz Spaces*; Lecture Notes in Mathematics; Springer: Cham, Switzerland, 2019; Volume 2236, p. x+167.
46. Musielak, J. *Orlicz Spaces and Modular Spaces*; Lecture Notes in Mathematics; Springer: Berlin, Germany, 1983; Volume 1034.
47. Stegliński, R. Infinitely many solutions for double phase problem with unbounded potential in $\mathbb{R}^N$. *Nonlinear Anal.* **2022**, *214*, 112580. [CrossRef]
48. Lin, X.; Tang, X.H. Existence of infinitely many solutions for p-Laplacian equations in $\mathbb{R}^N$. *Nonlinear Anal.* **2013**, *92*, 72–81. [CrossRef]
49. Simon, J. Regularite de la solution d'une equation non lineaire dans $\mathbb{R}^N$. In *Journées d'Analyse Non Linéaire*; Bénilan, P., Robert, J., Eds.; Lecture Notes in Mathematics; Springer: Berlin/Heidelberg, Germany, 1978; Volume 665.
50. Fabian, M.; Habala, P.; Hajék, P.; Montesinos, V.; Zizler, V. *Banach Space Theory: The Basis for Linear and Nonlinear Analysis*; Springer: New York, NY, USA, 2011.
51. Zhou, Y.; Wang, J.; Zhang, L. *Basic Theory of Fractional Differential Equations*, 2nd ed.; World Scientific Publishing Co. Pte. Ltd.: Singapore, 2017.
52. Alves, C.O.; Liu, S.B. On superlinear $p(x)$-Laplacian equations in $\mathbb{R}^N$. *Nonlinear Anal.* **2010**, *73*, 2566–2579. [CrossRef]
53. Zeidler, E. *Nonlinear Functional Analysis and Its Applications. II/B: Nonlinear Monotone Operators*; Springer: Berlin/Heidelberg, Germany, 1990.
54. Cen, J.; Vetro, C.; Zeng, S. A multiplicity theorem for double phase degenerate Kirchhoff problems. *Appl. Math. Lett.* **2023**, *146*, 108803. [CrossRef]

mathematics

MDPI

Article

Multivalued Contraction Fixed-Point Theorem in *b*-Metric Spaces

Bachir Slimani [1], John R. Graef [2,*] and Abdelghani Ouahab [1]

[1] Laboratory of Mathematics, University Sidi-Bel-Abbès, P.O. Box 89, Sidi-Bel-Abbès 2200, Algeria; bachir.slimani@univ-sba.dz (B.S.); ouahab@univ-sba.dz (A.O.)
[2] Department of Mathematics, University of Tennessee at Chattanooga, Chattanooga, TN 37403, USA
* Correspondence: john-graef@utc.edu

Abstract: The authors explore fixed-point theory in b-metric spaces and strong b-metric spaces. They wish to prove some new extensions of the Covitz and Nadler fixed-point theorem in b-metric spaces. In so doing, they wish to answer a question proposed by Kirk and Shahzad about Nadler's theorem holding in strong b-metric spaces. In addition, they offer an improvement to the fixed-point theorem proven by Dontchev and Hager.

Keywords: b-metric spaces; fixed-point theorems; multivalued maps; contractions

MSC: 47H04; 47H10

Citation: Slimani, B.; Graef, J.R.; Ouahab, A. Multivalued Contraction Fixed-Point Theorem in b-Metric Spaces. *Mathematics* **2024**, *12*, 567. https://doi.org/10.3390/math12040567

Academic Editor: Salvatore Sessa

Received: 4 January 2024
Revised: 9 February 2024
Accepted: 13 February 2024
Published: 13 February 2024

1. Introduction

Fixed-point theory is a major and important tool in the study of nonlinear phenomena. This theory has been applied in such diverse fields as topology, differential equations and inclusions, economics, game theory, engineering, physics, optimal control, and nonlinear functional analyses. Many authors are interested in fixed-point theorems in metric spaces. The concept of a b-metric space is an old notion that is used in many areas of mathematics. In 1970, Coifman and Guzffian [1] introduced a weaker notion of a metric space called a quasi-metric space; some researchers have used the notion of the b-distance in an attempt to include b-distance functions such as

$$d(x,y) = |x-y|^n, \quad x,\, y \in \mathbb{R}^n,$$

to resolve some central questions in harmonic analyses (see also [2–4]). The actual definition of a b-metric was introduced in 1979 by Madas and Segovia [5]. The notion of a b-metric was first used in fixed-point theory by Bakhtin [6] and extended by Czerwik [7]. Chapter 12, and in particular Section 12.1, of the monograph by Kirk and Shahzad [8] presents a nice introduction to the origin and history of this type of metric space as well as some elementary examples of such spaces.

Our aim in this work is to prove some new versions of the Covitz and Nadler fixed-point theorem [9,10] and to answer a question proposed by Kirk and Shahzad [8], namely, does Nadler's theorem hold in strong b-metric spaces [8] (page 128) (see Theorem 3 below)?

2. Preliminaries

We begin with some essential concepts and results. In what follows, $\mathcal{P}(X)$ denotes the set of all nonempty subsets of X so that $\mathcal{P}_{cl,b}(X)$ is the set of all nonempty closed and bounded subsets of X, and $\mathcal{P}_{cp}(X)$ is the set of all nonempty compact subsets of X.

Definition 1. *Let $A, B \in \mathcal{P}(X)$ and define:*

- $H_d^*(A,B) = \sup\{d(a,B) : a \in A\}$;

- $H_d^*(B,A) = \sup\{d(A,b) : b \in B\}$;
- $H_d(A,B) = \max(H_d^*(A,B), H_d^*(B,A))$ *(the b-Hausdorff distance between A and B).*

Remark 1. *For $\epsilon > 0$, let*

$$A_\epsilon = \{x \in X : d(x,A) < \epsilon\}.$$

Then,

$$H_d^*(A,B) = \inf\{\epsilon > 0 : A \subset B_\epsilon\}, \; H_d^*(B,A) = \inf\{\epsilon > 0 : B \subset A_\epsilon\}.$$

Next, we define what is meant by a b-metric space and a strong b-metric space.

Definition 2. *Let X be a nonempty set and $s \geq 1$. By a b-metric on X, we mean a map d: $X \times X \to [0,\infty)$ with the following properties for all x, y, $z \in X$:*

(i) $d(x,y) = 0$ if and only if $x = y$;
(ii) (Symmetry) $d(x,y) = d(y,x)$;
(iii) (s-relaxed triangle inequality) $d(x,y) \leq s[d(x,z) + d(z,y)]$.

The triple (X,d,s) is called a b-metric space.

Definition 3. *Let X be a nonempty set and $s \geq 1$. By a strong b-metric on X, we mean a map $d : X \times X \to [0,\infty)$ with the following properties for all x, y, $z \in X$:*

(i) $d(x,y) = 0$ if and only if $x = y$;
(ii) (Symmetry) $d(x,y) = d(y,x)$;
(iii) (s-relaxed triangle inequality) $d(x,y) \leq d(x,z) + sd(z,y)$.

The triple (X,d,s) is called a strong b-metric space.

A useful generalization of the s-relaxed triangle inequality is given in the following lemma.

Lemma 1. *Let (X,d,s) be a strong b-metric space. Then, for $x_0, x_1, \ldots, x_n \in X$, we have*

$$d(x_0,x_n) \leq \sum_{i=0}^{n-2} s^{i+1} d(x_i,x_{i+1}) + s^{n-1} d(x_{n-1},x_n).$$

The next two lemmas will be used in our proofs.

Lemma 2. *Let (X,d,s) be a strong b-metric space. Then, d is a continuous mapping.*

Proof. For any x, y, x_0, $y_0 \in X$,

$$\begin{aligned} d(x,y) &\leq sd(x,x_0) + d(x_0,y) \\ &\leq sd(x,x_0) + d(x_0,y_0) + sd(y_0,y). \end{aligned}$$

Hence,

$$d(x,y) - d(x_0,y_0) \leq sd(x,x_0) + sd(y_0,y).$$

Similarly,

$$d(x_0,y_0) - d(x,y) \leq sd(x,x_0) + sd(y_0,y). \tag{1}$$

This implies that

$$|d(x,y) - d(x_0,y_0)| \leq s[d(x,x_0) + d(y_0,y)],$$

and therefore d is continuous. □

Lemma 3 ([11]). *Let (X,d,s) be a b-metric space. Then, every sequence $(x_n)_{n\in\mathbb{N}} \subset X$ for which there exists $\gamma \in (0,1)$ such that*

$$d(x_n, x_{n+1}) \le \gamma d(x_n, x_{n-1}), \quad n \in \mathbb{N},$$

is a Cauchy sequence.

Lemma 4. *Let (X,d,s) be a b-metric space and A, $B \in \mathcal{P}_{cp}(X)$, which is the set of all nonempty compact subsets of X. If d is a continuous b-metric, then for any $x \in A$, there exists $y \in B$ such that*

$$d(x,y) \le d(x,B).$$

Proof. Let $x \in A$; then, for every $n \in \mathbb{N}$, there exists $y_n \in B$ with

$$d(x,y_n) \le d(x,B) + \frac{1}{n}. \tag{2}$$

Since B is compact, there exists a subsequence $(y_{n_k})_{k\in\mathbb{N}}$ of $(y_n)_{n\in\mathbb{N}}$ converging to $y \in B$. Since d is continuous, letting $n \to \infty$ in (2), we obtain

$$d(x,y) \le d(x,B) \le H_d(A,B),$$

which proves the lemma. □

3. Covitz–Nadler-Type Fixed-Point Theorems

In this section, we give versions of the Covitz and Nadler fixed-point theorem in b-metric spaces. They proved their classical fixed-point theorem in metric spaces for contraction multi-valued operators in 1970 (see [9,10]) (also see Deimling [12] (Theorem 11.1)).

Definition 4. *A mapping $F : X \to \mathcal{P}(X)$ is a multivalued map if for each $x \in X$, $F(x) \in \mathcal{P}(X)$. The point p is a fixed point of a multivalued map F if $p \in F(p)$. We will denote the set of fixed points of the mapping F by Fix F.*

We also have the notion of a contraction for multivalued maps.

Definition 5. *If the mapping F has a Lipschitz constant $c < 1$, then f is called a multivalued contraction mapping.*

The following lemma is referred to as the Covitz and Nadler fixed-point theorem [9].

Lemma 5. *Let (X,d) be a complete metric space. If $F : X \to P_{cl}(X)$ is a contraction, then Fix $X \neq \emptyset$.*

Our first result is contained in the following theorem.

Theorem 1. *Let (X,d,s) be a complete b-metric space and d be continuous. If $F : X \to \mathcal{P}_{cp}(X)$ is a contraction, then Fix $F \neq \emptyset$.*

Proof. Assume that $H_d(F(x), F(y)) \le Ld(x,y)$ for every $x, y \in X$, where $L \in [0,1)$, and let $x \in X$. Since $F(x)$ is compact, by Lemma 4, we can choose $x_1 \in F(x)$ such that

$$d(x,x_1) \le d(x,F(x)).$$

Then, we may choose $x_2 \in F(x_1)$ such that

$$d(x_1,x_2) \le d(x_1,F(x_1)) \text{ implies } d(x_1,x_2) \le H_d(F(x),F(x_1)).$$

This means that

$$d(x_1, x_2) \le Ld(x, F(x)).$$

Continuing this way, we can find a sequence $\{x_n : n \in \mathbb{N}\} \subset X$ with

$$d(x_n, x_{n+1}) \le d(x_n, F(x_n)).$$

Hence,

$$\begin{aligned} d(x_n, x_{n+1}) \le d(x_n, F(x_n)) &\le H_d(F(x_{n-1}), x_n) \\ &\le Ld(x_{n-1}, x_n) \le L^n d(x, F(x)). \end{aligned}$$

By Lemma 3, $\{x_n\}_{n\in\mathbb{N}}$ is a Cauchy sequence. Since X is complete, we let $\tilde{x} = \lim_{n\to\infty} x_n$. Then, $x_{n+1} \in F(x_n)$ for every $n \in \mathbb{N}$, and

$$0 \le d(\tilde{x}, F(\tilde{x})) \le s[d(x_{n+1}, \tilde{x}) + d(x_{n+1}, F(\tilde{x}))] \le s[d(x_{n+1}, \tilde{x}) + Ld(x_n, \tilde{x})].$$

Letting $n \to +\infty$ gives $\tilde{x} \in F(\tilde{x})$ as claimed, and this proves the theorem. □

As a direct consequence of Theorem 1, we are able to obtain the following generalization of Nadler's fixed-point theorem to strong b-metric spaces.

Corollary 1. *Let (X, d, s) be a complete strong b-metric space. If $F : X \to \mathcal{P}_{cp}(X)$ is an L-contraction, then Fix $F \neq \emptyset$.*

Proof. Since (X, d, s) is a complete strong b-metric space, it is complete. By Lemma 2, d is continuous. By Theorem 1, F has at least one fixed point, and this completes the proof. □

Our next result on the existence of a fixed point is contained in the following theorem.

Theorem 2. *Let (X, d, s) be a complete b-metric space and $F : X \to \mathcal{P}_{cl,b}(X)$ be an L-contraction multi-valued mapping. Then, F has a fixed point in X.*

Proof. We will employ a standard iterative procedure for contracting mappings. Let $L \in (0, 1)$ be such that

$$H_d(F(x), F(y)) \le Ld(x, y) \quad \text{for all } x, y \in X.$$

Let $x_0 \in X$ be fixed and choose $x_1 \in F(x_0)$ such that

$$d(x_1, x_0) \le d(x_0, F(x_0)) + L.$$

From the definition of the Hausdorff distance, we can find $x_2 \in F(x_1)$ with

$$d(x_1, x_2) \le d(x_1, F(x_1)) + L, \text{ which implies } d(x_1, x_2) \le H_d(F(x_0), F(x_1)) + L.$$

Similarly, we can find $x_3 \in F(x_2)$, with

$$d(x_3, x_2) \le H_d(F(x_2), F(x_1)) + L^2.$$

Continuing this process, we obtain a sequence $(x_n)_{n\in\mathbb{N}}$ in X such that $x_{i+1} \in (x_n)$ and

$$d(x_{i+1}, x_i) \le H_d(F(x_i), F(x_{i-1})) + L^i.$$

For fixed $m \in \mathbb{N}$,

$$
\begin{aligned}
d(x_m, x_{m+1}) &\leq H_d(F(x_m), F(x_{m-1})) + L^m \\
&\leq Ld(x_m, x_{m-1}) + L^m \\
&\leq LH_d(F(x_{m-1}), F(x_{m-2})) + 2L^m \\
&\leq L^2 d(x_{m-1}, x_{m-2}) + 2L^m \\
&\leq L^2(H_d(F(x_{m-2}), F(x_{m-3})) + L^{m-2}) + 2L^m \\
&\leq L^3 d(x_{m-2}, x_{m-3}) + 3L^m \\
&\ \ \vdots \\
&\leq L^m d(x_1, x_0) + mL^m.
\end{aligned}
$$

By the s-relaxed triangle inequality in b-metric spaces, for every $p \in \mathbb{N}$ and $q = [\log_2 p]$,

$$
\begin{aligned}
d(x_{m+1}, x_{m+p}) &\leq sd(x_{m+1}, x_{m+2}) + sd(x_{m+2}, x_{m+p}) \\
&\leq sd(x_{m+1}, x_{m+2}) + s^2 d(x_{m+2}, x_{m+2^2}) + s^2 d(x_{m+2^2}, x_{m+p}) \\
&\ \ \vdots \\
&\leq \sum_{n=1}^{q} s^n d(x_{m+2^{n-1}}, x_{m+2^n}) + s^{q+1} d(x_{m+2^q}, x_{m+p}).
\end{aligned}
$$

By Lemma 1, we obtain

$$
\begin{aligned}
d(x_{m+1}, x_{m+p}) \leq \sum_{n=1}^{q} s^{2n} &\sum_{i=m}^{m+2^{n-1}-1} d(x_{2^{n-1}+i}, x_{m+2^{n-1}+i+1}) \\
&+ s^{2(q+1)} \sum_{i=m}^{m+p-2^q-1} d(x_{2^q+i}, x_{2^q+i+1}).
\end{aligned}
$$

Consequently,

$$
\begin{aligned}
d(x_{m+1}, x_{m+p}) &\leq \sum_{n=1}^{q} s^{2n} \sum_{i=m}^{m+2^{n-1}-1} (L^{2^{n-1}+i} d(x_0, x_1) + (2^{n-1}+i)L^{2^{n-1}+i}) \\
&\quad + s^{2(q+1)} \sum_{i=m}^{m+p-2^q-1} (L^{2^q+i} d(x_0, x_1) + (2^q+i)L^{2^q+i}) \\
&\leq \sum_{n=1}^{q+1} s^{2n} \sum_{i=0}^{2^{n-1}-1} [L^{2^{n-1}+i+m} d(x_0, x_1) \\
&\quad + (2^{n-1}+i+m)L^{2^{n-1}+i+m}] \\
&\leq L^m \sum_{n=1}^{q+1} s^{2n} \sum_{i=0}^{2^{n-1}-1} L^{2^{n-1}+i} d(x_0, x_1) \\
&\quad + L^m \sum_{n=1}^{q+1} s^{2n} \sum_{i=0}^{2^{n-1}-1} (2^{n-1}+i)L^{2^{n-1}+i} \\
&\quad + mL^m \sum_{n=1}^{q+1} s^{2n} \sum_{i=0}^{2^{n-1}-1} (2^{n-1}+i)L^{2^{n-1}+i}.
\end{aligned}
$$

Using simple calculations, we can see that

$$
L^m \sum_{n=1}^{q+1} s^{2n} \sum_{i=0}^{2^{n-1}-1} L^{2^{n-1}+i} d(x_0, x_1) \leq \frac{L^m d(x_0, x_1)}{1-L} \sum_{n=1}^{q+1} L^{2n \log_L s + 2^{n-1}}, \tag{3}
$$

and

$$
\begin{aligned}
L^m \sum_{n=1}^{q+1} s^{2n} \sum_{i=0}^{2^{n-1}-1} (2^{n-1}+i)L^{2^{n-1}+i} \\
&\leq L^m \sum_{n=1}^{q+1} s^{2n} 2^{n-1} L^{2^{n-1}} \sum_{i=0}^{2^{n-1}-1} L^i + L^m \sum_{n=1}^{q+1} s^{2n} L^{2^{n-1}} \sum_{i=0}^{2^{n-1}-1} iL^i \\
&\leq \frac{2L^m}{1-L} \sum_{n=1}^{q+1} (2s)^{2n} L^{2^{n-1}} + L^m \sum_{i=0}^{\infty} iL^i \sum_{n=1}^{q+1} s^{2n} L^{2^{n-1}}.
\end{aligned}
$$

Then,

$$
\begin{aligned}
L^m \sum_{n=1}^{q+1} s^{2n} \sum_{i=0}^{2^{n-1}-1} (2^{n-1}+i)L^{2^{n-1}+i} \\
&\leq \frac{2L^m}{1-L} \sum_{n=1}^{q+1} L^{2n \log_L 2s + 2^{n-1}} + L^m \sum_{i=0}^{\infty} iL^i \sum_{n=1}^{q+1} L^{2n \log_L s + 2^{n-1}}.
\end{aligned}
$$

Hence,

$$
L^m \sum_{n=1}^{q+1} s^{2n} \sum_{i=0}^{2^{n-1}-1} 2^{n-1} L^{2^{n-1}+i} \leq \frac{2L^m}{1-L} \sum_{n=1}^{q+1} L^{2n \log_L 2s + 2^{n-1}}, \tag{4}
$$

and

$$
L^m \sum_{n=1}^{q+1} s^{2n} \sum_{i=0}^{2^{n-1}-1} iL^{2^{n-1}+i} \leq L^m \sum_{i=0}^{\infty} iL^i \sum_{n=1}^{q+1} L^{2n \log_L s + 2^{n-1}}. \tag{5}
$$

We observe that

$$
\lim_{n\to\infty} (2n \log_L s + 2^{n-1} - n) = \lim_{n\to\infty} (2n \log_L 2s + 2^{n-1} - n) = \infty.
$$

For a fixed $M > 0$, there exist $n_0 \in \mathbb{N}$ such that

$$
2n \log_L s + 2^{n-1} - n \geq M, \text{ and } 2n \log_L 2s + 2^{n-1} - n \geq M, \quad \text{for all } n \geq n_0.
$$

Then,

$$
L^{2n \log_L s + 2^{n-1}} \leq L^M L^n \text{ and } L^{2n \log_L 2s + 2^{n-1}} \leq L^n L^M,
$$

and since $\lim_{n\to\infty} \frac{(n+1)L^{n+1}}{nL^n} = L \in (0,1)$, we conclude that

$$
L_1 := \sum_{n=1}^{\infty} L^{2n \log_L s + 2^{n-1}}, \; L_2 := \sum_{n=1}^{\infty} L^{2n \log_L 2s + 2^{n-1}}, \; L_3 := \sum_{n=1}^{\infty} nL^n \tag{6}
$$

are convergent series. Using (3)–(6), we obtain

$$
d(x_{m+1}, x_{m+p}) \leq \frac{L^m L_1 d(x_1, x_0)}{1-L} + \frac{(2+(1-L)L_1)L_2(1+m)L^m}{1-L}.
$$

Thus, $(x_n)_{n\in\mathbb{N}}$ is a Cauchy sequence, and so $x_n \to x$ for some $x \in X$.
Next, we prove that $x \in F(x)$. For all $n \in \mathbb{N}$,

$$
\begin{aligned}
0 \leq d(x, F(x)) &\leq s[d(x, x_n) + d(x_n, F(x))] \\
&\leq s[d(x, x_n) + H_d(F(x_{n-1}), F(x))] \\
&\leq s[d(x, x_n) + Ld(x_{n-1}, x)].
\end{aligned}
$$

Letting $n \to \infty$, we see that

$$
d(x, F(x)) = 0,
$$

which implies $x \in F(x)$, and so x is a fixed point of F. This proves the theorem. □

Remark 2. *In [13], Czerwik obtained the result in Theorem 2 for b-metric spaces, but with the more restrictive condition that* $sL \in (0,1)$. *Kirk and Shahzad [8] (Theorem 12.5) relaxed the result for strong b-metric spaces with* $L \in (0,1)$. *Theorem 2 is an extension of the results of Czerwik and Kirk and Shahzad.*

4. Local Version of the Covitz–Nadler Theorem

For the next result, we give a version of the fixed-point theorems proved by Beer and Dontchev [14] (see Theorem 4) and Dontchev and Hager [15] in a strong b-metric space. Hence, we obtain a partial answer to the question raised by Kirk and Shahzad [8] (p. 128).

Theorem 3. *Let* (X,d,s) *be a complete strong b-metric space and* $F : X \to \mathcal{P}_{cp}(X)$. *Assume there exist* $x_0 \in X, r > 0$, *and* $sL \in (0,1)$ *such that*
(i) $d(x_0, F(x_0)) < r(1-sL)$;
(ii) $H_d^*(F(x) \cap \bar{B}(x_0,r), F(y)) \leq Ld(x,y)$ *for all* $x, y \in \bar{B}(x_0,r)$.
Then, F has a fixed point in $\bar{B}(x_0,r)$.

Proof. Since $F(x_0) \in \mathcal{P}_{cp}(X)$, there exists $x_1 \in F(x_0)$ with $x_1 \in B(x_0,r)$ such that

$$d(x_1,x_0) < r(1-sL) \tag{7}$$

and

$$H_d^*(F(x_0) \cap \bar{B}(x_0,r), F(x_1)) \leq Ld(x_1,x_0).$$

Since $x_1 \in F(x_0) \cap \bar{B}(x_0,r)$,

$$d(x_1,F(x_1)) \leq H_d^*(F(x_0) \cap \bar{B}(x_0,r), F(x_1)) \leq Ld(x_1,x_0) < r(1-sL)L.$$

Then, there exists $x_2 \in F(x_1)$ with

$$d(x_1,x_2) < r(1-sL)L,$$

so we have

$$d(x_0,x_2) \leq d(x_0,x_1) + sd(x_1,x_2) < r(1-sL) + sr(1-sL)L,$$

that is,

$$d(x_1,x_2) < r(1-sL)L, \ d(x_0,x_2) < r(1-(sL)^2), \ \text{and } x_2 \in \bar{B}(x_0,r). \tag{8}$$

Hence,

$$d(x_2,F(x_2)) \leq H_d^*(F(x_1) \cap \bar{B}(x_0,r), F(x_2)) \leq Ld(x_1,x_2) < rL^2(1-sL).$$

Then, there exists $x_3 \in F(x_2)$ such that

$$d(x_2,x_3) < rL^2(1-sL),$$

and so

$$\begin{aligned} d(x_0,x_3) \leq d(x_0,x_2) + sd(x_2,x_3) &\leq r(1-(sL)^2) + srL^2(1-sL) \\ &\leq r(1-(sL)^2) + srL^2(1-(sL)^2) \end{aligned}$$

since $sL < 1$. We then have

$$d(x_2,x_3) < rL^2(1-sL), \ d(x_0,x_3) < r(1-(sL)^4), \ \text{and } x_3 \in \bar{B}(x_0,r). \tag{9}$$

From (7)–(9), we can proceed by induction, so that there exist $(x_n)_{n\in\mathbb{N}} \subset \bar{B}(x_0, r)$ with $x_n \in F(x_{n-1})$, $n \in \mathbb{N}$, such that

$$d(x_n, x_{n+1}) < rL^n(1 - sL), \quad n \in \mathbb{N}_0.$$

By the s-relaxed triangular inequality, for $n \geq m$, we have

$$d(x_m, x_n) \leq s\sum_{i=m}^{n-1} d(x_i, x_{i+1}) \leq rs(1 - sL)\sum_{i=m}^{n-1} L^i \leq rs(1 - sL)L^m \sum_{i=0}^{\infty} L^i.$$

Therefore,

$$d(x_m, x_n) \leq \frac{rs(1 - sL)L^m}{1 - L} \to 0 \text{ as } m \to \infty,$$

which implies that $(x_n)_{n\in\mathbb{N}}$ is a Cauchy sequence in X. Since X is complete, there exists $x \in X$ such that $\lim_{n\to\infty} x_n = x \in \bar{B}(x_0, r)$. By condition (ii),

$$d(x_n, F(x)) \leq H_d^*(F(x_{n-1}) \cap \bar{B}(x_0, r), F(x)) \leq Ld(x_{n-1}, x).$$

The s-relaxed triangle inequality implies that

$$d(x, F(x)) \leq sd(x, x_n) + d(x_n, F(x)) \leq sd(x, x_n) + Ld(x_{n-1}, x) \to 0$$

as $n \to \infty$. Therefore, $d(x, F(x)) = 0$, and hence, x is a fixed point of F. This proves the theorem. □

A second result in the same direction is contained in the following theorem.

Theorem 4. *Let (X, d, s) be a complete strong b-metric space and $F : X \to \mathcal{P}_{cl}(X)$. Assume there exist $x_0 \in X$, $r > 0$, and $L \in (0, 1)$ such that*

(i) $d(x_0, F(x_0)) < \frac{r}{s}(1 - L)$;

(ii) $H_d^*(F(x) \cap \bar{B}(x_0, r), F(y)) \leq Ld(x, y)$ *for all* $x, y \in \bar{B}(x_0, r)$.

Then, F has a fixed point in $\bar{B}(x_0, r)$.

Proof. Since $F(x_0) \in \mathcal{P}_{cp}(X)$, there exists $x_1 \in F(x_0)$ with $x_1 \in \bar{B}(x_0, r)$ such that

$$d(x_1, x_0) < \frac{r}{s}(1 - L)$$

and

$$H_d^*(F(x_0) \cap \bar{B}(x_0, r), F(x_1)) \leq Ld(x_1, x_0).$$

Since $x_1 \in F(x_0) \cap \bar{B}(x_0, r)$,

$$d(x_1, F(x_1)) \leq H_d^*(F(x_0) \cap \bar{B}(x_0, r), F(x_1)) \leq Ld(x_1, x_0) < \frac{r}{s}(1 - L)L,$$

and so there exists $x_2 \in F(x_1)$ such that

$$d(x_1, x_2) < \frac{r}{s}(1 - L)L.$$

Hence, we have

$$d(x_0, x_2) \leq s[d(x_0, x_1) + d(x_1, x_2)] < r(1 - L) + r(1 - L)L = r(1 - L^2),$$

which means

$$d(x_1, x_2) < \frac{r}{s}(1 - L)L, \ d(x_0, x_2) < r(1 - L^2), \text{ and } x_2 \in \bar{B}(x_0, r).$$

Thus,

$$d(x_2, F(x_2)) \leq H_d^*(F(x_1) \cap \bar{B}(x_0, r), F(x_2)) \leq Ld(x_1, x_2) < \frac{r}{s} L^2(1 - L),$$

and so then there exists $x_3 \in F(x_2)$ such that

$$d(x_2, x_3) < \frac{r}{s} L^2(1 - L).$$

This implies

$$\begin{aligned} d(x_0, x_3) \leq d(x_0, x_2) + sd(x_2, x_3) &\leq r(1 - L^2) + rL^2(1 - L) \\ &\leq r(1 - L^2) + rL^2(1 - L^2) \end{aligned}$$

since $L < 1$. Thus, we have

$$d(x_2, x_3) < \frac{r}{s} L^2(1 - L), \;\; d(x_0, x_3) < r(1 - L^4), \;\; \text{and } x_3 \in \bar{B}(x_0, r).$$

Proceeding by induction, there exists $(x_n)_{n \in \mathbb{N}} \subset \bar{B}(x_0, r)$ with $x_n \in F(x_{n-1})$, $n \in \mathbb{N}$, such that

$$d(x_n, x_{n+1}) < \frac{r}{s} L^n(1 - L), \quad n \in \mathbb{N}_0.$$

As in the proof of Theorem 3, we again see that $(x_n)_{n \in \mathbb{N}_0}$ is a Cauchy sequence. Since X is complete, there exists $x \in \bar{B}(x_0, r)$ such that $\lim_{n \to \infty} x_n = x$ and $x \in F(x)$, which proves the theorem. □

The next result is our improvement of Dontchev and Hager's [15] (Lemma) fixed-point theorem.

Theorem 5. *Let (X, d, s) be a complete strong b-metric space and $F : X \to \mathcal{P}(X)$. Assume there exist $x_0 \in X$, $r > 0$, and $L \in (0, 1)$ such that*

(i) The set $\mathcal{G}r(F) \cap \bar{B}(x_0, r) \times \bar{B}(x_0, r)$ is a closed set;

(ii) $d(x_0, F(x_0)) < \frac{r}{s}(1 - L)$;

(iii) $H_d^*(F(x) \cap \bar{B}(x_0, r), F(y)) \leq Ld(x, y)$ for all $x, y \in \bar{B}(x_0, r)$.

Then, F has a fixed point in $\bar{B}(x_0, r)$.

Proof. Since $d(x_0, F(x_0)) < \frac{r}{s}(1 - L)$, there exists $x_1 \in F(x_0)$ with $x_1 \in \bar{B}(x_0, r)$ such that

$$d(x_1, x_0) < \frac{r}{s}(1 - L) \tag{10}$$

and

$$H_d^*(F(x_0) \cap \bar{B}(x_0, r), F(x_1)) \leq Ld(x_1, x_0).$$

Since $x_1 \in F(x_0) \cap \bar{B}(x_0, r)$,

$$d(x_1, F(x_1)) \leq H_d^*(F(x_0) \cap \bar{B}(x_0, r), F(x_1)) \leq Ld(x_1, x_0) < \frac{r}{s}(1 - L)L,$$

and so there exists $x_2 \in F(x_1)$ such that

$$d(x_1, x_2) < \frac{r}{s}(1 - L)L$$

and

$$d(x_0, x_2) \leq s[d(x_0, x_1) + d(x_1, x_2)] < r(1 - L) + r(1 - L)L = r(1 - L^2).$$

That is,

$$d(x_1, x_2) < \frac{r}{s}(1-L)L, \ d(x_0, x_2) < r(1-L^2), \ \text{and} \ x_2 \in \bar{B}(x_0, r). \tag{11}$$

Hence,

$$d(x_2, F(x_2)) \le H_d^*(F(x_1) \cap \bar{B}(x_0, r), F(x_2)) \le Ld(x_1, x_2) < \frac{r}{s}L^2(1-L),$$

so there exists $x_3 \in F(x_2)$ such that

$$d(x_2, x_3) < \frac{r}{s}L^2(1-L).$$

It follows that

$$\begin{aligned} d(x_0, x_3) \le d(x_0, x_2) + sd(x_2, x_3) &\le r(1-L^2) + rL^2(1-L) \\ &\le r(1-L^2) + rL^2(1-L^2), \end{aligned}$$

that is,

$$d(x_2, x_3) < \frac{r}{s}L^2(1-L), \ d(x_0, x_3) < r(1-L^4), \ \text{and} \ x_3 \in \bar{B}(x_0, r). \tag{12}$$

By induction, there exists

$$(x_n)_{n\in\mathbb{N}} \subset \bar{B}(x_0, r), \ x_n \in F(x_{n-1}), \ n \in \mathbb{N}, \tag{13}$$

with

$$d(x_n, x_{n+1}) < \frac{r}{s}L^n(1-L), \quad n \in \mathbb{N}_0.$$

As in the proof of Theorem 3, $(x_n)_{n\in\mathbb{N}_0}$ is a Cauchy sequence, and since X is complete, there exists $x \in \bar{B}(x_0, r)$ such that $\lim_{n\to\infty} x_n = x$. Hence, $(x_{n-1}, x_n) \to (x, x)$ as $n \to \infty$. From (13) and condition (i), we have

$$\{(x_{n-1}, x_n)\}_{n\in\mathbb{N}} \subset \mathcal{G}r(F) \cap \bar{B}(x_0, r) \times \bar{B}(x_0, r),$$

and so

$$(x, x) \in \mathcal{G}r(F) \cap \bar{B}(x_0, r) \times \bar{B}(x_0, r).$$

Therefore, $x \in F(x)$ and this completes the proof of the theorem. □

Author Contributions: Conceptualization, B.S., J.R.G. and A.O.; methodology, B.S., J.R.G. and A.O.; validation, B.S., J.R.G. and A.O.; formal analysis, B.S., J.R.G. and A.O.; investigation, B.S., J.R.G. and A.O.; writing—original draft preparation, B.S., J.R.G. and A.O.; writing—review and editing, B.S., J.R.G. and A.O.; project administration, B.S., J.R.G. and A.O. All authors have read and agreed to the published version of the manuscript.

Funding: This research received no external funding.

Data Availability Statement: No data sets were generated during this research.

Conflicts of Interest: The authors declare that there are no conflicts of interest.

References

1. Coifman, R.; de Guzman, M. Singular integrals and multipliers on homogeneous spaces. *Rev. Union Mat. Argent.* **1970**, *35*, 137–144.
2. Coifman, R.; Weiss, G. *Analyse Harmonique Non-Commutative sur Certains Spaces Homogenes, Etude de Certaines Integmles Singulieres*; Lecture Notes in Mathematics; Springer: Berlin, Germany, 1971; Volume 242.
3. Donggao, D.; Yongsheng, H. *Harmonic Analysis on Spaces of Homogeneous Type*; Lecture Notes in Mathematics; Springer: Berlin, Germany, 2009; Volume 1966.
4. Mitrea, D.; Mitrea, I.; Mitrea, M.; Monniaux, S. *Groupoid Metrization Theory, with Applications to Analysis on Quasi-Metric Spaces and Functional Analysis*; Applied and Numerical Harmonic Analysis; Birkhäuser: New York, NY, USA, 2013.

5. Macias, R.A.; Segovia, C. Lipschitz functions on spaces of homogeneous type. *Adv. Math.* **1979**, *33*, 257–270. [CrossRef]
6. Bakhtin, I.A. The contraction principle in quasimetric spaces. *Funct. Anal.* **1989**, *30*, 26–37.
7. Czerwik, S. Contraction mappings in *b*-metric spaces. *Acta Math. Inform. Univ. Ostrav.* **1993**, *1*, 5–11.
8. Kirk, W.; Shahzad, N. *Fixed Point Theory in Distance Spaces*; Springer: New York, NY, USA, 2014.
9. Covitz, H.; Nadler, S.B., Jr. Multi-valued contraction mappings in generalized metric spaces. *Isr. J. Math.* **1970**, *8*, 5–11. [CrossRef]
10. Nadler, S.B., Jr. Multi-valued contraction mappings. *Pac. J. Math.* **1969**, *30*, 475–488. [CrossRef]
11. Miculescu, R.; Mihail, A. New fixed point theorems for set-valued contractions in *b*-metric spaces. *J. Fixed Point Theory Appl.* **2017**, *19*, 2153–2163. [CrossRef]
12. Deimling, K. *Multi-Valued Differential Equations*; De Gruyter: Berlin, Germany; New York, NY, USA, 1992.
13. Czerwik, S. Nonlinear set-valued contraction mappings in *b*-metric spaces. *Atti Semin. Mat. Fis. Univ. Modena* **1998**, *46*, 263–276.
14. Beer, G.; Dontchev, A.L. The weak Ekeland variational principle and fixed points. *Nonlinear Anal.* **2014**, *102*, 91–96. [CrossRef]
15. Dontchev, A.L.; Hager, W.W. An inverse mapping theorem for setvalued maps. *Proc. Am. Math. Soc.* **1994**, *121*, 481–489. [CrossRef]

mathematics

MDPI

Article

Existence and Limit Behavior of Constraint Minimizers for a Varying Non-Local Kirchhoff-Type Energy Functional

Xincai Zhu * and Hanxiao Wu

School of Mathematics and Statistics, Xinyang Normal University, Xinyang 464000, China; wuhanxiao19991228@163.com
* Correspondence: zhuxc68@163.com

Abstract: In this paper, we study the constrained minimization problem for an energy functional which is related to a Kirchhoff-type equation. For $s = 1$, there many articles have analyzed the limit behavior of minimizers when $\eta > 0$ as $b \to 0^+$ or $b > 0$ as $\eta \to 0^+$. When the equation involves a varying non-local term $\left(\int_{\mathbb{R}^3} |\nabla u|^2 dx\right)^s$, we give a detailed limit behavior analysis of constrained minimizers for any positive sequence $\{\eta_k\}$ with $\eta_k \to 0^+$. The present paper obtains an interesting result on this topic and enriches the conclusions of previous works.

Keywords: Kirchhoff-type energy functional; constraint minimizer; limit behavior; varying non-local term

MSC: 32J20; 35J60; 35Q40; 46N50

Citation: Zhu, X.; Wu, H. Existence and Limit Behavior of Constraint Minimizers for a Varying Non-Local Kirchhoff-Type Energy Functional. *Mathematics* **2024**, *12*, 661. https://doi.org/10.3390/math12050661

Academic Editors: Lingju Kong and Min Wang

Received: 5 February 2024
Revised: 18 February 2024
Accepted: 19 February 2024
Published: 23 February 2024

1. Introduction and Main Results

We consider the following Kirchhoff-type equation with a varying non-local term

$$-\left(\eta + b\left(\int_{\mathbb{R}^3} |\nabla u|^2 dx\right)^s\right)\Delta u + V(x)u = \mu u + \lambda |u|^p u, \tag{1}$$

where $b > 0$ is a constant, parameters $\eta \geq 0, \lambda > 0$, exponents $s > 0, 0 < p < 4$ and μ is a Lagrange multiplier. The $b\left(\int_{\mathbb{R}^3} |\nabla u|^2 dx\right)^s$ in (1) arises as a varying non-local term.

In recent years, there have been many articles involved in different types of varying non-local problems similar to (1) such as the model

$$\begin{cases} -C\left(\int_\Omega |\nabla u|^2 dx\right)^s \Delta u = h(x,u)\left(\int_\Omega f(x,u)dx\right)^r, & x \in \Omega, \\ u = 0, & x \in \partial\Omega, \end{cases}$$

which mainly studied the existence of solutions by using variational theory and analytical methods, as seen in [1–4].

Especially for $s = 1$ in (1), the Kirchhoff-type constrained minimization problems are related to

$$-\left(\eta + b\int_{\mathbb{R}^3} |\nabla u|^2 dx\right)\Delta u + V(x)u = \mu u + \lambda |u|^p u$$

which have attracted a significant number of mathematicians to study their existence, non-existence, uniqueness and limit behavior of constraint minimizers. More detailed, for $V(x) = 0$, Ye [5,6] obtained some results of existence and nonexistence on constraint minimizers. Zeng and Zhang [7] proved the local uniqueness of minimizer, and then they [8] provided an analysis of asymptotic behavior for minimizers when $V(x)$ satisfies periodic potential. Guo, Zhang and Zhou [9] analyzed the existence and limit behavior of minimizers if the trapping potential $V(x) > 0$ satisfies $\liminf_{|x|\to+\infty} V(x) = \infty$. In papers [10–13], the authors studied the existence and non-existence of constraint minimizers for the Kirchhoff-type energy functional with a L^2-subcritical term. Also for $V(x)$ being a polynomial function, the articles [14,15] obtained the limit behavior of L^2-norm solutions when $\eta > 0$ as $b \to 0^+$ or $b > 0$ as $\eta \to 0^+$.

Coincidentally for $s = 0$ and $\mathbb{R}^3$ replaced by $\mathbb{R}^2$, the (1) comes from an interesting physical context, which is associated with the well known Bose–Einstein condensates (BECs). The mathematical theory study of BECs can be described by a Gross–Pitaevskii (GP) functional [16,17], which is related to the elliptic equation

$$\Delta u + V(x)u = \mu u + \lambda |u|^p u.$$

There are many researchers devoted to exploring the properties of the ground states for the GP functional related to the above elliptic equation. More precisely, when the external trapping potentials $V(x)$ are in the forms of polynomial, ring-shaped, multi-well, periodic and sinusoidal, the articles [18–22] gave the existence, non-existence and mass concentration behavior analysis of the ground states. If $V(x)$ behaves like logarithmic or homogeneous potential [23,24], the local uniqueness and refined spike profiles of ground states for the GP functional are analyzed when λ tends to a critical value λ^*.

However, as far as we know, there are few papers using the constrained variational approaches to study the varying non-local problem (1). Inspired by the above articles, the aim of the present paper is to study the following constrained minimization problem related to (1), which is defined by

$$I(\eta, s, \lambda) := \inf_{u \in \mathcal{U}} E(u), \tag{2}$$

where $E(u)$ fulfills

$$\begin{aligned} E(u) :&= \frac{\eta}{2} \int_{\mathbb{R}^3} |\nabla u|^2 dx + \frac{b}{2(s+1)} \Big(\int_{\mathbb{R}^3} |\nabla u|^2 dx \Big)^{s+1} \\ &+ \frac{1}{2} \int_{\mathbb{R}^3} V(x)|u|^2 dx - \frac{\lambda}{p+2} \int_{\mathbb{R}^3} |u|^{p+2} dx. \end{aligned} \tag{3}$$

The above $\mathcal{U}$ in (2) is restricted to meet

$$\mathcal{U} := \{ u \in \mathcal{H} \mid \int_{\mathbb{R}^3} |u|^2 dx = 1 \}, \tag{4}$$

where $\mathcal{H}$ satisfies

$$\mathcal{H} := \Big\{ u \in H^1(\mathbb{R}^3) \mid \int_{\mathbb{R}^3} V(x)|u|^2 dx < \infty \Big\}$$

as well as with the norm $\|u\|_{\mathcal{H}} := \Big(\int_{\mathbb{R}^3} |\nabla u|^2 dx + \int_{\mathbb{R}^3} (1 + V(x)|u|^2) dx \Big)^{\frac{1}{2}}$. Assume that the $V(x)$ in (1) satisfies

$$(V_1).\, V(x) \in L^\infty_{loc}(\mathbb{R}^3) \cap C^\alpha_{loc}(\mathbb{R}^3),\ \alpha \in (0,1),\ \lim_{|x| \to \infty} V(x) = +\infty \text{ and } \min_{\mathbb{R}^3} V(x) = 0.$$

To state our main results, we introduce an elliptic equation such as

$$-\frac{3p}{4} \Delta Q_p + \Big(1 - \frac{p}{4}\Big) Q_p - |Q_p|^p Q_p = 0,\ x \in \mathbb{R}^3,\ 0 < p < 4. \tag{5}$$

In fact, up to the translations, (5) has a unique positive radially symmetric solution $Q_p \in H^1(\mathbb{R}^3)$, as seen in [25]. For convenience, we denote a critical constant

$$\lambda^* := \frac{b}{(s+1)} \|Q\|_{L^2}^{\frac{4(s+1)}{3}},$$

where Q is the unique positive solution of (5) for $p = \frac{4(s+1)}{3}$. According to the above conditions, the existence and non-existence theorems on constraint minimizers for $I(\eta, s, \lambda)$ are established as follows:

Theorem 1. *For $\eta, s > 0$, $0 < p < 4$ and if (V_1) holds, then $I(\eta, s, \lambda)$ has at least one minimizer for $p < \frac{4(s+1)}{3}$ or $p = \frac{4(s+1)}{3}, 0 < \lambda \leq \lambda^*$. The $I(\eta, s, \lambda)$ has no minimizer for $p > \frac{4(s+1)}{3}$ or $p = \frac{4(s+1)}{3}, \lambda > \lambda^*$.*

Theorem 2. *For $\eta = 0$, $s > 0$, $p = \frac{4(s+1)}{3}$ and if (V_1) holds, then $I(\eta, s, \lambda)$ has at least one minimizer if $0 < \lambda < \lambda^*$. Moreover, $I(\eta, s, \lambda)$ has no minimizer for $\lambda \geq \lambda^*$*

Remark that similar conclusions appear elsewhere for studying different types of Kirchhoff equations, as seen in [7,12,14,15]. For convenience, we give a detailed proof of Theorems 1 and 2 in Section 3. In view of the above theorems, one knows that, for $\eta > 0$, $p = \frac{4(s+1)}{3}$ and $\lambda = \lambda^*$, the $I(\eta, s, \lambda)$ has at least one minimizer. However, for $\eta = 0$, $p = \frac{4(s+1)}{3}$ and $\lambda = \lambda^*$, the $I(\eta, s, \lambda^*)$ admits no minimizer. A nature question is what happens to constraint minimizers of $I(\eta, s, \lambda)$ when η tends to 0 from the right?

Suppose that u_η is a minimizer for $I(\eta, s, \lambda)$; then, one can restrict $u_\eta \geq 0$ due to $E(u) \geq E(|u|)$ for any $u \in \mathcal{U}$. At the same time, we always assume that $I(\eta, s, \lambda)$ admits a positive minimizer by applying the strong maximum principle to (1). In truth, for any positive sequence $\{\eta_k\}$ with $\eta_k \to 0^+$ as $k \to \infty$, one can verify that the positive constraint minimizers u_{η_k} satisfy $\int_{\mathbb{R}^3} |\nabla u_{\eta_k}|^2 dx \to +\infty$ as $k \to \infty$ (see Section 4); that is, the minimizers enact blow-up behavior as $\eta_k \to 0^+$. In order to obtain a more detailed limit behavior of the constraint minimizers, some appropriate assumptions on $V(x)$ are necessary. For this purpose, we assume that $V(x)$ is a form of polynomial function, and admits $n \geq 1$ isolated minima. More narrowly, there exist $n \geq 1$ distinct points $x_i \in \mathbb{R}^3$, numbers $q_i > 0$ and constant $\mathcal{M} > 0$ fulfilling

$$(V_2). \quad V(x) = C(x) \prod_{i=1}^{n} |x - x_i|^{q_i} \text{ with } \mathcal{M} < C(x) < \frac{1}{\mathcal{M}} \text{ for all } x \in \mathbb{R}^3;$$

here, $\lim_{x \to x_i} C(x)$ exists for all $1 \leq i \leq n$. For convenience, we denote

$$q = \max\{q_1, \cdots, q_n\} > 0, \tag{6}$$

$$\theta_i = \frac{1}{\|Q\|_{L^2}^2} \lim_{x \to x_i} \frac{V(x)}{|x - x_i|^q} \int_{\mathbb{R}^3} |x|^q |Q(x)|^2 dx > 0,$$

where $Q(x)$ satisfies (5) for $p = \frac{4(s+1)}{3}$. Moreover, let

$$\theta = \min\{\theta_1, \cdots \theta_n\} > 0 \tag{7}$$

and the set of flattest global minima for $V(x)$ is denoted by

$$W = \{x_i : \theta_i = \theta\}. \tag{8}$$

In light of Theorems 1 and 2, and inspired by [12,14,15,26], for any positive sequence $\{\eta_k\}$ and set u_{η_k} being the positive minimizers of $I(\eta_k, s, \lambda^*)$, we next establish the following theorem on limit behavior of constraint minimizers for $I(\eta_k, s, \lambda^*)$ when $p = \frac{4(s+1)}{3}$ and $\lambda = \lambda^*$ as $\eta_k \to 0^+$.

Theorem 3. *Assume that* (V_1) *and* (V_2) *hold. For* $p = \frac{4(s+1)}{3}$, $\lambda = \lambda^*$ *and any positive sequence* $\{\eta_k\}$ *with* $\eta_k \to 0^+$ *as* $k \to \infty$, *define* $\epsilon_{\eta_k} := \left(\int_{\mathbb{R}^3} |\nabla u_{\eta_k}|^2 dx \right)^{-\frac{1}{2}}$; *then, the following conclusions hold:*

(i) *The* u_{η_k} *has a unique local maximum* z_{η_k} *satisfying* $\lim_{k\to\infty} z_{\eta_k} = x_i$ *and* $x_i \in W$ *is a flattest global minimum of* $V(x)$. *Moreover, we have as* $k \to \infty$

$$\epsilon_{\eta_k}^{\frac{3}{2}} u_{\eta_k}(\epsilon_{\eta_k} x + z_{\eta_k}) \to \frac{Q(|x|)}{\|Q\|_2} \quad \textit{strongly in } H^1(\mathbb{R}^3),$$

where Q *denotes the unique positive solution of* (5) *for* $p = \frac{4(s+1)}{3}$.

(ii) *The* ϵ_{η_k} *fulfills as* $k \to \infty$

$$\epsilon_{\eta_k} \approx (q\theta)^{-\frac{1}{q+2}} (\eta_k)^{\frac{1}{q+2}}.$$

(iii) *The least energy* $I(\eta_k, s, \lambda^*)$ *satisfies as* $k \to \infty$

$$I(\eta_k, s, \lambda^*) \approx \left[\frac{1}{2} q^{\frac{2}{q+2}} + q^{\frac{-q}{q+2}}\right] \theta^{\frac{2}{q+2}} (\eta_k)^{\frac{q}{q+2}},$$

where q, θ *are stated by* (6) *and* (7).

Notice that the $f(\eta_k) \approx g(\eta_k)$ in Theorem 3 means $f/g \to 1$ as $k \to \infty$. In fact, for the case in which $s = 0$ and $V(x)$ behave in sinusoidal, ring-shaped, periodic and multi-well forms, the papers [19–22] widely studied the mass concentration behavior of the constrained minimizers.Particularly for $s = 1$, the authors in [14,15] also analyzed the limit behavior of minimizers when $\eta > 0$ as $b \to 0^+$ or $b > 0$ as $\eta \to 0^+$. As described in Theorem 3, our paper obtains an interesting result on this topic when it involves a varying non-local term, and it thus enriches the study of such issues.

The present paper is structured as follows. Section 3 shall establish the existence and non-existence proof of constrained minimizers for $I(\eta, s, \lambda)$ when the parameters η, λ and exponents s, p satisfy suitable range. For $p = \frac{4(s+1)}{3}$, $\lambda = \lambda^*$ and any positive sequence $\{\eta_k\}$ with $\eta_k \to 0^+$ as $k \to \infty$, in Section 4 we plan to give the accurate energy estimation of $I(\eta_k, s, \lambda^*)$, and then analyze the detailed limit behavior of positive constrained minimizers as $\eta_k \to 0^+$.

2. Preliminaries

In this paper, we shall make full use of the following notations:

- The $H^1(\mathbb{R}^3)$ is a Sobolev space with norm $\|u\|_{H^1} =: \left(\int_{\mathbb{R}^3} |\nabla u|^2 dx + \int_{\mathbb{R}^3} |u|^2 dx \right)^{\frac{1}{2}}$.
- On any compact support set of $\mathbb{R}^3$, the $L^\infty_{loc}(\mathbb{R}^3)$ denotes the essentially bounded measurable function space, and $C^\alpha_{loc}(\mathbb{R}^3)$ is a Hölder continuous function space.
- The $L^p(\mathbb{R}^3)$, $p \in (1, \infty)$ denotes a Sobolev space with norm $\|u\|_{L^p} =: \left(\int_{\mathbb{R}^3} |u|^p dx \right)^{\frac{1}{p}}$.
- The symbol $\to$ (resp. $\rightharpoonup$) means the strong (resp. weak) convergence.
- The letters $\mathcal{A}, \mathcal{C}, \mathcal{D}, \mathcal{E}, \mathcal{F}, \mathcal{K}$ and $\mathcal{M}$ represent different positive constants.

Moreover, we introduce the following equality, as seen in [9]:

$$\|\nabla Q_p\|_{L^2}^2 = \|Q_p\|_{L^2}^2 = \frac{2}{p+2} \|Q_p\|_{L^{p+2}}^{p+2}, \; 0 < p < 4. \tag{9}$$

Recall also from [27] (Proposition 4.1) that $Q_p(x)$ has the exponential decay property

$$|\nabla Q_p(x)|, Q_p(|x|) = O(|x|^{-1} e^{-|x|}) \quad \text{as } |x| \to \infty. \tag{10}$$

At last, we give a Gagliardo–Nirenberg (G-N)-type inequality [28] such as

$$\|u\|_{L^{2+p}}^{2+p} \leq \frac{p+2}{2\|Q_p\|_{L^2}^{p}} \|\nabla u\|_{L^2}^{\frac{3p}{2}} \|u\|_{L^2}^{2-\frac{p}{2}}, \ 0 < p < 4, \tag{11}$$

where Q_p is the unique positive solution of (5).

For proving the existence of constraint minimizers, the following compactness lemma is necessary:

Lemma 4 ([29] (Theorem 2.1)). *Suppose that* (V_1) *is holding; then, for any* $p \in (2,6)$, *the imbedding*

$$\mathcal{H} \hookrightarrow L^p(\mathbb{R}^3),$$

is compact, where $\mathcal{H}$ *is given by* (4).

3. Proof of Theorems 1 and 2

In this section, we shall give the proof of existence and non-existence on constraint minimizers for (2), which are divided into the following two parts:

Proof of Theorem 1. Under the assumption of Theorem 1, for any $u \in \mathcal{U}$, we deduce from G-N inequality (11) that for $\eta > 0$, $p < \frac{4(s+1)}{3}$

$$\begin{aligned} E(u) \geq &\frac{\eta}{2}\int_{\mathbb{R}^3} |\nabla u|^2 dx + \frac{b}{2(s+1)}\Big(\int_{\mathbb{R}^3} |\nabla u|^2 dx\Big)^{s+1} \\ &+ \frac{1}{2}\int_{\mathbb{R}^3} V(x)|u|^2 dx - \frac{\lambda}{2\|Q_p\|_{L^2}^{p}}\Big(\int_{\mathbb{R}^3} |\nabla u|^2 dx\Big)^{\frac{3p}{4}}. \end{aligned} \tag{12}$$

For $p = \frac{4(s+1)}{3}$ and $0 < \lambda \leq \lambda^* = \frac{b}{(s+1)}\|Q\|_{L^2}^{\frac{4(s+1)}{3}}$, one derives from (11) that

$$\begin{aligned} E(u) \geq &\frac{\eta}{2}\int_{\mathbb{R}^3} |\nabla u|^2 dx + \frac{b}{2(s+1)}\Big(\int_{\mathbb{R}^3} |\nabla u|^2 dx\Big)^{s+1} \\ &+ \frac{1}{2}\int_{\mathbb{R}^3} V(x)|u|^2 dx - \frac{\lambda}{2\|Q_p\|_{L^2}^{p}}\Big(\int_{\mathbb{R}^3} |\nabla u|^2 dx\Big)^{s+1} \\ \geq &\frac{\eta}{2}\int_{\mathbb{R}^3} |\nabla u|^2 dx + \frac{\lambda^* - \lambda}{2\|Q\|_{L^2}^{\frac{4(s+1)}{3}}}\Big(\int_{\mathbb{R}^3} |\nabla u|^2 dx\Big)^{s+1} + \frac{1}{2}\int_{\mathbb{R}^3} V(x)|u|^2 dx. \end{aligned} \tag{13}$$

Both $p < \frac{4(s+1)}{3}$ and $p = \frac{4(s+1)}{3}$, $0 < \lambda \leq \lambda^*$ hold, (12) and (13) yield a fact that, for any sequence $\{u_n\} \subseteq \mathcal{U}$, the $E(u_n)$ is bounded uniformly from below. Hence, there admits a minimization sequence $\{u_n\} \subseteq \mathcal{U}$ as fulfilling

$$I(\eta, s, \lambda) = \lim_{n\to\infty} E(u_n).$$

In truth, one can obtain from (12) and (13) that $\{u_n\}$ is bounded in $\mathcal{H}$. Applying the Lemma 4, there exists a $\bar{u} \in \mathcal{H}$, and $\{u_n\}$ has a subsequence $\{u_{n_k}\}$ such that as $k \to \infty$

$$u_{n_k} \rightharpoonup \bar{u} \text{ weakly in } \mathcal{H}, \quad u_{n_k} \to \bar{u} \text{ strongly in } L^{\nu}(\mathbb{R}^3),\ 2 < \nu < 6.$$

Using the weak lower semi-continuity, we obtain

$$\liminf_{k\to\infty} \int_{\mathbb{R}^3} |\nabla u_{n_k}|^2 dx \geq \int_{\mathbb{R}^3} |\nabla \bar{u}|^2 dx.$$

The above results give that

$$I(\eta,s,\lambda) = \liminf_{k\to\infty} E(u_{n_k}) \geq E(\bar{u}) \geq I(\eta,s,\lambda)$$

which then yields $E(\bar{u}) = I(\eta,s,\lambda)$. Hence, $\bar{u}$ is a minimizer for $I(\eta,s,\lambda)$.

The non-existence proof of constraint minimizer comes true by establishing energy estimation for $I(\eta,s,\lambda)$. To meet this goal, we choose a test function such as

$$u_t(x) := \frac{\mathcal{P}_t}{\|Q\|_{L^2}} t^{\frac{3}{2}} \Phi(x-x_i) Q(t|x-x_i|)(t>0), \tag{14}$$

where Q fulfills (5) for $p = \frac{4(s+1)}{3}$, and $x_i \in W$ satisfies $V(x_i) = 0$. The function $\Phi(x) \in C_0^\infty(\mathbb{R}^3)$ in (14) is chosen as

$$\begin{cases} \Phi(x) = 1, & |x| \leq 1, \\ 0 < \Phi(x) < 1, & 1 < |x| < 2, \\ |\Phi(x)| = 0, & |x| \geq 2, \\ |\nabla\Phi(x)| \leq C, & x \in \mathbb{R}^3. \end{cases}$$

Notice that $\mathcal{P}_t$ in (14) makes sure $\|u_t\|_{L^2}^2 = 1$. It is deduced from (10) and (14) that

$$1 \leq P_t \leq 1 + O(t^{-\infty}) \text{ and } \lim_{t\to+\infty} P_t = 1, \tag{15}$$

where $g(t) = O(t^{-\infty})$ means $\lim_{t\to+\infty} |g(t)|t^d = 0$ for any $d > 0$. One can attain from (9) that as $t \to \infty$

$$\begin{aligned} I(\eta,s,\lambda) \leq & \frac{\eta P_t^2 t^2}{2\|Q\|_{L^2}^2} \int_{\mathbb{R}^3} |\nabla Q|^2 dx + \frac{b P_t^{2(s+1)} t^{2(s+1)}}{2(s+1)\|Q\|_{L^2}^{2(s+1)}} \Big(\int_{\mathbb{R}^3} |\nabla Q|^2 dx \Big)^{s+1} \\ & - \frac{\lambda P_t^{p+2} t^{\frac{3p}{2}}}{(p+2)\|Q\|_{L^2}^{p+2}} \int_{\mathbb{R}^3} |Q|^{p+2} dx + V(x_0) + o(1) + O(t^{-\infty}) \end{aligned} \tag{16}$$

which yields that, for any $p > \frac{4(s+1)}{3}$, the $I(\eta,s,\lambda) \to -\infty$ as $t \to \infty$. For $\eta > 0$ and $p = \frac{4(s+1)}{3}$, we derive from (16) that

$$\begin{aligned} I(\eta,s,\lambda) & \leq \frac{\eta t^2}{2} + \frac{b t^{2(s+1)}}{2(s+1)} - \frac{\lambda t^{2(s+1)}}{2\|Q\|_{L^2}^{\frac{4(s+1)}{3}}} + o(1) + O(t^{-\infty}) \\ & = \frac{\eta t^2}{2} + \frac{(\lambda^* - \lambda) t^{2(s+1)}}{2\|Q\|_{L^2}^{\frac{4(s+1)}{3}}} + o(1) + O(t^{-\infty}) \to -\infty. \end{aligned} \tag{17}$$

We can deduce from (17) that for $\lambda > \lambda^*$, the $I(\eta,s,\lambda) \to -\infty$ as $t \to \infty$. Hence, for any $\eta > 0$, if either $p > \frac{4(s+1)}{3}$ or $p = \frac{4(s+1)}{3}$, $\lambda > \lambda^*$ holds, then $I(\eta,s,\lambda)$ has no minimizer. □

Proof of Theorem 2. Under the assumption of Theorem 2, for any $u \in \mathcal{U}$, one can derive from (11) that for $\eta = 0$ and $p = \frac{4(s+1)}{3}$ that

$$E(u) \geq \frac{\lambda^* - \lambda}{2\|Q\|_{L^2}^{\frac{4(s+1)}{3}}} \Big(\int_{\mathbb{R}^3} |\nabla u|^2 dx \Big)^{s+1} + \frac{1}{2} \int_{\mathbb{R}^3} V(x)|u|^2 dx. \tag{18}$$

If $0 < \lambda < \lambda^*$, repeating the proof of Theorem 1, one claims that $I(0,s,\lambda)$ has a minimizer.

The non-existence proof of constraint minimizer is established as follows: for $\eta = 0$ and $p = \frac{4(s+1)}{3}$, similar to the estimation of (17), one obtains that

$$I(0,s,\lambda) \leq E(u_t) = \frac{(\lambda^* - \lambda)t^{2(s+1)}}{2\|Q\|_{L^2}^{\frac{4(s+1)}{3}}} + o(1) + O(t^{-\infty}) \to -\infty \tag{19}$$

It then yields that $I(0,s,\lambda)$ has no minimizer due to $I(0,s,\lambda) = -\infty$ for $\lambda > \lambda^*$.

For $\eta = 0$ and $\lambda = \lambda^*$, one can obtain from (18) and (19) that $I(0,s,\lambda^*) = 0$. We next argue that $I(0,s,\lambda^*)$ has no minimizer by establishing a contradiction. If this is not true, suppose that $\hat{u} \in \mathcal{U}$ is a minimizer of $I(0,s,\lambda^*)$. As stated in Section 1, we may assume that $\hat{u}$ is positive. Since $V(x) \geq 0$ and $\int_{\mathbb{R}^3} |\hat{u}|^2 dx = 1$, the G-N inequality (11) then yields that

$$\frac{1}{(s+1)}\Big(\int_{\mathbb{R}^3} |\nabla \hat{u}|^2 dx\Big)^{s+1} = \frac{3\lambda^*}{2s+5}\int_{\mathbb{R}^3} |\hat{u}|^{\frac{4(s+1)}{3}+2} dx,$$

where the equality holds only for $\hat{u} = Q$, and Q is the unique positive solution of (5) for $p = \frac{4(s+1)}{3}$. One obtains from (12) that $\hat{u}$ satisfies

$$\int_{\mathbb{R}^3} V(x)\hat{u}^2 dx = \min_{\mathbb{R}^3} V(x) = 0.$$

However, the above two equalities cannot be held at the same time because the first one presents a fact that $\hat{u}$ has no compact support, and the second one needs $\hat{u} = Q$ to possess a compact support. Thus, one claims that $I(0,s,\lambda^*)$ has no minimizer. So far, the non-existence proof of constraint minimizer is completed. □

4. Proof of Theorem 3

In this section, for $p = \frac{4(s+1)}{3}$, $\lambda = \lambda^*$ and any positive sequence $\{\eta_k\}$ with $\eta_k \to 0^+$ as $k \to \infty$, we plan to analyze the limit behavior on minimizers u_{η_k} for $I(\eta_k, s, \lambda^*)$ as $\eta_k \to 0^+$. Before proving Theorem 3, some indispensable lemmas are necessary, which are stated as follows:

Lemma 5. *Under the assumption of Theorem 3, set* $\hat{v}_{\eta_k}(x) := \epsilon_{\eta_k}^{\frac{3}{2}} u_{\eta_k}(\epsilon_{\eta_k} x)$ *and* $\epsilon_{\eta_k} = \big(\int_{\mathbb{R}^3} |\nabla u_{\eta_k}|^2 dx\big)^{-\frac{1}{2}} > 0$*; then, as* $k \to \infty$*, the* $\epsilon_{\eta_k} \to 0$ *and* $\hat{v}_{\eta_k}$ *satisfy*

$$\int_{\mathbb{R}^3} |\nabla \hat{v}_{\eta_k}|^2 dx = 1, \quad \int_{\mathbb{R}^3} |\hat{v}_{\eta_k}|^{\frac{4(s+1)}{3}+2} \to \frac{b[2s+5]}{3(s+1)\lambda^*}.$$

Proof. If u_{η_k} are positive minimizers of (2), then u_{η_k} satisfies

$$-\Big(\eta_k + b\Big(\int_{\mathbb{R}^3} |\nabla u_{\eta_k}|^2 dx\Big)^s\Big)\Delta u_{\eta_k} + V(x)u_{\eta_k} = \mu_{\eta_k} u_{\eta_k} + \lambda^* |u_{\eta_k}|^{\frac{4(s+1)}{3}} u_{\eta_k} \tag{20}$$

here, $\mu_{\eta_k} \in \mathbb{R}$ denote Lagrange multipliers. Set

$$\hat{v}_{\eta_k}(x) := \epsilon_{\eta_k}^{\frac{3}{2}} u_{\eta_k}(\epsilon_{\eta_k} x), \tag{21}$$

where $\epsilon_{\eta_k} = \big(\int_{\mathbb{R}^3} |\nabla u_{\eta_k}|^2 dx\big)^{-\frac{1}{2}} > 0$. On the contrary, we assume that $\epsilon_{\eta_k} \nrightarrow 0$ as $\eta_k \to 0^+$; then, $\{u_{\eta_k}\}$ is bounded uniformly in $\mathcal{H}$. Similar to the proof of Theorems 1 and 2 in Section 3, one asserts that there exists a $u_0 \in \mathcal{U}$ and $\{u_{\eta_k}\}$ has a subsequence (still denoted by $\{u_{\eta_k}\}$) such that as $\eta_k \to 0^+$

$$u_{\eta_k} \rightharpoonup u_0 \text{ weakly in } \mathcal{H}, \quad u_{\eta_k} \to u_0 \text{ strongly in } L^p(\mathbb{R}^3),\ 2 < p < 6. \tag{22}$$

To obtain our result, we need to prove that $I(\eta_k, s, \lambda^*) \to 0$ as $\eta_k \to 0^+$. For this purpose, we choose a test function the same as (14). Based on (10), (14) and (15), one calculates that

$$\int_{\mathbb{R}^3} |\nabla u_t|^2 dx = \frac{P_t^2 t^2}{\|Q\|_{L^2}^2} \int_{\mathbb{R}^3} |\nabla Q|^2 dx + O(t^{-\infty})$$

and

$$\int_{\mathbb{R}^3} |u_t|^{\frac{4(s+1)}{3}+2} dx = \frac{P_t^{\frac{4(s+1)}{3}+2} t^{2(s+1)}}{\|Q\|_{L^2}^{\frac{4(s+1)}{3}+2}} \int_{\mathbb{R}^3} |Q|^{\frac{4(s+1)}{3}+2} dx + O(t^{-\infty}).$$

Since $V(x)$ satisfies (V_1) and (V_2), one obtains that as $t \to \infty$

$$\int_{\mathbb{R}^3} V(x)|u_t|^2 dx = V(x_i) + o(1) = o(1).$$

It thus follows from (9) that, for $p = \frac{4(s+1)}{3}$ and $\lambda = \lambda^*$ as $t \to +\infty$

$$\begin{aligned} I(\eta_k, s, \lambda^*) \le & \frac{\eta_k P_t^2 t^2}{2\|Q\|_{L^2}^2} \int_{\mathbb{R}^3} |\nabla Q|^2 dx + \frac{b P_t^{2(s+1)} t^{2(s+1)}}{2(s+1)\|Q\|_{L^2}^{2(s+1)}} \Big(\int_{\mathbb{R}^3} |\nabla Q|^2 dx \Big)^{s+1} \\ & - \frac{\lambda^* P_t^{p+2} t^4}{(p+2)\|Q\|_{L^2}^{p+2}} \int_{\mathbb{R}^3} |Q|^{p+2} dx + V(x_i) + o(1) + O(t^{-\infty}) \\ = & \frac{\eta_k t^2}{2} + \frac{b t^{2(s+1)}}{2(s+1)} - \frac{\lambda^* t^{2(s+1)}}{2\|Q\|_{L^2}^{\frac{4(s+1)}{3}}} + o(1) + O(t^{-\infty}) \\ = & \frac{\eta_k t^2}{2} + o(1) + O(t^{-\infty}). \end{aligned} \tag{23}$$

Taking $t = (\eta_k)^{-\frac{1}{3}}$ into (23), it yields that as $k, t \to \infty$

$$I(\eta_k, s, \lambda^*) \le E(u_t) = \frac{\eta_k^{\frac{1}{3}}}{2} + o(1) + O(t^{-\infty}) \to 0. \tag{24}$$

We can deduce from (3), (22) and (24) that

$$0 = I(0, s, \lambda^*) \le E(u_0) \le \liminf_{k \to \infty} E(u_{\eta_k}) = \lim_{k \to \infty} I(\eta_k, s, \lambda^*) = I(0, s, \lambda^*) = 0$$

which yields a fact that u_0 is a minimizer of $I(0, s, \lambda^*)$. However, this is a contradiction since Theorem 2 shows that $I(0, s, \lambda^*)$ has no minimizer. Thus, $\epsilon_{\eta_k} \to 0$ holds as $k \to \infty$.

By (21), we just have $\int_{\mathbb{R}^3} |\nabla \hat{v}_{\eta_k}|^2 dx = \epsilon_{\eta_k}^{-2} \int_{\mathbb{R}^3} |\nabla u_{\eta_k}|^2 dx = 1$. Since u_{η_k} are minimizers of $I(\eta_k, s, \lambda^*)$ for any $\eta_k > 0$, we can derive from (11) and (24) that as $k \to \infty$

$$0 \le E(u_{\eta_k}) = I(\eta_k, s, \lambda^*) \le E(u_t) \to 0$$

which yields that as $k \to \infty$

$$\frac{b}{2(s+1)} \Big(\int_{\mathbb{R}^3} |\nabla u_{\eta_k}|^2 dx \Big)^{2(s+1)} - \frac{3\lambda^*}{4s+10} \int_{\mathbb{R}^3} |u_{\eta_k}|^{\frac{4(s+1)}{3}+2} dx \to 0. \tag{25}$$

It hence follows from (21) and (25) that as $k \to \infty$

$$\frac{b}{2(s+1)} - \frac{3\lambda^*}{4s+10} \int_{\mathbb{R}^3} |\hat{v}_{\eta_k}|^{\frac{4(s+1)}{3}+2} dx \to 0,$$

which shows as $k \to \infty$
$$\int_{\mathbb{R}^3} |\hat{v}_{\eta_k}|^{\frac{4(s+1)}{3}+2} dx \to \frac{b[2s+5]}{3(s+1)\lambda^*}.$$
We have finished the proof of Lemma 5. □

Assume that u_{η_k} are positive minimizers of $I(\eta_k, s, \lambda^*)$ for any $\eta_k > 0$. Since $\int_{\mathbb{R}^3} |u_{\eta_k}|^2 dx = 1$, one has $u_{\eta_k}(x) \to 0$ as $|x| \to \infty$. This yields that $u_{\eta_k}(x)$ has at least one local maximum, which is denoted by z_{η_k}. We define a function

$$v_{\eta_k}(x) := \epsilon_{\eta_k}^{\frac{3}{2}} u_{\eta_k}(\epsilon_{\eta_k} x + z_{\eta_k}), \tag{26}$$

where ϵ_{η_k} is given in Lemma 5. We next establish the following lemma, which is related to convergence properties of v_{η_k} and z_{η_k}.

Lemma 6. *Under the assumption of Theorem 3, set z_{η_k} as a local maximum of u_{η_k} and v_{η_k} defined by (26); then, we have*

(i) There exist a finite ball $B_{2s}(0)$ and a constant $\mathcal{D} > 0$ such that
$$\liminf_{k\to\infty} \int_{B_{2s}(0)} |v_{\eta_k}(x)|^2 dx \geq \mathcal{D} > 0.$$

(ii) The z_{η_k} is a unique maximum of u_{η_k} and satisfies $z_{\eta_k} \to x_0$ for some $x_0 \in \mathbb{R}^3$ as $k \to \infty$. Furthermore, the x_0 is a minimum of $V(x)$, that is, $V(x_0) = 0$.

(iii) The function v_{η_k} satisfies
$$\lim_{k\to\infty} v_{\eta_k}(x) = \lim_{k\to\infty} \epsilon_{\eta_k}^{\frac{3}{2}} u_{\eta_k}(\epsilon_{\eta_k} x + z_{\eta_k}) = \frac{Q(|x|)}{\|Q\|_{L^2}} \text{ strongly in } H^1(\mathbb{R}^3),$$
where Q is the unique solution of (5) for $p = \frac{4(s+1)}{3}$.

Proof. (i) By (20), we see that v_{η_k} fulfills the elliptic equation

$$-\left(\eta_k \epsilon_{\eta_k}^{2s} + b\right)\Delta v_{\eta_k} + \epsilon_{\eta_k}^{2(s+1)} V(x) v_{\eta_k} = \epsilon_{\eta_k}^{2(s+1)} \mu_{\eta_k} v_{\eta_k} + \lambda^* |v_{\eta_k}|^{\frac{4(s+1)}{3}} v_{\eta_k}, \tag{27}$$

here, μ_{η_k} are Lagrange multipliers. In truth, (2) and (20) give that

$$\mu_{\eta_k} = 2I(\eta_k, s, \lambda^*) + \frac{sb}{s+1}\Big(\int_{\mathbb{R}^3} |\nabla u_{\eta_k}|^2 dx\Big)^{s+1} - \frac{2(s+1)\lambda^*}{2s+5} \int_{\mathbb{R}^3} |u_{\eta_k}|^{\frac{4(s+1)}{3}+2} dx. \tag{28}$$

Repeating the proof of (24), one obtains that as $k \to \infty$

$$\epsilon_{\eta_k}^{2(s+1)} I(\eta_k, s, \lambda^*) \to 0 \text{ and } \int_{\mathbb{R}^3} V(\epsilon_{\eta_k} x + z_{\eta_k}) v_{\eta_k}^2(x) dx \to 0. \tag{29}$$

Since $0 < p = \frac{4(s+1)}{3} < 4$ yields $0 < s < 2$, we can obtain from (28), (29) and Lemma 5 that as $k \to \infty$

$$\mu_{\eta_k} \epsilon_{\eta_k}^{2(s+1)} = 2\epsilon_{\eta_k}^{2(s+1)} I(\eta_k, s, \lambda^*) + \frac{sb}{s+1} - \frac{2b}{3} \to \frac{(s-2)b}{3(s+1)} < 0. \tag{30}$$

Since u_{η_k} take local maxima at $x = z_{\eta_k}$, it yields that v_{η_k} obtain local maxima at $x = 0$. We thus derive from (27) and (30) that there exists a constant $\mathcal{K} > 0$ satisfying as $k \to \infty$

$$v_{\eta_k}(0) \geq \mathcal{K} > 0. \tag{31}$$

Furthermore, one obtains from (27) that

$$-\Delta v_{\eta_k} - c(x)v_{\eta_k} \leq 0, \quad x \in \mathbb{R}^3, \tag{32}$$

where $c(x) = \lambda^*|v_{\eta_k}|^{\frac{4(s+1)}{3}}$. In view of the De Giorgi–Nash–Moser theory, as seen in [30] (Theorem 4.1), one declares that there exist a finite ball $B_{2s}(0) \subset \mathbb{R}^3$ and constant $\mathcal{C} > 0$ such that

$$\max_{B_s(0)} v_{\eta_k} \leq \mathcal{C}\Big(\int_{B_{2s}(0)} |v_{\eta_k}|^2 dx\Big)^{\frac{1}{2}}. \tag{33}$$

It hence yields from (31) and (33) that there exists a constant $\mathcal{D} > 0$ satisfying

$$\liminf_{k\to\infty} \int_{B_{2s}(0)} |v_{\eta_k}|^2 dx \geq \mathcal{D} > 0. \tag{34}$$

(ii) On the contrary, one may assume that $|z_{\eta_k}| \to \infty$ as $k \to \infty$. By applying (34) and Fatou's lemma, for any large constant $\mathcal{A}$, one has

$$\begin{aligned} &\liminf_{k\to\infty} \int_{\mathbb{R}^3} V(\epsilon_{\eta_k} x + z_{\eta_k})|v_{\eta_k}(x)|^2 dx \\ \geq &\int_{B_{2s}(0)} \liminf_{k\to\infty} V(\epsilon_{\eta_k} x + z_{\eta_k})|v_{\eta_k}(x)|^2 dx \geq \mathcal{A} > 0 \end{aligned} \tag{35}$$

which contradicts (29), and it hence shows that $|z_{\eta_k}|$ is bounded in $\mathbb{R}^3$. Taking a subsequence of $\{z_{\eta_k}\}$ if necessary (still denoted by $\{z_{\eta_k}\}$), there admits a $x_0 \in \mathbb{R}^3$ such that $z_{\eta_k} \to x_0$ as $k \to \infty$. In fact, one can claim that x_0 is a minimum of $V(x)$, that is, $V(x_0) = 0$. If not, repeating the proof of (35), it also yields a contradiction. Thus, we say that $z_{\eta_k} \to x_0$ as $k \to \infty$ and $V(x_0) = 0$.

(iii) The Lemma 5 shows that sequence $\{v_{\eta_k}\}$ is bounded in $H^1(\mathbb{R}^3)$, and under the sense of subsequence, there exists a $v_0 \in H^1(\mathbb{R}^3)$ such that $v_{\eta_k} \rightharpoonup v_0$ as $k \to \infty$. Using (30) and passing weak limit to (27), one obtains that v_0 satisfies

$$-\Delta v_0 + \frac{2-s}{3(s+1)} v_0 = \frac{\lambda^*}{b}|v_0|^{\frac{4(s+1)}{3}} v_0, \ x \in \mathbb{R}^3, \tag{36}$$

where $0 < s < 2$. By (34) and applying the strong maximum principle to (36), one has $v_0 > 0$. Taking $p = \frac{4(s+1)}{3}$ in (5), one knows that

$$-\Delta Q + \frac{2-s}{3(s+1)} Q = \frac{1}{s+1}|Q|^{\frac{4(s+1)}{3}} Q, \ x \in \mathbb{R}^3. \tag{37}$$

Due to the fact that (37) has a unique positive radially symmetric solution $Q \in H^1(\mathbb{R}^3)$, it hence yields from (36) that

$$v_0(x) = \frac{Q(|x-y_0|)}{\|Q\|_{L^2}} \text{ for some } y_0 \in \mathbb{R}^3. \tag{38}$$

Similar to the procedure of Theorem 1, one declares that as $k \to \infty$, $v_{\eta_k} \to v_0$ strongly in $H^1(\mathbb{R}^3)$. Using the standard elliptic regularity theory, we obtain from (27) that as $k \to \infty$

$$v_{\eta_k} \to v_0 \text{ in } C^{2,\alpha}_{loc}(\mathbb{R}^3), \ \alpha \in (0,1). \tag{39}$$

Applying the method [18] (Theorem 2), one knows that the $y_0 = 0$ in (38), and 0 is the unique global maximum of v_0. Therefore, v_0 behaves like

$$v_0(x) = \frac{Q(|x|)}{\|Q\|_{L^2}}, \ x \in \mathbb{R}^3. \tag{40}$$

By (39), using the technique of [19] (Theorem 1.2), we know that z_{η_k} is the unique global maximum of u_{η_k}. □

To obtain a more detailed description on limit behavior of constraint minimizers u_{η_k} as $\eta_k \to 0^+$, some precise energy estimation of $I(\eta_k, s, \lambda^*)$ as $\eta_k \to 0^+$ is necessary. Toward this aim, we begin with the upper-bound estimation of $I(\eta_k, s, \lambda)$, which is sated as the following lemma:

Lemma 7. *Assume that* (V_1) *and* (V_2) *hold. If* $p = \frac{4(s+1)}{3}$ *and* $\lambda = \lambda^*$*, then for any positive sequence* $\{\eta_k\}$ *with* $\eta_k \to 0^+$ *as* $k \to \infty$*, the* $I(\eta_k, s, \lambda)$ *satisfies as* $k \to \infty$

$$I(\eta_k, s, \lambda^*) \le \big[\frac{1}{2} q^{\frac{2}{q+2}} + q^{\frac{-q}{q+2}}\big] \theta^{\frac{2}{q+2}} (\eta_k)^{\frac{q}{q+2}} (1 + o(1)),$$

where q, θ *are defined by* (6) *and* (7).

Proof. Choosing (14), we can deduce from (9)–(11) that there exist positive constants d_1, d_2 such that as $t \to +\infty$

$$\begin{aligned} &\frac{b}{2(s+1)} \Big(\int_{\mathbb{R}^3} |\nabla u_t|^2 dx \Big)^{s+1} - \frac{3\lambda^*}{4s+10} \int_{\mathbb{R}^3} |u_t|^{\frac{4(s+1)}{3}+2} dx \\ \le &\frac{b t^{2(s+1)}}{2(s+1)} - \frac{\lambda^* t^{2(s+1)}}{2\|Q\|_{L^2}^{\frac{4(s+1)}{3}}} + d_1 e^{-d_2 t} = d_1 e^{-d_2 t} \end{aligned} \tag{41}$$

and there exist positive constants d_3, d_4 such that as $t \to +\infty$

$$\frac{\eta_k}{2} \int_{\mathbb{R}^3} |\nabla u_t|^2 dx = \frac{P_t^2 t^2}{\|Q\|_{L^2}^2} \int_{\mathbb{R}^3} |\nabla Q|^2 dx = \frac{\eta_k t^2}{2} + d_3 e^{-d_4 t}. \tag{42}$$

Since $V(x)$ satisfies (V_1) and (V_2), we derive that there exist positive constants d_5, d_6 such that as $t \to +\infty$

$$\begin{aligned} &\int_{\mathbb{R}^3} V(x) u_t^2 dx \le \frac{1}{\|Q\|_{L^2}^2} \int_{B_{\sqrt{t}}(0)} V(\frac{x}{t} + x_i) |Q|^2 dx + d_5 e^{-d_6 t} \\ =&\frac{1}{\|Q\|_{L^2}^2} \int_{B_{\sqrt{t}}(0)} C(\frac{x}{t} + x_i) \prod_{j=1}^{n} |\frac{x}{t} + x_i - x_j|^{q_j} |Q|^2 dx + d_5 e^{-d_6 t} \\ =&t^{-q} \frac{1}{\|Q\|_{L^2}^2} \lim_{x \to x_i} \frac{V(x)}{|x - x_i|^q} \int_{\mathbb{R}^3} |x|^q |Q(x)|^2 dx + o(t^{-q}) + d_5 e^{-d_6 t} \\ =&\theta t^{-q} + o(t^{-q}) + d_5 e^{-d_6 t}, \end{aligned} \tag{43}$$

where q, θ defined by (6) and (7). Using (41)–(43), we have

$$\begin{aligned} I(\eta_k, s, \lambda^*) \le &\frac{\eta_k t^2}{2} + \theta t^{-q} + o(t^{-q}) + d_1 e^{-d_2 t} + d_3 e^{-d_4 t} + d_5 e^{-d_6 t} \\ = &\frac{\eta_k t^2}{2} + \theta t^{-q} (1 + o(1)). \end{aligned} \tag{44}$$

Taking $t = (q\theta)^{\frac{1}{q+2}} (\eta_k)^{-\frac{1}{q+2}}$, one can deduce from (44) that as $\eta_k \to 0^+$

$$I(\eta_k, s, \lambda^*) \le \big[\frac{1}{2} q^{\frac{2}{q+2}} + q^{\frac{-q}{q+2}}\big] \theta^{\frac{2}{q+2}} (\eta_k)^{\frac{q}{q+2}} (1 + o(1)).$$

□

Proof of Theorem 3. According to the results of Lemmas 5–7, it remains to prove *(ii)* and *(iii)* in Theorem 3, which can be realized by establishing the precise lower energy estimation of $I(\eta_k, s, \lambda^*)$ as $\eta_k \to 0^+$. To meet this goal, we set $\{u_{\eta_k}\}$ as the positive minimizers of $I(\eta_k, s, \lambda^*)$, z_{η_k} being their unique global maxima, and we define v_{η_k} by (26). Using Lemma 6, one knows that for $\{z_{\eta_k}\}$, choosing a subsequence if necessary (still stated by $\{z_{\eta_k}\}$), the $z_{\eta_k} \to x_0$ and $V(x_0) = 0$.

In fact, we can go a step further, that is, we can come to the following conclusion:

$$z_{\eta_k} \to x_i \text{ and } \frac{|z_{\eta_k} - x_i|}{\epsilon_{\eta_k}} \text{ is bounded uniformly as } k \to \infty, \tag{45}$$

where $x_i \in W$ and x_i denotes a flattest global minimum of $V(x)$. To obtain (45), we firstly claim that

$$\frac{|z_{\eta_k} - x_0|}{\epsilon_{\eta_k}} \text{ is bounded uniformly as } k \to \infty. \tag{46}$$

If this is false, then we assume that $\frac{|z_{\eta_k} - x_0|}{\epsilon_{\eta_k}} \to \infty$ as $k \to \infty$. It then follows from (V_2) and Lemma 6 (i) that, for any large positive constant $\mathcal{F}$,

$$\begin{aligned} &\liminf_{k\to\infty} \frac{1}{\epsilon_{\eta_k}^{q_{i_0}}} \int_{\mathbb{R}^3} V(\epsilon_{\eta_k} x + z_{\eta_k}) v_{\eta_k}^2 dx \\ \geq &C \int_{B_{2s}(0)} \liminf_{k\to\infty} |x + \frac{z_{\eta_k} - x_0}{\epsilon_{\eta_k}}|^{q_{i_0}} \cdot \prod_{j=1, j\neq i_0}^{n} |\epsilon_{\eta_k} x + z_{\eta_k} - x_j|^{q_j} v_{\eta_k}^2 dx \geq \mathcal{F}. \end{aligned} \tag{47}$$

Recall from G-N inequality (11) that we also have for $p = \frac{4(s+1)}{3}$ and $\lambda = \lambda^*$

$$\liminf_{k\to\infty} \Big(\frac{b}{2(s+1)} \Big(\int_{\mathbb{R}^3} |\nabla u_{\eta_k}|^2 dx \Big)^{s+1} - \frac{\lambda^*}{p+2} \int_{\mathbb{R}^3} |u_{\eta_k}|^{p+2} dx \Big) \geq 0 \tag{48}$$

which together with (47) then gives

$$\liminf_{k\to\infty} I(\eta_k, s, \lambda^*) = \liminf_{k\to\infty} E(\eta_k) \geq \frac{\eta_k \epsilon_{\eta_k}^{-2}}{2} + \mathcal{D}\epsilon_{\eta_k}^{q_{i_0}} \geq \mathcal{E}\eta_k^{\frac{q_{i_0}}{q_{i_0}+2}}, \tag{49}$$

where $\mathcal{E}$ is a arbitrarily large constant. However, this is a contradiction with the upper energy in Lemma 7. Hence, (46) holds. In truth, the upper energy of $I(\eta_k, s, \lambda^*)$ also compels that $x_0 = x_i \in W$. If not, by repeating the proof process from (46) to (48), one still derives a contradiction. Thus, we complete the proof of *(i)* in Theorem 3.

Using (45) and similar to estimation of (47), one can deduce that there admits a $\hat{x} \in \mathbb{R}^3$ such that

$$\begin{aligned} &\liminf_{k\to\infty} \frac{1}{\epsilon_{\eta_k}^{q}} \int_{\mathbb{R}^3} V(\epsilon_{\eta_k} x + z_{\eta_k}) v_{\eta_k}^2 dx \\ = &\lim_{x\to x_i} \frac{V(x)}{|x - x_i|^q} \int_{\mathbb{R}^3} |x + \hat{x}|^q v_0^2 dx \\ \geq &\lim_{x\to x_i} \frac{V(x)}{|x - x_i|^q} \int_{\mathbb{R}^3} |x|^q v_0^2 dx = \theta, \end{aligned} \tag{50}$$

where θ, q given by (6) and (7). As a fact, the equality in (50) holds only for $\bar{x} = 0$. One then calculates from (49) and (50) that

$$\liminf_{k\to\infty} I(\eta_k, s, \lambda^*) = \liminf_{k\to\infty} E(\eta_k) \geq \frac{\eta_k \epsilon_{\eta_k}^{-2}}{2} + \theta\epsilon_{\eta_k}^{q}. \tag{51}$$

Due to the restriction of energy upper bound in Lemma 7, it yields that ϵ_{λ_k} is in the form of

$$\epsilon_{\eta_k} = (q\theta)^{-\frac{1}{q+2}}(\eta_k)^{\frac{1}{q+2}}$$

which shows a fact that the *(ii)* in Theorem 3 holds.

Taking the above ϵ_{η_k} into (51), we can obtain that

$$\liminf_{k\to\infty} I(\eta_k, s, \lambda^*) \geq \left[\frac{1}{2}q^{\frac{2}{q+2}} + q^{\frac{-q}{q+2}}\right]\theta^{\frac{2}{q+2}}(\eta_k)^{\frac{q}{q+2}}.$$

which together with Lemma 7 yields that as $k \to \infty$

$$I(\eta_k, s, \lambda^*) \approx \left[\frac{1}{2}q^{\frac{2}{q+2}} + q^{\frac{-q}{q+2}}\right]\theta^{\frac{2}{q+2}}(\eta_k)^{\frac{q}{q+2}}.$$

So far, we have finished the proof of *(iii)* in Theorem 3. □

5. Conclusions

There are many significant results for (2) when the exponent $s = 1$, and the readers are advised to refer to Section 1. In the present paper, we have studied the constrained minimization problem (2) with $s > 0$, which may be the first one studying the varying non-local problem by applying constrained variational methods. Under the assumptions of (V_1) and (V_2), our first conclusion is involved in the existence and non-existence of constraint minimizers for (2), which can be stated by Theorems 1 and 2. Furthermore, the second conclusion in Theorem 3 is concerned with the limit behavior of constraint minimizers as $\eta_k \to 0^+$. In detail, when the trapping potential $V(x)$ is a polynomial function and fulfills (V_1) and (V_2), we can prove that the mass of minimizers must concentrate (i.e., blow up) at some flattest global minimum of $V(x)$ as $\eta_k \to 0^+$. However, the local uniqueness of the constraint minimizer is hard to prove as $\eta_k \to 0^+$. Hence, in the future, we may try to overcome this problem.

Author Contributions: X.Z. and H.W. designed and drafted the manuscript. All participated in finalizing and approving the manuscript. All authors have read and agreed to the published version of the manuscript.

Funding: The research was supported by National Nature Science Foundation of China (NSFC), grant number 11901500; Nanhu Scholars Program for Young Scholars of XYNU.

Data Availability Statement: Data are contained within the article.

Acknowledgments: The authors are very grateful to Changjian Wang for his fruitful discussions on the present paper. We would like to express gratitude to the editors and the reviewers for their constructive comments.

Conflicts of Interest: The authors declare that there are no conflicts of interest regarding the publication of this paper.

References

1. Chabrowski, J. On bi-nonlocal problem for elliptic equations with Neumann boundary conditions. *J. Anal. Math.* **2018**, *134*, 303–334. [CrossRef]
2. Corrêa, F.J.S.A.; Figueiredo, G.M. Existence and multiplicity of nontrivial solutions for a bi-nonlocal equation. *Adv. Diff. Equ.* **2013**, *18*, 587–608. [CrossRef]
3. Mao, A.M.; Wang, W.Q. Signed and sign-changing solutions of bi-nonlocal fourth order elliptic problem. *J. Math. Phys.* **2019**, *60*, 051513. [CrossRef]
4. Tian, G.Q.; Suo, H.M.; An, Y.C. Multiple positive solutions for a bi-nonlocal Kirchhoff-Schrödinger-Poisson system with critical growth. *Electron. Res. Arch.* **2022**, *30*, 4493–4506. [CrossRef]
5. Ye, H.Y. The existence of normalized solutions for L^2-critical constrained problems related to Kirchhoff equations. *Z. Angew. Math. Phys.* **2015**, *66*, 1483–1497. [CrossRef]

6. Ye, H.Y. The sharp existence of constrained minimizers for a class of nonlinear Kirchhoff equations. *Math. Methods Appl. Sci.* **2015**, *38*, 2663–2679. [CrossRef]
7. Zeng, X.Y.; Zhang, Y.M. Existence and uniqueness of normalized solutions for the Kirchhoff equation. *Appl. Math. Lett.* **2017**, *74*, 52–59. [CrossRef]
8. Meng, X.Y.; Zeng, X.Y. Existence and asymptotic behavior of minimizers for the Kirchhoff functional with periodic potentials. *J. Math. Anal. Appl.* **2022**, *507*, 125727. [CrossRef]
9. Guo, H.L.; Zhang, Y.M.; Zhou, H.S. Blow-up solutions for a Kirchhoff type elliptic equation with trapping potential. *Commun. Pur. Appl. Anal.* **2018**, *17*, 1875–1897. [CrossRef]
10. Li, G.B.; Ye, H.Y. On the concentration phenomenon of L^2-subcritical constrained minimizers for a class of Kirchhoff equations with potentials. *J. Differ. Equ.* **2019**, *266*, 7101–7123. [CrossRef]
11. Li, Y.H.; Hao, X.C.; Shi, J.P. The existence of constrained minimizers for a class of nonlinear Kirchhoff-Schrödinger equations with doubly critical exponents in dimension four. *Nonlinear Anal.* **2019**, *186*, 99–112. [CrossRef]
12. Zhu, X.C.; Wang, C.J.; Xue, Y.F. Constraint minimizers of Kirchhoff-Schrödinger energy functionals with L^2-subcritical perturbation. *Mediterr. J. Math.* **2021**, *18*, 224. [CrossRef]
13. Zhu, X.C.; Zhang, S.; Wang, C.J.; He, C.X. Blow-up behavior of L^2-norm solutions for Kirchhoff equation in a bounded domain. *Bull. Malays. Math. Sci. Soc.* **2023**, *46*, 155. [CrossRef]
14. Guo, H.L.; Zhou, H.S. Properties of the minimizers for a constrained minimization problem arising in Kirchhoff equation. *Discret. Cont. Dyn. A* **2021**, *41*, 1023–1050. [CrossRef]
15. Hu, T.X.; Tang, C.L. Limiting behavior and local uniqueness of normalized solutions for mass critical Kirchhoff equations. *Calc. Var.* **2021**, *60*, 210. [CrossRef]
16. Bao, W.Z.; Cai, Y.Y. Mathematical theory and numerical methods for Bose-Einstein condensation. *Kinet. Relat. Model.* **2013**, *6*, 1–135. [CrossRef]
17. Dalfovo, F.; Giorgini, S.; Pitaevskii, L.P.; Stringari, S. Theory of Bose-Einstein condensation in trapped gases. *Rev. Mod. Phys.* **1999**, *71*, 463–512. [CrossRef]
18. Guo, Y.J.; Seiringer, R. On the mass concentration for Bose-Einstein condensates with attactive interactions. *Lett. Math. Phys.* **2014**, *104*, 141–156. [CrossRef]
19. Guo, Y.J.; Wang, Z.Q.; Zeng, X.Y.; Zhou, H.S. Properties of ground states of attractive Gross-Pitaevskii equations with multi-well potentials. *Nonlinearity* **2018**, 31, 957–979. [CrossRef]
20. Guo, Y.J.; Zeng, X.Y.; Zhou, H.S. Energy estimates and symmetry breaking in attractive Bose-Einstein condensates with ring-shaped potentials. *Ann. L'Insitut Henri Poincaré C Anal. Non Linéaire* **2016**, *33*, 809–828.
21. Wang, Q.X.; Zhao, D. Existence and mass concentration of 2D attractive Bose-Einstein condensates with periodic potentials. *J. Differ. Equ.* **2017**, *262*, 2684–2704. [CrossRef]
22. Zhu, X.C.; Wang, C.J. Mass concentration behavior of attractive Bose-Einstein condensates with sinusoidal potential in a circular region. *Mediterr. J. Math.* **2024**, *21*, 12. [CrossRef]
23. Guo, Y.J.; Liang, W.N.; Li, Y. Existence and uniqueness of constraint minimizers for the planar Schrödinger-Poisson system with logarithmic potentials. *J. Differ. Equ.* **2023**, *369*, 299–352. [CrossRef]
24. Guo, Y.J.; Lin, C.S.; Wei, J.C.Local uniqueness and refined spike profiles of ground states for two-dimensional attractive Bose-Einstein condensates. *SIAM J. Math. Anal.* **2017**, *49*, 3671–3715. [CrossRef]
25. Kwong, M.K. Uniqueness of positive solutions of $\Delta u - u + u^p = 0$ in $\mathbb{R}^N$. *Arch. Rational Mech. Anal.* **1989**, *105*, 243–266. [CrossRef]
26. Luo, Y.; Zhu, X.C. Mass concentration behavior of Bose-Einstein condensates with attractive interactions in bounded domains. *Anal. Appl.* **2020**, *99*, 2414–2427. [CrossRef]
27. Gidas, B.; Ni, W.M.; Nirenberg, L. Symmetry of positive solutions of nonlinear elliptic equations in $\mathbb{R}^n$. In *Mathematical Analysis and Applications Part A, Advances in Mathematics Supplementary Studies*; Academic Press: New York, NY, USA, 1981; Volume 7, pp. 369–402.
28. Weinstein, M.I. Nonlinear Schrödinger equations and sharp interpolations estimates. *Comm. Math. Phys.* **1983**, *87*, 567–576. [CrossRef]
29. Bartsch, T.; Wang, Z.Q. Existence and multiplicity results for some superlinear elliptic problems on $\mathbb{R}^n$. *Comm. Partial. Differ. Equ.* **1995**, *20*, 1725–1741. [CrossRef]
30. Han, Q.; Lin, F.H. *Elliptic Partial Differential Equations*; Courant Lecture Note in Mathematics 1; Courant Institute of Mathematical Science/AMS: New York, NY, USA, 2011.

mathematics

MDPI

Article

Chains with Connections of Diffusion and Advective Types

Sergey Kashchenko

Regional Scientific and Educational Mathematical Center "Centre of Integrable Systems", P. G. Demidov Yaroslavl State University, 150003 Yaroslavl, Russia; kasch@uniyar.ac.ru

Abstract: The local dynamics of a system of oscillators with a large number of elements and with diffusive- and advective-type couplings containing a large delay are studied. Critical cases in the problem of the stability of the zero equilibrium state are singled out, and it is shown that all of them have infinite dimensions. Applying special methods of infinite normalization, we construct quasinormal forms, namely, nonlinear boundary value problems of the parabolic type, whose nonlocal dynamics determine the behavior of the solutions of the initial system in a small neighborhood of the equilibrium state. These quasinormal forms contain either two or three spatial variables, which emphasizes the complexity of the dynamical properties of the original problem.

Keywords: boundary value problem; delay; stability; normal form; dynamics; asymptotics of solutions; bifurcations; singular perturbations; oscillators

MSC: 34K25

Citation: Kashchenko, S. Chains with Connections of Diffusion and Advective Types. *Mathematics* **2024**, *12*, 790. https://doi.org/10.3390/math12060790

Academic Editors: Lingju Kong and Min Wang

Received: 9 February 2024
Revised: 29 February 2024
Accepted: 6 March 2024
Published: 7 March 2024

1. Introduction

We consider the dynamics of chains with diffusive and advective couplings containing a large delay. The second-order equation with cubic nonlinearity,

$$\ddot{u} + a\dot{u} + u + f(u, \dot{u}) = 0, \tag{1}$$

$$f(u, \dot{u}) = b_1u^3 + b_2u^2\dot{u} + b_3u\dot{u}^2 + b_4\dot{u}^3, \tag{2}$$

serves as a basic example.

A chain of N equations of the form in (1) has the form

$$\ddot{u}_j + a\dot{u}_j + u_j + f(u_j, \dot{u}_j) = d\sum_{k=1}^{N} a_{j-k}u_k(t - T), \tag{3}$$

where $T > 0$ is the delay time, a_k denotes the coefficients of the couplings, and $u_k(t)$ denotes N-periodic functions of the index k:

$$u_{k\pm N} \equiv u_k.$$

The dynamics of chains of this kind have been studied by many authors, such as [1–3], where chains without a delay were considered, and [4–12], where chains with a delay were studied. The main assumption is that the number N of oscillators is sufficiently large; i.e., the value $\varepsilon = 2\pi N^{-1}$ is sufficiently small:

$$0 < \varepsilon \ll 1. \tag{4}$$

Functions $u_k(t)$ are conveniently associated with the values of a function of two variables, $u_k(t) = u(t, x_k)$, where x_k denotes points with angular coordinates uniformly distributed on some circle: $x_k = 2\pi kN^{-1}$. Condition (4) gives reason to transition from the system in (3) to the problem of studying functions of two variables, $u(t,x)$, with a continuous spatial variable $x \in (-\infty,\infty)$ and with the periodicity condition

$$u(t,x+2\pi) \equiv u(t,x), \tag{5}$$

for which

$$\frac{\partial^2 u}{\partial t^2} + a\frac{\partial u}{\partial t} + u + f\left(u, \frac{\partial u}{\partial t}\right) = d\int_{-\infty}^{\infty} \Phi(s,\varepsilon)u(t-T,x+s)ds. \tag{6}$$

The values of the function $\Phi(s,\varepsilon)$ are determined by coupling coefficients a_k. Let us describe the classes of functions $\Phi(s,\varepsilon)$ that will be studied in this paper. We arbitrarily set $\sigma > 0$ and introduce a Gaussian function:

$$F_\varepsilon(s) = \frac{1}{\sigma\varepsilon\sqrt{2\pi}} \exp\left(-\frac{(s-\varepsilon)^2}{2\varepsilon^2\sigma^2}\right).$$

Let $\Phi_0(s,\varepsilon)$ denote the function

$$\Phi_0(s,\varepsilon) = F_\varepsilon(s) - 2F_0(s) + F_{-\varepsilon}(s). \tag{7}$$

Due to the fact that, for every continuous function $u(x)$,

$$\lim_{\sigma\to 0}\int_{-\infty}^{\infty} \Phi_0(s,\varepsilon)u(x+s)ds = u(x+\varepsilon) - 2u(x) + u(x-\varepsilon), \tag{8}$$

it is natural to call (7) a diffusion-type coupling, since the right part of this equality resembles the expression for the standard difference approximation of the diffusion operator $\partial^2 u/\partial x^2$. Such couplings were used, for example, in [8,12–14]. Let us also note the work in [15], where chains of systems of laser equations were considered.

Let us introduce two more functions:

$$\Phi_1(s,\varepsilon) = F_\varepsilon(s) - F_{-\varepsilon}(s) \tag{9}$$

and

$$\Phi_2(s,\varepsilon) = F_\varepsilon(s) - F_0(s). \tag{10}$$

For each fixed continuous function $u(x)$ bounded on the interval $(-\infty,\infty)$, we have the following equations:

$$\lim_{\sigma\to 0}\int_{-\infty}^{\infty} \Phi_1(s,\varepsilon)u(x+s)ds = u(x+\varepsilon) - u(x-\varepsilon), \tag{11}$$

$$\lim_{\sigma\to 0}\int_{-\infty}^{\infty} \Phi_2(s,\varepsilon)u(x+s)ds = u(x+\varepsilon) - u(x). \tag{12}$$

The right-hand sides of (11) and (12) usually arise, for example, when applying the standard difference approximation of the advection (transfer) operator $\partial u/\partial x$. Therefore, it is natural to call the right-hand side in (6) an advection-type coupling.

Another assumption that paves the way for the application of asymptotic methods is that the value of T is sufficiently large: for some $c > 0$, we have

$$T = c\varepsilon^{-1}. \tag{13}$$

In Equation (6), we perform time normalization $t \to Tt$. As a result, we arrive at the singularly perturbed equation

$$\varepsilon^2 \frac{\partial^2 u}{\partial t^2} + \varepsilon a \frac{\partial u}{\partial t} + u + f\left(u, \varepsilon \frac{\partial u}{\partial t}\right) = d \int_{-\infty}^{\infty} \Phi(s,\varepsilon) u(t-c, x+s) ds. \quad (14)$$

Note that the degenerate at $\varepsilon = 0$ in Equation (14) does not give information about the behavior of solutions. We will use classical asymptotic methods based on the application of methods of many scales: methods characteristic of the theory of averaging (see, for example, [16]) and methods of singular perturbations [17–19]. In order to study the dynamical properties of solutions under conditions (4) and (13), we will use the special asymptotic methods of local analysis developed in [20,21].

Let us study the behavior of all solutions of the boundary value problem (14) as $t \to \infty$ with initial functions sufficiently small in the norm $C^1_{[-c,0]} \times C_{[0,2\pi]}$ and 2π-periodic in the spatial variable x.

In the study of the local—in the neighborhood of the zero equilibrium state—behavior of solutions, the linearized boundary value problem

$$\varepsilon^2 \frac{\partial^2 u}{\partial t^2} + \varepsilon a \frac{\partial u}{\partial t} + u = d \int_{-\infty}^{\infty} \Phi(s,\varepsilon) u(t-c, x+s) ds, \quad (15)$$

$$u(t, x+2\pi) \equiv u(t,x). \quad (16)$$

plays an important role. Its characteristic equation, which we obtain by substituting the Euler solutions $u = \exp(ikx + \lambda t)$ into (15), has the form

$$\varepsilon^2 \lambda^2 + \varepsilon a \lambda + 1 = d\gamma(z) \exp(-c\lambda), \quad (17)$$

where, in the case of diffusion coupling,

$$\gamma(z) = -4 \sin^2 \frac{z}{2} \cdot \exp\left(-\frac{1}{2}\sigma^2 z^2\right), \quad z = \varepsilon k, \quad k = 0, \pm 1, \pm 2, \ldots.$$

In advective coupling (9),

$$\gamma(z) = 2i \sin z, \quad (18)$$

and at the connection of the form in (10),

$$\gamma(z) = \exp(iz) - 1. \quad (19)$$

In the case where all roots of Equation (17), for all $k = 0, \pm 1, \pm 2, \ldots$, have negative real parts that move away from zero as $\varepsilon \to 0$, the solutions of the boundary value problem (15), (16) are asymptotically stable, and the solutions of (14), (16) with sufficiently small and ε-independent (by the norm $C^1_{[-c,0]} \times C_{[0,2\pi]}$) initial conditions tend to zero as $t \to \infty$. If Equation (17) has a root with a positive real part that moves away from zero as $\varepsilon \to 0$, then the solutions of (15), (16) are unstable, and the dynamics problem (14), (16) becomes nonlocal.

Here, we will consider the critical case where there are no roots with a positive real part that moves away from zero in (17), but there are roots that tend to the imaginary axis as $\varepsilon \to 0$. Note that, in the case of the finite dimensionality of the critical case, the methodology for the study of local dynamics is well known. It relies on the method of integral manifolds and the method of normal forms (see, e.g., [22,23]). A characteristic feature of all of the problems considered below is the fact that they realize infinite-dimensional critical cases when infinitely many roots of the characteristic equation tend to the imaginary axis as $\varepsilon \to 0$. Therefore, the methods of integral manifolds and normal forms are not directly applicable. The approach developed in [20,21], which is related to the construction of infinite-dimensional quasinormal forms, is essentially used here.

Let us briefly look at the research design used below. First, a linearized boundary value problem is considered, and its characteristic equation is studied. We determine those parameters at which a critical case occurs in the problem of the stability of solutions. Then, we obtain the asymptotics of those roots of the characteristic equation that tend to the imaginary axis as the small parameter tends to zero. Since there are infinitely many such roots, there are also infinitely many solutions corresponding to the linearized boundary value problem. The set of such solutions can be written in a special form using another spatial variable. Therefore, it is possible to determine the structure of the main approximation of solutions to a nonlinear boundary value problem. Let us denote it conditionally by εU_1.

The solutions of the nonlinear boundary value problem are then found in the form of a formal series in powers of ε, the coefficients of which are periodic in t. Since, for simplicity, there is no quadratic nonlinearity in the equation, then, as a consequence, there are no terms of order ε^2 in the formal asymptotic series. Substituting the formal series into the original equation, we obtain a special linear inhomogeneous boundary value problem for the elements of this series. Using the solvability conditions for the resulting equation, we arrive at an equation for the unknown slowly varying amplitudes included in U_1. These equations are called quasinormal forms. They describe the local behavior of the original boundary value problem.

Note that the form of the notation in (7) is convenient from a purely technical point of view. Below, we will use the equality

$$\int_{-\infty}^{\infty} F_{\pm}(s,\varepsilon)\exp(iks)ds = \exp(\pm ik\varepsilon)\exp\Big(-\frac{\sigma^2\varepsilon^2k^2}{2}\Big).$$

The σ parameter defines the set of chain elements that significantly affect each specific element. In addition, it also sets the strength of the corresponding influence: the farther the elements are from each other, the weaker this influence is.

At $\sigma = 0$, an additional critical case arises; therefore, this work examines the dynamics of the system under the condition $\sigma \ll 1$. As it turns out, in these cases, the quasinormal form acquires an additional spatial variable. It follows that, for $\sigma \to 0$, there is a tendency for the dynamic properties of solutions to become more complex.

The corresponding results are given in Sections 2.3 and 3.5.

Chains of this type without a delay were studied in [14]. The presence of a delay, on the one hand, allows one to obtain explicitly formal expressions for critical cases. On the other hand, the dimensionality of critical cases increases, and the corresponding quasinormal forms become even more complicated.

This paper consists of two parts. The first part studies diffusion-type couplings, whereas the second part deals with advection-type couplings.

2. Diffusion-Type Coupling

Linear analysis has a central role in the study of the boundary value problem (14), (16).

2.1. Linear Analysis

Let us consider the roots of the characteristic Equation (17). Recall that critical cases in the stability problem (15), (16) are realized when Equation (17) has a root with a zero or sufficiently close to zero real part for some k. In this connection, for some real value of ω, let us set $\lambda = i\omega\varepsilon^{-1}$ in (17). As a result, we obtain the following:

$$1-\omega^2+ia\omega = d\gamma(z)\exp\big(-i\omega\varepsilon^{-1}c\big), \quad z=\varepsilon k, \quad k=0,\pm1,\pm2,\dots. \tag{20}$$

Let $p(\omega)$ denote the modulus of the left part of (20):

$$p(\omega) = \left[(1-\omega^2)^2 + a^2\omega^2\right]^{1/2},$$

and let

$$p_0 = \min_{-\infty<\omega<\infty} p(\omega) = p(\omega_0).$$

Here,

$$\omega_0 = \begin{cases} 0, & \text{if } a^2 \geq 2, \\ \left(1 - \dfrac{a^2}{2}\right)^{1/2}, & \text{if } a^2 < 2, \end{cases} \qquad p_0 = \begin{cases} 1, & \text{if } a^2 \geq 2, \\ \dfrac{a^2}{2}(4-a^2)^{1/2}, & \text{if } a^2 < 2. \end{cases}$$

Note that $p_0 = 0$ for $a = 0$.

In this section, we will focus on the first case, where

$$\sigma > 0. \tag{21}$$

The case

$$\sigma = \varepsilon\sigma_1. \tag{22}$$

will be discussed in Section 2.3.

Let condition (21) be satisfied. For each fixed z and under the condition

$$d|\gamma(z)| < p_0$$

Equation (20) has no real roots. Below, we assume that

$$\gamma_0 = \max_{-\infty<z<\infty} \gamma(z) = \gamma(z_0) \quad (z_0 \geq 0). \tag{23}$$

The value of z_0 is defined in a unique way and is found simply. From the condition $\gamma'(z_0) = 0$, we find that z_0 is the first positive root of the equation

$$\frac{z}{2} = 2(\sigma^2 z)^{-1}.$$

Given $d|\gamma_0| < p_0$ and sufficiently small ε, all roots of Equation (17) have negative real parts that move away from zero as $\varepsilon \to 0$. Given $d|\gamma_0| > p_0$, we find z_0 such that Equation (17) has a root with a positive real part that moves away from zero as $\varepsilon \to 0$.

Let us restrict ourselves to the case where the parameter d is positive. The value of the parameter d_0, which distinguishes the critical case in the stability problem (15), (16), is determined by the equality

$$d_0 = p_0|\gamma_0|^{-1}.$$

In this connection, we assume below that, for an arbitrary fixed value d_1 for the parameter d, we have

$$d = d_0 + \varepsilon^2 d_1. \tag{24}$$

Under this condition, let us consider the asymptotics of all those roots of the characteristic Equation (17) whose real parts tend to zero as $\varepsilon \to 0$. We note at once that there are infinitely many such roots, so the critical case has infinite dimensionality.

Let us introduce some more notations. Let $\Omega_0 = \Omega_0(\omega_0)$ be a real value for which

$$1 - \omega_0^2 + i\omega = p_0 \exp(i\Omega_0).$$

We let $\theta_\omega = \theta_\omega(\varepsilon) \in [0, 2\pi)$ denote an expression that complements the value $\omega_0(c\varepsilon)^{-1}$ to an integer multiple of 2π. When $\omega_0 = 0$, then $\theta_\omega = 0$. We will similarly let $\theta_z = \theta_z(\varepsilon) \in [0, 1)$ denote an expression that complements the value $z_0\varepsilon^{-1}$ to an integer. Given $z_0 = 0$, we consider that $\theta_z = 0$.

Let us formulate two simple statements about the asymptotics of the roots of (17).

Lemma 1. *Let*

$$a^2 > 2. \tag{25}$$

Then, $d_0 = p_0 = 1, \omega_0 = 0$, *and for the roots* $\lambda_{kn}(\varepsilon)$ $(k, n = 0, \pm 1, \pm 2, \dots)$ *of* (17), *the real parts of which tend to zero as* $\varepsilon \to 0$, *the asymptotic equations*

$$\lambda_{kn}(\varepsilon) = \pi i c^{-1}(2n+1) + \varepsilon\lambda_{1kn} + \varepsilon^2\lambda_{2kn} + \dots, \tag{26}$$

are satisfied, where

$$\lambda_{1kn} = -c^{-2} i a \pi(2n+1),$$

$$\lambda_{2kn} = c^{-3}\left(1 - \frac{1}{2}a^2\right)(\pi(2n+1))^2 - ic^{-3}a^2\pi(2n+1) + c^{-1}d_1\gamma_0 p_0^{-1} +$$
$$+ \frac{1}{2}c^{-1}\gamma_0''(z_0)(\theta_z + k)^2(p_0\gamma_0)^{-1}.$$

Lemma 2. *Let*

$$0 < a^2 < 2. \tag{27}$$

Then, $\omega_0 > 0$, *and for the roots* $\lambda_{kn}(\varepsilon)$ $(k, n = 0, \pm 1, \pm 2, \dots)$ *of* (17) *whose real parts tend to zero as* $\varepsilon \to 0$, *the asymptotic equations*

$$\lambda_{kn}(\varepsilon) = i\frac{\omega_0}{\varepsilon} + \lambda_{0n} + \varepsilon\lambda_{1kn} + \varepsilon^2\lambda_{2kn} + \dots \tag{28}$$

hold, where

$$\lambda_{0n} = ic^{-1}\big[\pi(2n+1) + \theta_\omega - \Omega_0\big], \quad \varkappa = p_0\exp(i\Omega_0),$$
$$\lambda_{1kn} = ic^{-1}\varkappa^{-1}(2\omega_0 - ia)\lambda_{0n}, \tag{29}$$

$$\lambda_{2kn} = c^{-1}\bigg[\left(\varkappa^{-1} - \frac{1}{2}(-2\omega_0 + ia)^2\varkappa^{-2}\right)\lambda_{0n}^2 + d_1 p_0^{-1} -$$
$$+ \frac{1}{2}\gamma''(z_0)(\theta_z + k)^2(p_0\gamma_0)^{-1} - (c\varkappa)^{-1}2i\omega_0\varkappa^{-1}(2\omega_0 - ia)\lambda_{0n} - i\varkappa^{-1}a\lambda_{0n}\bigg].$$

Note that the following conditions hold:

$$\Re\left(\varkappa^{-1} - \frac{1}{2}(-2\omega_0 + ia)^2\varkappa^{-2}\right) < 0, \quad \Re\lambda_{1kn} = 0. \tag{30}$$

The first condition in (30) is obvious. Regarding the second equality in (30), it suffices to prove that the expression

$$(2\omega_0 - ia)\varkappa^{-1}$$

is purely imaginary. In this case, $P(\omega) = p(\omega)\exp(i\Omega(\omega))$ and $P'(\omega) = \Big(p'(\omega) + i\Omega'(\omega)p(\omega)\Big)$ $\exp\big(i\Omega(\omega)\big)$; hence,

$$P'(\omega) = i\Omega'(\omega_0)p_0\exp(i\Omega_0) = -2\omega_0 + ia.$$

Therefore, we conclude that $(-2\omega_0 + ia)\varkappa^{-1} = i\Omega'(\omega_0) = 2ia^{-1}$.

The roots $\lambda_{kn}(\varepsilon)$ of the characteristic Equation (17) allow us to determine solutions to the linear boundary value problem (15), (16):

$$u_{kn}(t, x, \varepsilon) = \exp\big(i(z_0\varepsilon^{-1} + \theta_z + k)x + \lambda_{kn}(\varepsilon)t\big),$$

and hence, the formal set of solutions is

$$u(t,x,\varepsilon) = \sum_{k,n=-\infty}^{\infty} \Big(\xi_{kn} u_{kn}(t,x,\varepsilon) + \bar{\xi}_{kn} \tilde{u}_{kn}(t,x,\varepsilon)\Big), \tag{31}$$

where ξ_{kn} denotes arbitrary complex constants.

Remark 1. *Together with the roots $\lambda_{kn}(\varepsilon)$ of Equation* (17)*, there are roots $\overline{\lambda}_{kn}(\varepsilon)$, which correspond to the solutions of the boundary value problem* (15), (16)*:*

$$\overline{u}_{kn}(t,x,\varepsilon) = \exp\big(-i(z_0\varepsilon^{-1} + \theta_z + k)x + \overline{\lambda}_{kn}(\varepsilon)t\big).$$

Note that for the parameters z and $-z$, the roots in (17) *are the same, since the dependence of the right-hand side of* (17) *on z is even. This means that for the modes of $-(z_0\varepsilon^{-1} + \theta_z + k)$, the roots are the same: $\lambda_{kn}(\varepsilon)$. Therefore, the problem* (15), (16) *has the solutions*

$$\tilde{u}_{kn}(t,x,\varepsilon) = \exp\big(-i(z_0\varepsilon^{-1} + \theta_z + k)x + \overline{\lambda}_{kn}(\varepsilon)t\big).$$

Under the conditions of Lemma 1, we have the following:

$$\tilde{u}_{kn}(t,x,\varepsilon) = \overline{u}_{kn}(t,x,\varepsilon),$$

which is not the case under the conditions of Lemma 2.

2.2. Nonlinear Analysis

We separately consider the cases where $a^2 > 2$ and where $0 < a^2 < 2$.

2.2.1. Case $a^2 > 2$

In this case, we have the equality $\omega_0 = 0, \Omega_0 = 0, p_0 = 1$. The critical case in the stability problem is defined by the equality

$$d_0|\gamma_0| = 1. \tag{32}$$

We will base the following on the representation in (31). Let us write it in a more convenient form:

$$u(t,x,\varepsilon) = E(x) \sum_{k,n=-\infty}^{\infty} \xi_{kn} \exp\big(ikx + ic^{-1}\pi(2n+1)(1-\varepsilon c^{-1}a)t + (\lambda_{2kn} + O(\varepsilon))\tau\big) =$$

$$= E(x) \sum_{k,n=-\infty}^{\infty} \xi_{kn}(\tau) \exp\big(ikx + i\pi(2n+1)x_1\big) = E(x)\xi(\tau,x,x_1), \tag{33}$$

where $\tau = \varepsilon^2 t$ is the "slow" time, $E(x) = \exp\big(i(z_0\varepsilon^{-1} + \theta_z)x\big)$, and $\xi_{kn}(\tau) = \xi_{kn} \exp\big((\lambda_{2kn} + O(\varepsilon))\tau\big)$ denotes the coefficients of the expansion $\xi(\tau,x,x_1)$ into a Fourier series by the 2π-periodic argument x and 1-antiperiodic argument $x_1 = c^{-1}(1-\varepsilon c^{-1}a)t$.

The solutions of the nonlinear boundary value problem (14), (16) are found in the form

$$u = \varepsilon\big(E(x)\xi(\tau,x,x_1) + \overline{cc}\big) + \varepsilon^3 u_3(\tau,x,x_1) + \dots. \tag{34}$$

Here and below, $\overline{cc}$ denotes the term that is complex conjugate to the previous one. The unknown complex function $\xi(\tau,x,x_1)$ is to be defined. Let us substitute (34) into (14) and equate the coefficients of the various powers of ε. Then, at the first degree of ε, we obtain the identity. Equating the coefficients of ε^3, we arrive at the equation

$$\begin{aligned} c\frac{\partial\xi}{\partial\tau} =&(2c^2)^{-1}(a^2-2)\frac{\partial^2\xi}{\partial x_1^2} + (2\gamma_0)^{-1}\gamma''(z_0)\frac{\partial^2\xi}{\partial x^2} - i\gamma_0^{-1}\gamma''(z_0)\theta_z\frac{\partial\xi}{\partial x} - \\ &- ac^{-2}\frac{\partial\xi}{\partial x_1} + \big((2\gamma_0)^{-1}\gamma''(z_0)\theta_z^2 - \gamma_0^{-1}d_1\big)\xi + 3b_1\xi|\xi|^2 \end{aligned} \tag{35}$$

with the boundary conditions

$$-\xi(\tau,x,x_1+1) \equiv \xi(\tau,x,x_1) \equiv \xi(\tau,x+2\pi,x_1). \tag{36}$$

Here, we take into account the relations

$$\begin{aligned} \frac{d\xi}{dt} =&\varepsilon^2\frac{\partial\xi}{\partial\tau} + \frac{\partial\xi}{\partial x_1}(1-\varepsilon ac^{-1}), \\ \xi_{t-c} =&\xi(\tau-\varepsilon^2 c, x, x_1 - c(1-\varepsilon ac^{-1})) = \\ =&\xi(\tau,x,x_1) - \varepsilon^2 c\frac{\partial\xi}{\partial\tau} + \varepsilon a\frac{\partial\xi}{\partial x_1} + \frac{1}{2}\varepsilon^2 a^2\frac{\partial^2\xi}{\partial x_1^2} + o(\varepsilon^2). \end{aligned}$$

Let us introduce the following notation. We arbitrarily fix the value $\theta_{0z} \in [0,1)$ and let $\varepsilon_n = \varepsilon_n(\theta_{0z})$ denote a sequence such that $\varepsilon_n \to 0$, for $n \to \infty$, and $\theta_z(\varepsilon_n,\theta_{0z}) = \theta_{0z}$. The above constructions justify the following result.

Theorem 1. *Let $a^2 > 2$ and conditions* (24) *and* (32) *be satisfied. Let $\theta_{0z} \in [0,1)$ be arbitrarily fixed, and let the boundary value problem* (35), (36) *for $\theta_z = \theta_{0z}$ have a bounded solution $\xi(\tau,x,x_1)$ for $\tau \to \infty$, $x \in [0,2\pi]$, $x_1 \in [0,1]$. Then, the function $u(t,x,\varepsilon) = \varepsilon\big(E(x)\xi(\tau,x,x_1) + \overline{cc}\big) + \varepsilon^3 u_3(\tau,x,x_1)$ satisfies the boundary value problem* (14), (16) *up to $o(\varepsilon^3)$.*

Thus, the parabolic boundary value problem (35), (36) is a quasinormal form for the boundary value problem (14), (16).

2.2.2. Case $0 < a^2 < 2$

The dynamical properties in this case are significantly more complicated. The principal parts of the roots $\lambda_{kn}(\varepsilon)$ of the characteristic equation are close to $i\omega_0\varepsilon^{-1}$: i.e., they are asymptotically large. Therefore, it is natural to expect that the oscillations in the boundary value problem (14), (16) will be rapid.

Note that, in this case,

$$\omega_0 = \left(1-\frac{a^2}{2}\right)^{1/2}, \quad p_0 = \frac{a^2}{2}(4-a^2)^{1/2}, \quad d_0 = p_0|\gamma_0|^{-1}. \tag{37}$$

The roots of $\lambda_{kn}(\varepsilon)$ correspond to the Euler solutions of the linear boundary value problem (15), (16):

$$u_{kn}^{\pm}(t,x,\varepsilon) = \exp\big(\pm i(z_0\varepsilon^{-1} + \theta_z + k)x + \lambda_{kn}(\varepsilon)t\big).$$

It is more convenient to write these functions in the form

$$u_{kn}^{\pm}(t,x,\varepsilon) = E^{\pm}(t,x)\exp\big(ikx + i\pi(2n+1)x_1 + (\lambda_{2kn} + O(\varepsilon))\tau\big),$$

where

$$\begin{aligned} E^{\pm}(t,x) =&\exp\big(\pm i(c^{-1}\omega_0\varepsilon^{-1} + c^{-1}(\theta_\omega - \Omega_0) + \varepsilon c^{-1}\varkappa^{-1}(2\omega_0 - ia)\cdot \\ &\cdot ic^{-1}(\theta_\omega - \Omega_0))t + i(z_0\varepsilon^{-1} + \theta_z)x\big), \end{aligned}$$

$$R = \varkappa^{-1}(2\omega_0 - ia) \cdot ic^{-1}(\theta_\omega - \Omega_0) = 2(ca)^{-1}, \quad \Im R = 0,$$

$\tau = \varepsilon^2 t$, $x_1 = c^{-1}(1 - \varepsilon c^{-1}R)t$. Hence, we find that

$$\sum_{k,n=-\infty}^{\infty} \xi_{kn}^{\pm} u_{kn}^{\pm}(t,x,\varepsilon) = E^{\pm}(t,x) \sum_{k,n=-\infty}^{\infty} \xi_{kn}^{\pm}(\tau) \exp\left(ikx + i\pi(2n+1)x_1\right) =$$
$$= E^{\pm}(t,x)\xi^{\pm}(\tau,x,x_1).$$

Here, $\xi_{kn}^{\pm}$ denotes arbitrary complex constants, and $\xi_{kn}^{\pm}(\tau) = \xi_{kn}^{\pm} \exp\left((\lambda_{2kn} + O(\varepsilon))\tau\right)$. The functions $\xi_{kn}^{\pm}(\tau)$ are the Fourier coefficients of the function $\xi^{\pm}(\tau,x,x_1)$, which is 2π-periodic with respect to x and 1-antiperiodic with respect to x_1.

The solutions of the nonlinear boundary value problem (14), (16) are found in the form

$$u(t,x) = u^{+}(t,x) + u^{-}(t,x), \tag{38}$$

$$u^{\pm}(t,x) = \varepsilon(\xi^{\pm}(\tau,x,x_1)E^{\pm}(t,x) + \overline{cc}) + \varepsilon^3 u_3(t,\tau,x,x_1) + \ldots,$$

where the dependence on t, x and x_1 is periodic.

Let us substitute (38) into (14) and equate the coefficients of the same powers ε. In the first step, we obtain the identity, and for ε^3, we obtain an equation for u_3. From the condition in the specified class of functions, we arrive at the relation. Let us substitute (38) into (14) and equate the coefficients of the same powers ε. In the first step, we obtain the identity, while, by equating the coefficients of ε^3, we obtain an equation for u_3. From its solvability condition in the specified class of functions, we arrive at the relation

$$\frac{\partial \xi^{\pm}}{\partial \tau} = A_1 \frac{\partial^2 \xi^{\pm}}{\partial x_1^2} + A_2 \frac{\partial \xi^{\pm}}{\partial x_1} + A_3 \xi^{\pm} + B_1 \frac{\partial^2 \xi^{\pm}}{\partial x^2} + B_2 \frac{\partial \xi^{\pm}}{\partial x} + c^{-1}\beta \xi^{\pm}(|\xi^{\pm}|^2 + 2|\xi^{\mp}|^2), \tag{39}$$

in which

$$\begin{aligned}
A_1 =& -c^{-3}\left[\varkappa^{-1} - \frac{1}{2}(ia - 2\omega_0)^2 \varkappa^{-2}\right],\\
A_2 =& c^{-3}\Big[-2(\varkappa^{-1} - \frac{1}{2}(ia - 2\omega_0)^2 \varkappa^{-2}(\theta_\omega - \Omega_0)) + c\varkappa^{-2} 2\omega_0(2\omega_0 - ia) +\\
&+ c^2 \varkappa^{-1} a(\theta_\omega - \Omega_0)\Big],\\
A_3 =& c^{-3}\left[\frac{1}{2}(ia - 2\omega_0)\varkappa^2(\theta_\omega - \Omega_0)^2 - \varkappa^{-1}\right] + d_1 c^{-1} p_0^{-1} +\\
&+ \frac{1}{2}\gamma''(z_0)c^{-1}\theta_z^2(p_0\gamma_0)^{-1} - i(c\varkappa)^{-2} 2i\omega_0(2\omega_0 - ia)\cdot\\
&\cdot(\theta_\omega - \Omega_0) - i(c\varkappa)^{-1} a(\theta_\omega - \Omega_0),\\
B_1 =& \frac{1}{2}c^{-1}\gamma''(z_0)(p_0\gamma_0)^{-1},\\
B_2 =& c^{-1}\gamma''(z_0)\theta_z(p_0\gamma_0)^{-1},\\
\beta =& b_1 + i\omega_0 b_2 - \omega_0^2 b_3 - i\omega_0^3 b_4.
\end{aligned}$$

Recall that the function $\xi(\tau,x,x_1)$ satisfies the boundary conditions

$$-\xi(\tau,x,x_1+1) \equiv \xi(\tau,x,x_1) \equiv \xi(\tau,x+2\pi,x_1). \tag{40}$$

In order to formulate the final result, we introduce some notations. We arbitrarily fix $\theta_{0\omega} \in [0,2\pi)$ and let the sequence $\varepsilon_s = \varepsilon_s(\theta_{0\omega})$ be defined by the condition $\theta_\omega(\varepsilon_s(\theta_{0\omega})) = \theta_{0\omega}$ $(s = 1,2,\ldots)$. Let $\Gamma(\theta_{0\omega})$ denote all limit points of the sequence $\theta_z(\varepsilon_s(\theta_{0\omega}))$ from the interval $[0,1]$. Let θ_{0z} denote the limit element of $\Gamma(\theta_{0\omega})$ and let the subsequence ε_{s_r} of the sequence ε_s be such that

$$\lim_{r\to\infty} \theta_z(\varepsilon_{s_r}) = \theta_{0z}.$$

Note that it is possible that the set $\Gamma(\theta_{0\omega})$ coincides with the segment $[0,1]$, and it is possible that this set consists of a single element.

Theorem 2. *Let $0 < a^2 < 2$ and $d_0 = p_0|\gamma_0|^{-1}$. We arbitrarily fix $\theta_{0\omega} \in [0,2\pi)$ and let $\theta_{0z} \in \Gamma(\theta_{0\omega})$. Let $\xi^{\pm}(\tau,x,x_1)$ be the solution of the boundary value problem (39), (40) that is bounded for $\tau \to \infty$, $x \in [0,2\pi]$, $x_1 \in [0,1]$. Then, the function*

$$u(t,x,\varepsilon) = \varepsilon\big(\xi^+(\tau,x,x_1)E^+(t,x) + \overline{cc} + \xi^-(\tau,x,x_1)E^-(t,x) + \overline{cc}\big) + \varepsilon^3 u_3(t,\tau,x,x_1)$$

satisfies the boundary value problem (14), (16) up to $o(\varepsilon_{s_r}^3)$ for $\tau = \varepsilon^2 t$, $x_1 = (1-\varepsilon c^{-1}R)t$, for the sequence $\varepsilon = \varepsilon_{s_r}$.

Thus, the boundary value problem (39), (40) is a quasinormal form for the original boundary value problem (14), (16) in this critical case.

2.3. Small Values of Parameter σ

Below, we will consider important questions about the dynamical properties of the boundary value problem (14), (16) for small values of σ. We will assume that for some fixed value of σ_1, equality (22) is satisfied.

The interest in this case is due to the fact that, first, as is shown above for small σ, the corresponding integral expressions in the boundary value problem (14), (16) are close to being written in the form of a finite difference on the spatial variable.

Second, it follows from (17) that the value of $\exp\big(-\sigma^2 z^2/2\big)$ on the right-hand side of (17) is small, and hence, the critical cases are determined by the periodic function $\gamma(z)$. Thus, the critical values of z_0 in (23) are obviously not unique. There are obviously infinitely many such values. This suggests that the quasinormal form becomes significantly more complex, and the dynamical properties more interesting and diverse.

Under condition (22) for the function $\gamma(z)$, we have the equality

$$\gamma(z) = -4\sin^2\left(\frac{z}{2}\right)\cdot \exp\left(-\frac{1}{2}\varepsilon^2\sigma_1^2 z^2\right).$$

Let

$$\gamma_0(z) = -4\sin^2\frac{z}{2}.$$

Then,

$$\gamma(z) = \gamma_0(z)\left(1 - \frac{1}{2}\varepsilon^2\sigma_1^2 z^2 + O(\varepsilon^4)\right).$$

The largest value $|\gamma_0(z)| = 4$, and for all values z_m at which this value is reached, we have the equations

$$z_m = \pi(2m+1), \quad m = 0, \pm1, \pm2, \ldots.$$

Recall that $\varepsilon = 2\pi N^{-1}$. Below, we will assume that the value N is even, so all values of $\pi(2m+1)\varepsilon^{-1}$ are integers for all integers m.

Consider the set of integers $\pi(2m+1)\varepsilon^{-1} + k$, $k, m = 0, \pm1, \pm2, \ldots$. Let $u_{kmn}(t,x)$ denote the Euler solutions of the linear problem (15), (16):

$$u_{kmn}(t,x) = \exp\left[i\big(\pi(2m+1)\varepsilon^{-1} + k\big)x + \lambda_{kmn}(\varepsilon)t\right].$$

Here, $\lambda_{kmn}(\varepsilon)$ represents the roots of the characteristic equation (17) whose real parts tend to zero as $\varepsilon \to 0$.

2.3.1. Building A Quasinormal Form For $A^2 > 2$

Recall that, given $a^2 > 2$, we have $\omega_0 = \Omega_0 = 0$, $p_0 = 1, |\gamma_0| = 4$, and $d_0 = 1/4$. Let us first consider the asymptotics of $\lambda_{kmn}(\varepsilon)$.

Lemma 3. *Let conditions* (22), (24) *and* (25) *be satisfied. Then, there are asymptotic equalities:*

$$\lambda_{kmn}(\varepsilon) = c^{-1}i\pi(2n+1) + \varepsilon\lambda_{1kmn} + \varepsilon^2\lambda_{2kmn} + \dots,$$

where

$$\begin{aligned}\lambda_{1kmn} =& iac^{-2}\pi(2n+1),\\ \lambda_{2kmn} =& \frac{1}{2}(2-a^2)c^{-3}\big(\pi(2n+1)\big)^2 - ia^2c^{-3}\pi(2n+1) + 4d_1 - \frac{1}{2}\sigma_1^2\big(\pi(2m+1)\big)^2 - \\ & - \frac{1}{4}(\theta_z + k)^2.\end{aligned}$$

The set of Euler solutions of the linear boundary value problem (15), (16)

$$u(t,x,\varepsilon) = \sum_{k,m,n=-\infty}^{\infty} \xi_{kmn} \exp\big(i(\pi(2m+1)\varepsilon^{-1} + k)x + \lambda_{kmn}(\varepsilon)t\big)$$

can be written in the form

$$\begin{aligned}u(t,x,\varepsilon) =& \sum_{k,m,n=-\infty}^{\infty} \xi_{kmn}(\tau) \exp\big(ikx + i\pi(2m+1)y + i\pi(2n+1)x_1\big) = \\ &= \xi(\tau,x,y,x_1).\end{aligned} \tag{41}$$

Here,

$$\xi_{kmn}(\tau) = \xi_{kmn} \exp\big(\lambda_{2kmn} + O(\varepsilon)\tau\big), \quad y = x\varepsilon^{-1}, \quad x_1 = (1 + \varepsilon ac^{-1})t.$$

Based on the representation in (41), we will look for solutions of the nonlinear boundary value problem (14), (16) of the form

$$u(t,x) = \varepsilon\xi(\tau,x,y,x_1) + \varepsilon^3 u_3(\tau,x,y,x_1) + \dots. \tag{42}$$

After substituting (42) into (14) and following the standard steps, we arrive at the boundary value problem for determining the unknown function $\xi(\tau,x,y,x_1)$:

$$\begin{aligned}\frac{\partial\xi}{\partial\tau} =& \frac{a^2-2}{2c}\cdot\frac{\partial^2\xi}{\partial x_1^2} - \frac{a^2}{c^2}\cdot\frac{\partial\xi}{\partial x_1} + \frac{\sigma_1}{2c}\cdot\frac{\partial^2\xi}{\partial y^2} + \frac{1}{4c}\cdot\frac{\partial^2\xi}{\partial x^2} - \frac{i\theta_z}{2c}\cdot\frac{\partial\xi}{\partial x} + \\ & + \left(\frac{4d_1}{c} - \frac{1}{4c}\theta_z^2\right)\xi + \frac{b_1}{c}\xi^3,\end{aligned} \tag{43}$$

$$-\xi(\tau,x,y+1,x_1) \equiv \xi(\tau,x,y,x_1) \equiv \xi(\tau,x+2\pi,y,x_1), \tag{44}$$

$$-\xi(\tau,x,y,x_1+1) \equiv \xi(\tau,x,y,x_1). \tag{45}$$

As a result of the above constructions, we come to the justification of the following result.

Theorem 3. *Let conditions* (22), (24) *and* (25) *be satisfied. Let $\theta_{z0} \in [0,1)$ be arbitrarily fixed, and let $\xi(\tau,x,y,x_1)$ be a solution of the boundary value problem* (43)–(45) *bounded for $\tau \to \infty$, $x \in [0,2\pi]$, $y \in [0,1]$, $x_1 \in [0,1]$. Then, for the sequence $\varepsilon_s(\theta_z(\varepsilon_s(\theta_{z0}) = \theta_{z0})$, the function*

$$u(t,x) = \varepsilon\xi(\tau,x,y,x_1) + \varepsilon^3 u_3(\tau,x,y,x_1)$$

satisfies the boundary value problem of (14), (16) *up to $o(\varepsilon_s^3)$ for $\theta_z = \theta_{z0}$.*

2.3.2. Building Quasinormal Forms for $0 < A^2 < 2$

Recall that, in this case, Equation (37) holds.

Let us consider the asymptotics of such roots of the characteristic Equation (17) whose real parts tend to zero as $\varepsilon \to 0$.

In the following, θ_ω denotes such a quantity that complements the expression $\omega_0\varepsilon^{-1}$ to a value that is an odd multiple of πc^{-1}.

Lemma 4. *Let $0 < a^2 < 2$ and let conditions (22) and (24) be satisfied. Then, for $\lambda_{kmn}(\varepsilon)$, $k, m, n = 0, \pm 1, \pm 2, \ldots$, the asymptotic equalities take place:*

$$\begin{aligned}
\lambda_{kmn}(\varepsilon) &= i(\omega\varepsilon^{-1} + \theta_\omega - c^{-1}\Omega_0 + c^{-1}\pi(2n+1)) + \varepsilon\lambda_{1kmn} + \varepsilon^2\lambda_{2kmn} + \ldots,\\
\lambda_{1kmn} &= -2i(ac)^{-1}K, \quad K = \theta_\omega - c^{-1}\Omega_0 + c^{-1}\pi(2n+1),\\
\lambda_{2kmn} &= -D_1K^2 + D_2K - \frac{1}{2}\sigma_1^2(\pi(2m+1))^2 + d_1d_0^{-1} - K^2,\\
D_1 &= 2a^{-2}c^{-3} - (1 + ia\omega_0 - \omega_0^2)^{-1}c^{-3},\\
D_2 &= 2i(2i\omega_0 + a)(p_0\exp(i\Omega_0)ca)^{-1}.
\end{aligned}$$

Note that $\Re D_1 > 0$.

The set of Euler solutions of the linear boundary value problem (15), (16) can then be represented as

$$\begin{aligned}
u(t,x) = &\sum_{k,m,n=-\infty}^{\infty} \xi_{kmn}\exp\left(i(\pi(2m+1)\varepsilon^{-1} + k)x + \lambda_{kmn}(\varepsilon)t\right) =\\
&= E(t)\sum_{k,m,n=-\infty}^{\infty} \xi_{kmn}(\tau)\exp\left(i\pi(2m+1)y + ikx + i\pi(2n+1)x_1\right) =\\
&= E(t)\xi(\tau, x, y, x_1).
\end{aligned} \tag{46}$$

Here, $\tau = \varepsilon^2 t$, $E(t) = \exp\left[i(\omega_0\varepsilon^{-1} + (\theta_\omega - c^{-1}\Omega_0)(1 - 2\varepsilon(ca)^{-1}))t\right]$, $\xi_{kmn}(\tau) = \xi_{kmn} \cdot \exp\left((\lambda_{2kmn} + O(\varepsilon))\tau\right)$, $y = x\varepsilon^{-1}$, $x_1 = c^{-1}(1 - 2\varepsilon(ca)^{-1})t$. Based on the representation in (46), we will look for solutions of the nonlinear boundary value problem (14), (16) of the form

$$u(t,x) = \varepsilon(\xi(\tau, x, y, x_1)E(t) + \overline{cc}) + \varepsilon^3 u_3(t, \tau, x, y, x_1) + \ldots, \tag{47}$$

where the dependence on x, y, x_1 and t is periodic.

By substituting (47) into (14) and performing some straightforward calculations, we arrive at an equation for u_3. From its solvability condition in the specified class of functions, we obtain

$$\begin{aligned}
\frac{\partial\xi}{\partial\tau} =& D_1\frac{\partial^2\xi}{\partial x_1^2} + i(2D_1 + D_2)\frac{\partial\xi}{\partial x_1}(\theta_\omega - c^{-1}\Omega_0) + \frac{1}{2c}\sigma_1^2\frac{\partial^2\xi}{\partial y^2} +\\
&+ \frac{1}{c}\frac{\partial^2\xi}{\partial x^2} + \left(-D_1(\theta_\omega - \Omega_0)^2 + D_2(\theta_\omega - \Omega_0)\right)\xi + c^{-1}\beta\xi|\xi|^2.
\end{aligned} \tag{48}$$

For this equation, the boundary conditions are satisfied:

$$-\xi(\tau, x, y, x_1 + 1) \equiv \xi(\tau, x, y, x_1) \equiv \xi(\tau, x + 2\pi, y, x_1), \tag{49}$$

$$-\xi(\tau, x, y + 1, x_1) \equiv \xi(\tau, x, y, x_1). \tag{50}$$

Let us summarize.

Theorem 4. *Let conditions* (22), (24) *and* (27) *be satisfied. We arbitrarily fix* $\theta_{0\omega} \in [0, c^{-1}\pi)$ *and let* $\xi(\tau, x, y, x_1)$ *be a solution of the boundary value problem* (48)–(50) *for* $\theta_\omega = \theta_{0\omega}$ *bounded for* $\tau \to \infty$, $x \in [0, 2\pi]$, $y \in [0, 1]$, $x_1 \in [0, 1]$. *Then, the function*

$$u(t, x) = \varepsilon\big(\xi(\tau, x, y, x_1)E(t) + \overline{cc}\big) + \varepsilon^3 u_3(t, \tau, x, y, x_1)$$

satisfies the boundary value problem (14), (16) *up to* $o(\varepsilon^3)$ *for* $\tau = \varepsilon^2 t$, $x_1 = c^{-1}(1 - 2\varepsilon(ca)^{-1})t$ *and* $\varepsilon = \varepsilon_s(\theta_{0\omega})$.

Thus, in this section, we construct quasinormal forms, namely, boundary value problems of the parabolic type, (43)–(45) and (48)–(50), with three spatial variables. They play the role of the normal forms of the original boundary value problem (14), (16) in the above critical cases.

3. Advective-Type Coupling

3.1. The Results of Linear Analysis in the Case $\Phi(s) = \Phi_1(s)$

At each fixed z and under the condition

$$d|\gamma(z)| < p_0$$

Equation (20) has no real roots. Let us assume that

$$\gamma_0 = \max_{-\infty < z < \infty} |\gamma(z)| = |\gamma(z_0)| \quad (z_0 \geq 0). \tag{51}$$

The value of z_0 is defined in a unique way and is found simply. From the condition $|\gamma(z_0)|' = 0$, we find that z_0 is the first positive root of equation

$$z = 2(\sigma^2 z)^{-1}. \tag{52}$$

Given $d|\gamma_0| < p_0$ and sufficiently small ε, all roots of Equation (17) have negative real parts that move away from zero as $\varepsilon \to 0$. Given $d|\gamma_0| > p_0$, we find a z_0 such that Equation (17) has a root with a positive real part that moves away from zero as $\varepsilon \to 0$.

Let us restrict ourselves to the case where the parameter d is positive. The value of the parameter d_0, which distinguishes the critical case in the stability problem (15), (16), is determined by the equality

$$d_0 = p_0|\gamma_0|^{-1}.$$

In this connection, we assume below that, for an arbitrary fixed value d_1 for the parameter d, we have

$$d = d_0 + \varepsilon^2 d_1. \tag{53}$$

Under this condition, let us consider the asymptotics of all those roots of the characteristic Equation (17) whose real parts tend to zero as $\varepsilon \to 0$. There are infinitely many such roots, so the critical case has infinite dimensionality.

Let us introduce some more notations. Let $\Omega_0 = \Omega_0(\omega_0)$ be a real value for which

$$1 - \omega_0^2 + i\omega = p_0 \exp(i\Omega_0).$$

As above, we let $\theta_\omega = \theta_\omega(\varepsilon) \in [0, 2\pi)$ denote an expression that complements the value of $c\omega_0\varepsilon^{-1}$ to an integer multiple of 2π. Given $\omega_0 = 0$, we consider $\theta_\omega = 0$. We similarly let $\theta_z = \theta_z(\varepsilon) \in [0, 1)$ denote an expression that complements the value of $z_0\varepsilon^{-1}$ to an integer. Given $z_0 = 0$, we consider that $\theta_z = 0$.

We shall now formulate a statement about the asymptotics of the roots of (17) in the case of (18).

Lemma 5. *Let* $\gamma(z) = \gamma_1(z)$ *and*

$$a^2 > 2. \tag{54}$$

Then, $d_0\gamma_0 = p_0 = 1, \omega_0 = 0$, and for the roots $\lambda_{kn}(\varepsilon)$ $(k, n = 0, \pm 1, \pm 2, \dots)$ of Equation (17), the real parts of which tend to zero as $\varepsilon \to 0$, the asymptotic equations are satisfied:

$$\lambda_{kn}(\varepsilon) = \pi i c^{-1}\Big(2n + \frac{1}{2}\Big) + \varepsilon\lambda_{1kn} + \varepsilon^2\lambda_{2kn} + \dots, \tag{55}$$

where

$$\lambda_{1kn} = -c^{-2} i a \pi\Big(2n + \frac{1}{2}\Big),$$

$$\lambda_{2kn} = c^{-3}\Big(1 - \frac{1}{2}a^2\Big)\Big(\pi\Big(2n + \frac{1}{2}\Big)\Big)^2 - ic^{-3}a^2\pi\Big(2n + \frac{1}{2}\Big) + c^{-1}d_1\gamma_0 p_0^{-1} + \\ + \frac{1}{2}c^{-1}\gamma_0''(z_0)(\theta_z + k)^2(p_0\gamma_0)^{-1}.$$

Lemma 6. *Let $\gamma(z) = \gamma_1(z)$ and*

$$0 < a^2 < 2. \tag{56}$$

Then, $\omega_0 > 0$, and for the roots $\lambda_{kn}(\varepsilon)$ $(k, n = 0, \pm 1, \pm 2, \dots)$ of Equation (17) whose real parts tend to zero as $\varepsilon \to 0$, the asymptotic equations are satisfied:

$$\lambda_{kn}(\varepsilon) = i\omega_0\varepsilon^{-1} + \lambda_{0n} + \varepsilon\lambda_{1kn} + \varepsilon^2\lambda_{2kn} + \dots, \tag{57}$$

where

$$\lambda_{0n} = ic^{-1}\Big[\pi\Big(2n + \frac{1}{2}\Big) + \theta_\omega - \Omega_0\Big], \quad \varkappa = p_0\exp(i\Omega_0),$$

$$\lambda_{1kn} = ic^{-1}\varkappa^{-1}(2\omega_0 - ia)\lambda_{0n}, \tag{58}$$

$$\lambda_{2kn} = c^{-1}\Big[\Big(\varkappa^{-1} - \frac{1}{2}(-2\omega_0 + ia)^2\varkappa^{-2}\Big)\lambda_{0n}^2 + d_1 p_0^{-1} - \\ + \frac{1}{2}\gamma''(z_0)(\theta_z + k)^2(p_0\gamma_0)^{-1} - (c\varkappa)^{-1}2i\omega_0\varkappa^{-1}(2\omega_0 - ia)\lambda_{0n} - i\varkappa^{-1}a\lambda_{0n}\Big].$$

Note that

$$\Re\Big(\varkappa^{-1} - \frac{1}{2}(-2\omega_0 + ia)^2\varkappa^{-2}\Big) < 0, \quad \Re\lambda_{1kn} = 0. \tag{59}$$

The roots $\lambda_{kn}(\varepsilon)$ of the characteristic Equation (17) allow us to determine solutions to the linear boundary value problem (15), (16):

$$u_{kn}(t, x, \varepsilon) = \exp\big(i(z_0\varepsilon^{-1} + \theta_z + k)x + \lambda_{kn}(\varepsilon)t\big),$$

and hence, the formal set of solutions is

$$u(t, x, \varepsilon) = \sum_{k,n=-\infty}^{\infty}\Big(\xi_{kn}u_{kn}(t, x, \varepsilon) + \bar{\xi}_{kn}\bar{u}_{kn}(t, x, \varepsilon)\Big), \tag{60}$$

where ξ_{kn} denotes arbitrary complex constants.

Remark 2. *Together with the roots $\lambda_{kn}(\varepsilon)$ of Equation (17), there are the roots $\overline{\lambda}_{kn}(\varepsilon)$, which correspond to the solutions of the boundary value problem (15), (16):*

$$\overline{u}_{kn}(t, x, \varepsilon) = \exp\big(-i(z_0\varepsilon^{-1} + \theta_z + k)x + \overline{\lambda}_{kn}(\varepsilon)t\big).$$

Note that for the parameters z and $-z$, the roots in (17) *are the same, since the dependence of the right-hand side of* (17) *on z is even. This means that for the modes of* $-(z_0\varepsilon^{-1}+\theta_z+k)$, *the roots are the same, i.e.,* $\lambda_{kn}(\varepsilon)$. *Therefore, the problem* (15), (16) *has the following solutions:*

$$\tilde{u}_{kn}(t,x,\varepsilon)=\exp\big(-i(z_0\varepsilon^{-1}+\theta_z+k)x+\overline{\lambda}_{kn}(\varepsilon)t\big).$$

Under the conditions of Lemma 5, we have

$$\tilde{u}_{kn}(t,x,\varepsilon)=\overline{u}_{kn}(t,x,\varepsilon),$$

and under the conditions of Lemma 6, this is no longer the case.

3.2. The Results of Linear Analysis in the Case $\Phi(s)=\Phi_2(s)$

In the case of (19), the value of $z_0>0$ is defined as the first positive root from the equation

$$\frac{z}{2}=(2\sigma^2 z)^{-1}. \tag{61}$$

Lemma 7. *Let condition* (19) *be satisfied and* $a^2>2$. *Then,* $d_0\gamma_0=p_0=1,\omega_0=0$, *and for the roots* $\lambda_{kn}(\varepsilon)$ $(k,n=0,\pm1,\pm2,\dots)$ *of Equation* (17) *whose real parts tend to zero as* $\varepsilon\to0$, *the asymptotic equations are satisfied:*

$$\lambda_{kn}(\varepsilon)=\left[i\pi\left(\frac{1}{2}+2n\right)+\frac{i}{2}(z_0+\varepsilon(\theta_z+k))\right]c^{-1}+\varepsilon\lambda_{1kn}+\varepsilon^2\lambda_{2kn}+\dots, \tag{62}$$

where

$$\lambda_{1kn}=-ic^{-2}a\left(\pi\left(\frac{1}{2}+2n\right)+\frac{z_0}{2}\right)-\frac{1}{2}c^{-1}(\theta_z+k),$$

$$\lambda_{2kn}=\left(\frac{2\pi n}{c}\right)^2\left[\frac{2-a^2}{c}\right]+\frac{2\pi n}{c}\left[\frac{\pi}{2c^2}(2-a^2)+\frac{z_0}{c^2}(2-a^2)+i\frac{a^2}{c}\right]+d_0c^{-1}\gamma''(z_0)k^2+$$
$$+2d_0c^{-1}\gamma''(z_0)\theta_z k+B_1,$$

$$B_1=c^{-1}d_1\gamma_0+c^{-1}d_0\gamma''(z_0)\theta_z^2+\frac{\pi^2}{4c^3}(2-a^2)+\frac{\pi^2}{2c^3}z_0(2-a^2)+\frac{z^2}{4c^3}(2-a^2)-\frac{ia^2}{2c^2}(\pi+z_0).$$

Lemma 8. *Let condition* (19) *be satisfied and*

$$0<a^2<2. \tag{63}$$

Then, $\omega_0>0$, *and for the roots* $\lambda_{kn}(\varepsilon)$ $(k,n=0,\pm1,\pm2,\dots)$ *of Equation* (17), *the real parts of which tend to zero as* $\varepsilon\to0$, *the asymptotic equations are fulfilled:*

$$\lambda_{kn}(\varepsilon)=i\left[\omega_0\varepsilon^{-1}+c^{-1}\lambda_{0n}\right]+\varepsilon\left(\frac{i}{2}c^{-1}(\theta_z+k)+\lambda_{1kn}\right)+\varepsilon^2\lambda_{2kn}+\dots, \tag{64}$$

where

$$\lambda_{0n}=\pi\left(2n+\frac{1}{2}\right)+\theta_\omega-\Omega_0+\frac{z_0}{2},\quad \varkappa=p_0\exp(i\Omega_0),$$

$$\lambda_{1kn}=-\frac{2i}{ac^2}\lambda_{0n}, \tag{65}$$

$$\lambda_{2kn}=-2c^{-3}a^{-2}\lambda_{0n}^2+d_1(cd_0)^{-1}+d_0(c\gamma_0)^{-1}\gamma''(z_0)(\theta_z+k)^2+$$
$$+(cp_0\exp(i\Omega_0))^{-1}\left[c^{-2}\lambda_{0n}^2-(2i\omega_0+a)\left(-\frac{2i}{ac}\lambda_{0n}+\frac{1}{2}(\theta_z+k)\right)\right].$$

Remark 3. *The roots $\lambda_{kn}(\varepsilon)$ of the characteristic Equation* (17) *allow us to determine solutions to the linear boundary value problem* (15), (16)*:*

$$u_{kn}(t,x,\varepsilon) = \exp\left(i(z_0\varepsilon^{-1} + \theta_z + k)x + \lambda_{kn}(\varepsilon)t\right),$$

and hence, the formal set of solutions is

$$u(t,x,\varepsilon) = \sum_{k,n=-\infty}^{\infty} \left(\xi_{kn}u_{kn}(t,x,\varepsilon) + \bar{\xi}_{kn}\bar{u}_{kn}(t,x,\varepsilon)\right), \tag{66}$$

where ξ_{kn} denotes arbitrary complex constants.

This remark applies to Lemmas 5–8.

3.3. Nonlinear Analysis for $\Phi(s) = \Phi_1(s)$

Consider the cases $a^2 > 2$ and $a^2 < 2$ separately.

3.3.1. Case $a^2 > 2$

In this case, we have the equality $\omega_0 = 0, \Omega_0 = 0, p_0 = 1$. The critical case in the stability problem is defined by the equality

$$d_0|\gamma_0| = 1. \tag{67}$$

The following will be based on the representation in (66). Let us write it in a more convenient form:

$$\begin{aligned} u(t,x,\varepsilon) = E(t,x) \sum_{k,n=-\infty}^{\infty} \xi_{kn} \exp\left(ikx + 2i\pi n c^{-1}(1-\varepsilon c^{-1}a)t + (\lambda_{2kn} + O(\varepsilon))\tau\right) = \\ = E(t,x)\xi(\tau,x,x_1), \end{aligned} \tag{68}$$

where $\tau = \varepsilon^2 t$ is the "slow" time, $E(t,x) = \exp(i(z_0\varepsilon^{-1} + \theta_z)x + i\pi(2c)^{-1}(1-\varepsilon a c^{-1})t)$, and $\xi_{kn}(\tau) = \xi_{kn}\exp\left((\lambda_{2kn} + O(\varepsilon))\tau\right)$ denotes coefficients of the expansion of $\xi(\tau,x,x_1)$ into a Fourier series with respect to the 2π-periodic argument x and the c-periodic argument $x_1 = (1-\varepsilon c^{-1}a)t$.

Solutions of the nonlinear boundary value problem (14), (16) are found in the form

$$u = \varepsilon\left(E(t,x)\xi(\tau,x,x_1) + \overline{cc}\right) + \varepsilon^3 u_3(\tau,x,x_1) + \dots. \tag{69}$$

Here and below, $\overline{cc}$ denotes the term that is complex conjugate to the previous one. The unknown complex function $\xi(\tau,x,x_1)$ is to be defined. Let us substitute (69) into (14) and collect the coefficients of the same powers of ε. Then, at the first power of ε, we obtain an identity. Equating the coefficients of ε^3, we arrive at the equation

$$\begin{aligned} c\frac{\partial\xi}{\partial\tau} =& \left(\frac{1}{2}a^2 - 1\right)\frac{\partial^2\xi}{\partial x_1^2} + (2\gamma_0)^{-1}\gamma''(z_0)\frac{\partial^2\xi}{\partial x^2} - i\gamma_0^{-1}\gamma''(z_0)\theta_z\frac{\partial\xi}{\partial x} + \\ &+ ic^{-1}\left(a^2 - \frac{\pi}{2}\left(1 - \frac{1}{2}a^2\right)\right)\frac{\partial\xi}{\partial x_1} + B_0\xi + 3b_1\xi|\xi|^2, \\ B_0 =& c^{-2}\pi^2\frac{1}{4}\left(1 - \frac{1}{2}a^2\right) + ia^2c^{-2}\frac{1}{2}\pi + \frac{1}{2}\gamma''(z_0)\theta_z^2 + 2d_1c^{-1}\gamma_0 \end{aligned} \tag{70}$$

with the boundary conditions

$$\xi(\tau,x,x_1+c) \equiv \xi(\tau,x,x_1) \equiv \xi(\tau,x+2\pi,x_1). \tag{71}$$

Here, the following relations are taken into account:

$$\begin{aligned}\frac{d\xi}{dt} =&\varepsilon^2\frac{\partial\xi}{\partial\tau}+\frac{\partial\xi}{\partial x_1}(1-\varepsilon ac^{-1}),\\ \xi_{t-c} =&\xi(\tau-\varepsilon^2 c, x, x_1-c(1-\varepsilon ac^{-1}))=\\ =&\xi(\tau,x,x_1)-\varepsilon^2 c\frac{\partial\xi}{\partial\tau}+\varepsilon a\frac{\partial\xi}{\partial x_1}+\frac{1}{2}\varepsilon^2 a^2\frac{\partial^2\xi}{\partial x_1^2}+o(\varepsilon^2).\end{aligned}$$

Let us introduce the following notation. We arbitrarily fix the value $\theta_{0z}\in[0,1)$ and let $\varepsilon_n=\varepsilon_n(\theta_{0z})$ denote a sequence for which $\varepsilon_n\to 0$ as $n\to\infty$ and $\theta_z(\varepsilon_n,\theta_{0z})=\theta_{0z}$. The above constructions justify the following result.

Theorem 5. *Let $a^2>2$ and conditions (53) and (67) be satisfied. Let $\theta_{0z}\in[0,1)$ be arbitrarily fixed, and let the boundary value problem (70), (71) at $\theta_z=\theta_{0z}$ have a bounded solution $\xi(\tau,x,x_1)$ as $\tau\to\infty$, $x\in[0,2\pi]$, $x_1\in[0,c]$. Then, the function $u(t,x,\varepsilon)=\varepsilon\big(E(t,x)\xi(\tau,x,x_1)+\overline{cc}\big)+\varepsilon^3 u_3(\tau,x,x_1)$ satisfies the boundary value problem (14), (16) with accuracy up to $o(\varepsilon^3)$.*

Thus, the parabolic boundary value problem (70), (71) is a quasinormal form for the boundary value problem (14), (16).

3.3.2. Case $a^2<2$

The dynamical properties in this case are much more complicated. The principal parts of the roots $\lambda_{kn}(\varepsilon)$ of the characteristic equation are close to $i\omega_0\varepsilon^{-1}$: i.e., they are asymptotically large. Therefore, the oscillations in the boundary value problem (14), (16) will be rapid.

Note that, in this case,

$$\omega_0=\left(1-\frac{a^2}{2}\right)^{1/2},\quad p_0=\frac{a^2}{2}(4-a^2)^{1/2},\quad d_0=p_0|\gamma_0|^{-1}. \tag{72}$$

The roots of $\lambda_{kn}(\varepsilon)$ correspond to the Euler solutions of the linear boundary value problem (15), (16):

$$u^{\pm}_{kn}(t,x,\varepsilon)=\exp\big(\pm i(z_0\varepsilon^{-1}+\theta_z+k)x+\lambda_{kn}(\varepsilon)t\big).$$

It is more convenient to write these functions in the form

$$u^{\pm}_{kn}(t,x,\varepsilon)=E^{\pm}(t,x)\exp\left(ikx+2i\pi nx_1+(\lambda_{2kn}+O(\varepsilon))\tau\right),$$

where

$$\begin{aligned}E^{\pm}(t,x)=&\exp\left(i(c^{-1}\omega_0\varepsilon^{-1}+c^{-1}\left(\theta_\omega-\Omega_0+\frac{\pi}{2}\right)+\varepsilon c^{-1}\varkappa^{-1}(2\omega_0-ia)\cdot\right.\\ &\left.\cdot ic^{-1}(\theta_\omega-\Omega_0))t\pm i(z_0\varepsilon^{-1}+\theta_z)x\right),\end{aligned}$$

$$R=\varkappa^{-1}(2\omega_0-ia)\cdot ic^{-1}(\theta_\omega-\Omega_0),\quad \Im R=0,$$

$\tau=\varepsilon^2 t$, $x_1=(1-\varepsilon c^{-1}R)t$. Hence, we find that

$$\begin{aligned}\sum_{k,n=-\infty}^{\infty}\xi^{\pm}_{kn}u^{\pm}_{kn}(t,x,\varepsilon)=E^{\pm}(t,x)\sum_{k,n=-\infty}^{\infty}\xi^{\pm}_{kn}(\tau)\exp\left(ikx+2i\pi nx_1\right)=\\ =E^{\pm}(t,x)\xi^{\pm}(\tau,x,x_1).\end{aligned}$$

Here, $\xi_{kn}^{\pm}$ denotes arbitrary complex constants, and $\xi_{kn}^{\pm}(\tau) = \xi_{kn}^{\pm}\exp\left((\lambda_{2kn} + O(\varepsilon))\tau\right)$. The functions $\xi_{kn}^{\pm}(\tau)$ are the Fourier coefficients of the function $\xi^{\pm}(\tau, x, x_1)$, which is 2π-periodic with respect to x and c-periodic with respect to x_1.

Solutions of the nonlinear boundary value problem (14), (16) are found in the form

$$u(t,x) = u^{+}(t,x) + u^{-}(t,x), \tag{73}$$

$$u^{\pm}(t,x) = \varepsilon\left(\xi^{\pm}(\tau,x,x_1)E^{\pm}(t,x) + \overline{cc}\right) + \varepsilon^3 u_3(t,\tau,x,x_1) + \ldots,$$

where the dependencies on t, x and x_1 are periodic.

Let us substitute (73) into (14) and equate the coefficients of the same powers of ε. In the first step, we obtain an identity, and by collecting the coefficients of ε^3, we obtain the equation for u_3. From its solvability condition in the specified class of functions, we arrive at the relation

$$\frac{\partial \xi^{\pm}}{\partial \tau} = A_1 \frac{\partial^2 \xi^{\pm}}{\partial x_1^2} + A_2 \frac{\partial \xi^{\pm}}{\partial x_1} + A_3 \xi^{\pm} + B_1 \frac{\partial^2 \xi^{\pm}}{\partial x^2} + B_2 \frac{\partial \xi^{\pm}}{\partial x} + c^{-1}\beta \xi^{\pm}(|\xi^{\pm}|^2 + 2|\xi^{\mp}|^2), \tag{74}$$

in which

$$\begin{aligned}
A_1 &= -c^{-3}\left[\varkappa^{-1} - \frac{1}{2}(ia - 2\omega_0)^2 \varkappa^{-2}\right],\\
A_2 &= c^{-3}\Big[-2(\varkappa^{-1} - \frac{1}{2}(ia - 2\omega_0)^2\varkappa^{-2}(\theta_\omega - \Omega_0)) + c\varkappa^{-2} 2\omega_0(2\omega_0 - ia) +\\
&\quad + c^2\varkappa^{-1} a(\theta_\omega - \Omega_0)\Big],\\
A_3 &= c^{-3}\left[\frac{1}{2}(ia - 2\omega_0)\varkappa^2(\theta_\omega - \Omega_0)^2 - \varkappa^{-1}\right] + d_1 c^{-1} p_0^{-1} +\\
&\quad + \frac{1}{2}\gamma''(z_0) c^{-1}\theta_z^2 (p_0\gamma_0)^{-1} - i(c\varkappa)^{-2} 2i\omega_0(2\omega_0 - ia)\cdot\\
&\quad \cdot(\theta_\omega - \Omega_0) - i(c\varkappa)^{-1} a(\theta_\omega - \Omega_0),\\
B_1 &= \frac{1}{2} c^{-1}\gamma''(z_0)(p_0\gamma_0)^{-1},\\
B_2 &= c^{-1}\gamma''(z_0)\theta_z(p_0\gamma_0)^{-1},\\
\beta &= b_1 + i\omega_0 b_2 - \omega_0^2 b_3 - i\omega_0^3 b_4.
\end{aligned}$$

Recall that the function $\xi(\tau, x, x_1)$ satisfies the boundary conditions

$$\xi(\tau, x, x_1 + c) \equiv \xi(\tau, x, x_1) \equiv \xi(\tau, x + 2\pi, x_1). \tag{75}$$

In order to formulate the final result, we introduce some notations. We arbitrarily fix $\theta_{0\omega} \in [0, 2\pi)$ and let the sequence $\varepsilon_s = \varepsilon_s(\theta_{0\omega})$ be defined by the condition $\theta_\omega(\varepsilon_s(\theta_{0\omega})) = \theta_{0\omega}$ $(s = 1, 2, \ldots)$. We let $\Gamma(\theta_{0\omega})$ denote all limit points of the sequence $\theta_z(\varepsilon_s(\theta_{0\omega}))$ from the interval $[0, 1]$. We let θ_{0z} denote the limit element of $\Gamma(\theta_{0\omega})$ and let the subsequence ε_{s_Γ} of the sequence ε_s be such that

$$\lim_{\Gamma \to \infty} \theta_z(\varepsilon_{s_\Gamma}) = \theta_{0z}.$$

Note that it is possible that the set $\Gamma(\theta_{0\omega})$ coincides with the segment $[0, 1]$, and it is possible that this set consists of a single element.

Theorem 6. *Let $0 < a^2 < 2$ and $d_0 = p_0|\gamma_0|^{-1}$. We arbitrarily fix $\theta_{0\omega} \in [0, 2\pi)$ and let $\theta_{0z} \in \Gamma(\theta_{0\omega})$. Let $\xi^{\pm}(\tau, x, x_1)$ be a bounded solution of the boundary value problem* (74), (75) *as $\tau \to \infty$, $x \in [0, 2\pi]$, $x_1 \in [0, c]$. Then, the function*

$$u(t,x,\varepsilon) = \varepsilon\left(\xi^{+}(\tau,x,x_1)E^{+}(t,x) + \overline{cc} + \xi^{-}(\tau,x,x_1)E^{-}(t,x) + \overline{cc}\right) + \varepsilon^3 u_3(t,\tau,x,x_1)$$

satisfies the boundary value problem (14), (16) *up to* $o(\varepsilon_{s_\Gamma}^3)$ *for* $\tau = \varepsilon^2 t$, $x_1 = (1 - \varepsilon c^{-1} R)t$, *for the sequence* $\varepsilon = \varepsilon_{s_\Gamma}$.

Thus, the boundary value problem (74), (75) is a quasinormal form for the original boundary value problem (14), (16) in this critical case.

3.4. Nonlinear Analysis for $\Phi(s) = \Phi_2(s)$

And here, we consider the cases $a^2 > 2$ and $a^2 < 2$ separately.

3.4.1. Case $a^2 > 2$

In this case, we have the equality $\omega_0 = 0, \Omega_0 = 0, p_0 = 1$. The critical case in the stability problem is defined by the equality

$$d_0|\gamma_0| = p_0. \tag{76}$$

The following will be based on the representation in (66). Let us write it in a more convenient form:

$$\begin{aligned} u(t,x,\varepsilon) = E(t,x) \sum_{k,n=-\infty}^{\infty} \xi_{kn} \exp\left(ikx + 2i\pi n c^{-1}(1 - \varepsilon c^{-1} a)t + (\lambda_{2kn} + O(\varepsilon))\tau\right) = \\ = E(t,x)\xi(\tau,x,x_1), \end{aligned} \tag{77}$$

where $\tau = \varepsilon^2 t$ is the "slow" time,

$$E(t,x) = \exp\left(i(\omega_0\varepsilon^{-1} + \theta_\omega - \Omega_0 + \frac{1}{2}(z_0 + \pi + \varepsilon\theta_z)) + i(z_0\varepsilon^{-1} + \theta_z)x + i\pi(2c)^{-1}(1 - \varepsilon a c^{-1})t\right),$$

and $\xi_{kn}(\tau) = \xi_{kn} \exp\left((\lambda_{2kn} + O(\varepsilon))\tau\right)$ denotes coefficients of the expansion of $\xi(\tau,x,x_1)$ into a Fourier series with respect to the 2π-periodic argument x and the c-periodic argument $x_1 = (1 - \varepsilon c^{-1} a)t$.

The solutions of the nonlinear boundary value problem (14), (16) are found in the form

$$u = \varepsilon\big(E(t,x)\xi(\tau,x,x_1) + \overline{cc}\big) + \varepsilon^3 u_3(\tau,x,x_1) + \ldots. \tag{78}$$

Here and below, $\overline{cc}$ denotes the term that is complex conjugate to the previous one. The unknown complex function $\xi(\tau,x,x_1)$ is to be defined. Let us substitute (78) into (14) and collect the coefficients of the same powers of ε. Then, at the first power of ε, we obtain an identity. Equating the coefficients of ε^3, we arrive at the equation

$$\begin{aligned} c\frac{\partial\xi}{\partial\tau} &= \left(\frac{1}{2}a^2 - 1\right)\frac{\partial^2\xi}{\partial x_1^2} + (2\gamma_0)^{-1}\gamma''(z_0)\frac{\partial^2\xi}{\partial x^2} - i\gamma_0^{-1}\gamma''(z_0)\theta_z\frac{\partial\xi}{\partial x} + \\ &+ ic^{-1}\left(a^2 - \frac{\pi}{2}\left(1 - \frac{1}{2}a^2\right)\right)\frac{\partial\xi}{\partial x_1} + B_0\xi + 3b_1\xi|\xi|^2, \\ B_0 &= c^{-2}\pi^2\frac{1}{4}\left(1 - \frac{1}{2}a^2\right) + ia^2c^{-2}\frac{1}{2}\pi + \frac{1}{2}\gamma''(z_0)\theta_z^2 + 2d_1c^{-1}\gamma_0 \end{aligned} \tag{79}$$

with the boundary conditions

$$\xi(\tau,x,x_1 + c) \equiv \xi(\tau,x,x_1) \equiv \xi(\tau,x + 2\pi,x_1). \tag{80}$$

Let us introduce some notation. We arbitrarily fix the value $\theta_{0z} \in [0,1)$ and let $\varepsilon_n = \varepsilon_n(\theta_{0z})$ denote a sequence for which $\varepsilon_n \to 0$ as $n \to \infty$ and $\theta_z(\varepsilon_n, \theta_{0z}) = \theta_{0z}$. The above constructions justify the following result.

Theorem 7. *Let* $a^2 > 2$ *and conditions* (53) *and* (76) *be satisfied. Let* $\theta_{0z} \in [0,1)$ *be arbitrarily fixed, and let the boundary value problem* (79), (80) *at* $\theta_z = \theta_{0z}$ *have a bounded solution* $\xi(\tau,x,x_1)$

as $\tau \to \infty$, $x \in [0, 2\pi]$, $x_1 \in [0, c]$. *Then, the function* $u(t, x, \varepsilon) = \varepsilon\big(E(t, x)\xi(\tau, x, x_1) + \overline{cc}\big) + \varepsilon^3 u_3(\tau, x, x_1)$ *satisfies the boundary value problem* (14), (16) *with accuracy up to* $o(\varepsilon^3)$.

Thus, the parabolic boundary value problem (79), (80) is a quasinormal form for the boundary value problem (14), (16).

3.4.2. Case $a^2 < 2$

The principal parts of the roots $\lambda_{kn}(\varepsilon)$ of the characteristic equation are close to $i\omega_0\varepsilon^{-1}$: i.e., they are asymptotically large. Therefore, the oscillations in the boundary value problem (14), (16) will be rapid.

Note that, in this case,

$$\omega_0 = \left(1 - \frac{a^2}{2}\right)^{1/2}, \quad p_0 = \frac{a^2}{2}(4 - a^2)^{1/2}, \quad d_0 = p_0|\gamma_0|^{-1}. \tag{81}$$

The roots of $\lambda_{kn}(\varepsilon)$ correspond to the Euler solutions of the linear boundary value problem (15), (16):

$$u^{\pm}_{kn}(t, x, \varepsilon) = \exp\big(\pm i(z_0\varepsilon^{-1} + \theta_z + k)x + \lambda_{kn}(\varepsilon)t\big).$$

It is more convenient to write these functions in the form

$$u^{\pm}_{kn}(t, x, \varepsilon) = E^{\pm}(t, x)\exp\big(ikx + 2i\pi n x_1 + (\lambda_{2kn} + O(\varepsilon))\tau\big),$$

where

$$E^{\pm}(t, x) = \exp\Bigg(i(c^{-1}\omega_0\varepsilon^{-1} + c^{-1}\left(\theta_\omega - \Omega_0 + \frac{\pi}{2}\right) + \varepsilon c^{-1}\varkappa^{-1}(2\omega_0 - ia)\cdot$$
$$\cdot ic^{-1}(\theta_\omega - \Omega_0))t \pm i(z_0\varepsilon^{-1} + \theta_z)x\Bigg),$$

$$R = \varkappa^{-1}(2\omega_0 - ia)\cdot ic^{-1}(\theta_\omega - \Omega_0) = \frac{2}{a}, \quad \Im R = 0,$$

$\tau = \varepsilon^2 t$, $x_1 = (1 - \varepsilon c^{-1}R)t$. Hence we find that

$$\sum_{k,n=-\infty}^{\infty} \xi^{\pm}_{kn} u^{\pm}_{kn}(t, x, \varepsilon) = E^{\pm}(t, x) \sum_{k,n=-\infty}^{\infty} \xi^{\pm}_{kn}(\tau)\exp\big(ikx + 2i\pi n x_1\big) =$$
$$= E^{\pm}(t, x)\xi^{\pm}(\tau, x, x_1).$$

Here, $\xi^{\pm}_{kn}$ denotes arbitrary complex constants, and $\xi^{\pm}_{kn}(\tau) = \xi^{\pm}_{kn}\exp\big((\lambda_{2kn} + O(\varepsilon))\tau\big)$. The functions $\xi^{\pm}_{kn}(\tau)$ are the Fourier coefficients of the function $\xi^{\pm}(\tau, x, x_1)$, which is 2π-periodic with respect to x and c-periodic with respect to x_1.

The solutions of the nonlinear boundary value problem (14), (16) are found in the form

$$u(t, x) = u^{+}(t, x) + u^{-}(t, x), \tag{82}$$
$$u^{\pm}(t, x) = \varepsilon\big(\xi^{\pm}(\tau, x, x_1)E^{\pm}(t, x) + \overline{cc}\big) + \varepsilon^3 u_3(t, \tau, x, x_1) + \ldots,$$

where the dependencies on t, x and x_1 are periodic.

Let us substitute (82) into (14) and equate the coefficients of the same powers of ε. In the first step, we obtain an identity, whereas, by collecting the coefficients of ε^3, we obtain the equation for u_3. From its solvability condition in the specified class of functions, we arrive at the relation

$$c\frac{\partial\xi^{\pm}}{\partial\tau} = A_1\frac{\partial^2\xi^{\pm}}{\partial x_1^2} + A_2\frac{\partial\xi^{\pm}}{\partial x_1} + A_3\frac{\partial^2\xi^{\pm}}{\partial x^2} + A_4\frac{\partial\xi^{\pm}}{\partial x} + A_5\xi + \beta\xi^{\pm}(|\xi^{\pm}|^2 + 2|\xi^{\mp}|^2), \tag{83}$$

in which

$$\begin{aligned}
A_1 &= 2a^2 - (p_0 \exp(i\Omega_0))^{-1}, \quad \Re A_1 > 0, \\
A_2 &= 2iA_1 l c^{-1} + 4a^{-2}, \\
A_3 &= d_0 \gamma_0^{-1} \gamma''(z_0), \\
A_4 &= -2i\theta_z d_0 \gamma_0^{-1} \gamma''(z_0) - 2(a^2 c)^{-1}, \\
A_5 &= A_1 l^2 + d_1 d_0^{-1} + d_0 \gamma_0^{-1} \gamma''(z_0) \theta_z^2 - 4i(a^2 c)^{-1} l + a^{-1} \theta_z, \\
l &= \theta_\omega - \Omega_0 + \frac{1}{2}(\pi + z_0), \\
\beta &= b_1 + i\omega_0 b_2 - \omega_0^2 b_3 - i\omega_0^3 b_4.
\end{aligned}$$

Recall that the function $\xi(\tau, x, x_1)$ satisfies the boundary conditions

$$\xi(\tau, x, x_1 + c) \equiv \xi(\tau, x, x_1) \equiv \xi(\tau, x + 2\pi, x_1). \tag{84}$$

In order to formulate the final result, we introduce some notations. We arbitrarily fix $\theta_{0\omega} \in [0, 2\pi)$ and let the sequence $\varepsilon_s = \varepsilon_s(\theta_{0\omega})$ be defined by the condition $\theta_\omega(\varepsilon_s(\theta_{0\omega})) = \theta_{0\omega}$ $(s = 1, 2, \ldots)$. Let $\Gamma(\theta_{0\omega})$ denote all limit points of the sequence $\theta_z(\varepsilon_s(\theta_{0\omega}))$ from the interval $[0, 1]$. Let θ_{0z} denote the limit element of $\Gamma(\theta_{0\omega})$, and let the subsequence ε_{s_Γ} of the sequence ε_s be such that

$$\lim_{\Gamma \to \infty} \theta_z(\varepsilon_{s_\Gamma}) = \theta_{0z}.$$

We formulate the final result.

Theorem 8. *Let $0 < a^2 < 2$ and $d_0 = p_0 |\gamma_0|^{-1}$. We arbitrarily fix $\theta_{0\omega} \in [0, 2\pi)$ and let $\theta_{0z} \in \Gamma(\theta_{0\omega})$. Let $\xi^{\pm}(\tau, x, x_1)$ be a bounded solution of the boundary value problem (74), (75) as $\tau \to \infty$, $x \in [0, 2\pi]$, $x_1 \in [0, c]$. Then, the function*

$$u(t, x, \varepsilon) = \varepsilon\big(\xi^+(\tau, x, x_1) E^+(t, x) + \overline{cc} + \xi^-(\tau, x, x_1) E^-(t, x) + \overline{cc}\big) + \varepsilon^3 u_3(t, \tau, x, x_1)$$

satisfies the boundary value problem (14), (16) up to $o(\varepsilon_{s_\Gamma}^3)$ for $\tau = \varepsilon^2 t$, $x_1 = (1 - \varepsilon c^{-1} R)t$, for the sequence $\varepsilon = \varepsilon_{s_\Gamma}$.

Thus, the boundary value problem (74), (75) is a quasinormal form for the original boundary value problem (14), (16) in this critical case.

3.5. Quasinormal Forms in the Case of Small Values of the Parameter σ

Here, we assume that for each fixed $\sigma_1 > 0$, the following condition is satisfied:

$$\sigma = \varepsilon \sigma_1. \tag{85}$$

Let us separately consider the cases where $\Phi(s) = \Phi_1(s)$ and $\Phi(s) = \Phi_2(s)$.

3.5.1. Building a Quasinormal Form under the Condition $\Phi(s) = \Phi_1(s)$ and $A^2 > 2$

Under condition (85) for the function $\gamma(z)$, we have the following:

$$\gamma(z) = 2i(\sin z) \cdot \exp\left(-\frac{1}{2}\varepsilon^2 \sigma_1^2 z^2\right).$$

Set

$$\gamma_0(z) = 2i \sin z.$$

Then,

$$\gamma(z) = \gamma_0(z)\left(1 - \frac{1}{2}\varepsilon^2 \sigma_1^2 z^2 + O(\varepsilon^4)\right).$$

The largest value $|\gamma_0(z)| = 2$, and for all values $z_m^{\pm}$ at which this value is reached, we have the equations

$$z_m^{\pm} = \pi\left(2m \pm \frac{1}{2}\right), \quad m = 0, \pm 1, \pm 2, \dots.$$

Recall that $\varepsilon = 2\pi N^{-1}$. Consider the sets of integers $\pi(2m \pm 1/2)\varepsilon^{-1} + k$, $k, m = 0, \pm 1, \pm 2, \dots$. We let $u_{kmn}(t, x)$ denote the Euler solutions of the linear problem (15), (16):

$$u_{kmn}^{\pm}(t, x) = \exp\left[i(\pi\left(2m + \frac{1}{2}\right)\varepsilon^{-1} + \theta_{zm} + k)x + \lambda_{kmn}^{\pm}(\varepsilon)t\right].$$

Here, $\lambda_{kmn}^{\pm}(\varepsilon)$ denotes the roots of the characteristic Equation (17) whose real parts tend to zero as $\varepsilon \to 0$. Note that

$$\theta_{zm} = \begin{cases} 0, & \mathrm{N} = 4\mathrm{P} \\ 3/4, & \mathrm{N} = 4\mathrm{P} + 1 \\ 1/2, & \mathrm{N} = 4\mathrm{P} + 2 \\ 1/4, & \mathrm{N} = 4\mathrm{P} + 3. \end{cases}$$

Recall that, for $a^2 > 2$, we have $\omega_0 = \Omega_0 = 0$, $p_0 = 1, |\gamma_0| = 2, d_0 = 1/2$. Let us first consider the asymptotics of $\lambda_{kmn}^{\pm}(\varepsilon)$.

Lemma 9. *Let conditions* (53), (54) *and* (85) *be satisfied. Then, there are the asymptotic relations*

$$\lambda_{kmn}^{\pm}(\varepsilon) = c^{-1}i\pi\left(2n \pm \frac{1}{2}\right) + \varepsilon\lambda_{1kmn}^{\pm} + \varepsilon^2\lambda_{2kmn}^{\pm} + \dots,$$

where

$$\begin{aligned} \lambda_{1kmn}^{\pm} =& iac^{-2}\pi\left(2n \pm \frac{1}{2}\right), \\ c\lambda_{2kmn}^{\pm} =& \frac{1}{2}(2 - a^2)c^{-2}\pi^2\left(2n \pm \frac{1}{2}\right)^2 - ia^2c^{-2}\pi\left(2n \pm \frac{1}{2}\right) + 4d_1 - \frac{1}{2}\sigma_1^2\pi^2\left(2m \pm \frac{1}{2}\right)^2 - \\ &- \frac{1}{4}(k \pm \theta_{zm})^2. \end{aligned}$$

The set of Euler solutions of the linear boundary value problem (15), (16)

$$u^{\pm}(t, x, \varepsilon) = \sum_{k,m,n=-\infty}^{\infty} \xi_{kmn}^{\pm} \exp\left[i\left(\pi\left(2m \pm \frac{1}{2}\right)\varepsilon^{-1} \pm \theta_{zm} + k\right)x + \lambda_{kmn}^{\pm}(\varepsilon)t\right]$$

can be written in the form

$$\begin{aligned} u^{\pm}(t, x, \varepsilon) =& E^{\pm}(t, x) \sum_{k,m,n=-\infty}^{\infty} \xi_{kmn}^{\pm}(\tau) \exp\left[ikx + 2i\pi nc^{-1}x_1 + 2i\pi my\right] = \\ &= \xi^{\pm}(\tau, x, x_1, y). \end{aligned} \tag{86}$$

Here,

$$E^{\pm}(t, x) = \exp\left[\pm i\frac{\pi}{2}\left(c^{-1}(1 - \varepsilon ac^{-1})t + (\varepsilon^{-1} + \theta_{zm})x\right)\right],$$

$$\xi_{kmn}^{\pm}(\tau) = \xi_{kmn}^{\pm} \exp\left(\lambda_{2kmn}^{\pm} + O(\varepsilon)\tau\right), \quad y = x\varepsilon^{-1}, \quad x_1 = (1 + \varepsilon ac^{-1})t.$$

Given that $E^-(t,x) = \overline{E}^+(t,x)$, we will look for solutions of the nonlinear boundary value problem (14), (16) in the form of

$$u(t,x) = \varepsilon\Big(E(t,x)\xi(\tau,x,x_1,y) + \overline{cc}\Big) + \varepsilon^3 u_3(\tau,x,x_1,y) + \dots. \tag{87}$$

Substituting (87) into (14) and performing the standard steps, we arrive at the boundary value problem for determining the unknown function $\xi(\tau,x,y,x_1)$:

$$c\frac{\partial\xi}{\partial\tau} = -\Big(1-\frac{1}{2}a^2\Big)\frac{\partial^2\xi}{\partial x_1^2} + \frac{\partial\xi}{\partial x_1}\Big(\frac{a^2}{c} - \frac{i\pi}{c}\Big(1-\frac{1}{2}a^2\Big)\Big) + \frac{\partial^2\xi}{\partial x^2} + i\theta_z\cdot\frac{\partial\xi}{\partial x} - \frac{\sigma_1^2}{2}\cdot\frac{\partial^2\xi}{\partial y^2} +$$
$$+ i\sigma_1^2\pi^2\cdot\frac{\partial\xi}{\partial y} + \Big(2d_1 + \frac{\pi^2}{4c^2}\Big(1-\frac{1}{2}a^2\Big) + i\frac{a^2\pi^2}{c^2} - \frac{1}{2}\theta_z^2 - \frac{1}{8}\sigma_1^2\pi^2\Big)\xi + b_1\xi|\xi|^2, \tag{88}$$

$$\xi(\tau,x+2\pi,x_1,y) \equiv \xi(\tau,x,x_1,y) \equiv \xi(\tau,x,x_1+c,y) \equiv \xi(\tau,x,x_1,y+1). \tag{89}$$

As a result of the above constructions, we come to the justification of the following result.

Theorem 9. *Let conditions* (53), (54) *and* (85) *be satisfied. Let $\theta_{z0} \in [0,1)$ be arbitrarily fixed, and let $\xi(\tau,x,x_1,y)$ be a bounded solution of the boundary value problem* (88)–(89) *as $\tau \to \infty$, $x \in [0,2\pi]$, $y \in [0,1]$, $x_1 \in [0,c]$. Then, for the sequence $\varepsilon_s(\theta_z(\varepsilon_s(\theta_{z0}) = \theta_{z0})$, the function*

$$u(t,x) = \varepsilon(E(t,x)\xi(\tau,x,x_1,y) + \overline{cc}) + \varepsilon^3 u_3(\tau,x,x_1,y)$$

satisfies the boundary value problem of (14), (16) *up to $o(\varepsilon_s^3)$ at $\theta_z = \theta_{z0}$.*

3.5.2. Building Quasinormal Forms under the Conditions $\Phi(s) = \Phi_2(s)$, $\sigma = \varepsilon\sigma_1$ and $A^2 > 2$

The values of the parameter z for which the critical cases are realized are determined by the following relation:

$$z_m = \pi(2m+1); \quad m = 0, \pm1, \pm2, \dots.$$

Thus, $\gamma_0(z_m) = -2$ and $p_0 = 1$, $\omega_0 = \Omega_0 = 0$, $d_0 = 1/2$. It follows from the condition $\varepsilon = 2\pi N^{-1}$ that

$$\theta_z = \theta_{zm} = \begin{cases} 0, & \text{if N} - \text{even}, \\ \frac{1}{2}, & \text{if N} - \text{odd}. \end{cases}$$

Below, we separately consider the cases where $\theta_z = 0$ and where $\theta_z = 1/2$.

3.5.3. Building Quasinormal Forms for $\theta_z = 0$

For the roots $\lambda_{kmn}(\varepsilon)$ $(k,m,n = 0,\pm1,\pm2,\dots)$ of the characteristic Equation (17) whose real parts tend to zero as $\varepsilon \to 0$, the following asymptotic equality takes place:

$$\lambda_{kmn}(\varepsilon) = i\pi(2n+1) + \varepsilon\lambda_{1kmn} + \varepsilon^2\lambda_{2kmn} + \dots, \tag{90}$$
$$\lambda_{1kmn} = -iac^{-2}\pi(2n+1) + \frac{1}{2}ic^{-1}k,$$
$$c\lambda_{2kmn} = \Big(1-\frac{1}{2}a^2\Big)(\pi(2n+1)c^{-1})^2 - \frac{1}{8}k^2 - \frac{1}{2}\sigma_1^2(\pi(2m+1))^2 - \frac{1}{2}a\pi(2n+1)k +$$
$$+ ia^2c^{-1}\pi(2n+1) - ia(2c)^{-1}k + 2d_1.$$

The solutions of the linear boundary value problem (15), (16) can then be written in the form

$$
\begin{aligned}
u(t,x) = &\sum_{k,m,n=-\infty}^{\infty} \xi_{kmn} \exp\left[i\pi(2m+1)\varepsilon^{-1}x + kx + \left(i\pi(2n+1)(1-\varepsilon ac^{-1}) - \right.\right.\\
&\left.\left. - \varepsilon a(2c)^{-1}k\right)t + (\lambda_{2kmn} + O(\varepsilon))\tau\right] = \\
&= \sum_{k,m,n=-\infty}^{\infty} \xi_{kmn}(\tau) \exp\left[i\pi(2m+1)y + i\pi(2n+1)x_1 + ikx_2\right] = \\
&= \xi(\tau, x_1, x_2, y),
\end{aligned} \tag{91}
$$

where

$$
\begin{aligned}
&\xi_{kmn}(\tau) = \xi_{kmn} \cdot \exp[(\lambda_{2kmn} + O(\varepsilon))\tau], \\
&x_1 = (1-\varepsilon ac^{-1})t, \quad x_2 = x - \varepsilon a(2c)^{-1}t, \quad y = x\varepsilon^{-1}.
\end{aligned} \tag{92}
$$

Based on equality (91), we seek solutions to the nonlinear boundary value problem (14), (16) of the form

$$
u(t,x,\varepsilon) = \varepsilon\xi(\tau,x_1,x_2,y) + \varepsilon u_3(\tau,x_1,x_2,y) + \dots .
$$

Substituting this expression into (14) and performing the standard steps, we arrive at the parabolic boundary value problem for finding a real function $\xi(\tau,x_1,x_2,y)$:

$$
\begin{aligned}
c\frac{\partial\xi}{\partial\tau} =& \left(\frac{1}{2}a^2 - 1\right)\frac{\partial^2\xi}{\partial x_1^2} + \frac{1}{8}\frac{\partial^2\xi}{\partial x_2^2} + \frac{\sigma_1^2}{2}\cdot\frac{\partial^2\xi}{\partial y^2} - \frac{1}{2}\frac{\partial^2\xi}{\partial x_1\partial x_2} + ac^{-1}\frac{\partial\xi}{\partial x_1} - \\
&- a(2c)^{-1}\frac{\partial\xi}{\partial x_2} + 2d_1\xi + b_1\xi|\xi|^2,
\end{aligned} \tag{93}
$$

with the boundary conditions

$$
-\xi(\tau,x_1+c,x_2,y) \equiv \xi(\tau,x_1,x_2,y) \equiv \xi(\tau,x_1,x_2+2\pi,y), \tag{94}
$$

$$
-\xi(\tau,x_1,x_2,y+1) \equiv \xi(\tau,x_1,x_2,y). \tag{95}
$$

This boundary value problem is a quasinormal form in the considered case.

3.5.4. Quasinormal Form for $\theta_z = 1/2$

In this case, let us give the following formulas for the elements of λ_{1kmn} and λ_{2kmn} :

$$
\begin{aligned}
\lambda_{1kmn} &= -iac^{-2}\pi(2n+1) + \frac{1}{2}ic^{-1}\left(\frac{1}{2}+k\right), \\
c\lambda_{2kmn} &= \left(1 - \frac{1}{2}a^2\right)(\pi(2n+1)c^{-1})^2 - \frac{1}{8}k^2 - \frac{1}{2}\sigma_1^2(\pi(2m+1))^2 - \\
&- \frac{1}{2}a\pi(2n+1)c^{-1}\left(\frac{1}{2}+k\right) + ia^2c^{-2}\pi(2n+1) - ia(2c)^{-1}\left(\frac{1}{2}+k\right) + 2d_1.
\end{aligned}
$$

The "critical" solutions of the linear boundary value problem (15), (16) can be written in the form

$$
\begin{aligned}
u(t,x) =& E(t,x)\sum_{k,m,n=-\infty}^{\infty} \xi_{kmn} \exp\left[i\pi(2m+1)y + i\pi(2n+1)x_1 + ikx_2\right] = \\
&= E(t,x)\xi(\tau,x_1,x_2,y),
\end{aligned}
$$

where

$$
E(t,x) = \exp\left[i\frac{1}{2}(x + \varepsilon(2c)^{-1}t)\right] = \exp\left[i\frac{1}{2}x_2\right].
$$

Therefore, solutions of the nonlinear boundary value problem (14), (16) are sought in the form

$$u(t,x,\varepsilon) = \varepsilon\big(E(t,x)\xi(\tau,x_1,x_2,y) + \overline{cc}\big) + \varepsilon^3 u_3(t,\tau,x_1,x_2,y) + \dots.$$

Let us substitute this expression into (14). After straightforward calculations, we obtain a parabolic boundary value problem, namely, a quasinormal form, for finding the complex function $\xi(\tau,x_1,x_2,y)$:

$$c\frac{\partial\xi}{\partial\tau} = \left(\frac{1}{2}a^2 - 1\right)\frac{\partial^2\xi}{\partial x_1^2} + \frac{1}{8}\frac{\partial^2\xi}{\partial x_2^2} + \frac{\sigma_1^2}{2}\cdot\frac{\partial^2\xi}{\partial y^2} - \frac{1}{2}\frac{\partial^2\xi}{\partial x_1\partial x_2} + \left(i\frac{a}{2} + ac^{-1}\right)\frac{\partial\xi}{\partial x_1} + \\ + \left(\frac{i}{8} - a(2c)^{-1}\right)\frac{\partial\xi}{\partial x_2} + \left(2d_1 - \frac{1}{32} - \frac{ia}{4c}\right)\xi + 3b_1\xi|\xi|^2 \qquad (96)$$

with boundary conditions (94) and (95).

Let us make one remark. In the right part of (96), there is no term of the form $Const\cdot E^2(t,x)\xi^3$. This is due to the fact that

$$E(t,x) = \exp\left[i\frac{1}{2}(x + (2c\varepsilon)^{-1}\tau)\right].$$

As a result of the principle of averaging over a rapidly oscillating periodic argument τ (see, e.g., [16,17]), the corresponding term in the principal term vanishes.

3.6. *Building a Quasinormal Form under the Conditions* $\Phi(s) = \Phi_2(s)$, $\sigma = \varepsilon\sigma_1$, $0 < a^2 < 2$

We first give the values of the coefficients $\lambda_{1,2,kmn}$ in formula (90) for the asymptotic representation of the roots $\lambda_{kmn}(\varepsilon)$ $(k,m,n = 0,\pm1,\pm2,\dots)$ of the characteristic Equation (17):

$$\lambda_{1kmn} = -2i(ac)^{-1}R + i(2c)^{-1}(\theta_z + k),$$
$$c\lambda_{2kmn} = -\frac{1}{2}\left(2a^{-1}R + \frac{1}{2}(\theta_z+k)\right)^2 + \frac{1}{2}\left(2a^{-1}R - \frac{1}{2}(\theta_z+k)\right)(\theta_z+k) - \\ - c^{-1}(\theta_z+k)^2 + (p_0\exp(i\Omega_0))^{-1}R^2 + 2\omega_0\left(2a^{-1}R - \frac{1}{2}(\theta_z+k)\right) - \\ - 2ic^{-1}R + ia(2c)^{-1}(\theta_z+k) - \frac{1}{2}\sigma_1^2\big(\pi(2m+1)\big)^2 + 2d_1p_0^{-1},$$

where $R = (\theta_\omega - \Omega_0 + \pi(2n+1))c^{-1}$.

Let us write the "critical" solutions of the linear boundary value problem (15), (16) in the form

$$u(t,x) = E(t,x)\sum_{k,m,n=-\infty}^{\infty}\xi_{kmn}\exp\left[i\pi(2n+1)x_1 + ikx_2 + i\pi(2m+1)y\right] = \\ = E(t,x)\xi(\tau,x_1,x_2,y),$$

where

$$E(t,x) = \exp\left[i(\omega_0\varepsilon^{-1} + (\theta_\omega - \Omega_0)c^{-1}(1 - 2\varepsilon ac^{-1}) + \varepsilon c^{-1}\theta_z)t + i\theta_z x\right],$$

and for $x_{1,2}$ and y, the relations in (92) hold. Then, the solutions of the nonlinear boundary value problem (14), (16) are found in the form

$$u(t,x,\varepsilon) = \varepsilon\big(E(t,x)\xi(\tau,x_1,x_2,y) + \overline{cc}\big) + \varepsilon^3 u_3(t,\tau,x_1,x_2,y) + \dots, \qquad (97)$$

and the dependence on t, x_1, x_2 and y is periodic. Let us substitute (97) into (14), and in the resulting formal identity, we will successively equate the coefficients of the same powers of ε. As a result, we arrive at an equation for u_3, from the solvability condition of which we obtain a boundary value problem for determining the unknown amplitude $\xi(\tau, x_1, x_2, y)$ in the specified class of functions:

$$c\frac{\partial\xi}{\partial\tau} = H_1\frac{\partial^2\xi}{\partial x_1^2} + H_2\frac{\partial\xi}{\partial x_1} - \frac{1}{8}\frac{\partial^2\xi}{\partial x_2^2} + H_3\frac{\partial\xi}{\partial x_2} + \left(\frac{1}{4} - a^{-1}\right)\frac{\partial^2\xi}{\partial x_1\partial x_2} + \\ + \frac{1}{2}\sigma_1^2\frac{\partial^2\xi}{\partial y^2} + H_4\xi + 3\beta\xi|\xi|^2 \quad (98)$$

with boundary conditions (94) and (95), where

$$H_1 = -\varkappa^{-1} + \frac{1}{2}(ia - 2\omega_0)^2\varkappa^{-2},$$
$$H_2 = c^{-1}\Big[-2(\varkappa^{-1} - \frac{1}{2}(ia - 2\omega_0)^2\varkappa^{-2}(\theta_\omega - \Omega_0)) + c\varkappa^{-2}2\omega_0(2\omega_0 - ia) + \\ + c^2\varkappa^{-1}a(\theta_\omega - \Omega_0)\Big],$$
$$H_3 = i\big[2\theta_z - \big(-(2a)^{-1}(\theta_\omega - \Omega_0) + a^{-1} - \omega_0 + ia(2c)^{-1}\big)\big],$$
$$H_4 = -\frac{1}{2}\left(2(\theta_\omega - \Omega_0) + \frac{1}{2}\theta_z\right)^2 + \frac{1}{2}\left(2a^{-1}(\theta_\omega - \Omega_0) - \frac{1}{2}\theta_z\right)\theta_z - c^{-1}\theta_z^2 + \\ + \left(p_0\exp(i\Omega_0)^{-1}(\theta_\omega - \Omega_0) + 2\omega_0(2a^{-1}(\theta_\omega - \Omega_0) - \frac{1}{2}\theta_z\right) + 2ic^{-1}(\theta_\omega - \Omega_0) + \\ + ia(2c)^{-1}\theta_z + 2d_1p_0^{-1},$$
$$\beta = b_1 + i\omega_0b_2 - \omega_0^2b_3 - i\omega_0^3b_4.$$

Recall that, depending on the evenness or oddness of N, the value of θ_z takes a value of 0 or 1/2.

The main result is that the boundary value problem (94), (95), (98) obtained here plays the role of a quasinormal form for the boundary value problem (14), (16) in the above critical case.

4. Conclusions

The local dynamics of a system of coupled identical oscillators are considered. The large number of oscillators gave grounds for the transition to the consideration of the boundary value problem with a continuous spatial variable. The presence of a large delay in the couplings made it possible to use special asymptotic methods [20,21].

Critical cases in the problem of the stability of the zero equilibrium state were singled out. It was shown that all of them have infinite dimensionality, so the known methods of local analysis based on the use of methods of invariant integral manifolds and methods of normal forms [22,23] are not directly applicable. This research is based on special infinite normalization methods [24,25]. The main results include the construction of the analogs of normal forms—quasinormal forms—nonlinear equations of the parabolic type containing no small parameters. Their nonlocal dynamics determine the local dynamics of the original problem. The corresponding quasinormal forms contain two or three spatial variables, so we can conclude that the dynamics of the problems under consideration are, in general, complex. Asymptotic formulas linking the solutions of quasinormal forms and solutions of the original equation were given.

We emphasize that asymptotic approximations were constructed on an infinite time interval. Therefore, a quasinormal form requires the existence of a bounded solution on the entire axis. Most often, "quasinormal forms" are boundary value problems of the parabolic type, which have the property of local solvability. Based on the known results of the numerical analysis of such problems (see, e.g., [26]), one can often conclude that solutions bounded on the entire axis exist. However, in the present paper, we do not talk about the asymptotics of exact solutions of the original system, but about the asymptotic approximation of functions satisfying the original system with a certain degree of accuracy. Of course, one can formulate conclusions about determining the asymptotics of solutions by means of solutions of a quasinormal form on a finite $O(\varepsilon^{-1})$-order time-varying interval, especially since the dependence on the time variable $x_1 = c^{-1}(1 - \varepsilon c^{-1}a)t$ is periodic.

It is interesting to note that, in the case of $a^2 > 2$, the quasinormal forms contain a coefficient at nonlinearity b_1 and do not contain the coefficients of b_2, b_3 or b_4. In the case of $a^2 < 2$, the quasinormal forms contain all coefficients of the function f.

The parameter a plays an important role in the dynamics of quasinormal forms. The structure of solutions in the case $a^2 < 2$ is much more complicated than in the case $a^2 > 2$, because quasinormal forms at $a^2 < 2$ are complex boundary value problems of the Ginzburg–Landau type, and the solutions contain rapidly oscillating t components. Explicit formulas are obtained that allow us to trace the role of the parameter c, included in the delay coefficient (13).

Quasinormal forms do not explicitly contain the parameter ε but depend essentially on ε through θ_ω and θ_z. As $\varepsilon \to 0$, these quantities run indefinitely from 0 to $c\omega_0$ and from 0 to 1, respectively. At the same time, unlimited alternations of forward and backward bifurcations can be observed in quasinormal forms. This indicates the high sensitivity of the dynamical properties to changes in the parameter ε and, hence, to changes in the values of N and T. In particular, even changing a large value of N to 1 can significantly affect the dynamics of the problem.

Cases where the parameter σ is small enough were considered. It was shown that quasinormal forms become even more complicated, since there appears a third spatial variable, and the dimensionality of the diffusion operator increases. It entails the complication of the dynamics of the initial problem. It is important to note that the condition $\sigma \ll 1$ is of special interest: the couplings between elements are more "close" to those that arise at standard approximations of the diffusion and advection operators (see (11), (12)).

It is interesting to note that, under the condition $T \gg 1$, we were able to obtain explicit formulas for all parameters defining the critical cases.

Let us focus on the most interesting differences in the structure of the solutions for the cases $\Phi(s) = \Phi_1(s)$ and $\Phi(s) = \Phi_2(s)$. The "critical" modes are adjacent to the values $z_0\varepsilon^{-1} + \theta_z$, and these values are determined by relations (52) and (61). When σ is small, these values are also different. In the first case, $z_m = \pi(m + 1/2)$, and in the second, $\pi(2m + 1)$ $(m = 0, \pm1, \pm2, \ldots)$. Not only are the coefficients and even the number of equations in the corresponding quasinormal forms different, but the boundary conditions (89) and (94), (95) are also different. Thus, the dynamics, even in the case of different advective-type couplings, can be essentially different.

The obtained results can be extended to other systems with diffusive, advective or other couplings (see, for example, [27]). We note that accounting for quadratic nonlinearities in (14) does not lead to additional difficulties.

It is important to emphasize that the principal terms of the asymptotics of the solutions of the original equation are determined by the solutions of the (nonlocal) quasinormal forms.

Funding: This work was supported by the Russian Science Foundation (project no. 21-71-30011), https://rscf.ru/en/project/21-71-30011/ (accessed on 25 December 2023).

Data Availability Statement: Data are contained within the article.

Conflicts of Interest: The author declares no conflicts of interest. The funder had no role in the design of the study; in the collection, analyses or interpretation of data; in the writing of the manuscript; or in the decision to publish the results.

References

1. Kuznetsov, A.P.; Kuznetsov, S.P.; Sataev, I.R.; Turukina, L.V. About Landau—Hopf scenario in a system of coupled self-oscillators. *Phys. Lett. A* **2013**, *377*, 3291–3295. [CrossRef]
2. Osipov, G.V.; Pikovsky, A.S.; Rosenblum, M.G.; Kurths, J. Phase synchronization effects in a lattice of nonidentical Rossler oscillators. *Phys. Rev. E* **1997**, *55*, 2353–2361. [CrossRef]
3. Pikovsky, A.S.; Rosenblum, M.G.; Kurths, J. *Synchronization: A Universal Concept in Nonlinear Sciences*; Cambridge University Press: Cambridge, UK, 2001.
4. Dodla, R.; Se, A.; Johnston, G.L. Phase-locked patterns and amplitude death in a ring of delay-coupled limit cycle oscillators. *Phys. Rev. E* **2004**, *69*, 12. [CrossRef] [PubMed]
5. Williams, C.R.S.; Sorrentino, F.; Murphy, T.E.; Roy, R. Synchronization states and multistability in a ring of periodic oscillators: Experimentally variable coupling delays. *Chaos Interdiscip. J. Nonlinear Sci.* **2013**, *23*, 43117. [CrossRef] [PubMed]
6. Rao, R.; Lin, Z.; Ai, X.; Wu, J. Synchronization of Epidemic Systems with Neumann Boundary Value under Delayed Impulse. *Mathematics* **2022**, *10*, 2064. [CrossRef]
7. Van Der Sande, G.; Soriano, M.C.; Fischer, I.; Mirasso, C.R. Dynamics, correlation scaling, and synchronization behavior in rings of delay-coupled oscillators. *Phys. Rev. E* **2008**, *77*, 55202. [CrossRef] [PubMed]
8. Klinshov, V.V.; Nekorkin, V.I. Synchronization of delay-coupled oscillator networks. *Physics-Uspekhi* **2013**, *56*, 1217–1229. [CrossRef]
9. Heinrich, G.; Ludwig, M.; Qian, J.; Kubala, B.; Marquardt, F. Collective dynamics in optomechanical arrays. *Phys. Rev. Lett.* **2011**, *107*, 043603. [CrossRef] [PubMed]
10. Zhang, M.; Wiederhecker, G.S.; Manipatruni, S.; Barnard, A.; McEuen, P.; Lipson, M. Synchronization of micromechanical oscillators using light. *Phys. Rev. Lett.* **2012**, *109*, 233906. [CrossRef] [PubMed]
11. Lee, T. E.; Sadeghpour, H.R. Quantum synchronization of quantum van der Pol oscillators with trapped ions. *Phys. Rev. Lett.* **2013**, *111*, 234101. [CrossRef] [PubMed]
12. Yanchuk, S.; Wolfrum, M. Instabilities of stationary states in lasers with longdelay optical feedback. *SIAM Appl. Dyn. Syst.* **2012**, *9*, 519–535. [CrossRef]
13. Kashchenko, S.A. Asymptotics of regular and irregular solutions in chains of coupled van der Pol equations. *Mathematics* **2023**, *11*, 2047. [CrossRef]
14. Kashchenko, S.A. Infinite Turing bifurcations in chains of van der Pol systems. *Mathematics* **2022**, *10*, 3769. [CrossRef]
15. Grigorieva, E.V.; Kashchenko, S.A. Phase-synchronized oscillations in a unidirectional ring of pump-coupled lasers. *Opt. Commun.* **2023**, *545*, 129688. [CrossRef]
16. Bogoliubov, N.N.; Mitropolsky, Y.A. *Asymptotic Methods in the Theory of Nonlinear Oscillations*; Hindustan Publishing Corporation: Delhi, India, 1961; 547p.
17. Kashchenko, S.A. Application of the averaging principle to the study of the dynamics of the delay logistic equation. *Math. Notes* **2018**, *104*, 231–243. [CrossRef]
18. Vasil'eva, A.B.; Butuzov, V.F. *Asymptotic Expansions of the Solutions of Singularly Perturbed Equations*; Nauka: Moscow, Russia, 1973; 272p.
19. Nefedov, N.N. Development of methods of asymptotic analysis of transition layers in reaction–diffusion–advection equations: Theory and applications. *Comput. Math. Math. Phys.* **2021**, *61*, 2068–2087. [CrossRef]
20. Kaschenko, S.A. Normalization in the systems with small diffusion. *Int. J. Bifurc. Chaos Appl. Sci. Eng.* **1996**, *6*, 1093–1109. [CrossRef]
21. Kashchenko, S.A. The Ginzburg–Landau equation as a normal form for a second-order difference-differential equation with a large delay. *Comput. Math. Math. Phys.* **1998**, *38*, 443–451.
22. Marsden, J.E.; McCracken, M.F. *The Hopf Bifurcation and Its Applications*; Springer: New York, NY, USA, 1976; 421p.
23. Hale, J.K. *Theory of Functional Differential Equations*, 2nd ed.; Springer: New York, NY, USA, 1977.
24. Kashchenko, S.A. On quasinormal forms for parabolic equations with small diffusion. *Sov. Math. Dokl.* **1988**, *37*, 510–513. Available online: Http://www.ams.org/mathscinet-getitem?mr=0947229 (accessed on 13 March 2017).
25. Grigorieva, E.V.; Haken, H.; Kashchenko, S.A. Complexity near equilibrium in model of lasers with delayed optoelectronic feedback. In Proceedings of the 1998 International Symposium on Nonlinear Theory and Its Applications, Crans-Montana, Switzerland, 14–17 September 1998; pp. 495–498.
26. Akhromeeva, T.S.; Kurdyumov, S.P.; Malinetskii, G.G.; Samarskii, A.A. *Nonstationary Structures and Diffusion Chaos*; Nauka: Moscow, Russia, 1992; 544p.
27. Kashchenko, S.A. Dynamics of chains of many oscillators with Unidirectional and bidirectional delay coupling. *Comput. Math. Math. Phys.* **2023**, *63*, 1817–1836. [CrossRef]

Σ mathematics MDPI

Article

Periodic Solutions to Nonlinear Second-Order Difference Equations with Two-Dimensional Kernel

Daniel Maroncelli

Department of Mathematics, College of Charleston, Charleston, SC 29424, USA; maroncellidm@cofc.edu

Abstract: In this work, we provide conditions for the existence of periodic solutions to nonlinear, second-order difference equations of the form $y(t+2) + by(t+1) + cy(t) = g(y(t))$, where b and c are real parameters, $c \neq 0$, and $g : \mathbb{R} \to \mathbb{R}$ is continuous.

Keywords: periodic difference equations; resonance; Lyapunov-Schmidt procedure; Schaefer's fixed point theorem

MSC: 39A23; 39A27

1. Introduction

In this work, we provide conditions for the existence of periodic solutions to nonlinear, second-order difference equations of the form

$$y(t+2) + by(t+1) + cy(t) = g(y(t)). \tag{1}$$

Throughout our discussion, we will assume that b and c are real parameters, $c \neq 0$, and $g : \mathbb{R} \to \mathbb{R}$ is continuous.

In the paper [1], the authors prove the existence of N-periodic solutions to (1) under various restrictions on the nonlinearity g, the parameters b and c, and the period N. Two of the most prominent results are the following:

Proposition 1. *Suppose that the following conditions hold:*

A1. $\lim_{r\to\infty} \frac{\|g\|_r}{r} = 0$, *where, for* $s > 0$, $\|g\|_s = \sup_{x\in[-s,s]} |g(x)|$;

A2. *there exists a positive number* $\hat{z}$ *such that* $xg(x) > 0$ *whenever* $|x| > \hat{z}$;

A3. *if* $N \arccos(-\frac{b}{2})$ *is a multiple of* 2π, *then* $c \neq 1$ *or* $2 \leq |b|$.

If N *is odd with* $N > 1$, *then (1) has a* N*-periodic solution.*

Proposition 2. *Suppose the following conditions hold:*

B1. $c = 1$, $|b| < 2$, *and* $N \arccos(-\frac{b}{2}) = 2\pi r$ *for some* $r \in \mathbb{N}$;

B2. *the function* g *is bounded, say by* K;

B3. *there are constants* $\hat{z}$ *and* $J > 0$ *such that for all* $x \in \mathbb{R}$ *with* $x \geq \hat{z}$, $g(-x) \leq -J < 0 < J \leq g(x)$;

B4. $\frac{N}{gcd(r,N)} \geq \max\left\{3, \frac{K}{J} + 1\right\}$, *where* $gcd(r,N)$ *denotes the greatest common divisor of* r *and* N.

If N *is odd, then (1) has a* N*-periodic solution.*

Clearly, the assumptions of Proposition 1 generate the existence of solutions to (1) for a more general class of nonlinearities, g, than do the assumptions of Proposition 2, since unbounded nonlinearities can easily satisfy the conditions of Proposition 1. For particular

Citation: Maroncelli, D. Periodic Solutions to Nonlinear Second-Order Difference Equations with Two-Dimensional Kernel. *Mathematics* **2024**, *12*, 849. https://doi.org/10.3390/math12060849

Academic Editors: Lingju Kong and Min Wang

Received: 19 February 2024
Revised: 9 March 2024
Accepted: 12 March 2024
Published: 14 March 2024

examples of such g, see [1]. Now, the reason that Proposition 2 requires stronger conditions on the nonlinearity, g, is simple. In Proposition 1, the assumption A3. ensures that the dimension of the solution space to the N-periodic homogeneous problem

$$y(t+2) + by(t+1) + cy(t) = 0 \tag{2}$$

is one-dimensional. In Proposition 2, condition B1. forces the solution space to (2) to be two-dimensional. See the appendix for the details. When the solution space of (2) is two-dimensional, the analysis of (1) is more complex, as the interaction of the solution space and the nonlinearity is much more complicated. For this reason, additional requirements were placed.

As a final remark at the end of [1], the authors left open the question of whether similar results to Proposition 2 hold without a boundedness assumption placed on g. In particular, they posed the question of whether the existence of solutions to (1) could be proved when condition B1. holds, but under assumptions "similar" to A1. and A2. In this paper, we show that this is indeed the case; that is, we prove the existence of solutions to (1) when B1. holds and assumptions A1. and A2. are valid. Interestingly, we will also show that this more general result holds when N is even, something that is not discussed in [1], where they always assume N is odd. We will also discuss the existence of solutions to (1) when $b = 0$, $c = -1$, and N is even with $N \geq 4$. As it turns out, see the appendix for the details, for real parameters b and c, the case when $b = 0$ and $c = -1$ is the only case in which condition B1. does not hold, and the solution space of (2) is two-dimensional. So, in this regard, this paper shows that conditions A1. and A2. of Proposition 1 are sufficient to prove the existence of solutions to (1) in all cases where the solution space of (2) is two-dimensional.

To provide a bit more concreteness to the discussion above, we list here, for reference, our main result, Theorem 2, which will be proved in Section 3.

Theorem (Theorem 2). *Suppose the following conditions hold:*

C1. *the solution space to* (2) *is two-dimensional;*

C2. $\lim_{s \to \infty} \frac{\|g\|_s}{s} = 0$, *where, for* $w > 0$, $\|g\|_w = \sup_{x \in [-w,w]} |g(x)|$;

C3. *there is a positive number* $\hat{z}$ *such that* $xg(x) > 0$ *whenever* $|x| > \hat{z}$.

Then (12) has a N-periodic solution.

Remark 1. *We would like to point out, while Propositions 1 and 2, and Theorem 2 are close by, that Theorem 2 is obviously a substantial generalization of Proposition 2; we will discuss the various "advantages" of Theorem 2 in more detail after the proof of Theorem 2. Additionally, Theorem 2 is also the "ideal" analog of Proposition 1 in the more complicated setting where the solution space to* (2) *is two-dimensional. However, as similar as the statements of Proposition 1 and Theorem 2 may be, their proofs take an entirely different route. In fact, the proof of Theorem 2 differs, almost in its entirety, from the original proofs of Propositions 1 and 2 (found in [1]), and it is this new approach that makes our work novel.*

The theory of periodic solutions to nonlinear differential/difference equations is extensive. Most of the deep results in this setting are for problems in which an associated linear homogeneous problem has at most a one-dimensional kernel. There are also some known results when the dimension of this solution space is odd but of a higher dimension. Very little is known in cases of resonance where the dimension of resonance is even. For those readers interested in known results in this area of study, we mention a few that are relevant to this work. In [2–5], periodic solutions are analyzed. In [6–11] the authors study the existence of solutions to nonlinear discrete Sturm-Liouville problems. Refs. [12–15] establish existence results for multi-point problems. Positive solutions are treated in [16–18]. Results regarding the existence of multiple solutions may be found in [19–21].

The paper is organized as follows: In Section 2, we introduce the preliminary ideas needed to study (1) from an operator theoretic point of view. Section 2 contains nothing novel and is included simply for completeness. Those familiar with the theory of linear difference equations at resonance can safely skim Section 2 and move directly to Section 3. Section 3 contains our main result, which is proved using Schaefer's fixed theorem. Section 4 contains an example showing the type of nonlinearities we had in mind when developing the main result, Theorem 2. Section 5 contains some concluding remarks. Lastly, in Appendix A, we conclude the paper with an appendix that contains calculations verifying the dimension of the solution space to (2) under various conditions on the real parameters b and c. The calculations in the appendix are not difficult; however, they are a bit tedious, which is why we have designated them as an appendix.

2. Preliminaries

We begin with several preliminary ideas that will be needed to develop our main result, Theorem 2. All of the statements in this section are well-known and can be found in [1]. We include these results to improve readability, especially for those who may not be experts in this area, and to make the document essentially self-contained.

Our approach to analyzing the nonlinear boundary value problem, (1), will be to view it as an operator problem for an equivalent system of difference equations. We start by defining

$$A = \begin{pmatrix} 0 & 1 \\ -c & -b \end{pmatrix},$$

and $f : \mathbb{R}^2 \to \mathbb{R}^2$ by

$$f(u,v) = \begin{pmatrix} 0 \\ g(u) \end{pmatrix}.$$

If we let $x(t)$ denote $\begin{pmatrix} y(t) \\ y(t+1) \end{pmatrix}$, then finding N-periodic solutions to (1) is equivalent to solving

$$x(t+1) = Ax(t) + f(x(t)) \tag{3}$$

subject to

$$x(0) - x(N) = 0. \tag{4}$$

To view our new system in an operator theoretic framework, we introduce the following function space and associated operators: First, we let

$$X_N = \Big\{ \varphi : \mathbb{N}_0 \to \mathbb{R}^2 | \varphi \text{ is } N\text{-periodic} \Big\}.$$

We view X_N as a finite-dimensional normed space using the supremum norm, which we will denote by $\|\cdot\|$. When needed, we will use $|\cdot|$ to denote the standard Euclidean norm on $\mathbb{R}^2$. We now define operators

$\mathcal{L}\colon X_N \to X_N$ by

$$(\mathcal{L}x)(t) = x(t+1) - Ax(t),$$

and

$\mathcal{F}\colon X_N \to X_N$ by

$$\mathcal{F}(x)(t) = f(x(t)).$$

It should be clear that finding N-periodic solutions to (1) is now equivalent to solving

$$\mathcal{L}x = \mathcal{F}(x). \tag{5}$$

As a first step in our analysis of the nonlinear boundary value problem (1), we analyze the linear nonhomogeneous problem $\mathcal{L}x = h$, where h is a N-periodic function. Our characterization of the $\mathrm{im}(\mathcal{L})$ (the image of $\mathcal{L}$) will then be used to create a projection scheme, often referred to as the Lyapunov-Schmidt projection scheme, which will be used to analyze (1). The characterization of the $\mathrm{im}(\mathcal{L})$ is straightforward; it depends to a large extent on the fact that the principal fundamental matrix solution to

$$x(t+1) = Ax(t) \tag{6}$$

is given by $\Phi(t) = A^t$, where t is as in (6). For those readers not familiar with this result, we suggest [22,23]. Ref. [23] is a great resource for those already familiar with many standard results from the theory of linear ordinary differential equations. Ref. [22] has a nice introduction to several standard topics in difference equations, their discussion of periodic linear systems being the one most relevant to the work of this paper.

As our first introductory result, we completely characterize the $\mathrm{im}(\mathcal{L})$. As is often the case for differential and difference operators, the image of our mapping is "essentially" an orthogonal complement. As a matter of notation, since it will appear several times moving forward, we point out, that for any matrix C, we will use C^T to denote its transpose.

Proposition 3. *An element $h \in X_N$ is contained in the $\mathrm{im}(\mathcal{L})$ if and only if*

$$A^N \sum_{i=0}^{N-1} A^{-(i+1)} h(i) \in \ker\left(\left(I - A^N\right)^T\right)^{\perp},$$

where for any subspace E of $\mathbb{R}^2$, $E^{\perp} = \{v \in \mathbb{R}^2 \mid v^T w = 0$ for all $w \in E\}$.

Proof. Suppose $\mathcal{L}x = h$ for some $x \in X_N$. Using the variation of parameters formula, we have

$$x(t) = A^t x(0) + A^t \sum_{i=0}^{t-1} A^{-(i+1)} h(i).$$

Since $x(0) = x(N)$, we must have that

$$x(0) = x(N) = A^N x(0) + A^N \sum_{i=0}^{N-1} A^{-(i+1)} h(i).$$

It now easily follows that $\mathcal{L}x = h$ if and only if $A^N \sum_{i=0}^{N-1} A^{-(i+1)} h(i) \in \mathrm{im}(I - A^N)$. The statement of the proposition is now a consequence of the fact that for any square matrix C, $\mathrm{im}(C) = \ker(C^T)^{\perp}$. □

We also have the following result regarding the linear homogeneous system, (6).

Corollary 1. *The $\ker(\mathcal{L})$ and $\ker\left(I - A^N\right)$ have the same dimension.*

Proof. From the proof of Proposition 3, $\mathcal{L}x = 0$ if and only if $x(t) = A^t v$ and $(I - A^N)v = 0$ for some $v \in \mathbb{R}^2$. □

Let W denote any matrix whose columns form a basis for $\ker((I - A^N)^T)$. It follows from Proposition 3 that $h \in \mathrm{im}(\mathcal{L})$ if and only

$$W^T A^N \sum_{i=0}^{N-1} A^{-(i+1)} h(i) = 0.$$

For $t \in \mathbb{N}_0$, we define $\Psi(t) = \begin{cases} (A^N)^T W & t = 0 \\ (A^{-(i+1)})^T (A^N)^T W & t > 0 \end{cases}$. It is then a routine verification to show that $\mathcal{L}x = h$ if and only if

$$\sum_{i=0}^{N-1} \Psi^T(i+1)h(i) = 0. \tag{7}$$

During the proof of Theorem 2, we will take advantage of the fact that the columns of Ψ span the solution space of the N-periodic linear homogeneous "adjoint" problem.

$$\mathcal{L}^* x = 0, \tag{8}$$

where $\mathcal{L}^* : X_N \to X_N$ is defined by

$$(\mathcal{L}^* x)(t) = x(t+1) - A^{-T}x(t).$$

As a reminder, $(\cdot)^T$ denotes transpose. If you know a bit about adjoint operators, $\mathcal{L}^*$ is the adjoint operator of $\mathcal{L}$. From the basic theory of linear difference equations, we have that any fundamental matrix solution to the "adjoint" problem, (8), is of the form $\Psi(t)D$, for some invertible matrix D. Using (7), we have that $\mathcal{L}x = h$ if and only if

$$\sum_{i=0}^{N-1} \Gamma^T(i+1)h(i) = 0 \tag{9}$$

for any fundamental matrix solution to (8), Γ.

We intend to prove the existence of solutions to (1) using a Schaefer fixed point argument. In this setting, it will be useful to know that the "adjoint" system produces periodic solutions to a scalar difference equation which is very similar to (1). In fact, in the cases of interest to this paper, the adjoint scalar difference equation and (1) agree. The derivation, regardless of the dimension of $\ker(\mathcal{L})$, proceeds along the following lines: Calculating A^{-T}, we get

$$A^{-T} = \frac{1}{c}\begin{pmatrix} -b & c \\ -1 & 0 \end{pmatrix}. \tag{10}$$

It is now easy to see that solving (8) is equivalent to

$$\begin{aligned} cx_1(t+1) &= -bx_1(t) + cx_2(t) \\ cx_2(t+1) &= -x_1(t) \end{aligned}$$

or

$$cx_2(t+2) + bx_2(t+1) + x_2(t) = 0.$$

Thus, the second component of a solution to the "adjoint" system is a N-periodic solution to

$$cy(t+2) + by(t+1) + y(t) = 0. \tag{11}$$

As was mentioned above, we intend to analyze the nonlinear periodic problem (1) using an alternative method in conjunction with Schaefer's fixed point theorem. Crucial to the use of this alternative method is the construction of projections onto the kernel and image of $\mathcal{L}$. The proofs of the following two results are trivial, so they are omitted. For readers interested in the proofs of Propositions 4 and 5, see [4].

Proposition 4. *Let V be the orthogonal projection onto $\ker(I - A^N)$. If we define $P : X_N \to X_N$ by $(Px)(t) = A^t V x(0)$, then P is a projection onto the $\ker(\mathcal{L})$.*

Proposition 5. *If we define* $Q : X_N \to X_N$ *by*

$$(Qh)(t) = \Psi(t)\left(\sum_{j=0}^{N-1} |\Psi(j)|^2\right)^{-1} \sum_{i=0}^{N-1} \Psi^T(i)h(i),$$

then Q *is a projection with* $\ker(Q) = \operatorname{im}(\mathcal{L})$.

The following is a formulation of the alternative method we will use to analyze (1). Since under our assumptions, $\ker(\mathcal{L})$ will be two-dimensional, $\mathcal{L}$ will not be invertible. When $\mathcal{L}$ is not invertible, using fixed point methods to analyze (1) is not straightforward. However, the development of the Lyapunov-Schmidt projection scheme will allow us to define a mapping, say H, on appropriate sequence spaces, for which the solutions to (1) are precisely the fixed points of H. For those readers interested in a more thorough treatment of alternative methods, we suggest [24]. Again, this result is well-known, we include the proof of this result for the benefit of the reader.

Proposition 6. *Solving* $\mathcal{L}x = \mathcal{F}(x)$ *is equivalent to solving the system*

$$\begin{cases} x = Px + M_p(I-Q)\mathcal{F}(x) \\ \text{and} \\ Q\mathcal{F}(x) = 0 \end{cases},$$

where M_p *is* $(\mathcal{L}_{|Ker(P)})^{-1}$.

Proof. $\mathcal{L}x = \mathcal{F}(x)$ for some $x \in X_N$ if and only if

$$\begin{cases} (I-Q)(\mathcal{L}x - \mathcal{F}(x)) = 0 \\ \text{and} \\ Q(\mathcal{L}x - \mathcal{F}(x)) = 0 \end{cases}.$$

Since $Q\mathcal{L}x = 0$, we conclude

$$\begin{cases} \mathcal{L}x - (I-Q)\mathcal{F}(x) = 0 \\ \text{and} \\ Q\mathcal{F}(x) = 0 \end{cases}.$$

Applying M_p to the first equation in the system gives

$$\begin{cases} M_p\mathcal{L}x - M_p(I-Q)\mathcal{F}(x) = 0 \\ \text{and} \\ Q\mathcal{F}(x) = 0 \end{cases},$$

which is equivalent to

$$\begin{cases} (I-P)x - M_p(I-Q)\mathcal{F}(x) = 0 \\ \text{and} \\ Q\mathcal{F}(x) = 0 \end{cases}.$$

□

Remark 2. *Since* $\ker(Q) = \operatorname{im}(\mathcal{L})$, $Q\mathcal{F}(x) = 0$ *if and only if*

$$\sum_{i=0}^{N-1} \Gamma^T(i+1)\begin{pmatrix} 0 \\ g(x(i)) \end{pmatrix} = 0$$

for all fundamental matrix solutions Γ *to (8). We will return to this idea shortly when constructing the mapping, H, mentioned above.*

3. Existence Results When $\dim(\ker(\mathcal{L})) = 2$

In this section, we prove our main existence theorem for the periodic difference Equation (1). As a reminder, we are interested in finding N-periodic solutions to

$$y(t+2) + by(t+1) + cy(t) = g(y(t)) \tag{12}$$

for $N \in \mathbb{N}$ with $N \geq 3$. Our interest will be limited to cases where the solution space is a linear, homogeneous problem

$$y(t+2) + by(t+1) + cy(t) = 0 \tag{13}$$

is two-dimensional, since in this case very little is known. As has been mentioned in the introduction and is proved in the appendix, the solution space to (13) is two-dimensional only in the following cases:

R1. $c = 1$, $|b| < 2$, and $N \arccos(-\frac{b}{2}) = 2\pi r$ for some $r \in \mathbb{N}$;
R2. $c = -1$, $b = 0$, and $N \in 2\mathbb{Z}$ with $N \geq 4$.

The analysis of (12) depends, to some extent, on which condition R1. or R2. holds, and so for the ease of the reader, we have broken the proof of our main result, Theorem 2, into two cases.

As has been mentioned in our earlier discussion of Theorem 2, we will prove the existence of solutions to (1) when B1. of Proposition 2 holds and assumptions A1. and A2. of Proposition 1 are valid. Existence will be proved using Schaefer's fixed point theorem, which we now state for the convenience of the reader.

Theorem 1 (Schaefer's Theorem). *Let X be a finite-dimensional Banach space, and for* $\nu > 0$, *let* $\overline{B}(0,\nu)$ *denote the closed ball of radius* ν *centered at the origin, with* $\partial\overline{B}(0,\nu)$ *denoting its boundary. Suppose* $T : X \to X$ *is a continuous mapping. If there exists an* $R > 0$ *such that* $S = \{(x,\lambda) \in \partial\overline{B}(0,R) \times (0,1) \mid x = \lambda T(x)\} = \varnothing$, *then T has a fixed point in* $\overline{B}(0,R)$.

We now come to our main result.

Theorem 2. *Suppose the following conditions hold:*

C1. the solution space to (2) is two-dimensional, that is, suppose either R1. or R2. holds;
C2. $\lim_{s\to\infty} \frac{\|g\|_s}{s} = 0$, *where, for* $w > 0$, $\|g\|_w = \sup_{x\in[-w,w]} |g(x)|$;
C3. There exists a positive number $\hat{z}$ *such that* $xg(x) > 0$ *whenever* $|x| > \hat{z}$.

Then (12) has a N-periodic solution.

Proof. *(The case R1.)* We start by assuming that condition R1. holds; that is, we will be assuming that $c = 1$, $|b| < 2$, N is a fixed natural number with $N \geq 3$, and $N\theta = 2\pi r$ for some natural number r, where $\theta = \arccos\left(-\frac{b}{2}\right)$. In this case, see the appendix, it follows that

$$\Phi(t) = \begin{pmatrix} \cos(\theta t) & \sin(\theta t) \\ \cos(\theta(t+1)) & \sin(\theta(t+1)) \end{pmatrix}$$

is a fundamental matrix solution to (6). Since $c = 1$, we have found that the periodic scalar problems (1) and (11) agree, so that

$$\Gamma(t) = \begin{pmatrix} -\cos(\theta t) & -\sin(\theta t) \\ \cos(\theta(t-1)) & \sin(\theta(t-1)) \end{pmatrix}$$

is a fundamental matrix solution to the adjoint system (8).

Let

$$H(\alpha,x) = \begin{pmatrix} \alpha - \sum_{j=0}^{N-1} e^{i\theta j} g(\langle \alpha, e^{i\theta j}\rangle + [x]_1(j)) \\ M_p(I-Q)\mathcal{F}(\Phi(\cdot)\alpha + x) \end{pmatrix},$$

whenever $\alpha \in \mathbb{R}^2$ and $x \in \mathrm{im}(I-P)$, where here $e^{i\theta j} = \begin{pmatrix} \cos(\theta j) \\ \sin(\theta j) \end{pmatrix}$. From Proposition 6, Remark 2, and the discussion above, it follows that the solutions to (12) are precisely the fixed points of H. We will show that H has a fixed point using Schaefer's fixed point theorem.

The norm generating the topology on $\mathbb{R}^2 \times \mathrm{im}(I-P)$ is not terribly important, but for concreteness we make $\mathbb{R}^2 \times \mathrm{im}(I-P)$ a Banach space under the topology generated by the norm

$$\|(\alpha,x)\| = \max\{|\alpha|, \|x\|\}.$$

Let $S = \{(\alpha,x) \in \mathbb{R}^2 \times \mathrm{im}(I-P) \mid (\alpha,x) = \lambda H(\alpha,x) \text{ for some } \lambda \in (0,1)\}$. We will show that S is a bounded set, and thus, by Schaefer's theorem, H will have a fixed point. To reach a contradiction, suppose that S is unbounded and choose sequences $(\alpha_n)_{n\in\mathbb{N}}, (x_n)_{n\in\mathbb{N}}, (\lambda_n)_{n\in\mathbb{N}}$ with $(\alpha_n, x_n) = \lambda_n H(\alpha_n, x_n)$, and $\|(\alpha_n,x_n)\| \to \infty$. By going to subsequences if needed, we may assume that there exist $\alpha_0 \in \mathbb{R}^2, x_0 \in \mathrm{im}(I-P)$, and $\lambda_0 \in [0,1]$, with $\frac{1}{\|(\alpha_n,x_n)\|}(\alpha_n,x_n) \to (\alpha_0,x_0)$ and $\lambda_n \to \lambda_0$.

To simplify notation, for $\alpha \in \mathbb{R}^2$ and $x \in \mathrm{im}(I-P)$, let

$$p(\alpha,x) = M_p(I-Q)\mathcal{F}(\Phi(\cdot)\alpha + x).$$

Observe that any $\alpha \in \mathbb{R}^2$ and any $x \in \mathrm{im}(I-P)$

$$|\langle \alpha, e^{i\theta k}\rangle + [x]_1(k)| \le |\alpha| + |[x]_1(k)| \le |\alpha| + \|x\| \le 2\|(\alpha,x)\|,$$

where $[x]_1$ is the first component of the vector x. Therefore,

$$\begin{aligned} \|p(\alpha,x)\| &= \|M_p(I-Q)\mathcal{F}(\Phi(\cdot)\alpha + x)\| \\ &\le \|M_p(I-Q)\|\|\mathcal{F}(\Phi(\cdot)\alpha + x)\| \\ &= \|M_p(I-Q)\| \sup_{k\in\mathbb{N}_0} |g(\langle \alpha, e^{i\theta k}\rangle + [x]_1(k))| \\ &\le \|M_p(I-Q)\|\|g\|_{2\|(\alpha,x)\|}, \end{aligned} \tag{14}$$

where $\|M_p(I-Q)\| = \sup_{\|z\|=1}\|M_p(I-Q)z\|$.

From (14) and C2., we see that

$$\frac{p(\alpha_n,x_n)}{\|(\alpha_n,x_n)\|} \to 0.$$

Under essentially the same reasoning, we conclude that

$$\frac{H(\alpha_n,x_n)}{\|(\alpha_n,x_n)\|} \to (\alpha_0, 0).$$

But $(\alpha_n,x_n) = \lambda_n H(\alpha_n,x_n)$, so that

$$(\alpha_0,x_0) = \lim_{n\to\infty} \frac{1}{\|(\alpha_n,x_n)\|}(\alpha_n,x_n) = \lim_{n\to\infty} \frac{1}{\|(\alpha_n,x_n)\|}\lambda_n H(\alpha_n,x_n) = \lambda_0(\alpha_0,0).$$

It follows that $\lambda_0 = 1$, $x_0 = 0$. Further, since $\|(\alpha_0,x_0)\| = 1$, we must have $|\alpha_0| = 1$.

Suppose for the moment that $\langle \alpha_0, e^{i\theta j} \rangle \neq 0$ for all $j \in \{0, \cdots, \frac{N}{gcd(r,N)} - 1\}$. Thus, $\frac{1}{\|(\alpha_n, x_n)\|}\langle \alpha_n, e^{i\theta j} \rangle \neq 0$ for all $j \in \{0, \cdots, \frac{N}{gcd(r,N)} - 1\}$ and large enough $n \in \mathbb{N}$. However, since $\frac{x_n}{\|(\alpha_n, x_n)\|} = \frac{\lambda_n p(\alpha_n, x_n)}{\|(\alpha_n, x_n)\|} \to 0$, we see that $\|(\alpha_n, x_n)\| = |\alpha_n|$ for large enough $n \in \mathbb{N}$. Since we are assuming that for every $j \in \{0, \cdots, \frac{N}{gcd(r,N)} - 1\}$ we have $\langle \alpha_0, e^{i\theta j} \rangle \neq 0$, it follows that $\langle \alpha_n, e^{i\theta j} \rangle + [x_n]_1(j) \to \pm\infty$ for all $j \in \{0, \cdots, \frac{N}{gcd(r,N)} - 1\}$ and that the sign (of $\pm\infty$) is that of $\langle \alpha_0, e^{i\theta j} \rangle$.

Since the collection $e^{i\theta j}, j = 0, \cdots, N-1$, is just $gcd(r, N)$ copies of the collection $e^{i\theta j}, j = 0, \cdots, \dfrac{N}{gcd(r, N)} - 1$, we easily deduce that $\langle \alpha_n, e^{i\theta j} \rangle + [x_n]_1(j) \to \pm\infty$ for each $j \in \{0, \cdots, N-1\}$ and that the sign is still the same as $\langle \alpha_0, e^{i\theta j} \rangle$. But then, for large enough $n \in \mathbb{N}$, we must have, using C3., that

$$\langle \alpha_n, e^{i\theta j} \rangle g(\langle \alpha_n, e^{i\theta j} \rangle + [x_n]_1(j)) > 0 \tag{15}$$

for all $j \in \mathbb{N}_0$, since the signs of $\langle \alpha_0, e^{i\theta j} \rangle$ and $\langle \alpha_n, e^{i\theta j} \rangle$ agree, at least for large enough $n \in \mathbb{N}$. It follows that for large enough $n \in \mathbb{N}$,

$$\begin{aligned} \left\langle \alpha_n, \sum_{j=0}^{N-1} e^{i\theta j} g(\langle \alpha_n, e^{i\theta j} \rangle + [x_n]_1(j)) \right\rangle &= \sum_{j=0}^{N-1} \langle \alpha_n, e^{i\theta j} \rangle g(\langle \alpha_n, e^{i\theta j} \rangle + [x_n]_1(j)) \\ &> 0. \end{aligned} \tag{16}$$

However, the result in (16) is contradictory, since from $(\alpha_n, x_n) = \lambda_n H(\alpha_n, x_n)$ we deduce

$$(1 - \lambda_n)\alpha_n + \lambda_n \sum_{j=0}^{N-1} e^{i\theta j} g(\langle \alpha_n, e^{i\theta j} \rangle + [x_n]_1(j)) = 0, \tag{17}$$

so that by taking an inner product of the expression in (17) and α_n, we see that

$$(1 - \lambda_n)|\alpha_n|^2 + \lambda_n \sum_{j=0}^{N-1} \langle \alpha_n, e^{i\theta j} \rangle g(\langle \alpha_n, e^{i\theta j} \rangle + [x_n]_1(j)) = 0, \tag{18}$$

which is not possible, since from (16), (18) is a sum of positive terms, at least for large $n \in \mathbb{N}$.

Our previous contradiction now forces $\langle \alpha_0, e^{i\theta j} \rangle = 0$ for some $j \in \{0, \cdots, \frac{N}{gcd(r,N)} - 1\}$. If we let $F = \{j \in \{0, \cdots, \frac{N}{gcd(r,N)} - 1\} \mid \langle \alpha_0, e^{i\theta j} \rangle \neq 0\}$, then

$$\begin{aligned} \sum_{j=0}^{N-1} \langle \alpha_0, e^{i\theta j} \rangle g(\langle \alpha_n, e^{i\theta j} \rangle + [x_n]_1(j)) &= gcd(r, N) \cdot \sum_{j \in F} \langle \alpha_0, e^{i\theta j} \rangle g(\langle \alpha_n, e^{i\theta j} \rangle + [x_n]_1(j)) \\ &> 0, \end{aligned}$$

whenever $F \neq \varnothing$, since as was just argued above, for all $j \in F$,

$$\langle \alpha_0, e^{i\theta j} \rangle g(\langle \alpha_n, e^{i\theta j} \rangle + [x_n]_1(j)) > 0,$$

whenever $n \in \mathbb{N}$ is large. Now it is entirely possible that $F = \varnothing$, but in this case, we trivially have

$$\sum_{j=0}^{N-1} \langle \alpha_0, e^{i\theta j} \rangle g(\langle \alpha_n, e^{i\theta j} \rangle + [x_n]_1(j)) = 0,$$

so that for all cases of N,

$$\sum_{j=0}^{N-1} \langle \alpha_0, e^{i\theta j} \rangle g(\langle \alpha_n, e^{i\theta j} \rangle + [x_n]_1(j)) \geq 0. \tag{19}$$

If we now have an inner product (17) with α_0, we deduce

$$(1-\lambda_n)\langle \alpha_0, \alpha_n \rangle + \lambda_n \sum_{j=0}^{N-1} \langle \alpha_0, e^{i\theta j} \rangle g(\langle \alpha_n, e^{i\theta j} \rangle + [x_n]_1(j)) = 0. \tag{20}$$

However, (20) also produces a contradiction for large enough $n \in \mathbb{N}$. Indeed, since $|\alpha_n| \to \infty$ and $\langle \alpha_0, \frac{\alpha_n}{|\alpha_n|} \rangle \to \langle \alpha_0, \alpha_0 \rangle = 1$, we must have

$$\langle \alpha_0, \alpha_n \rangle = |\alpha_n| \langle \alpha_0, \frac{\alpha_n}{|\alpha_n|} \rangle \to \infty.$$

Further, by (19), $\sum_{j=0}^{N-1} \langle \alpha_0, e^{i\theta j} \rangle g(\langle \alpha_n, e^{i\theta j} \rangle + [x_n]_1(j)) \geq 0$ whenever $n \in \mathbb{N}$ is large. Thus, (20) must be positive for large enough $n \in \mathbb{N}$.

Since a contradiction is produced for all choices of α_0, it must be that S is bounded and so, by Schaefer's fixed point theorem, H has a fixed point. This fixed point is our solution to (12), which proves the existence of a solution to (12) in the case where condition R1. holds.

(The case R2.)

The proof for the case when condition R2. holds is very similar to what was given for the case when condition R1. is valid. Due to the similarity, we will not provide a complete proof for this case, but we do want to point out the few differences. First, in the case where R1. holds, see Appendix A, we have that

$$\Phi(t) = \begin{pmatrix} 1 & (-1)^t \\ 1 & -(-1)^t \end{pmatrix}$$

is a fundamental matrix solution to (6). However, since $b = 0$ and $c = -1$, the periodic scalar problems (1) and (11) once again agree. It follows that

$$\Gamma(t) = \begin{pmatrix} 1 & (-1)^t \\ 1 & -(-1)^t \end{pmatrix}$$

is a fundamental matrix solution to (8).

Let

$$H(\alpha, x) = \begin{pmatrix} \alpha - \sum_{j=0}^{N-1} \begin{pmatrix} 1 \\ (-1)^j \end{pmatrix} g(\langle \alpha, \begin{pmatrix} 1 \\ (-1)^j \end{pmatrix} \rangle + [x]_1(j)) \\ M_p(I-Q)\mathcal{F}(\Phi(\cdot)\alpha + x) \end{pmatrix},$$

whenever $\alpha \in \mathbb{R}^2$ and $x \in \operatorname{im}(I-P)$. Once again, it follows that the solutions to (12) are precisely the fixed points of H. The proof now proceeds, essentially as in the case when R1. holds, by assuming

$$S = \{(\alpha, x) \in \mathbb{R}^2 \times \operatorname{im}(I-P) \mid (\alpha, x) = \lambda H(\alpha, x) \text{ for some } \lambda \in (0,1)\}$$

is unbounded and reaching a contradiction. The argument is almost identical; most of the changes consist of replacing $e^{i\theta j}$ by $\begin{pmatrix} 1 \\ (-1)^j \end{pmatrix}$ in the appropriate places. □

Remark 3. *Theorem 2 is a substantial generalization of Proposition 2, since if g is bounded, then certainly assumption C2. is valid. Additionally, C3. is clearly satisfied when B3. of Proposition 2 is. It is also extremely important to note that condition B4. of Proposition 2 is no longer required.*

Remark 4. *In Proposition 2, it is assumed that N is odd. In Theorem 2, we make no such assumption. Thus, Theorem 2 not only generalizes Proposition 2 in that it allows for much more general nonlinearities, but it also generalizes it to allow for many more cases of the period N.*

4. Example

The simplicity of the hypotheses of Theorem 2 makes it very easy to visualize examples of nonlinearities, g, which will allow periodic solutions to (1). We now provide an example of a nonlinearity that we had in mind when formulating Theorem 2. Suppose either R1. or R2. holds, and let

$$g(x) = \ln(1 + |x|)\arctan(x) + \sin(x).$$

Clearly, g is continuous. It is obvious that for this choice of g, C2. holds, since, with our notation as in theorem 2, we have, for $s > 0$,

$$\|g\|_s \leq \ln(1+s)\arctan(s) + 1.$$

It is also not hard to see that C3. holds. Thus, for this choice of g, (1) has a periodic solution under the conditions placed by either R1. or R2.

5. Concluding Remarks

We conclude our work, with the exception of the appendix, with a few closing remarks. First, even though it was not of interest to this paper, it is easy to establish that Proposition 1 can be extended from the assumption that N is odd to cases where N is even. This amounts to showing that $\ker(\mathcal{L})$ and $\ker(\mathcal{L}^*)$ have not changed in these cases where N is even. Lastly, there are several open questions in this setting that remain; I mention two that are of interest to the author. First, it is certainly of interest to know to what extent condition C2. of Theorem 2 can be weakened. Condition C2. is often referred to as a sublinear growth condition. It is currently an active area of research, in both nonlinear differential equations and nonlinear difference equations, to look for existence theorems under growth conditions on nonlinearities that are less stringent than sublinear growth. I encourage interested readers to look for existence results in this setting. Second, problem (1) is perfectly well-formulated when the parameters b and c are complex and the nonlinearity $g : \mathbb{C} \to \mathbb{C}$. The analysis in this complex setting is much more difficult, but it is certainly of interest to see to what extent Theorem 2 can be transferred to this complex setting.

Funding: This research received no external funding.

Data Availability Statement: No data sets were generated during this research.

Conflicts of Interest: The author declares no conflicts of interest.

Appendix A

In this final section, we present the characterizations of the $\ker(\mathcal{L})$ that were used in the proofs of our main result, Theorem 2. The calculations here are not difficult, but they do require a bit of tedious analysis, which is why they are deferred to this appendix.

As was shown in Proposition 1, $\mathcal{L}$ is singular if and only if $\ker(I - A^N)$ is singular, and in this case, $\dim(\ker(\mathcal{L}))$ is precisely equal to $\dim(\ker(I - A^N))$. In fact, in Proposition 1, we showed that if $\{v_1, \cdots, v_m\}$ is a basis for $\ker(I - A^N)$, then $\{\varphi_1, \cdots, \varphi_m\}$ is a basis of $\ker(\mathcal{L})$, where for $t \in \{0, \cdots, N\}$ and $k \in \{1, \cdots, m\}$, $\varphi_k(t) = A^t v_k$. Let us point out that since A is a 2×2 matrix, when $I - A^N$ is singular, we must have $m = 1$ or $m = 2$.

Now it is a simple characterization from linear algebra that $I - A^N$ is singular if and only if at least one eigenvalue of A is an Nth root of unity. However, since

$$A = \begin{pmatrix} 0 & 1 \\ -c & -b \end{pmatrix},$$

We know that the eigenvalues of A are precisely the roots of the characteristic polynomial $p(z) = z^2 + bz + c$. In what follows, we show that:

D1. The dimension of the kernel of $\mathcal{L}$ is precisely the number of roots of the characteristic polynomial, which are Nth roots of unity.

The Case of a Repeated Root Is Considered to Have One Nth Root of Unity

Suppose that λ_1 and λ_2 are the complex roots of the characteristic polynomial $p(z) = z^2 + bz + c$. Since $(z - \lambda_1)(z - \lambda_2) = z^2 - (\lambda_1 + \lambda_2)z + \lambda_1\lambda_2$, we see that $b = -(\lambda_1 + \lambda_2)$ and $c = \lambda_1\lambda_2$. Note that since $c \neq 0$, neither λ_1 nor λ_2 is zero. If neither λ_1 nor λ_2 is a Nth root of unity, then from our discussion above, $\mathcal{L}$ is invertible, and so A1. holds in this case.

Now, without loss of generality, assume that λ_1 is an Nth root of unity. At the moment, suppose that $\lambda_1 \neq \lambda_2$. It is well-known that when $\lambda_1 \neq \lambda_2$,

$$\varphi_1(t) = \begin{pmatrix} \lambda_1^t \\ \lambda_1^{t+1} \end{pmatrix} \text{ and } \varphi_2(t) = \begin{pmatrix} \lambda_2^t \\ \lambda_2^{t+1} \end{pmatrix}$$

are linearly independent solutions to (6). If $c_1\varphi_1 + c_2\varphi_2$ was N-periodic, then we would have

$$\begin{pmatrix} c_1 + c_2 \\ c_1\lambda_1 + c_2\lambda_2 \end{pmatrix} = \begin{pmatrix} c_1\lambda_1^N + c_2\lambda_2^N \\ c_1\lambda_1^{N+1} + c_2\lambda_2^{N+1} \end{pmatrix} = \begin{pmatrix} c_1 + c_2\lambda_2^N \\ c_1\lambda_1 + c_2\lambda_2^{N+1} \end{pmatrix},$$

since λ_1 is an Nth root of unity. Equivalently, we have

$$\begin{pmatrix} c_2(1 - \lambda_2^N) \\ c_2\lambda_2(1 - \lambda_2^N) \end{pmatrix} = \begin{pmatrix} 0 \\ 0 \end{pmatrix}.$$

If λ_2 is not an Nth root of unity, then $c_2 = 0$ and φ_1 must span $\ker(\mathcal{L})$. However, if λ_2 is an Nth root of unity, then φ_1, φ_2 must be a basis for $\ker(\mathcal{L})$. It follows that D1. holds for these cases of λ_1, λ_2.

The remaining case is when $\lambda_1 = \lambda_2$ and λ_1 is an Nth root of unity. As mentioned above, we are considering this case to have one Nth root of unity; D1. will be proved if we can show that $\dim(\ker(\mathcal{L})) = 1$ for this case. Now in the repeated roots case, it is well-known that

$$\varphi_1(t) = \begin{pmatrix} \lambda^t \\ \lambda^{t+1} \end{pmatrix} \text{ and } \varphi_2(t) = \begin{pmatrix} t\lambda^t \\ (t+1)\lambda^{t+1} \end{pmatrix}$$

are linearly independent solutions to (6), where $\lambda = \lambda_1 = \lambda_2$. If $c_1\varphi_1 + c_2\varphi_2$ was N-periodic, then we would have

$$\begin{pmatrix} c_1 \\ (c_1 + c_2)\lambda \end{pmatrix} = \begin{pmatrix} c_1 + Nc_2 \\ (c_1 + (N+1)c_2)\lambda \end{pmatrix},$$

since $\lambda^N = 1$. It follows easily that $c_2 = 0$ and that c_1 can be any complex constant; that is, φ_1 spans $\ker(\mathcal{L})$ and so $\dim(\ker(\mathcal{L})) = 1$.

From what was just shown, we know that $\dim(\ker(\mathcal{L})) = 2$ if and only if both roots of the characteristic polynomial $p(z) = z^2 + bz + c$ are roots of unity. We now look a bit more closely at these cases, under the assumptions that the coefficients b and c are real.

(Complex Roots)

If the parameters b and c are real, then in the case of complex roots, we must have that the roots are conjugate pairs. Thus, suppose that the roots of $z^2 + bz + c$ are λ and $\overline{\lambda}$, for some complex number λ. Here $\overline{\lambda}$ denotes the conjugate of λ. We then have that

$$z^2 + bz + c = (z - \lambda)(z - \overline{\lambda}) = z^2 - 2\,\mathrm{Re}(\lambda) + |\lambda|^2.$$

It follows that $b = -2\,\mathrm{Re}(\lambda)$ and $c = |\lambda|^2$.

Now λ is an Nth root of unity if and only if $\overline{\lambda}$ is an Nth root of unity, so if $\mathcal{L}$ (or equivalently $I - A^N$) is singular, then $|\lambda| = 1$. Since $c = |\lambda|^2$, we deduce that when $\mathcal{L}$ is singular, then $c = 1$. If we now write $\lambda = e^{i\theta}$ in polar form, then we also see that

$\text{Re}(\lambda) = \cos(\theta)$ and so $b = -2\cos(\theta)$. Thus, in this complex setting, we have deduced the following: if $\mathcal{L}$ is singular, then $c = 1$ and $-2 < b < 2$. We point out that these conditions on b and c are necessary conditions for $\mathcal{L}$ to be singular, but they are certainly not sufficient.

In fact, we can say a bit more. If $\lambda = e^{i\theta}$ is an Nth root of unity, then we may arrange (swap λ and $\overline{\lambda}$ if needed) so that $\theta = \frac{2\pi r}{N}$ for some natural number r with $0 < r < \frac{N}{2}$. Rearranging gives $N\theta = 2\pi r$, where, from above, we would have $\theta = \arccos(-\frac{b}{2})$. It is well known that in this complex case,

$$\Phi(t) = \begin{pmatrix} \cos(\theta t) & \sin(\theta t) \\ \cos(\theta(t+1)) & \sin(\theta(t+1)) \end{pmatrix}$$

is a fundamental matrix solution to (6), as was claimed in the proof of Theorem 2.

(Real Distinct Roots)

The final case in which we may have that $\dim(\ker(\mathcal{L})) = 2$ is when the roots of the characteristic polynomial $p(z) = z^2 + bz + c$ are real and distinct. So, suppose that λ_1 and λ_2 are distinct roots of the characteristic polynomial $p(z) = z^2 + bz + c$. Since $(z - \lambda_1)(z - \lambda_2) = z^2 - (\lambda_1 + \lambda_2)z + \lambda_1\lambda_2$, we see that $b = -(\lambda_1 + \lambda_2)$ and $c = \lambda_1\lambda_2$. If λ_1 and λ_2 are both roots of unity, then we may assume $\lambda_1 = 1$ and $\lambda_2 = -1$. This forces N to be even. Our characteristic polynomial becomes $z^2 - 1$, so that $c = -1$ and $b = 0$. It is a simple consequence of the theory of linear difference equations that, in this case,

$$\Phi(t) = \begin{pmatrix} 1 & (-1)^t \\ 1 & (-1)^{t+1} \end{pmatrix}$$

is a fundamental matrix solution to (6), as was claimed in the proof of Theorem 2.

References

1. Maroncelli, D.; Rodríguez, J. Periodic behaviour of nonlinear, second-order, discrete dynamical systems. *J. Differ. Equ. Appl.* **2015**, *22*, 280–294. [CrossRef]
2. Abernathy, Z.; Rodriguez, J. Existence of Periodic Solutions to Nonlinear Difference Equations at Full Resonance. *Commun. Math. Anal.* **2014**, *17*, 47–56. [CrossRef]
3. Etheridge, D.; Rodríguez, J. Periodic solutions of nonlinear discrete-time systems. *Appl. Anal.* **1996**, *62*, 119–137. [CrossRef]
4. Rodríguez, J.; Etheridge, D. Periodic solutions of nonlinear second-order difference equations. *Adv. Differ. Equ.* **2005**, *2005*, 718682. [CrossRef]
5. Zhou, Z.; Yu, J.; Guo, Z. Periodic solutions of higher-dimensional discrete systems. *Proc. R. Soc. Edinb. Sect. A Math.* **2004**, *134*, 1013–1022. [CrossRef]
6. Maroncelli, D.; Rodríguez, J. On the solvability of nonlinear discrete Sturm-Liouville problems at resonance. *Int. J. Differ. Equ.* **2017**, *12*, 119–129.
7. Ma, R. Nonlinear discrete Sturm-Liouville problems at resonance. *Nonlinear Anal.* **2007**, *67*, 3050–3057. [CrossRef]
8. Rodríguez, J. Nonlinear discrete Sturm-Liouville problems. *J. Math. Anal. Appl.* **2005**, *308*, 380–391. [CrossRef]
9. Rodríguez, J.; Abernathy, Z. Nonlinear discrete Sturm-Liouville problems with global boundary conditions. *J. Differ. Equ. Appl.* **2012**, *18*, 431–445. [CrossRef]
10. Rodríguez, J.; Suarez, A. On nonlinear perturbations of Sturm-Liouville problems in discrete and continuous settings. *Differ. Equ. Appl.* **2016**, *8*, 319–334. [CrossRef]
11. Gao, C.; Yang, E.; Li, H. Solutions to a discrete resonance problem with eigenparameter-dependent boundary conditions. *Electron. Res. Arch.* **2024**, *32*, 1692–1707. [CrossRef]
12. Maroncelli, D. Nonlinear scalar multipoint boundary value problems at resonance. *J. Differ. Equ. Appl.* **2018**, *24*, 1935–1952. [CrossRef]
13. Maroncelli, D.; Rodríguez, J. On the solvability of multipoint boundary value problems for discrete systems at resonance. *J. Differ. Equ. Appl.* **2013**, *20*, 24–35. [CrossRef]
14. Rodríguez, J.; Taylor, P. Scalar discrete nonlinear multipoint boundary value problems. *J. Math. Anal. Appl.* **2007**, *330*, 876–890. [CrossRef]
15. Zhang, G.; Medina, R. Three-point boundary value problems for difference equations. *Comput. Math. Appl.* **2004**, *48*, 1791–1799. [CrossRef]
16. Henderson, J.; Ntouyas, S.; Purnaras, I. Positive solutions for systems of three-point nonlinear discrete boundary value problems. *Neural Parallel Sci. Comput.* **2008**, *16*, 209–223.
17. Henderson, J.; Ntouyas, S.; Purnaras, I. Positive solutions for systems of nonlinear discrete boundary value problems. *J. Differ. Equ. Appl.* **2009**, *15*, 895–912. [CrossRef]

18. Henderson, J.; Luca, R. Positive solutions for a system of second-order multi-point discrete boundary value problems. *J. Differ. Equ. Appl.* **2012**, *18*, 1575–1592. [CrossRef]
19. Henderson, J.; Thompson, H.B. Existence of multiple solutions for second-order discrete boundary value problems. *Comput. Math. Appl.* **2002**, *43*, 1239–1248. [CrossRef]
20. Kong, L.; Wang, M. Multiple Solutions for a Nonlinear Discrete Problem of the Second Order. *Differ. Equ. Appl.* **2022**, *14*, 189–204. [CrossRef]
21. Liu, J.; Wang, S.; Zhang, J. Multiple solutions for boundary value problems of second order difference equations with resonance. *J. Math. Anal. Appl.* **2011**, *374*, 187–196. [CrossRef]
22. Elaydi, S. *An Introduction to Difference Equations*; Springer: Berlin/Heidelberg, Germany, 2005.
23. Kelley, W.G.; Peterson, A. *Difference Equations*; Academic Press: New York, NY, USA, 1978.
24. Chow, S.; Hale, J.K. *Methods of Bifurcation Theory*; Springer: Berlin, Germany, 1982.

mathematics

Article

A Signed Maximum Principle for Boundary Value Problems for Riemann–Liouville Fractional Differential Equations with Analogues of Neumann or Periodic Boundary Conditions

Paul W. Eloe [1,*], Yulong Li [1] and Jeffrey T. Neugebauer [2]

[1] Department of Mathematics, University of Dayton, Dayton, OH 45469, USA; yli004@udayton.edu
[2] Department of Mathematics and Statistics, Eastern Kentucky University, Richmond, KY 40475, USA; jeffrey.neugebauer@eku.edu
* Correspondence: peloe1@udayton.edu

Abstract: Sufficient conditions are obtained for a signed maximum principle for boundary value problems for Riemann–Liouville fractional differential equations with analogues of Neumann or periodic boundary conditions in neighborhoods of simple eigenvalues. The primary objective is to exhibit four specific boundary value problems for which the sufficient conditions can be verified. To show an application of the signed maximum principle, a method of upper and lower solutions coupled with monotone methods is developed to obtain sufficient conditions for the existence of a maximal solution and a minimal solution of a nonlinear boundary value problem. A specific example is provided to show that sufficient conditions for the nonlinear problem can be realized.

Keywords: fractional boundary value problem; signed maximum principle; fractional Neumann boundary conditions; fractional periodic boundary conditions

MSC: 34K37; 34A08; 34B27

Citation: Eloe, P.W.; Li, Y.; Neugebauer, J.T. A Signed Maximum Principle for Boundary Value Problems for Riemann–Liouville Fractional Differential Equations with Analogues of Neumann or Periodic Boundary Conditions. *Mathematics* **2024**, *12*, 1000. https://doi.org/10.3390/math12071000

Academic Editors: Lingju Kong and Min Wang

Received: 4 March 2024
Revised: 22 March 2024
Accepted: 26 March 2024
Published: 27 March 2024

1. Introduction

Applications of the maximum principle in functional analysis are well known and we refer the interested reader to the authoritative account [1]. In recent years, the maximum principle has become an important tool in the study of boundary value problems for fractional differential equations. Early applications appear in [2,3] where explicit Green's functions, expressed in terms of power functions, were constructed; sign properties of the Green's function were analyzed so that fixed point theorems could be applied to give sufficient conditions for the existence of positive solutions. More recently, Green's functions, expressed in terms of Mittag-Leffler functions, have been constructed so that fixed-point theorems and the maximum principle can be applied. See, for example, Refs. [4–7].

Credit for the discovery of an anti-maximum principle is given to Clément and Peletier [8]. Although primarily interested in partial differential equations, they initially illustrated the anti-maximum principle with the boundary value problem, $y'' + \lambda y = f$, $y'(0) = 0, y'(1) = 0$, with $0 < \lambda < \frac{\pi^2}{4}$. They showed, if $0 < \lambda < \Lambda = \frac{\pi^2}{4}$ and if $f \in \mathcal{L}[0,1]$, then the boundary value problem is uniquely solvable and $f \geq 0$ implies $y \geq 0$ where y is the unique solution associated with f.

At $\lambda = 0$, the boundary value problem, $y'' + \lambda y = f$, $y'(0) = 0$, $y'(1) = 0$, is at resonance, and $\lambda = 0$ is a simple eigenvalue of the homogeneous problem. Moreover, for $\lambda < 0$, then $f \geq 0$ implies $y \geq 0$; that is, for $\lambda < 0$, the boundary value problem obeys a maximum principle. Thus, there has been a change in the sign property, maximum principle or anti-maximum principle, through the simple eigenvalue $\lambda = 0$. In more succinct terms, if $0 < |\lambda| < \Lambda = \frac{\pi^2}{4}$, and if $f \in \mathcal{L}[0,1]$, then the boundary value problem is uniquely solvable and $f \geq 0$ implies $\lambda y \geq 0$ where y is the unique solution associated with f. Since the publication of [8], the change in behavior from maximum to anti-maximum principles as a function of the parameter has received considerable attention. For partial differential equations, see [9–16]. For ordinary differential equations, see [17–21]. More recently, this change in behavior from maximum to anti-maximum principles has also been noticed and studied in fractional differential equations. For equations analyzing the fractional $p-$Laplacian, see [22,23]; for fractional differential equations of one independent variable, see [24].

In [9], the authors studied the nature of the maximum principle for boundary value problems for an abstract differential equation, $(\mathcal{A} + \lambda\mathcal{I})y = f$, defined on $[0,1]$ with $f \in \mathcal{L}[0,1]$, under a fundamental assumption that $\lambda = 0$ was a simple eigenvalue for the homogeneous problem. Under mild sufficient conditions, they proved the existence of $\Lambda > 0$, and a constant $K > 0$, independent of f, such that

$$\lambda y(t) \geq K|f|_1, \quad \lambda \in [-\Lambda, \Lambda] \setminus \{0\}, \quad 0 \leq t \leq 1, \tag{1}$$

where y is the unique solution of the boundary value problem associated with $(\mathcal{A} + \lambda\mathcal{I})y = f$ and $|f|_1 = \int_0^1 |f(s)|ds$. If (1) holds and $\lambda < 0$, then $f \geq 0$ implies $y \leq 0$; that is, the boundary value problem for (1) obeys a maximum principle. If (1) holds and $\lambda > 0$, then $f \geq 0$ implies $y \geq 0$; that is, the boundary value problem for (1) obeys an anti-maximum principle [8].

The methods of [9] were recently adapted to apply to a boundary value problem with a parameter for a Riemann–Liouville fractional differential equation [24]. During the review process for [24], those authors were asked by one referee if the methods of [9] could be successfully adapted to apply to analogues of Neumann or periodic boundary value problems for Riemann–Liouville fractional differential equations. In [24], the eigenspace generated by $\lambda = 0$ is contained in the space of continuous functions on $[0,1]$. The corresponding eigenspace for boundary value problems analogous to Neumann or periodic type boundary value problems will contain a singularity. Thus, the question is interesting. The purpose of this study is to address that question with a positive response.

In Section 2, we shall introduce preliminary notations and concepts from fractional calculus. We shall also introduce four boundary value problems for which the general theorem, stated in Section 3, applies. In Section 3, we introduce the notations adapted from [9] and state and prove the abstract theorem. The proof of the abstract theorem closely models the proofs of analogous theorems in [9,24]; with subtle differences in the technical details due to the specific function space, we shall produce a proof here for the self-containment of the manuscript. In Section 4, we shall apply the abstract theorem to each of the four examples introduced in Section 2. In Section 5, to illustrate an application of the abstract theorem, we develop a monotone method motivated by the abstract theorem and apply the monotone method to a nonlinear problem related to one of the examples introduced in Section 2. The monotone method closely models one that has been developed in [24] with subtle differences in the convergence argument. In Section 6, we illustrate the monotone method with a specific example. In this example, a Green's function is constructed using Mittag-Leffler functions. The purpose of introducing the Green's function is not to produce an explicit function on which to analyze sign properties, as is the case in say, [2] or [3]; the purpose is to obtain a verifiable bound on Λ so that if $0 < |\lambda| < \Lambda$, then $f \geq 0$ implies $\lambda y \geq 0$.

2. Preliminaries

In this section, we introduce notations from fractional calculus and state common properties that we shall employ throughout. For authoritative accounts on the development of fractional calculus, we refer to the monographs [25–27].

Assume $\gamma > 0$. For $y \in \mathcal{L}[0,1]$, the space of Lebesgue integrable functions, a Riemann–Liouville fractional integral of y of order γ, is defined by

$$I_0^{\gamma} y(t) = \int_0^t \frac{(t-s)^{\gamma-1}}{\Gamma(\gamma)} y(s) ds, \quad 0 \le t \le 1,$$

where

$$\Gamma(z) = \int_0^{\infty} s^{z-1} e^{-s}, \quad Re\, z > 0,$$

denotes the special gamma function. For $\gamma = 0$, I_0^0 is defined to be the identity operator. Let n denote a positive integer and assume $n-1 < \alpha \le n$. A Riemann–Liouville fractional derivative of y of order α is defined by $D_0^{\alpha} y(t) = D^n I_0^{n-\alpha} y(t)$, where $D^n = \frac{d^n}{dt^n}$, if this expression exists. In the case α is a positive integer, we may write $D_0^{\alpha} y(t) = D^{\alpha} y(t)$ or $I_0^{\alpha} y(t) = I^{\alpha} y(t)$ since the Riemann–Liouville derivative or integral agrees with the classical derivative or integral if α is a positive integer.

For the sake of self-containment, we state properties that we shall employ in this study. It is well known that the Riemann–Liouville fractional integrals commute; that is, if $\gamma_1, \gamma_2 > 0$, and $y \in \mathcal{L}[0,1]$, then

$$I_0^{\gamma_1} I_0^{\gamma_2} y(t) = I_0^{\gamma_1+\gamma_2} y(t) = I_0^{\gamma_2} I_0^{\gamma_1} y(t).$$

A power rule is valid for the Riemann–Liouville fractional integral; if $\delta > -1$ and $\gamma \ge 0$, then

$$I_0^{\gamma} t^{\delta} = I_0^{\gamma} (t-0)^{\delta} = \frac{\Gamma(\delta+1)}{\Gamma(\delta+1+\gamma)} t^{\delta+\gamma}.$$

A power rule is valid for the Riemann–Liouville fractional derivative; if $\delta > -1$ and $\gamma \ge 0$, then

$$D_0^{\gamma} t^{\delta} = \frac{\Gamma(\delta+1)}{\Gamma(\delta+1-\gamma)} t^{\delta-\gamma}.$$

If $n-1 < \alpha \le n$, and if $D_0^{\alpha} y(t)$ exists, then $D_0^{\alpha-1} y(t)$ exists and

$$D_0^{\alpha} y(t) = D^n I_0^{n-\alpha} y(t) = D D^{n-1} I_0^{(n-1)-(\alpha-1)} y(t) = D D_0^{\alpha-1} y(t).$$

Thus, it is clear that for each $j \in \{1, \ldots, n-1\}$, $D_0^{\alpha-j} y(t)$ exists and

$$D_0^{\alpha} y(t) = D^j D_0^{\alpha-j} y(t).$$

A Green's function will be constructed in Section 6. The two-parameter Mittag-Leffler function

$$E_{\alpha,\beta}(z) = \sum_{n=0}^{\infty} \frac{z^n}{\Gamma(\alpha n + \beta)}, \quad Re(\alpha) > 0, \quad \beta \in \mathbb{C}, \quad z \in \mathbb{C},$$

will be employed in those calculations. Many properties and identities for the two-parameter Mittag-Leffler are derived in [26].

In [24], a boundary value problem,

$$D_0^{\alpha} y(t) + \beta D_0^{\alpha-1} y(t) = f(t), \quad 0 < t \le 1, \quad 1 < \alpha \le 2,$$

$$y(0) = 0, \quad D_0^{\alpha-1} y(0) = D_0^{\alpha-1} y(1),$$

was studied. This is an example of a boundary value problem at resonance since $< t^{\alpha-1} >$, the linear span of $t^{\alpha-1}$, denotes the solution space of the homogeneous problem, $D_0^{\alpha} y = 0$, with the given homogeneous boundary conditions; moreover, $\beta = 0$ is a simple eigenvalue of the homogeneous problem. There, an abstract theorem was proved that gave the existence of $\mathcal{B} > 0$, and a constant $K > 0$, independent of f, such that

$$\beta D_0^{\alpha-1}y(t) \geq K|f|_1, \quad \beta \in [-\mathcal{B}, \mathcal{B}] \setminus \{0\}, \quad 0 \leq t \leq 1, \tag{2}$$

where y is the unique solution associated with f. Thus, $f \geq 0$ implies $\beta D_0^{\alpha-1}y \geq 0$. It was also proved in [24] that $\beta D_0^{\alpha-1}y(t) \geq 0$, $y(0) = 0$, implies $\beta y \geq 0$. Thus, with control of the sign of both $\beta D_0^{\alpha-1}y$ and y, a monotone method was developed to obtain sufficient conditions for a solution of the nonlinear problem,

$$D_0^{\alpha}y(t) + \beta D_0^{\alpha-1}y(t) = f(t, y(t), D_0^{\alpha-1}y(t)), \quad 0 < t \leq 1, \quad 1 < \alpha \leq 2,$$

$$y(0) = 0, \quad D_0^{\alpha-1}y(0) = D_0^{\alpha-1}y(1).$$

Since the purpose of this study is to modify the methods developed in [9] to apply to Neumann-like or periodic-like boundary conditions, we shall focus on a differential equation,

$$D_0^{\alpha}y(t) + \lambda y(t) = f(t), \quad 0 < t \leq 1, \quad n-1 < \alpha \leq n,$$

where $n \geq 2$ is an integer.

Consider the fractional differential equation To study the Neumann-like boundary conditions, assume $1 < \alpha \leq 2$. Consider the fractional differential equation

$$D_0^{\alpha}y(t) + \lambda y(t) = f(t), \quad 0 < t \leq 1, \quad 1 < \alpha \leq 2, \tag{3}$$

We shall refer to the boundary conditions

$$D_0^{\alpha-1}y(0) = 0, \quad D_0^{\alpha-1}y(1) = 0, \tag{4}$$

as Neumann boundary conditions. The first exhibited boundary value problem is the boundary value problem, (3), (4).

To study periodic-like boundary conditions we shall consider a fractional differential equation

$$D_0^{\alpha}y(t) + aD_0^{\alpha-1}y(t) + \lambda y(t) = f(t), \quad 0 < t \leq 1, \quad 1 < \alpha \leq 2, \tag{5}$$

or

$$D_0^{\alpha}y(t) + \lambda y(t) = f(t), \quad 0 < t \leq 1, \quad n-1 < \alpha \leq n. \tag{6}$$

In the second exhibited example, we study the boundary value problem, (5), with boundary conditions

$$I_0^{n-\alpha}y(0) = I_0^{n-\alpha}y(1), \quad D_0^{\alpha-1}y(0) = D_0^{\alpha-1}y(1),$$

in the third exhibited example, we study the boundary value problem, (6), with the boundary conditions

$$I_0^{n-\alpha}y(0) = I_0^{n-\alpha}y(1), \quad D_0^{\alpha-j}y(0) = D_0^{\alpha-j}y(1), \quad j = 1, \ldots, n-1, \tag{7}$$

and in the final exhibited boundary value problem we study the boundary value problem, (6), with the boundary conditions

$$\lim_{t \to 0^+} t^{n-\alpha}y(t) = y(1), \quad D_0^{\alpha-j}y(0) = D_0^{\alpha-j}y(1), \quad j = 1, \ldots, n-1. \tag{8}$$

3. The Abstract Theorem

Let $C[0,1]$ denote the Banach space of continuous functions defined on $[0,1]$ with the supremum norm, $|\cdot|_0$, and let $\mathcal{L}[0,1]$ denote the space of Lebesgue integrable functions with the usual $\mathcal{L}_1$ norm. Let $n \geq 2$ denote an integer. Assume $n-1 < \alpha \leq n$. Employing notation introduced in [28], define

$$C_{\alpha-n}[0,1] = \{y : (0,1] \to \mathbb{R} : y(t) \text{ is continuous for } t \in (0,1], \text{ and } \lim_{t\to 0^+} t^{n-\alpha} y(t) \text{ exists }\}.$$

It is clear that $y \in C_{\alpha-n}[0,1]$ if, and only if, there exists $z \in C[0,1]$ such that $y(t) = t^{\alpha-n}z(t)$ for $t \in (0,1]$. Define $|y|_{\alpha-n} = |z|_0$ and $C_{\alpha-n}[0,1]$ with norm $|\cdot|_{\alpha-n}$ is a Banach space.

The following definition is motivated by Definition 1 found in [9].

Definition 1. *Assume $\mathcal{A}$ is a linear operator with Dom $(\mathcal{A}) \subset C_{\alpha-n}$ and Im $(\mathcal{A}) \subset \mathcal{L}[0,1]$. For $\lambda \in \mathbb{R}\setminus\{0\}$, the operator $\mathcal{A}+\lambda\mathcal{I}$, where $\mathcal{I}$ denotes the identity operator, satisfies a signed maximum principle in λy if for each $f \in \mathcal{L}[0,1]$, the equation*

$$(\mathcal{A}+\lambda\mathcal{I})y = f, \quad y \in \text{Dom }(\mathcal{A}),$$

has unique solution y, and $f \geq 0$, implies $\lambda y(t) \geq 0$, $0 < t \leq 1$. The operator $\mathcal{A}+\lambda\mathcal{I}$ satisfies a strong signed maximum principle in λy if $f \geq 0$, and $f(t) \neq 0$ a.e. implies $\lambda y(t) > 0$, $0 < t \leq 1$.

Remark 1. *In [9], the authors employed the phrase, maximum principle. We have taken the liberty to employ the phrase signed maximum principle to distinguish further from classical usage of maximum principle or anti-maximum principle.*

Remark 2. *The phrases "maximum principle" or "anti-maximum principle" are used loosely and we mean the following. Maximum principle means $f \geq 0$ implies $y \leq 0$. This is precisely the case for the classical second order ordinary differential equation with Dirichlet boundary conditions. Anti-maximum principle means $f \geq 0$ implies $y \geq 0$. This is the case observed in [8] for $\alpha = 2$, where the phrase anti-maximum principle was coined.*

For $f \in \mathcal{L}[0,1]$ (or $f \in C_{\alpha-n}[0,1]$), let $|f|_1 = \int_0^1 |f(s)|ds$ and define $\overline{f} = \int_0^1 f(t)dt$. Define

$$\tilde{C} \subset C_{\alpha-n}[0,1] = \{y \in C_{\alpha-n}[0,1] : \overline{y} = 0\}, \quad \tilde{\mathcal{L}} \subset \mathcal{L}[0,1] = \{f \in \mathcal{L}[0,1] : \overline{f} = 0\}.$$

Assume $\mathcal{A} :$ Dom $(\mathcal{A}) \to \mathcal{L}[0,1]$ denotes a linear operator satisfying

$$\text{Dom }(\mathcal{A}) \subset C_{\alpha-n}[0,1], \quad \text{Ker }(\mathcal{A}) = < t^{\alpha-n} >, \quad \text{Im }(\mathcal{A}) = \tilde{\mathcal{L}}, \tag{9}$$

where $< t^{\alpha-n} >$ denotes the linear span of $t^{\alpha-n}$. Assume further that for $\tilde{f} \in \tilde{\mathcal{L}}$, the problem $\mathcal{A}y = \tilde{f}$ is uniquely solvable with solution $\tilde{y} \in \text{Dom}(\mathcal{A})$ and such that $\int_0^1 \tilde{y}(t)dt = \overline{\tilde{y}} = 0$. In particular, define

$$\text{Dom }(\tilde{\mathcal{A}}) = \{\tilde{y} \in \text{ Dom }(\mathcal{A}) : \overline{\tilde{y}} = 0\} \subset \tilde{C}, \tag{10}$$

and then

$$\mathcal{A}|_{\text{ Dom }(\tilde{\mathcal{A}})} : \text{Dom }(\tilde{\mathcal{A}}) \to \tilde{\mathcal{L}}$$

is invertible. Moreover, if $\mathcal{A}\tilde{y} = \tilde{f}$ for $\tilde{f} \in \tilde{\mathcal{L}}$, $\tilde{y} \in \text{Dom}(\tilde{\mathcal{A}})$, assume there exists a constant $M > 0$ depending only on $\mathcal{A}$ such that

$$|\tilde{y}|_{\alpha-n} \leq M|\tilde{f}|_1. \tag{11}$$

For $f \in \mathcal{L}$, define

$$\tilde{f} = f - (\alpha - n + 1)\overline{f}t^{\alpha-n},$$

which implies $\tilde{f} \in \tilde{\mathcal{L}}$, and for $y \in$ Dom $(\mathcal{A})$ define

$$\tilde{y} = y - (\alpha - n + 1)\overline{y}t^{\alpha-n},$$

which implies $\tilde{y} \in \text{Dom}(\tilde{\mathcal{A}})$.

Since $\text{Ker}(\mathcal{A}) = < t^{\alpha-n} >$, with the decompositions $\tilde{f} = f - (\alpha - n + 1)\overline{f}t^{\alpha-n}$ and $\tilde{y} = y - (\alpha - n + 1)\overline{y}t^{\alpha-n}$, it follows that

$$\mathcal{A}y + \lambda y = f, \quad y \in \text{Dom}(\mathcal{A}), \tag{12}$$

which decouples as follows:

$$\mathcal{A}\tilde{y} + \lambda\tilde{y} = (\mathcal{A} + \lambda\mathcal{I})\tilde{y} = \tilde{f}, \tag{13}$$

$$\lambda(\alpha - n + 1)\overline{y}t^{\alpha-n} = (\alpha - n + 1)\overline{f}t^{\alpha-n}. \tag{14}$$

Denote the inverse of $(\mathcal{A} + \lambda\mathcal{I})$, if it exists, by $\mathcal{R}_\lambda$ and denote the inverse of

$$\mathcal{A}|_{\text{Dom}(\tilde{\mathcal{A}})}$$

by $\mathcal{R}_0$. So, $\mathcal{R}_0 : \tilde{\mathcal{L}} \to \tilde{\mathcal{C}}$ and

$$\tilde{y} = \mathcal{R}_0\tilde{f} \text{ if, and only if, } \mathcal{A}\tilde{y} = \tilde{f}. \tag{15}$$

Note that (15) implies that since $\tilde{y} \in \text{Dom}(\tilde{\mathcal{A}})$,

$$\tilde{y} = \mathcal{R}_0\mathcal{A}\tilde{y}. \tag{16}$$

Note that (11) implies that $\mathcal{R}_0 : \tilde{\mathcal{L}} \to \tilde{\mathcal{C}}$ is continuous, and hence, $\mathcal{R}_0 : \tilde{\mathcal{L}} \to \tilde{\mathcal{C}}$ is a bounded linear operator with $||\mathcal{R}_0||_{\tilde{\mathcal{L}}\to\tilde{\mathcal{C}}} \leq M$. To note the continuity, if $\mathcal{R}_0(\tilde{f}_n) = \tilde{y}_n, \mathcal{R}_0(\tilde{f}) = \tilde{y}$, and $|\tilde{f}_n - \tilde{f}|_1 \to 0$, as $n \to \infty$, then $|\tilde{y}_n - \tilde{y}|_{\alpha-n} \leq M|\tilde{f}_n - \tilde{f}|_1 \to 0$, as $n \to \infty$.

Since $\tilde{\mathcal{C}} \subset \tilde{\mathcal{L}}$, we can also consider $\mathcal{R}_0 : \tilde{\mathcal{C}} \to \tilde{\mathcal{C}}$. Equation (11) also implies that $\mathcal{R}_0 : \tilde{\mathcal{C}} \to \tilde{\mathcal{C}}$ is continuous and hence, bounded. To see this, assume $|\tilde{f}_n - \tilde{f}|_{\alpha-n} \to 0$, as $n \to \infty$. Then, $t^{2-\alpha}|\tilde{f}_n - \tilde{f}| \to 0$ uniformly as $n \to \infty$. For each $\epsilon > 0$, $|\tilde{f}_n - \tilde{f}|(t) < \epsilon t^{\alpha-2}$ and $|\tilde{f}_n - \tilde{f}|_1 < \frac{\epsilon}{\alpha-1}$, eventually; in particular, $|\tilde{f}_n - \tilde{f}|_1 \to 0$, as $n \to \infty$, which implies $|\tilde{y}_n - \tilde{y}|_{\alpha-n} \to 0$, as $n \to \infty$.

Theorem 1. *Assume $\mathcal{A}$: Dom $(\mathcal{A}) \to \mathcal{L}[0,1]$ denotes a linear operator satisfying* (9). *Define $\tilde{\mathcal{A}}$ by* (10) *and assume*

$$\mathcal{A}|_{\text{Dom}(\tilde{\mathcal{A}})} : \text{Dom}(\tilde{\mathcal{A}}) \to \tilde{\mathcal{L}}$$

is invertible. Finally, if $\mathcal{A}\tilde{y} = \tilde{f}$ for $\tilde{f} \in \tilde{\mathcal{L}}$, $\tilde{y} \in \text{Dom}(\tilde{\mathcal{A}})$, assume there exists a constant $M > 0$ depending only on $\mathcal{A}$ such that (11) *is satisfied. Then there exists $\Lambda_1 > 0$ such that if $0 < |\lambda| \leq \Lambda_1$, then $\mathcal{R}_\lambda : \tilde{\mathcal{C}} \to \tilde{\mathcal{C}}$, the inverse of $(\mathcal{A} + \lambda\mathcal{I})$, exists. Moreover, if $\tilde{f} \in \tilde{L}$, if $\Lambda_1||\mathcal{R}_0||_{\tilde{\mathcal{C}}\to\tilde{\mathcal{C}}} < 1$, where $\mathcal{R}_0$ denotes the inverse of $\mathcal{A}|_{\text{Dom}(\tilde{\mathcal{A}})}$, and if $0 < |\lambda| \leq \Lambda_1$, then*

$$|\mathcal{R}_\lambda\tilde{f}|_{\alpha-n} \leq \frac{||\mathcal{R}_0||_{\tilde{\mathcal{L}}\to\tilde{\mathcal{C}}}}{1 - \Lambda_1||\mathcal{R}_0||_{\tilde{\mathcal{C}}\to\tilde{\mathcal{C}}}}|\tilde{f}|_1. \tag{17}$$

Further, there exists $\Lambda \in (0, \Lambda_1)$ such that if $0 < |\lambda| \leq \Lambda$, then the operator $(\mathcal{A} + \lambda\mathcal{I})$ satisfies a strong signed maximum principle in λy.

Proof. Employ (16) and apply $\mathcal{R}_0$ to (13) to obtain

$$\tilde{y} + \lambda\mathcal{R}_0\tilde{y} = \mathcal{R}_0\tilde{f}.$$

It has been established that (11) implies that each of $\mathcal{R}_0 : \tilde{\mathcal{L}} \to \tilde{\mathcal{C}}$ and $\mathcal{R}_0 : \tilde{\mathcal{C}} \to \tilde{\mathcal{C}}$ are bounded linear operators. Since $|\lambda|||\mathcal{R}_0||_{\tilde{\mathcal{C}}\to\tilde{\mathcal{C}}} < 1$, it follows that $(\mathcal{I} + \lambda\mathcal{R}_0) : \tilde{\mathcal{C}} \to \tilde{\mathcal{C}}$ is invertible and

$$\tilde{y} = (\mathcal{I} + \lambda\mathcal{R}_0)^{-1}\mathcal{R}_0\tilde{f}.$$

Assume $0 < \Lambda_1 < \frac{1}{||\mathcal{R}_0||_{\tilde{C}\to\tilde{C}}}$ and assume $|\lambda| \leq \Lambda_1$. Then, $\mathcal{R}_\lambda = (\mathcal{I} + \lambda\mathcal{R}_0)^{-1}\mathcal{R}_0$ exists. Since $\Lambda_1||\mathcal{R}_0||_{\tilde{C}\to\tilde{C}} < 1$ and $0 < |\lambda| \leq \Lambda_1$, it follows that

$$|\tilde{y}|_{\alpha-n} - |\lambda\mathcal{R}_0\tilde{y}|_{\alpha-1} = \Big||\tilde{y}|_{\alpha-n} - |\lambda\mathcal{R}_0\tilde{y}|_{\alpha-1}\Big|$$

and so the triangle inequality implies

$$\begin{aligned}|\tilde{y}|_{\alpha-n} - \Lambda_1||\mathcal{R}_0||_{\tilde{C}\to\tilde{C}}|\tilde{y}|_{\alpha-n} &\leq |\tilde{y}|_{\alpha-n} - |\lambda|||\mathcal{R}_0||_{\tilde{C}\to\tilde{C}}|\tilde{y}|_{\alpha-n} \\ &\leq |(\mathcal{I} + \lambda\mathcal{R}_0)\tilde{y}|_{\alpha-n} = |\mathcal{R}_0\tilde{f}|_{\alpha-n} \leq ||\mathcal{R}_0||_{\tilde{\mathcal{L}}\to\tilde{C}}|\tilde{f}|_1.\end{aligned}$$

Thus, (17) is proved since $\mathcal{R}_0\tilde{f} = \tilde{y} \in C_{\alpha-n}[0,1]$.

Now assume $f \in \mathcal{L}[0,1]$ and assume $f \geq 0$ a.e. Then, $\overline{f} = |f|_1$. Let $0 < |\lambda| \leq \Lambda_1 < \frac{1}{||\mathcal{R}_0||_{\tilde{C}\to\tilde{C}}}$, write $f = (\alpha - n + 1)\overline{f}t^{\alpha-n} + \tilde{f}$, and consider

$$\lambda y = \lambda\mathcal{R}_\lambda f = \lambda\mathcal{R}_\lambda\Big((\alpha - n + 1)\overline{f}t^{\alpha-n} + \tilde{f}\Big).$$

Note that $\lambda\mathcal{R}_\lambda(\alpha - n + 1)\overline{f}t^{\alpha-n} = (\alpha - n + 1)\overline{f}t^{\alpha-n}$ since $(\mathcal{A} + \lambda\mathcal{I})(\alpha - n + 1)\overline{f}t^{\alpha-n} = \lambda(\alpha - (n-1))\overline{f}t^{\alpha-n}$. Thus,

$$\begin{aligned}\lambda y = \lambda\mathcal{R}_\lambda f &= \lambda\mathcal{R}_\lambda\Big((\alpha - n + 1)\overline{f}t^{\alpha-n} + \tilde{f}\Big) \\ &= (\alpha - n + 1)\overline{f}t^{\alpha-n} + \lambda\mathcal{R}_\lambda\tilde{f} \geq (\alpha - n + 1)|f|_1 - |\lambda||\mathcal{R}_\lambda\tilde{f}|_{\alpha-n}.\end{aligned}$$

Continuing to assume that $0 < |\lambda| \leq \Lambda_1$, it now follows from (17) that

$$\lambda y \geq (\alpha - (n-1))|f|_1 - |\lambda|\Big(\frac{||\mathcal{R}_0||_{\tilde{\mathcal{L}}\to\tilde{C}}}{1 - \Lambda_1||\mathcal{R}_0||_{\tilde{C}\to\tilde{C}}}\Big)|\tilde{f}|_1.$$

Since $\tilde{f} = f - (\alpha - n + 1)\overline{f}t^{\alpha-n}$, and $|\tilde{f}|_1 \leq |f|_1 + \overline{f} = 2|f|_1$, the theorem is proved with

$$\Lambda < \min\Big\{\Lambda_1, (\alpha - n + 1)\Big(\frac{1 - \Lambda_1||\mathcal{R}_0||_{\tilde{C}\to\tilde{C}}}{2||\mathcal{R}_0||_{\tilde{\mathcal{L}}\to\tilde{C}}}\Big)\Big\}.$$

In particular, if $0 < |\lambda| \leq \Lambda$, then

$$\lambda y(t) \geq K|f|_1 = (\alpha - n + 1)\Big(1 - \Lambda\Big(\frac{2||\mathcal{R}_0||_{\tilde{\mathcal{L}}\to\tilde{C}}}{1 - \Lambda_1||\mathcal{R}_0||_{\tilde{C}\to\tilde{C}}}\Big)\Big)|f|_1.$$

□

4. Four Examples

To apply Theorem 1, there are two primary tasks. First, if $\tilde{f} \in \tilde{\mathcal{L}}$, we must show there exists a unique solution $\tilde{y} \in$ Dom $(\mathcal{A})$ of $\mathcal{A}y = \tilde{f}$ satisfying $\overline{\tilde{y}} = 0$. In the case of ordinary differential equations or partial differential equations, one can often appeal to a Fredholm alternative to complete this task. For the Riemann–Liouville fractional differential equation, we only know to construct $\tilde{y}$ explicitly, and show uniqueness to complete this task. Second, we must show the existence of a constant $M > 0$ such that $|\tilde{y}|_{\alpha-n} \leq M|\tilde{f}|_1$. This will be a straightforward task since we will have constructed $\tilde{y}$ explicitly.

Example 1. *Let $1 < \alpha \leq 2$, and consider the linear boundary value problem, with a Riemann–Liouville analogue of Neumann boundary conditions, (3), (4); that is, consider,*

$$D_0^\alpha y(t) + \lambda y(t) = f(t), \quad 0 < t \leq 1,$$

$$D_0^{\alpha-1}y(0) = 0, \quad D_0^{\alpha-1}y(1) = 0.$$

For the boundary value problem (3), (4), $\mathcal{A} = D_0^\alpha$, and $Ker(\mathcal{A}) =< t^{\alpha-2} >$. We show that the operator $\mathcal{A}$ satisfies the hypotheses of Theorem 1.

One can show directly that $Im(\mathcal{A}) = \tilde{\mathcal{L}}$. If $f \in Im(\mathcal{A})$, then there exists a solution y of

$$D_0^\alpha y(t) = f(t), \quad 0 < t \le 1, \quad D_0^{\alpha-1}y(0) = 0, \quad D_0^{\alpha-1}y(1) = 0,$$

which implies

$$0 = D_0^{\alpha-1}y(1) - D_0^{\alpha-1}y(0) = \int_0^1 D_0^\alpha y(t)dt = \int_0^1 f(t)dt,$$

and $f \in \tilde{\mathcal{L}}$. Likewise, if $f \in \tilde{\mathcal{L}}$, then

$$\begin{aligned} \tilde{y}(t) &= \frac{1}{\Gamma(\alpha)} \int_0^t (t-s)^{\alpha-1} f(s)ds - \frac{(\alpha-1)t^{\alpha-2}}{\Gamma(\alpha+1)} \int_0^1 (1-s)^\alpha f(s)ds \\ &= I_0^\alpha f(t) - (\alpha-1) I_0^{\alpha+1} f(1) t^{\alpha-2} \in Dom\,(\mathcal{A}) \end{aligned} \tag{18}$$

is a solution of

$$D_0^\alpha y(t) = f(t), \quad 0 < t \le 1, \quad D_0^{\alpha-1}y(0) = 0, \quad D_0^{\alpha-1}y(1) = 0,$$

and $\overline{\tilde{y}} = 0$. To verify that $\tilde{y}$ satisfies these properties, note that any solution of $D_0^\alpha y(t) = f(t)$, $0 < t \le 1$, has the form, $I_0^\alpha f(t) + c_2 t^{\alpha-2} + c_1 t^{\alpha-1}$. Thus, $D_0^\alpha \tilde{y}(t) = f(t), 0 < t \le 1$. To see that the boundary conditions are satisfied, write

$$D_0^{\alpha-1} I_0^\alpha f(t) = D_0^{\alpha-1} I_0^{\alpha-1} I_0^1 f(t) = I_0^1 f(t) = \int_0^t f(s)ds,$$

and note that $D_0^{\alpha-1}t^{\alpha-2} = 0$. Thus, $D_0^{\alpha-1} I_0^\alpha f|_{t=0} = 0$, and $D_0^{\alpha-1} I_0^\alpha f|_{t=1} = 0$ since $f \in \tilde{\mathcal{L}}$; in particular, the boundary conditions are satisfied. To see that $\overline{\tilde{y}} = 0$, note that

$$I I_0^\alpha f(t) = I_0^{\alpha+1} f(t)$$

and so,

$$\overline{\tilde{y}} = \overline{I_0^\alpha f} - I_0^{\alpha+1} f(1) = I_0^{\alpha+1} f(1) - I_0^{\alpha+1} f(1) = 0.$$

To argue that $\mathcal{A}y = \tilde{f}$ is uniquely solvable with solution $\tilde{y} \in Dom\,(\tilde{\mathcal{A}})$, (18) implies the solvability. For uniqueness, if y_1 and y_2 are two such solutions, then $(y_1 - y_2)(t) = ct^{\alpha-2}$ and $\overline{y_1 - y_2} = 0$ implies $c = 0$.

Finally, (18) implies (11) is satisfied with $M = \frac{1}{\Gamma(\alpha)} + \frac{\alpha-1}{\Gamma(\alpha+1)} = \frac{2\alpha-1}{\Gamma(\alpha+1)}$.

Theorem 1 applies and there exists $\Lambda > 0$ such that if $0 < |\lambda| \le \Lambda$, then $(\mathcal{A} + \lambda\mathcal{I})$ satisfies a signed maximum principle in y; that is, $f \ge 0$ implies $\lambda y \ge 0$.

Example 2. *For the second example, let $1 < \alpha \le 2$, and let $a \in \mathbb{R}$. Consider the linear boundary value problem, with a Riemann–Liouville analogue of periodic boundary conditions, (5), (7); that is, consider,*

$$\begin{gathered} D_0^\alpha y(t) + aD_0^{\alpha-1}y(t) + \lambda y(t) = f(t), \quad 0 < t \le 1, \\ I_0^{2-\alpha}y(0) = I_0^{2-\alpha}y(1), \quad D_0^{\alpha-1}y(0) = D_0^{\alpha-1}y(1). \end{gathered}$$

Now, $\mathcal{A} = D_0^\alpha + aD_0^{\alpha-1}$, and $Ker(\mathcal{A}) =< t^{\alpha-2} >$. We show that the operator $\mathcal{A}$ satisfies the hypotheses of Theorem 1.

We show directly that $Im\,(\mathcal{A}) = \tilde{\mathcal{L}}$. If $f \in Im\,(\mathcal{A})$, then

$$\begin{aligned} If(t) &= I\Big(D_0^\alpha y(t) + aD_0^{\alpha-1}y(t)\Big) \\ &= \Big(D_0^{\alpha-1}y(t) - D_0^{\alpha-1}y(0)\Big) + a\Big(I_0^{2-\alpha}y(t) - I_0^{2-\alpha}y(0)\Big); \end{aligned}$$

thus, $If(1) = 0$ *since* y *satisfies the periodic boundary conditions. In particular,* $f \in \tilde{\mathcal{L}}$.

Now assume $f \in \tilde{\mathcal{L}}$. *We first construct a general solution of*

$$D_0^{\alpha}y(t) + aD_0^{\alpha-1}y(t) = f(t), \quad 0 < t \leq 1,$$

$$I_0^{2-\alpha}y(0) = I_0^{2-\alpha}y(1), \quad D_0^{\alpha-1}y(0) = D_0^{\alpha-1}y(1).$$

Since $D_0^{\alpha}y = DD_0^{\alpha-1}y$, *apply an integrating factor,* e^{at}, *and*

$$D(e^{at}D_0^{\alpha-1}y(t)) = e^{at}f(t),$$

which implies

$$D_0^{\alpha-1}y(t) = D_0^{\alpha-1}y(0)e^{-at} + \int_0^t e^{-a(t-s)}f(s)ds.$$

Then,

$$\begin{aligned} y(t) &= ct^{(\alpha-1)-1} + I_0^{\alpha-1}\left(D_0^{\alpha-1}y(0)e^{-at} + \int_0^t e^{-a(t-s)}f(s)ds\right) \\ &= ct^{\alpha-2} + D_0^{\alpha-1}y(0)I_0^{\alpha-1}e^{-at} + I_0^{\alpha-1}\left(\int_0^t e^{-a(t-s)}f(s)ds\right). \end{aligned}$$

Apply the periodic boundary conditions. Then,

$$D_0^{\alpha-1}y(t) = D_0^{\alpha-1}y(0)e^{-at} + \int_0^t e^{-a(t-s)}f(s)ds,$$

and the boundary condition $D_0^{\alpha-1}y(0) = D_0^{\alpha-1}y(1)$ *implies*

$$D_0^{\alpha-1}y(0) = \frac{1}{1-e^{-a}}\int_0^1 e^{-a(1-s)}f(s)ds$$

is uniquely determined. Now,

$$\begin{aligned} I_0^{2-\alpha}y(t) &= c\Gamma(\alpha-1) + D_0^{\alpha-1}y(0)Ie^{-at} + I\left(\int_0^t e^{-a(t-s)}f(s)ds\right) \\ &= c\Gamma(\alpha-1) + D_0^{\alpha-1}y(0)\int_0^t e^{-as}ds + \int_0^t\left(\int_0^s e^{-a(s-r)}f(r)dr\right)ds \\ &= c\Gamma(\alpha-1) + D_0^{\alpha-1}y(0)\frac{(1-e^{-at})}{a} - \int_0^t \frac{(e^{-a(t-s)}-1)}{a}f(s)ds. \end{aligned}$$

Thus, $I_0^{2-\alpha}y(0) = c\Gamma(\alpha-1)$ *and*

$$\begin{aligned} I_0^{2-\alpha}y(1) &= c\Gamma(\alpha-1) + D_0^{\alpha-1}y(0)\frac{(1-e^{-a})}{a} - \int_0^1 \frac{(e^{-a(1-s)}-1)}{a}f(s)ds \\ &= c\Gamma(\alpha-1) + \int_0^1 \frac{e^{-a(1-s)}}{a}f(s)ds - \int_0^1 \frac{e^{-a(1-s)}}{a}f(s)ds - \frac{1}{a}\int_0^1 f(s)ds \\ &= c\Gamma(\alpha-1). \end{aligned}$$

At this point in the construction, c is still undetermined and

$$y(t) = ct^{\alpha-2} + D_0^{\alpha-1}y(0)I_0^{\alpha-1}e^{-at} + I_0^{\alpha-1}\left(\int_0^t e^{-a(t-s)}f(s)ds\right)$$

is a general solution of

$$D_0^{\alpha}y(t) + aD_0^{\alpha-1}y(t) = f(t), \quad 0 < t \leq 1,$$

$$I_0^{2-\alpha}y(0) = I_0^{2-\alpha}y(1), \quad D_0^{\alpha-1}y(0) = D_0^{\alpha-1}y(1).$$

To obtain the parameter c uniquely, Theorem 1 requires that $\overline{y} = 0$. *Thus,*

$$0 = \frac{c}{\alpha - 1} + D_0^{\alpha-1}y(0)\overline{I_0^{\alpha-1}e^{-at}} + \overline{I_0^{\alpha-1}\int_0^t e^{-a(t-s)}f(s)ds}$$

and

$$c = (1-\alpha)D_0^{\alpha-1}y(0)\overline{I_0^{\alpha-1}e^{-at}} + \overline{I_0^{\alpha-1}\int_0^t e^{-a(t-s)}f(s)ds}$$

is uniquely determined.

Note that

$$D_0^{\alpha-1}y(0) = \frac{1}{1-e^{-a}}\int_0^1 e^{-a(1-s)}f(s)ds \text{ implies } |D_0^{\alpha-1}y(0)| \leq \frac{1}{1-e^{-a}}|f|_1.$$

Thus,

$$y(t) = ct^{\alpha-2} + D_0^{\alpha-1}y(0)I_0^{\alpha-1}e^{-at} + I_0^{\alpha-1}\Big(\int_0^t e^{-a(t-s)}f(s)ds\Big)$$

implies (11) is satisfied.

This concludes the second example.

Before proceeding to the third example, we observe that Theorem 1 does not apparently apply to a Neumann boundary value problem (5), (4) in the case $1 < \alpha \leq 2$, $a \neq 0$. *Assume* $f \in \tilde{\mathcal{L}}$ *and begin the construction of a general solution. As before, one obtains*

$$D_0^{\alpha-1}y(t) = D_0^{\alpha-1}y(0)e^{-at} + \int_0^t e^{-a(t-s)}f(s)ds = \int_0^t e^{-a(t-s)}f(s)ds.$$

Take for example, $f(t) = t - \frac{1}{2} \in \tilde{\mathcal{L}}$. *Then,* $D_0^{\alpha-1}y(1) \neq 0$.

Example 3. *For the third example, let* $n \geq 2$, *let* $n - 1 < \alpha \leq n$, *and consider the linear boundary value problem, with a Riemann–Liouville analogue of periodic boundary conditions, (6), (7); that is, consider,*

$$D_0^{\alpha}y(t) + \lambda y(t) = f(t), \quad 0 \leq t \leq 1,$$

$$I_0^{n-\alpha}y(0) = I_0^{n-\alpha}y(1), \quad D_0^{\alpha-j}y(0) = D_0^{\alpha-j}y(1), \quad j = 1, \ldots, n-1.$$

For the boundary value problem (6), (7), $\mathcal{A} = D_0^{\alpha}$ *and* $Ker(\mathcal{A}) = < t^{\alpha-n} >$. *Again, we show* $Im\ (\mathcal{A}) = \tilde{\mathcal{L}}$. *First, note that if the boundary value problem (6), (7) is solvable, then the boundary condition* $D_0^{\alpha-1}y(0) = D_0^{\alpha-1}y(1)$ *implies* $f \in \tilde{\mathcal{L}}$ *since* $If(t) = ID_0^{\alpha}y(t) = D_0^{\alpha-1}y(t) - D_0^{\alpha-1}y(0)$. *Thus,* $\int_0^1 f(t)dt = D_0^{\alpha-1}y(0) - D_0^{\alpha-1}y(0) = 0$.

Now assume $f \in \tilde{\mathcal{L}}$. *If* $\tilde{y} \in Dom\ (\tilde{\mathcal{A}})$, *then*

$$\tilde{y}(t) = I_0^{\alpha}f(t) + \sum_{j=1}^{n} c_{\alpha-j}t^{\alpha-j}.$$

We show the coefficients $c_{\alpha-j}$ *are uniquely determined. The condition* $D_0^{\alpha-1}\tilde{y}(0) = D_0^{\alpha-1}\tilde{y}(1)$ *implies*

$$If(0) + c_{\alpha-1}\Gamma(\alpha) = If(1) + c_{\alpha-1}\Gamma(\alpha)$$

which implies $c_{\alpha-1}$ *is undetermined at this point in the construction. Let* $k \in \{2, \ldots, n\}$. *Then,*

$$D_0^{\alpha-k}\tilde{y}(t) = I_0^k f(t) + \sum_{j=1}^{k} c_{\alpha-j}\frac{\Gamma(\alpha+1-j)}{\Gamma(k+1-j)}t^{k-j}. \tag{19}$$

Apply the boundary conditions $D_0^{\alpha-j}\tilde{y}(0) = D_0^{\alpha-j}\tilde{y}(1)$ *in the order* $j = 2, \ldots, n$. *At* $j = 2$,

$$I^2 f(0) + c_{\alpha-2}\Gamma(\alpha-1) = D_0^{\alpha-2}\tilde{y}(0) = D_0^{\alpha-2}\tilde{y}(1) = I^2 f(1) + c_{\alpha-2}\Gamma(\alpha-1) + c_{\alpha-1}\frac{\Gamma(\alpha)}{\Gamma(2)}.$$

Thus, $c_{\alpha-1} = -\frac{\Gamma(2)}{\Gamma(\alpha)} I^2 f(1)$ *is uniquely determined. Employ (19) inductively and for* $j = k$,

$$\begin{aligned} I^k f(0) + c_{\alpha-k}\Gamma(\alpha+1-k)) &= D_0^{\alpha-k}\tilde{y}(0) = D_0^{\alpha-k}\tilde{y}(1) \\ &= I^k f(1) + c_{\alpha-k}\Gamma(\alpha+1-k) + \sum_{j=1}^{k-1} c_{\alpha-j}\frac{\Gamma(\alpha+1-j)}{\Gamma(k+1-j)}. \end{aligned}$$

Inductively, $c_{\alpha-j}$, $j = 1, \ldots k-2$ *have been uniquely determined and so,*

$$c_{\alpha-(k-1)} = -\frac{\Gamma(2)}{\Gamma(\alpha-(k-2))}\left(I^k f(1) + \sum_{j=1}^{k-2} c_{\alpha-j}\frac{\Gamma(\alpha+1-j)}{\Gamma(k+1-j)}\right) \tag{20}$$

is uniquely determined. To summarize, the boundary conditions $D_0^{\alpha-j}y(0) = D_0^{\alpha-j}y(1), j = 1, \ldots, n-1$, *uniquely determine the coefficients,* $c_{\alpha-1}, \ldots, c_{\alpha-(n-2)}$.

To determine the coefficient, $c_{\alpha-(n-1)}$, *employ the boundary condition* $I_0^{n-\alpha}\tilde{y}(0) = I_0^{n-\alpha}\tilde{y}(1)$. *Since*

$$I_0^{n-\alpha}\tilde{y}(t) = I_0^n f(t) + \sum_{j=1}^{n} c_{\alpha-j}\frac{\Gamma(\alpha+1-j)}{\Gamma(n+1-j)} t^{n-j},$$

it follows that

$$c_{\alpha-(n-1)} = -\frac{\Gamma(2)}{\Gamma(\alpha-(n-2))}\left(I^n f(1) + \sum_{j=1}^{n-2} c_{\alpha-j}\frac{\Gamma(\alpha+1-j)}{\Gamma(n+1-j)}\right) \tag{21}$$

is uniquely determined.

Finally, the application of Theorem 1 requires that $\overline{\tilde{y}} = 0$. *Thus,*

$$0 = \overline{I_0^\alpha f} + \frac{c_{\alpha-n}}{\alpha+1-n} + \sum_{j=1}^{n-1} \frac{c_{\alpha-j}}{\alpha+1-j}.$$

Hence, $c_{\alpha-n}$ *is uniquely determined and the proof that* $f \in \tilde{\mathcal{L}}$ *implies* $\tilde{y} \in \mathrm{Dom}\,(\tilde{\mathcal{A}})$ *is uniquely determined is complete.*

To see that M *in (11) can be computed, recall that*

$$\tilde{y}(t) = I_0^\alpha f(t) + \sum_{j=1}^{n} c_{\alpha-j} t^{\alpha-j}.$$

and employ (20) and (21). Note that $c_{\alpha-1}$ *is a multiple of* $I^2 f(1)$, *which implies that* $c_{\alpha-k}$ *is a linear combination of* $I^k f(1), \ldots, I^2 f(1)$, *for* $k = 1, \ldots, n$. *Thus,* M *is computable. Thus, Theorem 1 applies and there exists* $\Lambda > 0$ *such that if* $0 < |\lambda| \leq \Lambda$, *then* $(\mathcal{A} + \lambda\mathcal{I})$ *satisfies the strong signed maximum principle in* y.

Example 4. *Theorem 1 can also apply to the boundary value problem with boundary conditions analogous to periodic boundary conditions, (6), (8); that is, consider,*

$$D_0^\alpha y(t) + \lambda y(t) = f(t), \quad 0 \leq t \leq 1,$$

$$\lim_{t\to 0^+} t^{n-\alpha}y(t) = y(1), \quad D_0^{\alpha-j}y(0) = D_0^{\alpha-j}y(1), \quad j = 1, \ldots, n-1.$$

The unique determination of $c_{\alpha-k}, k = 1, \ldots n-2$ proceeds precisely as in Example (3). Apply the boundary condition $\lim_{t\to 0^+} t^{n-\alpha}y(t) = y(1)$ to $\tilde{y}(t) = I_0^\alpha f(t) + \sum_{j=1}^{n} c_{\alpha-j}t^{\alpha-j}$ to obtain

$$c_{\alpha-n} = I^n f(1) + \sum_{j=1}^{n} c_{\alpha-j}$$

and $c_{\alpha-(n-1)} = -\left(I^n f(1) + \sum_{j=1}^{n-2} c_{\alpha-j}\right)$ is uniquely determined. Then, as in Example 3, $c_{\alpha-n}$ is uniquely determined by the requirement that $\bar{\tilde{y}} = 0$.

Thus, Theorem 1 applies and there exists $\Lambda > 0$ such that if $0 < |\lambda| \leq \Lambda$ then $(\mathcal{A} + \lambda\mathcal{I})$ satisfies the strong signed maximum principle in y.

5. A Monotone Method

The application of monotone methods in the presence of a maximum principle or in the presence of an anti-maximum principle to construct approximate solutions of initial value or boundary value type problems enjoys a long history. The purpose of this section is to employ (1) to quickly recognize the presence of the maximum principle or the anti-maximum principle. There are recent applications of monotone methods to periodic-like boundary value problems for Riemann–Liouville fractional differential equations; see, for example, [6,7]. In each of those application, $0 < \alpha \leq 1$, and the anti-maximum principle is observed by the explicit construction of a corresponding Green's function in terms of Mittag-Leffler functions.

Assume $f : (0,1] \times \mathbb{R} \to \mathbb{R}$ is continuous and consider the boundary value problem

$$D_0^\alpha y(t) = f(t, y(t)), \quad 0 < t \leq 1, \quad 1 < \alpha \leq 2, \tag{22}$$

$$D_0^{\alpha-1}y(0) = 0, \quad D_0^{\alpha-1}y(1) = 0. \tag{23}$$

Assume that

$$y(t) \in C_{\alpha-2}[0,1] \text{ implies } f(t, y(t)) \in C_{\alpha-2}[0,1], \tag{24}$$

and assume further that f satisfies the following monotonicity property,

$$f(t, y_1) < f(t, y_2) \text{ for } (t, y) \in (0,1] \times \mathbb{R}, \quad y_1 > y_2. \tag{25}$$

Thus, f is monotone decreasing in the second component.

Apply Theorem 1 and find $\Lambda > 0$ such that if $0 < \lambda \leq \Lambda$, then $(\mathcal{A} + \lambda\mathcal{I})$ satisfies a strong signed maximum principle in λy. Apply a shift [29] to (22) and consider the equivalent boundary value problem,

$$D_0^\alpha y(t) + \lambda y(t) = f(t, y(t)) + \lambda y(t), \quad 0 < t \leq 1,$$

with boundary conditions (23) where $-\Lambda \leq \lambda < 0$ and $\Lambda > 0$ is shown to exist in Theorem 1. Note that if $g(t,y) = f(t,y) + \lambda y$ and f satisfies (24) and (25), then g satisfies (24) and g satisfies (25) if $\lambda < 0$.

Assume the existence of solutions, $w_1, v_1 \in C_{\alpha-2}[0,1]$, of the following boundary value problems for differential inequalities

$$\begin{aligned} &D_0^\alpha w_1(t) \geq f(t, w_1(t)), \quad 0 < t \leq 1, && D_0^\alpha v_1(t) \leq f(t, v_1(t)), \quad 0 < t \leq 1, \\ &D_0^{\alpha-1}w_1(0) = 0, \quad D_0^{\alpha-1}w_1(1) = 0, && D_0^{\alpha-1}v_1(0) = 0, \quad D_0^{\alpha-1}v_1(1) = 0. \end{aligned} \tag{26}$$

Assume further that

$$v_1(t) - w_1(t) \geq 0, \quad 0 < t \leq 1. \tag{27}$$

Since $\lambda < 0$, define a partial order $\succeq_{\lambda<0}$ on $C_{\alpha-2}[0,1]$ by

$$u \succeq_{\lambda<0} 0 \Longleftrightarrow u(t) \leq 0, 0 < t \leq 1.$$

Then, the assumption (27) implies $w_1 \succeq_{\lambda<0} v_1$.

Define iteratively the sequences $\{v_k\}_{k=1}^{\infty}$, $\{w_k\}_{k=1}^{\infty}$, where

$$D_0^{\alpha} v_{k+1}(t) + \lambda v_{k+1}(t) = f(t, v_k(t)) + \lambda v_k(t), \quad 0 < t \leq 1, \qquad (28)$$
$$D_0^{\alpha-1} v_{k+1}(0) = 0, \quad D_0^{\alpha-1} v_{k+1}(1) = 0,$$

and

$$D_0^{\alpha} w_{k+1}(t) + \lambda w_{k+1}(t) = f(t, w_k(t)) + \lambda w_k(t), \quad 0 < t \leq 1, \qquad (29)$$
$$D_0^{\alpha-1} w_{k+1}(0) = 0, \quad D_0^{\alpha-1} w_{k+1}(1) = 0.$$

Inductively, Theorem 1 implies the existence of each v_{k+1}, w_{k+1} since $|\lambda| \leq \Lambda$ implies the inverse of $(\mathcal{A} + \lambda \mathcal{I})$ exists, and, for example, $f(t, v_k(t)) + \lambda v_k(t) \in C_{\alpha-2}[0,1]$.

Theorem 2. *Assume $f : (0,1] \times \mathbb{R} \to \mathbb{R}$ is continuous, assume that f satisfies* (24)*, and assume f satisfies the monotonicity properties* (25)*. Assume the existence of functions $v_1, w_1 \in C_{\alpha-2}[0,1]$ satisfying* (26) *and* (27)*. Define the sequences of iterates $\{v_k\}_{k=1}^{\infty}$, $\{w_k\}_{k=1}^{\infty}$ by* (28) *and* (29)*, respectively. Then, for each positive integer k,*

$$w_k \succeq_{\lambda<0} w_{k+1} \succeq_{\lambda<0} v_{k+1} \succeq_{\lambda<0} v_k. \qquad (30)$$

Moreover, $\{v_k\}_{k=1}^{\infty}$ converges in $C_{\alpha-2}$ to a solution $v \in C_{\alpha-2}[0,1]$ of the boundary value problem (22), (23) *and $\{w_k\}_{k=1}^{\infty}$ converges in $C_{\alpha-2}[0,1]$ to a solution $w \in C_{\alpha-2}[0,1]$ of the boundary value problem* (22), (23) *satisfying*

$$w_k \succeq_{\lambda<0} w_{k+1} \succeq_{\lambda<0} w \succeq_{\lambda<0} v \succeq_{\lambda<0} v_{k+1} \succeq_{\lambda<0} v_k. \qquad (31)$$

Proof. Since v_1 satisfies a differential inequality given in (27), then for $0 < t \leq 1$,

$$D_0^{\alpha} v_2(t) + \lambda v_2(t) = f(t, v_1(t)) + \lambda v_1(t) \geq D_0^{\alpha} v_1(t) + \lambda v_1(t).$$

Set $u = v_2 - v_1$ and u satisfies a boundary value problem for a differential inequality,

$$D_0^{\alpha} u(t) + \lambda u(t) \geq 0, \quad 0 < t \leq 1, \quad D_0^{\alpha-1} u(0) = 0, \quad D_0^{\alpha-1} u(1) = 0.$$

The signed maximum principle applies and $u \succeq_{\lambda<0} 0$; in particular, $v_2 \succeq_{\lambda<0} v_1$. Similarly, $w_1 \succeq_{\lambda<0} w_2$. Now set $u = w_2 - v_2$ and

$$D_0^{\alpha} u(t) + \lambda u(t) = \Big(f(t, w_1(t)) - f(t, v_1(t))\Big) + \lambda(w_1(t) - v_1(t)), \quad 0 < t \leq 1,$$
$$D_0^{\alpha-1} u(0) = 0, \quad D_0^{\alpha-1} u(1) = 0.$$

Since f satisfies (25) and $w_1 \succeq_{\lambda<0} v_1$, then

$$D_0^{\alpha} u(t) + \lambda u(t) \geq 0, \quad 0 \leq t \leq 1,$$

and again the signed maximum principle applies and $u \succeq_{\lambda<0} 0$. In particular, $w_2 \succeq_{\lambda<0} v_2$. Thus, (30) is proved for $k = 1$.

Before applying a straightforward induction to obtain (30), we must show $D_0^{\alpha} w_2(t) \geq f(t, w_2(t))$, and $D_0^{\alpha} v_2(t) \leq f(t, v_2(t))$, for $0 < t \leq 1$. Since $f(t, v_1(t)) \leq f(t, v_2(t))$, $\lambda < 0$ and $(v_1 - v_2)(t) \geq 0$, it follows that

$$D_0^{\alpha} v_2(t) = f(t, v_1(t)) + \lambda(v_1 - v_2)(t) \leq f(t, v_2(t)).$$

Similarly, $D_0^{\alpha} w_2(t) \geq f(t, w_2(t))$ and (30) is valid.

To obtain the existence of limiting solutions v and w satisfying (31), note that the sequence $\{v_k\}$ is monotone decreasing and bounded below by $\{w_1\}$. Thus, the sequence $\{v_k\}$ is converging pointwise to some $v(t)$ for each $t \in (0,1]$. Moreover, if

$$z_k(t) = t^{2-\alpha} v_k \in C[0,1], \quad z_k(0) = a_k,$$

the sequence $\{z_k\}$ is converging pointwise to some $z(t) = t^{2-\alpha}v(t)$, $z(0) = a_0$ where a_k converges monotonically to a_0. At this point in the argument, the convergence is pointwise. Since

$$D_0^\alpha v_{k+1}(t) = f(t, v_k(t)) + \lambda(v_k(t) - v_{k+1}(t)), \quad 0 < t \le 1,$$

if follows that $\{D_0^\alpha v_k\}$ is converging pointwise to $g(t) = f(t, v(t))$ for each $t \in (0,1]$. Since $D_0^{\alpha-1} v_k(0) = 0$,

$$v_k(t) = a_k t^{\alpha-2} + I_0^\alpha D_0^\alpha v_k(t), \quad 0 < t \le 1.$$

Thus, by the dominated convergence theorem

$$v(t) = a_0 t^{\alpha-2} + I_0^\alpha g(t), \quad 0 < t \le 1;$$

in particular,

$$D_0^\alpha v(t) = g(t) = f(t, v(t)), \quad 0 < t \le 1,$$

and v satisfies the fractional differential equation. To see that v satisfies the Neumann type boundary conditions, again observe

$$D_0^\alpha v_{k+1}(t) = f(t, v_k(t)) + \lambda(v_k(t) - v_{k+1}(t)), \quad 0 < t \le 1,$$

$$D_0^{\alpha-1} v_k(0) = 0, \quad D_0^{\alpha-1} v_k(1) = 0.$$

Since $0 = D_0^{\alpha-1} v_k(1) - D_0^{\alpha-1} v_k(0) = \int_0^1 D_0^\alpha v_{k+1}(s) ds$, it follows that

$$\int_0^1 \Big(f(s, v_k(s)) + \lambda(v_k(s) - v_{k+1}(s)) \Big) ds = 0.$$

Again, the dominated convergence theorem implies that $\int_0^1 f(s, v(s)) ds = 0$. Thus,

$$D_0^{\alpha-1} v(t) = \int_0^t f(s, v(s)) ds$$

which implies $D_0^{\alpha-1} v(0) = 0$ and $D_0^{\alpha-1} v(1) = \int_0^1 f(s, v(s)) ds = 0$.

Note that since $w_1(t) \le v(t) \le v_1(t)$ on $(0,1]$ and $D_0^{\alpha-1} v(t) = \int_0^t f(s, v(s)) ds$, then $D_0^{\alpha-1} v$ is uniformly continuous on any compact subinterval of $(0,1]$. Thus,

$$v(t) = a_0 t^{\alpha-2} + I_0^{\alpha-1} D_0^{\alpha-1} v(t), \quad 0 < t \le 1,$$

implies $v \in C_{\alpha-2}[0,1]$ and

$$w_k \succeq_{\lambda<0} v \succeq_{\lambda<0} v_k$$

for each k. Moreover, Dini's theorem now applies and the convergence of $t^{2-\alpha} v_k(t)$ is uniform.

Similar details apply to $\{w_k\}$ and the theorem is proved. □

Suppose now f satisfies the "anti"-inequalities to (25); that is, suppose f satisfies

$$f(t, y_1) > f(t, y_2) \text{ for } (t, y) \in (0,1] \times \mathbb{R}, \quad y_1 > y_2. \tag{32}$$

One can appeal to the signed maximum principle, apply a shift to (22), and consider the equivalent boundary value problem, $D_0^\alpha y(t) + \lambda y(t) = f(t, y(t)) + \lambda y(t)$, $0 < t \le 1$, where

$0 < \lambda \leq \Lambda$, and $\Lambda > 0$ is given by Theorem 1. Note, if f satisfies (32) and $\lambda > 0$, then $g(t,y) = f(t,y) + \lambda y$ satisfies (32).

Now, assume the existence of solutions, $w_1, v_1 \in C_{\alpha-2}[0,1]$, of the following differential inequalities

$$\begin{aligned} D_0^\alpha w_1(t) &\leq f(t, w_1(t)), \quad 0 < t \leq 1, & D_0^\alpha v_1(t) &\geq f(t, v_1(t)), \quad 0 < t \leq 1, \\ D_0^{\alpha-1} w_1(0) &= 0, \quad D_0^{\alpha-1} w_1(1) = 0, & D_0^{\alpha-1} v_1(0) &= 0, \quad D_0^{\alpha-1} v_1(1) = 0. \end{aligned} \tag{33}$$

Assume further that

$$(v_1(t) - w_1(t)) \geq 0, \quad 0 < t \leq 1. \tag{34}$$

Noting that $\lambda > 0$ defines a partial order $\succeq_{\lambda>0}$ on $C_{\alpha-2}[0,1]$ by

$$u \succeq_{\lambda>0} 0 \Longleftrightarrow u(t) \geq 0, 0 < t \leq 1.$$

In particular, in (34), assume $v_1 \succeq_{\lambda>0} w_1$.

Theorem 3. *Assume $f : (0,1] \times \mathbb{R} \to \mathbb{R}$ is continuous, assume that f satisfies* (24), *and assume f satisfies the monotonicity properties,* (32). *Assume the existence of $w_1, v_1 \in C_{\alpha-2}[0,1]$ satisfying* (33) *and* (34). *Define the sequences of iterates $\{v_k\}_{k=1}^\infty$, $\{w_k\}_{k=1}^\infty$ by* (28) *and* (29), *respectively. Then, for each positive integer k,*

$$v_k \succeq_{\lambda>0} v_{k+1} \succeq_{\lambda>0} w_{k+1} \succeq_{\lambda>0} w_k.$$

Moreover, $\{v_k\}_{k=1}^\infty$ converges in $C_{\alpha-2}$ to a solution $v \in C_{\alpha-2}[0,1]$ of the boundary value problem (22), (23) *and $\{w_k\}_{k=1}^\infty$ converges in $C_{\alpha-2}[0,1]$ to a solution $w \in C_{\alpha-2}[0,1]$ of the boundary value problem* (22), (23) *satisfying*

$$v_k \succeq_{\lambda>0} v_{k+1} \succeq_{\lambda>0} v \succeq_{\lambda>0} w \succeq_{\lambda>0} w_{k+1} \succeq_{\lambda>0} w_k. \tag{35}$$

6. Example

We close the article with an example in which Theorem 3 applies and in which upper and lower solutions, v_1 and w_1, are explicitly produced. To do so, we construct an explicit Green's function to obtain an estimate on $\Lambda > 0$, and we exhibit verifiable conditions on f so that (24) is satisfied.

The two-parameter Mittag-Leffler function

$$E_{\alpha,\beta}(z) = \sum_{n=0}^{\infty} \frac{z^n}{\Gamma(\alpha n + \beta)}, \quad Re(\alpha) > 0, \quad \beta \in \mathbb{C}, \quad z \in \mathbb{C}$$

will be employed to construct an appropriate Green's function.

Assume $1 < \alpha < 2$, assume $\lambda \neq 0$, and consider a Neumann boundary value problem for nonhomogenous linear Equations (3) and (4). We restate the boundary value problem for convenience.

$$D_0^\alpha y(t) + \lambda y(t) = f(t), \quad 0 < t \leq 1, \quad 1 < \alpha < 2,$$

$$D_0^{\alpha-1} y(0) = 0, \quad D_0^{\alpha-1} y(1) = 0.$$

Thus, $y(t) = -\lambda I_0^\alpha y(t) + I_0^\alpha f(t) + ct^{\alpha-2}$ where c is still undetermined or

$$(I + \lambda I_0^\alpha) y(t) = I_0^\alpha f(t) + ct^{\alpha-2}.$$

Employ the Neumann series to see that if $(I+\lambda I_0^\alpha)y(t)=h(t)$, then

$$\begin{aligned} y(t) &= \sum_{n=0}^{\infty}(-\lambda)^n I_0^{\alpha n}h(t) = \Big(I+\sum_{n=1}^{\infty}(-\lambda)^n I_0^{\alpha n}\Big)h(t) \\ &= h(t) + \int_0^t \sum_{n=1}^{\infty}(-\lambda)^n \frac{(t-s)^{\alpha n-1}}{\Gamma(\alpha n)}h(s)ds \\ &= h(t) - \lambda\int_0^t (t-s)^{\alpha-1}\sum_{n=0}^{\infty}\frac{(-\lambda(t-s)^\alpha)^n}{\Gamma(\alpha n+\alpha)}h(s)ds \\ &= h(t) - \lambda\int_0^t (t-s)^{\alpha-1}E_{\alpha,\alpha}(-\lambda(t-s)^\alpha)h(s)ds. \end{aligned}$$

Thus,

$$y(t) = h(t) + (-\lambda)\int_0^t (t-s)^{\alpha-1}E_{\alpha,\alpha}(-\lambda(t-s)^\alpha))h(s)ds,$$

where $h(t)=I_0^\alpha f(t)+ct^{\alpha-2}$. Employ the identity

$$\int_a^b (t-a)^\beta(x-t)^{n-1}dt = \frac{\Gamma(\beta+1)\Gamma(n)}{\Gamma(\beta+1+n)}(x-a)^{n+\beta}$$

and note that

$$\begin{aligned} & t^{\alpha-2} + (-\lambda)\int_0^t (t-s)^{\alpha-1}E_{\alpha,\alpha}(-\lambda(t-s)^\alpha)s^{\alpha-2}ds \\ &= \Gamma(\alpha-1)\frac{t^{\alpha-2}}{\Gamma(\alpha-1)} + \sum_{n=0}^{\infty}(-\lambda)^{n+1}\int_0^t \frac{(t-s)^{\alpha n+\alpha-1}s^{\alpha-2}}{\Gamma(\alpha n+\alpha)}dt \\ &= \Gamma(\alpha-1)\frac{t^{\alpha-2}}{\Gamma(\alpha-1)} + \sum_{n=0}^{\infty}(-\lambda)^{n+1}\frac{\Gamma(\alpha-1)}{\Gamma(\alpha(n+1)+\alpha-1)}t^{\alpha(n+1)+\alpha-2} \\ &= \Gamma(\alpha-1)t^{\alpha-2}E_{\alpha,\alpha-1}(-\lambda t^\alpha). \end{aligned}$$

Thus,

$$\begin{aligned} y(t) = I_0^\alpha f(t) + (-\lambda)\int_0^t (t-s)^{\alpha-1}E_{\alpha,\alpha}(-\lambda(t-s)^\alpha))I_0^\alpha f(s)ds \\ + c\Gamma(\alpha-1)t^{\alpha-2}E_{\alpha,\alpha-1}(-\lambda t^\alpha). \end{aligned} \tag{36}$$

To calculate $D_0^{\alpha-1}y(t)$, we have $D_0^{\alpha-1}I_0^\alpha f(t)=I^1 f(t)$,

$$\begin{aligned} D_0^{\alpha-1}t^{\alpha-2}E_{\alpha,\alpha-1}(-\lambda t^\alpha) &= t^{-1}E_{\alpha,0}(-\lambda t^\alpha) \\ &= t^{-1}\sum_{n=0}^{\infty}\frac{(-\lambda t^\alpha)^n}{\Gamma(\alpha n)} = t^{-1}\sum_{n=1}^{\infty}\frac{(-\lambda t^\alpha)^n}{\Gamma(\alpha n)} \\ &= (-\lambda)t^{\alpha-1}\sum_{n=0}^{\infty}\frac{(-\lambda t^\alpha)^n}{\Gamma(\alpha n+\alpha)} = (-\lambda)t^{\alpha-1}E_{\alpha,\alpha}(-\lambda t^\alpha), \end{aligned}$$

and

$$\begin{aligned}
D_0^{\alpha-1} t^{\alpha-2} & \int_0^t (t-s)^{\alpha-1} E_{\alpha,\alpha}(-\lambda(t-s)^{\alpha})) I_0^{\alpha} f(s) ds \\
&= D I_0^{2-\alpha} t^{\alpha-2} \int_0^t (t-s)^{\alpha-1} E_{\alpha,\alpha}(-\lambda(t-s)^{\alpha})) I_0^{\alpha} f(s) ds \\
&= \int_0^t E_{\alpha,1}(-\lambda(t-s)^{\alpha}) I_0^{\alpha} f(s) ds \\
&= \int_0^t E_{\alpha,1}(-\lambda(t-r)^{\alpha}) \int_0^r \frac{(r-s)^{\alpha-1}}{\Gamma(\alpha)} f(s) ds dr \\
&= \int_0^t \Big(\int_s^t \sum_{n=0}^{\infty} \frac{(-\lambda(t-r)^{\alpha})^n}{\Gamma(\alpha n+1)} \frac{(r-s)^{\alpha-1}}{\Gamma(\alpha)} dr \Big) f(s) ds \\
&= \int_0^t (\sum_{n=0}^{\infty} \frac{(-\lambda)^n (t-s)^{\alpha n+\alpha}}{\Gamma(\alpha n+\alpha+1)} (t-s)^{\alpha n+\alpha}) f(s) ds \\
&= \int_0^t (t-s)^{\alpha} E_{\alpha,\alpha+1}(-\lambda(t-s)^{\alpha}) f(s) ds.
\end{aligned}$$

Thus,

$$\begin{aligned}
D_0^{\alpha-1} y(1) = I^1 f(1) + (-\lambda) \int_0^1 (1-s)^{\alpha} E_{\alpha,\alpha+1}(-\lambda(1-s)^{\alpha})) f(s) ds \\
- \lambda c \Gamma(\alpha-1) E_{\alpha,\alpha}(-\lambda).
\end{aligned}$$

Employ the boundary condition $D_0^{\alpha-1} y(1) = 0$ and obtain

$$c = \frac{\int_0^1 f(s) ds - \lambda \int_0^1 (1-s)^{\alpha} E_{\alpha,\alpha+1}(-\lambda(1-s)^{\alpha}) f(s) ds}{\lambda \Gamma(\alpha-1) E_{\alpha,\alpha}(-\lambda)},$$

if $E_{\alpha,\alpha}(-\lambda) \neq 0$.

The solution y in (36) satisfies $\lambda y = -\lambda D_0^{\alpha} y + f$ or

$$\begin{aligned}
y &= \frac{1}{\lambda} \Big(\lambda \int_0^t (t-s)^{\alpha-1} E_{\alpha,\alpha}(-\lambda(t-s)^{\alpha}) f(s) ds + \lambda c \Gamma(\alpha-1) t^{\alpha-2} E_{\alpha,\alpha-1}(-\lambda t^{\alpha}) \Big) \\
&= \int_0^t (t-s)^{\alpha-1} E_{\alpha,\alpha}(-\lambda(t-s)^{\alpha}) f(s) ds + c \Gamma(\alpha-1) t^{\alpha-2} E_{\alpha,\alpha-1}(-\lambda t^{\alpha})
\end{aligned}$$

Define

$$\begin{aligned}
g(\alpha,\lambda;t,s) &= \frac{t^{\alpha-2} E_{\alpha,\alpha-1}(-\lambda t^{\alpha}) \Big(1 - \lambda(1-s)^{\alpha} E_{\alpha,\alpha+1}(-\lambda(1-s)^{\alpha}) \Big)}{\lambda E_{\alpha,\alpha}(-\lambda)} \\
&= \frac{t^{\alpha-2} E_{\alpha,\alpha-1}(-\lambda t^{\alpha}) E_{\alpha,1}(-\lambda(1-s)^{\alpha}) \Big)}{\lambda E_{\alpha,\alpha}(-\lambda)},
\end{aligned}$$

where an identity $E_{\alpha,\beta}(z) = \frac{1}{\Gamma(\beta)} + z E_{\alpha,\alpha+\beta}$ has been employed. Then,

$$y(t) = \int_0^1 G(\alpha,\lambda;t,s) f(s) ds,$$

where

$$G(\alpha,\lambda;t,s) = \begin{cases} g(\alpha,\lambda;t,s), & 0 \le t \le s \le 1, \\ g(\alpha,\lambda;t,s) + (t-s)^{\alpha-1} E_{\alpha,\alpha}(-\lambda(t-s)^{\alpha}), & 0 \le s < t \le 1. \end{cases}$$

One can see from this construction that a maximum principle will be valid for $\lambda \in (-\infty, 0)$. For the anti-maximum principle, it is shown in ([30], Corollary 3) that $E_{\alpha,\alpha}(-z)$ has the smallest in modulus root which is a positive root. From the identity,

$$I_0^{\alpha-1} E_{\alpha,1}(-\lambda t^\alpha) = t^{\alpha-1} E_{\alpha,\alpha}(-\lambda t^\alpha),$$

and integrating from 0 to 1, it is clear that $E_{\alpha,1}(-z)$ has the smallest positive root which is smaller than the smallest root of $E_{\alpha,\alpha}(-z)$. Then, the identity

$$I_0^{2-\alpha} t^{\alpha-2} E_{\alpha,\alpha-1}(-\lambda t^\alpha) = E_{\alpha,1}(-\lambda t^\alpha),$$

implies that $E_{\alpha,\alpha-1}(-z)$ has the smallest positive root which is smaller than the smallest positive root of $E_{\alpha,1}(-z)$. Thus, from the construction, an anti-maximum principle will be valid for $\lambda \in (0, \lambda_0)$, where λ_0 is the smallest positive real root of the Mittag-Leffler function, $E_{\alpha,\alpha-1}(-z)$.

Now, consider a boundary value problem for nonlinear fractional differential Equations (22) and (23). Assume $f : (0,1] \times \mathbb{R} \to \mathbb{R}$ is continuous, assume f satisfies the monotonicity property (25), and assume there exists $\lambda < 0$ such that $f(t,s) = g(t,s) - \lambda s$ and $g(t,s)$ is bounded and continuous on $(0,1] \times \mathbb{R}$. Then, f satisfies (24).

Corollary 1. *Assume $1 < \alpha < 2$. Assume $f : (0,1] \times \mathbb{R} \to \mathbb{R}$ is continuous, and assume f satisfies the monotonicity property (25). Assume there exists $\lambda < 0$ such that $f(t,s) = g(t,s) - \lambda s$ and $g(t,s)$ is bounded and continuous on $(0,1] \times \mathbb{R}$. Then, there exists a solution of the boundary value problem*

$$D_0^\alpha y(t) = f(t, y(t)), \quad 0 < t \le 1,$$
$$D_0^{\alpha-1} y(0) = 0, \quad D_0^{\alpha-1} y(1) = 0.$$

Proof. As noted above, the boundedness condition on g implies that f satisfies (24). Let $(-\lambda)M$ denote an upper bound on $|g|$. Set $v_1(t) = Mt^{\alpha-2}$ and set $w_1(t) = -Mt^{\alpha-2}$. Thus, v_1 and w_1 satisfy the boundary conditions (4). Moreover,

$$D^\alpha v_1(t) + \lambda v_1(t) = \lambda M t^{\alpha-2} \le \lambda M \le -|g(t, Mt^{\alpha-2})| \le f(t, v_1(t)) + \lambda v_1(t),$$

or $D^\alpha v_1(t) \le f(t, v_1(t))$. Similarly, $D^\alpha w_1(t) \ge f(t, w_1(t))$ and Theorem 2 applies. □

Corollary 2. *Assume $1 < \alpha < 2$. Assume $f : (0,1] \times \mathbb{R} \to \mathbb{R}$ is continuous and assume f satisfies the monotonicity property (32). Let $\lambda_0 > 0$ denote the smallest positive real root of $E_{\alpha,\alpha-1}(-z)$. Assume there exists $\lambda \in (0, \lambda_0)$ such that $f(t,s) = g(t,s) - \lambda s$ and $g(t,s)$ is bounded and continuous on $(0,1] \times \mathbb{R}$. Then, there exists a solution of the boundary value problem*

$$D_0^\alpha y(t) = f(t, y(t)), \quad 0 < t \le 1,$$

$$D_0^{\alpha-1} y(0) = 0, \quad D_0^{\alpha-1} y(1) = 0.$$

Proof. Let λM denote an upper bound on $|g|$. Set $v_1(t) = Mt^{\alpha-2}$ and set $w_1(t) = -Mt^{\alpha-2}$. v_1 and w_1 satisfy (33) and Theorem 3 applies. □

7. Conclusions

In this paper, we study a λ dependent boundary value problem for a Riemann–Liouville fractional differential equation. Denoting the boundary value problem abstractly as $Ay + \lambda y = f$, $\lambda = 0$ is assumed to be a simple eigenvalue. Sufficient conditions are obtained to show the existence of $\Lambda > 0$ such that if $|\lambda| \in (0, \Lambda)$, then $(A + \lambda I)$ is invertible and $f \ge 0$ implies $\lambda y \ge 0$ where y denotes the unique solution of $(A + \lambda I)y = f$. Four examples are produced illustrating the abstract result. An application of monotone methods and the method of upper and lower solutions is produced for a nonlinear boundary value problem.

Author Contributions: Conceptualization, P.W.E., Y.L. and J.T.N.; methodology, P.W.E., Y.L. and J.T.N.; investigation, P.W.E., Y.L. and J.T.N.; writing—original draft preparation, P.W.E.; writing—review and editing, P.W.E., Y.L. and J.T.N.; project administration, P.W.E., Y.L. and J.T.N. All authors have read and agreed to the published version of the manuscript.

Funding: This research received no external funding.

Data Availability Statement: No data sets were generated during this research.

Conflicts of Interest: The authors declare no conflicts of interest.

References

1. Protter, M.H.; Weinberger, H. *Maximum Principles in Differential Equations*; Prentice Hall: Englewoods Cliffs, NJ, USA, 1967.
2. Zhang, S.Q. The existence of a positive solution for a nonlinear fractional differential equation. *J. Math. Anal. Appl.* **2000**, *252*, 804–812. [CrossRef]
3. Bai, Z.; Lü, H. Positive solutions for boundary value problem of nonlinear fractional differential equation. *J. Math. Anal. Appl.* **2005**, *311*, 495–505. [CrossRef]
4. Nieto, J. Maximum principles for fractional differential equations derived from Mittag-Leffler functions. *Appl. Math. Lett.* **2010**, *23*, 1248–1251. [CrossRef]
5. Cabada, A.; Kisela, T. Existence of positive periodic solutions of some nonlinear fractional differential equations. *Commun. Nonlinear Sci. Numer. Simul.* **2017**, *50*, 51–67. [CrossRef]
6. Wei, Z.; Dong W.; Che, J. Periodic boundary value problems for fractional differential equations involving a Riemann-Liouville fractional derivative. *Nonlinear Anal.* **2010**, *73*, 3232–3238. [CrossRef]
7. Ding, Y.; Li, Y. Monotone iterative technique for periodic problem involving Riemann-Liouville fractional derivatives in Banach spaces. *Bound. Value Probl.* **2018**, *2018*, 119. [CrossRef]
8. Clément, P.; Peletier, L.A. An anti-maximum principle for second-order elliptic operators. *J. Differ. Equ.* **1979**, *34*, 218–229. [CrossRef]
9. Campos, J.; Mawhin, J.; Ortega, R. Maximum principles around an eigenvalue with constant eigenfunctions. *Commun. Contemp. Math.* **2008**, *10*, 1243–1259. [CrossRef]
10. Alziary, B.; Fleckinger, J.; Takáč, P. An extension of maximum and anti-maximum principles to a Schrödinger equation in $\mathbb{R}^2$. *J. Differ. Equ.* **1999**, *156*, 122–152. [CrossRef]
11. Arcoya, D.; Gámez, J.L. Bifurcation theory and related problems: Anti-maximum principle and resonance. *Comm. Partial Differ. Equ.* **2001**, *26*, 1879–1911. [CrossRef]
12. Clément, P.; Sweers, G. Uniform anti-maximum principles. *J. Differ. Equ.* **2000**, *164*, 118–154. [CrossRef]
13. Hess, P. An antimaximum principle for linear elliptic equations with an indefinite weight function. *J. Differ. Equ.* **1981**, *41*, 369–374. [CrossRef]
14. Mawhin, J. Partial differential equations also have principles: Maximum and antimaximum. *Contemp. Math.* **2011**, *540*, 1–13.
15. Pinchover, Y. Maximum and anti-maximum principles and eigenfunctions estimates via perturbation theory of positive solutions of elliptic equations. *Math. Ann.* **1999**, *314*, 555–590 [CrossRef]
16. Takáč, P. An abstract form of maximum and anti-maximum principles of Hopf's type. *J. Math. Anal. Appl.* **1996**, *201*, 339–364. [CrossRef]
17. Barteneva, I.V.; Cabada, A.; Ignatyev, A.O. Maximum and anti-maximum principles for the general operator of second order with variable coefficients. *Appl. Math. Comput.* **2003**, *134*, 173–184. [CrossRef]
18. Cabada, A.; Cid, J.Á. On comparison principles for the periodic Hill's equation. *J. Lond. Math. Soc.* **2012**, *86*, 272–290. [CrossRef]
19. Cabada, A.; Cid, J.Á.; López-Somoza, L. *Maximum Principles for the Hill's Equation*; Academic Press: London, UK, 2018.
20. Cabada, A.; Cid, J.Á.; Tvrdý, M. A generalized anti-maximum principle for the periodic on-dimensional $p-$Laplacian with sign changing potential. *Nonlinear Anal.* **2010**, *72*, 3434–3446. [CrossRef]
21. Zhang, M. Optimal conditions for maximum and antimaximum principles of the periodic solution problem. *Bound. Value Probl.* **2010**, *2010*, 410986. [CrossRef]
22. Del Pezzo, L.M.; Quaas, A. Non-resonant Fredholm alternative and anti-maximum principle for the fractional $p-$Laplacian. *J. Fixed Point Theory Appl.* **2017**, *19*, 939–958. [CrossRef]
23. Asso, O.; Cuesta, M.; Doumaté, J.T.; Leadi, L. Maximum and anti-maximum principle for fractional $p-$Laplacian with indefinite weights. *J. Math. Anal. Appl.* **2024**, *529*, 127626. [CrossRef]
24. Eloe, P.; Neugebauer, J.T. Maximum and anti-maximum principles and monotone methods for boundary value problems for Riemann-Liouville fractional differential equations in neighborhoods of simple eigenvalues. *Cubo* **2023**, *25*, 251–272. [CrossRef]
25. Diethelm, K. *The Analysis of Fractional Differential Equations. An Application-Oriented Exposition Using Differential Operators of Caputo Type*; Lecture Notes in Mathematics; No. 2004; Springer: Berlin/Heidelberg, Germany, 2010.

26. Kilbas, A.A.; Srivastava, H.M.; Trujillo, J.J. *Theory and Applications of Fractional Differential Equations*; North-Holland Mathematics Studies 204; Elsevier Science: Amsterdam, The Netherlands, 2006.
27. Samko, S.G.; Kilbas, A.A.; Marichev, O.I. *Fractional Integrals and Derivatives: Theory and Applications*; Gordon and Breach Science Publishers: Yverdon, Switzerland, 1993.
28. Webb, J.R.L. Initial value problems for Caputo fractional equations with singular nonlinearities. *Electron. J. Differ. Equ.* **2019**, *2019*, 1–32.
29. Infante, G.; Pietramala, P.; Tojo, F.A.F. Nontrivial solutions of local and nonlocal Neumann boundary value problems. *Proc. R. Soc. Edinb. Sect. A* **2016**, *146*, 337–369. [CrossRef]
30. Li, Y.; Telyakovsiy, A.S.; Çelik, E. Analysis of one-sided 1-D fractional diffusion operator. *Commun. Pure Appl. Anal.* **2022**, *21*, 1673–1690. [CrossRef]

Article

The Blow-Up of the Local Energy Solution to the Wave Equation with a Nontrivial Boundary Condition

Yulong Liu

School of Mathematics and Statistics, Taiyuan Normal University, Jinzhong 030619, China; liuylmath@139.com

Abstract: In this study, we examine the wave equation with a nontrivial boundary condition. The main target of this study is to prove the local-in-time existence and the blow-up in finite time of the energy solution. Through the construction of an auxiliary function and the imposition of appropriate conditions on the initial data, we establish the both lower and upper bounds for the blow-up time of the solution. Meanwhile, based on these estimates, we obtain the result of the local-in-time existence and the blow-up of the energy solution. This approach enhances our understanding of the dynamics leading to blow-up in the considered condition.

Keywords: positive initial energy; boundary value problem; auxiliary function; lower and upper bounds

MSC: 35B35; 35L05; 35L20

1. Introduction

In this paper, we are concerned with the local-in-time existence of the energy solution to the following wave equation:

$$\begin{cases} u''(x,t) - \mu(t)\triangle u(x,t) + h(u(x,t)) = 0 & \text{in } \Omega \times (0,+\infty) \\ u(x,t) = 0 & \text{on } \Gamma_0 \times (0,+\infty) \\ \mu(t)\frac{\partial u}{\partial \nu} + g(u') = |u|^\gamma u & \text{on } \Gamma_1 \times (0,+\infty) \\ u(x,0) = u_0(x), u'(x,0) = u_1(x) & \text{in } \Omega \end{cases} \quad (1)$$

where Ω is a bounded domain of $\mathbb{R}^n (n = 1,2,3)$ with boundary $\Gamma = \Gamma_0 \cup \Gamma_1$ of class C^2. Here, $\Gamma_0 \neq \emptyset$, Γ_0 and Γ_1 are closed and disjoint. Let ν be the outward normal to Γ; $\triangle$ stands for the Laplace operator.

System (1) has been studied in [1]. When μ, γ and g satisfy appropriate assumptions, the solution of System (1) will blow up within a finite time. In this article, based on the solution blow-up, we will continue to study the upper and lower bounds for the blow-up time of System (1). Based on these estimates, we will obtain the result of the local-in-time existence of the energy solution. There is relatively little existing literature on the problem of calculating the upper and lower bounds of the blow-up time, but accurately calculating the blow-up time has significant practical significance in specific engineering problems. The authors of Ref. [2] study a nonlinear viscoelastic wave equation with damping and source terms. By using the concavity method, it shows a finite time blow-up result and obtains the upper bound for the blow-up time. Ref. [3] deals with a nonlinear viscoelastic wave equation with strong damping. By means of a first-order differential inequality technique, the estimate the lower bound for the blow-up time is obtained. Ref. [4] deals with the blow-up for a class of nonlinear viscoelastic wave equations. Based on a first-order differential inequality technique and some Sobolev-type inequality, a lower bound for blow-up time is obtained. However, each reference listed above has the Dirichlet's boundary condition. The previous studies that have been performed related to trivial boundary conditions. More importantly, the problem with nontrivial boundary conditions has extremely few

Citation: Liu, Y. The Blow-Up of the Local Energy Solution to the Wave Equation with a Nontrivial Boundary Condition. *Mathematics* **2024**, *12*, 1317. https://doi.org/10.3390/math12091317

Academic Editor: Luís Castro

Received: 6 March 2024
Revised: 21 April 2024
Accepted: 23 April 2024
Published: 25 April 2024

Copyright: © 2024 by the author. Licensee MDPI, Basel, Switzerland. This article is an open access article distributed under the terms and conditions of the Creative Commons Attribution (CC BY) license (https://creativecommons.org/licenses/by/4.0/).

results. In the references above, it always assumes that $u = 0$ on $\partial\Omega$, which greatly reduces the difficulty of estimating the blow-up time boundary. Unlike the previous literature, our article considers nontrivial boundary conditions, and these boundary conditions are nonlinear, increasing the difficulty of estimating the blow-up time. In addition, nontrivial boundary conditions can also cause difficulties in inequality estimation and auxiliary function construction. Therefore, our research can fill the gap in this area of study. There are still many other studies on handling blow-up time under trivial boundary conditions, for example, G.A. Philippin [5] explores the lower bounds for the blow-up time in the context of the wave equation with trivial boundary conditions. However, this study does not currently address the upper bounds for blow-up time. Future research endeavors may extend the investigation to include upper bounds and further enrich our understanding of the dynamics in this particular scenario. J. Zhou [6] considered the blow-up time with three different ranges of initial energy under the condition of atrivial boundary. Furthermore, considering positive initial energy and nonlinear boundary damping, T.G.Ha [1,7] established the blow-up of solutions for the semilinear wave equation. However, the specific determination of the blow-up time is not addressed within the current scope of the research. Investigating the blow-up time in this context could provide valuable insights into the temporal evolution of the solutions.

On the other hand, the blow-up behavior of solutions to the wave equation is not only related to the interaction between damping terms and source terms, but also to the sign of the system's initial energy. Generally speaking, negative initial energy is more likely to cause system solution blow-up, while positive initial energy requires stricter conditions for system solution blow-up. This article has already addressed the issue of system solution blow-up under positive initial energy, and we further estimate the upper and lower bounds of the solution blow-up time. Considerable progress has been made in demonstrating to the wave equation, especially in cases where the initial energy is negative, the conclusions about blow-up solution have been proved [8–15]. Meanwhile, many similar results also have been found when the initial energy is positive (see [16–19]). However, the problem of computing exact blow-up time T has not been considered. In instances where the solution of the wave equation experiences blow-up, the exact computation of the blow-up time T is often not feasible. So figuring out the bounds for T is valuable in practical applications. In recent years, there have been some advances in research on the bounds of blow-up time. However, a great deal of research work has focused on parabolic equations [20–25]. Very few researchers have focused their work on hyperbolic equations with nontrivial boundary conditions [5]. In addition, the above literature only obtained the bounds of blow-up time, but did not analyze the sharpness of blow-up time. In [26,27], not only the limit of blasting time is obtained, but also the sharpness of blasting time is analyzed.

Compared to existing literature results, this paper addresses a notable gap in the existing research, as minimal attention has been dedicated to investigating the lower and upper bounds for the blow-up time of the wave equation with weak boundary damping and source term. The primary focus of this work is to contribute to this specific aspect of the field.

This paper aims to investigate how the interaction between the damping term and source term influences the occurrence of blow-up in the solution. Specifically, the focus is on demonstrating that the blow-up and blow-up time are intricately controlled by the interplay of these two terms. Building upon the findings of [7], the objective is to extend and generalize the results by precisely computing both lower and upper bounds for the blow-up time T in the context of the wave equation with weak boundary damping and source term. Therefore, the motivation of this paper is to generalize the results under trivial boundary conditions, and further solve the problem of constructing new auxiliary functions to estimate the bounds of blow-up time under nontrivial boundary conditions.

This paper follows a structured organization. Section 2 provides a review of notation, hypotheses, and crucial preliminary steps. It also introduces the blow-up solution for Equation (1). Moving on to Section 3, the main result is presented, and the paper precisely computes both lower and upper bounds for the blow-up time T in the context of problem (1). This organization ensures a clear and systematic presentation of the research.

2. Preliminaries

Before delving into our principal discovery, it is crucial to take a moment to revisit the extant body of research pertaining to the local existence, uniqueness, and blow-up of the solution. This foundational understanding will provide a solid foundation for our forthcoming discussion and findings. We begin this part by outlining a few theories and some necessary results. To be more precise, we have the following hypotheses:

Hypothesis 1. *$\Omega \subset \mathbb{R}^n$ is a bounded domain, $n \geq 1$, where the boundary of Ω is $\Gamma = \Gamma_0 \cup \Gamma_1$ of class C^2.*

Here, $\Gamma_0 \neq \emptyset$, Γ_0 and Γ_1 are closed and disjoint, satisfying the following conditions:

$$m(x) \cdot \nu(x) \geq \sigma > 0 \text{ on } \Gamma_1, m(x) \cdot \nu(x) \leq 0 \text{ on } \Gamma_0,$$

$$m(x) = x - x^0 \ (x^0 \in \mathbb{R}^n) \text{ and } R = max_{x \in \overline{\Omega}} |m(x)|,$$

where ν represents the unit outward normal vector to Γ. We assume that

$$\mu(0)\frac{\partial u_0}{\partial \nu} + g(u_1) = |u_0|^{\gamma} u_0 \text{ on } \Gamma_1.$$

Hypothesis 2. *Assume $\mu \in W^{2,\infty}(0,T) \cap W^{2,1}(0,T)$, and $\mu(t) > 0$ is monotonic decreasing. Meanwhile, $h : \mathbb{R} \to \mathbb{R}$ is a continuous function and $h(s)s \geq 0$ for all $s \in \mathbb{R}$.*

Hypothesis 3. *Assume γ is a constant and satisfies requirements:*

$$\begin{cases} 0 \leq \gamma < 1, & \text{if } n = 3, \\ \gamma \geq 0, & \text{if } n = 1,2. \end{cases}$$

Hypothesis 4. *Assume g is a monotone increasing function and satisfies $g(0) = 0$. There exist a non-negative constant m and a strictly increasing and odd function β of C^1 class on $[-1, 1]$ such that*

$$|\beta(s)| \leq |g(s)| \leq |\beta^{-1}(s), \text{ if } |s| \leq 1,$$
$$C_1|s|^{m+1} \leq |g(s)| \leq C_2|s|^{m+1}, \text{ if } |s| > 1,$$

where β^{-1} denotes the inverse function of β and C_1 and C_2 are positive constants.

2.1. Wellposedness Result

First of all, one can define the energy $E(t)$ associated with system (1).

$$E(t) = \frac{1}{2}\|u'\|_2^2 + \int_{\Omega} \Psi(u(x,t))dx + \frac{1}{2}\mu(t)\|\nabla u\|_2^2 - \frac{1}{\gamma+2}\|u\|_{\gamma+2,\Gamma_1}^{\gamma+2}, \tag{2}$$

where $\Psi(t) = \int_0^t h(s)dx$. By calculation, we can obtain

$$E'(t) = \mu'(t)\|\nabla u\| - \int_{\Gamma_1} g(u')u'd\Gamma, \tag{3}$$

where ∇ is the gradient operator. According to the Hypothesis 2, $E(t)$ is monotone decreasing function.

Remark 1. *The proof of the energy identity (2)–(3) will be proved in (7)–(8).*

With the notion we set, the following conclusion will be obtained [28].

Theorem 1. *Assume Hypotheses 1–4 hold and*

$$m \geq \gamma \text{ or } (u_0, u_1) \in \{(u_0, u_1) \in H^1_{\Gamma_0}(\Omega) \times L^2(\Omega);\ \|\nabla u\| < \lambda_0,\ E(0) < d\}.$$

Then, the problem (1) has a unique local solution

$$u \in C^0(0, T; H^1_{\Gamma_0}(\Omega)) \cap C^1(0, T; L^2(\Omega)).$$

2.2. Blow-Up Solution

Next, we have the corresponding blow-up result.

Theorem 2. *Assume Hypotheses 1–4 hold and $m < \gamma$. Meanwhile, to System (1), we suppose that*

$$(u_0, u_1) \in \{(u_0, u_1) \in H^1_{\Gamma_0}(\Omega) \times L^2(\Omega); \|\nabla u_0\|_2 > \lambda_0, E(0) < E_1 < d, E_1 \in \mathbb{R}\}$$

and

$$\beta^{-1} \leq \left(\frac{(\gamma+2)(\mu_0 \gamma \lambda_0 - 2(\gamma+2)E_1)^2}{8(\gamma+1) meas(\Gamma_1)(\mu_0 \lambda_0^2 - 2E_1)} \right)^{\frac{\gamma+1}{\gamma+2}}.$$

Consequently, the solution $u(t)$ blows up.

The result of Theorem 2 has been obtained in [7]. We can now report our primary finding in the next section.

3. The Bounds for T

In this section, we turn our attention to examining the lower bound of the blow-up time for the blow-up solution of Equation (1). Prior to presenting and demonstrating our primary result, we require the following lemma that plays a pivotal role in establishing the upper bounds for the blow-up time T.

Lemma 1. *In the case of the assumptions specified in Theorem 2, the solution to system (1) yields the following result*

$$\|\nabla u(t)\|_2 > \lambda_0.$$

Lemma 1 closely parallels Lemma 1 in [1]. Therefore, the proof will be omitted for brevity.

Theorem 3. *Assume Hypotheses 1–4 hold. Under the result in Theorem 2, the solution $u(x,t)$ to System (1) will blow up at a finite T, and blow-up time T satisfies*

$$\int_{F(0)}^{F(T^-)} \frac{dy}{y + 2\mathbf{k} + C_0 y^{\frac{2\gamma+3}{2\gamma+4}} (meas(\Gamma_1))^{\frac{1}{2\gamma+4}}} \leq T \leq \frac{1-\overline{\chi}}{C_7 [L(0)]^{\frac{\overline{\chi}}{1-\overline{\chi}}}},$$

where C_0, C_7 is a positive constant, $0 < \overline{\chi} < \chi < \frac{\gamma - m}{(m+2)(\gamma+2)}$ and

$$\begin{aligned} F(0) &= \int_\Omega |u_0|^2 dx + \int_{\partial\Omega} |u_0|^{\gamma+2} d\Gamma + t^* \int_{\partial\Omega} |u_1|^{\gamma+2} d\Gamma, \\ \mathbf{k} &:= \frac{1}{2}\|u_1\|^2 + \int_\Omega \Psi(u_0) dx + \frac{1}{2}\mu(t)\|\nabla u_0\|_2^2 - \frac{1}{\gamma+2}\|u_0\|_{\gamma+2,\Gamma_1}^{\gamma+2}. \end{aligned} \quad (4)$$

Proof. (i): In this section, we initiate the estimation of the upper bound of time T using auxiliary function that allows us to establish an upper bound

E_1 is a constant and satisfies $E(0) < E_1 < d$; then, we define $H(t)$ as follows:

$$H(t) = E_1 - E(t).$$

Subsequently, we obtain

$$H'(t) = 0 - E'(t) = -E'(t) \geq 0.$$

It is straightforward to derive that $H(t)$ is nondecreasing. Meanwhile, we have,

$$H(t) \geq H_0 := E_1 - E(0) \geq 0, \; for \; all \; t \geq 0.$$

According to Lemma 1 and Hypothesis 2, we obtain

$$\begin{aligned} H(t) &\leq E_1 - \frac{1}{2}\mu(0)\|\nabla u\|_2^2 + \frac{1}{\gamma+2}\|u(t)\|_{\gamma+2,\Gamma_1}^{\gamma+2} \\ &< d - \frac{1}{2}\mu(0)\lambda_0^2 + \frac{1}{\gamma+2}\|u(t)\|_{\gamma+2,\Gamma_1}^{\gamma+2} \\ &\leq \frac{1}{\gamma+2}\|u(t)\|_{\gamma+2,\Gamma_1}^{\gamma+2}. \end{aligned}$$

Afterward, we will examine:

$$I = \frac{d}{dt}\int_\Omega u'udx = (\frac{\Phi'(t)}{2})'.$$

By similar calculation as in [1,7], we can see that the following estimate holds:

$$\begin{aligned} I &= \|u'\|_2^2 - \int_\Omega h(u)udx - \mu(t)\|\nabla u\|_2^2 + \|u\|_{\gamma+2,\Gamma_1}^{\gamma+2} - \int_{\Gamma_1} g(u')ud\Gamma + \theta E(t) - \theta E(t) \\ &\geq \left(1+\frac{\theta}{2}\right)\|u'\|_2^2 - \mu_0\left(\frac{\theta}{2}-1\right)\|\nabla u\|_2^2 - \theta E_1 + \left(1-\frac{\theta}{\gamma+1}\right)\|u\|_{\gamma+2,\Gamma_1}^{\gamma+2} \\ &+ \theta H(t) - \int_{\Gamma_1} g(u')ud\Gamma \\ &\geq C_5\left(\|u'\|_2^2 + \|u(t)\|_{\gamma+2,\Gamma_1}^{\gamma+2} + H(t) - H'(t)H_0^{\overline{\chi}-\chi}H^{-\overline{\chi}(t)}\right), \end{aligned} \tag{5}$$

where $0 < \overline{\chi} < \chi < \frac{\gamma-m}{(m+2)(\gamma+2)}$ and $C_5 > 0$.

To derive the corresponding estimate, we construct an auxiliary function that allows us to establish the upper bound for T.

$$L(t) = H^{1-\overline{\chi}}(t) + \delta\Phi'(t),$$

where $\Phi(t) = \|u(t)\|_2^2$.

By taking the derivative of $L(t)$ and utilizing (5), we obtain:

$$\begin{aligned} L'(t) &= (1-\overline{\chi})H^{-\overline{\chi}}(t)H'(t) + \delta\Phi''(t) \\ &\geq \left(1-\overline{\chi}-2C_5\delta H^{\overline{\chi}-\chi}\right)H^{-\overline{\chi}}H'(t) + 2C_5\delta\left(\|u'\|_2^2 + \|u(t)\|_{\gamma+2,\Gamma_1}^{\gamma+2} + H(t)\right). \end{aligned}$$

Choosing $0 < \overline{\chi} < min\{\frac{1}{2}, \chi\}$ and making δ sufficiently small, we establish

$$L'(t) \geq C_6\left(\|u'\|_2^2 + \|u(t)\|_{\gamma+2,\Gamma_1}^{\gamma+2} + H(t)\right),$$

where C_6 is a positive number, so $L(t) > 0$ is an increasing function. Using the same reasoning as in [1], we establish:

$$L'(t) \geq C_7 L^{\frac{1}{1-\overline{\chi}}}(t), \qquad for \; all \; t \in [0,T], \tag{6}$$

where $C_7 > 0$ is constant and satisfies $1 < \frac{1}{1-\overline{\chi}} < 2$.

Then, a straightforward integration of (6) over $(0, T)$ produces

$$L^{\frac{\overline{\chi}}{1-\overline{\chi}}} \geq \frac{1}{L^{\frac{-\overline{\chi}}{1-\overline{\chi}}}(0) - C_7 T \frac{\overline{\chi}}{1-\overline{\chi}}},$$

therefore $L(t)$ blows up in time

$$T \leq \frac{1-\overline{\chi}}{C_7 \overline{\chi} [L(0)]^{\frac{\overline{\chi}}{1-\overline{\chi}}}}.$$

(ii): In this section, we initiate the estimation of the lower bound of time T using a series of energy mode estimation and inequality reduction techniques.

By multiplying both sides of the first equation by u' and integrating over the domain, we obtain the following energy mode estimate:

$$\int_\Omega (u''u' - \mu(t)\triangle u u' + h(u)u')dx = 0$$

by Green's formulas we have

$$\int_\Omega u''u'dx - \mu(t)(\int_{\partial\Omega} u' \frac{\partial u}{\partial v} d\Gamma - \int_\Omega \nabla u \nabla u' dx) + \int_\Omega h(u)u'dx = 0$$

Because of the bound condition of Γ in Equation (1), we obtain

$$\int_\Omega u''u'dx - \int_{\Gamma_1} |u|^{\gamma+1} u u' d\Gamma + \int_{\Gamma_1} u' g(u') d\Gamma + \mu(t) \int_\Omega \nabla u \nabla u' dx + \int_\Omega h(u)u'dx = 0.$$

It is straightforward to derive that

$$\begin{aligned} &\frac{d}{dt}\left(\frac{1}{2}\int_\Omega |u'|^2 dx - \frac{1}{\gamma+2}\int_{\Gamma_1} |u|^{\gamma+2} d\Gamma + \frac{1}{2}\mu(t)\int_\Omega |\nabla u|^2 dx + \int_\Omega \int_0^u h(s) ds dx\right) \\ =&\frac{1}{2}\mu'(t)\int_\Omega |\nabla u|^2 dx - \int_{\Gamma_1} g(u')u' d\Gamma. \end{aligned} \tag{7}$$

Through the above calculation, we can deduce the result (2), and

$$E'(t) = \frac{1}{2}\mu'(t)\int_\Omega |\nabla u|^2 dx - \int_{\Gamma_1} g(u')u' d\Gamma \leq 0. \tag{8}$$

So

$$E(t) \leq E(0) = \mathbf{k}.$$

It is straightforward to derive that

$$\begin{aligned} &2E(t) + \frac{2}{\gamma+2}\|u\|_{\gamma+2,\Gamma_1}^{\gamma+2} \\ &\leq 2\mathbf{k} + \frac{2}{\gamma+2}\|u\|_{\gamma+2,\Gamma_1}^{\gamma+2}. \end{aligned} \tag{9}$$

Next, we will define an auxiliary function as follows:

$$F(t) = \int_\Omega |u|^2 dx + \int_{\partial\Omega} |u|^{\gamma+2} d\Gamma + (t^* - t)\int_{\partial\Omega} |u_1|^{2\gamma+3} d\Gamma,$$

where $t^* > 0$ is a time large enough; furthermore, we can set $t^* = \frac{1-\overline{\chi}}{C_7\overline{\chi}[L(0)]^{\frac{\overline{\chi}}{1-\overline{\chi}}}}$, then

$$F'(t) = 2\int_\Omega uu'dx + (\gamma+2)\int_{\partial\Omega}|u|^\gamma uu'd\Gamma - \int_{\partial\Omega}|u_1|^{2\gamma+3}d\Gamma.$$

By using a series of inequality reduction techniques, we have

$$\begin{aligned}
F'(t) &\leq \int_\Omega |u|^2dx + \int_\Omega |u'|^2dx + \varepsilon\int_{\partial\Omega}|u'|^{2\gamma+3}d\Gamma \\
&+ C_\varepsilon\int_{\partial\Omega}|u|^{(\gamma+1)\frac{2\gamma+3}{2\gamma+2}}d\Gamma - \int_{\partial\Omega}|u_1|^{2\gamma+3}d\Gamma \\
&\leq \int_\Omega |u|^2dx + \int_\Omega |u'|^2dx + \varepsilon\int_{\partial\Omega}|u'|^{2\gamma+3}d\Gamma \\
&+ C_\varepsilon\left(\int_{\partial\Omega}|u|^{\gamma+2}d\Gamma\right)^{\frac{2\gamma+3}{2\gamma+4}}(meas(\Gamma))^{\frac{1}{2\gamma+4}} - \int_{\partial\Omega}|u_1|^{2\gamma+3}d\Gamma,
\end{aligned}$$

where C_ε is a constant depending on ε. Furthermore we choose $\varepsilon = \frac{\int_{\partial\Omega}|u_1|^{2\gamma+3}d\Gamma}{2\int_{\partial\Omega}|u'|^{2\gamma+3}d\Gamma}$ small enough so that

$$\varepsilon\int_{\partial\Omega}|u'|^{2\gamma+3}d\Gamma - \int_{\partial\Omega}|u_1|^{2\gamma+3}d\Gamma \leq 0,$$

then, we have

$$F'(t) \leq \int_\Omega |u|^2dx + \int_\Omega |u'|^2dx + C_\varepsilon\left(\int_{\partial\Omega}|u|^{\gamma+2}d\Gamma\right)^{\frac{2\gamma+3}{2\gamma+4}}(meas(\Gamma_1))^{\frac{1}{2\gamma+4}}.$$

Through (9) we obtain

$$\begin{aligned}
F'(t) &\leq \int_\Omega |u|^2dx + 2\mathbf{k} + \frac{2}{\gamma+2}\|u\|^{\gamma+2}_{\gamma+2,\Gamma_1} \\
&+ C_\varepsilon\left(\int_{\partial\Omega}|u|^{\gamma+2}d\Gamma\right)^{\frac{2\gamma+3}{2\gamma+4}}(meas(\Gamma_1))^{\frac{1}{2\gamma+4}} \\
&\leq \int_\Omega |u|^2dx + 2\mathbf{k} + \frac{2}{\gamma+2}\|u\|^{\gamma+2}_{\gamma+2,\Gamma_1} \\
&+ C_\varepsilon\left(\int_{\partial\Omega}|u|^{\gamma+2}d\Gamma\right)^{\frac{2\gamma+3}{2\gamma+4}}(meas(\Gamma_1))^{\frac{1}{2\gamma+4}} + (t^*-t)\int_{\partial\Omega}|u_1|^{\frac{\gamma+2}{2}}d\Gamma \\
&\leq \int_\Omega |u|^2dx + \|u\|^{\gamma+2}_{\gamma+2,\Gamma_1} + (t^*-t)\int_{\partial\Omega}|u_1|^{\frac{\gamma+2}{2}}d\Gamma + 2\mathbf{k} \\
&+ C_\varepsilon(F(t))^{\frac{2\gamma+3}{2\gamma+4}}(meas(\Gamma_1))^{\frac{1}{2\gamma+4}} \\
&\leq F(t) + 2\mathbf{k} + C_0(F(t))^{\frac{2\gamma+3}{2\gamma+4}}(meas(\Gamma_1))^{\frac{1}{2\gamma+4}},
\end{aligned} \tag{10}$$

where $C_0 = \text{Max}_{t\in(0,T)}\{C_\varepsilon\}$.

From Theorem 2, it is straightforward to derive that the solution of System (1) blows up; as a consequence, we concluded that

$$\lim_{t\to T^-} F(t) = \infty$$

and by (10), we have

$$\int_{F(0)}^\infty \frac{dy}{y + 2\mathbf{k} + C_0y^{\frac{2\gamma+3}{2\gamma+4}}(meas(\Gamma_1))^{\frac{1}{2\gamma+4}}} \leq T.$$

Finally, we complete the proof of Theorem 3. □

Remark 2. *Theorem 3 gives an upper and lower bound on the blow-up time, but does not analyze the sharpness of the blow-up time. According to (10), we have*

$$F'(t) \leq F(t) + C_a(F(t))^{\frac{2\gamma+3}{2\gamma+4}}$$

with $p = \frac{2\gamma+3}{2\gamma+4}$. *This differential inequality may be reduced to a linear differential inequality by the process of solving the Bernoulli equation. Moreover, we can obtain*

$$(F(t))^{1-p} \geq (F(0))^{1-p} + C_a e^{(1-p)t} - C_a,$$

where C_a *is a positive constant. Hence,* $F(t)$ *bounded for* $t \in [0, T)$ *with*

$$\frac{1}{1-p}(log\{1 + \frac{1}{C_a}(F(0))^{1-p}\}) \leq T$$

if we let

$$u(x,0) = \varepsilon_1 u_0(x), u'(x,0) = \varepsilon_2 u_1(x),$$

where ε_1 *and* ε_2 *are small parameters. Then, we can determine the sharpness of the lower bound*

$$C_m log(1 + \varepsilon_0^{2-2p}) \leq T(\varepsilon_0)$$

where $\varepsilon_0 = max\{\varepsilon_1, \varepsilon_2\}$ *and* C_m *is a positive constant independent of* ε_0.

In the same way, we can obtain the sharpness of the upper bound

$$T(\varepsilon_0) \leq C_M \varepsilon_0^{\gamma+2-\frac{\gamma-m}{m+2}}.$$

where C_M *is a positive constant independent of* ε_0.

4. Conclusions

The present paper substantially expands upon T.G. Ha's findings on the blow-up solution to the wave equation with damping and source terms, which were initially introduced in 2015. The main conclusions of this article are as follows: Firstly, through a series of energy mode estimations and auxiliary function techniques, the result of both upper and lower bounds for blow-up time is obtained. Based on these estimates, we obtain the result of the local-in-time existence of the energy solution. In comparison to previous studies, the most original contribution of this paper is the construction of a new auxiliary function under nontrivial boundary conditions, which solves the problem of estimating the bounds of blow-up time. Second, this work also delves deeper into how the source term and damping term impact blow-up time, revealing their effects more comprehensively. These insights provide valuable theoretical support and reference points for real-world engineering applications. Moving forward, we will study the effect of increasing the viscoelastic term and the time delay term on the blasting of the equation solution, and then estimate the upper and lower bounds of the blow-up time. Therefore, estimating the upper and lower bounds of the blow-up time under the influence of the viscoelastic term and the time delay term within the domain will be the focus of our next research.

Funding: This research was funded by the Shanxi Province Higher Education Science and Technology Innovation Project (No. 2022L406).

Data Availability Statement: No new data were created or analyzed in this study.

Conflicts of Interest: The author declares no conflicts of interest.

References

1. Ha, T.G. Blow-up for semilinear wave equation with boundary damping and source terms. *J. Math. Anal. Appl.* **2012**, *390*, 328–334. [CrossRef]

2. Benkouider, S.; Ranmoune, A. The exponential growth of solution, upper and lower bounds for the blow-up time for a viscoelastic wave equation with variable exponent nonlinearities. *Wseas Trans. Math.* **2023**, *22*, 451–465. [CrossRef]
3. Peng, X; Shang, Y.D.; Zheng, X.X. Lower bounds for the blow-up time to a nonlinear viscoelastic wave equation with strong damping. *Appl. Math. Lett.* **2018**, *76*, 66–73. [CrossRef]
4. Yang, L.; Liang, F.; Guo, Z.H. Lower bounds for blow-up time of a nonlinear viscoelastic wave equation. *Bound. Value Probl.* **2015**, *219*, 1–6.
5. Philippin, G.A. Lower bounds for blow-up time in a class of nonlinear wave equation. *Z. Angew. Math. Phys.* **2015**, *66*, 129–134. [CrossRef]
6. Zhou, J. Global existence and blow-up of solution for a kirchhoff type plate equation with damping. *Appl. Math. Comput.* **2015**, *265*, 807–818. [CrossRef]
7. Ha, T.G. Blow-up for wave equation with weak boundary damping and source terms. *Appl. Math. Lett.* **2015**, *49*, 166–172. [CrossRef]
8. Erhan, P.; Veysel, B. Blow up of solutions for viscoelastic wave equations of kirchhoff type with variable exponents. *Al-Qadisiyah J. Pure Sci.* **2022**, *27*, 11.
9. Tebba, Z.; Degaichia, H. Blow-up of solutions for a class quasilinear wave equation with nonlinearity variable exponents. *J. Funct. Spaces* **2021**, *2021*, 5546630. [CrossRef]
10. Ren, C.; Ming, S.; Fan, X.M.; Du, J.Y. Blow-up of solutions to the semilinear wave equation with scale invariant damping on exterior domain. *Bound. Value Probl.* **2023**, *2023*, 36. [CrossRef]
11. Levine, H.A.; Serrin, J. Global nonexistence theorem for quasilinear evolution equation with dissipation. *J. Math. Anal. Appl.* **1997**, *137*, 341–361. [CrossRef]
12. Shakhmurov, V.; Shahmurov, R. The regularity properties and blow-up of solutions for nonlocal wave equations and applications. *Results Math* **2022**, *77*, 229. [CrossRef]
13. Pitts, D.R.; Rammaha, M.A. Global existence and non-existence theorems for nonlinear wave equations. *Indiana Univ. Math. J.* **2002**, *51*, 1479–1509. [CrossRef]
14. Rammaha, M.A. The influence of damping and source terms on solutions of nonlinear wave equations. *Bol. Soc. Parana. Mat.* **2007**, *25*, 77–90. [CrossRef]
15. Rammaha, M.A.; Strei, T.A. Global existence and nonexistence for nonlinear wave equations with damping and source terms. *Trans. Amer. Math. Soc.* **2002**, *354*, 3621–3637. [CrossRef]
16. Alves, C.O.; Cavalcanti, M.M. On existence, uniform decay rates and blow up for solutions of the 2-d wave equation with exponential source. *Calc. Var. Partial. Differ. Equ.* **2009**, *34*, 377–411. [CrossRef]
17. Zu, G.; Sun, L.L.; Wu, J.C. Global existence and blow-up for wave equation of p-laplacian type. *Anal. Math. Phys.* **2023**, *13*, 53. [CrossRef]
18. Zu, G.; Guo, B.; Gao, W.J. Decay estimate and blow-up for a damped wave equation with supercritical sources. *Acta Appl. Math.* **2022**, *177*, 8. [CrossRef]
19. Todorova, G.; Vitillaro, E. Blow-up for nonlinear dissipative wave equations in R^n. *J. Math. Anal. Appl.* **2005**, *303*, 242–257. [CrossRef]
20. Baghaei, K.; Hesaaraki, M. Lower bounds for the blow-up time in the higher-dimensional non- linear divergence form parabolic equations. *C. R. Acad. Paris Ser. I* **2013**, *351*, 731–735. [CrossRef]
21. Bao, A.; Song, X. Bounds for the blowup time of the solutions to quasi-linear parabolic problems. *Z. Angew. Math. Phys.* **2014**, *65*, 115–123. [CrossRef]
22. Liu, Y. Lower bounds for the blow-up time in a non-local reaction diffusion problem under nonlinear boundary conditions. *Math. Comput. Model.* **2013**, *57*, 926–931. [CrossRef]
23. Payne, L.E.; Schaefer, P.W. Bounds for blow-up time for the heat equation under nonlinear boundary conditions. *Proc. Roy. Soc. Edinburgh Sect. A* **2009**, *139*, 1289–1296. [CrossRef]
24. Payne, L.E.; Philippin, G.A. Blow-up phenomena in parabolic problems with time dependent coefficients under dirichlet boundary conditions. *Proc. Amer. Math. Soc.* **2013**, *141*, 2309–2318. [CrossRef]
25. Song, J.C. Lower bounds for the blow-up time in a non-local reaction diffusion problem. *Appl. Math. Lett.* **2014**, *24*, 793–796. [CrossRef]
26. Zhou, Y.; Han, W. Sharpness on the lower bound of the lifespan of solutions to nonlinear Wave Equations. *Chin. Ann. Math.* **2011**, *32*, 521–526. [CrossRef]
27. Takamura, H.; Wakasa, K. The sharp upper bound of the lifespan of solutions to critical semilinear wave equations in high dimensions. *J. Differ. Equ.* **2011**, *251*, 1157–1171. [CrossRef]
28. Ha, T.G. Asymptotic stability of the semilinear wave equation with boundary damping and source term. *C. R. Acad. Sci. Paris Ser. I* **2014**, *352*, 213–218. [CrossRef]

Article

Bifurcation Analysis for an OSN Model with Two Delays

Liancheng Wang * and Min Wang

Department of Mathematics, Kennesaw State University, Marietta, GA 30060, USA; mwang23@kennesaw.edu
* Correspondence: lwang5@kennesaw.edu

Abstract: In this research, we introduce and analyze a mathematical model for online social networks, incorporating two distinct delays. These delays represent the time it takes for active users within the network to begin disengaging, either with or without contacting non-users of online social platforms. We focus particularly on the user prevailing equilibrium (UPE), denoted as P^*, and explore the role of delays as parameters in triggering Hopf bifurcations. In doing so, we find the conditions under which Hopf bifurcations occur, then establish stable regions based on the two delays. Furthermore, we delineate the boundaries of stability regions wherein bifurcations transpire as the delays cross these thresholds. We present numerical simulations to illustrate and validate our theoretical findings. Through this interdisciplinary approach, we aim to deepen our understanding of the dynamics inherent in online social networks.

Keywords: online social network; stability region; Hopf bifurcation

MSC: 34D20; 34D23; 34K18

Citation: Wang, L.; Wang, M. Bifurcation Analysis for an OSN Model with Two Delays. *Mathematics* **2024**, *12*, 1321. https://doi.org/10.3390/math12091321

Academic Editor: Jaume Giné

Received: 20 March 2024
Revised: 10 April 2024
Accepted: 24 April 2024
Published: 26 April 2024

Copyright: © 2024 by the authors. Licensee MDPI, Basel, Switzerland. This article is an open access article distributed under the terms and conditions of the Creative Commons Attribution (CC BY) license (https://creativecommons.org/licenses/by/4.0/).

1. Introduction

The emergence of online social networks (OSNs) has significantly reshaped the landscape of information dissemination and interpersonal connectivity over the last two decades. Platforms like Facebook, Twitter, and Instagram have revolutionized how individuals exchange ideas and interact, profoundly influencing daily life. OSNs serve as virtual spaces where users can present themselves, engage with others, and forge connections irrespective of geographical boundaries. Their widespread adoption, particularly among tech-savvy generations, has had far-reaching implications across various domains, such as education, elections, and information dissemination. Understanding the intricate ways in which OSNs influence societal, political, and economic realms, as well as individual behaviors, has become increasingly imperative.

To better comprehend the dynamics of OSNs, mathematical models have been developed, offering profound insights into how social networks shape opinions and behaviors. Noteworthy contributions include seminal works by, for example [1–11]. Many of these models draw inspiration from SIR/SEIR disease-type models, providing a framework to study OSN dynamics effectively. Interested readers can delve into classic and advanced results on SIR/SEIR mathematical models and SIR/SEIR mathematical models with delays in works such as those by [12–24] and references therein. Most recently, Barman and Mishra [25,26] introduced a graph Laplacian diffusion into SIR/SEIR type network models and carried out Hopf bifurcation analysis.

In the realm of OSN modeling, the total population $N(t)$ at time t is often partitioned into three distinct sub-classes representing key populations within OSN dynamics: potential users, active users, and individuals opposed to OSNs, denoted by $x(t)$, $y(t)$, and $z(t)$, respectively. Cannarella and Spechler [2] introduced the "infectious recovery" SIR-type model to analyze user adoption and abandonment of OSNs, later extended in ordinary, fractional, and stochastic differential equation models as given in [3,5,6]. Graef et al. [5] explored the following OSN model with demography to examine adoption and abandonment dynamics, conducting both local and global stability analyses.

$$\begin{cases} x' = \Lambda - \alpha xy - \mu x, \\ y' = \alpha xy - \eta yz - (\mu + \delta)y, \\ z' = \eta yz + \delta y - \mu z. \end{cases} \tag{1}$$

Motivated by existing research and the nuanced complexities of OSNs, Wang and Wang [27] proposed a dynamic mathematical model capturing unique characteristics such as users' varying interests and the impact of time delays. Their model accounts for the transition of potential users to active ones and the eventual abandonment of OSNs by active users due to disinterest or interaction with those opposed to OSNs. This interaction is described by a system of differential equations as follows:

$$\begin{cases} x' &= A - \alpha xy - \mu x, \\ y' &= \alpha xy - \eta y(t)z(t) - \delta y(t-\tau) - \mu y, \\ z' &= B + \eta y(t)z(t) + \delta y(t-\tau) - \mu z, \end{cases} \tag{2}$$

where the parameters $A > 0$ and $B \geq 0$ represent the rates that newcomers come into the community as either potential online network users or as people who are never interested in OSNs. $\alpha > 0$ denotes the contact rate between the potential and active OSN users; $\mu > 0$ is the death rate for all people; $\eta > 0$ is the contact rate between active users and people who are opposed to OSNs; $\delta > 0$ is the transferring rate describing the rate the active users lose their interest and become opposing to OSNs; and $\tau \geq 0$ is the time delay that represents the time for active users to starting abandoning the network. Wang and Wang [27] performed a detailed analysis for System (2), including local and global analysis for user free equilibrium (UFE) and UPE. Hopf bifurcation was also carried out using the delay τ as the bifurcating parameter. Conditions and critical values were found that guarantee the occurrence of Hopf bifurcation.

Building upon prior work, considering the fact that it will take some time for active users to disengage after interacting with non-users, we introduce the following refined model that accounts for this time delay. Our proposed system of equations incorporates a time delay ρ, representing the period for active users to abandon OSNs after contact with non-users. This addition of a new time delay can indeed make it more representative of real-world situations and more accurately representing real-world dynamics and improving the reliability of predictions and control strategies. Notably, our model encompasses previous formulations as special cases, offering a comprehensive framework to study the evolving dynamics of OSNs

$$\begin{cases} x' &= A - \alpha xy - \mu x, \\ y' &= \alpha xy - \eta y(t-\rho)z(t-\rho) - \delta y(t-\tau) - \mu y, \\ z' &= B + \eta y(t-\rho)z(t-\rho) + \delta y(t-\tau) - \mu z. \end{cases} \tag{3}$$

For System (3), define

$$f(z) = A\alpha(\delta + \eta z) \tag{4}$$

and

$$g(z) = \mu\eta(\alpha + \eta)z^2 + [\mu(\mu + \delta)(\alpha + \eta) + \eta(\mu\delta - B\alpha)]z + (\mu + \delta)(\mu\delta - B\alpha). \tag{5}$$

Let R_0 be the basic reproduction number defined by

$$R_0 = \frac{A\alpha}{B\eta + \mu(\mu + \delta)}. \tag{6}$$

The following results are established by Wang and Wang [27].

Theorem 1. *Let R_0 be defined by (6). If $R_0 \leq 1$, then System (3) has a unique user free equilibrium $P_0 = (A/\mu, 0, B/\mu)$ and it exists for all parameter values. If $R_0 > 1$, then System (3) has two equilibria: P_0 and a unique user prevailing equilibrium $P^* = (x^*, y^*, z^*)$, where z^* is the unique positive root of the equation $f(z) = g(z)$, such that $z^* > B/\mu$, and x^* and y^* are given by*

$$x^* = \frac{\mu + \delta}{\alpha} + \frac{\eta}{\alpha} z^*, \tag{7}$$

and

$$y^* = \frac{\mu z^* - B}{\delta + \eta z^*}. \tag{8}$$

Theorem 2. *Let R_0 be defined by (6) and assume that $\tau = \rho = 0$. If $R_0 < 1$, P_0 is locally asymptotically stable; if $R_0 = 1$, P_0 is neutrally stable; and if $R_0 > 1$, P_0 becomes unstable, and P^* emerges and it is locally asymptotically stable.*

The following result was established by Ruan and Wei [28] and will be used in this research.

Lemma 1. *Consider the following exponential polynomial:*

$$\begin{aligned} P(\lambda, \tau_1, \tau_2, \cdots, \tau_m) &= \lambda^n + a_1^{(0)} \lambda^{n-1} + \cdots + a_n^{(0)} \\ &+ [a_1^{(1)} \lambda^{n-1} + \cdots + a_n^{(1)}] e^{-\lambda \tau_1} \\ &+ \cdots \\ &+ [a_1^{(m)} \lambda^{n-1} + \cdots + a_n^{(m)}] e^{-\lambda \tau_m}, \end{aligned}$$

where $\tau_i \geq 0$ $(i = 1, 2, \cdots, m)$ and $a_j^{(i)}$ $(i = 0, 1, 2, \cdots, m; j = 1, 2, \cdots, n)$ are constants. As $(\tau_1, \tau_2, \cdots, \tau_m)$ changes, the sum of the orders of the zeros of P in the open right half plane can change only if a zero appears on or crosses the imaginary axis.

In this research, we were interested in finding out what network user dynamics the new model presents, in particular, whether or not a Hopf bifurcation will occur for this new OSN model after adding a time delay. In doing so, we performed a Hopf bifurcation analysis for System (3) using two delays τ and ρ as bifurcating parameters. We investigated the Hopf bifurcations at the unique user prevailing equilibrium point when $R_0 > 1$. Stability regions were established in terms of two delays τ and ρ. Conditions and critical curves were obtained so that the Hopf bifurcation occurs as (τ, ρ), passing through the boundary of the stability regions.

The remainder of the manuscript is structured as follows: In Section 2, we delve into Hopf bifurcation analysis concerning the interplay of two delays. We explore the establishment of stability regions and identify critical values under scenarios where either one delay is absent, or both delays are concurrently present. Our investigation delves into the conditions conducive to Hopf bifurcations and delineates the associated implications. To augment our theoretical insights, we present numerical simulations aimed at illustrating the dynamics of the system under consideration.

Finally, Section 3 encapsulates our findings and conclusions drawn from the preceding analyses. We synthesize the key insights gleaned from our study and discuss their broader implications in understanding the dynamics of online social networks.

2. Hopf Bifurcation

From Wang and Wang [27], we know that the dynamics of System (3) is completely determined by the basic reproduction number R_0 when delays $\rho = \tau = 0$. In particular, we know that when $R_0 > 1$, the unique user prevailing equilibrium P^* is locally asymptotically stable. We are interested in the question of whether the delays ρ and τ could cause the stability of the UPE P^* to switch as they increase. In this section, we study the occurrence of Hopf bifurcations using the delays ρ and τ as the bifurcation parameters. Note that when $R_0 > 1$ there is a unique UPE $P^* = (x^*, y^*, z^*)$. For this section, we always assume that $R_0 > 1$.

The characteristic equation of System (3) at the unique equilibrium P^* when $\rho, \tau \geq 0$ is the determinant of the matrix

$$J^* = \begin{pmatrix} \lambda + \alpha y^* + \mu & \alpha x^* & 0 \\ -\alpha y^* & \lambda + \mu - \alpha x^* + \eta z^* e^{-\lambda\rho} + \delta e^{-\lambda\tau} & \eta y^* e^{-\lambda\rho} \\ 0 & -\eta z^* e^{-\lambda\rho} - \delta e^{-\lambda\tau} & \lambda + \mu - \eta y^* e^{-\lambda\rho} \end{pmatrix},$$

which is

$$(\lambda + \mu)(\lambda^2 + a\lambda + b + \eta(c\lambda + d)e^{-\lambda\rho} + \delta(\lambda + h)e^{-\lambda\tau}) = 0, \tag{9}$$

where

$$\begin{aligned} a &= 2\mu + \alpha y^* - \alpha x^*, \\ b &= \mu(\mu + \alpha y^* - \alpha x^*), \\ c &= z^* - y^*, \\ d &= (z^* - y^*)(\mu + \alpha y^*) + \alpha x^* y^*, \\ h &= \mu + \alpha y^*, \end{aligned} \tag{10}$$

and x^*, y^*, and z^* are given in Theorem 1.

One root of Equation (9) is $\lambda = -\mu < 0$. The other roots are determined by the transcendental equation:

$$\lambda^2 + a\lambda + b + \eta(c\lambda + d)e^{-\lambda\rho} + \delta(\lambda + h)e^{-\lambda\tau} = 0. \tag{11}$$

We know that if $R_0 > 1$ and $\rho = \tau = 0$, all roots of Equation (11) have negative real parts and P^* is locally asymptotically stable. Our interest is to see whether or not the delays ρ and τ cause the stability of P^* to switch as ρ and τ increase while R_0 remains larger than the unity. Due to Lemma 1, we need to investigate if a zero of Equation (11) appears on or crosses the imaginary axis as ρ and τ increases. Keep in mind that when $R_0 > 1$, $z^* > B/\mu$, see [27].

From (10) and using the expressions given in (7) and (8), we can obtain

$$b + \eta d + \delta h = \frac{(\mu z^* - B)\left(\alpha\left(\eta\left(B + \eta(z^*)^2\right) + \delta^2 + \delta(\mu + 2\eta z^*)\right) + \eta(\delta + \eta z^*)^2\right)}{(\delta + \eta z^*)^2} > 0$$

since $z^* > B/\mu$. Therefore, $\lambda = 0$ is not a root of (11). Therefore, there are no zero-Hopf bifurcations.

2.1. *Hopf Bifurcation When* $\rho = 0$

For the case that $\rho = 0$, the Hopf bifurcation analysis was carried out completely by Wang and Wang [27]. For completeness, we only cite key definitions and results here. We refer readers to [27] for a detailed analysis. When $\rho = 0$, Equation (11) becomes

$$\lambda^2 + a_1\lambda + b_1 + (\delta\lambda + c_1)e^{-\lambda\tau} = 0, \tag{12}$$

where

$$\begin{aligned} a_1 &= 2\mu + \alpha y^* + \eta z^* - \alpha x^* - \eta y^*, \\ b_1 &= \mu^2 + \mu(\alpha y^* + \eta z^* - \alpha x^* - \eta y^*) + \alpha\eta y^*(x^* + z^* - y^*), \\ c_1 &= \delta(\mu + \alpha y^*). \end{aligned} \tag{13}$$

Now, let $\lambda = \omega i$ ($\omega > 0$) be a root to Equation (12). Plug it into (12), then ω has to satisfy the following equation:

$$\omega^4 + (a_1^2 - \delta^2 - 2b_1)\omega^2 + b_1^2 - c_1^2 = 0.$$

Let $p = w^2$ and denote $a_2 = a_1^2 - \delta^2 - 2b_1$ and $b_2 = b_1^2 - c_1^2$. Then, the above equation can be rewritten as:

$$p^2 + a_2 p + b_2 = 0. \tag{14}$$

The following result is well known.

Lemma 2. *For Equation (14), we have*

(a) *If $b_2 < 0$ or if $b_2 = 0$ and $a_2 < 0$, then it has a unique positive root.*
(b) *If $a_2 \geq 0$ and $b_2 \geq 0$, then it has no positive roots.*
(c) *If $a_2 < 0$ and $b_2 > 0$, then it has no positive roots if $a_2^2 - 4b_2 < 0$; one positive root if $a_2^2 - 4b_2 = 0$; and two positive roots if $a_2^2 - 4b_2 > 0$.*

Plug a_1, b_1, c_1, given in (13) and x^*, and y^*, given in (7) and (8), into a_2 and b_2, and we have

$$a_2 = a_1^2 - \delta^2 - 2b_1 = \frac{1}{(\delta + \eta z^*)^2} P_1(z^*), \tag{15}$$

$$b_2 = b_1^2 - c_1^2 = \frac{(\mu z^* - B)}{(\delta + \eta z^*)^4} P_2(z^*) P_3(z^*), \tag{16}$$

where

$$\begin{aligned} P_1(z) &= -2\eta^2\mu(\alpha + \eta)z^3 + (2B\eta^2(\alpha + \eta) + \mu(\alpha^2\mu - 4\alpha\delta\eta - 2\alpha\delta\eta^2))z^2 \\ &\quad + (B(4\alpha\delta\eta + 2\delta\eta^2 - 2\alpha\mu) - 2\alpha\delta^2\mu)z \\ &\quad + B^2(\eta^2 + \alpha^2) + \delta^2\mu^2 + 2B\delta(\alpha\delta + \eta\mu), \end{aligned} \tag{17}$$

$$\begin{aligned} P_2(z) &= (\alpha\eta^2 + \eta^3)z^2 + (2\alpha\delta\eta + 2\delta\eta^2)z + \alpha\delta^2 + \alpha\delta\mu + \alpha B\eta + \delta^2\eta, \\ P_3(z) &= (\alpha\eta^2\mu + \eta^3\mu)z^3 - (\alpha B\eta^2 + B\eta^3)z^2 \\ &\quad + (-\alpha\delta^2\mu + \alpha\delta\mu^2 + \alpha B\eta\mu - 2B\delta\eta^2 - 3\delta^2\eta\mu)z \\ &\quad - \alpha B^2\eta + \alpha B\delta^2 - \alpha B\delta\mu - B\delta^2\eta - 2\delta^3\mu. \end{aligned} \tag{18}$$

We then have the following results; see Wang and Wang [27].

Theorem 3. *Let $R_0 > 1$, and let a_2, b_2, P_1 and P_3 be defined by (15), (16), (17), and (18). Assume that P_1 and P_3 have unique positive roots z_1 and z_2, respectively.*

(I) *When any of the following conditions is satisfied, Equation (14) has no positive roots.*
   (1) *$z_1 = z_2$ and $z^* = z_1$;*
   (2) *$z_1 > z_2$ and $z_2 \leq z^* \leq z_1$;*
   (3) *$z^* > \max\{z_1, z_2\}$ and $a_2^2 - 4b_2 < 0$.*
(II) *When any of the following conditions is satisfied, Equation (14) has a unique positive root.*
   (1) *$z_1 < z_2$ and $z^* \leq z_2$;*
   (2) *$z_1 \geq z_2$ and $z^* < z_2$;*
   (3) *$z^* > \max\{z_1, z_2\}$ and $a_2^2 - 4b_2 = 0$.*
(III) *Equation (14) has two positive roots if $z^* > \max\{z_1, z_2\}$ and $a_2^2 - 4b_2 > 0$.*

Now assume that $R_0 > 1$ and Equation (14) has at least one positive root. Solving p from Equation (14) for the positive roots gives

$$p^{\pm} = \frac{1}{2}\left[-(a_1^2 - \delta^2 - 2b_1) \pm \sqrt{(a_1 - \delta^2 - 2b_1)^2 - 4(b_1^2 - c_1^2)} \right].$$

Note that if Equation (14) has a unique positive root, then it is p^+. Let $\omega^{\pm} = \sqrt{p^{\pm}}$ and define

$$f_1(\omega) = \frac{c_1\omega^2 - a_1\delta\omega^2 - b_1c_1}{c_1^2 + \delta^2\omega^2}$$

and

$$f_2(\omega) = \frac{\omega(a_1c_1 - b_1\delta + \delta\omega^2)}{c_1^2 + \delta^2\omega^2}.$$

Also define $\tau_n^{\pm}, n = 0, 1, 2, \cdots$, as

$$\tau_n^{\pm} = \begin{cases} \frac{1}{\omega^{\pm}}(\arccos f_1(\omega^{\pm}) + 2n\pi) & \text{if } f_2(\omega^{\pm}) > 0, \\ \frac{1}{\omega^{\pm}}(2\pi - \arccos f_1(\omega^{\pm}) + 2n\pi) & \text{if } f_2(\omega^{\pm}) \leq 0. \end{cases} \tag{19}$$

Hence, $\tau_n^{\pm} > 0$ and Equation (11) has a pair of purely imaginary roots $\pm i\omega^{\pm}$ when $\tau = \tau_n^{\pm}$ for $n = 0, 1, 2, \cdots$.

Theorem 4. *Assume that $R_0 > 1$ and let $a_2, b_2, P_1, P_3, z^*, \omega^+, \tau_0^+$ be defined above. Assume that P_1 and P_3 have unique positive roots z_1 and z_2, respectively. We then have the following results.*

(I) *All roots of Equation (12) have negative real parts for all delay $\tau \geq 0$, if*
   (1) $z_1 = z_2$ *and* $z^* = z_1$, *or*
   (2) $z_1 > z_2$ *and* $z_2 \leq z^* \leq z_1$, *or*
   (3) $z^* > \max\{z_1, z_2\}$ *and* $a_2^2 - 4b_2 < 0$.
   Therefore, P^* is locally asymptotically stable for all $\tau \geq 0$.

(II) *There is a $\tau_0^+ > 0$, such that all roots of Equation (12) have negative real parts for all $\tau \in [0, \tau_0^+)$. It has a pair of purely imaginary roots $\pm i\omega^+$, and all other roots have negative real parts when $\tau = \tau_0^+$, if*
   (1) $z_1 < z_2$ *and* $z^* \leq z_2$, *or*
   (2) $z_1 \geq z_2$ *and* $z^* < z_2$, *or*
   (3) $z^* > \max\{z_1, z_2\}$ *and* $a_2^2 - 4b_2 \geq 0$.
   Therefore, P^* is locally asymptotically stable for all $\tau < \tau_0^+$. Hopf bifurcation occurs as τ passes through $\tau = \tau_0^+$.

We use one numerical simulation to illustrate the above theoretical results. If we choose $A = 10, B = 0.2, \alpha = 0.1, \eta = 0.5, \mu = 0.2, \delta = 0.4$. Then we have $P^* = (43.239, 0.3127, 7.4479)$, i.e., $z^* = 7.4479$. Calculations show that $R_0 = 4.54545 > 1$, and

$$a_1 = 0.325082, \quad b_1 = 0.682603, \quad c_1 = 0.092508.$$

Two polynomials P_1 and P_3 can be found:

$$\begin{aligned} P_1(z) &= 0.0392 + 0.0488z + 0.0044z^2 - 0.06z^3, \\ P_3(z) &= -0.042 - 0.0876z - 0.03z^2 + 0.03z^3. \end{aligned}$$

By Descartes' Rule of Signs, both P_1 and P_3 have a unique positive root and they are

$$z_1 = 1.20208, \qquad z_2 = 2.43518.$$

We also find that

$$a_2 = -1.41953, \qquad b_2 = 0.457389.$$

Thus

$$a_2^2 - 4b_2 = 0.185503 > 0.$$

Therefore, Condition (II)(3) of Theorem 4 is satisfied and a $\tau_0^+ > 0$ exists. Using (19), we find that

$$\tau_0^+ = 0.440535.$$

According to Theorem 4, all roots of Equation (11) have negative real parts for all $\tau < \tau_0^+$, thus P^* is locally asymptotically stable for all $\tau < \tau_0^+$. When $\tau = \tau_0^+$, Equation (11) has a pair of purely imaginary roots, and all other roots have negative real parts. Hopf bifurcation occurs as τ passes across $\tau = \tau_0^+$. See Figure 1 for solutions to converge to P^* for $\tau = 0.2 < \tau_0^+$, Figure 2 for Hopf bifurcations to occur and periodic solutions to appear when $\tau = \tau_0^+ = 0.440535$, and Figure 3 for solutions blow out when τ moves to the right of $\tau_0^+ = 0.440535$.

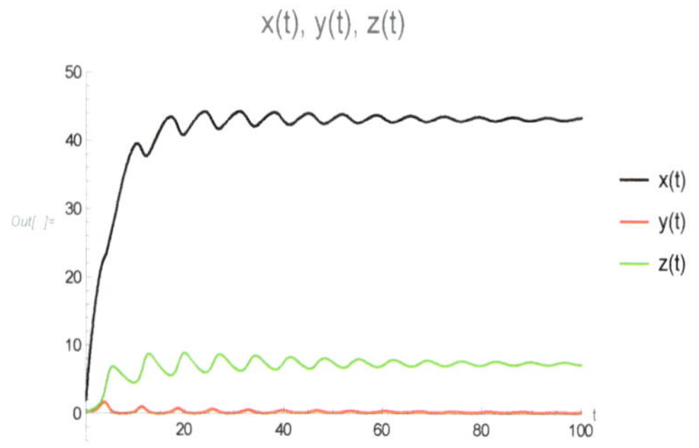

Figure 1. $\tau = 0.2 < \tau_0^+$. Solutions converge to P^*.

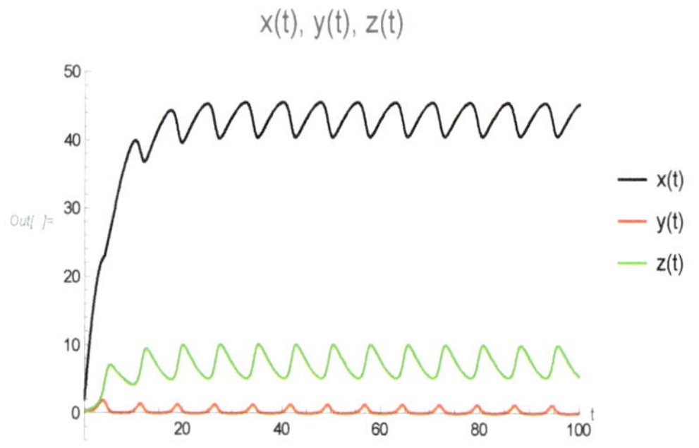

Figure 2. $\tau = \tau_0^+ = 0.440535$. Periodic solutions appear.

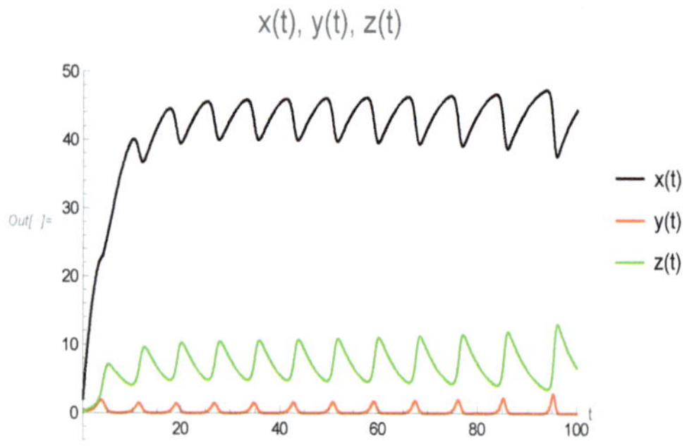

Figure 3. $\tau = 0.4406 > \tau_0^+$. Solutions go to infinity.

2.2. Hopf Bifurcation When $\tau = 0$

When $\tau = 0$, Equation (11) becomes

$$\lambda^2 + a_3\lambda + b_3 + \eta(c_3\lambda + d_3)e^{-\lambda\rho} = 0, \tag{20}$$

where

$$\begin{aligned} a_3 &= 2\mu + \delta + \alpha y^* - \alpha x^*, \\ b_3 &= \mu(\mu + \alpha y^* - \alpha x^*) + \delta(\mu + \alpha y^*), \\ c_3 &= z^* - y^*, \\ d_3 &= (z^* - y^*)(\mu + \alpha y^*) + \alpha x^* y^*. \end{aligned} \tag{21}$$

Now, let $\lambda = \omega i$ ($\omega > 0$) be a root to Equation (20). When plugged into (20), separating the real and imaginary parts gives

$$d_3\eta\cos(\omega\rho) + \eta c_3\omega\sin(\omega\rho) = \omega^2 - b_3, \tag{22}$$

$$\eta c_3\omega\cos(\omega\rho) - d_3\eta\sin(\omega\rho) = -a_3\omega. \tag{23}$$

Squaring both sides and adding them together yields

$$\omega^4 + (a_3^2 - \eta^2 c_3^2 - 2b_3)\omega^2 + b_3^2 - \eta^2 d_3^2 = 0.$$

Let $q = \omega^2$ and denote $a_4 = a_3^2 - \eta^2 c_3^2 - 2b_3$ and $b_4 = b_3^2 - \eta^2 d_3^2$. Then, the above equation can be rewritten as:

$$q^2 + a_4 q + b_4 = 0. \tag{24}$$

Plug a_3, b_3, c_3 and d_3 given in (21) and x^* and y^* given in (7) and (8) into a_4 and b_4, calculations yield

$$a_4 = a_3^2 - \eta^2 c_3^2 - 2b_3 = \frac{1}{(\delta + \eta z^*)^2} Q_1(z^*), \tag{25}$$

$$b_4 = b_3^2 - \eta^2 d_3^2 = \frac{(\mu z^* - B)}{(\delta + \eta z^*)^4} Q_2(z^*) Q_3(z^*), \tag{26}$$

where Q_1, Q_2 and Q_3 are polynomials of z, such that

$$\begin{aligned} Q_1(z) &= 2\eta^2\mu(\eta - \alpha)z^3 + (\mu\left(\alpha^2\mu - 4\alpha\delta\eta + 2\delta\eta^2\right) + 2B\eta^2(\alpha - \eta))z^2 \\ &\quad -2\left(\delta\mu(\alpha\delta - \eta\mu) + B\left(\alpha^2\mu - 2\alpha\delta\eta + \eta^2(\delta - \mu)\right)\right)z \\ &\quad +B^2\left(\alpha^2 - \eta^2\right) + 2\alpha B\delta^2 + \delta^2\mu^2, \end{aligned} \tag{27}$$

$$\begin{aligned} Q_2(z) &= \alpha\delta^2 + \alpha\delta\mu + \alpha B\eta + \delta^2\eta + \alpha\eta^2 z^2 + \eta^3 z^2 + 2\alpha\delta\eta z + 2\delta\eta^2 z, \\ Q_3(z) &= -\eta^2\mu(\alpha + 3\eta)z^3 + \eta(2\mu(\alpha\mu - 3\delta\eta) + B\eta(\alpha + \eta))z^2 \\ &\quad +\delta\mu(\alpha(\delta + \mu) - 3\delta\eta) + B\eta(2\delta\eta - 3\alpha\mu)z \\ &\quad +B\left(\delta^2\eta - \alpha\left(-B\eta + \delta^2 + \delta\mu\right)\right). \end{aligned} \tag{28}$$

Note that $Q_1(z)$ is a degree three polynomial with $Q_1(B/\mu) = B^2\eta^2 + 2B\delta\eta\mu + \delta^2\mu^2 > 0$. Obviously, $Q_2(z^*) > 0$, and $\mu z^* - B > 0$ as $z^* > B/\mu$ if $R_0 > 1$. $Q_3(z)$ is also a degree three polynomial of z, such that

$$Q_3(B/\mu) = -\frac{2B^3\eta^3}{\mu^2} - \frac{4B^2\delta\eta^2}{\mu} - 2B\delta^2\eta \leq 0$$

and

$$Q_3(B/\mu) < 0$$

if $B > 0$.

Applying the results of Lemma 2, we have the following results.

Theorem 5. *Let $R_0 > 1$, and let Q_1 and Q_3 be defined by (27), and (28). We then have:*

(I) *If $Q_1(z^*) \geq 0$ and $Q_3(z^*) \geq 0$, then Equation (24) has no positive roots.*
(II) *If $Q_3(z^*) < 0$, or if $Q_3(z^*) = 0$ and $Q_1(z^*) < 0$, then Equation (24) has a unique positive root.*

Now assume that $R_0 > 1$ and Equation (24) has at least one positive root. Solving q from Equation (24) for the positive roots gives

$$q^{\pm} = \frac{1}{2}\left[-(a_3^2 - \eta^2 c_3^2 - 2b_3) \pm \sqrt{(a_3 - \eta^2 c_3^2 - 2b_3)^2 - 4(b_3^2 - \eta^2 d_3^2)} \right].$$

Note that if Equation (24) has a unique positive root, then it is q^+. Let $\omega^{\pm} = \sqrt{q^{\pm}}$. Solving for $\sin(\omega\rho)$ and $\cos(\omega\rho)$ from (22) and (23), we obtain

$$\cos(\omega\rho) = \frac{(d_3 - a_3 c_3)\omega^2 - b_3 d_3}{\eta\left(c_3^2\omega^2 + d_3^2\right)} = g_1(\omega)$$

and

$$\sin(\omega\rho) = \frac{\omega\left(c_3\omega^2 + a_3 d_3 - b_3 c_3\right)}{\eta\left(c_3^2\omega^2 + d_3^2\right)} = g_2(\omega).$$

Define $\rho_n^{\pm}, n = 0, 1, 2, \cdots$, as

$$\rho_n^{\pm} = \begin{cases} \frac{1}{\omega^{\pm}}(\arccos g_1(\omega^{\pm}) + 2n\pi) & \text{if } g_2(\omega^{\pm}) > 0, \\ \frac{1}{\omega^{\pm}}(2\pi - \arccos g_1(\omega^{\pm}) + 2n\pi) & \text{if } g_2(\omega^{\pm}) \leq 0. \end{cases} \tag{29}$$

Hence, $\rho_n^{\pm} > 0$ and Equation (20) has a pair of purely imaginary roots $\pm i\omega^{\pm}$ when $\rho = \rho_n^{\pm}$ for $n = 0, 1, 2, \cdots$. Next, we attempt to establish the transversality condition for Hopf bifurcation. For $\rho > 0$, let

$$\lambda(\rho) = \alpha(\rho) + iw(\rho) \tag{30}$$

be the root of Equation (20), satisfying

$$\alpha(\rho_n^{\pm}) = 0, \quad w(\rho_n^{\pm}) = w^{\pm}.$$

Differentiating both sides of Equation (20) with respect to ρ gives

$$\text{Re}\left(\frac{d\lambda}{d\rho}\right)^{-1}_{\rho=\rho_n^{\pm}} = \frac{\pm\sqrt{a_4^2 - 4b_4}}{d_3^2 + c_3^2\omega^2}. \tag{31}$$

Note that $a_4^2 - 4b_4 > 0$ since in this case Equation (24) has two positive roots. We thus established that $\text{Re}\left(\frac{d\lambda}{d\rho}\right)^{-1}_{\rho=\rho_n^+} > 0$ and $\text{Re}\left(\frac{d\lambda}{d\rho}\right)^{-1}_{\rho=\rho_n^-} < 0$. The discussion above establishes the following stability and Hopf bifurcation results.

Theorem 6. *Assume that $R_0 > 1$ and let $a_4, b_4, Q_1, Q_3, z^*, \omega^+, \rho_0^+$ be defined above. We then have the following results.*

(I) *If $Q_1(z^*) \geq 0$ and $Q_3(z^*) \geq 0$, then all roots of Equation (20) have negative real parts for all delay $\rho \geq 0$. Therefore, P^* is locally asymptotically stable for all $\rho \geq 0$.*

(II) *If $Q_3(z^*) < 0$, or if $Q_3(z^*) = 0$ and $Q_1(z^*) < 0$, then there is a $\rho_0^+ > 0$, such that all roots of Equation (20) have negative real parts for all $\rho \in [0, \rho_0^+)$. It has a pair of purely imaginary roots $\pm i\omega^+$, and all other roots have negative real parts when $\rho = \rho_0^+$. Therefore, P^* is locally asymptotically stable for all $\rho < \rho_0^+$, and is unstable for all $\rho > \rho_0^+$. Hopf bifurcation occurs as ρ passes through $\rho = \rho_0^+$.*

If we choose the same parameter values as in Section 2.1, i.e., $A = 10, B = 0.2, \alpha = 0.1$, $\eta = 0.5, \mu = 0.2, \delta = 0.4$. Then we have $P^* = (43.239, 0.3127, 7.4479)$, i.e., $z^* = 7.4479$. We also have $R_0 = 4.54545 > 1$, and calculations give

$$
\begin{aligned}
Q_1(z) &= 0.0032 + 0.0048z - 0.0156z^2 + 0.04z^3, \\
Q_3(z) &= 0.0132 - 0.0092z - 0.086z^2 - 0.08z^3.
\end{aligned}
$$

Therefore, $Q_1(z^*) = 15.6992$, $Q_3(z^*) = -37.87 < 0$, which means that the condition (II) of Theorem 6 is satisfied, and a $\rho_0^+ > 0$ exists. Actually, calculations yield

$$\rho_0^+ = 0.0474351.$$

That means that all roots of Equation (20) have negative real parts when $\rho < \rho_0^+$; therefore, P^* is locally asymptotically stable for all $\rho < \rho_0^+$. When $\rho = \rho_0^+$, Equation (20) has a pair of purely imaginary roots, and all other roots have negative real parts. Hopf bifurcation occurs as ρ passes across $\rho = \rho_0^+$. See Figure 4 for solutions to converge to P^* for $\rho = 0.02 < \rho_0^+$, Figure 5 for Hopf bifurcations to occur and periodic solutions to appear when $\rho = \rho_0^+ = 0.0474351$, and Figure 6 for solutions blow out when ρ moves to the right of $\rho_0^+ = 0.0474351$.

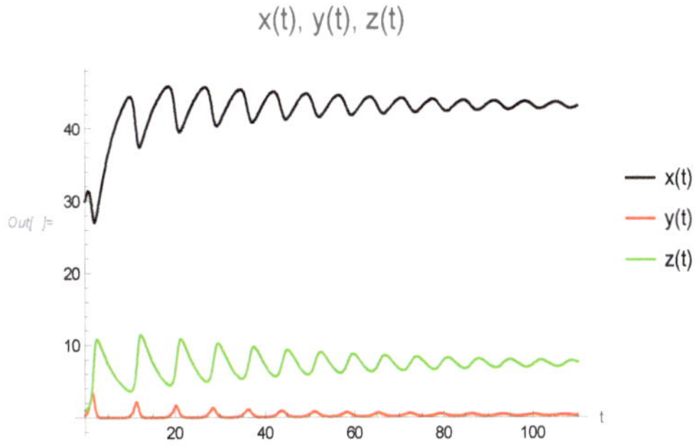

Figure 4. $\rho = 0.02 < \rho_0^+$. Solutions converge to P^*.

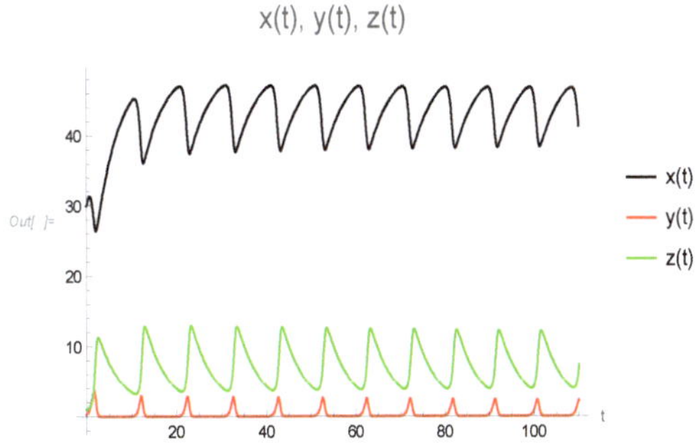

Figure 5. $\rho = \rho_0^+ = 0.0474351$. Periodic solutions appear.

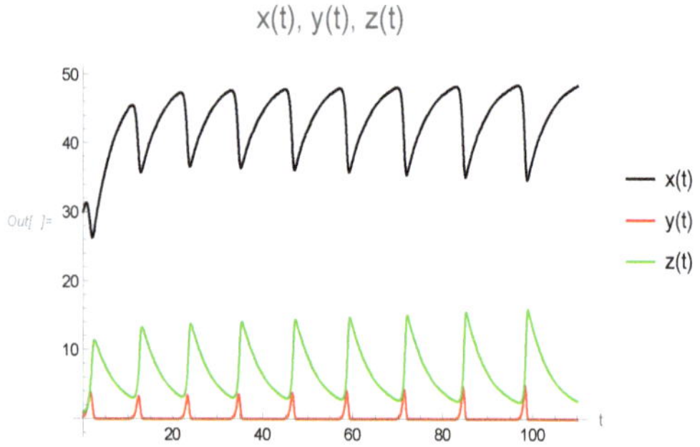

Figure 6. $\rho = 0.05 > \rho_0^+$. Solutions go to infinity.

2.3. *Hopf Bifurcation When $\rho > 0$ and $\tau > 0$*

Now, assume that $\rho \geq 0$ and $\tau \geq 0$. Let $\lambda = \omega i$ ($\omega > 0$) be a root to Equation (11). Plug it into (11), and separate the real and imaginary parts, we obtain

$$c\eta\omega \sin(\rho\omega) + d\eta \cos(\rho\omega) = \omega^2 - b - \delta\omega \sin(\tau\omega) - \delta h \cos(\tau\omega), \tag{32}$$
$$c\eta\omega \cos(\rho\omega) - d\eta \sin(\rho\omega) = -a\omega - \delta\omega \cos(\tau\omega) + \delta h \sin(\tau\omega). \tag{33}$$

Squaring both sides and adding them together yields

$$\begin{aligned} & 2\delta[\omega(ah - b + \omega^2)\sin(\tau\omega) + (\omega^2(h-a) - bh)\cos(\tau\omega)] \\ = \; & \omega^4 + (a^2 + \delta^2 - 2b - c^2\eta^2)\omega^2 + b^2 + h^2\delta^2 - d^2\eta^2 \end{aligned}$$

which is equivalent to

$$\sin(\theta + \omega\tau) = \frac{\omega^4 + (a^2 + \delta^2 - 2b - c^2\eta^2)\omega^2 + b^2 + h^2\delta^2 - d^2\eta^2}{2\delta\sqrt{(h^2+\omega^2)(a^2\omega^2 + (\omega^2 - b)^2)}},$$

where

$$\theta = \arcsin \frac{(h-a)\omega^2 - bh}{\sqrt{(h^2+\omega^2)(a^2\omega^2 + (\omega^2 - b)^2)}}.$$

Let

$$F(\omega) = \sin(\theta + \omega\tau) \tag{34}$$

and

$$G(\omega) = \frac{\omega^4 + (a^2 + \delta^2 - 2b - c^2\eta^2)\omega^2 + b^2 + h^2\delta^2 - d^2\eta^2}{2\delta\sqrt{(h^2+\omega^2)(a^2\omega^2 + (\omega^2 - b)^2)}}. \tag{35}$$

Now, we study the existence of positive solutions to the equation

$$F(\omega) = G(\omega)$$

when $\tau \geq 0$. First, note that if $\omega = 0$, then we have

$$\frac{(h-a)\omega^2 - bh}{\sqrt{(h^2+\omega^2)(a^2\omega^2 + (\omega^2 - b)^2)}} = \frac{-b}{|b|} = \begin{cases} 1, & \text{if } b < 0, \\ -1, & \text{if } b > 0. \end{cases}$$

Therefore, it follows that

$$F(0) = \begin{cases} 1, & \text{if } b < 0, \\ -1, & \text{if } b > 0. \end{cases}$$

we also have

$$G(0) = \frac{b^2 + h^2\delta^2 - d^2\eta^2}{2\delta h|b|} = \frac{b^2 + h^2\delta^2}{2\delta h|b|} - \frac{d^2\eta^2}{2\delta h|b|}$$

and $G(\omega) \to \infty$ as $\omega \to \infty$. Also note that F has a sine-shaped curve. If the equation $F(\omega) = G(\omega)$ has positive solutions, it has only a finite number of solutions.

Solving Equations (32) and (33) for $\cos(\omega\rho)$ and $\sin(\omega\rho)$, we obtain

$$\cos(\omega\rho) = -\frac{ac\omega^2+bd+\delta\cos(\tau\omega)\left(c\omega^2+dh\right)+\delta\omega(d-ch)\sin(\tau\omega)-d\omega^2}{\eta(c^2\omega^2+d^2)} = h_1(\omega) \quad (36)$$

$$\sin(\omega\rho) = \frac{ad\omega-bc\omega-\delta\sin(\tau\omega)\left(c\omega^2+dh\right)+\delta\omega(d-ch)\cos(\tau\omega)+c\omega^3}{\eta(c^2\omega^2+d^2)} = h_2(\omega). \quad (37)$$

For values of τ, such that $F(\omega) = G(\omega)$ has positive roots, assume that $0 < \omega_1 < \omega_2 < \cdots < \omega_m$ are the roots, and define $\rho_{jk}^+, j = 1, 2, \cdots, m$, and $k = 0, 1, 2, \cdots$, as

$$\rho_{jk}^+ = \begin{cases} \frac{1}{\omega_j}[2k\pi + \arccos h_1(\omega_j)] & \text{if} \quad h_2(\omega_j) > 0, \\ \frac{1}{\omega_j}[2\pi(k+1) - \arccos h_1(\omega_j)] & \text{if} \quad h_2(\omega_j) \le 0. \end{cases} \quad (38)$$

It follows that for every $1 \le j \le m$, $k = 0, 1, 2, \cdots$, $\rho_{jk}^+ > 0$ is a function of τ on some interval and for each j, ρ_{jk}^+ are defined on the same interval for all k. There are a number of different cases in terms of functions ρ_{jk}^+. We list a couple of cases here. For more information regarding the stability regions if a system has two delays, see Hale and Huang [29] and Wang [30].

Theorem 7. *Assume that $R_0 > 1$. Let a, b, c, d, and h be defined by (10), and a_1, b_1, and c_1 be defined by (13). Also let F, G be defined in (34) and (35). We then have the following results.*

(I) *Equation (14) has no positive roots. Then*
- *If the equation $F(\omega) = G(\omega)$ has no positive solutions for any $\tau \ge 0$, then all roots of Equation (11) have negative real parts for all delays $\rho \ge 0$ and $\tau \ge 0$. Therefore, P^* is locally asymptotically stable for all $\rho \ge 0$ and $\tau \ge 0$. The stability region of P^* is the whole first quadrant of the (τ, ρ) plane.*
- *If the equation $F(\omega) = G(\omega)$ has positive solutions for some $\tau \ge 0$, then there exists a $\rho(\tau) > 0$, such that all roots of Equation (11) have negative real parts for all delays $0 \le \rho < \rho(\tau)$. When $\rho = \rho(\tau)$, it has a pair of imaginary roots $\pm i\omega$, and all other roots have negative real parts. Therefore, P^* is locally asymptotically stable for all $\rho < \rho(\tau)$, and Hopf bifurcations occur as ρ passes through $\rho(\tau)$. The stability region of P^* is the region given by*

$$\{(\tau, \rho) : 0 \le \tau < \infty, 0 \le \rho < \rho(\tau).\}$$

(II) *Equation (14) has positive roots. Thus, a $\tau_0^+ > 0$ exists and is given by (19). Then*
- *If the equation $F(\omega) = G(\omega)$ has no positive solutions for any $0 \le \tau < \tau_0^+$, then all roots of Equation (11) have negative real parts for all delays $\rho \ge 0$ and $0 \le \tau < \tau_0^+$. Therefore, P^* is locally asymptotically stable for all (τ, ρ) in the region $\{(\tau, \rho) : \tau < \tau_0^+, \rho \ge 0\}$.*
- *If the equation $F(\omega) = G(\omega)$ has one positive solution for all $0 \le \tau < \tau_0^+$, then there exists a $\rho(\tau) > 0$, such that all roots of Equation (11) have negative real parts for all delays (τ, ρ) in the region $R = \{(\tau, \rho) : 0 \le \tau < \tau_0^+, \rho < \rho(\tau)\}$. When $\rho = \rho(\tau)$, it has a pair of imaginary roots $\pm i\omega$, and all other roots have negative real parts. Therefore, P^* is locally asymptotically stable for all (τ, ρ) in R, and Hopf bifurcations occur as (τ, ρ) crosses through the curve given by $\rho = \rho(\tau)$.*

Again, we perform some numerical simulations to illustrate our theoretical results. First, if we choose the same parameter values as in Sections 2.1 and 2.2 as $A = 10$, $B = 0.2$, $\alpha = 0.1, \eta = 0.5, \mu = 0.2, \delta = 0.4$. Then, we have $P^* = (43.239, 0.3127, 7.4479)$, $R_0 = 4.54545 > 1$. In this case, both $\tau_0^+ > 0$ and $\rho_0^+ > 0$ exist, and they are

$$\tau_0^+ = 0.440535, \qquad \rho_0^+ = 0.047453.$$

A function $\rho(\tau) > 0$ as a function of τ can be found using (38), such that the stability region S in the $\tau\rho$-space can be identified. P^* is locally asymptotically stable for all (τ, ρ) in the interior of S, and Hopf bifurcation occurs as (τ, ρ) passes across the boundary of S, where

$$S = \{(\tau, \rho) : 0 \leq \tau \leq \tau_0^+, 0 \leq \rho \leq \rho(\tau)\}.$$

See Figure 7 for the stability region S and Figure 8 for solutions to converge to P^* when $(\tau, \rho) = (0.1, 0.1)$ is in the interior of S. Also see Figure 9 for Hopf bifurcations to occur and periodic solutions to appear when $(\tau, \rho) = (0.2, 0.0314633)$ is on the boundary of the stability region S, and Figure 10 for solutions blow out when (τ, ρ) moves out of the stability region S.

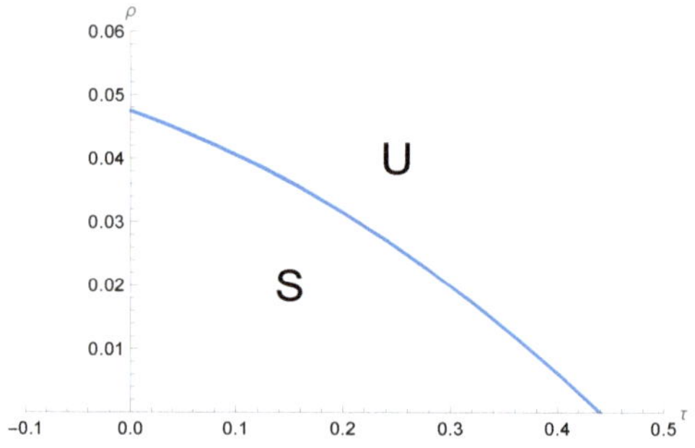

Figure 7. The stability region.

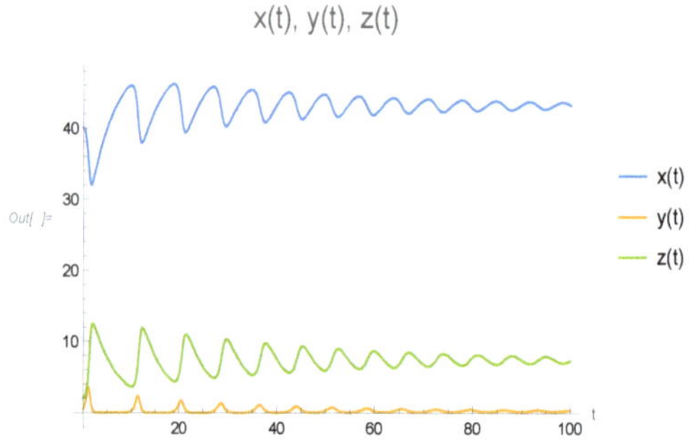

Figure 8. $\tau = 0.1, \rho = 0.01$, $(\tau, \rho) \in S$. Solutions converge to P^*.

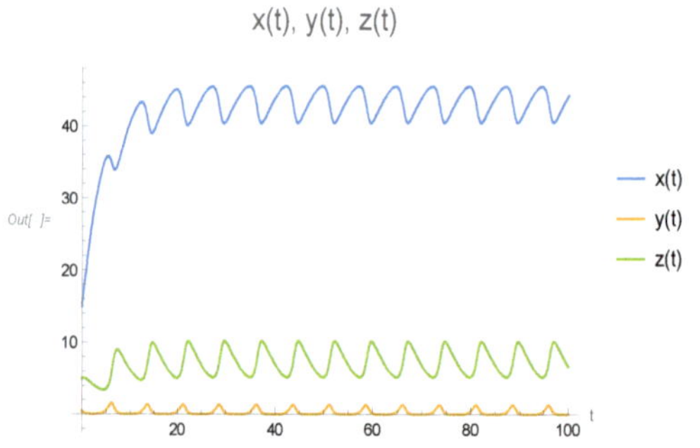

Figure 9. $\tau = 0.2, \rho = 0.0314633$. (τ, ρ) is on the boundary of S. Periodic solutions appear.

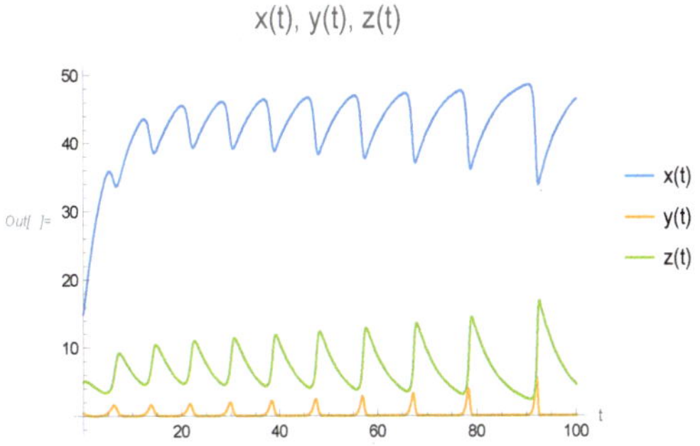

Figure 10. $\tau = 0.2, \rho = 0.04$. (τ, ρ) is outside of S. Solutions go to infinity.

Next, if we choose the parameter values as $A = 2, B = 0.2, \alpha = 0.3, \eta = 0.5, \mu = 0.3, \delta = 0.1$, then we have $P^* = (4.8471, 0.37484, 2.1094)$, and $R_0 = 2.72727 > 1$. In this case, calculations show that:

$$a_2 = 0.629726, \qquad b_2 = 0.0992197.$$

So, Equation (14) has no positive roots, and that implies that $\tau_0^+ > 0$ does not exist. But in this case, $\rho_0^+ > 0$ exists, and

$$\rho_0^+ = 0.325204.$$

A function of $\rho(\tau) > 0$ as a function of τ can be found using (38), such that the stability region S in the $\tau\rho$-space can be identified. P^* is locally asymptotically stable for all (τ, ρ) in the interior of S; Hopf bifurcation occurs as (τ, ρ) passing across the boundary of S, where

$$S = \{(\tau, \rho) : 0 \le \tau, 0 \le \rho \le \rho(\tau)\}$$

See Figure 11 for the stability region S, Figure 12 for solutions to converge to P^* when $(\tau, \rho) = (0.1, 0.1)$ is in the interior of S, and Figure 13 for Hopf bifurcations to occur and periodic solutions to appear when $(\tau, \rho) = (1, 0.2413)$ is on the boundary of the stability region S. As (τ, ρ) moves out of the stability region S, solutions will blow out to infinity. It's similar to cases above, so we omit a numerical simulation here.

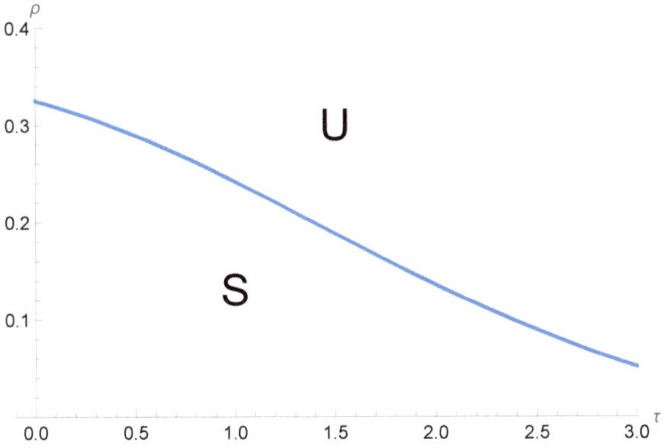

Figure 11. The stability region.

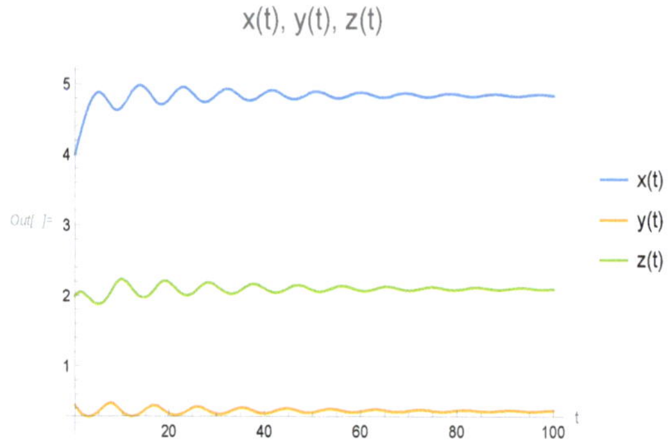

Figure 12. $\tau = 1, \rho = 0.18$, $(\tau, \rho) \in S$. Solutions converge to P^*.

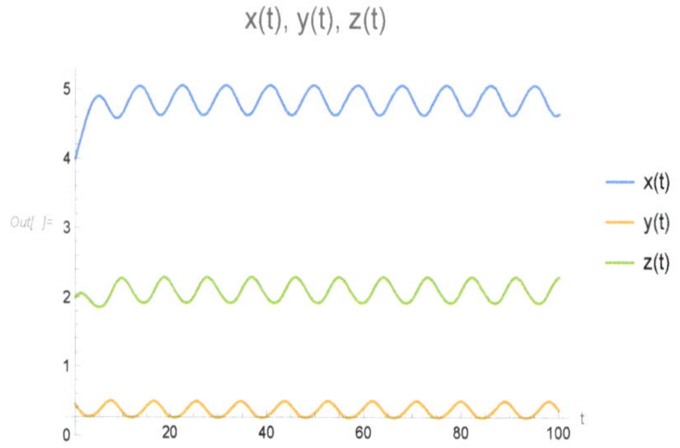

Figure 13. $\tau = 1, \rho = 0.2413$. (τ, ρ) is on the boundary of S. Periodic solutions appear.

3. Discussion

In this paper, we introduced and explored a mathematical model for online social networks, wherein the population is categorized into three distinct sub-classes: potential network users, active users, and individuals opposed to networks. Diverging from existing literature, our model accounts for the presence of individuals who will never express interest in using online networks. Additionally, active online social network users may exhibit a tendency to lose interest and subsequently abandon the platform over time, with or without interacting with non-users.

Assuming that the basic reproduction number R_0 exceeds unity, we delved into an investigation of whether time delays affecting active users' abandonment of the network can induce a switch in the stability of the unique user prevailing equilibrium (UPE) denoted as P^*. We established conditions ensuring the asymptotic stability of P^* for all delays $\tau \geq 0$ and $\rho \geq 0$, enabling individuals across all three sub-classes to settle into equilibrium over time. Furthermore, we identified stability regions and associated conditions under which Hopf bifurcations occur as the delays (τ, ρ) traverse the boundaries of these regions. Consequently, periodic solutions emerged, leading to oscillations in the populations of the three sub-classes.

To validate our theoretical findings, we conducted numerical simulations, providing empirical evidence to support the dynamics predicted by our model. Through this comprehensive analysis, we shed light on the complex dynamics inherent in online social networks and elucidate the role of time delays in shaping equilibrium states and oscillatory behavior. Our study contributes to a deeper understanding of the underlying mechanisms driving the evolution of online social networks, with implications for diverse fields including sociology, network science, and computational modeling.

Author Contributions: Conceptualization, L.W. and M.W.; methodology, L.W. and M.W.; software, L.W.; validation, L.W.; formal analysis, L.W.; investigation, L.W.; resources, L.W. and M.W.; writing—original draft preparation, L.W.; writing—review and editing, L.W. and M.W.; project administration, L.W. All authors have read and agreed to the published version of the manuscript.

Funding: This research received no external funding.

Data Availability Statement: No data sets were generated during this research.

Conflicts of Interest: The authors declare no conflicts of interest.

References

1. Bettencourt, L.M.; Cintrn-Arias, A.; Kaiser, D.I.; Castillo-Chvez, C. The power of a good idea: Quantitative modeling of the spread of ideas from epidemiological models. *Phys. A Stat. Mech. Its Appl.* **2006**, 364, 513–536. [CrossRef]
2. Cannarella, J.; Spechler, J. Epidemiological modeling of online network dynamics. *arXiv* **2014**, arXiv:1401.4208.
3. Chen, R.; Kong, L.; Wang, M. Stability analysis of an online social network model. *Rocky Mt. J. Math.* **2003**, *53*, 1019–1041. [CrossRef]
4. Dai, G.; Ma, R.; Wang, H.; Wang, F.; Xu, K. Partial differential equations with Robin boundary conditions in online social networks. *Discret. Contin. Dyn. Syst. Ser. B* **2015**, *20*, 1609–1624. [CrossRef]
5. Graef, J. R.; Kong, L.; Ledoan, A.; Wang, M. Stability analysis of a fractional online social network model, *Math. Comput. Simulat.* **2020**, *178*, 625–645. [CrossRef]
6. Kong L.; Wang, M. Deterministic and stochastic online social network models with varying population size. *Dcdis Ser. A Math. Anal.* **2023**, 30, 253–275.
7. Kong, L.; Wang, M. Optimal control for an ordinary differential equation online social network model. *Differ. Equ. Appl.* **2022**, *14*, 205–214. [CrossRef]
8. Lei, C.; Lin, Z.; Wang, H. The free boundary problem describing information diffusion in online social networks. *J. Differ. Equ.* **2013**, *254*, 1326–1341. [CrossRef]
9. Liu, X.; Li, T.; Cheng, X.; Liu, W.; Xu, H. Spreading dynamics of a preferential information model with hesitation psychology on scale-free networks. *Adv. Differ. Equ.* **2019**, *2019*, 279. [CrossRef]
10. Liu, X.; Li, T.; Tian, M. Rumor spreading of a SEIR model in complex social networks with hesitating mechanism. *Adv. Differ. Equ.* **2018**, *2018*, 391. [CrossRef]
11. Wang, F.; Wang, H.; Xu, K. Diffusion logistic model towards predicting information diffusion in online social networks. In Proceedings of the 2012 32nd International Conference on Distributed Computing Systems Workshops (ICDCSW), Macau, China, 18–21 June 2012; pp. 133–139.
12. Anderson, R.M.; May, R.M. Population biology of infectious diseases: Part I. *Nature* **1979**, *280*, 361–367. [CrossRef] [PubMed]
13. Bernoussi, A. Stability analysis of an SIR epidemic model with homestead-isolation on the susceptible and infectious, immunity, relapse and general incidence rate. *Int. J. Biomath.* **2023**, *16*, 2250102. [CrossRef]
14. Han, Z.; Wang, Y.; Gao, S.; Sun, G.; Wang, H. Final epidemic size of a two-community SIR model with asymmetric coupling. *J. Math. Biol.* **2024**, *88*, 51. [CrossRef] [PubMed]
15. Hill, A.; Glasser, J.; Feng, Z. Implications for infectious disease models of heterogeneous mixing on control thresholds. *J. Math. Biol.* **2023**, *86*, 53. [CrossRef]
16. Li, A.; Zou, X. R_0 May Not Tell Us Everything: Transient Disease Dynamics of Some SIR Models Over Patchy Environments. *Bull. Math. Biol.* **2024**, 41. [CrossRef] [PubMed]
17. Kermack, W.; McKendrick, A. A Contribution to the Mathematical Theory of Epidemics. *Proc. R. Soc. Lond. Ser. A Contain. Pap. Math. Phys. Character* **1927**, *115*, 700–721.
18. Li, M.Y.; Graef, J.R.; Wang, L.; Karsai, J. Global dynamics of an SEIR model with vertical transmission. *SIAM J. Appl. Math.* **1999**, *160*, 191–213. [CrossRef]
19. Li, M.Y.; Smith, H.L.; Wang, L. Global dynamics of a SEIR model with a varying total population size. *Math. Biosci.* **2001**, *62*, 58–69. [CrossRef]
20. Llibre J.; Salhi, T. Phase portraits of an SIR epidemic model. *Appl. Anal.* **2024**, *103*, 1165–1175. [CrossRef]
21. Wang, L.; Li, M.Y.; Kirschner, D. Mathematical analysis of the global dynamics of a model for HTLV-I infection and ATL progression. *Math. Biosci.* **2002**, *179*, 207–217. [CrossRef]
22. Wang, L.; Wu, X. Stability and Hopf Bifurcation for an SEIR Epidemic Model with Delay. *Adv. Theory Nonl. Anal. Its Appl.* **2018**, *2*, 113–127. [CrossRef]
23. Xie, J.; Guo, H.; Zhang, M. Dynamics of an SEIR model with media coverage mediated nonlinear infectious force. *Math. Biosci. Eng.* **2023**, *20*, 14616–14633. [CrossRef] [PubMed]
24. Zhang, J.; Qiao, Y. Bifurcation analysis of an SIR model considering hospital resources and vaccination. *Math. Comput. Simul.* **2023**, *208*, 157–185. [CrossRef]
25. Barman, M.; Mishra, N. Hopf bifurcation analysis for a delayed nonlinear-SEIR epidemic model on networks. *Chaos Solitons Fractals* **2024**, *178*, 114351. [CrossRef]

26. Barman, M.; Mishra, N. Hopf bifurcation in a networked delay SIR epidemic model. *J. Math. Anal. Appl.* **2023**, *525*, 127131. [CrossRef]
27. Wang, L.; Wang, M. Stability and Bifurcation Analysis For An OSN Model with Delay. *Adv. Theory Nonl. Anal. Its Appl.* **2023**, *7*, 413–427. [CrossRef]
28. Ruan, S.; Wei, J. On the zeros of transcendental functions with applications to stability of delay differential equations with two delays. *Dyn. Contin. Discret. Impuls. Syst.* **2003**, *10*, 863–874.
29. Hale, J.; Huang, W. Global geometry of the stable regions for two delay differential equations. *Math. Anal. Appl.* **1993**, *178*, 344–362. [CrossRef]
30. Wang, L. Stability and bifurcation analysis for a general differential equation with two delays. *Pan-Am. Math. J.* **2021**, *31*, 55–78.

mathematics

MDPI

Article

Existence of Solutions to a System of Fractional q-Difference Boundary Value Problems

Alexandru Tudorache [1] **and Rodica Luca** [2,*]

[1] Department of Computer Science and Engineering, Gh. Asachi Technical University, 700050 Iasi, Romania; alexandru-gabriel.tudorache@academic.tuiasi.ro
[2] Department of Mathematics, Gh. Asachi Technical University, 700506 Iasi, Romania
* Correspondence: rluca@math.tuiasi.ro

Abstract: We are investigating the existence of solutions to a system of two fractional $\mathfrak{q}$-difference equations containing fractional $\mathfrak{q}$-integral terms, subject to multi-point boundary conditions that encompass $\mathfrak{q}$-derivatives and fractional $\mathfrak{q}$-derivatives of different orders. In our main results, we rely on various fixed point theorems, such as the Leray–Schauder nonlinear alternative, the Schaefer fixed point theorem, the Krasnosel'skii fixed point theorem for the sum of two operators, and the Banach contraction mapping principle. Finally, several examples are provided to illustrate our findings.

Keywords: fractional $\mathfrak{q}$-difference equations; coupled multi-point boundary conditions; fractional $\mathfrak{q}$-integrals; existence; uniqueness

MSC: 39A13; 39A27; 33D05

Citation: Tudorache, A.; Luca, R. Existence of Solutions to a System of Fractional q-Difference Boundary Value Problems. *Mathematics* **2024**, *12*, 1335. https://doi.org/10.3390/math12091335

Academic Editors: Lingju Kong and Min Wang

Received: 8 April 2024
Revised: 24 April 2024
Accepted: 26 April 2024
Published: 27 April 2024

1. Introduction

We examine the system of fractional $\mathfrak{q}$-difference equations

$$\begin{cases} (\mathrm{D}_{\mathfrak{q}}^{\alpha}\mathrm{u})(\nu)+\mathcal{F}\left(\nu,\mathrm{u}(\nu),\mathrm{v}(\nu),\mathrm{I}_{\mathfrak{q}}^{\delta_1}\mathrm{u}(\nu),\mathrm{I}_{\mathfrak{q}}^{\gamma_1}\mathrm{v}(\nu)\right)=0, \;\; \nu\in(0,1), \\ \left(\mathrm{D}_{\mathfrak{q}}^{\beta}\mathrm{v}\right)(\nu)+\mathcal{G}\left(\nu,\mathrm{u}(\nu),\mathrm{v}(\nu),\mathrm{I}_{\mathfrak{q}}^{\delta_2}\mathrm{u}(\nu),\mathrm{I}_{\mathfrak{q}}^{\gamma_2}\mathrm{v}(\nu)\right)=0, \;\; \nu\in(0,1), \end{cases} \tag{1}$$

subject to the multi-point boundary conditions

$$\begin{cases} \mathrm{D}_{\mathfrak{q}}^{i}\mathrm{u}(0)=0, \;\; i=0,\dots,n-2, \;\; \mathrm{D}_{\mathfrak{q}}^{\varsigma}\mathrm{u}(1)=\sum_{i=1}^{\mathfrak{a}}a_i\mathrm{D}_{\mathfrak{q}}^{\varrho_i}\mathrm{u}(\xi_i)+\sum_{i=1}^{\mathfrak{b}}b_i\mathrm{D}_{\mathfrak{q}}^{\sigma_i}\mathrm{v}(\omega_i), \\ \mathrm{D}_{\mathfrak{q}}^{i}\mathrm{v}(0)=0, \;\; i=0,\dots,m-2, \;\; \mathrm{D}_{\mathfrak{q}}^{\vartheta}\mathrm{v}(1)=\sum_{i=1}^{\mathfrak{c}}c_i\mathrm{D}_{\mathfrak{q}}^{\eta_i}\mathrm{u}(\zeta_i)+\sum_{i=1}^{\mathfrak{d}}d_i\mathrm{D}_{\mathfrak{q}}^{\rho_i}\mathrm{v}(\theta_i). \end{cases} \tag{2}$$

Here, $\mathfrak{q}\in(0,1)$, $\alpha,\beta\in\mathbb{R}$, $\alpha\in(n-1,n]$, $\beta\in(m-1,m]$, $n,m\in\mathbb{N}$, $n,m\geq 2$; $\mathfrak{a},\mathfrak{b},\mathfrak{c},\mathfrak{d}\in\mathbb{N}$; $\varsigma,\varrho_i,\eta_k\in[0,\alpha-1)$; $\vartheta,\sigma_j,\rho_\iota\in[0,\beta-1)$; $a_i,b_j,c_k,d_\iota\in\mathbb{R}$; $\xi_i,\omega_j,\zeta_k,\theta_\iota\in(0,1)$; $\mathrm{D}_{\mathfrak{q}}^{\kappa}$ is the fractional $\mathfrak{q}$-derivative of order κ, for $\kappa=\alpha,\beta,\varsigma,\vartheta,\varrho_i,\sigma_j,\eta_k,\rho_\iota$, for all $i=1,\dots,\mathfrak{a}$, $j=1,\dots,\mathfrak{b}$, $k=1,\dots,\mathfrak{c}$, $\iota=1,\dots,\mathfrak{d}$; $\mathrm{D}_{\mathfrak{q}}^{p}$ represents the $\mathfrak{q}$-derivative of order p, for $p=0,\dots,n-2$ and $p=0,\dots,m-2$; $\delta_r,\gamma_r>0$ for $r=1,2$; $\mathrm{I}_{\mathfrak{q}}^{\kappa}$ is the fractional $\mathfrak{q}$-integral of order κ, for $\kappa=\delta_i,\gamma_i$, $i=1,2$, and $\mathcal{F},\mathcal{G}$ are nonlinear functions satisfying some assumptions.

In this paper, we aim to set forth conditions on the functions $\mathcal{F}$ and $\mathcal{G}$ that guarantee the existence of at least one solution to problem (1), (2). Our proofs will make use of various fixed-point theorems, including the Leray–Schauder nonlinear alternative, the Schaefer fixed-point theorem, the Krasnosel'skii fixed-point theorem for the sum of two operators, and the Banach contraction mapping principle. Furthermore, we will include references to relevant literature closely associated with our investigated problem. In [1], the author studied the existence, uniqueness, and multiplicity of positive solutions for problem (1), (2) under different assumptions than those used in our present paper. The associated Green functions are constructed, and some of their properties are presented. For the proof of the principal findings, the author employed in [1] a range of fixed point theorems, including the Schauder fixed point theorem, the Leggett–Williams fixed point theorem, and the Guo–Krasnosel'skii fixed point theorem. Therefore, the methods used in [1] are distinct from those we will apply in our paper. In [2], the authors investigated the system of nonlinear fractional q-difference equations

$$\begin{cases} (D_q^{\alpha_1}u)(t) + P(t, u(t), v(t), I_q^{\omega_1}u(t), I_q^{\delta_1}v(t)) = 0, \ \ t \in (0,1), \\ (D_q^{\alpha_2}v)(t) + Q(t, u(t), v(t), I_q^{\omega_2}u(t), I_q^{\delta_2}v(t)) = 0, \ \ t \in (0,1), \end{cases} \tag{3}$$

with the coupled nonlocal boundary conditions

$$\begin{cases} D_q^i u(0) = 0, \ \ i = 0, \dots, m-2, \ \ D_q^{\zeta_0}u(1) = \int_0^1 D_q^{\zeta}v(t)\, d_qH(t), \\ D_q^i v(0) = 0, \ \ i = 0, \dots, n-2, \ \ D_q^{\xi_0}v(1) = \int_0^1 D_q^{\xi}u(t)\, d_qK(t), \end{cases} \tag{4}$$

where $q \in (0,1)$, $\alpha_1, \alpha_2 \in \mathbb{R}$, $\alpha_1 \in (m-1, m]$, $\alpha_2 \in (n-1, n]$, $m, n \in \mathbb{N}$, $m \geq 2$, $n \geq 2$, $\omega_i > 0$, $\delta_i > 0$, $i = 1, 2$, $\zeta \in [0, \alpha_2 - 1)$, $\xi \in [0, \alpha_1 - 1)$, $\zeta_0 \in [0, \alpha_1 - 1)$, $\xi_0 \in [0, \alpha_2 - 1)$, the integrals from (4) are Riemann–Stieltjes integrals, and H and K are bounded variation functions. Utilizing diverse fixed-point theorems, they established results affirming the existence and uniqueness of solutions to problem (3), (4). In [3], the authors analyzed the existence of solutions to the fractional q-difference equation subject to nonlocal boundary conditions

$$\begin{cases} ({}^{C}D_q^{\beta}u)(t) = f(t, u(t)), \ \ \text{for a.e. } t \in (0, T), \\ u(0) - u'(0) = \int_0^T h(s, u(s))\, ds, \ \ u(T) + u'(T) = \int_0^T g(s, u(s))\, ds, \end{cases} \tag{5}$$

where $T > 0$, $q \in (0,1)$, $\beta \in (1,2]$, and ${}^{C}D_q^{\alpha}$ is the Caputo fractional q-derivative of order α. In demonstrating the main result, they employed the Mönch fixed-point theorem, and the method of measures of noncompactness. In [4], the authors examined the existence, uniqueness and multiplicity of positive solutions to the fractional q-difference equation supplemented with nonlocal boundary conditions

$$\begin{cases} (D_q^{\beta}u)(t) + g(t, u(t)) = 0, \ \ t \in (0,1), \\ (D_q^i u)(0) = 0, \ \ i = 0, \dots, m-2, \ \ (D_q^{\gamma}u)(1) = a(D_q^{\gamma}u)(\eta), \end{cases} \tag{6}$$

where $q \in (0,1)$, $\beta \in (m-1, m]$, $m > 2$, $\gamma \in [1, m-2]$, $\eta \in (0,1)$, $a \in [0,1]$, and $g : [0,1] \times [0, \infty) \to [0, \infty)$ satisfies Caratheodory type conditions. In proving the main theorems, they utilized multiple fixed-point theorems. In [5], based on the Guo–Krasnosel'skii fixed point theorem, the author explored the existence of positive solutions for the fractional q-difference equation subject to boundary conditions

$$\begin{cases} (D_q^{\gamma}v)(t) = -g(t, v(t)), \ \ t \in (0,1), \\ v(0) = (D_q v)(0) = 0, \ \ (D_q v)(1) = \beta, \end{cases} \tag{7}$$

where $q \in (0,1)$, $\gamma \in (2,3]$, $\beta \geq 0$, and $g : [0,1] \times \mathbb{R} \to \mathbb{R}$ is a nonnegative continuous function. In [6], the author studied the existence of nontrivial solutions for the nonlinear q-fractional boundary value problem

$$\begin{cases} (D_q^{\gamma}v)(t) = -g(t, v(t)), \ \ t \in (0,1), \\ v(0) = v(1) = 0, \end{cases} \tag{8}$$

where $\mathfrak{q} \in (0,1)$, $\gamma \in (1,2]$, and $g : [0,1] \times \mathbb{R} \to \mathbb{R}$ is a nonnegative continuous function. To prove the main results, he also used the Guo–Krasnosel'skii fixed point theorem. For other research works that investigate fractional $\mathfrak{q}$-difference equations and systems of fractional $\mathfrak{q}$-difference equations with either coupled or uncoupled boundary conditions, we refer the reader to the following papers [7–14].

The domain of $\mathfrak{q}$-difference calculus, commonly known as quantum calculus, finds its roots in the seminal contributions of Jackson [15,16]. For a comprehensive exploration of diverse applications within this field, readers are encouraged to delve into the research conducted by Ernst [17]. The inception of fractional $\mathfrak{q}$-difference calculus can be traced back to the works of Al-Salam [18] and Agarwal [19]. To stay updated on advancements in this subfield, covering $\mathfrak{q}$-analogs of integral and differential fractional operators, along with properties such as $\mathfrak{q}$-analogs of Cauchy's formula, the fractional Leibniz $\mathfrak{q}$-formula, $\mathfrak{q}$-Taylor's formula, $\mathfrak{q}$-Laplace transform, and $\mathfrak{q}$-analogs of the Mittag–Leffler function, see the papers [19–31].

The novelty aspects of our problem (1), (2), compared to that examined in [1] are the following. In our paper, we study the existence of solutions for problem (1), (2), in contrast to [1], where the author investigated the existence of positive solutions for (1), (2). For this reason, the assumptions on the orders of the fractional derivatives in [1] are stronger than those used here, and they assure the nonnegativity of the associated Green functions. Indeed, in [1], the orders ς and ϑ must be greater than or equal to 1, an assumption that does not appear in our present work. In addition, in [1], there are connections between ς, ϱ_i and η_k for $i = 1, \ldots, \mathfrak{a}$ and $k = 1, \ldots, \mathfrak{c}$, on the one hand, and ϑ, σ_j and ρ_ι for $j = 1, \ldots, \mathfrak{b}$ and $\iota = 1, \ldots, \mathfrak{d}$, on the other hand. Namely, ϱ_i and η_k are less than or equal to ς, for $i = 1, \ldots, \mathfrak{a}$ and $k = 1, \ldots, \mathfrak{c}$, and σ_j and ρ_ι are less than or equal to ϑ, for $j = 1, \ldots, \mathfrak{b}$ and $\iota = 1, \ldots, \mathfrak{d}$. These last conditions are not used in our paper. Furthermore, the theorems applied in the present paper are different than those utilized in [1]. Related to paper [2], the differences between [2] and our paper are in the form of boundary conditions, which in our case (boundary conditions (2)) are more general than the conditions (4); our conditions (2) are generalized coupled boundary conditions.

Our paper is structured as follows: Section 2 presents auxiliary results essential for the subsequent sections. In Section 3, we unveil the primary existence results for the problem (1), (2). Moving on, Section 4 offers illustrative examples to showcase the applicability of our theorems. Finally, Section 5 concludes the paper by providing a summary of the findings and presenting comprehensive conclusions.

2. Auxiliary Results

This section provides initial findings that will be utilized in subsequent sections. We begin by examining the linear system associated with our given problem (1), (2), namely

$$\begin{cases} (D_{\mathfrak{q}}^{\alpha}u)(\nu) + h(\nu) = 0, \ \nu \in (0,1), \\ (D_{\mathfrak{q}}^{\beta}v)(\nu) + k(\nu) = 0, \ \nu \in (0,1), \end{cases} \tag{9}$$

with the boundary conditions (2), where $h, k \in C[0,1]$.

We introduce the constants

$$\begin{aligned} &\Lambda_1 = \frac{\Gamma_{\mathfrak{q}}(\alpha)}{\Gamma_{\mathfrak{q}}(\alpha-\varsigma)} - \sum_{i=1}^{\mathfrak{a}} a_i \frac{\Gamma_{\mathfrak{q}}(\alpha)}{\Gamma_{\mathfrak{q}}(\alpha-\varrho_i)} \xi_i^{\alpha-\varrho_i-1}, \\ &\Lambda_2 = \sum_{i=1}^{\mathfrak{b}} b_i \frac{\Gamma_{\mathfrak{q}}(\beta)}{\Gamma_{\mathfrak{q}}(\beta-\sigma_i)} \omega_i^{\beta-\sigma_i-1}, \ \Lambda_3 = \sum_{i=1}^{\mathfrak{c}} c_i \frac{\Gamma_{\mathfrak{q}}(\alpha)}{\Gamma_{\mathfrak{q}}(\alpha-\eta_i)} \zeta_i^{\alpha-\eta_i-1}, \\ &\Lambda_4 = \frac{\Gamma_{\mathfrak{q}}(\beta)}{\Gamma_{\mathfrak{q}}(\beta-\vartheta)} - \sum_{i=1}^{\mathfrak{d}} d_i \frac{\Gamma_{\mathfrak{q}}(\beta)}{\Gamma_{\mathfrak{q}}(\beta-\rho_i)} \theta_i^{\beta-\rho_i-1}, \\ &\Delta = \Lambda_1\Lambda_4 - \Lambda_2\Lambda_3. \end{aligned} \tag{10}$$

Lemma 1 ([1]). *If $\Delta \neq 0$, then the solution $(\mathrm{u}(\nu), \mathrm{v}(\nu))$, $\nu \in [0,1]$ of problem (9), (2) is given by*

$$\begin{aligned}
\mathrm{u}(\nu) &= -\frac{1}{\Gamma_{\mathrm{q}}(\alpha)}\int_0^{\nu}(\nu-\mathrm{q}\tau)^{(\alpha-1)}h(\tau)\,d_{\mathrm{q}}\tau \\
&+\frac{\nu^{\alpha-1}}{\Delta}\left[\frac{\Lambda_4}{\Gamma_{\mathrm{q}}(\alpha-\varsigma)}\int_0^1(1-\mathrm{q}\tau)^{(\alpha-\varsigma-1)}h(\tau)\,d_{\mathrm{q}}\tau\right. \\
&-\Lambda_4\sum_{i=1}^{\mathfrak{a}}\frac{a_i}{\Gamma_{\mathrm{q}}(\alpha-\varrho_i)}\int_0^{\xi_i}(\xi_i-\mathrm{q}\tau)^{(\alpha-\varrho_i-1)}h(\tau)\,d_{\mathrm{q}}\tau \\
&\left.-\Lambda_2\sum_{i=1}^{\mathfrak{c}}\frac{c_i}{\Gamma_{\mathrm{q}}(\alpha-\eta_i)}\int_0^{\zeta_i}(\zeta_i-\mathrm{q}\tau)^{(\alpha-\eta_i-1)}h(\tau)\,d_{\mathrm{q}}\tau\right] \\
&+\frac{\nu^{\alpha-1}}{\Delta}\left[-\Lambda_4\sum_{i=1}^{\mathfrak{b}}\frac{b_i}{\Gamma_{\mathrm{q}}(\beta-\sigma_i)}\int_0^{\omega_i}(\omega_i-\mathrm{q}\tau)^{(\beta-\sigma_i-1)}k(\tau)\,d_{\mathrm{q}}\tau\right. \\
&+\frac{\Lambda_2}{\Gamma_{\mathrm{q}}(\beta-\vartheta)}\int_0^1(1-\mathrm{q}\tau)^{(\beta-\vartheta-1)}k(\tau)\,d_{\mathrm{q}}\tau \\
&\left.-\Lambda_2\sum_{i=1}^{\mathfrak{d}}\frac{d_i}{\Gamma_{\mathrm{q}}(\beta-\rho_i)}\int_0^{\theta_i}(\theta_i-\mathrm{q}\tau)^{(\beta-\rho_i-1)}k(\tau)\,d_{\mathrm{q}}\tau\right],\quad \nu\in[0,1], \\
\mathrm{v}(\nu) &= \frac{\nu^{\beta-1}}{\Delta}\left[-\Lambda_1\sum_{i=1}^{\mathfrak{c}}\frac{c_i}{\Gamma_{\mathrm{q}}(\alpha-\eta_i)}\int_0^{\zeta_i}(\zeta_i-\mathrm{q}\tau)^{(\alpha-\eta_i-1)}h(\tau)\,d_{\mathrm{q}}\tau\right. \\
&+\frac{\Lambda_3}{\Gamma_{\mathrm{q}}(\alpha-\varsigma)}\int_0^1(1-\mathrm{q}\tau)^{(\alpha-\varsigma-1)}h(\tau)\,d_{\mathrm{q}}\tau \\
&\left.-\Lambda_3\sum_{i=1}^{\mathfrak{a}}\frac{a_i}{\Gamma_{\mathrm{q}}(\alpha-\varrho_i)}\int_0^{\xi_i}(\xi_i-\mathrm{q}\tau)^{(\alpha-\varrho_i-1)}h(\tau)\,d_{\mathrm{q}}\tau\right] \\
&-\frac{1}{\Gamma_{\mathrm{q}}(\beta)}\int_0^{\nu}(\nu-\mathrm{q}\tau)^{(\beta-1)}k(\tau)\,d_{\mathrm{q}}\tau \\
&+\frac{\nu^{\beta-1}}{\Delta}\left[\frac{\Lambda_1}{\Gamma_{\mathrm{q}}(\beta-\vartheta)}\int_0^1(1-\mathrm{q}\tau)^{(\beta-\vartheta-1)}k(\tau)\,d_{\mathrm{q}}\tau\right. \\
&-\Lambda_1\sum_{i=1}^{\mathfrak{d}}\frac{d_i}{\Gamma_{\mathrm{q}}(\beta-\rho_i)}\int_0^{\theta_i}(\theta_i-\mathrm{q}\tau)^{(\beta-\rho_i-1)}k(\tau)\,d_{\mathrm{q}}\tau \\
&\left.-\Lambda_3\sum_{i=1}^{\mathfrak{b}}\frac{b_i}{\Gamma_{\mathrm{q}}(\beta-\sigma_i)}\int_0^{\omega_i}(\omega_i-\mathrm{q}\tau)^{(\beta-\sigma_i-1)}k(\tau)\,d_{\mathrm{q}}\tau\right],\quad \nu\in[0,1].
\end{aligned} \tag{11}$$

By the definition of fractional q-integrals, we obtain the next lemma.

Lemma 2. *The following relations are satisfied:*

(a) $\frac{1}{\Gamma_{\mathrm{q}}(\alpha)}\int_0^{\nu}(\nu-\mathrm{q}\tau)^{(\alpha-1)}\,d_{\mathrm{q}}\tau = \frac{\nu^{\alpha}}{\Gamma_{\mathrm{q}}(\alpha+1)}\ (=(I_{\mathrm{q}}^{\alpha}1)(\nu)),\ \nu\geq 0,$

(b) $\frac{1}{\Gamma_{\mathrm{q}}(\beta)}\int_0^{\nu}(\nu-\mathrm{q}\tau)^{(\beta-1)}\,d_{\mathrm{q}}\tau = \frac{\nu^{\beta}}{\Gamma_{\mathrm{q}}(\beta+1)}\ \left(=(I_{\mathrm{q}}^{\beta}1)(\nu)\right),\ \nu\geq 0,$

(c) $\frac{1}{\Gamma_{\mathrm{q}}(\alpha-\varsigma)}\int_0^1(1-\mathrm{q}\tau)^{(\alpha-\varsigma-1)}\,d_{\mathrm{q}}\tau = \frac{1}{\Gamma_{\mathrm{q}}(\alpha-\varsigma+1)},$

(d) $\frac{1}{\Gamma_{\mathrm{q}}(\beta-\vartheta)}\int_0^1(1-\mathrm{q}\tau)^{(\beta-\vartheta-1)}\,d_{\mathrm{q}}\tau = \frac{1}{\Gamma_{\mathrm{q}}(\beta-\vartheta+1)},$

(e) $\frac{1}{\Gamma_{\mathrm{q}}(\alpha-\varrho_i)}\int_0^{\xi_i}(\xi_i-\mathrm{q}\tau)^{(\alpha-\varrho_i-1)}\,d_{\mathrm{q}}\tau = \frac{\xi_i^{\alpha-\varrho_i}}{\Gamma_{\mathrm{q}}(\alpha-\varrho_i+1)},\ i=1,\ldots,\mathfrak{a},$

(f) $\frac{1}{\Gamma_{\mathrm{q}}(\alpha-\eta_i)}\int_0^{\zeta_i}(\zeta_i-\mathrm{q}\tau)^{(\alpha-\eta_i-1)}\,d_{\mathrm{q}}\tau = \frac{\zeta_i^{\alpha-\eta_i}}{\Gamma_{\mathrm{q}}(\alpha-\eta_i+1)},\ i=1,\ldots,\mathfrak{c},$

(g) $\frac{1}{\Gamma_{\mathrm{q}}(\beta-\sigma_i)}\int_0^{\omega_i}(\omega_i-\mathrm{q}\tau)^{(\beta-\sigma_i-1)}\,d_{\mathrm{q}}\tau = \frac{\omega_i^{\beta-\sigma_i}}{\Gamma_{\mathrm{q}}(\beta-\sigma_i+1)},\ i=1,\ldots,\mathfrak{b},$

(h) $\frac{1}{\Gamma_{\mathrm{q}}(\beta-\rho_i)}\int_0^{\theta_i}(\theta_i-\mathrm{q}\tau)^{(\beta-\rho_i-1)}\,d_{\mathrm{q}}\tau = \frac{\theta_i^{\beta-\rho_i}}{\Gamma_{\mathrm{q}}(\beta-\rho_i+1)},\ i=1,\ldots,\mathfrak{d}.$

Lemma 3 ([1]). *If* $\mathrm{w} \in C[0,1]$*, then for* $\kappa > 0$*, we have*

$$|\mathrm{I}_{\mathrm{q}}^{\kappa}\mathrm{w}(\nu)| \leq \frac{\|\mathrm{w}\|}{\Gamma_{\mathrm{q}}(\kappa+1)}, \quad \forall \nu \in [0,1], \tag{12}$$

where $\|\mathrm{w}\| = \sup_{\nu\in[0,1]} |\mathrm{w}(\nu)|$.

We consider now the Banach space $\mathcal{U} = C([0,1],\mathbb{R})$ with the supremum norm $\|\mathrm{u}\| = \sup_{\nu\in[0,1]} |\mathrm{u}(\nu)|$, and the Banach space $\mathcal{V} = \mathcal{U}\times\mathcal{U}$ with the norm $\|(\mathrm{u},\mathrm{v})\|_{\mathcal{V}} = \|\mathrm{u}\| + \|\mathrm{v}\|$. We define the operator $\mathcal{E} : \mathcal{V} \to \mathcal{V}$, $\mathcal{E}(\mathrm{u},\mathrm{v}) = (\mathcal{E}_1(\mathrm{u},\mathrm{v}), \mathcal{E}_2(\mathrm{u},\mathrm{v}))$, with $\mathcal{E}_1, \mathcal{E}_2 : \mathcal{V} \to \mathcal{U}$ given by

$$\begin{aligned}
\mathcal{E}_1(\mathrm{u},\mathrm{v})(\nu) &= -\frac{1}{\Gamma_{\mathrm{q}}(\alpha)}\int_0^{\nu}(\nu-\mathrm{q}\tau)^{(\alpha-1)}\mathcal{F}_{\mathrm{uv}}(\tau)\,d_{\mathrm{q}}\tau \\
&+\frac{\nu^{\alpha-1}}{\Delta}\Bigg[\frac{\Lambda_4}{\Gamma_{\mathrm{q}}(\alpha-\varsigma)}\int_0^1(1-\mathrm{q}\tau)^{(\alpha-\varsigma-1)}\mathcal{F}_{\mathrm{uv}}(\tau)\,d_{\mathrm{q}}\tau \\
&-\Lambda_4\sum_{i=1}^{\mathfrak{a}}\frac{a_i}{\Gamma_{\mathrm{q}}(\alpha-\varrho_i)}\int_0^{\xi_i}(\xi_i-\mathrm{q}\tau)^{(\alpha-\varrho_i-1)}\mathcal{F}_{\mathrm{uv}}(\tau)\,d_{\mathrm{q}}\tau \\
&-\Lambda_2\sum_{i=1}^{\mathfrak{c}}\frac{c_i}{\Gamma_{\mathrm{q}}(\alpha-\eta_i)}\int_0^{\zeta_i}(\zeta_i-\mathrm{q}\tau)^{(\alpha-\eta_i-1)}\mathcal{F}_{\mathrm{uv}}(\tau)\,d_{\mathrm{q}}\tau\Bigg] \\
&+\frac{\nu^{\alpha-1}}{\Delta}\Bigg[-\Lambda_4\sum_{i=1}^{\mathfrak{b}}\frac{b_i}{\Gamma_{\mathrm{q}}(\beta-\sigma_i)}\int_0^{\omega_i}(\omega_i-\mathrm{q}\tau)^{(\beta-\sigma_i-1)}\mathcal{G}_{\mathrm{uv}}(\tau)\,d_{\mathrm{q}}\tau \\
&+\frac{\Lambda_2}{\Gamma_{\mathrm{q}}(\beta-\vartheta)}\int_0^1(1-\mathrm{q}\tau)^{(\beta-\vartheta-1)}\mathcal{G}_{\mathrm{uv}}(\tau)\,d_{\mathrm{q}}\tau \\
&-\Lambda_2\sum_{i=1}^{\mathfrak{d}}\frac{d_i}{\Gamma_{\mathrm{q}}(\beta-\rho_i)}\int_0^{\theta_i}(\theta_i-\mathrm{q}\tau)^{(\beta-\rho_i-1)}\mathcal{G}_{\mathrm{uv}}(\tau)\,d_{\mathrm{q}}\tau\Bigg], \quad \nu\in[0,1], \\
\mathcal{E}_2(\mathrm{u},\mathrm{v})(\nu) &= \frac{\nu^{\beta-1}}{\Delta}\Bigg[-\Lambda_1\sum_{i=1}^{\mathfrak{c}}\frac{c_i}{\Gamma_{\mathrm{q}}(\alpha-\eta_i)}\int_0^{\zeta_i}(\zeta_i-\mathrm{q}\tau)^{(\alpha-\eta_i-1)}\mathcal{F}_{\mathrm{uv}}(\tau)\,d_{\mathrm{q}}\tau \\
&+\frac{\Lambda_3}{\Gamma_{\mathrm{q}}(\alpha-\varsigma)}\int_0^1(1-\mathrm{q}\tau)^{(\alpha-\varsigma-1)}\mathcal{F}_{\mathrm{uv}}(\tau)\,d_{\mathrm{q}}\tau \\
&-\Lambda_3\sum_{i=1}^{\mathfrak{a}}\frac{a_i}{\Gamma_{\mathrm{q}}(\alpha-\varrho_i)}\int_0^{\xi_i}(\xi_i-\mathrm{q}\tau)^{(\alpha-\varrho_i-1)}\mathcal{F}_{\mathrm{uv}}(\tau)\,d_{\mathrm{q}}\tau\Bigg] \\
&-\frac{1}{\Gamma_{\mathrm{q}}(\beta)}\int_0^{\nu}(\nu-\mathrm{q}\tau)^{(\beta-1)}\mathcal{G}_{\mathrm{uv}}(\tau)\,d_{\mathrm{q}}\tau \\
&+\frac{\nu^{\beta-1}}{\Delta}\Bigg[\frac{\Lambda_1}{\Gamma_{\mathrm{q}}(\beta-\vartheta)}\int_0^1(1-\mathrm{q}\tau)^{(\beta-\vartheta-1)}\mathcal{G}_{\mathrm{uv}}(\tau)\,d_{\mathrm{q}}\tau \\
&-\Lambda_1\sum_{i=1}^{\mathfrak{d}}\frac{d_i}{\Gamma_{\mathrm{q}}(\beta-\rho_i)}\int_0^{\theta_i}(\theta_i-\mathrm{q}\tau)^{(\beta-\rho_i-1)}\mathcal{G}_{\mathrm{uv}}(\tau)\,d_{\mathrm{q}}\tau \\
&-\Lambda_3\sum_{i=1}^{\mathfrak{b}}\frac{b_i}{\Gamma_{\mathrm{q}}(\beta-\sigma_i)}\int_0^{\omega_i}(\omega_i-\mathrm{q}\tau)^{(\beta-\sigma_i-1)}\mathcal{G}_{\mathrm{uv}}(\tau)\,d_{\mathrm{q}}\tau\Bigg], \quad \nu\in[0,1],
\end{aligned} \tag{13}$$

for $(\mathrm{u},\mathrm{v}) \in \mathcal{V}$, where $\mathcal{F}_{\mathrm{uv}}(\tau) = \mathcal{F}(\tau,\mathrm{u}(\tau),\mathrm{v}(\tau),\mathrm{I}_{\mathrm{q}}^{\delta_1}\mathrm{u}(\tau),\mathrm{I}_{\mathrm{q}}^{\gamma_1}\mathrm{v}(\tau))$, $\mathcal{G}_{\mathrm{uv}}(\tau) = \mathcal{G}(\tau,\mathrm{u}(\tau),\mathrm{v}(\tau),\mathrm{I}_{\mathrm{q}}^{\delta_2}\mathrm{u}(\tau),\mathrm{I}_{\mathrm{q}}^{\gamma_2}\mathrm{v}(\tau))$, for any $\tau \in [0,1]$.

By Lemma 1, we see that (u,v) is a solution of problem (1), (2) if and only if (u,v) is a fixed point of operator $\mathcal{E}$.

3. Existence of Solutions

In this section, we will outline the principal existence results for the problem defined by Equations (1) and (2).

We introduce the fundamental assumptions that form the basis of our theorems.

(J1) $\mathfrak{q} \in (0,1)$, α, $\beta \in \mathbb{R}$, $\alpha \in (n-1,n]$, $\beta \in (m-1,m]$, $n,m \in \mathbb{N}$, $n,m \geq 2$; $\mathfrak{a},\mathfrak{b},\mathfrak{c},\mathfrak{d} \in \mathbb{N}$; $\varsigma, \varrho_i, \eta_k \in [0,\alpha-1)$; $\vartheta, \sigma_j, \rho_\iota \in [0,\beta-1)$; $a_i, b_j, c_k, d_\iota \in \mathbb{R}$; $\xi_i, \omega_j, \zeta_k, \theta_\iota \in (0,1)$, for all $i = 1,\dots,\mathfrak{a}$, $j = 1,\dots,\mathfrak{b}$, $k = 1,\dots,\mathfrak{c}$, $\iota = 1,\dots,\mathfrak{d}$; $\delta_\kappa, \gamma_\kappa > 0$ for $\kappa = 1,2$; $\Delta \neq 0$ (given by (10)).

We also define the constants

$$\begin{aligned}
\Upsilon_1 &= \frac{1}{\Gamma_\mathfrak{q}(\alpha+1)} + \frac{1}{|\Delta|}\left[|\Lambda_4|\frac{1}{\Gamma_\mathfrak{q}(\alpha-\varsigma+1)} + |\Lambda_4|\sum_{i=1}^{\mathfrak{a}}|a_i|\frac{\xi_i^{\alpha-\varrho_i}}{\Gamma_\mathfrak{q}(\alpha-\varrho_i+1)}\right.\\
&\left.+|\Lambda_2|\sum_{i=1}^{\mathfrak{c}}|c_i|\frac{\zeta_i^{\alpha-\eta_i}}{\Gamma_\mathfrak{q}(\alpha-\eta_i+1)}\right],\\
\Upsilon_2 &= \frac{1}{|\Delta|}\left[|\Lambda_2|\frac{1}{\Gamma_\mathfrak{q}(\beta-\vartheta+1)} + |\Lambda_4|\sum_{i=1}^{\mathfrak{b}}|b_i|\frac{\omega_i^{\beta-\sigma_i}}{\Gamma_\mathfrak{q}(\beta-\sigma_i+1)}\right.\\
&\left.+|\Lambda_2|\sum_{i=1}^{\mathfrak{d}}|d_i|\frac{\theta_i^{\beta-\rho_i}}{\Gamma_\mathfrak{q}(\beta-\rho_i+1)}\right]\\
\Upsilon_3 &= \frac{1}{|\Delta|}\left[|\Lambda_3|\frac{1}{\Gamma_\mathfrak{q}(\alpha-\varsigma+1)} + |\Lambda_3|\sum_{i=1}^{\mathfrak{a}}|a_i|\frac{\xi_i^{\alpha-\varrho_i}}{\Gamma_\mathfrak{q}(\alpha-\varrho_i+1)}\right.\\
&\left.+|\Lambda_1|\sum_{i=1}^{\mathfrak{c}}|c_i|\frac{\zeta_i^{\alpha-\eta_i}}{\Gamma_\mathfrak{q}(\alpha-\eta_i+1)}\right],\\
\Upsilon_4 &= \frac{1}{\Gamma_\mathfrak{q}(\beta+1)} + \frac{1}{|\Delta|}\left[|\Lambda_1|\frac{1}{\Gamma_\mathfrak{q}(\beta-\vartheta+1)} + |\Lambda_3|\sum_{i=1}^{\mathfrak{b}}|b_i|\frac{\omega_i^{\beta-\sigma_i}}{\Gamma_\mathfrak{q}(\beta-\sigma_i+1)}\right.\\
&\left.+|\Lambda_1|\sum_{i=1}^{\mathfrak{d}}|d_i|\frac{\theta_i^{\beta-\rho_i}}{\Gamma_\mathfrak{q}(\beta-\rho_i+1)}\right].
\end{aligned} \tag{14}$$

Under assumption (J1), we remark that $\Upsilon_1 > 0$, $\Upsilon_2 \geq 0$, $\Upsilon_3 \geq 0$, $\Upsilon_4 > 0$, and so $\Upsilon_1 + \Upsilon_3 > 0$, $\Upsilon_2 + \Upsilon_4 > 0$.

The initial existence and uniqueness theorem for problem (1), (2) is as follows, relying on the Banach contraction mapping principle, as detailed in [32].

Theorem 1. *Suppose that (J1) holds. In addition, we assume that the functions $\mathcal{F}, \mathcal{G} : [0,1] \times \mathbb{R}^4 \to \mathbb{R}$ are continuous and satisfy the condition*

(J2) There exist the functions $\mathcal{H}_i$, $\mathcal{K}_i \in C([0,1],\mathbb{R}_+)$, $i = 1,\dots,4$, ($\mathbb{R}_+ = [0,\infty)$), such that

$$\begin{aligned}
|\mathcal{F}(\nu,\mathrm{u}_1,\mathrm{u}_2,\mathrm{u}_3,\mathrm{u}_4) - \mathcal{F}(\nu,\mathrm{v}_1,\mathrm{v}_2,\mathrm{v}_3,\mathrm{v}_4)| &\leq \sum_{i=1}^{4}\mathcal{H}_i(\nu)|\mathrm{u}_i - \mathrm{v}_i|,\\
|\mathcal{G}(\nu,\mathrm{u}_1,\mathrm{u}_2,\mathrm{u}_3,\mathrm{u}_4) - \mathcal{G}(\nu,\mathrm{v}_1,\mathrm{v}_2,\mathrm{v}_3,\mathrm{v}_4)| &\leq \sum_{i=1}^{4}\mathcal{K}_i(\nu)|\mathrm{u}_i - \mathrm{v}_i|,
\end{aligned} \tag{15}$$

for all $\nu \in [0,1]$ and $\mathrm{u}_i, \mathrm{v}_i \in \mathbb{R}$, $i = 1,\dots,4$.

If

$$\Theta_0 < 1, \tag{16}$$

where $\Theta_0 = \max\{\Theta_1,\Theta_2\}$,

$$\begin{aligned}
\Theta_1 &= \left(\mathfrak{h}_1^* + \frac{\mathfrak{h}_3^*}{\Gamma_\mathfrak{q}(\delta_1+1)}\right)(\Upsilon_1+\Upsilon_3) + \left(\mathfrak{k}_1^* + \frac{\mathfrak{k}_3^*}{\Gamma_\mathfrak{q}(\delta_2+1)}\right)(\Upsilon_2+\Upsilon_4),\\
\Theta_2 &= \left(\mathfrak{h}_2^* + \frac{\mathfrak{h}_4^*}{\Gamma_\mathfrak{q}(\gamma_1+1)}\right)(\Upsilon_1+\Upsilon_3) + \left(\mathfrak{k}_2^* + \frac{\mathfrak{k}_4^*}{\Gamma_\mathfrak{q}(\gamma_2+1)}\right)(\Upsilon_2+\Upsilon_4),
\end{aligned} \tag{17}$$

and $\mathfrak{h}_i^* = \sup_{\nu\in[0,1]} \mathcal{H}_i(\nu)$, $\mathfrak{k}_i^* = \sup_{\nu\in[0,1]} \mathcal{K}_i(\nu)$, $i = 1,\ldots,4$, *then the boundary value problem (1), (2) has a unique solution* $(\mathrm{u}(\nu),\mathrm{v}(\nu))$, $\nu \in [0,1]$.

Proof. We denote by $\Xi_1 = \sup_{\nu\in[0,1]} |\mathcal{F}(\nu,0,0,0,0)|$ and $\Xi_2 = \sup_{\nu\in[0,1]} |\mathcal{G}(\nu,0,0,0,0)|$. We consider the positive number

$$R \geq \frac{\Xi_1(\mathrm{Y}_1+\mathrm{Y}_3)+\Xi_2(\mathrm{Y}_2+\mathrm{Y}_4)}{1-\Theta_0}, \tag{18}$$

and let the set $\Omega = \{(\mathrm{u},\mathrm{v}) \in \mathcal{V},\ \|(\mathrm{u},\mathrm{v})\|_{\mathcal{V}} \leq R\}$.

We will show firstly that $\mathcal{E}(\Omega) \subset \Omega$. For this, let $(\mathrm{u},\mathrm{v}) \in \Omega$, that is $\|\mathrm{u}\| + \|\mathrm{v}\| \leq R$. Then, by $(J1)$ and Lemma 3, we obtain for all $\nu \in [0,1]$

$$\begin{aligned}
|\mathcal{F}_{\mathrm{uv}}(\nu)| &= |\mathcal{F}(\nu,\mathrm{u}(\nu),\mathrm{v}(\nu),\mathrm{I}_{\mathrm{q}}^{\delta_1}\mathrm{u}(\nu),\mathrm{I}_{\mathrm{q}}^{\gamma_1}\mathrm{v}(\nu))| \\
&\leq |\mathcal{F}(\nu,\mathrm{u}(\nu),\mathrm{v}(\nu),\mathrm{I}_{\mathrm{q}}^{\delta_1}\mathrm{u}(\nu),\mathrm{I}_{\mathrm{q}}^{\gamma_1}\mathrm{v}(\nu)) - \mathcal{F}(\nu,0,0,0,0)| + |\mathcal{F}(\nu,0,0,0,0)| \\
&\leq \mathcal{H}_1(\nu)|\mathrm{u}(\nu)| + \mathcal{H}_2(\nu)|\mathrm{v}(\nu)| + \mathcal{H}_3(\nu)|\mathrm{I}_{\mathrm{q}}^{\delta_1}\mathrm{u}(\nu)| + \mathcal{H}_4(\nu)|\mathrm{I}_{\mathrm{q}}^{\gamma_1}\mathrm{v}(\nu)| + \Xi_1 \\
&\leq \mathfrak{h}_1^*\|\mathrm{u}\| + \mathfrak{h}_2^*\|\mathrm{v}\| + \mathfrak{h}_3^*\frac{\|\mathrm{u}\|}{\Gamma_{\mathrm{q}}(\delta_1+1)} + \mathfrak{h}_4^*\frac{\|\mathrm{v}\|}{\Gamma_{\mathrm{q}}(\gamma_1+1)} + \Xi_1 \\
&= \left(\mathfrak{h}_1^* + \frac{\mathfrak{h}_3^*}{\Gamma_q(\delta_1+1)}\right)\|\mathrm{u}\| + \left(\mathfrak{h}_2^* + \frac{\mathfrak{h}_4^*}{\Gamma_q(\gamma_1+1)}\right)\|\mathrm{v}\| + \Xi_1 =: A_{\mathrm{uv}}, \\
|\mathcal{G}_{\mathrm{uv}}(\nu)| &= |\mathcal{G}(\nu,\mathrm{u}(\nu),\mathrm{v}(\nu),\mathrm{I}_{\mathrm{q}}^{\delta_2}\mathrm{u}(\nu),\mathrm{I}_{\mathrm{q}}^{\gamma_2}\mathrm{v}(\nu))| \\
&\leq |\mathcal{G}(\nu,\mathrm{u}(\nu),\mathrm{v}(\nu),\mathrm{I}_{\mathrm{q}}^{\delta_2}\mathrm{u}(\nu),\mathrm{I}_{\mathrm{q}}^{\gamma_2}\mathrm{v}(\nu)) - \mathcal{G}(\nu,0,0,0,0)| + |\mathcal{G}(\nu,0,0,0,0)| \\
&\leq \mathcal{K}_1(\nu)|\mathrm{u}(\nu)| + \mathcal{K}_2(\nu)|\mathrm{v}(\nu)| + \mathcal{K}_3(\nu)|\mathrm{I}_{\mathrm{q}}^{\delta_2}\mathrm{u}(\nu)| + \mathcal{K}_4(\nu)|\mathrm{I}_{\mathrm{q}}^{\gamma_2}\mathrm{v}(\nu)| + \Xi_2 \\
&\leq \mathfrak{k}_1^*\|\mathrm{u}\| + \mathfrak{k}_2^*\|\mathrm{v}\| + \mathfrak{k}_3^*\frac{\|\mathrm{u}\|}{\Gamma_{\mathrm{q}}(\delta_2+1)} + \mathfrak{k}_4^*\frac{\|\mathrm{v}\|}{\Gamma_{\mathrm{q}}(\gamma_2+1)} + \Xi_2 \\
&= \left(\mathfrak{k}_1^* + \frac{\mathfrak{k}_3^*}{\Gamma_q(\delta_2+1)}\right)\|\mathrm{u}\| + \left(\mathfrak{k}_2^* + \frac{\mathfrak{k}_4^*}{\Gamma_q(\gamma_2+1)}\right)\|\mathrm{v}\| + \Xi_2 =: B_{\mathrm{uv}}.
\end{aligned} \tag{19}$$

Therefore, we find

$$\begin{aligned}
|\mathcal{E}_1(\mathrm{u},\mathrm{v})(\nu)| &\leq \frac{1}{\Gamma_{\mathrm{q}}(\alpha)}\int_0^{\nu}(\nu-\mathrm{q}\tau)^{(\alpha-1)}|\mathcal{F}_{\mathrm{uv}}(\tau)|\,d_{\mathrm{q}}\tau \\
&+\frac{1}{|\Delta|}\left[|\Lambda_4|\frac{1}{\Gamma_q(\alpha-\varsigma)}\int_0^1(1-\mathrm{q}\tau)^{(\alpha-\varsigma-1)}|\mathcal{F}_{\mathrm{uv}}(\tau)|\,d_{\mathrm{q}}\tau\right. \\
&+|\Lambda_4|\sum_{i=1}^{\mathfrak{a}}\frac{|a_i|}{\Gamma_{\mathrm{q}}(\alpha-\varrho_i)}\int_0^{\xi_i}(\xi_i-\mathrm{q}\tau)^{(\alpha-\varrho_i-1)}|\mathcal{F}_{\mathrm{uv}}(\tau)|\,d_{\mathrm{q}}\tau \\
&\left.+|\Lambda_2|\sum_{i=1}^{\mathfrak{c}}\frac{|c_i|}{\Gamma_q(\alpha-\eta_i)}\int_0^{\zeta_i}(\zeta_i-\mathrm{q}\tau)^{(\alpha-\eta_i-1)}|\mathcal{F}_{\mathrm{uv}}(\tau)|\,d_{\mathrm{q}}\tau\right] \\
&+\frac{1}{|\Delta|}\left[|\Lambda_4|\sum_{i=1}^{\mathfrak{b}}\frac{|b_i|}{\Gamma_q(\beta-\sigma_i)}\int_0^{\omega_i}(\omega_i-\mathrm{q}\tau)^{(\beta-\sigma_i-1)}|\mathcal{G}_{\mathrm{uv}}(\tau)|\,d_{\mathrm{q}}\tau\right. \\
&+|\Lambda_2|\frac{1}{\Gamma_{\mathrm{q}}(\beta-\vartheta)}\int_0^1(1-\mathrm{q}\tau)^{(\beta-\vartheta-1)}|\mathcal{G}_{\mathrm{uv}}(\tau)|\,d_{\mathrm{q}}\tau \\
&\left.+|\Lambda_2|\sum_{i=1}^{\mathfrak{d}}\frac{|d_i|}{\Gamma_{\mathrm{q}}(\beta-\rho_i)}\int_0^{\theta_i}(\theta_i-\mathrm{q}\tau)^{(\beta-\rho_i-1)}|\mathcal{G}_{\mathrm{uv}}(\tau)|\,d_{\mathrm{q}}\tau\right] \\
&\leq A_{\mathrm{uv}}\left\{\frac{1}{\Gamma_{\mathrm{q}}(\alpha)}\int_0^{\nu}(\nu-\mathrm{q}\tau)^{(\alpha-1)}\,d_{\mathrm{q}}\tau + \frac{1}{|\Delta|}\left[|\Lambda_4|\frac{1}{\Gamma_{\mathrm{q}}(\alpha-\varsigma)}\int_0^1(1-\mathrm{q}\tau)^{(\alpha-\varsigma-1)}\,d_{\mathrm{q}}\tau\right.\right.
\end{aligned}$$

$$
\begin{aligned}
&+|\Lambda_4|\sum_{i=1}^{\mathfrak{a}}\frac{|a_i|}{\Gamma_{\mathrm{q}}(\alpha-\varrho_i)}\int_0^{\xi_i}(\xi_i-\mathrm{q}\tau)^{(\alpha-\varrho_i-1)}\,d_{\mathrm{q}}\tau\\
&+|\Lambda_2|\sum_{i=1}^{\mathfrak{c}}\frac{|c_i|}{\Gamma_{\mathrm{q}}(\alpha-\eta_i)}\int_0^{\zeta_i}(\zeta_i-\mathrm{q}\tau)^{(\alpha-\eta_i-1)}\,d_{\mathrm{q}}\tau\Bigg]\Bigg\}\\
&+B_{\mathrm{uv}}\frac{1}{|\Delta|}\Bigg[|\Lambda_4|\sum_{i=1}^{\mathfrak{b}}\frac{|b_i|}{\Gamma_{\mathrm{q}}(\beta-\sigma_i)}\int_0^{\omega_i}(\omega_i-\mathrm{q}\tau)^{(\beta-\sigma_i-1)}\,d_{\mathrm{q}}\tau\\
&+|\Lambda_2|\frac{1}{\Gamma_{\mathrm{q}}(\beta-\vartheta)}\int_0^{1}(1-\mathrm{q}\tau)^{(\beta-\vartheta-1)}\,d_{\mathrm{q}}\tau\\
&+|\Lambda_2|\sum_{i=1}^{\mathfrak{d}}\frac{|d_i|}{\Gamma_{\mathrm{q}}(\beta-\rho_i)}\int_0^{\theta_i}(\theta_i-\mathrm{q}\tau)^{(\beta-\rho_i-1)}\,d_{\mathrm{q}}\tau\Bigg] \qquad (20)\\
&=A_{\mathrm{uv}}\Bigg\{\frac{\nu^{\alpha}}{\Gamma_{\mathrm{q}}(\alpha+1)}+\frac{1}{|\Delta|}\Bigg[|\Lambda_4|\frac{1}{\Gamma_{\mathrm{q}}(\alpha-\varsigma+1)}+|\Lambda_4|\sum_{i=1}^{\mathfrak{a}}|a_i|\frac{\xi_i^{\alpha-\varrho_i}}{\Gamma_{\mathrm{q}}(\alpha-\varrho_i+1)}\\
&+|\Lambda_2|\sum_{i=1}^{\mathfrak{c}}|c_i|\frac{\zeta_i^{\alpha-\eta_i}}{\Gamma_{\mathrm{q}}(\alpha-\eta_i+1)}\Bigg]\Bigg\}\\
&+B_{\mathrm{uv}}\frac{1}{|\Delta|}\Bigg[|\Lambda_4|\sum_{i=1}^{\mathfrak{b}}|b_i|\frac{\omega_i^{\beta-\sigma_i}}{\Gamma_{\mathrm{q}}(\beta-\sigma_i+1)}+|\Lambda_2|\frac{1}{\Gamma_{\mathrm{q}}(\beta-\vartheta+1)}\\
&+|\Lambda_2|\sum_{i=1}^{\mathfrak{d}}|d_i|\frac{\theta_i^{\beta-\rho_i}}{\Gamma_{\mathrm{q}}(\beta-\rho_i+1)}\Bigg]\le A_{\mathrm{uv}}\Upsilon_1+B_{\mathrm{uv}}\Upsilon_2,\ \ \forall\nu\in[0,1],
\end{aligned}
$$

and

$$
\begin{aligned}
&|\mathcal{E}_2(\mathrm{u},\mathrm{v})(\nu)|\le\frac{1}{|\Delta|}\Bigg[|\Lambda_1|\sum_{i=1}^{\mathfrak{c}}\frac{|c_i|}{\Gamma_{\mathrm{q}}(\alpha-\eta_i)}\int_0^{\zeta_i}(\zeta_i-\mathrm{q}\tau)^{(\alpha-\eta_i-1)}|\mathcal{F}_{\mathrm{uv}}(\tau)|\,d_{\mathrm{q}}\tau\\
&+|\Lambda_3|\frac{1}{\Gamma_{\mathrm{q}}(\alpha-\varsigma)}\int_0^{1}(1-\mathrm{q}\tau)^{(\alpha-\varsigma-1)}|\mathcal{F}_{\mathrm{uv}}(\tau)|\,d_{\mathrm{q}}\tau\\
&+|\Lambda_3|\sum_{i=1}^{\mathfrak{a}}\frac{|a_i|}{\Gamma_{\mathrm{q}}(\alpha-\varrho_i)}\int_0^{\xi_i}(\xi_i-\mathrm{q}\tau)^{(\alpha-\varrho_i-1)}|\mathcal{F}_{\mathrm{uv}}(\tau)|\,d_{\mathrm{q}}\tau\Bigg]\\
&+\frac{1}{\Gamma_{\mathrm{q}}(\beta)}\int_0^{\nu}(\nu-\mathrm{q}\tau)^{(\beta-1)}|\mathcal{G}_{\mathrm{uv}}(\tau)|\,d_{\mathrm{q}}\tau\\
&+\frac{1}{|\Delta|}\Bigg[|\Lambda_1|\frac{1}{\Gamma_{\mathrm{q}}(\beta-\vartheta)}\int_0^{1}(1-\mathrm{q}\tau)^{(\beta-\vartheta-1)}|\mathcal{G}_{\mathrm{uv}}(\tau)|\,d_{\mathrm{q}}\tau\\
&+|\Lambda_1|\sum_{i=1}^{\mathfrak{d}}\frac{|d_i|}{\Gamma_{\mathrm{q}}(\beta-\rho_i)}\int_0^{\theta_i}(\theta_i-\mathrm{q}\tau)^{(\beta-\rho_i-1)}|\mathcal{G}_{\mathrm{uv}}(\tau)|\,d_{\mathrm{q}}\tau\\
&+|\Lambda_3|\sum_{i=1}^{\mathfrak{b}}\frac{|b_i|}{\Gamma_{\mathrm{q}}(\beta-\sigma_i)}\int_0^{\omega_i}(\omega_i-\mathrm{q}\tau)^{(\beta-\sigma_i-1)}|\mathcal{G}_{\mathrm{uv}}(\tau)|\,d_{\mathrm{q}}\tau\Bigg] \qquad (21)\\
&\le A_{\mathrm{uv}}\frac{1}{|\Delta|}\Bigg[|\Lambda_1|\sum_{i=1}^{\mathfrak{c}}\frac{|c_i|}{\Gamma_{\mathrm{q}}(\alpha-\eta_i)}\int_0^{\zeta_i}(\zeta_i-\mathrm{q}\tau)^{(\alpha-\eta_i-1)}\,d_{\mathrm{q}}\tau\\
&+|\Lambda_3|\frac{1}{\Gamma_{\mathrm{q}}(\alpha-\varsigma)}\int_0^{1}(1-\mathrm{q}\tau)^{(\alpha-\varsigma-1)}\,d_{\mathrm{q}}\tau\\
&+|\Lambda_3|\sum_{i=1}^{\mathfrak{a}}\frac{|a_i|}{\Gamma_{\mathrm{q}}(\alpha-\varrho_i)}\int_0^{\xi_i}(\xi_i-\mathrm{q}\tau)^{(\alpha-\varrho_i-1)}\,d_{\mathrm{q}}\tau\Bigg]\\
&+B_{\mathrm{uv}}\Bigg\{\frac{1}{\Gamma_{\mathrm{q}}(\beta)}\int_0^{\nu}(\nu-\mathrm{q}\tau)^{(\beta-1)}\,d_{\mathrm{q}}\tau+\frac{1}{|\Delta|}\Bigg[|\Lambda_1|\frac{1}{\Gamma_{\mathrm{q}}(\beta-\vartheta)}\int_0^{1}(1-\mathrm{q}\tau)^{(\beta-\vartheta-1)}\,d_{\mathrm{q}}\tau\\
&+|\Lambda_1|\sum_{i=1}^{\mathfrak{d}}\frac{|d_i|}{\Gamma_{\mathrm{q}}(\beta-\rho_i)}\int_0^{\theta_i}(\theta_i-\mathrm{q}\tau)^{(\beta-\rho_i-1)}\,d_{\mathrm{q}}\tau\\
&+|\Lambda_3|\sum_{i=1}^{\mathfrak{b}}\frac{|b_i|}{\Gamma_{\mathrm{q}}(\beta-\sigma_i)}\int_0^{\omega_i}(\omega_i-\mathrm{q}\tau)^{(\beta-\sigma_i-1)}\,d_{\mathrm{q}}\tau\Bigg]\Bigg\}
\end{aligned}
$$

$$
\begin{aligned}
&= A_{\mathrm{uv}}\frac{1}{|\Delta|}\left[|\Lambda_1|\sum_{i=1}^{\mathfrak{c}}|c_i|\frac{\zeta_i^{\alpha-\eta_i}}{\Gamma_{\mathrm{q}}(\alpha-\eta_i+1)}+|\Lambda_3|\frac{1}{\Gamma_{\mathrm{q}}(\alpha-\varsigma+1)}\right.\\
&\left.+|\Lambda_3|\sum_{i=1}^{\mathfrak{a}}|a_i|\frac{\xi_i^{\alpha-\varrho_i}}{\Gamma_{\mathrm{q}}(\alpha-\varrho_i+1)}\right]\\
&+B_{\mathrm{uv}}\left\{\frac{\nu^{\beta}}{\Gamma_{\mathrm{q}}(\beta+1)}+\frac{1}{|\Delta|}\left[|\Lambda_1|\frac{1}{\Gamma_{\mathrm{q}}(\beta-\vartheta+1)}+|\Lambda_1|\sum_{i=1}^{\mathfrak{d}}|d_i|\frac{\theta_i^{\beta-\rho_i}}{\Gamma_{\mathrm{q}}(\beta-\rho_i+1)}\right.\right.\\
&\left.\left.+|\Lambda_3|\sum_{i=1}^{\mathfrak{b}}|b_i|\frac{\omega_i^{\beta-\sigma_i}}{\Gamma_{\mathrm{q}}(\beta-\sigma_i+1)}\right]\right\}\leq A_{\mathrm{uv}}\mathrm{Y}_3+B_{\mathrm{uv}}\mathrm{Y}_4,\ \ \forall\nu\in[0,1].
\end{aligned}
$$

Therefore, by (20), (21) and (18), we deduce

$$
\begin{aligned}
&\|\mathcal{E}(\mathrm{u},\mathrm{v})\|_{\mathcal{V}}=\|\mathcal{E}_1(\mathrm{u},\mathrm{v})\|+\|\mathcal{E}_2(\mathrm{u},\mathrm{v})\|\leq A_{\mathrm{uv}}(\mathrm{Y}_1+\mathrm{Y}_3)+B_{\mathrm{uv}}(\mathrm{Y}_2+\mathrm{Y}_4)\\
&=\left[\left(\mathfrak{h}_1^*+\frac{\mathfrak{h}_3^*}{\Gamma_{\mathrm{q}}(\delta_1+1)}\right)\|\mathrm{u}\|+\left(\mathfrak{h}_2^*+\frac{\mathfrak{h}_4^*}{\Gamma_{\mathrm{q}}(\gamma_1+1)}\right)\|\mathrm{v}\|+\Xi_1\right](\mathrm{Y}_1+\mathrm{Y}_3)\\
&+\left[\left(\mathfrak{k}_1^*+\frac{\mathfrak{k}_3^*}{\Gamma_{\mathrm{q}}(\delta_2+1)}\right)\|\mathrm{u}\|+\left(\mathfrak{k}_2^*+\frac{\mathfrak{k}_4^*}{\Gamma_{\mathrm{q}}(\gamma_2+1)}\right)\|\mathrm{v}\|+\Xi_2\right](\mathrm{Y}_2+\mathrm{Y}_4)\\
&=\left[\left(\mathfrak{h}_1^*+\frac{\mathfrak{h}_3^*}{\Gamma_{\mathrm{q}}(\delta_1+1)}\right)(\mathrm{Y}_1+\mathrm{Y}_3)+\left(\mathfrak{k}_1^*+\frac{\mathfrak{k}_3^*}{\Gamma_{\mathrm{q}}(\delta_2+1)}\right)(\mathrm{Y}_2+\mathrm{Y}_4)\right]\|\mathrm{u}\|\\
&+\left[\left(\mathfrak{h}_2^*+\frac{\mathfrak{h}_4^*}{\Gamma_{\mathrm{q}}(\gamma_1+1)}\right)(\mathrm{Y}_1+\mathrm{Y}_3)+\left(\mathfrak{k}_2^*+\frac{\mathfrak{k}_4^*}{\Gamma_{\mathrm{q}}(\gamma_2+1)}\right)(\mathrm{Y}_2+\mathrm{Y}_4)\right]\|\mathrm{v}\|\\
&+\Xi_1(\mathrm{Y}_1+\mathrm{Y}_3)+\Xi_2(\mathrm{Y}_2+\mathrm{Y}_4)\\
&=\Theta_1\|\mathrm{u}\|+\Theta_2\|\mathrm{v}\|+\Xi_1(\mathrm{Y}_1+\mathrm{Y}_3)+\Xi_2(\mathrm{Y}_2+\mathrm{Y}_4)\\
&\leq\Theta_0\|(\mathrm{u},\mathrm{v})\|_{\mathcal{V}}+\Xi_1(\mathrm{Y}_1+\mathrm{Y}_3)+\Xi_2(\mathrm{Y}_2+\mathrm{Y}_4)\\
&\leq\Theta_0R+\Xi_1(\mathrm{Y}_1+\mathrm{Y}_3)+\Xi_2(\mathrm{Y}_2+\mathrm{Y}_4)\leq R.
\end{aligned}
\tag{22}
$$

Therefore, we conclude that $\mathcal{E}(\Omega)\subset\Omega$.

Subsequently, we will prove that $\mathcal{E}$ is a contraction. For this, let $(\mathrm{u}_1,\mathrm{v}_1)$, $(\mathrm{u}_2,\mathrm{v}_2)\in\mathcal{V}$. By relations (15), we find for any $\tau\in[0,1]$

$$
\begin{aligned}
&|\mathcal{F}_{\mathrm{u}_1\mathrm{v}_1}(\tau)-\mathcal{F}_{\mathrm{u}_2\mathrm{v}_2}(\tau)|\leq\mathcal{H}_1(\tau)|\mathrm{u}_1(\tau)-\mathrm{u}_2(\tau)|+\mathcal{H}_2(\tau)|\mathrm{v}_1(\tau)-\mathrm{v}_2(\tau)|\\
&\quad+\mathcal{H}_3(\tau)|\mathrm{I}_{\mathrm{q}}^{\delta_1}\mathrm{u}_1(\tau)-\mathrm{I}_{\mathrm{q}}^{\delta_1}\mathrm{u}_2(\tau)|+\mathcal{H}_4(\tau)|\mathrm{I}_{\mathrm{q}}^{\gamma_1}\mathrm{v}_1(\tau)-\mathrm{I}_{\mathrm{q}}^{\gamma_1}\mathrm{v}_2(\tau)|\\
&\leq\mathfrak{h}_1^*\|\mathrm{u}_1-\mathrm{u}_2\|+\mathfrak{h}_2^*\|\mathrm{v}_1-\mathrm{v}_2\|+\frac{\mathfrak{h}_3^*}{\Gamma_{\mathrm{q}}(\delta_1+1)}\|\mathrm{u}_1-\mathrm{u}_2\|+\frac{\mathfrak{h}_4^*}{\Gamma_{\mathrm{q}}(\gamma_1+1)}\|\mathrm{v}_1-\mathrm{v}_2\|\\
&=\left(\mathfrak{h}_1^*+\frac{\mathfrak{h}_3^*}{\Gamma_{\mathrm{q}}(\delta_1+1)}\right)\|\mathrm{u}_1-\mathrm{u}_2\|+\left(\mathfrak{h}_2^*+\frac{\mathfrak{h}_4^*}{\Gamma_{\mathrm{q}}(\gamma_1+1)}\right)\|\mathrm{v}_1-\mathrm{v}_2\|=:C_{\mathrm{uv}},\\
&|\mathcal{G}_{\mathrm{u}_1\mathrm{v}_1}(\tau)-\mathcal{G}_{\mathrm{u}_2\mathrm{v}_2}(\tau)|\leq\mathcal{K}_1(\tau)|\mathrm{u}_1(\tau)-\mathrm{u}_2(\tau)|+\mathcal{K}_2(\tau)|\mathrm{v}_1(\tau)-\mathrm{v}_2(\tau)|\\
&\quad+\mathcal{K}_3(\tau)|\mathrm{I}_{\mathrm{q}}^{\delta_2}\mathrm{u}_1(\tau)-\mathrm{I}_{\mathrm{q}}^{\delta_2}\mathrm{u}_2(\tau)|+\mathcal{K}_4(\tau)|\mathrm{I}_{\mathrm{q}}^{\gamma_2}\mathrm{v}_1(\tau)-\mathrm{I}_{\mathrm{q}}^{\gamma_2}\mathrm{v}_2(\tau)|\\
&\leq\mathfrak{k}_1^*\|\mathrm{u}_1-\mathrm{u}_2\|+\mathfrak{k}_2^*\|\mathrm{v}_1-\mathrm{v}_2\|+\frac{\mathfrak{k}_3^*}{\Gamma_{\mathrm{q}}(\delta_2+1)}\|\mathrm{u}_1-\mathrm{u}_2\|+\frac{\mathfrak{k}_4^*}{\Gamma_{\mathrm{q}}(\gamma_2+1)}\|\mathrm{v}_1-\mathrm{v}_2\|\\
&=\left(\mathfrak{k}_1^*+\frac{\mathfrak{k}_3^*}{\Gamma_{\mathrm{q}}(\delta_2+1)}\right)\|\mathrm{u}_1-\mathrm{u}_2\|+\left(\mathfrak{k}_2^*+\frac{\mathfrak{k}_4^*}{\Gamma_{\mathrm{q}}(\gamma_2+1)}\right)\|\mathrm{v}_1-\mathrm{v}_2\|=:D_{\mathrm{uv}}.
\end{aligned}
\tag{23}
$$

Then, for any $\nu\in[0,1]$, we obtain

$$
\begin{aligned}
&|\mathcal{E}_1(\mathrm{u}_1,\mathrm{v}_1)(\nu)-\mathcal{E}_1(\mathrm{u}_2,\mathrm{v}_2)(\nu)|\\
&\leq\frac{1}{\Gamma_{\mathrm{q}}(\alpha)}\int_0^{\nu}(\nu-\mathrm{q}\tau)^{(\alpha-1)}|\mathcal{F}_{\mathrm{u}_1\mathrm{v}_1}(\tau)-\mathcal{F}_{\mathrm{u}_2\mathrm{v}_2}(\tau)|\,d_{\mathrm{q}}\tau\\
&\quad+\frac{1}{|\Delta|}\left[\frac{|\Lambda_4|}{\Gamma_{\mathrm{q}}(\alpha-\varsigma)}\int_0^1(1-\mathrm{q}\tau)^{(\alpha-\varsigma-1)}|\mathcal{F}_{\mathrm{u}_1\mathrm{v}_1}(\tau)-\mathcal{F}_{\mathrm{u}_2\mathrm{v}_2}(\tau)|\,d_{\mathrm{q}}\tau\right.\\
&\quad+|\Lambda_4|\sum_{i=1}^{\mathfrak{a}}\frac{|a_i|}{\Gamma_{\mathrm{q}}(\alpha-\varrho_i)}\int_0^{\xi_i}(\xi_i-\mathrm{q}\tau)^{\alpha-\varrho_i-1)}|\mathcal{F}_{\mathrm{u}_1\mathrm{v}_1}(\tau)-\mathcal{F}_{\mathrm{u}_2\mathrm{v}_2}(\tau)|\,d_{\mathrm{q}}\tau\\
&\quad\left.+|\Lambda_2|\sum_{i=1}^{\mathfrak{c}}\frac{|c_i|}{\Gamma_{\mathrm{q}}(\alpha-\eta_i)}\int_0^{\zeta_i}(\zeta_i-\mathrm{q}\tau)^{(\alpha-\eta_i-1)}|\mathcal{F}_{\mathrm{u}_1\mathrm{v}_1}(\tau)-\mathcal{F}_{\mathrm{u}_2\mathrm{v}_2}(\tau)|\,d_{\mathrm{q}}\tau\right]
\end{aligned}
$$

$$
\begin{aligned}
&+\frac{1}{|\Delta|}\Bigg[|\Lambda_4|\sum_{i=1}^{\mathfrak{b}}\frac{|b_i|}{\Gamma_q(\beta-\sigma_i)}\int_0^{\omega_i}(\omega_i-q\tau)^{(\beta-\sigma_i-1)}|\mathcal{G}_{u_1v_1}(\tau)-\mathcal{G}_{u_2v_2}(\tau)|\,d_q\tau\\
&+\frac{|\Lambda_2|}{\Gamma_q(\beta-\vartheta)}\int_0^1(1-q\tau)^{(\beta-\vartheta-1)}|\mathcal{G}_{u_1v_1}(\tau)-\mathcal{G}_{u_2v_2}(\tau)|\,d_q\tau\\
&+|\Lambda_2|\sum_{i=1}^{\mathfrak{d}}\frac{|d_i|}{\Gamma_q(\beta-\rho_i)}\int_0^{\theta_i}(\theta_i-q\tau)^{(\beta-\rho_i-1)}|\mathcal{G}_{u_1v_1}(\tau)-\mathcal{G}_{u_2v_2}(\tau)|\,d_q\tau\Bigg]\\
&\le C_{uv}\Bigg\{\frac{1}{\Gamma_q(\alpha)}\int_0^{\nu}(\nu-q\tau)^{(\alpha-1)}\,d_q\tau+\frac{1}{|\Delta|}\Bigg[\frac{|\Lambda_4|}{\Gamma_q(\alpha-\varsigma)}\int_0^1(1-q\tau)^{(\alpha-\varsigma-1)}\,d_q\tau\\
&+|\Lambda_4|\sum_{i=1}^{\mathfrak{a}}\frac{|a_i|}{\Gamma_q(\alpha-\varrho_i)}\int_0^{\xi_i}(\xi_i-q\tau)^{(\alpha-\varrho_i-1)}\,d_q\tau\\
&+|\Lambda_2|\sum_{i=1}^{\mathfrak{c}}\frac{|c_i|}{\Gamma_q(\alpha-\eta_i)}\int_0^{\zeta_i}(\zeta_i-q\tau)^{(\alpha-\eta_i-1)}\,d_q\tau\Bigg]\Bigg\}\\
&+D_{uv}\frac{1}{|\Delta|}\Bigg[|\Lambda_4|\sum_{i=1}^{\mathfrak{b}}\frac{|b_i|}{\Gamma_q(\beta-\sigma_i)}\int_0^{\omega_i}(\omega_i-q\tau)^{(\beta-\sigma_i-1)}\,d_q\tau\\
&+\frac{|\Lambda_2|}{\Gamma_q(\beta-\vartheta)}\int_0^1(1-q\tau)^{(\beta-\vartheta-1)}\,d_q\tau\\
&+|\Lambda_2|\sum_{i=1}^{\mathfrak{d}}\frac{|d_i|}{\Gamma_q(\beta-\rho_i)}\int_0^{\theta_i}(\theta_i-q\tau)^{(\beta-\rho_i-1)}\,d_q\tau\Bigg]\le C_{uv}Y_1+D_{uv}Y_2.
\end{aligned}
\tag{24}
$$

In a similar manner, for any $\nu\in[0,1]$, we deduce

$$
|\mathcal{E}_2(u_1,v_1)(\nu)-\mathcal{E}_2(u_2,v_2)(\nu)|\le C_{uv}Y_3+D_{uv}Y_4. \tag{25}
$$

Then, by (24), (25) and (17), we conclude that

$$
\begin{aligned}
&\|\mathcal{E}(u_1,v_1)-\mathcal{E}(u_2,v_2)\|_{\mathcal{V}}=\|\mathcal{E}_1(u_1,v_1)-\mathcal{E}_1(u_2,v_2)\|+\|\mathcal{E}_2(u_1,v_1)-\mathcal{E}_2(u_2,v_2)\|\\
&\le C_{uv}(Y_1+Y_3)+D_{uv}(Y_2+Y_4)\\
&=\left(\mathfrak{h}_1^*+\frac{\mathfrak{h}_3^*}{\Gamma_q(\delta_1+1)}\right)(Y_1+Y_3)\|u_1-u_2\|+\left(\mathfrak{h}_2^*+\frac{\mathfrak{h}_4^*}{\Gamma_q(\gamma_1+1)}\right)(Y_1+Y_3)\|v_1-v_2\|\\
&+\left(\mathfrak{k}_1^*+\frac{\mathfrak{k}_3^*}{\Gamma_q(\delta_2+1)}\right)(Y_2+Y_4)\|u_1-u_2\|+\left(\mathfrak{k}_2^*+\frac{\mathfrak{k}_4^*}{\Gamma_q(\gamma_2+1)}\right)(Y_2+Y_4)\|v_1-v_2\|\\
&=\left[\left(\mathfrak{h}_1^*+\frac{\mathfrak{h}_3^*}{\Gamma_q(\delta_1+1)}\right)(Y_1+Y_3)+\left(\mathfrak{k}_1^*+\frac{\mathfrak{k}_3^*}{\Gamma_q(\delta_2+1)}\right)(Y_2+Y_4)\right]\|u_1-u_2\|\\
&+\left[\left(\mathfrak{h}_2^*+\frac{\mathfrak{h}_4^*}{\Gamma_q(\gamma_1+1)}\right)(Y_1+Y_3)+\left(\mathfrak{k}_2^*+\frac{\mathfrak{k}_4^*}{\Gamma_q(\gamma_2+1)}\right)(Y_2+Y_4)\right]\|v_1-v_2\|\\
&=\Theta_1\|u_1-u_2\|+\Theta_2\|v_1-v_2\|\le\Theta_0(\|u_1-u_2\|+\|v_1-v_2\|)\\
&=\Theta_0\|(u_1,v_1)-(u_2,v_2)\|_{\mathcal{V}}.
\end{aligned}
\tag{26}
$$

By (16) and (26), we deduce that $\mathcal{E}$ is a contraction operator. Therefore, by the Banach contraction mapping principle, the operator $\mathcal{E}$ has a unique fixed point $(u^*,v^*)\in\Omega$. Therefore, problem (1), (2) has a unique solution $(u^*(\nu),v^*(\nu))$, $\nu\in[0,1]$ with $\|u^*\|+\|v^*\|\le R$. Moreover, for any $(u_0,v_0)\in\Omega$, the sequence $((u_n,v_n))_{n\ge0}$ defined by $(u_n,v_n)=\mathcal{E}(u_{n-1},v_{n-1})$ for $n\ge1$ converges to (u^*,v^*) as $n\to\infty$. By the proof of Banach theorem, we obtain the error estimate

$$
\|(u_n,v_n)-(u^*,v^*)\|_{\mathcal{V}}\le\frac{\Theta_0^n}{1-\Theta_0}\|(u_1,v_1)-(u_0,v_0)\|_{\mathcal{V}}. \tag{27}
$$

□

Corollary 1. *Suppose that* $(J1)$ *holds. In addition, we assume that the functions* $\mathcal{F}$, $\mathcal{G}:[0,1]\times\mathbb{R}^4\to\mathbb{R}$ *are continuous and*

$(J2)'$ *There exist* $L_i \geq 0,\ M_i \geq 0, i = 1, \ldots, 4$ *such that*

$$\begin{aligned}
|\mathcal{F}(\nu, \mathrm{u}_1, \mathrm{u}_2, \mathrm{u}_3, \mathrm{u}_4) - \mathcal{F}(\nu, \mathrm{v}_1, \mathrm{v}_2, \mathrm{v}_3, \mathrm{v}_4)| &\leq \sum_{i=1}^{4} L_i |\mathrm{u}_i - \mathrm{v}_i|, \\
|\mathcal{G}(\nu, \mathrm{u}_1, \mathrm{u}_2, \mathrm{u}_3, \mathrm{u}_4) - \mathcal{G}(\nu, \mathrm{v}_1, \mathrm{v}_2, \mathrm{v}_3, \mathrm{v}_4)| &\leq \sum_{i=1}^{4} M_i |\mathrm{u}_i - \mathrm{v}_i|,
\end{aligned} \tag{28}$$

for all $\nu \in [0, 1]$ *and* $\mathrm{u}_i, \mathrm{v}_i \in \mathbb{R}, i = 1, \ldots, 4.$

If $\Theta_0 < 1$, *where* $\Theta_0 = \max\{\Theta_1, \Theta_2\}$,

$$\begin{aligned}
\Theta_1 &= \left(L_1 + \frac{L_3}{\Gamma_q(\delta_1 + 1)} \right)(\mathrm{Y}_1 + \mathrm{Y}_3) + \left(M_1 + \frac{M_3}{\Gamma_q(\delta_2 + 1)} \right)(\mathrm{Y}_2 + \mathrm{Y}_4), \\
\Theta_2 &= \left(L_2 + \frac{L_4}{\Gamma_q(\gamma_1 + 1)} \right)(\mathrm{Y}_1 + \mathrm{Y}_3) + \left(M_2 + \frac{M_4}{\Gamma_q(\gamma_2 + 1)} \right)(\mathrm{Y}_2 + \mathrm{Y}_4),
\end{aligned} \tag{29}$$

then the boundary value problem (1), (2) has a unique solution $(\mathrm{u}(\nu), \mathrm{v}(\nu)),\ \nu \in [0, 1]$.

The following two outcomes regarding the existence of solutions to problem (1), (2) rely on the Krasnosel'skii fixed point theorem applied to the combination of two operators (refer to [33] for details).

Theorem 2. *Suppose that assumptions* $(J1)$ *and* $(J2)$ *hold. In addition, we assume that the functions* $\mathcal{F}, \mathcal{G} : [0, 1] \times \mathbb{R}^4 \to \mathbb{R}$ *are continuous and*

$(J3)$ *There exist the functions* $\Phi, \Psi \in C([0, 1], \mathbb{R}_+)$ *such that*

$$|\mathcal{F}(\nu, \mathrm{u}_1, \mathrm{u}_2, \mathrm{u}_3, \mathrm{u}_4)| \leq \Phi(\nu), \ |\mathcal{G}(\nu, \mathrm{u}_1, \mathrm{u}_2, \mathrm{u}_3, \mathrm{u}_4)| \leq \Psi(\nu), \tag{30}$$

for all $\nu \in [0, 1]$, $\mathrm{u}_i \in \mathbb{R}, i = 1, \ldots, 4.$

If

$$\mathfrak{L}_0 < 1, \tag{31}$$

where $\mathfrak{L}_0 = \max\{\mathfrak{L}_1, \mathfrak{L}_2\}$ *with*

$$\begin{aligned}
\mathfrak{L}_1 &= \left(\mathfrak{h}_1^* + \frac{\mathfrak{h}_3^*}{\Gamma_q(\delta_1 + 1)} \right)\left(\mathrm{Y}_1 + \mathrm{Y}_3 - \frac{1}{\Gamma_q(\alpha + 1)} \right) \\
&\quad + \left(\mathfrak{k}_1^* + \frac{\mathfrak{k}_3^*}{\Gamma_q(\delta_2 + 1)} \right)\left(\mathrm{Y}_2 + \mathrm{Y}_4 - \frac{1}{\Gamma_q(\beta + 1)} \right), \\
\mathfrak{L}_2 &= \left(\mathfrak{h}_2^* + \frac{\mathfrak{h}_4^*}{\Gamma_q(\gamma_1 + 1)} \right)\left(\mathrm{Y}_1 + \mathrm{Y}_3 - \frac{1}{\Gamma_q(\alpha + 1)} \right) \\
&\quad + \left(\mathfrak{k}_2^* + \frac{\mathfrak{k}_4^*}{\Gamma_q(\gamma_2 + 1)} \right)\left(\mathrm{Y}_2 + \mathrm{Y}_4 - \frac{1}{\Gamma_q(\beta + 1)} \right),
\end{aligned} \tag{32}$$

then problem (1), (2) has at least one solution $(\mathrm{u}(\nu), \mathrm{v}(\nu)),\ \nu \in [0, 1]$.

Proof. We define the number $r > 0$, which satisfies the condition

$$r \geq (\mathrm{Y}_1 + \mathrm{Y}_3)\|\Phi\| + (\mathrm{Y}_2 + \mathrm{Y}_4)\|\Psi\|, \tag{33}$$

and the closed set $\Omega_0 = \{(\mathrm{u}, \mathrm{v}) \in \mathcal{V},\ \|(\mathrm{u}, \mathrm{v})\|_{\mathcal{V}} \leq r\}$. We shall verify the assumptions of the Krasnosel'skii fixed point theorem for the sum of two operators. We split the operator

$\mathcal{E}$ defined on Ω_0, as $\mathcal{E} = \mathcal{P} + \mathcal{Q}$, $\mathcal{P} = (\mathcal{P}_1, \mathcal{P}_2)$, $\mathcal{Q} = (\mathcal{Q}_1, \mathcal{Q}_2)$, where $\mathcal{P}_i$, $\mathcal{Q}_i$, $i = 1, 2$ are defined by

$$\begin{aligned}
\mathcal{P}_1(\mathrm{u},\mathrm{v})(\nu) &= -\frac{1}{\Gamma_{\mathrm{q}}(\alpha)}\int_0^{\nu}(\nu - \mathrm{q}\tau)^{(\alpha-1)}\mathcal{F}_{\mathrm{uv}}(\tau)\, d_{\mathrm{q}}\tau,\\
\mathcal{Q}_1(\mathrm{u},\mathrm{v})(\nu) &= \mathcal{E}_1(\mathrm{u},\mathrm{v})(\nu) - \mathcal{P}_1(\mathrm{u},\mathrm{v})(\nu),\\
\mathcal{P}_2(\mathrm{u},\mathrm{v})(\nu) &= -\frac{1}{\Gamma_{\mathrm{q}}(\beta)}\int_0^{\nu}(\nu - \mathrm{q}\tau)^{(\beta-1)}\mathcal{G}_{\mathrm{uv}}(\tau)\, d_{\mathrm{q}}\tau,\\
\mathcal{Q}_2(\mathrm{u},\mathrm{v})(\nu) &= \mathcal{E}_2(\mathrm{u},\mathrm{v})(\nu) - \mathcal{P}_2(\mathrm{u},\mathrm{v})(\nu),
\end{aligned} \tag{34}$$

for all $\nu \in [0,1]$ and $(\mathrm{u},\mathrm{v}) \in \Omega_0$.

Firstly, we will prove that $\mathcal{P}(\mathrm{u}_1,\mathrm{v}_1) + \mathcal{Q}(\mathrm{u}_2,\mathrm{v}_2) \in \Omega_0$ for all $(\mathrm{u}_1,\mathrm{v}_1)$, $(\mathrm{u}_2,\mathrm{v}_2) \in \Omega_0$. For this, let $(\mathrm{u}_1,\mathrm{v}_1)$, $(\mathrm{u}_2,\mathrm{v}_2) \in \Omega_0$. Then, we find

$$\begin{aligned}
&|\mathcal{P}_1(\mathrm{u}_1,\mathrm{v}_1)(\nu) + \mathcal{Q}_1(\mathrm{u}_2,\mathrm{v}_2)(\nu)| \le \frac{1}{\Gamma_{\mathrm{q}}(\alpha)}\int_0^{\nu}(\nu - \mathrm{q}\tau)^{(\alpha-1)}|\mathcal{F}_{\mathrm{u}_1\mathrm{v}_1}(\nu)|\, d_{\mathrm{q}}\nu\\
&+\frac{\nu^{\alpha-1}}{|\Delta|}\Bigg[\frac{|\Lambda_4|}{\Gamma_{\mathrm{q}}(\alpha-\varsigma)}\int_0^1(1-\mathrm{q}\tau)^{(\alpha-\varsigma-1)}|\mathcal{F}_{\mathrm{u}_2\mathrm{v}_2}(\tau)|\, d_{\mathrm{q}}\tau\\
&+|\Lambda_4|\sum_{i=1}^{\mathfrak{a}}\frac{|a_i|}{\Gamma_{\mathrm{q}}(\alpha-\varrho_i)}\int_0^{\xi_i}(\xi_i - \mathrm{q}\tau)^{(\alpha-\varrho_i-1)}|\mathcal{F}_{\mathrm{u}_2\mathrm{v}_2}(\tau)|\, d_{\mathrm{q}}\tau\\
&+|\Lambda_2|\sum_{i=1}^{\mathfrak{c}}\frac{|c_i|}{\Gamma_{\mathrm{q}}(\alpha-\eta_i)}\int_0^{\zeta_i}(\zeta_i - \mathrm{q}\tau)^{(\alpha-\eta_i-1)}|\mathcal{F}_{\mathrm{u}_2\mathrm{v}_2}(\tau)|\, d_{\mathrm{q}}\tau\Bigg]\\
&+\frac{\nu^{\alpha-1}}{|\Delta|}\Bigg[|\Lambda_4|\sum_{i=1}^{\mathfrak{b}}\frac{|b_i|}{\Gamma_{\mathrm{q}}(\beta-\sigma_i)}\int_0^{\omega_i}(\omega_i - \mathrm{q}\tau)^{(\beta-\sigma_i-1)}|\mathcal{G}_{\mathrm{u}_2\mathrm{v}_2}(\tau)|\, d_{\mathrm{q}}\tau\\
&+\frac{|\Lambda_2|}{\Gamma_{\mathrm{q}}(\beta-\vartheta)}\int_0^1(1-\mathrm{q}\tau)^{(\beta-\vartheta-1)}|\mathcal{G}_{\mathrm{u}_2\mathrm{v}_2}(\tau)|\, d_{\mathrm{q}}\tau\\
&+|\Lambda_2|\sum_{i=1}^{\mathfrak{d}}\frac{|d_i|}{\Gamma_{\mathrm{q}}(\beta-\rho_i)}\int_0^{\theta_i}(\theta_i - \mathrm{q}\tau)^{(\beta-\rho_i-1)}|\mathcal{G}_{\mathrm{u}_2\mathrm{v}_2}(\tau)|\, d_{\mathrm{q}}\tau\Bigg]\\
&\le \|\Phi\|\Bigg\{\frac{1}{\Gamma_{\mathrm{q}}(\alpha)}\int_0^{\nu}(\nu-\mathrm{q}\tau)^{(\alpha-1)}\, d_{\mathrm{q}}\tau + \frac{1}{|\Delta|}\Bigg[\frac{|\Lambda_4|}{\Gamma_{\mathrm{q}}(\alpha-\varsigma)}\int_0^1(1-\mathrm{q}\tau)^{(\alpha-\varsigma-1)}\, d_{\mathrm{q}}\tau\\
&+|\Lambda_4|\sum_{i=1}^{\mathfrak{a}}\frac{|a_i|}{\Gamma_{\mathrm{q}}(\alpha-\varrho_i)}\int_0^{\xi_i}(\xi_i-\mathrm{q}\tau)^{(\alpha-\varrho_i-1)}\, d_{\mathrm{q}}\tau\\
&+|\Lambda_2|\sum_{i=1}^{\mathfrak{c}}\frac{|c_i|}{\Gamma_{\mathrm{q}}(\alpha-\eta_i)}\int_0^{\zeta_i}(\zeta_i-\mathrm{q}\tau)^{(\alpha-\eta_i-1)}\, d_{\mathrm{q}}\tau\Bigg]\Bigg\}\\
&+\|\Psi\|\frac{1}{|\Delta|}\Bigg[|\Lambda_4|\sum_{i=1}^{\mathfrak{b}}\frac{|b_i|}{\Gamma_{\mathrm{q}}(\beta-\sigma_i)}\int_0^{\omega_i}(\omega_i-\mathrm{q}\tau)^{(\beta-\sigma_i-1)}\, d_{\mathrm{q}}\tau\\
&+\frac{|\Lambda_2|}{\Gamma_{\mathrm{q}}(\beta-\vartheta)}\int_0^1(1-\mathrm{q}\tau)^{(\beta-\vartheta-1)}\, d_{\mathrm{q}}\tau\\
&+|\Lambda_2|\sum_{i=1}^{\mathfrak{d}}\frac{|d_i|}{\Gamma_{\mathrm{q}}(\beta-\rho_i)}\int_0^{\theta_i}(\theta_i-\mathrm{q}\tau)^{(\beta-\rho_i-1)}\, d_{\mathrm{q}}\tau\Bigg]\\
&= \|\Phi\|\Bigg\{\frac{\nu^{\alpha}}{\Gamma_{\mathrm{q}}(\alpha+1)} + \frac{1}{|\Delta|}\Bigg[\frac{|\Lambda_4|}{\Gamma_{\mathrm{q}}(\alpha-\varsigma+1)} + |\Lambda_4|\sum_{i=1}^{\mathfrak{a}}|a_i|\frac{\xi_i^{\alpha-\varrho_i}}{\Gamma_{\mathrm{q}}(\alpha-\varrho_i+1)}\\
&+|\Lambda_2|\sum_{i=1}^{\mathfrak{c}}|c_i|\frac{\zeta_i^{\alpha-\eta_i}}{\Gamma_{\mathrm{q}}(\alpha-\eta_i+1)}\Bigg]\Bigg\}\\
&+\|\Psi\|\frac{1}{|\Delta|}\Bigg[|\Lambda_4|\sum_{i=1}^{\mathfrak{b}}|b_i|\frac{\omega_i^{\beta-\sigma_i}}{\Gamma_{\mathrm{q}}(\beta-\sigma_i+1)} + |\Lambda_2|\frac{1}{\Gamma_{\mathrm{q}}(\beta-\vartheta+1)}\\
&+|\Lambda_2|\sum_{i=1}^{\mathfrak{d}}|d_i|\frac{\theta_i^{\beta-\rho_i}}{\Gamma_{\mathrm{q}}(\beta-\rho_i+1)}\Bigg] \le \|\Phi\|\mathrm{Y}_1 + \|\Psi\|\mathrm{Y}_2,\ \ \forall\, \nu \in [0,1].
\end{aligned} \tag{35}$$

In a similar manner, we obtain

$$|\mathcal{P}_2(\mathrm{u}_1,\mathrm{v}_1)(\nu) + \mathcal{Q}_2(\mathrm{u}_2,\mathrm{v}_2)(\nu)| \le \|\Phi\|\mathrm{Y}_3 + \|\Psi\|\mathrm{Y}_4,\ \ \forall\, \nu \in [0,1]. \tag{36}$$

Therefore, we deduce

$$\begin{aligned} &\|\mathcal{P}(u_1,v_1)+\mathcal{Q}(u_2,v_2)\|_{\mathcal{V}} = \|\mathcal{P}_1(u_1,v_1)+\mathcal{Q}_1(u_2,v_2)\| + \|\mathcal{P}_2(u_1,v_1)+\mathcal{Q}_2(u_2,v_2)\| \\ &\le (\Upsilon_1+\Upsilon_3)\|\Phi\| + (\Upsilon_2+\Upsilon_4)\|\Psi\| \le r, \end{aligned} \tag{37}$$

that is, $\mathcal{P}(u_1,v_1)+\mathcal{Q}(u_2,v_2) \in \Omega_0$.

Subsequently, we will show that operator $\mathcal{Q}$ is a contraction mapping. Indeed, for all (u_1,v_1), $(u_2,v_2) \in \Omega_0$, by using assumption $(J2)$, we obtain

$$\begin{aligned} &|\mathcal{Q}_1(u_1,v_1)(\nu) - \mathcal{Q}_1(u_2,v_2)(\nu)| \le C_{uv}\left(\Upsilon_1 - \frac{1}{\Gamma_q(\alpha+1)}\right) + D_{uv}\Upsilon_2, \ \forall \nu \in [0,1], \\ &|\mathcal{Q}_2(u_1,v_1)(\nu) - \mathcal{Q}_2(u_2,v_2)(\nu)| \le C_{uv}\Upsilon_3 + D_{uv}\left(\Upsilon_4 - \frac{1}{\Gamma_q(\beta+1)}\right), \ \forall \nu \in [0,1]. \end{aligned} \tag{38}$$

Therefore, we find

$$\begin{aligned} &\|\mathcal{Q}(u_1,v_1) - \mathcal{Q}(u_2,v_2)\|_{\mathcal{V}} \\ &\le C_{uv}\left(\Upsilon_1+\Upsilon_3 - \frac{1}{\Gamma_q(\alpha+1)}\right) + D_{uv}\left(\Upsilon_2+\Upsilon_4 - \frac{1}{\Gamma_q(\beta+1)}\right) \\ &= \left[\left(\mathfrak{h}_1^* + \frac{\mathfrak{h}_3^*}{\Gamma_q(\delta_1+1)}\right)\|u_1-u_2\| + \left(\mathfrak{h}_2^* + \frac{\mathfrak{h}_4^*}{\Gamma_q(\gamma_1+1)}\right)\|v_1-v_2\|\right] \\ &\quad \times\left(\Upsilon_1+\Upsilon_3 - \frac{1}{\Gamma_q(\alpha+1)}\right) \\ &\quad + \left[\left(\mathfrak{k}_1^* + \frac{\mathfrak{k}_3^*}{\Gamma_q(\delta_2+1)}\right)\|u_1-u_2\| + \left(\mathfrak{k}_2^* + \frac{\mathfrak{k}_4^*}{\Gamma_q(\gamma_2+1)}\right)\|v_1-v_2\|\right] \\ &\quad \times\left(\Upsilon_2+\Upsilon_4 - \frac{1}{\Gamma_q(\beta+1)}\right) \\ &= \left[\left(\mathfrak{h}_1^* + \frac{\mathfrak{h}_3^*}{\Gamma_q(\delta_1+1)}\right)\left(\Upsilon_1+\Upsilon_3 - \frac{1}{\Gamma_q(\alpha+1)}\right)\right. \\ &\quad \left. + \left(\mathfrak{k}_1^* + \frac{\mathfrak{k}_3^*}{\Gamma_q(\delta_2+1)}\right)\left(\Upsilon_2+\Upsilon_4 - \frac{1}{\Gamma_q(\beta+1)}\right)\right]\|u_1-u_2\| \\ &\quad + \left[\left(\mathfrak{h}_2^* + \frac{\mathfrak{h}_4^*}{\Gamma_q(\gamma_1+1)}\right)\left(\Upsilon_1+\Upsilon_3 - \frac{1}{\Gamma_q(\alpha+1)}\right)\right. \\ &\quad \left. + \left(\mathfrak{k}_2^* + \frac{\mathfrak{k}_4^*}{\Gamma_q(\gamma_2+1)}\right)\left(\Upsilon_2+\Upsilon_4 - \frac{1}{\Gamma_q(\beta+1)}\right)\right]\|v_1-v_2\| \\ &= \mathfrak{L}_1\|u_1-u_2\| + \mathfrak{L}_2\|v_1-v_2\| \le \mathfrak{L}_0\|(u_1,v_1)-(u_2,v_2)\|_{\mathcal{V}}. \end{aligned} \tag{39}$$

By condition (31), we conclude that operator $\mathcal{Q}$ is a contraction.

The operators $\mathcal{P}_1$, $\mathcal{P}_2$ and $\mathcal{P}$ are continuous by the continuity of functions $\mathcal{F}$ and $\mathcal{G}$. Moreover, $\mathcal{P}$ is uniformly bounded on Ω_0, because

$$\begin{aligned} &\|\mathcal{P}_1(u,v)\| \le \frac{1}{\Gamma_q(\alpha)} \sup_{\nu\in[0,1]}\left(\int_0^\nu (\nu - q\tau)^{(\alpha-1)}|\mathcal{F}_{uv}(\tau)|\, d_q\tau\right) \\ &\le \sup_{\nu\in[0,1]}\Phi(\nu)\frac{1}{\Gamma_q(\alpha)}\sup_{\nu\in[0,1]}\int_0^\nu (\nu - q\tau)^{(\alpha-1)}\, d_q\tau \\ &= \|\Phi\|\sup_{\nu\in[0,1]}\frac{\nu^\alpha}{\Gamma_q(\alpha+1)} = \frac{1}{\Gamma_q(\alpha+1)}\|\Phi\|, \ \forall (u,v) \in \Omega_0, \\ &\|\mathcal{P}_2(u,v)\| \le \frac{1}{\Gamma_q(\beta)} \sup_{\nu\in[0,1]}\left(\int_0^\nu (\nu - q\tau)^{(\beta-1)}|\mathcal{G}_{uv}(\tau)|\, d_q\tau\right) \\ &\le \sup_{\nu\in[0,1]}\Psi(\nu)\frac{1}{\Gamma_q(\beta)}\sup_{\nu\in[0,1]}\int_0^\nu (\nu - q\tau)^{(\beta-1)}\, d_q\tau \\ &= \|\Psi\|\sup_{\nu\in[0,1]}\frac{\nu^\beta}{\Gamma_q(\beta+1)} = \frac{1}{\Gamma_q(\beta+1)}\|\Psi\|, \ \forall (u,v) \in \Omega_0, \end{aligned} \tag{40}$$

and then

$$\|\mathcal{P}(\mathrm{u},\mathrm{v})\| \leq \frac{1}{\Gamma_{\mathrm{q}}(\alpha+1)}\|\Phi\| + \frac{1}{\Gamma_{\mathrm{q}}(\beta+1)}\|\Psi\|, \ \forall (\mathrm{u},\mathrm{v}) \in \Omega_0. \tag{41}$$

In the last part of the proof, we will prove that $\mathcal{P}$ is compact. Let $\nu_1, \nu_2 \in [0,1], \nu_1 < \nu_2$. Then for all $(\mathrm{u},\mathrm{v}) \in \Omega_0$, we obtain

$$\begin{aligned}
&|\mathcal{P}_1(\mathrm{u},\mathrm{v})(\nu_2) - \mathcal{P}_1(\mathrm{u},\mathrm{v})(\nu_1)| \\
&= \left| -\frac{1}{\Gamma_{\mathrm{q}}(\alpha)} \int_0^{\nu_2} (\nu_2 - \mathrm{q}\tau)^{(\alpha-1)} \mathcal{F}_{\mathrm{uv}}(\tau)\, d_{\mathrm{q}}\tau + \frac{1}{\Gamma_{\mathrm{q}}(\alpha)} \int_0^{\nu_1} (\nu_1 - \mathrm{q}\tau)^{(\alpha-1)} \mathcal{F}_{\mathrm{uv}}(\tau)\, d_{\mathrm{q}}\tau \right| \\
&\leq \frac{1}{\Gamma_{\mathrm{q}}(\alpha)} \int_0^{\nu_1} \left[(\nu_2 - \mathrm{q}\tau)^{(\alpha-1)} - (\nu_1 - \mathrm{q}\tau)^{(\alpha-1)} \right] |\mathcal{F}_{\mathrm{uv}}(\tau)|\, d_{\mathrm{q}}\tau \\
&\quad + \frac{1}{\Gamma_{\mathrm{q}}(\alpha)} \int_{\nu_1}^{\nu_2} (\nu_2 - \mathrm{q}\tau)^{(\alpha-1)} |\mathcal{F}_{\mathrm{uv}}(\tau)|\, d_{\mathrm{q}}\tau \\
&\leq \|\Phi\| \left\{ \frac{1}{\Gamma_{\mathrm{q}}(\alpha)} \int_0^{\nu_1} \left[(\nu_2 - \mathrm{q}\tau)^{(\alpha-1)} - (\nu_1 - \mathrm{q}\tau)^{(\alpha-1)} \right] d_{\mathrm{q}}\tau \right. \\
&\quad \left. + \frac{1}{\Gamma_{\mathrm{q}}(\alpha)} \int_{\nu_1}^{\nu_2} (\nu_2 - \mathrm{q}\tau)^{(\alpha-1)}\, d_{\mathrm{q}}\tau \right\} \\
&= \|\Phi\| \frac{1}{\Gamma_{\mathrm{q}}(\alpha)} \left(\int_0^{\nu_2} (\nu_2 - \mathrm{q}\tau)^{(\alpha-1)}\, d_{\mathrm{q}}\tau - \int_0^{\nu_1} (\nu_1 - \mathrm{q}\tau)^{(\alpha-1)}\, d_{\mathrm{q}}\tau \right) \\
&= \|\Phi\| \frac{1}{\Gamma_{\mathrm{q}}(\alpha+1)} (\nu_2^{\alpha} - \nu_1^{\alpha}),
\end{aligned} \tag{42}$$

which tends to 0 as $\nu_2 \to \nu_1$, independently of $(\mathrm{u},\mathrm{v}) \in \Omega_0$.

In a similar manner, we find

$$|\mathcal{P}_2(\mathrm{u},\mathrm{v})(\nu_2) - \mathcal{P}_2(\mathrm{u},\mathrm{v})(\nu_1)| \leq \|\Psi\| \frac{1}{\Gamma_{\mathrm{q}}(\beta+1)} \left(\nu_2^{\beta} - \nu_1^{\beta} \right), \tag{43}$$

which tends to 0 as $\nu_2 \to \nu_1$, independently of $(\mathrm{u},\mathrm{v}) \in \Omega_0$.

Therefore, the operators $\mathcal{P}_1$, $\mathcal{P}_2$ and $\mathcal{P}$ are equicontinuous. Using the Arzela–Ascoli theorem, we deduce that $\mathcal{P}$ is compact on Ω_0. Then, by the Krasnosel'skii fixed point theorem (see [33]), we conclude that problem (1), (2) has at least one solution $(\mathrm{u}(\nu), \mathrm{v}(\nu))$, $\nu \in [0,1]$. □

Theorem 3. *Suppose that* $(J1)$ *holds and the functions* $\mathcal{F}, \mathcal{G} : [0,1] \times \mathbb{R}^4 \to \mathbb{R}$ *are continuous and satisfy the assumptions* $(J2)$ *and* $(J3)$. *If*

$$\mathfrak{M}_0 < 1, \tag{44}$$

where $\mathfrak{M}_0 = \max\{\mathfrak{M}_1, \mathfrak{M}_2\}$ *with*

$$\begin{aligned}
\mathfrak{M}_1 &= \frac{1}{\Gamma_{\mathrm{q}}(\alpha+1)} \left(\mathfrak{h}_1^* + \frac{\mathfrak{h}_3^*}{\Gamma_{\mathrm{q}}(\delta_1+1)} \right) + \frac{1}{\Gamma_{\mathrm{q}}(\beta+1)} \left(\mathfrak{k}_1^* + \frac{\mathfrak{k}_3^*}{\Gamma_{\mathrm{q}}(\delta_2+1)} \right), \\
\mathfrak{M}_2 &= \frac{1}{\Gamma_{\mathrm{q}}(\alpha+1)} \left(\mathfrak{h}_2^* + \frac{\mathfrak{h}_4^*}{\Gamma_{\mathrm{q}}(\gamma_1+1)} \right) + \frac{1}{\Gamma_{\mathrm{q}}(\beta+1)} \left(\mathfrak{k}_2^* + \frac{\mathfrak{k}_4^*}{\Gamma_{\mathrm{q}}(\gamma_2+1)} \right),
\end{aligned} \tag{45}$$

then problem (1), (2) has at least one solution $(\mathrm{u}(\nu), \mathrm{v}(\nu))$, $\nu \in [0,1]$.

Proof. We consider again, similar to the proof of Theorem 2, the positive number $r \geq (\Upsilon_1 + \Upsilon_3)\|\Phi\| + (\Upsilon_2 + \Upsilon_4)\|\Psi\|$, and the closed set $\Omega_0 = \{(\mathrm{u},\mathrm{v}) \in \mathcal{V},\ \|(\mathrm{u},\mathrm{v})\|_{\mathcal{V}} \leq r\}$. We also split the operator $\mathcal{E}$ defined on Ω_0 as $\mathcal{E} = \mathcal{P} + \mathcal{Q}$, $\mathcal{P} = (\mathcal{P}_1, \mathcal{P}_2)$, $\mathcal{Q} = (\mathcal{Q}_1, \mathcal{Q}_2)$, where $\mathcal{P}_i$, $\mathcal{Q}_i$, $i = 1,2$ are given by (34). For $(\mathrm{u}_1, \mathrm{v}_1), (\mathrm{u}_2, \mathrm{v}_2) \in \Omega_0$, we deduce, as in the first part of the proof of Theorem 2, that $\|\mathcal{P}(\mathrm{u}_1, \mathrm{v}_1) + \mathcal{Q}(\mathrm{u}_2, \mathrm{v}_2)\|_{\mathcal{V}} \leq r$.

In what follows we will show that the operator $\mathcal{P}$ is a contraction. Indeed, for (u_1, v_1), $(u_2, v_2) \in \Omega_0$, we obtain

$$
\begin{aligned}
&|\mathcal{P}_1(u_1,v_1)(\nu) - \mathcal{P}_1(u_2,v_2)(\nu)| \\
&= \left| -\frac{1}{\Gamma_q(\alpha)} \int_0^\nu (\nu - q\tau)^{(\alpha-1)} \mathcal{F}_{u_1v_1}(\tau)\, d_q\tau + \frac{1}{\Gamma_q(\alpha)} \int_0^\nu (\nu - q\tau)^{(\alpha-1)} \mathcal{F}_{u_2v_2}(\tau)\, d_q\tau \right| \\
&\leq \frac{1}{\Gamma_q(\alpha)} \int_0^\nu (\nu - q\tau)^{(\alpha-1)} |\mathcal{F}_{u_1v_1}(\tau) - \mathcal{F}_{u_2v_2}(\tau)|\, d_q\tau \\
&\leq C_{uv} \frac{1}{\Gamma_q(\alpha)} \int_0^\nu (\nu - q\tau)^{(\alpha-1)}\, d_q\tau = C_{uv} \frac{\nu^\alpha}{\Gamma_q(\alpha+1)} \leq \frac{C_{uv}}{\Gamma_q(\alpha+1)}, \quad \forall \nu \in [0,1], \\
&|\mathcal{P}_2(u_1,v_1)(\nu) - \mathcal{P}_2(u_2,v_2)(\nu)| \\
&= \left| -\frac{1}{\Gamma_q(\beta)} \int_0^\nu (\nu - q\tau)^{(\beta-1)} \mathcal{G}_{u_1v_1}(\tau)\, d_q\tau + \frac{1}{\Gamma_q(\beta)} \int_0^\nu (\nu - q\tau)^{(\beta-1)} \mathcal{G}_{u_2v_2}(\tau)\, d_q\tau \right| \\
&\leq \frac{1}{\Gamma_q(\beta)} \int_0^\nu (\nu - q\tau)^{(\beta-1)} |\mathcal{G}_{u_1v_1}(\tau) - \mathcal{G}_{u_2v_2}(\tau)|\, d_q\tau \\
&\leq D_{uv} \frac{1}{\Gamma_q(\beta)} \int_0^\nu (\nu - q\tau)^{(\beta-1)}\, d_q\tau = D_{uv} \frac{\nu^\beta}{\Gamma_q(\beta+1)} \leq \frac{D_{uv}}{\Gamma_q(\beta+1)}, \quad \forall \nu \in [0,1],
\end{aligned}
\tag{46}
$$

where C_{uv}, D_{uv} are given by (23).

So we conclude that

$$
\begin{aligned}
&\|\mathcal{P}(u_1,v_1) - \mathcal{P}(u_2,v_2)\|_\mathcal{V} \\
&\leq \left[\frac{1}{\Gamma_q(\alpha+1)} \left(\mathfrak{h}_1^* + \frac{\mathfrak{h}_3^*}{\Gamma_q(\delta_1+1)} \right) + \frac{1}{\Gamma_q(\beta+1)} \left(\mathfrak{k}_1^* + \frac{\mathfrak{k}_3^*}{\Gamma_q(\delta_2+1)} \right) \right] \|u_1 - u_2\| \\
&\quad + \left[\frac{1}{\Gamma_q(\alpha+1)} \left(\mathfrak{h}_2^* + \frac{\mathfrak{h}_4^*}{\Gamma_q(\gamma_1+1)} \right) + \frac{1}{\Gamma_q(\beta+1)} \left(\mathfrak{k}_2^* + \frac{\mathfrak{k}_4^*}{\Gamma_q(\gamma_2+1)} \right) \right] \|v_1 - v_2\| \\
&= \mathcal{M}_1 \|u_1 - u_2\| + \mathcal{M}_2 \|v_1 - v_2\| \leq \mathcal{M}_0 \|(u_1,v_1) - (u_2,v_2)\|_\mathcal{V},
\end{aligned}
\tag{47}
$$

that is, by (44), the operator $\mathcal{P}$ is a contraction.

By the continuity of the functions $\mathcal{F}$ and $\mathcal{G}$, the operators $\mathcal{Q}_1$, $\mathcal{Q}_2$ and $\mathcal{Q}$ are continuous. In addition, $\mathcal{Q}$ is uniformly bounded on Ω_0, because we have

$$
\begin{aligned}
|\mathcal{Q}_1(u,v)(\nu)| &\leq \frac{1}{|\Delta|} \left[\frac{|\Lambda_4|}{\Gamma_q(\alpha-\varsigma)} \int_0^1 (1 - q\tau)^{(\alpha-\varsigma-1)} |\mathcal{F}_{uv}(\tau)|\, d_q\tau \right. \\
&\quad + |\Lambda_4| \sum_{i=1}^{\mathfrak{a}} \frac{|a_i|}{\Gamma_q(\alpha-\varrho_i)} \int_0^{\xi_i} (\xi_i - q\tau)^{(\alpha-\varrho_i-1)} |\mathcal{F}_{uv}(\tau)|\, d_q\tau \\
&\quad \left. + |\Lambda_2| \sum_{i=1}^{\mathfrak{c}} \frac{|c_i|}{\Gamma_q(\alpha-\eta_i)} \int_0^{\zeta_i} (\zeta_i - q\tau)^{(\alpha-\eta_i-1)} |\mathcal{F}_{uv}(\tau)|\, d_q\tau \right] \\
&\quad + \frac{1}{|\Delta|} \left[|\Lambda_4| \sum_{i=1}^{\mathfrak{b}} \frac{|b_i|}{\Gamma_q(\beta-\sigma_i)} \int_0^{\omega_i} (\omega_i - q\tau)^{(\beta-\sigma_i-1)} |\mathcal{G}_{uv}(\tau)|\, d_q\tau \right. \\
&\quad + \frac{|\Lambda_2|}{\Gamma_q(\beta-\vartheta)} \int_0^1 (1 - q\tau)^{(\beta-\vartheta-1)} |\mathcal{G}_{uv}(\tau)|\, d_q\tau \\
&\quad \left. + |\Lambda_2| \sum_{i=1}^{\mathfrak{d}} \frac{|d_i|}{\Gamma_q(\beta-\rho_i)} \int_0^{\theta_i} (\theta_i - q\tau)^{(\beta-\rho_i-1)} |\mathcal{G}_{uv}(\tau)|\, d_q\tau \right] \\
&\leq \|\Phi\| \frac{1}{|\Delta|} \left[\frac{|\Lambda_4|}{\Gamma_q(\alpha-\varsigma+1)} + |\Lambda_4| \sum_{i=1}^{\mathfrak{a}} |a_i| \frac{\xi_i^{\alpha-\varrho_i}}{\Gamma_q(\alpha-\varrho_i+1)} \right. \\
&\quad \left. + |\Lambda_2| \sum_{i=1}^{\mathfrak{c}} |c_i| \frac{\zeta_i^{\alpha-\eta_i}}{\Gamma_q(\alpha-\eta_i+1)} \right] \\
&\quad + \|\Psi\| \frac{1}{|\Delta|} \left[|\Lambda_4| \sum_{i=1}^{\mathfrak{b}} |b_i| \frac{\omega_i^{\beta-\sigma_i}}{\Gamma_q(\beta-\sigma_i+1)} + \frac{|\Lambda_2|}{\Gamma_q(\beta-\vartheta+1)} \right. \\
&\quad \left. + |\Lambda_2| \sum_{i=1}^{\mathfrak{d}} |d_i| \frac{\theta_i^{\beta-\rho_i}}{\Gamma_q(\beta-\rho_i+1)} \right] \\
&= \|\Phi\| \left(\Upsilon_1 - \frac{1}{\Gamma_q(\alpha+1)} \right) + \|\Psi\| \Upsilon_2, \quad \forall \nu \in [0,1], \quad (u,v) \in \Omega_0,
\end{aligned}
\tag{48}
$$

and

$$\begin{aligned}
|\mathcal{Q}_2(\mathrm{u},\mathrm{v})(\nu)| \leq \frac{1}{|\Delta|}\Bigg[&|\Lambda_1|\sum_{i=1}^{\mathfrak{c}}\frac{|c_i|}{\Gamma_\mathrm{q}(\alpha-\eta_i)}\int_0^{\zeta_i}(\zeta_i-\mathrm{q}\tau)^{(\alpha-\eta_i-1)}|\mathcal{F}_{\mathrm{uv}}(\tau)|\,d_\mathrm{q}\tau \\
&+|\Lambda_3|\frac{1}{\Gamma_\mathrm{q}(\alpha-\varsigma)}\int_0^1(1-\mathrm{q}\tau)^{(\alpha-\varsigma-1)}|\mathcal{F}_{\mathrm{uv}}(\tau)|\,d_\mathrm{q}\tau \\
&+|\Lambda_3|\sum_{i=1}^{\mathfrak{a}}|a_i|\frac{1}{\Gamma_\mathrm{q}(\alpha-\varrho_i)}\int_0^{\xi_i}(\xi_i-\mathrm{q}\tau)^{(\alpha-\varrho_i-1)}|\mathcal{F}_{\mathrm{uv}}(\tau)|\,d_\mathrm{q}\tau\Bigg] \\
&+\frac{1}{|\Delta|}\Bigg[\frac{|\Lambda_1|}{\Gamma_\mathrm{q}(\beta-\vartheta)}\int_0^1(1-\mathrm{q}\tau)^{(\beta-\vartheta-1)}|\mathcal{G}_{\mathrm{uv}}(\tau)|\,d_\mathrm{q}\tau \\
&+|\Lambda_1|\sum_{i=1}^{\mathfrak{d}}\frac{|d_i|}{\Gamma_\mathrm{q}(\beta-\rho_i)}\int_0^{\theta_i}(\theta_i-\mathrm{q}\tau)^{(\beta-\rho_i-1)}|\mathcal{G}_{\mathrm{uv}}(\tau)|\,d_\mathrm{q}\tau \\
&+|\Lambda_3|\sum_{i=1}^{\mathfrak{b}}|b_i|\frac{1}{\Gamma_\mathrm{q}(\beta-\sigma_i)}\int_0^{\omega_i}(\omega_i-\mathrm{q}\tau)^{(\beta-\sigma_i-1)}|\mathcal{G}_{\mathrm{uv}}(\tau)|\,d_\mathrm{q}\tau\Bigg] \\
\leq \|\Phi\|\frac{1}{|\Delta|}\Bigg[&|\Lambda_1|\sum_{i=1}^{\mathfrak{c}}|c_i|\frac{\zeta_i^{\alpha-\eta_i}}{\Gamma_\mathrm{q}(\alpha-\eta_i+1)}+\frac{|\Lambda_3|}{\Gamma_\mathrm{q}(\alpha-\varsigma+1)} \\
&+|\Lambda_3|\sum_{i=1}^{\mathfrak{a}}|a_i|\frac{\xi_i^{\alpha-\varrho_i}}{\Gamma_\mathrm{q}(\alpha-\varrho_i+1)}\Bigg] \\
&+\|\Psi\|\frac{1}{|\Delta|}\Bigg[\frac{|\Lambda_1|}{\Gamma_\mathrm{q}(\beta-\vartheta+1)}+|\Lambda_1|\sum_{i=1}^{\mathfrak{d}}|d_i|\frac{\theta_i^{\beta-\rho_i}}{\Gamma_\mathrm{q}(\beta-\rho_i+1)} \\
&+|\Lambda_3|\sum_{i=1}^{\mathfrak{b}}|b_i|\frac{\omega_i^{\beta-\sigma_i}}{\Gamma_\mathrm{q}(\beta-\sigma_i+1)}\Bigg] \\
= \|\Phi\|\mathrm{Y}_3+\|\Psi\|&\left(\mathrm{Y}_4-\frac{1}{\Gamma_\mathrm{q}(\beta+1)}\right),\ \forall\nu\in[0,1],\ (\mathrm{u},\mathrm{v})\in\Omega_0.
\end{aligned} \tag{49}$$

Therefore we deduce

$$\begin{aligned}
&\|\mathcal{Q}_1(\mathrm{u},\mathrm{v})\|\leq\|\Phi\|\left(\mathrm{Y}_1-\frac{1}{\Gamma_\mathrm{q}(\alpha+1)}\right)+\|\Psi\|\mathrm{Y}_2,\ \forall(\mathrm{u},\mathrm{v})\in\Omega_0, \\
&\|\mathcal{Q}_2(\mathrm{u},\mathrm{v})\|\leq\|\Phi\|\mathrm{Y}_3+\|\Psi\|\left(\mathrm{Y}_4-\frac{1}{\Gamma_\mathrm{q}(\beta+1)}\right),\ \forall(\mathrm{u},\mathrm{v})\in\Omega_0,
\end{aligned} \tag{50}$$

and then

$$\|\mathcal{Q}(\mathrm{u},\mathrm{v})\|_\mathcal{V}\leq\|\Phi\|\left(\mathrm{Y}_1+\mathrm{Y}_3-\frac{1}{\Gamma_\mathrm{q}(\alpha+1)}\right)+\|\Psi\|\left(\mathrm{Y}_2+\mathrm{Y}_4-\frac{1}{\Gamma_\mathrm{q}(\beta+1)}\right),\ \forall(\mathrm{u},\mathrm{v})\in\Omega_0, \tag{51}$$

that is, $\mathcal{Q}$ is uniformly bounded on Ω_0.

We finally prove that operator $\mathcal{Q}$ is compact. Let $\nu_1,\nu_2\in[0,1]$, $\nu_1<\nu_2$. Then for all $(\mathrm{u},\mathrm{v})\in\Omega_0$, we find

$$\begin{aligned}
&|\mathcal{Q}_1(\mathrm{u},\mathrm{v})(\nu_2)-\mathcal{Q}_1(\mathrm{u},\mathrm{v})(\nu_1)| \\
&\leq\frac{\nu_2^{\alpha-1}-\nu_1^{\alpha-1}}{|\Delta|}\|\Phi\|\Bigg[\frac{|\Lambda_4|}{\Gamma_\mathrm{q}(\alpha-\varsigma)}\int_0^1(1-\mathrm{q}\tau)^{(\alpha-\varsigma-1)}\,d_\mathrm{q}\tau \\
&\quad+|\Lambda_4|\sum_{i=1}^{\mathfrak{a}}\frac{|a_i|}{\Gamma_\mathrm{q}(\alpha-\varrho_i)}\int_0^{\xi_i}(\xi_i-\mathrm{q}\tau)^{(\alpha-\varrho_i-1)}\,d_\mathrm{q}\tau \\
&\quad+|\Lambda_2|\sum_{i=1}^{\mathfrak{c}}\frac{|c_i|}{\Gamma_\mathrm{q}(\alpha-\eta_i)}\int_0^{\zeta_i}(\zeta_i-\mathrm{q}\tau)^{(\alpha-\eta_i-1)}\,d_\mathrm{q}\tau\Bigg] \\
&\quad+\frac{\nu_2^{\alpha-1}-\nu_1^{\alpha-1}}{|\Delta|}\|\Psi\|\Bigg[|\Lambda_4|\sum_{i=1}^{\mathfrak{b}}\frac{|b_i|}{\Gamma_\mathrm{q}(\beta-\sigma_i)}\int_0^{\omega_i}(\omega_i-\mathrm{q}\tau)^{(\beta-\sigma_i-1)}\,d_\mathrm{q}\tau \\
&\quad+\frac{|\Lambda_2|}{\Gamma_\mathrm{q}(\beta-\vartheta)}\int_0^1(1-\mathrm{q}\tau)^{(\beta-\vartheta-1)}\,d_\mathrm{q}\tau
\end{aligned} \tag{52}$$

$$+|\Lambda_2|\sum_{i=1}^{\mathfrak{d}}\frac{|d_i|}{\Gamma_q(\beta-\rho_i)}\int_0^{\theta_i}(\theta_i-q\tau)^{(\beta-\rho_i-1)}\,d_q\tau\Bigg]$$
$$=\frac{\nu_2^{\alpha-1}-\nu_1^{\alpha-1}}{|\Delta|}\|\Phi\|\Bigg[\frac{|\Lambda_4|}{\Gamma_q(\alpha-\varsigma+1)}+|\Lambda_4|\sum_{i=1}^{\mathfrak{a}}|a_i|\frac{\xi_i^{\alpha-\varrho_i}}{\Gamma_q(\alpha-\varrho_i+1)}$$
$$+|\Lambda_2|\sum_{i=1}^{\mathfrak{c}}|c_i|\frac{\zeta_i^{\alpha-\eta_i}}{\Gamma_q(\alpha-\eta_i+1)}\Bigg]$$
$$+\frac{\nu_2^{\alpha-1}-\nu_1^{\alpha-1}}{|\Delta|}\|\Psi\|\Bigg[|\Lambda_4|\sum_{i=1}^{\mathfrak{b}}|b_i|\frac{\omega_i^{\beta-\sigma_i}}{\Gamma_q(\beta-\sigma_i+1)}+\frac{|\Lambda_2|}{\Gamma_q(\beta-\vartheta+1)}$$
$$+|\Lambda_2|\sum_{i=1}^{\mathfrak{d}}|d_i|\frac{\theta_i^{\beta-\rho_i}}{\Gamma_q(\beta-\rho_i+1)}\Bigg]$$
$$=(\nu_2^{\alpha-1}-\nu_1^{\alpha-1})\left[\|\Phi\|\left(\mathrm{Y}_1-\frac{1}{\Gamma_q(\alpha+1)}\right)+\|\Psi\|\mathrm{Y}_2\right],$$

which tends to zero as $\nu_2\to\nu_1$, independently of $(\mathrm{u},\mathrm{v})\in\Omega_0$.

In a similar manner, we obtain

$$\begin{aligned}&|\mathcal{Q}_2(\mathrm{u},\mathrm{v})(\nu_2)-\mathcal{Q}_2(\mathrm{u},\mathrm{v})(\nu_1)|\\&\le(\nu_2^{\beta-1}-\nu_1^{\beta-1})\left[\|\Phi\|\mathrm{Y}_3+\|\Psi\|\left(\mathrm{Y}_4-\frac{1}{\Gamma_q(\beta+1)}\right)\right],\end{aligned}\tag{53}$$

which tends to zero as $\nu_2\to\nu_1$, independently of $(\mathrm{u},\mathrm{v})\in\Omega_0$.

Therefore the operators $\mathcal{Q}_1$, $\mathcal{Q}_2$ and $\mathcal{Q}$ are equicontinuous. Utilizing the Arzela–Ascoli theorem, we ascertain the compactness of $\mathcal{Q}$ on Ω_0. Consequently, employing the Krasnosel'skii fixed-point theorem, we deduce the existence of at least one solution $(\mathrm{u}(\nu),\mathrm{v}(\nu))$ $\nu\in[0,1]$ to problem (1), (2) □

The forthcoming result relies on the Schaefer fixed-point theorem (refer to [34]).

Theorem 4. *Suppose that assumption* $(J1)$ *holds. In addition, we assume that the functions* $\mathcal{F},\mathcal{G}:[0,1]\times\mathbb{R}^4\to\mathbb{R}$ *are continuous and satisfy the condition*

$(J4)$ *There exist positive constants* T_1, T_2 *such that*

$$\begin{aligned}&|\mathcal{F}(\nu,\mathrm{x}_1,\mathrm{x}_2,\mathrm{x}_3,\mathrm{x}_4)|\le T_1,\ \ |\mathcal{G}(\nu,\mathrm{x}_1,\mathrm{x}_2,\mathrm{x}_3,\mathrm{x}_4)|\le T_2,\\&\forall\nu\in[0,1],\ \mathrm{x}_i\in\mathbb{R},\ i=1,\dots,4.\end{aligned}\tag{54}$$

Then, there exists at least one solution $(\mathrm{u}(\nu),\mathrm{v}(\nu))$, $\nu\in[0,1]$ *of problem (1), (2).*

Proof. We prove firstly that operator $\mathcal{E}$ is completely continuous. Operator $\mathcal{E}$ is continuous. Indeed, let $(\mathrm{u}_n,\mathrm{v}_n)\in\mathcal{V}$, $n\in\mathbb{N}$, with $(\mathrm{u}_n,\mathrm{v}_n)\to(\mathrm{u},\mathrm{v})$, as $n\to\infty$ in $\mathcal{V}$. Then, for each $\nu\in[0,1]$, we deduce, as in the proof of Theorem 1, that

$$\begin{aligned}&|\mathcal{E}_1(\mathrm{u}_n,\mathrm{v}_n)(\nu)-\mathcal{E}_1(\mathrm{u},\mathrm{v})(\nu)|\\&\le\frac{1}{\Gamma_q(\alpha)}\int_0^{\nu}(\nu-q\tau)^{(\alpha-1)}|\mathcal{F}_{\mathrm{u}_n\mathrm{v}_n}(\tau)-\mathcal{F}_{\mathrm{uv}}(\tau)|\,d_q\tau\\&+\frac{1}{|\Delta|}\Bigg[\frac{|\Lambda_4|}{\Gamma_q(\alpha-\varsigma)}\int_0^1(1-q\tau)^{(\alpha-\varsigma-1)}|\mathcal{F}_{\mathrm{u}_n\mathrm{v}_n}(\tau)-\mathcal{F}_{\mathrm{uv}}(\tau)|\,d_q\tau\\&+|\Lambda_4|\sum_{i=1}^{\mathfrak{a}}\frac{|a_i|}{\Gamma_q(\alpha-\varrho_i)}\int_0^{\xi_i}(\xi_i-q\tau)^{(\alpha-\varrho_i-1)}|\mathcal{F}_{\mathrm{u}_n\mathrm{v}_n}(\tau)-\mathcal{F}_{\mathrm{uv}}(\tau)|\,d_q\tau\\&+|\Lambda_2|\sum_{i=1}^{\mathfrak{c}}\frac{|c_i|}{\Gamma_q(\alpha-\eta_i)}\int_0^{\zeta_i}(\zeta_i-q\tau)^{(\alpha-\eta_i-1)}|\mathcal{F}_{\mathrm{u}_n\mathrm{v}_n}(\tau)-\mathcal{F}_{\mathrm{uv}}(\tau)|\,d_q\tau\Bigg]\\&+\frac{1}{|\Delta|}\Bigg[|\Lambda_4|\sum_{i=1}^{\mathfrak{b}}\frac{|b_i|}{\Gamma_q(\beta-\sigma_i)}\int_0^{\omega_i}(\omega_i-q\tau)^{(\beta-\sigma_i-1)}|\mathcal{G}_{\mathrm{u}_n\mathrm{v}_n}(\tau)-\mathcal{G}_{\mathrm{uv}}(\tau)|\,d_q\tau\end{aligned}\tag{55}$$

$$+\frac{|\Lambda_2|}{\Gamma_q(\beta-\vartheta)}\int_0^1(1-q\tau)^{(\beta-\vartheta-1)}|\mathcal{G}_{u_nv_n}(\tau)-\mathcal{G}_{uv}(\tau)|\,d_q\tau$$
$$+|\Lambda_2|\sum_{i=1}^{\mathfrak{d}}\frac{|d_i|}{\Gamma_q(\beta-\rho_i)}\int_0^{\theta_i}(\theta_i-q\tau)^{(\beta-\rho_i-1)}|\mathcal{G}_{u_nv_n}(\tau)-\mathcal{G}_{uv}(\tau)|\,d_q\tau\Bigg],$$

and

$$\begin{aligned}
&|\mathcal{E}_2(u_n,v_n)(\nu)-\mathcal{E}_2(u,v)(\nu)|\\
&\leq\frac{1}{|\Delta|}\Bigg[|\Lambda_1|\sum_{i=1}^{\mathfrak{c}}\frac{|c_i|}{\Gamma_q(\alpha-\eta_i)}\int_0^{\zeta_i}(\zeta_i-q\tau)^{(\alpha-\eta_i-1)}|\mathcal{F}_{u_nv_n}(\tau)-\mathcal{F}_{uv}(\tau)|\,d_q\tau\\
&+\frac{|\Lambda_3|}{\Gamma_q(\alpha-\varsigma)}\int_0^1(1-q\tau)^{(\alpha-\varsigma-1)}|\mathcal{F}_{u_nv_n}(\tau)-\mathcal{F}_{uv}(\tau)|\,d_q\tau\\
&+|\Lambda_3|\sum_{i=1}^{\mathfrak{a}}\frac{|a_i|}{\Gamma_q(\alpha-\varrho_i)}\int_0^{\xi_i}(\xi_i-q\tau)^{(\alpha-\varrho_i-1)}|\mathcal{F}_{u_nv_n}(\tau)-\mathcal{F}_{uv}(\tau)|\,d_q\tau\Bigg]\\
&+\frac{1}{\Gamma_q(\beta)}\int_0^{\nu}(\nu-q\tau)^{(\beta-1)}|\mathcal{G}_{u_nv_n}(\tau)-\mathcal{G}_{uv}(\tau)|\,d_q\tau\\
&+\frac{1}{|\Delta|}\Bigg[\frac{|\Lambda_1|}{\Gamma_q(\beta-\vartheta)}\int_0^1(1-q\tau)^{(\beta-\vartheta-1)}|\mathcal{G}_{u_nv_n}(\tau)-\mathcal{G}_{uv}(\tau)|\,d_q\tau\\
&+|\Lambda_1|\sum_{i=1}^{\mathfrak{d}}\frac{|d_i|}{\Gamma_q(\beta-\rho_i)}\int_0^{\theta_i}(\theta_i-q\tau)^{(\beta-\rho_i-1)}|\mathcal{G}_{u_nv_n}(\tau)-\mathcal{G}_{uv}(\tau)|\,d_q\tau\\
&+|\Lambda_3|\sum_{i=1}^{\mathfrak{b}}\frac{|b_i|}{\Gamma_q(\beta-\sigma_i)}\int_0^{\omega_i}(\omega_i-q\tau)^{(\beta-\sigma_i-1)}|\mathcal{G}_{u_nv_n}(\tau)-\mathcal{G}_{uv}(\tau)|\,d_q\tau\Bigg].
\end{aligned}\tag{56}$$

Because $\mathcal{F}$ and $\mathcal{G}$ are continuous, we obtain

$$\begin{aligned}
&|\mathcal{F}_{u_nv_n}(\tau)-\mathcal{F}_{uv}(\tau)|=|\mathcal{F}(\tau,u_n(\tau),v_n(\tau),I_q^{\delta_1}u_n(\tau),I_q^{\gamma_1}v_n(\tau))\\
&\quad-\mathcal{F}(\tau,u(\tau),v(\tau),I_q^{\delta_1}u(\tau),I_q^{\gamma_1}v(\tau))|\to 0,\\
&|\mathcal{G}_{u_nv_n}(\tau)-\mathcal{G}_{uv}(\tau)|=|\mathcal{G}(\tau,u_n(\tau),v_n(\tau),I_q^{\delta_2}u_n(\tau),I_q^{\gamma_2}v_n(\tau))\\
&\quad-\mathcal{G}(\tau,u(\tau),v(\tau),I_q^{\delta_2}u(\tau),I_q^{\gamma_2}v(\tau))|\to 0,
\end{aligned}\tag{57}$$

as $n\to\infty$, for all $\tau\in[0,1]$. Therefore, by the inequalities (55)–(57), we find

$$\|\mathcal{E}_1(u_n,v_n)-\mathcal{E}_1(u,v)\|\to 0,\ \ \|\mathcal{E}_2(u_n,v_n)-\mathcal{E}_2(u,v)\|\to 0,\ \text{ as } n\to\infty,\tag{58}$$

and then

$$\|\mathcal{E}(u_n,v_n)-\mathcal{E}(u,v)\|_{\mathcal{V}}\to 0,\ \text{ as } n\to\infty,\tag{59}$$

that is, $\mathcal{E}$ is a continuous operator.

In what follows, we prove that $\mathcal{E}$ maps bounded sets into bounded sets in $\mathcal{V}$. For $R>0$, let $\Omega_1=\{(u,v)\in\mathcal{V},\ \|(u,v)\|_{\mathcal{V}}\leq R\}$. Then, by using the inequalities (54) and similar computations as those from the first part of the proof of Theorem 1, we obtain

$$|\mathcal{E}_1(u,v)(\nu)|\leq T_1Y_1+T_2Y_2,\ \ |\mathcal{E}_2(u,v)(\nu)|\leq T_1Y_3+T_2Y_4,\tag{60}$$

for all $\nu\in[0,1]$ and $(u,v)\in\Omega_1$. Then, we deduce

$$\|\mathcal{E}(u,v)\|_{\mathcal{V}}\leq T_1(Y_1+Y_3)+T_2(Y_2+Y_4),\ \ \forall\,(u,v)\in\Omega_1,\tag{61}$$

that is, $\mathcal{E}(\Omega_1)$ is bounded.

Subsequently, we will demonstrate that $\mathcal{E}$ transforms bounded sets into equicontinuous sets. To illustrate this, consider $\nu_1,,\nu_2\in[0,1]$ with $\nu_1<\nu_2$ and $(u,v)\in\Omega_1$. Employing computations akin to those found in the proofs of Theorems 2 and 3, we arrive at the following conclusions

$$
\begin{aligned}
&|\mathcal{E}_1(u,v)(\nu_2)-\mathcal{E}_1(u,v)(\nu_1)| \\
&\le |\mathcal{P}_1(u,v)(\nu_2)-\mathcal{P}_1(u,v)(\nu_1)|+|\mathcal{Q}_1(u,v)(\nu_2)-\mathcal{Q}_1(u,v)(\nu_1)| \\
&\le \frac{T_1}{\Gamma_q(\alpha+1)}(\nu_2^{\alpha}-\nu_1^{\alpha})+\left[T_1\left(Y_1-\frac{1}{\Gamma_q(\alpha+1)}\right)+T_2Y_2\right](\nu_2^{\alpha-1}-\nu_1^{\alpha-1})\to 0, \\
&|\mathcal{E}_2(u,v)(\nu_2)-\mathcal{E}_2(u,v)(\nu_1)| \\
&\le |\mathcal{P}_2(u,v)(\nu_2)-\mathcal{P}_2(u,v)(\nu_1)|+|\mathcal{Q}_2(u,v)(\nu_2)-\mathcal{Q}_2(u,v)(\nu_1)| \\
&\le \frac{T_2}{\Gamma_q(\beta+1)}(\nu_2^{\beta}-\nu_1^{\beta})+\left[T_1Y_3+T_4\left(Y_4-\frac{1}{\Gamma_q(\beta+1)}\right)\right](\nu_2^{\beta-1}-\nu_1^{\beta-1})\to 0,
\end{aligned}
\tag{62}
$$

as $\nu_2 \to \nu_1$, independently of $(u,v) \in \Omega_2$.

Therefore, the operators $\mathcal{E}_1$ and $\mathcal{E}_2$ are equicontinuous, and so $\mathcal{E}$ is also an equicontinuous operator on Ω_2. Then, the operator $\mathcal{E} : \Omega_2 \to \mathcal{V}$ is completely continuous using the Arzela–Ascoli theorem.

In the concluding section of the proof, we establish the boundedness of the set $\mathcal{Z} = \{(u,v) \in \mathcal{V},\ (u,v) = \lambda\mathcal{E}(u,v),\ 0 \le \lambda \le 1\}$. Take $(u,v) \in \mathcal{V}$, implying there exists $\lambda \in [0,1]$ such that $(u,v) = \lambda\mathcal{E}(u,v)$ or $u(\nu) = \lambda\mathcal{E}_1(u,v)(\nu)$ and $v(\nu) = \lambda\mathcal{E}_2(u,v)(\nu)$ for all $\nu \in [0,1]$. Utilizing $(J4)$, we infer, similarly to the initial part of this proof, that

$$
\begin{aligned}
|u(\nu)| &= \lambda|\mathcal{E}_1(u,v)(\nu)| \le |\mathcal{E}_1(u,v)(\nu)| \le T_1Y_1+T_2Y_2,\ \ \forall \nu \in [0,1], \\
|v(\nu)| &= \lambda|\mathcal{E}_2(u,v)(\nu)| \le |\mathcal{E}_2(u,v)(\nu)| \le T_1Y_3+T_2Y_4,\ \ \forall \nu \in [0,1],
\end{aligned}
\tag{63}
$$

and then

$$
\|(u,v)|_{\mathcal{V}} = \|u\| + \|v\| \le T_1(Y_1+Y_3)+T_2(Y_2+Y_4). \tag{64}
$$

This final inequality indicates the boundedness of the set $\mathcal{Z}$. Consequently, employing the Schaefer fixed-point theorem, we establish the existence of at least one fixed point for the operator $\mathcal{E}$. Thus, problem (1), (2) possesses at least one solution. This concludes the proof. □

In the subsequent existence theorem, we will employ the Leray–Schauder nonlinear alternative (refer to [35]).

Theorem 5. *Assume that assumption $(J1)$ holds. In addition, we suppose that the functions $\mathcal{F},\mathcal{G} : [0,1] \times \mathbb{R}^4 \to \mathbb{R}$ are continuous and the following conditions are satisfied*

$(J5)$ *There exist the functions φ_1, $\varphi_2 \in C([0,1],\mathbb{R}_+)$ and the functions ψ_1, $\psi_2 \in C((\mathbb{R}_+)^4,\mathbb{R}_+)$ nondecreasing in each of variables such that*

$$
\begin{aligned}
|\mathcal{F}(\nu,x_1,x_2,x_3,x_4)| &\le \varphi_1(\nu)\psi_1(|x_1|,|x_2|,|x_3|,|x_4|), \\
|\mathcal{G}(\nu,x_1,x_2,x_3,x_4)| &\le \varphi_2(\nu)\psi_2(|x_1|,|x_2|,|x_3|,|x_4|),
\end{aligned}
\tag{65}
$$

for all $\nu \in [0,1]$, $x_i \in \mathbb{R}$, $i = 1,\dots,4$.

$(J6)$ *There exists a positive constant V such that*

$$
\begin{aligned}
&\|\varphi_1\|\psi_1\left(V,V,\frac{V}{\Gamma_q(\delta_1+1)},\frac{V}{\Gamma_q(\gamma_1+1)}\right)(Y_1+Y_3) \\
&+\|\varphi_2\|\psi_2\left(V,V,\frac{V}{\Gamma_q(\delta_2+1)},\frac{V}{\Gamma_q(\gamma_2+1)}\right)(Y_2+Y_4) < V.
\end{aligned}
\tag{66}
$$

Then, the q-fractional boundary value problem (1), (2) has at least one solution $(u(\nu),v(\nu))$, $\nu \in [0,1]$.

Proof. We define the set $\mathcal{W} = \{(\mathrm{u},\mathrm{v}) \in \mathcal{V},\ \|(\mathrm{u},\mathrm{v})\|_{\mathcal{V}} < V\}$, where V is the constant given by (66). The operator $\mathcal{E} : \overline{\mathcal{W}} \to \mathcal{V}$ is completely continuous. We suppose that there exist $(\mathrm{u},\mathrm{v}) \in \partial\mathcal{W}$ such that $(\mathrm{u},\mathrm{v}) = \mu\mathcal{E}(\mathrm{u},\mathrm{v})$ for some $\mu \in (0,1)$. Then, we obtain

$$\begin{aligned}
|\mathrm{u}(\nu)| &= \mu|\mathcal{E}_1(\mathrm{u},\mathrm{v})(\nu)| \le |\mathcal{E}_1(\mathrm{u},\mathrm{v})(\nu)| \\
&\le \|\varphi_1\|\,\psi_1\left(\|\mathrm{u}\|,\|\mathrm{v}\|,\frac{\|\mathrm{u}\|}{\Gamma_q(\delta_1+1)},\frac{\|\mathrm{v}\|}{\Gamma_q(\gamma_1+1)}\right)\mathrm{Y}_1 \\
&\quad+\|\varphi_2\|\,\psi_2\left(\|\mathrm{u}\|,\|\mathrm{v}\|,\frac{\|\mathrm{u}\|}{\Gamma_q(\delta_2+1)},\frac{\|\mathrm{v}\|}{\Gamma_q(\gamma_2+1)}\right)\mathrm{Y}_2, \\
|\mathrm{v}(\nu)| &= \mu|\mathcal{E}_2(\mathrm{u},\mathrm{v})(\nu)| \le |\mathcal{E}_2(\mathrm{u},\mathrm{v})(\nu)| \\
&\le \|\varphi_1\|\,\psi_1\left(\|\mathrm{u}\|,\|\mathrm{v}\|,\frac{\|\mathrm{u}\|}{\Gamma_q(\delta_1+1)},\frac{\|\mathrm{v}\|}{\Gamma_q(\gamma_1+1)}\right)\mathrm{Y}_3 \\
&\quad+\|\varphi_2\|\,\psi_2\left(\|\mathrm{u}\|,\|\mathrm{v}\|,\frac{\|\mathrm{u}\|}{\Gamma_q(\delta_2+1)},\frac{\|\mathrm{v}\|}{\Gamma_q(\gamma_2+1)}\right)\mathrm{Y}_4,
\end{aligned} \tag{67}$$

for all $\nu \in [0,1]$, and so we find

$$\begin{aligned}
\|(\mathrm{u},\mathrm{v})\|_{\mathcal{V}} &= \|\mathrm{u}\| + \|\mathrm{v}\| \\
&\le \|\varphi_1\|\,\psi_1\left(\|\mathrm{u}\|,\|\mathrm{v}\|,\frac{\|\mathrm{u}\|}{\Gamma_q(\delta_1+1)},\frac{\|\mathrm{v}\|}{\Gamma_q(\gamma_1+1)}\right)(\mathrm{Y}_1+\mathrm{Y}_3) \\
&\quad+\|\varphi_2\|\,\psi_2\left(\|\mathrm{u}\|,\|\mathrm{v}\|,\frac{\|\mathrm{u}\|}{\Gamma_q(\delta_2+1)},\frac{\|\mathrm{v}\|}{\Gamma_q(\gamma_2+1)}\right)(\mathrm{Y}_2+\mathrm{Y}_4) \\
&\le \|\varphi_1\|\,\psi_1\left(\|(\mathrm{u},\mathrm{v})\|_{\mathcal{V}},\|(\mathrm{u},\mathrm{v})\|_{\mathcal{V}},\frac{\|(\mathrm{u},\mathrm{v})\|_{\mathcal{V}}}{\Gamma_q(\delta_1+1)},\frac{\|(\mathrm{u},\mathrm{v})\|_{\mathcal{V}}}{\Gamma_q(\gamma_1+1)}\right)(\mathrm{Y}_1+\mathrm{Y}_3) \\
&\quad+\|\varphi_2\|\,\psi_2\left(\|(\mathrm{u},\mathrm{v})\|_{\mathcal{V}},\|(\mathrm{u},\mathrm{v})\|_{\mathcal{V}},\frac{\|(\mathrm{u},\mathrm{v})\|_{\mathcal{V}}}{\Gamma_q(\delta_2+1)},\frac{\|(\mathrm{u},\mathrm{v})\|_{\mathcal{V}}}{\Gamma_q(\gamma_2+1)}\right)(\mathrm{Y}_2+\mathrm{Y}_4).
\end{aligned} \tag{68}$$

Therefore, we deduce

$$\begin{aligned}
V\Big/\Bigg[&\|\varphi_1\|\,\psi_1\left(V,V,\frac{V}{\Gamma_q(\delta_1+1)},\frac{V}{\Gamma_q(\gamma_1+1)}\right)(\mathrm{Y}_1+\mathrm{Y}_3) \\
&+\|\varphi_2\|\,\psi_2\left(V,V,\frac{V}{\Gamma_q(\delta_2+1)},\frac{V}{\Gamma_q(\gamma_2+1)}\right)(\mathrm{Y}_2+\mathrm{Y}_4)\Bigg] \le 1,
\end{aligned} \tag{69}$$

which, by (66), is a contradiction.

We conclude that there is no $(\mathrm{u},\mathrm{v}) \in \partial\mathcal{W}$ such that $(\mathrm{u},\mathrm{v}) = \mu\mathcal{E}(\mathrm{u},\mathrm{v})$ for some $\mu \in (0,1)$. Consequently, by employing the Leray–Schauder nonlinear alternative, we infer that $\mathcal{E}$ possesses a fixed point $(\mathrm{u},\mathrm{v}) \in \overline{\mathcal{W}}$, serving as a solution to problem (1), (2). This concludes the proof. □

4. Examples

Let $q = \frac{1}{2}$, $\alpha = \frac{5}{2}$, $n = 3$, $\beta = \frac{10}{3}$, $m = 4$, $\delta_1 = \frac{34}{11}$, $\gamma_1 = \frac{71}{25}$, $\delta_2 = \frac{48}{13}$, $\gamma_2 = \frac{95}{32}$, $\varsigma = \frac{6}{5}$, $\vartheta = \frac{9}{7}$, $\mathfrak{a} = \mathfrak{b} = \mathfrak{c} = \mathfrak{d} = 1$, $\varrho_1 = \frac{2}{9}$, $\sigma_1 = \frac{5}{4}$, $\eta_1 = \frac{2}{3}$, $\rho_1 = \frac{21}{10}$, $\xi_1 = \frac{1}{8}$, $\omega_1 = \frac{1}{2}$, $\zeta_1 = \frac{1}{4}$, $\theta_1 = \frac{1}{16}$, $a_1 = 3$, $b_1 = -\frac{7}{12}$, $c_1 = \frac{4}{15}$, $d_1 = -2$.

We consider the system of $\mathfrak{q}$-difference equations

$$\begin{cases}
(D_{1/2}^{5/2}\mathrm{u})(\nu) + \mathcal{F}\left(\nu,\mathrm{u}(\nu),\mathrm{v}(\nu),I_{1/2}^{34/11}\mathrm{u}(\nu),I_{1/2}^{71/25}\mathrm{v}(\nu)\right) = 0, & \nu \in (0,1), \\
(D_{1/2}^{10/3}\mathrm{v})(\nu) + \mathcal{G}\left(\nu,\mathrm{u}(\nu),\mathrm{v}(\nu),I_{1/2}^{48/13}\mathrm{u}(\nu),I_{1/2}^{95/32}\mathrm{v}(\nu)\right) = 0, & \nu \in (0,1),
\end{cases} \tag{70}$$

with the boundary conditions

$$\begin{cases}
\mathrm{u}(0) = D_{1/2}\mathrm{u}(0) = 0,\ D_{1/2}^{6/5}\mathrm{u}(1) = 3D_{1/2}^{2/9}\mathrm{u}\left(\frac{1}{8}\right) - \frac{7}{12}D_{1/2}^{5/4}\mathrm{v}\left(\frac{1}{2}\right), \\
\mathrm{v}(0) = D_{1/2}\mathrm{v}(0) = D_{1/2}^{2}\mathrm{v}(0) = 0,\ D_{1/2}^{9/7}\mathrm{v}(1) = \frac{4}{15}D_{1/2}^{2/3}\mathrm{u}\left(\frac{1}{4}\right) - 2D_{1/4}^{21/10}\mathrm{v}\left(\frac{1}{16}\right).
\end{cases} \tag{71}$$

By using the Mathematica program, we obtain $\Lambda_1 \approx 1.05480868$, $\Lambda_2 \approx -0.48038739$, $\Lambda_3 \approx 0.10410274$, $\Lambda_4 \approx 3.76405767$, and $\Delta \approx 4.02037036 \neq 0$. Therefore, assumption $(J1)$ is satisfied.

In addition, after some computations, we find $\Upsilon_1 \approx 1.37638598$, $\Upsilon_2 \approx 0.16737542$, $\Upsilon_3 \approx 0.02789379$, and $\Upsilon_4 \approx 0.49956085$.

Example 1. *We consider the functions*

$$\begin{aligned}
&\mathcal{F}(\nu,\mathrm{u},\mathrm{v},\mathrm{x},\mathrm{y}) = \frac{\sin(3\nu+2)}{\sqrt[4]{\nu^3+2}} + \frac{1}{9}e^{-(\nu-1)^2}\sqrt{\mathrm{u}^2+1} - \frac{1}{17}e^{-2\nu^3+1}\arctan \mathrm{v} \\
&+\frac{\nu}{4(\nu^2+1)}\sin \mathrm{x} - \frac{3\nu}{25}\cos^2 \mathrm{y}, \\
&\mathcal{G}(\nu,\mathrm{u},\mathrm{v},\mathrm{x},\mathrm{y}) = -\nu^2+5+\frac{1}{8(\nu+1)}\sin^2 \mathrm{u} - \frac{2}{31(\nu^2+4)}\frac{|\mathrm{v}|}{1+|\mathrm{v}|} - \frac{1}{2}\mathrm{x} \\
&+\frac{1}{6(\nu^3+1)}\frac{\mathrm{y}}{\mathrm{y}^2+1},
\end{aligned} \tag{72}$$

for all $\nu \in [0,1]$, $\mathrm{u},\mathrm{v},\mathrm{x},\mathrm{y} \in \mathbb{R}$.

For these continuous functions, we obtain the following inequalities

$$\begin{aligned}
&|\mathcal{F}(\nu,\mathrm{u}_1,\mathrm{v}_1,\mathrm{x}_1,\mathrm{y}_1) - \mathcal{F}(\nu,\mathrm{u}_2,\mathrm{v}_2,\mathrm{x}_2,\mathrm{y}_2)| \\
&\leq \mathcal{H}_1(\nu)|\mathrm{u}_1-\mathrm{u}_2| + \mathcal{H}_2(\nu)|\mathrm{v}_1-\mathrm{v}_2| + \mathcal{H}_3(\nu)|\mathrm{x}_1-\mathrm{x}_2| + \mathcal{H}_4(\nu)|\mathrm{y}_1-\mathrm{y}_2|, \\
&|\mathcal{G}(\nu,\mathrm{u}_1,\mathrm{v}_1,\mathrm{x}_1,\mathrm{y}_1) - \mathcal{G}(\nu,\mathrm{u}_2,\mathrm{v}_2,\mathrm{x}_2,\mathrm{y}_2)| \\
&\leq \mathcal{K}_1(\nu)|\mathrm{u}_1-\mathrm{u}_2| + \mathcal{K}_2(\nu)|\mathrm{v}_1-\mathrm{v}_2| + \mathcal{K}_3(\nu)|\mathrm{x}_1-\mathrm{x}_2| + \mathcal{K}_4(\nu)|\mathrm{y}_1-\mathrm{y}_2|,
\end{aligned} \tag{73}$$

for all $\nu \in [0,1]$, $\mathrm{u}_i,\mathrm{v}_i,\mathrm{x}_i,\mathrm{y}_i \in \mathbb{R}$, $i=1,2$, *where*

$$\begin{aligned}
&\mathcal{H}_1(\nu) = \frac{1}{9}e^{-(\nu-1)^2}, \ \mathcal{H}_2(\nu) = \frac{1}{17}e^{-2\nu^3+1}, \ \mathcal{H}_3(\nu) = \frac{\nu}{4(\nu^2+1)}, \ \mathcal{H}_4(\nu) = \frac{6\nu}{25}, \\
&\mathcal{K}_1(\nu) = \frac{1}{4(\nu+1)}, \ \mathcal{K}_2(\nu) = \frac{2}{31(\nu^2+4)}, \ \mathcal{K}_3(\nu) = \frac{1}{2}, \ \mathcal{K}_4(\nu) = \frac{1}{6(\nu^3+1)},
\end{aligned} \tag{74}$$

for all $\nu \in [0,1]$. *The functions* $\mathcal{H}_i$, $\mathcal{K}_i$, $i=1,\dots,4$ *are continuous, and we find* $\mathfrak{h}_1^* \approx 0.11111111$, $\mathfrak{h}_2^* \approx 0.15989893$, $\mathfrak{h}_3^* = 0.125$, $\mathfrak{h}_4^* = 0.24$, $\mathfrak{k}_1^* = 0.25$, $\mathfrak{k}_2^* \approx 0.01612903$, $\mathfrak{k}_3^* = 0.5$, *and* $\mathfrak{k}_4^* \approx 0.16666667$. *In addition, we obtain* $\Theta_1 \approx 0.46864611$, $\Theta_2 \approx 0.41971398$, *and so* $\Theta_0 = \Theta_1 < 1$. *Therefore, assumption* $(J2)$ *and condition (16) are satisfied. Then, by Theorem 1, we deduce that problem (70), (71) with the functions* $\mathcal{F}$ *and* $\mathcal{G}$ *given by (72) has a unique solution* $(\mathrm{u}(\nu),\mathrm{v}(\nu))$, $\nu \in [0,1]$.

Example 2. *We consider the functions*

$$\begin{aligned}
&\mathcal{F}(\nu,\mathrm{u},\mathrm{v},\mathrm{x},\mathrm{y}) = \frac{\cos(\nu^3+7)}{2\nu+5} - \frac{1}{\nu^2+6}\frac{4\mathrm{u}^4+1}{\mathrm{u}^4+3} + \frac{(\nu^5+2)e^{-3\nu+1}}{6(\nu^4+27)}\sin \mathrm{v} \\
&-\frac{\nu}{8(\nu^2+1)}\cos^2 \mathrm{x} + \frac{1}{\nu+4}\frac{|\mathrm{y}|}{1+3|\mathrm{y}|}, \\
&\mathcal{G}(\nu,\mathrm{u},\mathrm{v},\mathrm{x},\mathrm{y}) = -\frac{e^{-\nu+4}}{3\nu^2+1} + \frac{1}{\nu^2+7}\frac{\mathrm{u}}{\mathrm{u}^2+1} - \frac{\nu+1}{9\sqrt{\nu^4+5}}e^{-\mathrm{v}^2} \\
&+\frac{2}{11}\sin^2 \mathrm{x} - \frac{\nu|\mathrm{y}|}{6(1+4|\mathrm{y}|)},
\end{aligned} \tag{75}$$

for all $\nu \in [0,1]$, $\mathrm{u},\mathrm{v},\mathrm{x},\mathrm{y} \in \mathbb{R}$. *For these continuous functions, we obtain the following inequalities*

$$\begin{aligned}
&|\mathcal{F}(\nu,\mathrm{u},\mathrm{v},\mathrm{x},\mathrm{y})| \leq \frac{1}{2\nu+5} + \frac{4}{\nu^2+6} + \frac{(\nu^5+2)e^{-3\nu+1}}{6(\nu^4+27)} + \frac{\nu}{8(\nu^2+1)} + \frac{1}{3(\nu+4)} =: \Phi(\nu), \\
&|\mathcal{G}(\nu,\mathrm{u},\mathrm{v},\mathrm{x},\mathrm{y})| \leq \frac{e^{-\nu+4}}{3\nu^2+1} + \frac{1}{2(\nu^2+7)} + \frac{\nu+1}{9\sqrt{\nu^4+5}} + \frac{2}{11} + \frac{\nu}{24} =: \Psi(\nu),
\end{aligned} \tag{76}$$

for all $\nu \in [0,1]$, $\mathrm{u}, \mathrm{v}, \mathrm{x}, \mathrm{y} \in \mathbb{R}$. *In addition, we find*

$$\begin{aligned} &|\mathcal{F}(\nu, \mathrm{u}_1, \mathrm{v}_1, \mathrm{x}_1, \mathrm{y}_1) - \mathcal{F}(\nu, \mathrm{u}_2, \mathrm{v}_2, \mathrm{x}_2, \mathrm{y}_2)| \\ &\leq \mathcal{H}_1(\nu)|\mathrm{u}_1 - \mathrm{u}_2| + \mathcal{H}_2(\nu)|\mathrm{v}_1 - \mathrm{v}_2| + \mathcal{H}_3(\nu)|\mathrm{x}_1 - \mathrm{x}_2| + \mathcal{H}_4(\nu)|\mathrm{y}_1 - \mathrm{y}_2|, \\ &|\mathcal{G}(\nu, \mathrm{u}_1, \mathrm{v}_1, \mathrm{x}_1, \mathrm{y}_1) - \mathcal{G}(\nu, \mathrm{u}_2, \mathrm{v}_2, \mathrm{x}_2, \mathrm{y}_2)| \\ &\leq \mathcal{K}_1(\nu)|\mathrm{u}_1 - \mathrm{u}_2| + \mathcal{K}_2(\nu)|\mathrm{v}_1 - \mathrm{v}_2| + \mathcal{K}_3(\nu)|\mathrm{x}_1 - \mathrm{x}_2| + \mathcal{K}_4(\nu)|\mathrm{y}_1 - \mathrm{y}_2|, \end{aligned} \tag{77}$$

for all $\nu \in [0,1]$, $\mathrm{u}_i, \mathrm{v}_i, \mathrm{x}_i, \mathrm{y}_i \in \mathbb{R}$, $i = 1,2$, *where*

$$\begin{aligned} &\mathcal{H}_1(\nu) = \frac{2.9678}{\nu^2+6}, \ \mathcal{H}_2(\nu) = \frac{(\nu^5+2)e^{-3\nu+1}}{6(\nu^4+27)}, \ \mathcal{H}_3(\nu) = \frac{\nu}{4(\nu^2+1)}, \ \mathcal{H}_4(\nu) = \frac{1}{\nu+4}, \\ &\mathcal{K}_1(\nu) = \frac{1}{\nu^2+7}, \ \mathcal{K}_2(\nu) = \frac{0.8578(\nu+1)}{9\sqrt{\nu^4+5}}, \ \mathcal{K}_3(\nu) = \frac{4}{11}, \ \mathcal{K}_4(\nu) = \frac{\nu}{6}, \end{aligned} \tag{78}$$

for all $\nu \in [0,1]$. *Therefore, assumptions* $(J2)$ *and* $(J3)$ *are satisfied. In addition, we obtain* $\mathfrak{h}_1^* \approx 0.49463333$, $\mathfrak{h}_2^* \approx 0.03355903$, $\mathfrak{h}_3^* = 0.125$, $\mathfrak{h}_4^* = 0.25$, $\mathfrak{k}_1^* \approx 0.14285714$, $\mathfrak{k}_2^* \approx 0.07782119$, $\mathfrak{k}_3^* \approx 0.36363636$, $\mathfrak{k}_4^* \approx 0.16666667$, *and so* $\mathfrak{L}_1 \approx 0.56557327$, $\mathfrak{L}_2 \approx 0.25625052$, *and* $\mathfrak{L}_0 = \mathfrak{L}_1 < 1$. *Then, condition (31) is also satisfied. Therefore, by Theorem 2, we conclude that problem (70), (71) with functions (75) has at least one solution* $(\mathrm{u}(\nu), \mathrm{v}(\nu))$, $\nu \in [0,1]$.

Example 3. *We consider the functions*

$$\begin{aligned} &\mathcal{F}(\nu, \mathrm{u}, \mathrm{v}, \mathrm{x}, \mathrm{y}) = \frac{e^{-4\nu+3}}{\sqrt{\nu^3+1}} \cos(\mathrm{uv} + \mathrm{x}^2 - \mathrm{y}) - \frac{1}{6}\sqrt[3]{\nu^2+12}, \\ &\mathcal{G}(\nu, \mathrm{u}, \mathrm{v}, \mathrm{x}, \mathrm{y}) = \frac{1}{2(\nu+1)} e^{-(\mathrm{u}+\mathrm{v})^2} - \arctan\sqrt{\mathrm{x}^2+2} + \frac{\nu^2}{\nu^5+3}\frac{4\mathrm{y}^2+1}{\mathrm{y}^2+3} - \sin(2\nu+1), \end{aligned} \tag{79}$$

for all $\nu \in [0,1]$, $\mathrm{u}, \mathrm{v}, \mathrm{x}, \mathrm{y} \in \mathbb{R}$. *For these continuous functions, we obtain the following inequalities*

$$|\mathcal{F}(\nu, \mathrm{u}, \mathrm{v}, \mathrm{x}, \mathrm{y})| < 20.4919 = T_1, \ |\mathcal{G}(\nu, \mathrm{u}, \mathrm{v}, \mathrm{x}, \mathrm{y})| < 4.0708 = T_2. \tag{80}$$

Therefore, assumption $(J4)$ *is satisfied. Then, by Theorem 4 we infer that problem (70), (71) with functions (79) has at least one solution* $(\mathrm{u}(\nu), \mathrm{v}(\nu))$, $\nu \in [0,1]$.

Example 4. *We consider the functions*

$$\begin{aligned} &\mathcal{F}(\nu, \mathrm{u}, \mathrm{v}, \mathrm{x}, \mathrm{y}) = \frac{2}{\nu^3+5}\left(\frac{\mathrm{u}-3\mathrm{x}+1}{34}\sin(\mathrm{u}^2 - 8\mathrm{v} + \mathrm{x}^3) - \frac{\sqrt{\mathrm{v}^2+4\mathrm{y}^2}}{27}\arctan\frac{\mathrm{u}+\mathrm{xy}}{\mathrm{y}^2+3} + \frac{1}{9}\right), \\ &\mathcal{G}(\nu, \mathrm{u}, \mathrm{v}, \mathrm{x}, \mathrm{y}) = \frac{3\nu}{\nu^4+71}\left(\frac{4\mathrm{u}-5\mathrm{y}}{43}\cos(\mathrm{ux} - 3\mathrm{vy}) - \frac{\mathrm{v}+7\mathrm{x}}{11}e^{-(\mathrm{u}+3\mathrm{y})^2} - \frac{2}{15}\right), \end{aligned} \tag{81}$$

for all $\nu \in [0,1]$, $\mathrm{u}, \mathrm{v}, \mathrm{x}, \mathrm{y} \in \mathbb{R}$. *For these continuous functions, we obtain the inequalities*

$$\begin{aligned} &|\mathcal{F}(\nu, \mathrm{u}, \mathrm{v}, \mathrm{x}, \mathrm{y})| \leq \frac{2}{\nu^3+5}\left(\frac{|\mathrm{u}|}{34} + \frac{\pi|\mathrm{v}|}{54} + \frac{3|\mathrm{x}|}{34} + \frac{\pi|\mathrm{y}|}{27} + \frac{43}{306}\right), \\ &|\mathcal{G}(\nu, \mathrm{u}, \mathrm{v}, \mathrm{x}, \mathrm{y})| \leq \frac{3\nu}{\nu^4+71}\left(\frac{4|\mathrm{u}|}{43} + \frac{|\mathrm{v}|}{11} + \frac{7|\mathrm{x}|}{11} + \frac{5|\mathrm{y}|}{43} + \frac{2}{15}\right), \end{aligned} \tag{82}$$

for all $\nu \in [0,1]$, $\mathrm{u}, \mathrm{v}, \mathrm{x}, \mathrm{y} \in \mathbb{R}$. *Therefore, the continuous functions* φ_i, ψ_i, $i = 1,2$ *from (65) are given by*

$$\begin{aligned} &\varphi_1(\nu) = \frac{2}{\nu^3+5}, \ \psi_1(a,b,c,d) = \frac{a}{34} + \frac{\pi b}{54} + \frac{3c}{34} + \frac{\pi d}{27} + \frac{43}{306}, \\ &\varphi_2(\nu) = \frac{3\nu}{\nu^4+71}, \ \psi_2(a,b,c,d) = \frac{4a}{43} + \frac{b}{11} + \frac{7c}{11} + \frac{5d}{43} + \frac{2}{15}, \end{aligned} \tag{83}$$

for all $\nu \in [0,1]$ *and* $a,b,c,d \in \mathbb{R}_+$; *that is, assumption* $(J5)$ *is satisfied. In addition, we find* $\|\varphi_1\| = \frac{2}{5}$ *and* $\|\varphi_2\| = \frac{3}{72}$. *If* $V \geq 0.1$, *then assumption* $(J6)$ *is also satisfied. Therefore, by Theorem 5, we conclude the existence of at least one solution* $(u(\nu), v(\nu))$, $\nu \in [0,1]$ *for problem (70), (71) with functions (81).*

5. Conclusions

In this study, we explored the existence and uniqueness of solutions to a system of fractional q-difference equations with fractional q-integral terms (1), subject to the multi-point boundary conditions (2), which encompass q-derivatives and fractional q-derivatives of diverse orders. We associated an operator ($\mathcal{E}$) on the space $\mathcal{V}$ with our problem, where the solutions of (1) and (2) correspond to the fixed points of this operator. Consequently, our main results involved the utilization of various fixed-point theorems, including the Banach contraction mapping principle (employed in Theorem 1), the Krasnosel'skii fixed-point theorem for the sum of two operators (applied in Theorems 2 and 3), the Schaefer fixed-point theorem (utilized in Theorem 4), and the Leray–Schauder nonlinear alternative (employed in Theorem 5). To exemplify our findings, we concluded by presenting several illustrative examples.

Author Contributions: Conceptualization, R.L.; formal analysis, A.T. and R.L.; methodology, A.T. and R.L. All authors have read and agreed to the published version of the manuscript.

Funding: This research received no external funding.

Data Availability Statement: Data are contained within the article.

Conflicts of Interest: The authors declare no conflicts of interest.

References

1. Luca, R. Positive solutions for a system of fractional q-difference equations with multi-point boundary conditions. *Fractal Fract.* **2024**, *8*, 70. [CrossRef]
2. Yu, C.; Wang, S.; Wang, J.; Li, J. Solvability criterion for fractional q-integro-difference system with Riemann-Stieltjes integrals conditions. *Fractal Fract.* **2022**, *6*, 554. [CrossRef]
3. Allouch, N.; Graef, J.R.; Hamani, S. Boundary value problem for fractional q-difference equations with integral conditions in Banach spaces. *Fractal Fract.* **2022**, *6*, 237. [CrossRef]
4. Yu, C.; Wang, J. Positive solutions of nonlocal boundary value problem for high-order nonlinear fractional q-difference equations. *Abstr. Appl. Anal.* **2013**, *2013*, 928147. [CrossRef]
5. Ferreira, R.A.C. Positive solutions for a class of boundary value problems with fractional q-differences. *Comput. Math. Appl.* **2011**, *61*, 367–373. [CrossRef]
6. Ferreira, R.A.C. Nontrivial solutions for fractional q-difference boundary value problems. *Electr. J. Qual. Theory Differ. Equ.* **2010**, *2010*, 1–10.
7. Alsaedi, A.; Al-Hutami, H.; Ahmad, B.; Agarwal, R.P. Existence results for a coupled system of nonlinear fractional q-integro-difference equations with q-integral-coupled boundary conditions. *Fractals* **2022**, *30*, 2240042. [CrossRef]
8. Bai, C.; Yang, D. The iterative positive solution for a system of fractional q-difference equations with four-point boundary conditions. *Discret. Dyn. Nat. Soc.* **2020**, *2020*, 3970903. [CrossRef]
9. Boutiara, A.; Benbachir, M.; Kaabar, M.K.A.; Martinez, F.; Samei, M.E.; Kaplan, M. Explicit iteration and unbounded solutions for fractional q-difference equations with boundary conditions on an infinite interval. *J. Ineq. Appl.* **2022**, *2022*, 1–27. [CrossRef]
10. Jiang, M.; Huang, R. Existence and stability results for impulsive fractional q-difference equation. *J. Appl. Math. Phys.* **2020**, *8*, 1413–1423. [CrossRef]
11. Li, X.; Han, Z.; Sun, S.; Sun, L. Eigenvalue problems of fractional q-difference equations with generalized p-Laplacian. *Appl. Math. Lett.* **2016**, *57*, 46–53. [CrossRef]
12. Li, Y.; Liu, J.; O'Regan, D.; Xu, J. Nontrivial solutions for a system of fractional q-difference equations involving q-integral boundary conditions. *Mathematics* **2020**, *8*, 828. [CrossRef]
13. Suantai, S.; Ntouyas, S.K.; Asawasamrit, S.; Tariboon, J. A coupled system of fractional q-integro-difference equations with nonlocal fractional q-integral boundary conditions. *Adv. Differ. Equ.* **2015**, *2015*, 124. [CrossRef]
14. Zhai, C.; Ren, J. The unique solution for a fractional q-difference equation with three-point boundary conditions. *Indag. Math.* **2018**, *29*, 948–961. [CrossRef]
15. Jackson, F.H. On q-functions and a certain difference operator. *Trans. Roy. Soc. Edinburg* **1908**, *46*, 253–281. [CrossRef]
16. Jackson, F.H. On q-definite integrals. *Quart. J. Pure Appl. Math.* **1910**, *41*, 193–203.
17. Ernst, T. *The History of q-Calculus and a New Method*; UUDM Report 2000:16; Department of Mathematics, Uppsala University: Uppsala, Sweden, 2000; ISSN 1101-3591.
18. Al-Salam, W.A. Some fractional q-integrals and q-derivatives. *Proc. Edinb. Math. Soc.* **1966**, *15*, 135–140. [CrossRef]

19. Agarwal, R.P. Certain fractional q-integrals and q-derivatives. *Proc. Camb. Philos. Soc.* **1969**, *66*, 365–370. [CrossRef]
20. Al-Salam, W.A. q-Analogues of Cauchy's formulas. *Proc. Amer. Math. Soc.* **1966**, *17*, 616–621.
21. Al-Salam, W.A.; Verma, A. A fractional Leibniz q-formula. *Pac. J. Math.* **1975**, *60*, 1–9. [CrossRef]
22. Atici, F.M.; Eloe, P.W. Fractional q-calculus on a time scale. *J. Nonlinear Math. Phys.* **2007**, *14*, 341–352. [CrossRef]
23. Kac, V.; Cheung, P. *Quantum Calculus*; Springer: New York, NY, USA, 2002.
24. Rajkovic, P.M.; Marinkovic, S.D.; Stankovic, M.S. Fractional integrals and derivatives in q-calculus. *Appl. Anal. Discret. Math.* **2007**, *1*, 311–323.
25. Rajkovic, P.M.; Marinkovic, S.D.; Stankovic, M.S. On q-analogues of Caputo derivative and Mittag-Leffler function. *Fract. Calc. Appl. Anal.* **2007**, *10*, 359–373.
26. Jia, Z.; Khan, B.; Hu, Q.; Niu, D. Applications of generalized q-difference equations for general q-polynomials. *Symmetry* **2021**, *13*, 1222. [CrossRef]
27. Arjika, S. q-difference equations for homogeneous q-difference operators and their applications. *J. Differ. Equ. Appl.* **2020**, *26*, 987–999. [CrossRef]
28. Ruan, Y.B.; Wen, Y.X. Quantum K-theory and q-difference equations. *Acta Math. Sin. Engl. Ser.* **2022**, *38*, 1677–1704. [CrossRef]
29. Cao, T.B.; Dai, H.X.; Wang, J. Nevanlinna theory for Jackson difference operators and entire solutions of q-difference equations. *Anal. Math.* **2021**, *47*, 529–557. [CrossRef]
30. Semary, M.S.; Hassan, H.N. The homotopy analysis method for q-difference equations. *Ain Shams Eng. J.* **2018**, *9*, 415–421. [CrossRef]
31. Laledj, N.; Salim, A.; Lazreg, J.E.; Abbas, S.; Ahmad, B.; Benchohra, M. On implicit fractional q-difference equations: Analysis and stability. *Math. Methods Appl. Sci.* **2022**, *45*, 10775–10797. [CrossRef]
32. Deimling, K. *Nonlinear Functional Analysis*; Springer: New York, NY, USA, 1985.
33. Krasnoselskii, M.A. Two remarks on the method of successive approximations. *Uspekhi Mat. Nauk* **1955**, *10*, 123–127.
34. Smart, D.R. *Fixed Point Theory*; Cambridge University Press: Cambridge, UK, 1974.
35. Granas, A.; Dugundji, J. *Fixed Point Theory*; Springer: New York, NY, USA, 2003.

mathematics

MDPI

Article

Kamenev-Type Criteria for Testing the Asymptotic Behavior of Solutions of Third-Order Quasi-Linear Neutral Differential Equations

Hail S. Alrashdi [1], Wedad Albalawi [2,*], Ali Muhib [1], Osama Moaaz [3] and Elmetwally M. Elabbasy [1]

[1] Department of Mathematics, Faculty of Science, Mansoura University, Mansoura 35516, Egypt; hailaldyabai@std.mans.edu.eg (H.S.A.); muhib39@students.mans.edu.eg (A.M.); emelabbasy@mans.edu.eg (E.M.E.)
[2] Department of Mathematical Sciences, College of Science, Princess Nourah bint Abdulrahman University, P.O. Box 84428, Riyadh 11671, Saudi Arabia
[3] Department of Mathematics, College of Science, Qassim University, P.O. Box 6644, Buraydah 51452, Saudi Arabia; o_moaaz@mans.edu.eg
* Correspondence: wsalbalawi@pnu.edu.sa

Abstract: This paper aims to study the asymptotic properties of nonoscillatory solutions (eventually positive or negative) of a class of third-order canonical neutral differential equations. We use Riccati substitution to reduce the order of the considered equation, and then we use the Philos function class to obtain new criteria of the Kamenev type, which guarantees that all nonoscillatory solutions converge to zero. This approach is characterized by the possibility of applying its conditions to a wider area of equations. This is not the only aspect that distinguishes our results; we also use improved relationships between the solution and the corresponding function, which in turn is reflected in a direct improvement of the criteria. The findings in this article extend and generalize previous findings in the literature and also improve some of these findings.

Keywords: quasi-linear differential equations; asymptotic and oscillatory analysis; third-order; neutral delay arguments

MSC: 34C10; 34K11

Citation: Alrashdi, H.S.; Albalawi, W.; Muhib, A.; Moaaz, O.; Elabbasy, E.M. Kamenev-Type Criteria for Testing the Asymptotic Behavior of Solutions of Third-Order Quasi-Linear Neutral Differential Equations. *Mathematics* **2024**, *12*, 1734. https://doi.org/10.3390/math12111734

Academic Editors: Lingju Kong and Min Wang

Received: 7 November 2023
Revised: 21 January 2024
Accepted: 2 February 2024
Published: 3 June 2024

Correction Statement: This article has been republished with a minor change. The change does not affect the scientific content of the article and further details are available within the backmatter of the website version of this article.

1. Introduction

One type of functional differential equation (FDE) that accounts for the temporal memory of phenomena is the delay differential equation (DDE). Thus, it is simple to understand how these equations are applied in a wide spectrum of fields, including as biological, engineering, and physical models, as well as in other sciences [1,2].

A variety of inquiries concerning oscillatory behavior and asymptotic features of DDE solutions are addressed by oscillation theory, a subfield of qualitative theory. The basic task of oscillation theory is to identify the criteria that eliminate the nonoscillatory solutions. A variety of findings, techniques, and strategies for examining the oscillation of DDEs were gathered in monographs [3–6].

The investigation of oscillation for solutions of ordinary, partial, and fractional FDEs with delay, neutral delay (NDDE), mixed delay, and damping is a recent, significant expansion and enhancement of the oscillation theory. It is known that differential equations with delay have received the most attention, particularly for non-canonical cases. For instance, refer to [7–15] for delay, advanced, and neutral equations, respectively. Furthermore, Refs. [16–21] show how investigations of odd-order equations have evolved. Moreover, one may trace the variation of fractional DDEs in Survey [22]. Whereas [23–25] dealt with damping equations, and [26–29] studied mixed equations. Over the past 20 years, functional dynamic equations have also drawn a lot of attention; see, for instance, [30–32].

In this paper, we present new criteria for the oscillation of quasi-linear third-order neutral DDEs:

$$\left(a(\mathrm{s})\left((x(\mathrm{s})+\eta(\mathrm{s})x(g(\mathrm{s})))''\right)^r\right)'+q(\mathrm{s})x^r(\tau(\mathrm{s}))=0, \tag{1}$$

where $\mathrm{s}\geq \mathrm{s}_0,$ and r is the ratio of any two positive odd integers. Here, in this work, the following assumptions are satisfied:

(I) $a\in C^1([\mathrm{s}_0,\infty),(0,\infty))$, $a'(\mathrm{s})\geq 0$, and $\mathcal{T}(\mathrm{s}_0,\infty)=\infty$, where

$$\mathcal{T}(l,\mathrm{s})=\int_l^{\mathrm{s}}\frac{1}{a^{1/r}(\theta)}\mathrm{d}\theta; \tag{2}$$

(II) $\eta,q\in C([\mathrm{s}_0,\infty),[0,\infty))$ with $0\leq\eta(\mathrm{s})\leq\eta_0<\infty$ and $q(\mathrm{s})$ does not vanish eventually;

(III) $g,\tau\in C([\mathrm{s}_0,\infty),\mathbb{R})$, $g(\mathrm{s})\leq \mathrm{s}$, $\tau(\mathrm{s})\leq \mathrm{s}$, and $\lim_{\mathrm{s}\to\infty}g(\mathrm{s})=\lim_{\mathrm{s}\to\infty}\tau(\mathrm{s})=\infty$.

For the solution of (1) on $[\mathrm{s}_x,\infty)$, we refer to a real-valued function $x\in C([\mathrm{s}_x,\infty),\mathbb{R})$, $\mathrm{s}_x\geq\mathrm{s}_0$, which satisfies (1) on $[\mathrm{s}_x,\infty)$, and has the properties $(x+\eta\cdot(x\circ g))\in C^2([\mathrm{s}_x,\infty),\mathbb{R})$ and $\left(a\cdot\left((x+\eta\cdot(x\circ g))''\right)^r\right)\in C([\mathrm{s}_x,\infty),\mathbb{R})$. We only consider those solutions $x(\mathrm{s})$ of (1) satisfying $\sup\{|x(\mathrm{s})|:\mathrm{s}\geq \mathrm{S}\}>0$ for all $\mathrm{S}\geq\mathrm{s}_x$, and we assume that (1) has such solutions. A solution of (1) is said to be oscillatory if it has arbitrarily large zeros in $[\mathrm{s}_0,\infty)$, and is called nonoscillatory otherwise. Equation (1) is said to be oscillatory if all of its solutions are oscillatory.

In the study of neutral equations, the corresponding function z to the solution x, defined as

$$z(\mathrm{s}):=x(\mathrm{s})+\eta(\mathrm{s})x(g(\mathrm{s})), \tag{3}$$

is vital.

Numerous studies have been conducted on third-order functional differential equations and the oscillation behavior of solutions; see [33–40]. There exists a theoretical and applicable interest in the problem of oscillatory properties of neutral DDEs; see Hale [1] for some important applications in various applied sciences.

In what follows, we survey some of the most important research that handles the study of third-order NDDEs using different techniques and some different restrictions to obtain conditions that ensure that the solution is oscillatory or tends to zero to cover the the largest area when applied to special cases.

Baculikova and Dzurina [41] tested the asymptotic features of a pair of third-order NDDEs,

$$\left(a(\mathrm{s})\left((x(\mathrm{s})\pm\eta(\mathrm{s})x(g(\mathrm{s})))''\right)^r\right)'+q(\mathrm{s})x^r(\tau(\mathrm{s}))=0,\ \mathrm{s}\geq\mathrm{s}_0, \tag{4}$$

where $0\leq\eta(\mathrm{s})\leq\eta<1$. They established novel sufficient conditions that confirm that all nonoscillatory solutions of (4) converge to zero.

Thandapani and Li [42] studied the oscillatory features of the third-order NDDE (1), where $g'(\mathrm{s})\geq g_0>0$, $\tau\circ g=g\circ\tau$ and $0\leq\eta(\mathrm{s})\leq\eta<\infty$. By using the Riccati transformation, they established some sufficient criteria, which confirm that any solution of (1) is oscillatory or tends to zero.

Graef et al. [43] discussed the oscillatory properties of a class of solutions of third-order nonlinear NDDEs:

$$\left(\left((x(\mathrm{s})+\eta(\mathrm{s})x(g(\mathrm{s})))''\right)^r\right)'+q(\mathrm{s})x^r(\tau(\mathrm{s}))=0$$

where $a=1$ and $\eta(\mathrm{s})\geq 1$. They presented novel sufficient criteria for any solution of the studied equation to be either oscillating or converging to zero.

Kumar and Ganesan [44] discussed the third-order nonlinear NDDE in the form

$$\left(a(\mathrm{s})\varphi(z''(\mathrm{s}))\right)'+q(\mathrm{s})\varphi(x(\tau(\mathrm{s})))=0,\ \mathrm{s}\geq\mathrm{s}_0>0, \tag{5}$$

where $\varphi(u) = |u|^{r-1}u$, $g'(s) \geq g_0 > 0$ and $\tau \circ g = g \circ \tau$. The third- and first-order equation comparison principles provide the foundation for the obtained results. Below, we present some results obtained in previous studies to facilitate the reader's understanding.

Theorem 1 ([42]). *Let $r \geq 1$, $\tau \in C^1([s_0, \infty))$ and $\tau' > 0$. Assume that*

$$\int_{s_0}^{\infty} \int_{v}^{\infty} \left(\frac{1}{a(g(u))} \int_{u}^{\infty} Q(\theta) d\theta \right)^{1/r} du dv = \infty,$$

holds and $\tau(s) \leq g(s)$. Moreover, assuming there is a function $\rho \in C^1([s_0, \infty), (0, \infty))$, for all $s_1 \geq s_0$ large enough, there exists $s_1 \geq s_0$ where

$$\limsup_{s \to \infty} \int_{s_2}^{s} \left(\frac{\rho(l)Q(l)}{2^{r+1}} - \frac{\left(1 + \frac{\eta_0^r}{g_0}\right)\left((\rho'(l))_+\right)^{r+1}}{(r+1)^{r+1}(\rho(l)\beta_1(\tau(l), s_1)\tau'(l))^r} \right) dl = \infty,$$

for Q =min$\{q(s), q(g(s))\}$, $(\rho'(s))_+ := \max\{0, \rho'(s)\}$ and $\beta_1(s, s_1) = \int_{s_1}^{s} 1 l a^{1/r}(\theta) d\theta$. Then, (1) is almost oscillatory.

Theorem 2 ([44]). *Let $\tau(s) \leq g(s) \leq 1$. Assuming that $0 < r \leq 1$,*

$$\int_{s_1}^{s} g'(v) \int_{v}^{\infty} \left(\frac{g'(u)}{a(g(u))} \int_{u}^{\infty} Q(t) dt \right)^{1/r} du dv = \infty$$

and the first-order DDE

$$w'(s) + \frac{g_0}{g_o + \eta_0^r} Q_1(s) w\left(g^{-1}(\tau(s))\right) = 0$$

oscillates, then any positive solution of (5) meets $\lim_{s \to \infty} x(s) = 0$, where $g^{-1}(s)$ is an inverse function of $g(s)$, and

$$Q_1(s) = Q(s)\left(\int_{s_1}^{\tau(s)} (\mathcal{T}(l, t) - \mathcal{T}(l, t_1)) dt\right).$$

Our goal in this study was to examine the asymptotic properties of a class of neutral third-order NDDEs. Based on the improved relationship between x and z that was derived in [45], we obtained new relationships between x and z. The new relationship is characterized by taking into account both cases $\eta \leq 1$ and $\eta > 1$; this was not common in previous third-order studies. We present Kamenev-type criteria that ensure that all solutions of the neutral DDE, (1), either converge to zero or are oscillatory. We begin by deducing some new relationships that help improve the approach. Then, we use the Philos function class to obtain the required conditions. The criteria we obtain improve and extend some results from previous studies. Finally, we employ the results in the special case of our studied equation.

2. Preliminaries

We begin with lemmas, notations that are required throughout this paper. For convenience, we use the symbol $\mathcal{P}$ to state the category of all eventually positive solutions to (1), the symbol $\mathcal{P}_{\downarrow}$ to denote the class of solutions $x \in \mathcal{P}$, whose corresponding function confirms $z'(t) < 0$, and the symbol $\mathcal{P}_{\uparrow}$ to denote the class of solutions $x \in \mathcal{P}$ whose corresponding function confirms $z'(t) > 0$.

Lemma 1 ([41] (Lemma 1)). *Assume that $x \in \mathcal{P}$. Then, z meets one of the following possible cases, eventually:*

(i) $z > 0$, $z' > 0$ *and* $z'' > 0$;

(ii) $z > 0,\ z' < 0$ *and* $z'' > 0$.

Lemma 2 ([41] (Lemma 2)). *Suppose that* $x \in \mathcal{P}_{\downarrow}$. *If*

$$\int_{s_0}^{\infty}\int_{v}^{\infty}\left(\frac{1}{a(u)}\int_{u}^{\infty}q(\theta)\mathrm{d}\theta\right)^{1/r}\mathrm{d}u\mathrm{d}v = \infty, \tag{6}$$

then $\lim_{s\to\infty} x(s) = \lim_{s\to\infty} z(s) = 0$.

Lemma 3 ([41] (Lemma 3)). *Suppose that* $u \in C^2([s_0,\infty),\mathbb{R})$. *Assume that* $u(s) > 0,\ u'(s) \geq 0$ *and* $u''(s) \leq 0$, *on* $[s_0,\infty)$. *Then, there exist a* $s_1 \geq s_0$ *for each* $k_1 \in (0,1)$ *such that*

$$\frac{u(\tau(s))}{u(s)} \geq k_1\frac{\tau(s)}{s},$$

where $s \geq s_1$.

Lemma 4 ([46]). *Suppose that* $u \in C^{m+1}([s_0,\infty),\mathbb{R})$, $u^{(j)}(s) > 0$, *for* $j = 0,1,\ldots,m$, *and* $u^{(m+1)}(s) \leq 0$. *Then, there exist a* $s_1 \geq s_0$, *for each* $k_2 \in (0,1)$, *such that*

$$\frac{u(s)}{u'(s)} \geq \frac{k_2}{m}s,$$

where $s \geq s_1$.

Notation 1. *For simplicity, let* $G^{[0]}(s) := s$, $G^{[j]}(s) = G\left(G^{[j-1]}(s)\right)$, $G^{[-j]}(s) = G^{-1}\left(G^{[-j+1]}(s)\right)$, *for* $j = 1,2,\ldots$.

Lemma 5 ([45]). *Suppose that* $x \in \mathcal{P}_{\uparrow} \cup \mathcal{P}_{\downarrow}$. *Then,*

$$x > \sum_{k=0}^{m}\left(\prod_{n=0}^{2k}\eta\left(g^{[n]}\right)\right)\left(\frac{z\left(g^{[2k]}\right)}{\eta\left(g^{[2k]}\right)} - z\left(g^{[2k+1]}\right)\right), \tag{7}$$

eventually, where $m > 0,\ m \in \mathbb{Z}$.

Let $\Re$ be class of functions, the function $\mathcal{K} \in \Re$, where $\mathcal{K} \in C(H,\mathbb{R})$, $H = \{(s,\theta,\ell) : s_0 \leq \ell \leq \theta \leq s \leq \infty\}$, if $\mathcal{K}$ satisfies the following hypotheses:

(1) $\mathcal{K}(s,s,\ell) = 0,\ \mathcal{K}(s,\ell,\ell) = 0,\ \mathcal{K}(s,\theta,\ell) \neq 0$, for $\ell < \theta < s$;
(2) $\mathcal{K}(s,\theta,\ell)$ possesses the partial derivative $\partial\mathcal{K}/\partial\theta$ on H with the condition that $\partial\mathcal{K}/\partial\theta$ can be integrated locally in terms of θ in H and

$$\frac{\partial\mathcal{K}(s,\theta,\ell)}{\partial\theta} = h(s,\theta,\ell)\mathcal{K}(s,\theta,\ell), \tag{8}$$

for some $h \in C(H,\mathbb{R})$.

This class of functions is defined by Philos [47].

Notation 2. *During the main results, we need to define the following abbreviations:*

$$\psi(s) = \int_{s_0}^{s}\mathcal{T}(s_0,u)\mathrm{d}u,$$

$$\Theta_1(s) = \sum_{k=0}^{m}\left(\prod_{n=0}^{2k}\eta\left(g^{[n]}(\tau(s))\right)\right)\left(\frac{1}{\eta(g^{[2k]}(\tau(s)))} - 1\right)\frac{\psi\left(g^{[2k]}(\tau(s))\right)}{\psi(\tau(s))},$$

$$\Theta_2(s) = \sum_{k=1}^{m}\left(\prod_{j=1}^{2k-1}\frac{1}{\eta(g^{[-j]}(\tau(s)))}\right)\left(1-\frac{1}{\eta(g^{[-2k]}(\tau(s)))}\frac{\psi\left(g^{[-2k]}(\tau(s))\right)}{\psi(g^{[-2k+1]}(\tau(s)))}\right),$$

$$\Theta(s) = \begin{cases} 1, & \textit{for } \eta = 0 \\ \Theta_1(s), & \textit{for } 0 < \eta < 1 \\ \Theta_2(s), & \textit{for } \eta > \psi\left(g^{[-2k]}(\tau(s))\right)/\psi\left(g^{[-2k+1]}(\tau(s))\right), \end{cases}$$

and

$$M_0 = \sum_{j=0}^{r+1}\binom{r+1}{r-j+1}(-1)^{r-j+1}\gamma^{r-j+1}\lambda^j\frac{\Gamma(\gamma+j-r)\Gamma(\lambda-j+1)}{\Gamma(\gamma+\lambda-r+1)}, \textit{ for } r \in \mathbb{Z}^+,$$

where $\gamma, \lambda \in (r, \infty)$,

$$\Gamma(\theta) = \int_0^{+\infty} x^{\theta-1}e^{-x}dx,\ \theta > 0,$$

and

$$k_0 = \frac{1}{(r+1)^{(r+1)}}.$$

3. Main Results

We present new conditions that guarantee that each solution to DDE (1) oscillates or converges to zero.

Theorem 3. *Suppose that (6) holds and the function $\mathcal{K} \in \Re$. In the event that a function, $\rho \in C^1([s_0, \infty), \mathbb{R}^+)$, is present and satisfies $\rho'(s) \geq 0$ such that*

$$\limsup_{s\to\infty}\int_\ell^s \mathcal{K}(s,\theta,\ell)\rho(\theta)\left(k_1^r k_2^r\frac{\tau^{2r}(\theta)}{(2\theta)^r}q(\theta)\Theta^r(\theta) - k_0 a(\theta)\left(h(s,\theta,\ell)+\frac{\rho'(\theta)}{\rho(\theta)}\right)^{r+1}\right)d\theta > 0, \tag{9}$$

for any $k_1, k_2 \in (0,1)$, then the solution $x(s)$ oscillates or tends to zero.

Proof. Suppose that $x \in \mathcal{P}$. Suppose that there is an $s \geq s_1$ such that $x(s) > 0$, $x(g(s)) > 0$, and $x(\tau(s)) > 0$. Clearly, $z(s) > 0$, $s \geq s_1$. From Lemma 1, we can see that (i) or (ii) is satisfied.

Assume that (ii) is satisfied. Since (6) holds, following from Lemma 2 that $\lim_{s\to\infty} x(s) = 0$. Now, assume that (i) is satisfied. We have

$$\begin{aligned} z'(s) &\geq \int_{s_0}^s \frac{a^{1/r}(u)z''(u)}{a^{1/r}(u)}du \geq a^{1/r}(s)z''(s)\int_{s_0}^s \frac{1}{a^{1/r}(u)}du \\ &\geq a^{1/r}(s)z''(s)\mathcal{T}(s_0,s),\ s \geq s_1 \end{aligned}$$

therefore, we find

$$\left(\frac{z'(s)}{\mathcal{T}(s_0,s)}\right)' = \frac{\mathcal{T}(s_0,s)z''(s) - z'(s)a^{-1/r}(s)}{\mathcal{T}^2(s_0,s)} = \frac{a^{1/r}(s)\mathcal{T}(s_0,s)z''(s) - z'(s)}{a^{1/r}(s)\mathcal{T}^2(s_0,s)} \leq 0,\ s \geq s_1. \tag{10}$$

Since

$$z(s) \geq \int_{s_0}^s \frac{\mathcal{T}(s_0,u)z'(u)}{\mathcal{T}(s_0,u)}du, \text{ for } s \geq s_1$$

by using (10), we obtain

$$z(s) \geq \frac{z'(s)}{\mathcal{T}(s_0,s)}\int_{s_0}^s \mathcal{T}(s_0,u)du \geq \frac{z'(s)}{\mathcal{T}(s_0,s)}\psi(s)$$

and so

$$\left(\frac{z(s)}{\psi(s)}\right)' = \frac{\psi(s)z'(s) - z(s)\mathcal{T}(s_0,s)}{\psi^2(s)} = \frac{\mathcal{T}^{-1}(s_0,s)\psi(s)z'(s) - z(s)}{\mathcal{T}^{-1}(s_0,s)\psi^2(s)} \leq 0,\ s \geq s_1. \tag{11}$$

From (3), we have

$$x(s) = z(s) - \eta(s)x(g(s)).$$

Now, assume that $\eta < 1$. Since $z(s)$ satisfies (i), following Lemma 5, that (7) holds. Using $g^{[2k+1]}(s) \leq g^{[2k]}(s) \leq s$, $z'(s) > 0$ and (11), we obtain

$$z\left(g^{[2k+1]}(s)\right) \leq z\left(g^{[2k]}(s)\right) \leq z(s),\ s \geq s_1$$

and

$$z\left(g^{[2k]}(s)\right) \geq \frac{\psi\left(g^{[2k]}(s)\right)z(s)}{\psi(s)},\ \text{for } k = 0,1,\ldots.$$

Thus, we see that (7) becomes

$$\begin{aligned}
x(s) &> \sum_{k=0}^{m}\left(\prod_{n=0}^{2k}\eta\left(g^{[n]}(s)\right)\right)\left(\frac{z\left(g^{[2k]}(s)\right)}{\eta(g^{[2k]}(s))} - z\left(g^{[2k]}(s)\right)\right)\\
&> \sum_{k=0}^{m}\left(\prod_{n=0}^{2k}\eta\left(g^{[n]}(s)\right)\right)\left(\frac{1}{\eta(g^{[2k]}(s))} - 1\right)z\left(g^{[2k]}(s)\right)\\
&> z(s)\sum_{k=0}^{m}\left(\prod_{n=0}^{2k}\eta\left(g^{[n]}(s)\right)\right)\left(\frac{1}{\eta(g^{[2k]}(s))} - 1\right)\frac{\psi\left(g^{[2k]}(s)\right)}{\psi(s)},\ s \geq s_1.
\end{aligned}$$

Using this inequality in (1), we obtain

$$\left(a(s)\left(\left(x(s) + \eta(s)x(g(s))\right)''\right)^r\right)' \leq -q(s)z^r(\tau(s))\Theta^r(s),\ s \geq s_1. \tag{12}$$

Now, assume that $\eta > 1$. It follows from the (3) that

$$\begin{aligned}
x(s) &= \frac{1}{\eta(g^{-1}(s))}\left(z\left(g^{-1}(s)\right) - x\left(g^{-1}(s)\right)\right)\\
&= \frac{z(g^{-1}(s))}{\eta(g^{-1}(s))} - \frac{1}{\eta(g^{-1}(s))\eta(g^{[-2]}(s))}\left(z\left(g^{[-2]}(s)\right) - x\left(g^{[-2]}(s)\right)\right)\\
&= \frac{z(g^{-1}(s))}{\eta(g^{-1}(s))}\\
&\quad -\frac{1}{\eta(g^{-1}(s))\eta(g^{[-2]}(s))}\left(z\left(g^{[-2]}(s)\right) - \frac{1}{\eta(g^{[-3]}(s))}\left(z\left(g^{[-3]}(s)\right) - x\left(g^{[-3]}(s)\right)\right)\right)\\
&= \frac{z(g^{-1}(s))}{\prod_{j=1}^{1}\eta(g^{[-j]}(s))} - \frac{z\left(g^{[-2]}(s)\right)}{\prod_{j=1}^{2}\eta(g^{[-j]}(s))}\\
&\quad +\frac{1}{\prod_{j=1}^{3}\eta(g^{[-j]}(s))}\left(z\left(g^{[-3]}(s)\right) - x\left(g^{[-3]}(s)\right)\right),\ s \geq s_1,
\end{aligned}$$

and so on. Thus, we have

$$x(s) > \sum_{k=1}^{m}\left(\prod_{j=1}^{2k-1}\frac{1}{\eta(g^{[-j]}(s))}\right)\left(z\left(g^{[-2k+1]}(s)\right) - \frac{1}{\eta(g^{[-2k]}(s))}z\left(g^{[-2k]}(s)\right)\right),\ s \geq s_1. \tag{13}$$

From the facts that $g^{[-2k]} \geq g^{[-2k+1]} \geq s$, $z' > 0$ and (11), we arrive at

$$z\left(g^{[-2k+1]}(s)\right) \geq z(s),\ s \geq s_1 \tag{14}$$

and

$$z\left(g^{[-2k]}(s)\right) \leq \frac{\psi\left(g^{[-2k]}(s)\right) z\left(g^{[-2k+1]}(s)\right)}{\psi\left(g^{[-2k+1]}(s)\right)},\ s \geq s_1. \tag{15}$$

Using (14) and (15) in (13), we obtain

$$x(s) > z(s) \sum_{k=1}^{m} \left(\prod_{j=1}^{2k-1} \frac{1}{\eta\left(g^{[-j]}(s)\right)} \right) \left(1 - \frac{1}{\eta\left(g^{[-2k]}(s)\right)} \frac{\psi\left(g^{[-2k]}(s)\right)}{\psi\left(g^{[-2k+1]}(s)\right)} \right),\ s \geq s_1$$

and so

$$x(\tau(s)) > z(\tau(s)) \sum_{k=1}^{m} \left(\prod_{j=1}^{2k-1} \frac{1}{\eta\left(g^{[-j]}(\tau(s))\right)} \right) \left(1 - \frac{1}{\eta\left(g^{[-2k]}(\tau(s))\right)} \frac{\psi\left(g^{[-2k]}(\tau(s))\right)}{\psi\left(g^{[-2k+1]}(\tau(s))\right)} \right),\ s \geq s_1.$$

From the above inequality and (1), we obtain (12), therefore,

$$\left(a(s)\left(\left(x(s) + \eta(s)x(g(s))\right)''\right)^r\right)' \leq 0. \tag{16}$$

Using (16), $a'(s) \geq 0$, and $z''(s) > 0$, we have $z'''(s) \leq 0$. Therefore, there exists an $s_2 \geq s_1$ such that $z(s)$ satisfies

$$z(\tau(s)) > 0,\ z'(s) > 0,\ z''(s) > 0,\ z'''(s) \leq 0,\ s \geq s_2.$$

We define $\omega(s)$ as follow:

$$\omega(s) = \rho(s) \frac{a(s)(z''(s))^r}{(z'(s))^r},\ s \geq s_2. \tag{17}$$

We see that $\omega(s) > 0$ and

$$\begin{aligned} \omega'(s) &= \rho'(s) \frac{a(s)(z''(s))^r}{(z'(s))^r} \\ &\quad + \frac{\rho(s)(z'(s))^r \left(a(s)(z''(s))^r\right)' - r\rho(s)a(s)(z''(s))^r (z'(s))^{r-1} z''(s)}{(z'(s))^{2r}},\ s \geq s_2. \end{aligned}$$

By using (12) and (17), we have

$$\omega'(s) \leq \rho'(s) \frac{\omega(s)}{\rho(s)} - \rho(s) \frac{q(s) z^r(\tau(s)) \Theta^r(s)}{(z'(s))^r} - r \frac{\omega^{(r+1)/r}(s)}{a^{1/r}(s) \rho^{1/r}(s)},\ s \geq s_2. \tag{18}$$

By using Lemma 3 with $u(s) = z'(s)$, there exists a $s_3 \geq s_2$ such that

$$\frac{z'(\tau(s))}{z'(s)} \geq k_1 \frac{\tau(s)}{s},\ s \geq s_3 \geq s_2. \tag{19}$$

By using Lemma 4, we have

$$\frac{z(s)}{z'(s)} \geq \frac{1}{2} k_2 s,\ s \geq s_3. \tag{20}$$

From (19) and (20), we obtain

$$\frac{1}{z'(s)} \geq k_1 \frac{\tau(s)}{sz'(\tau(s))} \geq k_1 k_2 \frac{\tau^2(s)}{2s} \frac{1}{z(\tau(s))}, \ s \geq s_3. \tag{21}$$

Using (18) and (21), we obtain

$$\omega'(s) \leq \rho'(s)\frac{\omega(s)}{\rho(s)} - k_1^r k_2^r \frac{\tau^{2r}(s)}{(2s)^r}\rho(s)q(s)\Theta^r(s) - r\frac{\omega^{(r+1)/r}(s)}{a^{1/r}(s)\rho^{1/r}(s)}, \ s \geq s_3$$

and so

$$k_1^r k_2^r \frac{\tau^{2r}(s)}{(2s)^r}\rho(s)q(s)\Theta^r(s) \leq -\omega'(s) + \rho'(s)\frac{\omega(s)}{\rho(s)} - r\frac{\omega^{(r+1)/r}(s)}{a^{1/r}(s)\rho^{1/r}(s)}, \ s \geq s_3. \tag{22}$$

Multiplying the above inequality by $\mathcal{K}(s,\theta,\ell)$ and integrating from $\ell \geq s_3$ to s, we obtain

$$\begin{aligned} &\int_\ell^s \mathcal{K}(s,\theta,\ell)k_1^r k_2^r \frac{\tau^{2r}(\theta)}{(2\theta)^r}\rho(\theta)q(\theta)\Theta^r(\theta)d\theta \\ \leq\ & -\int_\ell^s \mathcal{K}(s,\theta,\ell)\omega'(\theta)d\theta + \int_\ell^s \mathcal{K}(s,\theta,\ell)\rho'(\theta)\frac{\omega(\theta)}{\rho(\theta)}d\theta \\ & -r\int_\ell^s \frac{\mathcal{K}(s,\theta,\ell)\omega^{(r+1)/r}(\theta)}{a^{1/r}(\theta)\rho^{1/r}(\theta)}d\theta, \ \ell \geq s_3. \end{aligned} \tag{23}$$

By using (8), for all $s \geq \ell$, we have

$$\begin{aligned} &\int_\ell^s \mathcal{K}(s,\theta,\ell)k_1^r k_2^r \frac{\tau^{2r}(\theta)}{(2\theta)^r}\rho(\theta)q(\theta)\Theta^r(\theta)d\theta \\ \leq\ & \int_\ell^s \mathcal{K}(s,\theta,\ell)\left(\left(h(s,\theta,\ell) + \frac{\rho'(\theta)}{\rho(\theta)}\right)\omega(\theta) - r\frac{\omega^{(r+1)/r}(\theta)}{a^{1/r}(\theta)\rho^{1/r}(\theta)}\right)d\theta, \ s \geq \ell. \end{aligned} \tag{24}$$

Set

$$F(\vartheta) = \left(h(s,\theta,\ell) + \frac{\rho'(\theta)}{\rho(\theta)}\right)\vartheta - r\frac{\vartheta^{(r+1)/r}}{a^{1/r}(\theta)\rho^{1/r}(\theta)}, \ s \geq \ell.$$

A simple calculation implies when

$$\vartheta = k_0\rho(\theta)a(\theta)\left(h(s,\theta,\ell) + \frac{\rho'(\theta)}{\rho(\theta)}\right)^r, \ s \geq \ell$$

$F(\vartheta)$ has the maximum

$$k_0\rho(\theta)a(\theta)\left(h(s,\theta,\ell) + \frac{\rho'(\theta)}{\rho(\theta)}\right)^{r+1}, \ s \geq \ell$$

that is,

$$F(\vartheta) \leq F_{\max} = k_0\rho(\theta)a(\theta)\left(h(s,\theta,\ell) + \frac{\rho'(\theta)}{\rho(\theta)}\right)^{r+1}, \ s \geq \ell. \tag{25}$$

Using (24) and (25), we have

$$\begin{aligned} 0 \ \geq\ & \int_\ell^s \mathcal{K}(s,\theta,\ell)k_1^r k_2^r \frac{\tau^{2r}(\theta)}{(2\theta)^r}\rho(\theta)q(\theta)\Theta^r(\theta)d\theta \\ & -\int_\ell^s \mathcal{K}(s,\theta,\ell)k_0\rho(\theta)a(\theta)\left(h(s,\theta,\ell) + \frac{\rho'(\theta)}{\rho(\theta)}\right)^{r+1}d\theta, \ s \geq \ell \end{aligned}$$

and so

$$\int_{\ell}^{s} \mathcal{K}(s,\theta,\ell)\rho(\theta)\left(k_1^r k_2^r \frac{\tau^{2r}(\theta)}{(2\theta)^r} q(\theta)\Theta^r(\theta) - k_0 a(\theta)\left(h(s,\theta,\ell) + \frac{\rho'(\theta)}{\rho(\theta)}\right)^{r+1}\right) d\theta \leq 0,\ s \geq \ell.$$

Taking the super limit, we obtain

$$\limsup_{s\to\infty} \int_{\ell}^{s} \mathcal{K}(s,\theta,\ell)\rho(\theta)\left(k_1^r k_2^r \frac{\tau^{2r}(\theta)}{(2\theta)^r} q(\theta)\Theta^r(\theta) - k_0 a(\theta)\left(h(s,\theta,\ell) + \frac{\rho'(\theta)}{\rho(\theta)}\right)^{r+1}\right) d\theta \leq 0,\ s \geq \ell.$$

This contradicts (9) and the proof is complete. □

Theorem 4. *Assume that (6) holds and*

$$\mathcal{K}(s,\theta,\ell) = (s-\theta)^{\sigma}(\theta-\ell)^{\vartheta},$$

where σ, ϑ are constants greater than r. If there is a $\rho \in C^1([s_0,\infty),\mathbb{R}^+)$ satisfying $\rho'(s) \geq 0$ such that

$$\limsup_{s\to\infty} \int_{\ell}^{s} (s-\theta)^{\sigma}(\theta-\ell)^{\vartheta}\rho(\theta)\Phi(s,l,\theta) d\theta > 0 \tag{26}$$

for any $k_1, k_2 \in (0,1)$, then, the solution $x(s)$ is oscillatory or converges to zero, where

$$\Phi(s,l,\theta) := k_1^r k_2^r \frac{\tau^{2r}(\theta)}{(2\theta)^r} q(\theta)\Theta^r(\theta) - k_0 a(\theta)\left(\frac{\vartheta s - (\sigma+\vartheta)\theta + \sigma\ell}{(s-\theta)(\theta-\ell)} + \frac{\rho'(\theta)}{\rho(\theta)}\right)^{r+1}.$$

Proof. Suppose that $x \in \mathcal{P}$. Suppose that there is an $s \geq s_1$ such that $x(s) > 0$, $x(g(s)) > 0$, and $x(\tau(s)) > 0$. Clearly, $z(s) > 0$, $s \geq s_1$. Since

$$\mathcal{K}(s,\theta,\ell) = (s-\theta)^{\sigma}(\theta-\ell)^{\vartheta},\ s \geq \ell,$$

by using (8), we have

$$h(s,\theta,\ell) = \frac{\vartheta s - (\sigma+\vartheta)\theta + \sigma\ell}{(s-\theta)(\theta-\ell)},\ s \geq \ell.$$

Now, as in the proof of Theorem 3, we arrive at

$$\limsup_{s\to\infty} \int_{\ell}^{s} (s-\theta)^{\sigma}(\theta-\ell)^{\vartheta}\rho(\theta)\Phi(s,l,\theta) d\theta \leq 0,\ s \geq \ell.$$

This contradicts (26) and the proof is complete. □

Theorem 5. *Assume that (6) holds and*

$$\mathcal{K}(s,\theta,\ell) = (\mathcal{T}(s_0,s) - \mathcal{T}(s_0,\theta))^{\gamma}(\mathcal{T}(s_0,\theta) - \mathcal{T}(s_0,\ell))^{\lambda},$$

where γ, λ are constants greater than r. If there exists a function $\rho \in C^1([s_0,\infty),\mathbb{R}^+)$ satisfying $\rho'(s) \geq 0$ such that

$$\limsup_{s\to\infty} \int_{\ell}^{s} (\mathcal{T}(s_0,s) - \mathcal{T}(s_0,\theta))^{\gamma}(\mathcal{T}(s_0,\theta) - \mathcal{T}(s_0,\ell))^{\lambda}\rho(\theta)\Psi(s,l,\theta) d\theta > 0 \tag{27}$$

for any $k_1, k_2 \in (0,1)$, *then, the solution* $x(s)$ *is oscillatory or converges to zero, where*

$$\Psi(s,l,\theta) \ : \ = k_1^r k_2^r \frac{\tau^{2r}(\theta)}{(2\theta)^r} q(\theta)\Theta^r(\theta) \\ -k_0 a(\theta)\left(\frac{\lambda\mathcal{T}(s_0,s) - (\gamma+\lambda)\mathcal{T}(s_0,\theta) + \gamma\mathcal{T}(s_0,\ell)}{a^{1/r}(\theta)(\mathcal{T}(s_0,s) - \mathcal{T}(s_0,\theta))(\mathcal{T}(s_0,\theta) - \mathcal{T}(s_0,\ell))} + \frac{\rho'(\theta)}{\rho(\theta)}\right)^{r+1}.$$

Proof. Suppose that $x \in \mathcal{P}$. Suppose that there is an $s \geq s_1$ such that $x(s) > 0$, $x(g(s)) > 0$, and $x(\tau(s)) > 0$. Clearly, $z(s) > 0$, $s \geq s_1$. Since

$$\mathcal{K}(s,\theta,\ell) = (\mathcal{T}(s_0,s) - \mathcal{T}(s_0,\theta))^{\gamma}(\mathcal{T}(s_0,\theta) - \mathcal{T}(s_0,\ell))^{\lambda}, \ s \geq \ell,$$

by using (8), we have

$$h(s,\theta,\ell) = \frac{\lambda\mathcal{T}(s_0,s) - (\gamma+\lambda)\mathcal{T}(s_0,\theta) + \gamma\mathcal{T}(s_0,\ell)}{a^{1/r}(\theta)(\mathcal{T}(s_0,s) - \mathcal{T}(s_0,\theta))(\mathcal{T}(s_0,\theta) - \mathcal{T}(s_0,\ell))}, \ s \geq \ell.$$

Now, as in the proof of Theorem 3, we arrive at

$$\limsup_{s\to\infty} \int_{\ell}^{s} (\mathcal{T}(s_0,s) - \mathcal{T}(s_0,\theta))^{\gamma}(\mathcal{T}(s_0,\theta) - \mathcal{T}(s_0,\ell))^{\lambda}\rho(\theta)\Psi(s,l,\theta)d\theta \leq 0, \ s \geq \ell.$$

This contradicts (27) and the proof is complete. □

Corollary 1. *Suppose that (6) holds, r is an odd natural number and* $\rho(s) = 1$. *If there exist two constants* $\gamma, \lambda > r$ *such that*

$$\limsup_{s\to\infty} \frac{\int_{\ell}^{s} (\mathcal{T}(s_0,s) - \mathcal{T}(s_0,\theta))^{\gamma}(\mathcal{T}(s_0,\theta) - \mathcal{T}(s_0,\ell))^{\lambda} k_1^r k_2^r \frac{\tau^{2r}(\theta)}{(2\theta)^r} q(\theta)\Theta^r(\theta)d\theta}{(\mathcal{T}(s_0,s) - \mathcal{T}(s_0,\ell))^{\gamma+\lambda-r}} > k_0 M_0 \tag{28}$$

for any $k_1, k_2 \in (0,1)$, *then, the solution* $x(s)$ *is oscillatory or converges to zero.*

Proof. As in Theorem 5 with $\rho(s) = 1$, we have to sufficiently prove that (28) leads to (27). From

$$\int_0^1 y^{\gamma-1}(1-y)^{\lambda-1}dy = \frac{\Gamma(\gamma)\Gamma(\lambda)}{\Gamma(\gamma+\lambda)}.$$

Using $y = \varrho/\delta$, we obtain

$$\int_0^{\delta} (\delta-\varrho)^{\gamma+j-r-1}\varrho^{\lambda-j}d\varrho = \int_0^1 \delta^{\gamma+\lambda-r}(1-y)^{\gamma+j-r-1}y^{\lambda-j}dy \\ = \delta^{\gamma+\lambda-r}\frac{\Gamma(\gamma+j-r)\Gamma(\lambda-j+1)}{\Gamma(\gamma+\lambda-r+1)}. \tag{29}$$

Let $\varrho = \mathcal{T}(s_0,\theta) - \mathcal{T}(s_0,\ell)$ and $\delta = \mathcal{T}(s_0,s) - \mathcal{T}(s_0,\ell)$. Then, by (9),

$$\int_{\ell}^{s} a(\theta)(\mathcal{T}(s_0,s) - \mathcal{T}(s_0,\theta))^{\gamma}(\mathcal{T}(s_0,\theta) - \mathcal{T}(s_0,\ell))^{\lambda}\digamma(s,l,\theta)d\theta \\ = \int_0^{\delta} (\delta-\varrho)^{\gamma-r-1}\varrho^{\lambda-r-1}(\lambda(\delta-\varrho) - \gamma\varrho)^{r+1}d\varrho, \tag{30}$$

where

$$\digamma(s,l,\theta) := \left(\frac{\lambda\mathcal{T}(s_0,s) - (\gamma+\lambda)\mathcal{T}(s_0,\theta) + \gamma\mathcal{T}(s_0,\ell)}{a^{1/r}(\theta)(\mathcal{T}(s_0,s) - \mathcal{T}(s_0,\theta))(\mathcal{T}(s_0,\theta) - \mathcal{T}(s_0,\ell))}\right)^{r+1}, \ s \geq \ell,$$

and

$$(\lambda(\delta-\varrho)-\gamma\varrho)^{r+1}=\sum_{j=0}^{r+1}(-1)^{j}\binom{r+1}{j}(\lambda(\delta-\varrho))^{j}(\gamma\varrho)^{r+1-j}. \tag{31}$$

From (30) and (31), we have

$$\begin{aligned}&\int_{\ell}^{s}a(\theta)(\mathcal{T}(s_0,s)-\mathcal{T}(s_0,\theta))^{\gamma}(\mathcal{T}(s_0,\theta)-\mathcal{T}(s_0,\ell))^{\lambda}F(s,l,\theta)d\theta\\ =\;&\sum_{j=0}^{r+1}\binom{r+1}{r-j+1}(-1)^{r-j+1}\gamma^{r-j+1}\lambda^{j}\int_{0}^{\delta}\varrho^{\lambda-j}(\delta-\varrho)^{\gamma+j-r-1}d\varrho\\ =\;&(\mathcal{T}(s_0,s)-\mathcal{T}(s_0,\ell))^{\gamma+\lambda-r}M_0,\; s\geq\ell.\end{aligned} \tag{32}$$

Hence, by (28) and (32), (27) holds. The proof is complete. □

Corollary 2. *Suppose that (6) holds, r is an odd natural number, and* $\rho(s)=1$. *If there exist two constants* $\gamma,\lambda>r$ *such that*

$$\limsup_{s\to\infty}\frac{\int_{\ell}^{s}(\mathcal{T}(s_0,s)-\mathcal{T}(s_0,\theta))^{\gamma}(\mathcal{T}(s_0,\theta)-\mathcal{T}(s_0,\ell))^{\lambda}\frac{\tau^{2r}(\theta)}{\theta^{r}}q(\theta)\Theta^{r}(\theta)d\theta}{(\mathcal{T}(s_0,s)-\mathcal{T}(s_0,\ell))^{\gamma+\lambda-r}}>2^{r}k_0M_0, \tag{33}$$

then, the solution $x(s)$ *is oscillatory or converges to zero.*

Proof. We shall show (33) implies (28). Note that (33) implies

$$\left(\frac{k_1k_2}{2}\right)^{r}q(s)\Theta^{r}(\theta)\left(\frac{\tau^{2}(s)}{s}\right)^{r}=\left(\frac{k}{2}\right)^{r}q(s)\Theta^{r}(\theta)\left(\frac{\tau^{2}(s)}{s}\right)^{r}, \tag{34}$$

where $k=k_1k_2$. Conversely, (33) suggests, for $k\in(0,1)$,

$$\limsup_{s\to\infty}\frac{\int_{\ell}^{s}(\mathcal{T}(s_0,s)-\mathcal{T}(s_0,\theta))^{\gamma}(\mathcal{T}(s_0,\theta)-\mathcal{T}(s_0,\ell))^{\lambda}\frac{\tau^{2r}(\theta)}{\theta^{r}}q(\theta)\Theta^{r}(\theta)d\theta}{(\mathcal{T}(s_0,s)-\mathcal{T}(s_0,\ell))^{\gamma+\lambda-r}}>\frac{1}{k^{r}}2^{r}k_0M_0,\; s\geq\ell. \tag{35}$$

Combining (34) and (35), we obtain that (28) holds. Hence, by Corollary 1, we complete the proof. □

Example 1. *For the third-order NDDE*

$$\left(x(s)+\frac{1}{2}x\left(\frac{s}{2}\right)\right)'''+\frac{\kappa}{s^{3}}x\left(\frac{s}{2}\right)=0,\; s>1. \tag{36}$$

Note that $r=1$, $a(s)=1$, $\eta(s)=1/2<1$, $q(s)=\kappa/s^{3}$, $\kappa>0$, $g(s)=s/2$, *and* $\tau(s)=s/2$. *Condition (6) is satisfied, where*

$$\int_{s_0}^{\infty}\int_{v}^{\infty}\left(\frac{1}{a(u)}\int_{u}^{\infty}q(\theta)d\theta\right)^{1/r}dudv=\int_{s_0}^{\infty}\int_{v}^{\infty}\int_{u}^{\infty}\frac{\kappa}{\theta^{3}}d\theta dudv=\infty.$$

Note that

$$\mathcal{T}(s_0,s)=\int_{s_0}^{s}\frac{d\theta}{a^{1/r}(\theta)}=\int_{s_0}^{s}d\theta=(s-s_0)=(s-1).$$

We may choose $\gamma = 4,\ \lambda = 5$, *then*

$$\begin{aligned} M_0 &= \sum_{j=0}^{r+1} \binom{r+1}{r-j+1} (-1)^{r-j+1} \gamma^{r-j+1} \lambda^j \frac{\Gamma(\gamma+j-r)\Gamma(\lambda-j+1)}{\Gamma(\gamma+\lambda-r+1)} \\ &= \sum_{j=0}^{1+1} C_{1+1}^{1-j+1} (-1)^{1-j+1} 4^{1-j+1} 5^j \frac{\Gamma(4+j-1)\Gamma(5-j+1)}{\Gamma(4+5-1+1)} = 4.1664 \times 10^{-2} \end{aligned}$$

and so

$$2^r k_0 M_0 = (2)\left(\frac{1}{4}\right)\left(4.1664 \times 10^{-2}\right) = 2.0832 \times 10^{-2}.$$

Now,

$$\psi\left(g^{[2k]}(\tau(\mathrm{s}))\right) = \frac{\mathrm{s}^2}{2^{4k+3}},$$

$$\begin{aligned} \Theta_1(\mathrm{s}) &= \sum_{k=0}^{m} \left(\prod_{n=0}^{2k} \eta\left(g^{[n]}(\tau(\mathrm{s}))\right) \right) \left(\frac{1}{\eta\left(g^{[2k]}(\tau(\mathrm{s}))\right)} - 1 \right) \frac{\psi\left(g^{[2k]}(\tau(\mathrm{s}))\right)}{\psi(\tau(\mathrm{s}))} \\ &= \sum_{k=0}^{20} \left(\frac{1}{2}\right)^{2k+1} (1) \frac{\mathrm{s}^2}{2^{4k+3}} \frac{2^3}{\mathrm{s}^2} = \sum_{k=0}^{20} \left(\frac{1}{2}\right)^{2k+1} \frac{1}{2^{4k}} \\ &\approx 0.50794 := \mu_0, \end{aligned}$$

Moreover, for $\mathrm{s} > \ell > 1$, *the left side of (33) is*

$$\begin{aligned} &\limsup_{\mathrm{s}\to\infty} \frac{\int_\ell^{\mathrm{s}} (\mathcal{T}(\mathrm{s}_0,\mathrm{s}) - \mathcal{T}(\mathrm{s}_0,\theta))^\gamma (\mathcal{T}(\mathrm{s}_0,\theta) - \mathcal{T}(\mathrm{s}_0,\ell))^\lambda \frac{\tau^{2r}(\theta)}{\theta^r} q(\theta) \Theta^r(\theta) \mathrm{d}\theta}{(\mathcal{T}(\mathrm{s}_0,\mathrm{s}) - \mathcal{T}(\mathrm{s}_0,\ell))^{\gamma+\lambda-r}} \\ = &\limsup_{\mathrm{s}\to\infty} \frac{\mu_0 \kappa}{4(\mathrm{s}-\ell)^8} \int_\ell^{\mathrm{s}} \frac{(\mathrm{s}-\theta)^4 (\theta-\ell)^5}{\theta^2} \mathrm{d}\theta \\ = &\frac{\mu_0}{1120}\kappa. \end{aligned}$$

Therefore, from Corollary 2, it confirms that every positive solution of (36) approaches zero and that $\kappa \gtrapprox 45.934$.

Example 2. *Consider the third-order NDDE*

$$\left(\mathrm{s}\left(\left(x(\mathrm{s}) + \frac{1}{3} x\left(\frac{\mathrm{s}}{2}\right) \right)''' \right)^3 \right)' + \frac{\kappa}{\mathrm{s}^6} x^3\left(\frac{\mathrm{s}}{2}\right) = 0,\ \mathrm{s} > 1. \tag{37}$$

Note that $r = 3,\ a(\mathrm{s}) = \mathrm{s},\ \eta(\mathrm{s}) = 1/3 < 1,\ q(\mathrm{s}) = \kappa/\mathrm{s}^6,\ \kappa > 0, g(\mathrm{s}) = \mathrm{s}/2$, *and* $\tau(\mathrm{s}) = \mathrm{s}/2$. *Condition (6) is satisfied, where*

$$\int_{\mathrm{s}_0}^\infty \int_v^\infty \left(\frac{1}{a(u)} \int_u^\infty q(\theta) \mathrm{d}\theta \right)^{1/r} \mathrm{d}u \mathrm{d}v = \int_{\mathrm{s}_0}^\infty \int_v^\infty \left(\frac{1}{u} \int_u^\infty \frac{\kappa}{{}^6} \mathrm{d}\theta \right)^{1/3} \mathrm{d}u \mathrm{d}v = \infty.$$

Note that

$$\mathcal{T}(\mathrm{s}_0,\mathrm{s}) = \int_{\mathrm{s}_0}^{\mathrm{s}} \frac{\mathrm{d}\theta}{a^{1/r}(\theta)} = \frac{3}{2}\left(\mathrm{s}^{2/3} - 1\right).$$

We may choose $\gamma = 4,\ \lambda = 5$, *then*

$$\begin{aligned} M_0 &= \sum_{j=0}^{r+1} \binom{r+1}{r-j+1} (-1)^{r-j+1} \gamma^{r-j+1} \lambda^j \frac{\Gamma(\gamma+j-r)\Gamma(\lambda-j+1)}{\Gamma(\gamma+\lambda-r+1)} \\ &= \sum_{j=0}^{3+1} C_{3+1}^{3-j+1} (-1)^{3-j+1} 4^{3-j+1} 5^j \frac{\Gamma(4+j-3)\Gamma(5-j+1)}{\Gamma(4+5-3+1)} = 27.5 \end{aligned}$$

and so

$$2^r k_0 M_0 = 2^3 \frac{1}{(4)^4}(27.5) = 0.85938.$$

Now,

$$\psi\left(g^{[2k]}(\tau(\mathrm{s}))\right) = \frac{9}{10} \frac{\mathrm{s}^{5/3}}{2^{(10k+5)/3}},$$

$$\begin{aligned} \Theta_1(\mathrm{s}) &= \sum_{k=0}^{m} \left(\prod_{n=0}^{2k} \eta\left(g^{[n]}(\tau(\mathrm{s}))\right) \right) \left(\frac{1}{\eta\left(g^{[2k]}(\tau(\mathrm{s}))\right)} - 1 \right) \frac{\psi\left(g^{[2k]}(\tau(\mathrm{s}))\right)}{\psi(\tau(\mathrm{s}))} \\ &= \sum_{k=0}^{20} \left(\frac{1}{3}\right)^{2k+1} (2) \frac{\mathrm{s}^{5/3}}{2^{(10k+5)/3}} \frac{2^{5/3}}{\mathrm{s}^{5/3}} = \sum_{k=0}^{20} \left(\frac{1}{3}\right)^{2k+1} (2) \frac{1}{2^{10k/3}} \\ &\approx 0.67410 := \mu_0, \end{aligned}$$

and, for $\mathrm{s} > \ell > 1$, *the left side of (33) takes*

$$\begin{aligned} &\limsup_{\mathrm{s}\to\infty} \frac{\int_\ell^{\mathrm{s}} (\mathcal{T}(\mathrm{s}_0,\mathrm{s}) - \mathcal{T}(\mathrm{s}_0,\theta))^\gamma (\mathcal{T}(\mathrm{s}_0,\theta) - \mathcal{T}(\mathrm{s}_0,\ell))^\lambda \frac{\tau^{2r}(\theta)}{\theta^r} q(\theta) \Theta^r(\theta) \mathrm{d}\theta}{(\mathcal{T}(\mathrm{s}_0,\mathrm{s}) - \mathcal{T}(\mathrm{s}_0,\ell))^{\gamma+\lambda-r}} \\ = &\limsup_{\mathrm{s}\to\infty} \left(\frac{3}{2}\right)^9 \frac{\mu_0^3 \kappa}{2^6 \left(\mathrm{s}^{2/3} - \ell^{2/3}\right)^6} \int_\ell^{\mathrm{s}} \frac{\left(\mathrm{s}^{2/3} - \theta^{2/3}\right)^4 \left(\theta^{2/3} - \ell^{2/3}\right)^5}{\theta^3} \mathrm{d}\theta \\ = &\left(\frac{3}{2}\right)^9 \frac{\mu_0^3 \kappa}{2^6 (20)}. \end{aligned}$$

Hence, by Corollary 2, it confirms that every nonoscillatory solution of (37) converges to zero provided that $\kappa \gtrapprox 93.412$.

Remark 1. *Consider the NDDE*

$$\left(x(\mathrm{s}) + \frac{1}{2} x\left(\frac{\mathrm{s}}{4}\right) \right)''' + \frac{\kappa}{\mathrm{s}^3} x\left(\frac{\mathrm{s}}{2}\right) = 0,\ \mathrm{s} > 1. \tag{38}$$

We find that Theorem 1 in [42] and Theorem 2 in [44] cannot be applied to this equation because $\tau(\mathrm{s}) = \mathrm{s}/2 > g(\mathrm{s}) = \mathrm{s}/4$. *While using the results we obtained, we find that the solutions of (38) are oscillatory or tend to zero. Therefore, our results improve the results in [42,44].*

Remark 2. *We note that additional conditions were mentioned in [42,44], including the composition condition* $(\tau \circ g = g \circ \tau)$, *which is a harsh condition on the delay functions, while we were able to dispense with these conditions in our results. We also note that the results we obtained are considered an expansion and extension of both [41,43], as we find that in [41], (1) was studied when* $0 \le \eta(\mathrm{s}) \le \eta < 1$, *and we find in [43] that Equation (1) was studied when* $a = 1$ *and* $\eta(\mathrm{s}) \ge 1$, *while in our study, Equation (1) was studied when* $0 \le \eta(\mathrm{s}) \le \eta_0 < \infty$.

Remark 3. *From Example 1 in [41], we find that every nonoscillatory solution of (37) converges to zero provided that* $\kappa > 9^3/2$. *However, by using our criterion (33), we find that every nonoscillatory* *solution of (37) converges to zero provided that* $\kappa > 93.412$. *Hence, our findings enhance those presented in [41].*

4. Conclusions

It is known that studying the solution behavior of odd-order differential equations is more difficult than studying even-order equations. This is due to several reasons, one of which is the ability to obtain relationships between the different derivatives of positive solutions, as well as the multiplicity of derivative possibilities for positive solutions. Based on the improved relationship between x and z that was derived in [45], we obtained new relationships between x and z. The new relationship takes into account the cases $\eta \leq 1$ and $\eta > 1$, and this was not usual in previous studies of neutral third-order differential equations. Using the appropriate Riccati substitution, we obtained the Riccati inequality and then applied the Philos approach to obtain new criteria for the asymptotic behavior of the studied equation. The new criteria ensure that all nonoscillatory solutions converge to zero. The results provided in this work improve and extend the well-known results in previous works; for instance, see [41–44]. It would also be of interest to use this approach to study the equation

$$\left(a(\mathrm{s})\left(\left(x(\mathrm{s})+\eta(\mathrm{s})x(g(\mathrm{s}))\right)^{(n-1)}\right)^{r}\right)' + q(\mathrm{s})x^{r}(\tau(\mathrm{s})) = 0,$$

where $n \geq 3$.

Author Contributions: Conceptualization, H.S.A., W.A., A.M., O.M. and E.M.E.; Methodology, H.S.A., W.A., A.M., O.M. and E.M.E.; Investigation, H.S.A., W.A., A.M., O.M. and E.M.E.; Writing—original draft, H.S.A. and A.M.; Writing—review & editing, W.A., O.M. and E.M.E. All authors have read and agreed to the published version of the manuscript.

Funding: This research is funded by Princess Nourah bint Abdulrahman University Researchers Supporting Project number (PNURSP2024R157), Princess Nourah bint Abdulrahman University, Riyadh, Saudi Arabia.

Data Availability Statement: Data are contained within the article.

Acknowledgments: The authors gratefully acknowledge the editor and the anonymous reviewers for their comments that improved the final version of the manuscript. Princess Nourah bint Abdulrahman University Researchers Supporting Project number (PNURSP2024R157), Princess Nourah bint Abdulrahman University, Riyadh, Saudi Arabia.

Conflicts of Interest: The authors declare no conflicts of interest.

References

1. Hale, J.K. Functional differential equations. In *Oxford Applied Mathematical Sciences*; Springer: New York, NY, USA, 1971; Volume 3.
2. Rihan, F.A. *Delay Differential Equations and Applications to Biology*; Springer Nature Singapore Pte Ltd.: Singapore, 2021.
3. Ladde, G.S.; Lakshmikantham, V.; Zhang, B.G. *Oscillation Theory of Differential Equations with Deviating Arguments*; Marcel Dekker: New York, NY, USA, 1987.
4. Gyori, I.; Ladas, G. *Oscillation Theory of Delay Differential Equations with Applications*; Clarendon Press: Oxford, UK, 1991.
5. Erbe, L.H.; Kong, Q.; Zhong, B.G. *Oscillation Theory for Functional Differential Equations*; Marcel Dekker: New York, NY, USA, 1995.
6. Agarwal, R.P.; Grace, S.R.; O'Regan, D. *Oscillation Theory for Second Order Linear, Half-Linear, Superlinear and Sublinear Dynamic Equations*; Kluwer Academic Publishers: Dordrecht, The Netherlands, 2002.
7. Dzurina, J.; Jadlovska, I. A sharp oscillation result for second-order half-linear noncanonical delay differential equations. *Electron. J. Qual. Theory Differ. Equ.* **2020**, *46*, 1–14. [CrossRef]
8. Dzurina, J.; Jadlovska, I. Kneser-type oscillation criteria for second-order half-linear delay differential equations. *Appl. Math. Comput.* **2020**, *380*, 125289.
9. Jadlovska, I. Oscillation criteria of Kneser-type for second-order half-linear advanced differential equations. *Appl. Math. Lett.* **2020**, *106*, 106354. [CrossRef]
10. Jadlovska, I. New criteria for sharp oscillation of second-order neutral delay differential equations. *Mathematics* **2021**, *9*, 2089. [CrossRef]
11. Dzurina, J.; Grace, S.R.; Jadlovska, I.; Li, T. Oscillation criteria for second-order Emden-Fowler delay differential equations with a sublinear neutral term. *Math. Nachr.* **2020**, *5*, 910–922. [CrossRef]

12. Thandapani, E.; Tamilvanan, S.; Jambulingam, E.S. Oscillation of third order half linear neutral delay differential equations. *Int. J. Pure Appl. Math.* **2012**, *77*, 359–368.
13. Bohner, M.; Grace, S.R.; Jadlovska, I. Oscillation criteria for second-order neutral delay differential equations. *Electron. J. Qual. Theory Differ. Equ.* **2017**, *60*, 1–12. [CrossRef]
14. Bohner, M.; Grace, S.R.; Jadlovská, I. Sharp oscillation criteria for second-order neutral delay differential equations. *Math. Methods Appl. Sci.* **2020**, *17*, 10041–10053. [CrossRef]
15. Moaaz, O.; Ramos, H.; Awrejcewicz, J. Second-order Emden–Fowler neutral differential equations: A new precise criterion for oscillation. *Appl. Math. Lett.* **2021**, *118*, 107172. [CrossRef]
16. Almarri, B.; Moaaz, O.; Anis, M.; Qaraad, B. Third-Order Neutral Differential Equation with a Middle Term and Several Delays: Asymptotic Behavior of Solutions. *Axioms* **2023**, *12*, 166. [CrossRef]
17. Gopal, T.; Ayyappan, G.; Graef, J.R.; Thandapani, E. Oscillatory and asymptotic behavior of solutions of third-order quasi-linear neutral difference equations. *Math. Slovaca* **2022**, *72*, 411–418. [CrossRef]
18. Jadlovska, I.; Chatzarakis, G.E.; Dzurina, J.; Grace, S.R. On sharp oscillation criteria for general third-order delay differential equations. *Mathematics* **2021**, *9*, 1675. [CrossRef]
19. Thandapani, E.; Göktürk, B.; Özdemir, O.; Tunç, E. Oscillatory behavior of semi-canonical nonlinear neutral differential equations of third-order via comparison principles. *Qualit. Theo. Dyn. Syst.* **2023**, *22*, 30. [CrossRef]
20. Dzurina, J.; Thapani, E.; Tamilvanan, S. Oscillation of solutions to third order half-linear neutral differential equations. *Electron. J. Differ. Equ.* **2012**, *2012*, 29.
21. Su, M.; Xu, Z. Oscillation criteria of certain third order neutral differential equations. *Differ. Equ. Appl.* **2012**, *4*, 221–232. [CrossRef]
22. Alzabut, J.; Agarwal, R.P.; Grace, S.R.; Jonnalagadda, J.M.; Selvam, A.G.M.; Wang, C. A survey on the oscillation of solutions for fractional difference equations. *Mathematics* **2022**, *10*, 894. [CrossRef]
23. Graef, J.R.; Özdemir, O.; Kaymaz, A.; Tunc, E. Oscillation of damped second-order linear mixed neutral differential equations. *Monatsh. Math.* **2021**, *194*, 85–104. [CrossRef]
24. Yang, D.; Bai, C. On the oscillation criteria for fourth-order p-Laplacian differential equations with middle term. *J. Funct. Space* **2021**, *2021*, 1–10. [CrossRef]
25. Zeng, Y.; Li, Y.; Luo, L.; Luo, Z. Oscillation of generalized neutral delay differential equations of Emden-Fowler type with with damping. *J. Zhejiang Univ.-Sci. A* **2016**, *43*, 394–400.
26. Santra, S.S.; Scapellato, A. Some conditions for the oscillation of second-order differential equations with several mixed delays. *J. Fix. Point. Theory. A* **2022**, *24*, 18. [CrossRef]
27. Santra, S.S.; El-Nabulsi, R.A.; Khedher, K.M. Oscillation of second-order differential equations with multiple and mixed delays under a canonical operator. *Mathematics* **2021**, *9*, 1323. [CrossRef]
28. Santra, S.S.; Khedher, K.M.; Yao, S.W. New aspects for oscillation of differential systems with mixed delays and impulses. *Symmetry* **2021**, *13*, 780. [CrossRef]
29. Tunç, E.; Özdemir, O. Comparison theorems on the oscillation of even order nonlinear mixed neutral differential equations. *Math. Method. Appl. Sci.* **2023**, *46*, 631–640. [CrossRef]
30. Hassan, T.S.; Sun, Y.; Menaem, A.A. Improved oscillation results for functional nonlinear dynamic equations of second order. *Mathematics* **2020**, *8*, 1897. [CrossRef]
31. O'Regan, D.; Hassan, T.S. Oscillation criteria for solutions to nonlinear dynamic equations of higher order. *Hacet. J. Math. Stat.* **2016**, *45*, 417–427. [CrossRef]
32. Hassan, A.M.; Ramos, H.; Moaaz, O. Second-Order Dynamic Equations with Noncanonical Operator: Oscillatory Behavior. *Fractal Fract.* **2023**, *7*, 134. [CrossRef]
33. Chatzarakis, G.E.; Grace, S.R.; Jadlovská, I.; Li, T.; Tun ç, E. Oscillation criteria for third-order Emden–Fowler differential equations with unbounded neutral coefficients. *Complexity* **2019**, *2019*, 5691758. [CrossRef]
34. Dzurina, J.; Grace, S.R.; Jadlovska, I. On nonexistence of Kneser solutions of third-order neutral delay differential equations. *Appl. Math. Lett.* **2019**, **88**, 193–200. [CrossRef]
35. Moaaz, O.; Alnafisah, Y. An improved approach to investigate the oscillatory properties of third-order neutral differential equations. *Mathematics* **2023**, *11*, 2290. [CrossRef]
36. Moaaz, O.; Awrejcewicz, J.; Muhib, A. Establishing new criteria for oscillation of odd-order nonlinear differential equations. *Mathematics* **2020**, **8**, 937. [CrossRef]
37. Moaaz, O.; Dassios, I.; Muhsin, W.; Muhib, A. Oscillation theory for non-linear neutral delay differential equations of third order. *Appl. Sci.* **2020**, *10*, 4855. [CrossRef]
38. Moaaz, O.; Qaraad, B.; El-Nabulsi, R.A.; Bazighifan, O. New results for kneser solutions of third-order nonlinear neutral differential equations. *Mathematics* **2020**, *8*, 686. [CrossRef]
39. Muhib, A.; Abdeljawad, T.; Moaaz, O.; Elabbasy, E.M. Oscillatory properties of odd-order delay differential equations with distribution deviating arguments. *Appl. Sci.* **2020**, *10*, 5952. [CrossRef]
40. Pátíková, Z.; Fišnarová, S. Use of the modified Riccati technique for neutral half-linear differential equations. *Mathematics* **2021**, *9*, 235. [CrossRef]
41. Baculíková, B.; Džurina, J. Oscillation of third-order neutral differential equations. *Math. Comput. Model.* **2010**, *52*, 215–226. [CrossRef]

42. Thandapani, E.; Li, T. On the oscillation of third-order quasi-linear neutral functional differential equations. *Arch. Math.* **2011**, *47*, 181–199.
43. Graef, J.R.; Tunç, E.; Grace, S. Oscillatory and asymptotic behavior of a third-order nonlinear neutral differential equation. *Opusc. Math.* **2017**, *37*, 839–852. [CrossRef]
44. Kumar, M.S.; Ganesan, V. On the oscillatory behavior of solutions of third order nonlinear neutral differential equations. *Malaya J. Mat.* **2019**, *2019*, 596–599.
45. Moaaz, O.; Cesarano, C.; Almarri, B. An improved relationship between the solution and its corresponding function in neutral fourth-order differential equations and its applications. *Mathematics* **2023**, *11*, 1708. [CrossRef]
46. Kiguradze, I.T.; Chanturia, T.A. *Asymptotic Properties of Solutions of Nonautonomous Ordinary Diferential Equations*; Trans lated from the 1985 Russian original; Kluwer Academic: Dordrecht, The Netherlands, 1993.
47. Philos, C.G. Oscillation theroms for linear differential equations of second order. *Arch. Math.* **1989**, *53*, 482–492. [CrossRef]

mathematics

Article

Differentiation of Solutions of Caputo Boundary Value Problems with Respect to Boundary Data

Jeffrey W. Lyons

Department of Mathematical Sciences, The Citadel, 171 Moultrie Street, Charleston, SC 29409, USA; jlyons3@citadel.edu

Abstract: Under suitable continuity and uniqueness conditions, solutions of an α order Caputo fractional boundary value problem are differentiated with respect to boundary values and boundary points. This extends well-known results for nth order boundary value problems. The approach used applies a standard algorithm to achieve the result and makes heavy use of recent results for differentiation of solutions of Caputo fractional intial value problems with respect to initial conditions and continuous dependence for Caputo fractional boundary value problems.

Keywords: Caputo fractional differential equation; boundary value problem; continuous dependence; variational equation

MSC: 26A33; 34A08; 34B15

Citation: Lyons, J.W. Differentiation of Solutions of Caputo Boundary Value Problems with Respect to Boundary Data. *Mathematics* **2024**, *12*, 1790. https://doi.org/10.3390/math12121790

Academic Editors: Lingju Kong and Min Wang

Received: 14 May 2024
Revised: 3 June 2024
Accepted: 7 June 2024
Published: 8 June 2024

1. Introduction

Let $n \in \mathbb{N}$ with $\alpha \in (n-1, n)$ and $a < t_0 < b$ in $\mathbb{R}$. Our concern is characterizing partial derivatives with respect to the boundary data for solutions to the Caputo fractional boundary value problem

$$D^{\alpha}_{*t_0}x(t) = f(t, x(t), x'(t), \dots, x^{(n-1)}(t)), \quad a < t_0 < t < b, \tag{1}$$

satisfying conjugate boundary conditions

$$x(t_i) = x_i \tag{2}$$

where $D^{\alpha}_{*t_0}x$ is the Caputo fractional derivative of order α of the function $x(t)$ and $a < t_0 \leq t_1 < t_2 < \dots < t_n < b$ and $x_i \in \mathbb{R}$ for $1 \leq i \leq n$. These partial derivatives solve the associated Caputo fractional variational equation.

Definition 1. *The α order Caputo fractional variational equation of* (1) *along a solution $x(t)$ is the differential equation*

$$D^{\alpha}_{*t_0}z(t) = \sum_{j=0}^{n-1} \frac{\partial f}{\partial x_j}(t, x(t), x'(t), \dots, x^{(n-1)}(t))z^{(j)}. \tag{3}$$

In this paper, we impose suitable continuity and uniqueness hypotheses so that given a solution of (1), (2), one may take the derivative with respect to the boundary data. This derivative solves the variational Equation (3) with interesting boundary data where all but one of the boundary values are zero. Colloquially, we refer to this as studying the smoothness of conditions.

The history of initial and boundary data smoothness dates back to Peano and his work on the smoothness of initial conditions as cited by Hartman [1]. Subsequently, Peterson [2], Spencer [3], and Sukup [4] were among the first to shift to studying the smoothness of boundary conditions. In the following decade, these results were then extended by Henderson to right-focal boundary conditions [5,6] and conjugate-type boundary conditions [7]. Over the next several decades, results were introduced for nonlocal boundary conditions [8–10], difference equations [11–13], dynamic equations on time scales [14–16], and researchers incorporated parameters into the nonlinearity [15,17].

With this work, we broaden the scope even further by analyzing smoothness of solutions to Caputo fractional boundary value problems. Research into fractional differential equations has seen an explosion of articles in the past decade that seek to generalize results for integer order differential equations to fractional order. To name a few, we cite [18–27]. In fact, there also seem to be a limitless number of different ways to define a fractional derivative. However, two definitions have become the source of focus amongst a broad range of researchers in the field; namely the Riemann-Liouville and Caputo fractional derivatives. Brief definitions may be found in Section 2. For expository material on fractional differential equations, we refer the reader to [28–31].

The theorems and proof in this article are novel as no other research to date has attempted to extend boundary data smoothness to fractional differential equations. The reason is that the results found in this article rely heavily upon two recent results for Caputo fractional differential equations. The first establishes differentiation of solutions of Caputo initial value problems with respect to the initial data [22], and the second establishes the continuous dependence on boundary conditions for Caputo boundary value problems [32].

The idea behind the proof of our main result is to first assume a unique solution to a Caputo boundary value problem. Then, we define a difference quotient with respect to the boundary point or boundary value of interest. We view this difference quotient in terms of an initial value problem and apply Theorem 3.2 from [22]. This yields that the difference quotient solves the variational equation. Finally, we take a limit by applying the continuous dependence result, Theorem 4.2, from [32] which yields the desired result.

The remainder of the paper is organized as follows. In Section 2, one will find brief definitions of fractional integrals and derivatives. Section 3 is where we establish our sufficient hypotheses. For Section 4, we present important recent results in continuous dependence and smoothness of initial conditions. Following this, we have Section 5 that contains the main result and its proof. Finally, we conclude with a summary of project and thoughts on future research avenues.

2. Fractional Derivatives

Let $\alpha > 0$. The Riemann-Liouville fractional integral of a function x of order α, denoted $I^{\alpha}_{t_0}x$, is defined as

$$I^{\alpha}_{t_0}x(t) = \frac{1}{\Gamma(\alpha)}\int_{t_0}^{t}(t-s)^{\alpha-1}x(s)ds, \quad t_0 \leq t,$$

provided the right-hand side exists. Moreover, let $n \in \mathbb{N}$ denote a positive integer and assume $n-1 < \alpha \leq n$. The Riemann-Liouville fractional derivative of order α of the function x, denoted $D^{\alpha}_{t_0}x$, is defined as

$$D^{\alpha}_{t_0}x(t) = D^{n}I^{n-\alpha}_{t_0}x(t),$$

provided the right-hand side exists. If a function x is such that

$$D^{\alpha}_{t_0}\left(x(t) - \sum_{i=0}^{n-1}x^{(i)}(t_0)\frac{(t-t_0)^i}{i!}\right)$$

exists, then the Caputo fractional derivative of order α of x is defined by

$$D^{\alpha}_{*t_0}x(t) = D^{\alpha}_{t_0}\left(x(t) - \sum_{i=0}^{n-1}x^{(i)}(t_0)\frac{(t-t_0)^i}{i!}\right).$$

Remark 1. *A sufficient condition to guarantee the existence of the Caputo fractional derivative is the absolute continuity of the $(n-1)$st derivative of $x(t)$. See Theorem 3.1 in [28] and discussion thereafter.*

3. Preliminaries

Throughout this work, we make use of the following assumptions which are required to apply the continuous dependence and differentiation results from [22,32]

(1) $f : (a,b) \times \mathbb{R}^n \to \mathbb{R}$ is continuous;
(2) for $1 \le i \le n$, $\partial f(t, x_1, \ldots, x_n)/\partial x_i : (a,b) \times \mathbb{R}^n \to \mathbb{R}$ is continuous; and
(3) solutions to initial value problems for (1) are unique on (a,b);

Next, we present two more hypotheses which establish a uniqueness condition for (1) and (3), respectively.

(4) Given points $a < t_0 \le t_1 < t_2 < \ldots < t_n < b$, if y and z are solutions of (1) such that for $1 \le i \le n$, $y(t_i) = z(t_i)$, then $y(t) = z(t)$ on $[t_0, b)$; and
(5) given points $a < t_0 \le t_1 < t_2 < \ldots < t_n < b$, if u is a solution of (3) along (1) such that for $1 \le i \le n$, $u(t_i)$=0, then $u(t) \equiv 0$ on $[t_0, b)$.

Next, we present two crucial results that make this work possible.
Let $[c,d] \subset \mathbb{R}$ and for $x \in C[c,d]$, define

$$\|x\|_{0,[c,d]} = \max_{t \in [c,d]} |x(t)|.$$

If $k \in \mathbb{N}$, for $x \in C^k[c,d]$, define

$$\|x\|_{k,[c,d]} = \max\{\|x\|_{0,[c,d]}, \|x'\|_{0,[c,d]}, \ldots, \|x^{(k)}\|_{0,[c,d]}\}.$$

We seek a boundary value problem result as an analog of the initial value problem result from Eloe et al. [22].

Theorem 1. *Assume that hypotheses* (1)–(3) *hold. Let $y(t) := y(t; t_0, y_0, \ldots, y_{n-1})$ be the unique solution of the initial value problem* (1) *satisfying*

$$y^{(i)}(t_0) = y_i,\ i = 0, \ldots, n-1, \tag{4}$$

with maximal interval of existence $[t_0, \omega)$. Choose $[c,d] \subset [t_0, \omega)$. Then,

(a) for each $0 \le j \le n-1$, $\gamma_j(t) := \partial y(t)/\partial y_j$ exists and is the solution of the variational Equation (3) *along $y(t)$ on $[c,d]$ and hence, $[t_0, \omega)$ satisfying the initial conditions*

$$\gamma_j^{(i)}(t_0) = \delta_{ij},\ 0 \le i \le n-1;$$

(b) if, in addition, f has a continuous first derivative with respect to t and

$$f(t_0, y_0, y_1, \ldots, y_{n-1}) = 0,$$

then $\beta(t) := \partial y(t)/\partial t_0$ exists and is the solution of the variational Equation (3) *along $y(t)$ on $[c,d]$ and hence, $[t_0, \omega)$ satisfying the initial conditions*

$$\beta^{(i)}(t_0) = -y^{(i+1)}(t_0),\ 0 \le i \le n-1; \text{ and}$$

(c) Under the additional in (b), $\beta(t) = -\sum_{i=0}^{n-1} y^{(i+1)}(t_0)\gamma_i(t)$.

We also use recent continuous dependence on boundary conditions results for Caputo fractional differential equations [32]. The first one is if the left-most boundary condition is to the right of the starting point of the Caputo fractional derivative; namely $t_0 < t_1$, and the second is if they are equal; namely $t_0 = t_1$. Note that the second result has an additional condition to establish continuous dependence to the left of t_0.

Theorem 2. *[Case when $t_0 < t_1$] Assume that hypotheses* (1), (3), *and* (4) *hold. Let $x(t)$ be a solution of* (1) *on $[t_0, b)$, $[c, d] \subset [t_0, b)$ with points $t_0 \leq c < t_1 < t_2 < \ldots < t_n < d$, and $\epsilon > 0$. Then, there exists a $\delta(\epsilon, [c, d]) > 0$ such that if for $1 \leq i \leq n$, $|t_i - \tau_i| < \delta$ with $c < \tau_1 < \tau_2 < \tau_3 < \ldots \tau_n < d$ and $|x(t_i) - y_i| < \delta$ with $y_i \in \mathbb{R}$, then there exists a solution $y(t)$ of* (1) *satisfying $y(\tau_i) = y_i$. Also,*

$$||x(t) - y(t)||_{n-1,[c,d]} < \epsilon.$$

Theorem 3. *[Case when $t_0 = t_1$] Assume that hypotheses* (1), (3), *and* (4) *hold. Let $x(t)$ be a solution of* (1) *on $[t_1, b)$, $[c, d] \subset [t_1, b)$ with points $c = t_1 < t_2 < \ldots < t_n < d$, and $\epsilon > 0$. Then, there exists a $\delta(\epsilon, [c, d]) > 0$ such that if for $2 \leq i \leq n$, $|t_i - \tau_i| < \delta$ with $c < \tau_2 < \tau_3 < \ldots \tau_n < d$ and for $1 \leq i \leq n$, $|x(t_i) - y_i| < \delta$ with $y_i \in \mathbb{R}$, then there exists a solution $y(t)$ of* (1) *satisfying $y(t_1) = y_1$ and for $2 \leq i \leq n$, $y(\tau_i) = y_i$. Also,*

$$||x(t) - y(t)||_{n-1,[c,d]} < \epsilon.$$

Additionally, if $f_k : (a, b) \times \mathbb{R}^n \to \mathbb{R}$ is a sequence of continuous functions that converge uniformly to f on compact subsets of $[c, d] \times \mathbb{R}^n$ and for $k \geq 1$, t_1^k is an increasing sequence such that $t_1^k \uparrow t_1^-$ as $k \to \infty$, then there exists a K such that if $k \geq K$, then

$$||x_k(t) - x(t)||_{n-1,[c,d]} \to 0 \quad as \quad k \to \infty.$$

4. Main Results

In this section, we present our boundary value problem analog. First, we state and prove the result when $t_0 < t_1$.

Theorem 4. *[Case when $t_0 < t_1$] Assume conditions* (1)–(5) *are satisfied and that $t_0 < t_1$. Let $x(t) := x(t, t_1, \ldots, t_n, x_1, \ldots, x_n)$ be a solution of* (1) *satisfying $x(t_i) = x_i$ for $1 \leq i \leq n$ on $[t_0, \omega) \subset (a, b)$. Then,*

(a) *for each $1 \leq j \leq n$, $z_j(t) := \partial x(t)/\partial x_j$ exists and is the solution of the variational Equation* (3) *along $x(t)$ on $[c, d]$ and hence, $[t_0, \omega)$ satisfying the boundary conditions*

$$z_j(t_i) = \delta_{ij},\ 1 \leq i \leq n;$$

(b) *if f has a continuous first derivative with respect to t and for each $1 \leq j \leq n$,*

$$f\left(t_j, x(t_j), x'(t_j), \ldots, x^{(n-1)}(t_j)\right) = 0,$$

then $w_j(t) := \partial x(t)/\partial t_j$ exists and is the solution of the variational Equation (3) *along $x(t)$ on $[c, d]$ and hence, $[t_0, \omega)$ satisfying the boundary conditions*

$$w_j(t_i) = -x'(t_i)\delta_{ij},\ 1 \leq i \leq n; \text{ and}$$

(c) *Under the conditions of (b), for each $1 \leq j \leq n$, $w_j(t) = -x'(t_j)z_j(t)$.*

Proof. We will only prove part (a) as the proof of part (b) is similar. Part (c) is an immediate consequence from parts (a) and (b) when coupled with hypothesis (5).

Let $1 \leq j \leq n$, and consider $\partial x(t)/\partial x_j$. In the interests of conserving space and lessening the tedious notation, we denote $x(t; t_1, \ldots, t_n, x_1, \ldots, x_j, \ldots, x_n)$ by $x(t; x_j)$ as x_j is the boundary value of interest.

Let $\delta > 0$ be as in Theorem 2, $0 < |h| < \delta$ be given, and define the difference quotient with respect to x_j by

$$z_{jh}(t) = \frac{1}{h}[x(t; x_j + h) - x(t; x_j)].$$

Note that for every $h \neq 0$,

$$\begin{aligned} z_{jh}(t_j) &= \frac{1}{h}[x(t_j; x_j + h) - x(t_j; x_j)] \\ &= \frac{1}{h}[(x_j + h) - x_j] \\ &= \frac{1}{h}[h] \\ &= 1. \end{aligned}$$

Also, for every $h \neq 0,\ 1 \leq k \leq n$ with $k \neq j$,

$$\begin{aligned} z_{jh}(t_k) &= \frac{1}{h}[x(t_k; x_j + h) - x(t_k; x_j)] \\ &= \frac{1}{h}[x_k - x_k] \\ &= 0. \end{aligned}$$

Now that we have established the boundary conditions for $z_{jh}(t)$, we show that $z_{jh}(t)$ solves the variational equation. To that end, for $1 \leq i \leq n-1$, let

$$v_i = x^{(i)}(t_j; x_j)$$

and

$$\epsilon_i = \epsilon_i(h) = x^{(i)}(t_j; x_j + h) - v_i.$$

By Theorem 2, for $1 \leq i \leq n-1$, $\epsilon_i = \epsilon_i(h) \to 0$ as $h \to 0$. Using the notation of Theorem 1 for solutions of initial value problems for (1), viewing $x(t)$ as the solution of an initial value problem, and denoting the solution $x(t)$ by $y(t; t_j, x_j, v_1, \ldots, v_{n-1})$, we have

$$z_{jh}(t) = \frac{1}{h}[y(t; t_j, x_j + h, v_1 + \epsilon_1, \ldots, v_{n-1} + \epsilon_{n-1}) - y(t; t_j, x_j, v_1, \ldots, v_{n-1})].$$

Then, by utilizing telescoping sums, we have

$$\begin{aligned} z_{jh}(t) =& \frac{1}{h}\Big\{[y(t; t_j, x_j + h, v_1 + \epsilon_1, \ldots, v_{n-1} + \epsilon_{n-1}) - y(t; t_j, x_j, v_1 + \epsilon_1, \ldots, v_{n-1} + \epsilon_{n-1})] \\ &+ [y(t; t_j, x_j, v_1 + \epsilon_1, \ldots, v_{n-1} + \epsilon_{n-1}) - y(t; t_j, x_j, v_1, \ldots, v_{n-1} + \epsilon_{n-1})] \\ &+ [y(t; t_j, x_j, v_1, \ldots, v_{n-1} + \epsilon_{n-1})) - \cdots] \\ &+ [y(t; t_j, x_j, v_1, \ldots, v_{n-1} + \epsilon_{n-1})) - y(t; t_j, x_j, v_1, \ldots, v_{n-1})]\Big\}. \end{aligned}$$

By Theorem 1 and the Mean Value Theorem, we obtain

$$\begin{aligned} z_{jh}(t) =& \frac{1}{h}\Big[\gamma_0(t, y(t; t_j, x_j + \bar{h}, v_1 + \epsilon_1, \ldots, v_{n-1} + \epsilon_{n-1}))(x_j + h - x_j) \\ &+ \gamma_1(t, y(t; t_j, x_j, v_1 + \bar{\epsilon}_1, \ldots, v_{n-1} + \epsilon_{n-1}))(v_1 + \epsilon_1 - v_1) + \cdots \\ &+ \gamma_{n-1}(t, y(t; t_j, x_j, v_1, \ldots, v_{n-1} + \bar{\epsilon}_{n-1}))(v_{n-1} + \epsilon_{n-1} - v_{n-1})\Big] \\ =& \gamma_0(t, y(t; t_j, x_j + \bar{h}, v_1 + \epsilon_1, \ldots, v_{n-1} + \epsilon_{n-1})) \\ &+ \frac{\epsilon_1}{h}\gamma_1(t, y(t; t_j, x_j, v_1 + \bar{\epsilon}_1, \ldots, v_{n-1} + \epsilon_{n-1})) + \cdots \\ &+ \frac{\epsilon_{n-1}}{h}\gamma_{n-1}(t, y(t; t_j, x_j, v_1, \ldots, v_{n-1} + \bar{\epsilon}_{n-1})) \end{aligned}$$

where, for $0 \le k \le n-1$, $\gamma_k(t, y(\cdot))$ is the solution of the variational Equation (3) along $y(\cdot)$ satisfying

$$\gamma_k^{(i)}(t_j) = \delta_{ik}, \ \ 0 \le i \le n-1.$$

Furthermore, for each $1 \le i \le n-1$, $v_i + \bar{\epsilon}_i$ is between v_i and $v_i + \epsilon_i$. Thus, to show $\lim_{h\to 0} z_{jh}(x)$ exists, it suffices to show, for each $1 \le i \le n-1$, $\lim_{h\to 0} \epsilon_i/h$ exists.

Now, from the construction of $z_{jh}(t)$, we have

$$z_{jh}(t_k) = 0, \ 1 \le k \le n \text{ with } k \ne j.$$

Hence, for $1 \le k \le n$ with $k \neq j$, we have a system of $n-1$ linear equations with $n-1$ unknowns:

$$\begin{aligned} &-\gamma_0(t_k, y(t; t_j, x_j + \bar{h}, v_1 + \epsilon_1, \ldots, v_{n-1} + \epsilon_{n-1})) \\ &= \frac{\epsilon_1}{h}\gamma_1(t_k, y(t; t_j, x_j, v_1 + \bar{\epsilon}_1, \ldots, v_{n-1} + \epsilon_{n-1})) + \cdots \\ &+ \frac{\epsilon_{n-1}}{h}\gamma_{n-1}(t_k, y(t; t_j, x_j, v_1, \ldots, v_{n-1} + \bar{\epsilon}_{n-1})). \end{aligned}$$

In the system of equations above, we notice that $y(\cdot)$ is not always the same. Therefore, we consider the coefficient matrix M based on $y(t)$

$$M := \begin{pmatrix} \gamma_1(t_1, y(t)) & \gamma_2(t_1, y(t)) & \cdots & \gamma_{n-1}(t_1, y(t)) \\ \gamma_1(t_2, y(t)) & \gamma_2(t_2, y(t)) & \cdots & \gamma_{n-1}(t_2, y(t)) \\ \vdots & \vdots & \ddots & \vdots \\ \gamma_1(t_{j-1}, y(t)) & \gamma_2(t_{j-1}, y(t)) & \cdots & \gamma_{n-1}(t_{j-1}, y(t)) \\ \gamma_1(t_{j+1}, y(t)) & \gamma_2(t_{j+1}, y(t)) & \cdots & \gamma_{n-1}(t_{j+1}, y(t)) \\ \vdots & \vdots & \ddots & \vdots \\ \gamma_1(t_n, y(t)) & \gamma_2(t_n, y(t)) & \cdots & \gamma_{n-1}(t_n, y(t))) \end{pmatrix}.$$

We claim $\det(M) \neq 0$. Suppose to the contrary that $\det(M) = 0$. Then, there exist $p_i \in \mathbb{R}$ for $1 \le i \le n-1$ not all zero such that

$$p_1 \begin{pmatrix} \gamma_1(t_1, y(t)) \\ \gamma_1(t_2, y(t)) \\ \vdots \\ \gamma_1(t_{j-1}, y(t)) \\ \gamma_1(t_{j+1}, y(t)) \\ \vdots \\ \gamma_1(t_n, y(t)) \end{pmatrix} + \cdots + p_{n-1} \begin{pmatrix} \gamma_{n-1}(t_1, y(t)) \\ \gamma_{n-1}(t_2, y(t)) \\ \vdots \\ \gamma_{n-1}(t_{j-1}, y(t)) \\ \gamma_{n-1}(t_{j+1}, y(t)) \\ \vdots \\ \gamma_{n-1}(t_n, y(t)) \end{pmatrix} = \begin{pmatrix} 0 \\ 0 \\ \vdots \\ 0 \\ 0 \\ \vdots \\ 0 \end{pmatrix}.$$

Set

$$w(t,y(t)) := p_1\gamma_1(t,y(t)) + \cdots + p_{n-1}\gamma_{n-1}(t,y(t)).$$

Then, $w(t,y(t))$ is a nontrivial solution of the variational Equation (3). However, $w(t_j,y(t))$ = 0, and for $1 \le k \le n-1$ with $k \ne j$, $w(x_k,y(t)) = 0$. By hypothesis (5), $w(t,y(t)) = 0$. Thus, $p_1 = p_2 = \cdots = p_{n-1} = 0$ which is a contradiction to the choice of the p_i's. Hence, $\det(M) \ne 0$.

As a result of continuous dependence, for $h \ne 0$ and sufficiently small, $\det(M(h)) \ne 0$ implying $M(h)$ has an inverse where $M(h)$ is the appropriately defined matrix from the system of equations. Therefore, for each $1 \le i \le n-1$, we are able to find ϵ_i/h using Cramer's rule.

Note as $h \to 0$, $\det(M(h)) \to \det(M)$, and so for $1 \le i \le n-1$, $\epsilon_i(h)/h \to \det(M_i)/\det M := B_i$ as $h \to 0$, where M_i is the $n-1 \times n-1$ matrix found by replacing the appropriate column of the matrix defining M by

$$\text{col}\Big[-\gamma_0(t_1,x(t)), -\gamma_0(t_2,x(t)), \ldots, -\gamma_0(t_{j-1},x(t)), -\gamma_0(t_{j+1},x(t)), \ldots, -\gamma_0(t_k,x(t))\Big].$$

Now, let $z_j(t) = \lim_{h\to 0} z_{jh}(t)$, and by construction of $z_{jh}(t)$,

$$z_j(t) = \frac{\partial x}{\partial x_j}(t).$$

Furthermore,

$$z_j(t) = \lim_{h\to 0} z_{jh}(t) = \gamma_0(t,x(t)) + \sum_{i=1}^{n-1} B_i\gamma_i(t,x(t))$$

which is a solution of the variational Equation (3) along $x(t)$. In addition, for $1 \le j \le n$,

$$z_j(x_k) = \lim_{h\to 0} z_{jh}(x_k) = \delta_{jk}.$$

This completes the argument for $\partial x(t)/\partial x_j$. □

Next, with the additional assumption from Theorem 3, the same result is established for $t_0 = t_1$ and the proof remains the same. Without this additional assumption, the derivative at t_1 would only be a right-hand derivative but the result still holds.

Theorem 5. *[Case when $t_0 = t_1$] Assume conditions* (1)–(5) *are satisfied and that $t_0 = t_1$. Let $x(t) := x(t,t_1,\ldots,t_n,x_1,\ldots,x_n)$ be a solution of* (1) *satisfying $x(t_i) = x_i$ for $1 \le i \le n$ on $[t_0,\omega) \subset (a,b)$. Then,*

(a) for each $1 \le j \le n$, $z_j(t) := \partial x(t)/\partial x_j$ exists and is the solution of the variational Equation (3) *along $x(t)$ on $[c,d]$ and hence, $[t_0,\omega)$ satisfying the boundary conditions*

$$z_j(t_i) = \delta_{ij},\ 1 \le i \le n;$$

(b) if f has a continuous first derivative with respect to t,

$$f\Big(t_1, x(t_1), x'(t_1), \ldots, x^{(n-1)}(t_1)\Big) = 0,$$

and additionally, $f_k : (a,b) \times \mathbb{R}^n \to \mathbb{R}$ is a sequence of continuous functions that converge uniformly to f on compact subsets of $[c,d] \times \mathbb{R}^n$ and for $k \ge 1$, t_1^k is an increasing sequence such that $t_1^k \uparrow t_1^-$ as $k \to \infty$, then $w_1(t) := \partial x(t)/\partial t_1$ exists and is the solution of the variational Equation (3) *along $x(t)$ on $[c,d]$ and hence, $[t_0,\omega)$ satisfying the boundary conditions*

$$w_1(t_i) = -x'(t_i)\delta_{i1},\ 1 \le i \le n;$$

(c) *for each* $2 \leq j \leq n$, *if* f *has a continuous first derivative with respect to* t *and*

$$f\left(t_j, x(t_j), x'(t_j), \ldots, x^{(n-1)}(t_j)\right) = 0,$$

then $w_j(t) := \partial x(t)/\partial t_j$ *exists and is the solution of the variational Equation* (3) *along* $x(t)$ *on* $[c, d]$ *and hence,* $[t_0, \omega)$ *satisfying the boundary conditions*

$$w_j(t_i) = -x'(t_i)\delta_{ij},\ 1 \leq i \leq n;\ and$$

(d) *Under the conditions of (b) and (c), for each* $1 \leq j \leq n$, $w_j(t) = -x'(t_j)z_j(t)$.

5. Conclusions

In this paper, we showed that under suitable continuity and uniqueness conditions that a solution Caputo fractional conjugate boundary value problem may be differentiated with respect to the boundary points and the boundary values. The resulting function solves the Caputo fractional version of the variational equation. This work only recently became possible as its proof relies extensively upon the differentiation of a solution to a Caputo fractional initial value problem [22] and the continuous dependence of solutions to Caputo fractional boundary value problems with respect to boundary data [32].

The results contained herein are novel and have not been explored or considered previously. We believe this result is foundational in smoothness of solutions for Caputo fractional boundary value problems and the proof sets a template for how to proceed for several future research avenues such as Caputo fractional differential equations with varying types of boundary conditions including parameter dependence, Caputo fractional difference equations, and Caputo fractional dynamic equations.

When looking at the wide breadth and depth of research conducted for smoothness of solutions for integer order differential, difference, and dynamic equations, it is clear there is a lot of work to be done in this area.

Other future work could entail loosening the hypothesis that the nonlinearity be continuously differentiable. This was posited for future study in [22]. Another avenue would be finding sufficient conditions to guarantee the uniqueness condition in hypothesis (3) in certain contexts.

Funding: This research received no external funding.

Data Availability Statement: No new data were created or analyzed in this study.

Conflicts of Interest: The author declares no conflicts of interest.

References

1. Hartman, P. *Ordinary Differential Equations*; Wiley: New York, NY, USA, 1964; 612p.
2. Peterson, A. Comparison theorems and existence theorems for ordinary differential equations. *J. Math. Anal. Appl.* **1976**, *55*, 773–784. [CrossRef]
3. Spencer, J.D. Relations between boundary value functions for a nonlinear differential equation and its variational equations. *Can. Math. Bull.* **1975**, *18*, 269–276. [CrossRef]
4. Sukup, D. On the existence of solutions to multipoint boundary value problems. *Rocky Mt. J. Math.* **1976**, *6*, 357–375. [CrossRef]
5. Henderson, J. Existence of solutions of right focal point boundary value problems for ordinary differential equations. *Nonlin. Anal.* **1981**, *5*, 989–1002. [CrossRef]
6. Henderson, J. Right focal point boundary value problems for ordinary differential equations and variational equations. *J. Math. Anal. Appl.* **1984**, *98*, 363–377. [CrossRef]
7. Henderson, J. Disconjugacy, disfocality, and differentiation with respect to boundary conditions. *J. Math. Anal. Appl.* **1987**, *121*, 1–9. [CrossRef]
8. Henderson, J.; Hopkins, B.; Kim, E.; Lyons, J.W. Boundary data smoothness for solutions of nonlocal boundary value problems for n-th order differential equations. *Involve* **2008**, *1*, 167–181. [CrossRef]
9. Henderson, J.; Karna, B.; Tisdell, C.C. Existence of solutions for three-point boundary value problems for second order equations. *Proc. Am. Math. Soc.* **2005**, *133*, 1365–1369. [CrossRef]

10. Janson, A.F.; Juman, B.T.; Lyons, J.W. The connections between variational equations and solutions of second order nonlocal integral boundary value problems. *Dynam. Syst. Appl.* **2014**, *23*, 493–503.
11. Datta, A.; Henderson, J. Differentiation of solutions of difference equations with respect to right focal boundary values. *Panamer. Math. J.* **1992**, *2*, 1–16.
12. Henderson, J.; Jiang, X. Differentiation with respect to parameters of solutions of nonlocal boundary value problems for difference equations. *Involve* **2015**, *8*, 629–636. [CrossRef]
13. Henderson, J.; Lee, L. Continuous dependence and differentiation of solutions of finite difference equations. *Int. J. Math. Math. Sci.* **1991**, *14*, 747–756. [CrossRef]
14. Baxter, L.H.; Lyons, J.W.; Neugebauer, J.T. Differentiating solutions of a boundary value problem on a time scale. *Bull. Aust. Math. Soc.* **2016**, *94*, 101–109. [CrossRef]
15. Jensen, W.M.; Lyons, J.W.; Robinson, R. Delta derivatives of the solution to a third-order parameter dependent boundary value problem on an arbitrary time scale. *Differ. Equ. Appl.* **2022**, *14*, 291–304. [CrossRef]
16. Lyons, J.W. Derivatives of solutions of nth order dynamic equations on time scales. *Sarajevo J. Math.* **2023**, *19*, 193–205.
17. Lyons, J.W.; Miller, J.K. The derivative of a solution to a second order parameter dependent boundary value problem with a nonlocal integral boundary condition. *J. Math. Stat. Sci.* **2015**, 43–50.
18. Abbas, S.; Benchohra, M.; Nieto, J.J. Caputo-Fabrizio fractional differential equations with non instantaneous impulses. *Rend. Circ. Mat. Palermo Ser. 2* **2022**, *71*, 131–144. [CrossRef]
19. Ahmad, B.; Alghanmi, M.; Ntouyas, S.K.; Alsaedi, A. A study of fractional differential equations and inclusions involving generalized Caputo-type derivative equipped with generalized fractional integral boundary conditions. *AIMS Math.* **2019**, *4*, 26–42. [CrossRef]
20. Bohner, M.; Hristova, S. Stability for generalized Caputo proportional fractional delay integro-differential equations. *Bound. Value Probl.* **2022**, *2022*, 14. [CrossRef]
21. Das, P.; Rana, S.; Ramos, H. Homotopy perturbation method for solving Caputo-type fractional-order Volterra-Fredholm integro-differential equations. *Comput. Math. Methods* **2019**, *1*, e1047. [CrossRef]
22. Eloe, P.W.; Lyons, J.W.; Neugebauer, J.T. Differentiation of solutions of Caputo initial value problems with respect to initial data. *PanAmer. Math. J.* **2020**, *30*, 71–80.
23. Eloe, P.W.; Masthay, T. Initial value problems for Caputo fractional differential equations. *J. Fract. Calc. Appl.* **2018**, *9*, 178–195.
24. Lan, K. Equivalence of higher order linear Riemann-Liouville fractional differential and integral equations. *Proc. Am. Math. Soc.* **2020**, *148*, 5225–5234. [CrossRef]
25. Tisdell, C.C. Basic existence and a priori bound results for solutions to systems of boundary value problems for fractional differential equations. *Electron. J. Differ. Equations* **2016**, *2016*, 1–9.
26. Wang, Y.; Li, X.; Huang, Y. The Green's function for Caputo fractional boundary value problem with a convection term. *AIMS Math.* **2022**, *7*, 4887–4897. [CrossRef]
27. Zhou, Y. Existence and uniqueness of solutions for a system of fractional differential equations. *Fract. Calc. Appl. Anal.* **2009**, *12*, 195–204.
28. Diethelm, K. *The Analysis of Fractional Differential Equations. An Application-Oriented Exposition Using Differential Operators of Caputo Type*; Lecture Notes in Mathematics; Springer: Berlin, Germany, 2010; 247p.
29. Kilbas, A.A.; Srivastava, H.M.; Trujillo, J.J. *Theory and Applications of Fractional Differential Equations*; North-Holland Mathematics Studies, 204; Elsevier Science B.V.: Amsterdam, The Netherlands, 2006; 523p.
30. Kiryakova, V. *Generalized Fractional Calculus and Applications*; Longman-Wiley: New York, NY, USA, 1994; 338p.
31. Podlubny, I. *Fractional Differential Equations*; Academic Press Inc.: San Diego, CA, USA, 1999; 340p.
32. Lyons, J.W. Continuous dependence on boundary conditions for Caputo fractional differential equations. *Rocky Mt. J. Math.* 2024, *in press*. Available online: https://projecteuclid.org/journals/rmjm/rocky-mountain-journal-of-mathematics/DownloadAcceptedPapers/220531-Lyons.pdf (accessed on 14 May 2024).

mathematics

Article

Stability and Bifurcation Analysis in a Discrete Predator–Prey System of Leslie Type with Radio-Dependent Simplified Holling Type IV Functional Response

Luyao Lv and Xianyi Li *

Department of Big Data Science, School of Science, Zhejiang University of Science and Technology, Hangzhou 310023, China; 212109701012@zust.edu.cn
* Correspondence: mathxyli@zust.edu.cn

Abstract: In this paper, we use a semi-discretization method to consider the predator–prey model of Leslie type with ratio-dependent simplified Holling type IV functional response. First, we discuss the existence and stability of the positive fixed point in total parameter space. Subsequently, through using the central manifold theorem and bifurcation theory, we obtain sufficient conditions for the flip bifurcation and Neimark–Sacker bifurcation of this system to occur. Finally, the numerical simulations illustrate the existence of Neimark–Sacker bifurcation and obtain some new dynamical phenomena of the system—the existence of a limit cycle. Corresponding biological meanings are also formulated.

Keywords: discrete predator–prey system of Leslie type; Holling type IV functional response; semi-discretization method; flip bifurcation; Neimark–Sacker bifurcation

MSC: 39A28; 39A30

Citation: Lv, L.; Li, X. Stability and Bifurcation Analysis in a Discrete Predator–Prey System of Leslie Type with Radio-Dependent Simplified Holling Type IV Functional Response. *Mathematics* **2024**, *12*, 1803. https://doi.org/10.3390/math12121803

Academic Editors: Lingju Kong and Min Wang

Received: 13 May 2024
Revised: 31 May 2024
Accepted: 4 June 2024
Published: 10 June 2024

1. Introduction and Preliminaries

In the past few decades, mathematical models have played a crucial role in the study of biology. According to different application environments, the interaction between populations can be expressed as consumer–resource [1], plant–herbivore [2], parasite–host [3], etc. Predator–prey models are the building blocks of ecosystems, as biomass grows from resource masses. This topic plays an important role in ecology [4–16].

Two of the most famous predator–prey dynamical models are the Lotka–Volterra model and the Leslie type model. Based on these models, subsequent scholars have considered more influencing factors, such as the fear effect [9], the Allee effect [12], super-predators [13], etc.

In [4], Leslie first proposed that the carrying capacity of the environment for the predator is proportional to the number of prey. So, this form of predator growth is also called Leslie–Gower type and can be represented as

$$\frac{dy}{dt} = sy(1 - \frac{y}{hx})$$

Therefore, the dynamical relationship between prey and predator may be expressed as

$$\begin{cases} \frac{dx}{dt} = g(x)x - f(x,y)y \\ \frac{dy}{dt} = sy(1 - \frac{y}{hx}) \end{cases} \quad (1)$$

where x and y represent prey and predator population sizes or densities, respectively; the function $g(x)$ characterizes the growth rate of prey in the absence of a predator, and may be represented through logistic growth $g(x) = r(1 - \frac{x}{k})$; $f(x,y)$ is a functional response curve and has many different forms, such as Holling types I–IV [17,18], Beddington–DeAngelis type [19,20], Hassell–Varley type [15,21], etc.; the parameter s signifies the intrinsic growth rate of the predator; and k and h denote the carrying capacity of the prey and predator provided by the environment, respectively.

As is well-known, the generalized Holling-IV response function is $f(x,y) = \frac{mx}{ax^2+bx+1}$. There is far less research on the Holling-IV response function than on the Holling-I–III response functions. Here, we assume that the prey growth follows logistic growth, and the functional response $f(x,y)$ is taken as a Holling-IV response function. Then, the system (1) can be reformulated as

$$\begin{cases} \frac{dx}{dt} = rx(1-\frac{x}{k}) - \frac{mx}{a+x^2}y \\ \frac{dy}{dt} = sy(1-\frac{y}{hx}) \end{cases} \tag{2}$$

Here, m and a are positive constants, the parameter m is the maximal predator per capita consumption rate, the parameter a is the number of prey necessary to achieve half of the maximum rate m, and the parameter r signifies the intrinsic growth rate of prey.

If one takes the functional response $f(x,y)$ as the ratio-dependent type, i.e., $f(x,y) = \frac{m\frac{x}{y}}{a+(\frac{x}{y})^2}$, then one has

$$\begin{cases} \frac{dx}{dt} = rx(1-\frac{x}{k}) - \frac{mxy^2}{ay^2+x^2} \\ \frac{dy}{dt} = sy(1-\frac{y}{hx}) \end{cases} \tag{3}$$

For the sake of the simplicity of mathematical analysis, we now non-dimensionalize the system (3). To accomplish this, let $\frac{x}{k} \to u, \frac{y}{l} \to v, rt \to \tau, hk \to l, \frac{k^2r}{m} \to \alpha, \frac{a}{k^2} \to \beta$, and $\frac{s}{r} \to \delta$. Then, one can derive an equivalent to the system (3) as follows:

$$\begin{cases} \frac{du}{d\tau} = u(1-u) - \frac{\alpha uv^2}{\beta v^2+u^2} \\ \frac{dv}{d\tau} = \delta v(1-\frac{v}{u}) \end{cases} \tag{4}$$

This continuous system has been discussed in [18], whereas its discrete version has not been found to be investigated yet. It is very difficult to solve a complicated continuous equation or system without using a computer. Meanwhile, many models in nature look more reasonable in their discrete forms. So, it is crucial to consider the discrete version corresponding to a continuous model.

Now, we use a semi-discretization method to discretize the system (4). Let $[t]$ denote the greatest integer not exceeding t. Consider the average change rate of the system (4) at integer number points, namely, the following model:

$$\begin{cases} \frac{1}{u(\tau)}\frac{du}{d\tau} = 1 - u([\tau]) - \frac{\alpha v^2([\tau])}{\beta v^2([\tau])+u^2([\tau])} \\ \frac{1}{v(\tau)}\frac{dv}{d\tau} = \delta(1-\frac{v([\tau])}{u([\tau])}) \end{cases} \tag{5}$$

One can see that a solution $(u(\tau), v(\tau))$ of the system (5) for $\tau \in [0,+\infty)$ has the following characteristics:

1. On the interval $[0,+\infty)$, $u(\tau)$ and $v(\tau)$ are continuous;
2. $\frac{du(\tau)}{d\tau}$ and $\frac{dv(\tau)}{d\tau}$ exist everywhere when $\tau \in [0,+\infty)$, possibly except at the points $\{0,1,2,3,\cdots\}$;
3. The system (5) is true on any interval $[n, n+1)$ with $n = 0,1,2,\cdots$.

The following system can be obtained by integrating the system (5) over the interval [n,τ] for any $\tau \in [n,n+1)$ and $n = 0,1,2,\cdots$

$$\begin{cases} ln\frac{u(\tau)}{u(n)} = \left(1 - u_n - \frac{\alpha(v_n)^2}{\beta(v_n)^2+(u_n)^2}\right)(\tau - n), \\ ln\frac{v(\tau)}{v(n)} = \delta(1-\frac{v_n}{u_n})(\tau - n) \end{cases} \tag{6}$$

Subsequently, we simultaneously take the exponent with e as the base for Equation (6):

$$\begin{cases} u(\tau) = u_n e^{\left(1-u_n-\frac{\alpha(v_n)^2}{\beta(v_n)^2+(u_n)^2}\right)(\tau-n)} \\ v(\tau) = v_n e^{\delta(1-\frac{v_n}{u_n})(\tau-n)} \end{cases} \tag{7}$$

where $u_n = u(n)$ and $v_n = v(n)$. Letting $\tau \to (n+1)^-$ in the system (7) produces

$$\begin{cases} u_{n+1} = u_n e^{1-u_n-\frac{\alpha(v_n)^2}{\beta(v_n)^2+(u_n)^2}} \\ v_{n+1} = v_n e^{\delta(1-\frac{v_n}{u_n})} \end{cases} \tag{8}$$

where the parameters $\alpha, \beta, \delta > 0$, and they are the same as in (4). The system (8) will be considered in the sequel.

The rest of this paper is organized as follows. In Section 2, we discuss the existence and stability of the positive fixed point because of the biological significance. In Section 3, we provide the sufficient conditions for the existence of the flip bifurcation and Neimark–Sacker bifurcation. In Section 4, we illustrate the theoretical results derived with numerical simulations. Finally, some conclusions and discussions are stated in Section 5.

2. Existence and Stability of Fixed Points

We discuss the existence and stability of non-negative fixed points of the system (8) in this section. The fixed point of the system (8) satisfies the following equation:

$$u - ue^{1-u-\frac{\alpha v^2}{\beta v^2+u^2}} = 0, v - ve^{\delta(1-\frac{v}{u})} = 0$$

It is easy to show that the system (8) has two non-negative fixed points $E_1 = (1,0)$ and $E_2 = (u^*, v^*)$ for $\alpha < \beta + 1$, where

$$u^* = \frac{1+\beta-\alpha}{1+\beta}, v^* = u^*$$

The Jacobian matrix of the system (8) at a fixed point $E(x,y)$ is

$$J(E) = \begin{pmatrix} \left(1-u+\frac{2\alpha u^2v^2}{(u^2+\beta v^2)^2}\right)e^{1-u-\frac{\alpha v^2}{\beta v^2+u^2}} & -\frac{2\alpha u^3 v}{(u^2+\beta v^2)^2}e^{1-u-\frac{\alpha v^2}{\beta v^2+u^2}} \\ \frac{\delta v^2}{u^2}e^{\delta(1-\frac{v}{u})} & \left(1-\frac{\delta v}{u}\right)e^{\delta(1-\frac{v}{u})} \end{pmatrix}$$

and its characteristic equation is

$$F(\lambda) = \lambda^2 - Tr(J(E))\lambda + Det(J(E)) = 0$$

where

$$Tr(J(E)) = \left(1-u+\frac{2\alpha u^2v^2}{(u^2+\beta v^2)^2}\right)e^{1-u-\frac{\alpha v^2}{\beta v^2+u^2}} + \left(1-\frac{\delta v}{u}\right)e^{\delta(1-\frac{v}{u})}$$

$$Det(J(E)) = \left[\left(1-u+\frac{2\alpha u^2v^2}{(u^2+\beta v^2)^2}\right)(1-\frac{v}{u}) + \frac{2\alpha uv^3}{(u^2+\beta v^2)^2}\right]e^{1-u-\frac{\alpha v^2}{\beta v^2+u^2}+\delta(1-\frac{v}{u})}$$

Before analyzing the properties of the fixed points of the system (8), we provide the following definition and Lemma [22–25].

Definition 1. *Let $E(x,y)$ be a fixed point of the system (8) with multipliers λ_1 and λ_2.*

(i) If $|\lambda_1| < 1$ and $|\lambda_2| < 1$, $E(x,y)$ is called sink, then a sink is locally asymptotically stable.

(ii) If $|\lambda_1| > 1$ and $|\lambda_2| > 1$, $E(x,y)$ is called source, then a source is locally asymptotically unstable.

(iii) If $|\lambda_1| < 1$ and $|\lambda_2| > 1$ (or $|\lambda_1| > 1$ and $|\lambda_2| < 1$), then $E(x,y)$ is called saddle.

(iv) If either $|\lambda_1| = 1$ or $|\lambda_2| = 1$, then $E(x, y)$ is called to be non-hyperbolic.

Lemma 1. *Let $F(\lambda) = \lambda^2 + B\lambda + C$, where B and C are two real constants. Suppose λ_1 and λ_2 are two roots of $F(\lambda) = 0$. Then, the following statements hold.*
(i) If $F(1) > 0$, then
(i.1) $|\lambda_1| < 1$ and $|\lambda_2| < 1$ if and only if $F(-1) > 0$ and $C < 1$;
(i.2) $\lambda_1 = -1$ and $\lambda_2 \neq -1$ if and only if $F(-1) = 0$ and $B \neq 2$;
(i.3) $|\lambda_1| < 1$ and $|\lambda_2| > 1$ if and only if $F(-1) < 0$;
(i.4) $|\lambda_1| > 1$ and $|\lambda_2| > 1$ if and only if $F(-1) > 0$ and $C > 1$;
(i.5) λ_1 and λ_2 are a pair of conjugate complex roots and $|\lambda_1| = |\lambda_2| = 1$ if and only if $-2 < B < 2$ and $C = 1$;
(i.6) $\lambda_1 = \lambda_2 = -1$ if and only if $F(-1) = 0$ and $B = 2$.
(ii) If $F(1) = 0$, namely, 1 is one root of $F(\lambda) = 0$, then another root λ satisfies $|\lambda| = (<, >)1$ if and only if $|C| = (<, >)1$.
(iii) If $F(1) < 0$, then $F(\lambda) = 0$ has one root lying in $(1, \infty)$. Moreover
(iii.1) the other root λ satisfies $\lambda < (=) - 1$ if and only if $F(-1) < (=)0$;
(iii.2) the other root $-1 < \lambda < 1$ if and only if $F(-1) > 0$.

Due to biological significance, we only consider E_2. By using Definition 1 and Lemma 1, the following result can be obtained.

Theorem 1. *For $\alpha < 1 + \beta$, $E_2 = (u^*, v^*) = (\frac{1+\beta-\alpha}{1+\beta}, \frac{1+\beta-\alpha}{1+\beta})$ is a positive fixed point of the system* (8).

Let $\delta_1 = 2 + \frac{4\alpha}{(1+\alpha+\beta)(1+\beta)}$ and $\delta_2 = \frac{3+\beta}{1+\beta} - \frac{1+\beta}{\alpha}$. The following statements are true about the positive fixed point E_2.
Case 1. When $0 < \alpha \leq \frac{(1+\beta)^2}{3+\beta}$, $\delta_2 \leq 0 < \delta_1$:
(1) if $0 < \delta < \delta_1$, then E_2 is a sink;
(2) if $\delta = \delta_1$, then E_2 is non-hyperbolic;
(3) if $\delta > \delta_1$, then E_2 is a saddle.
Case 2. When $\frac{(1+\beta)^2}{3+\beta} < \alpha < 1 + \beta$, $0 < \delta_2 < \delta_1$:
(1) if $0 < \delta < \delta_2$, then E_2 is a sink;
(2) if $\delta = \delta_2$, then E_2 is non-hyperbolic;
(3) if $\delta_2 < \delta < \delta_1$, then E_2 is a source;
(4)if $\delta = \delta_1$, then E_2 is non-hyperbolic;
(5) if $\delta > \delta_1$, then E_2 is a saddle.

Proof. The Jacobian matrix $J(E)$ of the system (8) at E_2 is

$$J(E_2) = \begin{pmatrix} \frac{\alpha}{1+\beta} + \frac{2\alpha}{(1+\beta)^2} & -\frac{2\alpha}{(1+\beta)^2} \\ \delta & 1 - \delta \end{pmatrix}$$

whose characteristic polynomial can be written as

$$F(\lambda) = \lambda^2 - P\lambda + Q \tag{9}$$

with

$$P = \frac{\alpha}{1+\beta} + \frac{2\alpha}{(1+\beta)^2} + 1 - \delta$$

$$\begin{aligned} Q &= \left(\frac{\alpha}{1+\beta} + \frac{2\alpha}{(1+\beta)^2}\right)(1-\delta) + \frac{2\delta\alpha}{(1+\beta)^2} \\ &= \frac{\alpha}{1+\beta}\left(\frac{3+\beta}{1+\beta} - \delta\right) \end{aligned}$$

□

It is easy to see that $F(1) = \delta(1 - \frac{\alpha}{1+\beta}) > 0$ always holds for $\alpha < 1+\beta$. Simple calculations display that

$$
\begin{aligned}
F(-1) &= 2[1 + \frac{\alpha}{1+\beta} + \frac{2\alpha}{(1+\beta)^2}] - \delta(1 + \frac{\alpha}{1+\beta}) \\
&= \frac{1+\alpha+\beta}{1+\beta}(\delta_1 - \delta) \\
Q - 1 &= \frac{\alpha}{1+\beta} + \frac{2\alpha}{(1+\beta)^2} - \frac{\delta\alpha}{1+\beta} - 1 \\
&= \frac{\alpha}{1+\beta}(\delta_2 - \delta)
\end{aligned}
$$

We can see that when $\delta > (=,<)\delta_1$, then $F(-1) < (=,>)0$, and when $\delta > (=,<)\delta_2$, then $Q < (=,>)1$.

Case 1. If $0 < \alpha \leq \frac{(1+\beta)^2}{3+\beta}$, then $\delta_2 \leq 0 < \delta_1$.

If $0 < \delta < \delta_1$, then $F(-1) > 0$. But $Q - 1 = \frac{\alpha}{1+\beta}(\delta_2 - \delta) < 0$, namely, $Q < 1$. Lemma 1 (i.1) states that E_2 is a stable node, i.e., a sink. If $\delta = \delta_1$, then $F(-1) = 0$; hence, E_2 is non-hyperbolic. If $\delta > \delta_1$, then $F(-1) < 0$, then Lemma 1 (i.3) says that E_2 is a saddle.

Case 2. If $\frac{(1+\beta)^2}{3+\beta} < \alpha < 1+\beta$, then $0 < \delta_2 < \delta_1$.

When $0 < \delta < \delta_2$, then $F(-1) > 0$ and $Q > 1$. By Lemma 1 (i.4), $|\lambda_1| > 1$ and $|\lambda_2| > 1$; therefore, E_2 is an unstable node, i.e., a source. When $\delta = \delta_2$, $F(-1) = 0$ and $Q = 1$. On one hand, the following applies:

$$
\begin{aligned}
P + 2 &= \frac{\alpha}{1+\beta} + \frac{2\alpha}{(1+\beta)^2} + 1 - \left(\frac{3+\beta}{1+\beta} - \frac{1+\beta}{\alpha}\right) + 2 \\
&= \frac{\alpha}{1+\beta} + \frac{2\alpha}{(1+\beta)^2} + \frac{2\beta}{1+\beta} + \frac{1+\beta}{\alpha} > 0
\end{aligned}
$$

So, $P > -2$. On the other hand, the following applies:

$$
\begin{aligned}
P - 2 &= \frac{\alpha}{1+\beta} + \frac{2\alpha}{(1+\beta)^2} - \left(\frac{3+\beta}{1+\beta} - \frac{1+\beta}{\alpha}\right) - 1 \\
&= \frac{\alpha}{1+\beta} + \frac{2\alpha}{(1+\beta)^2} - \frac{4+2\beta}{1+\beta} + \frac{1+\beta}{\alpha} \\
&= \frac{1}{\alpha(1+\beta)}\left(\frac{3+\beta}{1+\beta}\alpha^2 - 2(1+\beta)\alpha + (1+\beta)^2\right) \\
&< 0 \text{ because } \frac{(1+\beta)^2}{3+\beta} < \alpha < 1+\beta
\end{aligned}
$$

Hence, $P < 2$. Accordingly, $-2 < P < 2$. By Lemma 1 (i.5), Equation (9) has a pair of conjugate complex roots $\lambda_1$and λ_1 with $|\lambda_1| = |\lambda_2| = 1$, implying that E_2 is non-hyperbolic. When $\delta_2 < \delta < \delta_1$, $Q < 1$. Lemma 1 (i.1) tells us that $|\lambda_1| < 1$ and $|\lambda_2| < 1$, so E_2 is a stable node, i.e., a sink.

When $\delta = \delta_1$, then $F(-1) = 0$ and E_2 is non-hyperbolic.

When $\delta > \delta_1$, according to Lemma 1 (i.3), $|\lambda_1| < 1$ and $|\lambda_2| > 1$. Therefore, E_2 is a saddle. Summarizing the above discussions, we obtain the following Table 1.

Table 1. Type of the fixed point E_2.

Conditions		Eigenvalues	Properties
$0 < \alpha \leq \frac{(1+\beta)^2}{3+\beta}$	$0 < \delta < \delta_1$	$\lvert\lambda_1\rvert < 1, \lvert\lambda_2\rvert < 1$	sink (stable node)
	$\delta = \delta_1$	$\lambda_1 = -1, \lambda_2 \neq -1$	non-hyperbolic
	$\delta > \delta_1$	$\lvert\lambda_1\rvert < 1, \lvert\lambda_2\rvert > 1$	saddle
$\frac{(1+\beta)^2}{3+\beta} < \alpha < 1+\beta$	$0 < \delta < \delta_2$	$\lvert\lambda_1\rvert > 1, \lvert\lambda_2\rvert > 1$	source (unstable node)
	$\delta = \delta_2$	$\lvert\lambda_1\rvert = \lvert\lambda_2\rvert = 1$	non-hyperbolic
	$\delta_2 < \delta < \delta_1$	$\lvert\lambda_1\rvert < 1, \lvert\lambda_2\rvert < 1$	sink (stable node)
	$\delta = \delta_1$	$\lambda_1 = -1, \lambda_2 \neq -1$	non-hyperbolic
	$\delta > \delta_1$	$\lvert\lambda_1\rvert < 1, \lvert\lambda_2\rvert > 1$	saddle

3. Bifurcation Analysis

In this section, we employ the center manifold theorem and bifurcation theory to research the local bifurcation problems of the system (8) at the fixed point E_2.

3.1. Main Results

One can see from Theorem 1 that the fixed point E_2 is a non-hyperbolic fixed point when $\delta = \delta_1$. As soon as the parameter δ goes through the critical value δ_1, a flip bifurcation probably occurs near the fixed point E_2. Namely, the bifurcation probably occurs in the space of parameters

$$(\alpha, \beta) \in \Omega_1 = \left\{(\alpha, \beta) \in R_+^2 \mid 0 < \alpha < 1+\beta, \beta > 0\right\}$$

In fact, a result is obtained as follows.

Theorem 2. *Suppose the paramenters* $(\alpha, \beta) \in \Omega_1$. *Let* $\delta_1 = 2 + \frac{4\alpha}{(1+\alpha+\beta)(1+\beta)}$. *Assume* $c_{200}^2 + c_{300} \neq 0$*, where* c_{200} *and* c_{300} *will be defined in the sequel. If the parameter* δ *varies in a small neighborhood of the critical value* δ_1*, then the system* (8) *experiences a flip bifurcation at the fixed point* E_2.

When $\delta = \delta_2$, there is a pair of conjugate imaginary roots with $|\lambda_1| = |\lambda_2| = 1$, which ensures the necessary condition for a Neimark–Sacker bifurcation to occur. The following result may be obtained.

Theorem 3. *Suppose we have the following parameters:*

$$(\alpha, \beta) \in \Omega_2 = \left\{(\alpha, \beta) \in R_+^2 \mid \frac{(1+\beta)^2}{3+\beta} < \alpha < 1+\beta, \beta > 0\right\}$$

Let $\delta_2 = \frac{3+\beta}{1+\beta} - \frac{1+\beta}{\alpha}$*, and let L be defined in (18). Then, the system* (8) *undergoes a Neimark–Sacker bifurcation at the fixed point* E_2 *when the parament* δ *varies in a small neighborhood of the critical value* δ_2*. Moreover, if* $L < (>) 0$*, then a (an) stable (unstable) invariant closed orbit is bifurcated out from the fixed point* E_2 *of the system* (8).

3.2. Proof of Main Results

Proof of Theorem 2. First, let $X_n = u_n - u^*$ and $Y_n = v_n - u^*$, which transforms the fixed point E_2 to the origin. Then, the system (8) becomes

$$\begin{cases} X_{n+1} = (X_n + u^*)e^{1-X_n-u^*-\frac{\alpha(Y_n+u^*)^2}{\beta(Y_n+u^*)^2+(X_n+u^*)^2}} - u^* \\ Y_{n+1} = (Y_n + u^*)e^{\delta(1-\frac{Y_n+u^*}{X_n+u^*})} - u^* \end{cases} \tag{10}$$

Second, giving a small perturbation δ^* of the parameter δ around δ_1, i.e., $\delta^* = \delta - \delta_1$ with $0 < |\delta^*| \ll 1$, and letting $\delta^*_{n+1} = \delta^*_n = \delta^*$, the system (10) is perturbed into

$$\begin{cases} X_{n+1} = (X_n + u^*)e^{1-X_n-u^*-\frac{\alpha(Y_n+u^*)^2}{\beta(Y_n+u^*)^2+(X_n+u^*)^2}} - u^* \\ Y_{n+1} = (Y_n + u^*)e^{(\delta_1+\delta^*_n)(1-\frac{Y_n+u^*}{X_n+u^*})} - u^* \\ \delta^*_{n+1} = \delta^*_n \end{cases} \tag{11}$$

Using the Taylor expansion of the system (11) at $(X_n, Y_n, \delta^*_n) = (0, 0, 0)$, one has

$$\begin{cases} X_{n+1} = & a_{100}X_n + a_{010}Y_n + a_{200}X_n^2 + a_{020}Y_n^2 + a_{110}X_nY_n \\ & +a_{300}X_n^3 + a_{030}Y_n^3 + a_{210}X_n^2Y_n + a_{120}X_nY_n^2 + o(\rho_1^3) \\ Y_{n+1} = & b_{100}X_n + b_{010}Y_n + b_{001}\delta^*_n + b_{200}X_n^2 + b_{020}Y_n^2 + b_{002}(\delta^*_n)^2 \\ & +b_{110}X_nY_n + b_{101}X_n\delta^*_n + b_{011}Y_n\delta^*_n + b_{300}X_n^3 + b_{030}Y_n^3 \\ & +b_{003}(\delta^*_n)^3 + b_{210}X_n^2Y_n + b_{201}X_n^2\delta^*_n + b_{120}X_nY_n^2 + b_{021}Y_n^2\delta^*_n \\ & +b_{102}X_n(\delta^*_n)^2 + b_{012}Y_n(\delta^*_n)^2 + b_{111}X_nY_n\delta^*_n + o(\rho_1^3) \end{cases} \tag{12}$$

where $\rho_1 = \sqrt{X_n^2 + Y_n^2 + (\delta^*_n)^2}$.

$$a_{100} = \frac{\alpha}{1+\beta} + \frac{2\alpha}{(1+\beta)^2}, a_{010} = -\frac{2\alpha}{(1+\beta)^2}$$

$$a_{200} = \frac{2\alpha}{u^*(1+\beta)^2}\left(1 + \frac{\alpha}{(1+\beta)^2} - \frac{u^*}{2}\right) + \frac{\alpha(\beta-3)}{u^*(1+\beta)^3}$$

$$a_{020} = \frac{2\alpha^2}{u^*(1+\beta)^4} + \frac{\alpha(3\beta-1)}{u^*(1+\beta)^3}$$

$$a_{110} = -\frac{2\alpha}{(1+\beta)^2}\left(\frac{2\alpha}{u^*(1+\beta)^2} - \frac{\alpha}{1+\beta}\right) + \frac{4\alpha(1-\beta)}{u^*(1+\beta)^3}$$

$$\begin{aligned} a_{300} = & \frac{4u^*}{3}\left(\frac{\alpha}{u^*(1+\beta)^2} - \frac{1}{2}\right)^3 + 2\left(\frac{\alpha}{u^*(1+\beta)^2} - \frac{1}{2}\right)^2 - \frac{2\alpha}{(u^*)^2(1+\beta)^3} \\ & + \frac{2\alpha(\beta-3)}{(u^*)^2(1+\beta)^3}\left(\frac{\alpha}{u^*(1+\beta)^2} - \frac{1}{2}\right) + \frac{\alpha(\beta-3)}{1+\beta}\left(\frac{1}{(u^*)^2(1+\beta)^2} - \frac{2(u^*)^2}{\beta(1-3\beta)}\right) \end{aligned}$$

$$a_{030} = \frac{\alpha(3\beta-1)}{(u^*)^2(1+\beta)^3}\left(\frac{\alpha}{(1+\beta)^2} + \frac{2}{1+\beta} + \alpha\right) + \frac{2\alpha}{(u^*)^2(1+\beta)^3}\left(\frac{2\alpha}{3(1+\beta)^3} - 1\right)$$

$$\begin{aligned} a_{210} = & \frac{4\alpha}{u^*(1+\beta)^2}\left(\frac{u^*-\beta}{u^*(1+\beta)} + \frac{1}{2}\right) + \frac{\alpha\beta}{(1+\beta)^3}\left(16 - \frac{3\beta}{(u^*)^2}\right) \\ & - \frac{4\alpha}{3(1+\beta)^2}\left(\frac{\alpha}{u^*(1+\beta)^2} - \frac{1}{2}\right)^2 + \frac{2\alpha(\beta-3)}{(u^*)^2(1+\beta)^3}\left(1 - \frac{\beta}{1+\beta} - \frac{\alpha}{(1+\beta)^2}\right) \\ & + \frac{4(1-\beta)}{u^*(1+\beta)^2}\left(\frac{\alpha}{1+\beta} - 2\right)\left(\frac{\alpha}{u^*(1+\beta)^2} - \frac{1}{2}\right) \end{aligned}$$

$$\begin{aligned} a_{120} = & \left(\frac{10\alpha^2}{3u^*(1+\beta)^4} + \frac{(\alpha+1)(3\beta-1)}{u^*(1+\beta)^3}\right)\left(\frac{\alpha}{u^*(1+\beta)^2} - \frac{1}{2}\right) \\ & + \frac{16\alpha\beta}{(u^*)^2(1+\beta)^3}\left(\frac{\beta}{(u^*)^2(1+\beta)} - 1\right) + \frac{\alpha(3\beta-1)}{(u^*)^2(1+\beta)^3}\left(\frac{2\beta}{1+\beta} + 1\right) \end{aligned}$$

$$+\frac{2\alpha}{(u^*)^2(1+\beta)^2}\left(\frac{\alpha}{(1+\beta)^2}-\frac{\beta}{(u^*)^2(1+\beta)}+1\right)$$
$$+\frac{\alpha^2}{(u^*)^2(1+\beta)^5}\left(\frac{(\beta-3)}{3u^*(1+\beta)^2}-8(1+\beta)\right)$$
$$b_{001}=b_{002}=b_{003}=b_{102}=b_{012}=0, b_{100}=m\delta_1, b_{010}=1-\delta_1, b_{200}=-\frac{\delta_1(2-\delta_1)}{2u^*}$$

$$b_{020}=-\frac{\delta_1(2-\delta_1)}{2u^*}, b_{110}=\frac{\delta_1(2-\delta_1)}{u^*}, b_{101}=1, b_{011}=-1, b_{030}=\frac{\delta_1^2(3-\delta_1)}{6(u^*)^2}$$
$$b_{300}=\frac{\delta_1}{2(u^*)^2}\left(2-\delta_1-\frac{\delta_1(3-\delta_1)}{3}\right), b_{210}=\frac{\delta_1}{(u^*)^2}\left(-\frac{\delta_1^2}{2}+\frac{5\delta_1}{2}-2\right), b_{201}=\frac{(\delta_1-1)}{u^*}$$
$$b_{120}=\frac{\delta_2}{(u^*)^2}\left(\frac{\delta_1^2}{2}-2\delta_1+1\right), b_{021}=\frac{\delta_1-1}{u^*}, b_{111}=\frac{2(1-\delta_1)}{u^*}$$

Therefore, we obtain the Jacobian matrix of the system (11) at the fixed point E_2

$$J(E_2)=\begin{pmatrix}\frac{\alpha}{1+\beta}+\frac{2\alpha}{(1+\beta)^2} & -\frac{2\alpha}{(1+\beta)^2} & 0\\ \delta_1 & 1-\delta_1 & 0\\ 0 & 0 & 1\end{pmatrix}$$

and its eigenvalues

$$\lambda_1=-1, \lambda_2=a_{100}+2-\delta_1, \lambda_3=1$$

with corresponding eigenvectors

$$\xi_1=\begin{pmatrix}1\\ M\\ 0\end{pmatrix}, \xi_2=\begin{pmatrix}1\\ N\\ 0\end{pmatrix}, \xi_3=\begin{pmatrix}0\\ 0\\ 1\end{pmatrix}$$

where $M=1+\frac{(1+\beta)(1+\alpha+\beta)}{2\alpha}$ and $N=\frac{2(1+\beta)}{1+\alpha+\beta}$.

Set $T=(\xi_1,\xi_2,\xi_3)$, i.e.

$$T=\begin{pmatrix}1 & 1 & 0\\ M & N & 0\\ 0 & 0 & 1\end{pmatrix}$$

then

$$T^{-1}=\begin{pmatrix}\frac{N}{N-M} & -\frac{1}{N-M} & 0\\ -\frac{M}{N-M} & \frac{1}{N-M} & 0\\ 0 & 0 & 1\end{pmatrix}$$

Taking the transformation

$$(X_n, Y_n, \delta_n^*)^T=T(l_n, m_n, \omega_n)^T$$

the system (11) is changed into the following form:

$$\begin{pmatrix}l_{n+1}\\ m_{n+1}\\ \omega_{n+1}\end{pmatrix}=\begin{pmatrix}-1 & 0 & 0\\ 0 & \lambda_2 & 0\\ 0 & 0 & 1\end{pmatrix}\begin{pmatrix}l_n\\ m_n\\ \omega_n\end{pmatrix}+\begin{pmatrix}g_1(l_n,m_n,\omega_n)+o(\rho_2^3)\\ g_2(l_n,m_n,\omega_n)+o(\rho_2^3)\\ 0\end{pmatrix} \tag{13}$$

where $\rho_2=\sqrt{l_n^2+m_n^2+\omega_n^2}$.

$$g_1(l_n,m_n,\omega_n)=c_{200}l_n^2+c_{020}m_n^2+c_{002}\omega_n^2+c_{110}l_nm_n+c_{101}l_n\omega_n+c_{011}m_n\omega_n$$

$$
\begin{aligned}
&+ c_{300}l_n^3 + c_{030}m_n^3 + c_{003}\omega_n^3 + c_{210}l_n^2 m_n + c_{201}l_n^2\omega_n + c_{120}l_n m_n^2 \\
&+ c_{102}l_n\omega_n^2 + c_{012}m_n\omega_n^2 + c_{021}m_n^2\omega_n + c_{111}l_n m_n\omega_n \\
g_2(l_n, m_n, \omega_n) = &\, d_{200}l_n^2 + d_{020}m_n^2 + d_{002}\omega_n^2 + d_{110}l_n m_n + d_{101}l_n\omega_n + d_{011}m_n\omega_n \\
&+ d_{300}l_n^3 + d_{030}m_n^3 + d_{003}\omega_n^3 + d_{210}l_n^2 m_n + d_{201}l_n^2\omega_n + d_{120}l_n m_n^2 \\
&+ d_{102}l_n\omega_n^2 + d_{012}m_n\omega_n^2 + d_{021}m_n^2\omega_n + d_{111}l_n m_n\omega_n
\end{aligned}
$$

$$
\begin{aligned}
&c_{102} = c_{012} = c_{002} = c_{003} = 0 \\
&c_{200} = \gamma a_{200} + \mu b_{200} + M(\gamma a_{110} + \mu b_{110}) + M^2(\gamma a_{020} + \mu b_{020}) \\
&c_{110} = 2(\gamma a_{200} + \mu b_{200}) + (M+N)(\gamma a_{110} + \mu b_{110}) + 2MN(\gamma a_{020} + \mu b_{020}) \\
&c_{020} = \gamma a_{200} + \mu b_{200} + N(\gamma a_{110} + \mu b_{110}) + N^2(\gamma a_{020} + \mu b_{020}) \\
&c_{101} = \mu M b_{011} + \mu b_{101},\ c_{011} = \mu N b_{011} + \mu b_{101} \\
&c_{300} = \gamma a_{300} + \mu b_{300} + M^3(\gamma a_{030} + \mu b_{030}) + M(\gamma a_{210} + \mu b_{210}) \\
&\quad + M^2(\gamma a_{120} + \mu b_{120}),\ c_{030} = \gamma a_{300} + \mu b_{300} + N^3(\gamma a_{030} + \mu b_{030}) \\
&\quad + N(\gamma a_{210} + \mu b_{210}) + N^2(\gamma a_{120} + \mu b_{120}) \\
&c_{210} = 3(\gamma a_{300} + \mu b_{300}) + 3M^2N(\gamma a_{030} + \mu b_{030}) + (2M+N)(\gamma a_{210} + \mu b_{210}) \\
&\quad + (M^2 + 2MN)(\gamma a_{120} + \mu b_{120}),\ c_{120} = 3(\gamma a_{300} + \mu b_{300}) + 3MN^2(\gamma a_{030} + \mu b_{030}) \\
&\quad + (M+2N)(\gamma a_{210} + \mu b_{210}) + (N^2 + 2MN)(\gamma a_{120} + \mu b_{120}) \\
&c_{201} = \mu b_{201} + \mu M^2 b_{021} + \mu M b_{111},\ c_{021} = \mu b_{201} + \mu N^2 b_{021} + \mu N b_{111} \\
&c_{111} = \mu b_{201} + \mu MN b_{021} + \frac{\mu(M+N)b_{111}}{2} \\
&d_{102} = d_{012} = d_{002} = d_{003} = 0 \\
&d_{200} = \epsilon a_{200} - \mu b_{200} + M(\epsilon a_{110} - \mu b_{110}) + M^2(\epsilon a_{020} - \mu b_{020}) \\
&d_{110} = 2(\epsilon a_{200} - \mu b_{200}) + (M+N)(\epsilon a_{110} - \mu b_{110}) + 2MN(\epsilon a_{020} - \mu b_{020}) \\
&d_{020} = \epsilon a_{200} - \mu b_{200} + N(\epsilon a_{110} - \mu b_{110}) + N^2(\epsilon a_{020} + \mu b_{020}) \\
&d_{101} = -\mu M b_{011} - \mu b_{101},\ c_{011} = -\mu N b_{011} - \mu b_{101} \\
&d_{300} = \epsilon a_{300} - \mu b_{300} + M^3(\epsilon a_{030} - \mu b_{030}) + M(\epsilon a_{210} - \mu b_{210}) \\
&\quad + M^2(\epsilon a_{120} - \mu b_{120}),\ d_{030} = \epsilon a_{300} - \mu b_{300} + N^3(\epsilon a_{030} - \mu b_{030}) \\
&\quad + N(\epsilon a_{210} - \mu b_{210}) + N^2(\epsilon a_{120} - \mu b_{120}) \\
&d_{210} = 3(\epsilon a_{300} - \mu b_{300}) + 3M^2N(\epsilon a_{030} - \mu b_{030}) + (2M+N)(\epsilon a_{210} - \mu b_{210}) \\
&\quad + (M^2 + 2MN)(\epsilon a_{120} - \mu b_{120}),\ d_{120} = 3(\epsilon a_{300} - \mu b_{300}) + 3MN^2(\epsilon a_{030} - \mu b_{030}) \\
&\quad + (M+2N)(\epsilon a_{210} - \mu b_{210}) + (M^2 + 2MN)(\epsilon a_{120} - \mu b_{120}) \\
&d_{201} = -\mu b_{201} - \mu M^2 b_{021} - \mu M b_{111},\ d_{021} = -\mu b_{201} - \mu N^2 b_{021} - \mu N b_{111} \\
&d_{111} = -\mu b_{201} - \mu MN b_{021} - \frac{\mu(M+N)b_{111}}{2} \\
&\gamma = \frac{N}{N-M},\ \epsilon = -\frac{M}{N-M},\ \mu = -\frac{1}{N-M}
\end{aligned}
$$

Assume on the center manifold that

$$
m_n = h(l_n, \omega_n) = h_{20}l_n^2 + h_{11}l_n\omega_n + h_{02}\omega_n^2 + o(\rho_3^2)
$$

where $\rho_3 = \sqrt{l_n^2 + \omega_n^2}$. Then, according to (13), we obtain

$$
\begin{aligned}
m_{n+1} = &h(l_{n+1}, \omega_{n+1}) = \lambda_2 h(l_n, \omega_n) + g_2(l_n, h(l_n, \omega_n), \omega_n) + o(\rho_3^3) \\
h(l_{n+1}, \omega_{n+1}) &= h_{20}(-l_n + g_1(l_n, h(l_n, \omega_n), \omega_n))^2
\end{aligned}
$$

$$+h_{11}(-l_n+g_1(l_n,h(l_n,\omega_n),\omega_n))\omega_n+h_{02}\omega_n^2+o(\rho_3^3)$$

Comparing the corresponding coefficients of terms in the above center manifold equation, it is easy to derive that

$$h_{20}=\frac{d_{200}}{1-\lambda_2},h_{11}=\frac{d_{101}}{1-\lambda_2},h_{02}=0$$

So, the system (13) restricted to the center manifold is given by

$$\begin{aligned}l_{n+1}&=f(l_n,\omega_n)=:-l_n+g_1(l_n,h(l_n,\omega_n),\omega_n)+o(\rho_3^3)\\&=-l_n+c_{20}l_n^2+c_{11}l_n\omega_n+c_{30}l_n^3+c_{21}l_n^2\omega_n+c_{12}l_n\omega_n^2+o(\rho_3^3)\end{aligned}$$

Accordingly, we have the following:

$$f^2(l_n,\omega_n)=l_n-2c_{11}l_n\omega_n-2(c_{20}^2+c_{30})l_n^3+(c_{11}^2-2c_{12})l_n\omega_n^2-c_{11}c_{20}l_n^2\omega_n+o(\rho_3^3)$$

with $c_{20}=c_{200}$, $c_{11}=c_{101}$, $c_{30}=c_{300}$, $c_{21}=c_{100}h_{11}+c_{011}h_{20}+c_{201}$, and $c_{12}=c_{011}$.

It is not difficult to calculate

$$\begin{aligned}f(l_n,\omega_n)|_{(0,0)}&=0,\ \frac{\partial f}{\partial l_n}|_{(0,0)}=-1,\ \frac{\partial f^2}{\partial \omega_n}|_{(0,0)}=0,\ \frac{\partial^2 f^2}{\partial l_n^2}|_{(0,0)}=0\\ \frac{\partial^2 f^2}{\partial l_n\partial\omega_n}|_{(0,0)}&=-2c_{11}=-2c_{101}=-2\mu(1-M)\\&=\frac{2(1+\beta)(1+\alpha+\beta)^2}{2\alpha(1+\beta-\alpha)-(1+\beta)(1+\alpha+\beta)^2}\\&=\frac{2(1+\beta)(1+\alpha+\beta)^2}{-2\alpha(\beta^2+\beta+1)-(1+\beta)((1+\beta)^2+\alpha^2)}<0(\neq 0)\\ \frac{\partial^3 f^2}{\partial l_n^3}|_{(0,0)}&=-12(c_{20}^2+c_{30})=-12(c_{200}^2+c_{300})\neq 0\end{aligned}$$

According to (21.1.43)–(21.1.46) in [26], p. 507, all conditions are valid for a flip bifurcation to occur; hence, the system (8) undergoes a flip bifurcation at the fixed point E_2. The proof is complete. □

Next, we provide a proof for Theorem 3.

Proof of Theorem 3. First, give a small perturbation δ^{**} of the parameter δ around δ_2 in the system (10), i.e., $\delta^{**}=\delta-\delta_2$ with $0<|\delta^{**}|\ll 1$. Under the perturbation, the system (10) is

$$\begin{cases}X_{n+1}=(X_n+u^*)e^{1-X_n-u^*-\frac{\alpha(Y_n+u^*)^2}{\beta(Y_n+u^*)^2+(X_n+u^*)^2}}-u^*\\ Y_{n+1}=(Y_n+u^*)e^{(\delta_2+\delta^{**})(1-\frac{Y_n+u^*}{X_n+u^*})}-u^*\end{cases}\tag{14}$$

The characteristic equation of the linearized equation of the system (14) at the origin (0,0) is

$$F(\lambda)=\lambda^2-p(\delta^{**})\lambda+q(\delta^{**})=0\tag{15}$$

where

$$\begin{aligned}p(\delta^{**})&=\frac{\alpha(3+\beta)}{1+\beta}+1-\delta_2\\ q(\delta^{**})&=\frac{\alpha(3+\beta)}{1+\beta}(1-\delta_2-\delta^{**})+\frac{\alpha(\delta_2-\delta^{**})}{(1+\beta)^2}\end{aligned}$$

Notice that $p^2(0) - 4q(0) = \left(2 + \frac{\alpha\delta_2}{1+\beta} - \delta_2\right)^2 - 4 < 0$; so, for $0 < |\delta^{**}| \ll 1$, the two roots of $F(\lambda) = 0$ in (15) are

$$\lambda_{1,2}(\delta^{**}) = \frac{p(\delta^{**}) \pm i\sqrt{4q(\delta^{**}) - p^2(\delta^{**})}}{2}$$

The occurrence of a Neimark–Sacker bifurcation requires the following two conditions to be satisfied [26]:

1. $\left(\frac{d|\lambda_{1,2}(\delta^{**})|}{d\delta^{**}}\right)\Big|_{\delta^{**}=0} \neq 0$;
2. $\lambda_{1,2}^i(0) \neq 1, i = 1,2,3,4$.

It is easy to observe that $|\lambda_{1,2}(\delta^{**})| = \sqrt{q(\delta^{**})}$ and $(|\lambda_{1,2}(\delta^{**})|)|_{\delta^{**}=0} = \sqrt{q(0)} = 1$. Therefore

$$\left(\frac{d|\lambda_{1,2}(\delta^{**})|}{d\delta^{**}}\right)\Big|_{\delta^{**}=0} = -\frac{\alpha(2+\beta)^2}{(1+\beta)^2} < 0(\neq 0)$$

Obviously, $\lambda_{1,2}^i(0) \neq 1$ for $i = 1,2,3,4$,; so, the two conditions are satisfied.

Second, in order to derive the normal form of the system (14), one expands (14) in a power series up to the third-order term around the origin to obtain

$$\begin{cases} X_{n+1} = & s_{10}X_n + s_{01}Y_n + s_{20}X_n^2 + s_{11}X_nY_n + s_{02}Y_n^2 \\ & +s_{30}X_n^3 + s_{21}X_n^2Y_n + s_{12}X_nY_n^2 + s_{03}Y_n^3 + o(\rho_7^3) \\ Y_{n+1} = & t_{10}X_n + t_{01}Y_n + t_{20}X_n^2 + t_{11}X_nY_n + t_{02}Y_n^2 \\ & +t_{30}X_n^3 + t_{21}X_n^2Y_n + t_{12}X_nY_n^2 + t_{03}Y_n^3 + o(\rho_7^3) \end{cases} \quad (16)$$

where $\rho_7 = \sqrt{X_n^2 + Y_n^2}$.

$$\begin{aligned} & s_{10} = a_{100},\ s_{01} = a_{010},\ s_{20} = a_{200},\ s_{11} = a_{110} \\ & s_{02} = a_{020},\ s_{30} = a_{300},\ s_{21} = a_{210},\ s_{12} = a_{120},\ s_{03} = a_{030} \\ & t_{10} = \delta_2,\ t_{01} = 1 - \delta_2,\ t_{20} = \frac{\delta_2(\delta_2 - 2)}{2u^*},\ t_{02} = \frac{\delta_2(\delta_2 - 2)}{2u^*} \\ & t_{11} = -\frac{\delta_2(\delta_2 - 2)}{u^*},\ t_{30} = \frac{m\delta_2(\delta_2^2 - 6\delta_2 + 6)}{6(u^*)^2} \\ & t_{03} = -\frac{\delta_2^2(\delta_2 - 3)}{6(u^*)^2},\ t_{12} = \frac{\delta_2(\delta_2^2 - 2\delta_2 + 2)}{2(u^*)^2} \\ & b_{21} = -\frac{\delta_2(\delta_2^2 - 5\delta_2 + 4)}{2(u^*)^2} \end{aligned}$$

Take matrix

$$T = \begin{pmatrix} 0 & s_{01} \\ \eta & 1-\zeta \end{pmatrix},\ \text{then } T^{-1} = \begin{pmatrix} \frac{\zeta-1}{\eta_{01}} & \frac{1}{\eta} \\ \frac{1}{s_{01}} & 0 \end{pmatrix}$$

Make a change in variables

$$(X, Y)^T = T(M, N)^T$$

Then, the system (16) is changed to the following form:

$$\begin{pmatrix} M \\ N \end{pmatrix} \to \begin{pmatrix} \zeta & -\eta \\ \eta & \zeta \end{pmatrix}\begin{pmatrix} M \\ N \end{pmatrix} + \begin{pmatrix} g_3(M,N) + o(\rho_8^4) \\ g_4(M,N) + o(\rho_8^4) \end{pmatrix} \quad (17)$$

where $\rho_8 = \sqrt{M^2 + N^2}$.

$$g_3(M,N) = j_{20}X^2 + j_{11}XY + j_{02}Y^2 + j_{30}X^3 + j_{21}X^2v + j_{12}XY^2 + j_{03}Y^3$$

$$g_4(M,N) = k_{20}X^2 + k_{11}XY + k_{02}Y^2 + k_{30}X^3 + k_{21}X^2Y + k_{12}XY^2 + k_{03}Y^3$$
$$X = s_{01}N, Y = \eta M + (1-\zeta)N$$

$$j_{20} = \frac{s_{20}(\zeta-1)}{\eta s_{01}} + \frac{t_{20}}{\eta},\ j_{02} = \frac{s_{02}(\zeta-1)}{\eta a_{01}} + \frac{t_{02}}{\eta},\ j_{11} = \frac{s_{11}(\zeta-1)}{\eta s_{01}} + \frac{t_{11}}{\eta}$$
$$j_{30} = \frac{s_{30}(\zeta-1)}{\eta s_{01}} + \frac{t_{30}}{\eta},\ j_{03} = \frac{s_{03}(\zeta-1)}{\eta s_{01}} + \frac{t_{03}}{\eta},\ j_{12} = \frac{s_{12}(\zeta-1)}{\eta a_{01}} + \frac{t_{12}}{\eta}$$
$$j_{21} = \frac{s_{21}(\zeta-1)}{\eta s_{01}} + \frac{t_{21}}{\eta}, k_{20} = \frac{s_{20}}{s_{01}}, k_{02} = \frac{s_{02}}{s_{01}}, k_{11} = \frac{s_{11}}{s_{01}}, k_{30} = \frac{s_{30}}{s_{01}}$$
$$k_{03} = \frac{s_{03}}{s_{01}}, k_{12} = \frac{s_{12}}{s_{01}}, k_{21} = \frac{s_{21}}{s_{01}}$$

Furthermore

$$F_{XX}|_{(0,0)} = 2j_{02}\eta^3, F_{XY}|_{(0,0)} = j_{11}s_{01}\eta + 2j_{02}\eta(1-\zeta)$$
$$F_{YY}|_{(0,0)} = 2j_{02}s_{01}^2 + 2j_{11}s_{01}(1-\zeta), F_{XXX}|_{(0,0)} = 6j_{03}\eta^3$$
$$F_{XXY}|_{(0,0)} = 2j_{21}s_{01}\eta^2 + 6j_{03}\eta^2(1-\zeta)$$
$$F_{XYY}|_{(0,0)} = 2j_{21}s_{01}^2\eta + 4j_{12}s_{01}\eta(1-\zeta) + 6j_{03}\eta(1-\zeta)^2$$
$$F_{YYY}|_{(0,0)} = 4(1-\zeta)^3 + 6j_{30}s_{01}^3 + 4j_{21}s_{01}^2(1-\zeta) + 6j_{12}s_{01}(1-\zeta)^2$$
$$G_{XX}|_{(0,0)} = 2k_{02}\eta^3, G_{XY}|_{(0,0)} = k_{11}s_{01}\eta + 2k_{02}\eta(1-\zeta)$$
$$G_{YY}|_{(0,0)} = 2k_{02}s_{01}^2 + 2k_{11}s_{01}(1-\zeta), G_{XXX}|_{(0,0)} = 6j_{03}\eta^3$$
$$G_{XXY}|_{(0,0)} = 2k_{21}s_{01}\eta^2 + 6k_{03}\eta^2(1-\zeta)$$
$$G_{XYY}|_{(0,0)} = 2k_{21}s_{01}^2\eta + 4k_{12}s_{01}\eta(1-\zeta) + 6k_{03}\eta(1-\zeta)^2$$
$$G_{YYY}|_{(0,0)} = 4(1-\zeta)^3 + 6k_{30}s_{01}^3 + 4k_{21}s_{01}^2(1-\zeta) + 6k_{12}s_{01}(1-\zeta)^2$$

To determine the stability and direction of the bifurcation curve (closed orbit) for the system (8), the discriminating quantity L should be calculated and not be zero, where

$$L = -Re\Big(\frac{(1-2\lambda_1)\lambda_2^2}{1-\lambda_1}\theta_{20}\theta_{11}\Big) - \frac{1}{2}|\theta_{11}|^2 - |\theta_{02}|^2 + Re(\lambda_2\theta_{21}) \tag{18}$$

$$\theta_{20} = \frac{1}{8}[F_{XX} - F_{YY} + 2G_{XY} + i(G_{XX} - G_{YY} - 2F_{XY})]|_{(0,0)}$$

$$\theta_{11} = \frac{1}{4}[F_{XX} + F_{YY} + i(G_{XX} + G_{YY})]|_{(0,0)}$$

$$\theta_{02} = \frac{1}{8}[F_{XX} - F_{YY} - 2G_{XY} + i(G_{XX} - G_{YY} + 2F_{XY})]|_{(0,0)}$$

$$\theta_{21} = \frac{1}{16}[F_{XXX} + F_{XYY} + G_{XXY} + G_{YYY} + i(G_{XXX} + G_{XYY} - F_{XXY} - F_{YYY})]|_{(0,0)}$$

Based on [26–28], we see that if $L < (>)0$, then an attracting (a repelling) invariant closed curve bifurcates from the fixed point.

The proof is then complete. □

4. Numerical Simulation

In this section, by using the software Matlab, we obtain the bifurcation diagrams and phase portraits of the system (8) at the fixed point E_2, which illustrate our theoretical results previously derived and reveal some new dynamical behaviors.

First, vary δ in the range $(2.7, 3)$ and $(0.35, 0.6)$, respectively, and fix $\alpha = 0.8, \beta = 0.5$ with the initial value $(x_0, y_0) = (0.4667, 0.4667)$. Figure 1a shows the existence of a flip bifurcation at the fixed point $E_2 = (0.4667, 0.4667)$ when $\delta = \delta_1 = 2 + \frac{4\alpha}{(1+\alpha+\beta)(1+\beta)} \approx 2.93$ and indicates the periodic orbits and chaos in the system (8) as δ increases. Meanwhile, we can calculate that $c_{200}^2 + c_{300} \approx -10.92 < 0$ and $-\frac{\partial^2 f^2}{\partial l_n \partial \omega_n} / \frac{\partial^3 f^2}{\partial l_n^3}|_{(0,0)} > 0$, which means that the direction of the flip bifurcation is on the right side of the critical value. Furthermore, according to Case 2, we can clearly see that the nature of the system (8) changes from unstable to stable near δ_2. This change is shown in Figure 1b, and the periodic orbit is simulated in Figure 2b. This agrees with the conclusion in Theorem 2.

Then, we choose different values of the parameter δ. The corresponding phase portraits are plotted in Figures 3 and 4, respectively. Figure 3 implies that the closed curve is stable inside, while Figure 4 indicates that the closed curve is stable outside. That is to say, there occurs a stable invariant closed curve around the fixed point E_2. This agrees with the conclusion in Theorem 3.

Finally, take initial values $(x_0, y_0) = (0.43, 0.43)$ in Figure 2a and $(0.4667, 0.4667)$ in Figure 2b. One finds a new dynamical phenomenon—the existence of a limit cycle. This means that the system produces periodic oscillations here.

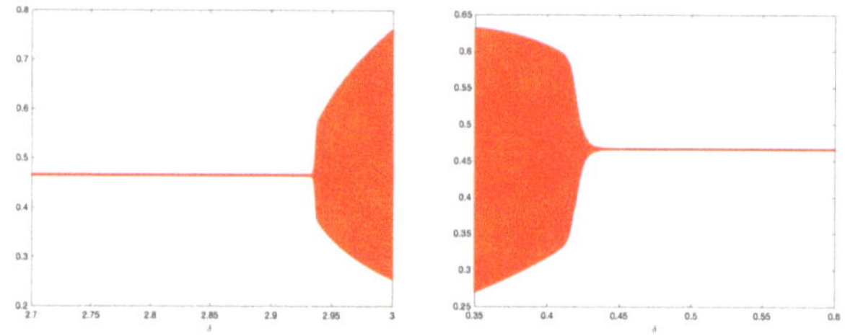

(**a**) $\delta \in (2.7, 3)$ (**b**) $\delta \in (0.35, 0.6)$

Figure 1. Bifurcation of the system (8) in (δ, x)-plane with $\alpha = 0.8, \beta = 0.5$, and the initial value $(x_0, y_0) = (0.4667, 0.4667)$.

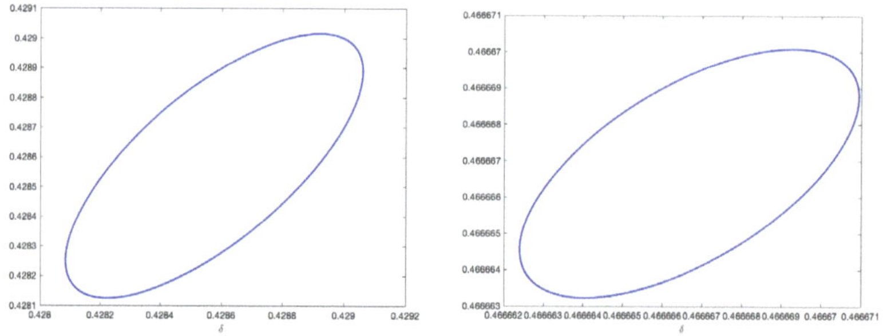

(**a**) $\delta = 0.67857$ (**b**) $\delta = 0.45833$

Figure 2. Phase portraits of the system (8) with different parameter values: (**a**) $\alpha = 0.8$, $\beta = 0.4$, and $\delta = 0.67857$; and (**b**) $\alpha = 0.8, \beta = 0.5$, and $\delta = 0.45833$. Different initial values: (**a**) $(x_0, y_0) = (0.43, 0.43)$ and (**b**) $(x_0, y_0) = (0.4667, 0.4667)$.

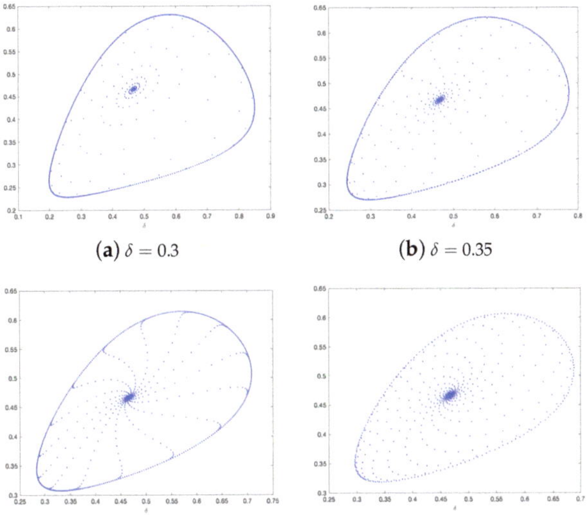

(**a**) $\delta = 0.3$ (**b**) $\delta = 0.35$

(**c**) $\delta = 0.39$ (**d**) $\delta = 0.4$

Figure 3. Phase portraits for the system (8) with $\alpha = 0.8, \beta = 0.5$, and different δ with the initial value $(x_0, y_0) = (0.4667, 0.4667)$ inside the closed orbit.

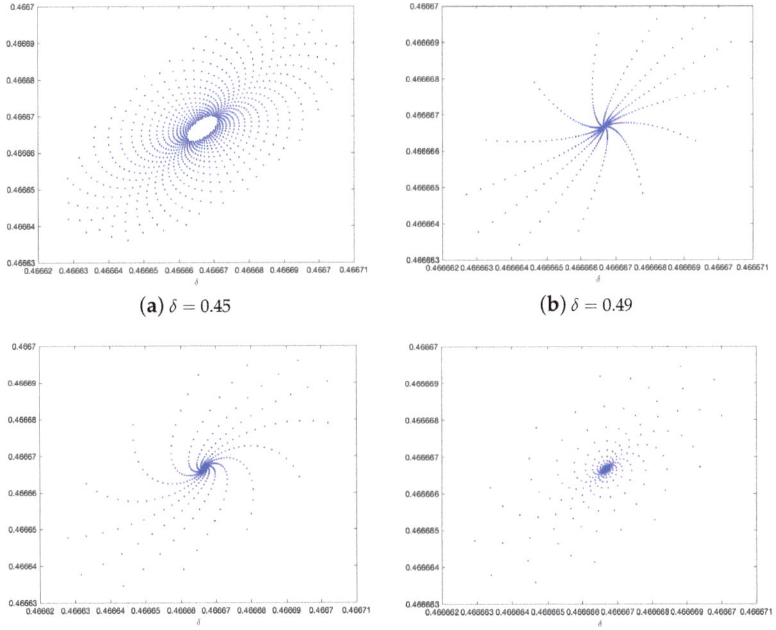

(**a**) $\delta = 0.45$ (**b**) $\delta = 0.49$

(**c**) $\delta = 0.5$ (**d**) $\delta = 0.52$

Figure 4. Phase portraits for the system (8) with $\alpha = 0.8, \beta = 0.5$, and different δ with the initial value $(x_0, y_0) = (0.4667, 0.4667)$ outside the closed orbit.

5. Conclusions and Discussion

In this paper, we analyze a predator–prey model of Leslie type with ratio-dependent simplified Holling type IV functional response. By using the semi-discretization method, the system (4) is transformed to the discrete system (8). At first, one considers the existence and stability of the positive fixed point $E_2 = (\frac{1+\beta-\alpha}{1+\beta}, \frac{1+\beta-\alpha}{1+\beta})$. Subsequently, one studies the existence conditions of the flip bifurcation and Neimark–Sacker bifurcation of the system (8) at the fixed point E_2 by using the center manifold theorem and bifurcation theory. In the end, we confirm the correctness of the theoretical results previously derived through numerical simulations. In the process of simulation, the existence of a limit cycle is also found.

As for the biological significance, our results indicate that a limit cycle will occur when the parameter δ is small. This means that the interaction between prey and predator leads to periodic oscillations, indicating the rich dynamic properties of the system. When appropriately adding the value of the parameter δ, the prey and predator populations will coexist and the limit cycle will be eliminated. Our studies provide a theoretical basis for the stable coexistence of predator and prey.

However, there still are some questions worth investigating. For example, we only know of the existence and bifurcation of the system (3) at the fixed point E_2 when $0 < \alpha < 1 + \beta$. How about the case when $\alpha \geq 1 + \beta$? Are there more interesting dynamical properties if we discuss the impact of seasonality on the system's behavior? How about using discrete methods other than the semi-discretization method that we use in this paper? We hope that interested readers consider these questions.

Author Contributions: L.L. and X.L. contributed equally and significantly in writing this paper. All authors have read and agreed to the published version of the manuscript.

Funding: This work is partly supported by the National Natural Science Foundation of China (61473340) and the Distinguished Professor Foundation of Qianjiang Scholar in Zhejiang Province (F708108P02).

Data Availability Statement: There are no applicable data associated with this manuscript.

Conflicts of Interest: The authors declare that they have no competing interests.

References

1. Holland, J.N.; DeAngelis, D.L. Consumer-resource theory predicts dynamic transitions between outcomes of interspecific interactions. *Ecol. Lett.* **2009**, *12*, 1357–1366. [CrossRef] [PubMed]
2. Kang, Y.; Armbruster, D.; Kuang, Y. Dynamics of a plant-herbivore model. *J. Biol. Dyn.* **2008**, *2*, 89–101. [CrossRef] [PubMed]
3. Westwood, J.H. The physiology of the established parasite-host association. In *Parasitic Orobanchaceae: Parasitic Mechanisms and Control Strategies*; Springer: Berlin/Heidelberg, Germany, 2013; pp. 87–114.
4. Leslie, P.H. Some further notes on the use of matrices in population mathematics. *Biometrika* **1948**, *35*, 213–245. [CrossRef]
5. Kuto, K.; Yamada, Y. Multiple coexistence states for a prey-predator system with cross-diffusion. *J. Differ. Equ.* **2004**, *197*, 315–348. [CrossRef]
6. Jiang, G.; Lu, Q.; Qian, L. Complex dynamics of a Holling type II prey-predator system with state feedback control. *Chaos Solitons Fractals* **2007**, *31*, 448–461. [CrossRef]
7. Peng, R.; Wang, M. Global stability of the equilibrium of a diffusive Holling–Tanner prey-predator model. *Appl. Math. Lett.* **2007**, *20*, 664–670. [CrossRef]
8. Khaliq, A.; Ibrahim, T.F.; Alotaibi, A.M.; Shoaib, M.; El-Moneam, M.A. Dynamical analysis of Discrete-Time Two-Predators One-Prey Lotka–Volterra model. *Mathematics* **2022**, *10*, 4015. [CrossRef]
9. Chen, J.; He, X.; Chen, F. The Influence of fear effect on a Discrete-Time Predator-Prey system with predator has other food resource. *Mathematics* **2021**,*9*, 865. [CrossRef]
10. Hauzy, C.; Hulot, F.D.; Gins, A.; Loreau, M. Intra- and interspecific density-dependent dispersal in an aquatic prey-predator system. *J. Anim. Ecol.* **2007**, *76*, 552–558. [CrossRef]
11. Li, B.; Kuang, Y. Heteroclinic bifurcation in the Michaelis-Menten-type ratio-dependent predator-prey system. *SIAM J. Appl. Math.* **2007**, *67*, 1453–1464. [CrossRef]
12. Sen, M.; Banerjee, M.; Morozov, A. Bifurcation analysis of a ratio-dependent prey-predator model with the Allee effect. *Ecol. Complex.* **2012**, *11*, 12–27. [CrossRef]
13. Mbava, W.; Mugisha, J.Y.T.; Gonsalves, J.W. Prey, predator and super-predator model with disease in the super-predator. *Appl. Math. Comput.* **2017**, *297*, 92–114. [CrossRef]
14. Yang, R.; Wei, J. Stability and bifurcation analysis of a diffusive prey-predator system in Holling type III with a prey refuge. *Nonlinear Dyn.* **2015**, *79*, 631–646. [CrossRef]

15. Chen, X.; Du, Z. Existence of Positive Periodic Solutions for a Neutral Delay Predator-Prey Model with Hassell–Varley Type Functional Response and Impulse. *Qual. Theory Dyn. Syst.* **2017**, *17*, 67–80. [CrossRef]
16. Arditi, R.; Ginzburg, L.R. Coupling in predator-prey dynamics: Ratio-dependence. *J. Theor. Biol.* **1989**, *139*, 311–326. [CrossRef]
17. Gao, Y.; Yao, S. Dynamical analysis of a modified Leslie-Gower Holling-type II predator-prey stochastic model in polluted environments with interspecific competition and impulsive toxicant input. *J. Biol. Dyn.* **2022**, *16*, 840–858. [CrossRef] [PubMed]
18. Amirabad, H.Q.; Rabieimotlagh, O.; Mohammadinejad, H. M. Permanency in predator-prey models of Leslie type with ratio-dependent simplified Holling type-IV functional response. *Math. Comput. Simul.* **2019**, *157*, 63–76. [CrossRef]
19. Negi, K.; Gakkhar, S. Dynamics in a Beddington–DeAngelis prey-predator system with impulsive harvesting. *Ecol. Model.* **2007**, *206*, 421–430. [CrossRef]
20. Tripathi, J.P.; Abbas, S.; Thakur, M. Dynamical analysis of a prey-predator model with Beddington–DeAngelis type function response incorporating a prey refuge. *Nonlinear Dyn.* **2015**, *80*, 177–196. [CrossRef]
21. Xu, C.; Li, P. Oscillations for a delayed predator-prey model with Hassell–Varley-type functional response. *C. R. Biol.* **2015**, *338*, 227–240. [CrossRef]
22. Liu, Y.; Li, X. Dynamics of a discrete predator-prey model with Holling-II functional response. *Int. J. Biomath.* **2021**, *18*, 2150068. [CrossRef]
23. Yao, W.; Li, X. Bifurcation difference induced by different discrete methods in a discrete predator-prey model. *J. Nonlinear Model. Anal.* **2022**, *4*, 64–79.
24. Dong, J.; Li, X. Bifurcation of a discrete predator-prey model with increasing functional response and constant-yield prey harvesting. *Electron. Res. Arch.* **2022**, *30*, 3930–3948. [CrossRef]
25. Li, X.; Shao, X. Flip bifurcation and Neimark-Sacker bifurcation in a discrete predator-prey model with Michaelis-Menten functional response. *Electron. Res. Arch.* **2022**, *31*, 37–57. [CrossRef]
26. Wiggins, S. *Introduction to Applied Nonlinear Dynamical Systems and Chaos*; Springer: NewYork, NY, USA, 2003.
27. Carr, J. *Application of Center Manifold Theory*; Springer: NewYork, NY, USA, 1981.
28. Guckenheimer, J.; Holmes, P. *Nonlinear Oscillations, Dynamical Systems, and Bifurcation of Vector Fields*; Springer: New York, NY, USA, 1983.

mathematics

MDPI

Article

Global Existence of Small Data Solutions to Weakly Coupled Systems of Semi-Linear Fractional σ–Evolution Equations with Mass and Different Nonlinear Memory terms

Seyyid Ali Saiah [1], Abdelatif Kainane Mezadek [1,*], Mohamed Kainane Mezadek [1], Abdelhamid Mohammed Djaouti [2,3,*], Ashraf Al-Quran [2,3] and Ali M. A. Bany Awad [4]

1 Laboratory of Mathematics and Applications, Department of Mathematics, Faculty of Exact Sciences and Informatics, Hassiba Benbouali University, Ouled Fares, Chlef 021800, Algeria; a.saiahseyyid@univ-chlef.dz (S.A.S.); med.kainane@univ-chlef.dz (M.K.M.)
2 Preparatory Year, King Faisal University, Hofuf 31982, Saudi Arabia
3 Department of Mathematics and Statistics, Faculty of Sciences, King Faisal University, Hofuf 31982, Saudi Arabia
4 Deanship of Development and Quality Assurance, King Faisal University, Al-Ahsa 31982, Saudi Arabia
* Correspondence: adjaout@kfu.edu.sa (A.M.D.); a.kainane@univ-chlef.dz (A.K.M.)

Abstract: We study in this paper the long-term existence of solutions to the system of weakly coupled equations with fractional evolution and various nonlinearities. Our objective is to determine the connection between the regularity assumptions on the initial data, the memory terms, and the permissible range of exponents in a specific equation. Using $L^p - L^q$ estimates for solutions to the corresponding linear fractional σ–evolution equations with vanishing right-hand sides, and applying a fixed-point argument, the existence of small data solutions is established for some admissible range of powers $(p_1, p_2, \ldots, p_k)$.

Keywords: σ–evolution equations; small data solutions; global in time existence; fractional equations; nonlinear memory; weakly coupled system; loss of decay

MSC: 35R11; 35A01

Citation: Saiah, S.A.; Kainane Mezadek, A.; Kainane Mezadek, M.; Mohammed Djaouti, A.; Al-Quran, A.; Bany Awad, A.M.A. Global Existence of Small Data Solutions to Weakly Coupled Systems of Semi-Linear Fractional σ–Evolution Equations with Mass and Different Nonlinear Memory terms. *Mathematics* **2024**, *12*, 1942. https://doi.org/10.3390/math12131942

Academic Editors: Lingju Kong and Min Wang

Received: 4 May 2024
Revised: 14 June 2024
Accepted: 18 June 2024
Published: 22 June 2024

1. Introduction

This paper is devoted to the weakly coupled system of k semi-linear fractional σ–evolution equations. The system incorporates mass terms and different memory terms and our focus is on small data solutions to the corresponding Cauchy problem.

$$\begin{cases} \partial_t^{1+\alpha_1} u_1 + (-\Delta)^{\sigma_1} u_\ell + M_1^2 u_1 = F_{\mu_1,p_1}(u_k), \\ \partial_t^{1+\alpha_2} u_2 + (-\Delta)^{\sigma_2} u_2 + M_2^2 u_2 = F_{\mu_2,p_2}(u_1), \\ \quad\quad\quad\quad\quad . \\ \quad\quad\quad\quad\quad . \\ \partial_t^{1+\alpha_k} u_k + (-\Delta)^{\sigma_k} u_k + M_k^2 u_k = F_{\mu_k,p_k}(u_{k-1}), \\ u_\ell(0,x) = u_{0l}(x), \partial_t u_\ell(0,x) = 0, \;\; \ell = 1,2,...,k, \end{cases} \tag{1}$$

where $k \geq 2$, for $l = 1, \cdots, k$, $\alpha_l \in (0,1)$, $\mu_l \in (0,1)$, $p_l > 1$, $M_l > 0$, $\sigma_l \geq 1$, $(t,x) \in [0,\infty) \times \mathbb{R}^d$, with

$$F_{\mu,p}(u)(t,x) := \int_0^t (t-s)^{-\mu} |u(s,x)|^p ds. \tag{2}$$

The fractional derivative is defined as follows: $\partial_t^{1+\alpha_l} u = D_t^{\alpha_l}(u_t)$, where

$$D_t^{\alpha_l}(f) = \partial_t (I_t^{1-\alpha_l} f) \quad \text{and} \quad I_t^{\beta} f = \frac{1}{\Gamma(\beta)} \int_0^t (t-s)^{\beta-1} f(s)\, ds \ \text{ for } \beta > 0.$$

Here, $D_t^{\alpha}(f)$ and $I_t^{\beta} f$ denote the fractional Riemann–Liouville derivative and the fractional Riemann–Liouville integral, respectively, of f in $[0,t]$, and Γ is the Euler Gamma function.

In this discussion, we will illustrate two distinct Cauchy problems: the semi-linear heat equation and the semi-linear wave equation.

Firstly, let us consider the semi-linear heat equation:

$$u_t - \Delta u = |u|^p, \quad u(0,x) = u_0(x).$$

According to Fujita's results in [1], the critical exponent for this equation is defined as $p_{\mathrm{Fuj}} := 1 + \frac{2}{n}$. It is noteworthy that for $p > p_{\mathrm{Fuj}}$, small initial data solutions exist globally (in time), while for $1 < p < p_{\mathrm{Fuj}}$, a blow-up phenomenon occurs. The critical case $p = p_{\mathrm{Fuj}}$ was further studied in [2,3], where it was shown that blow-up does indeed occur.

Moving on, let us shift our focus to the semi-linear wave equation:

$$u_{tt} - \Delta u = |u|^p, \quad u(0,x) = u_0(x), \quad u_t(0,x) = u_1(x).$$

For the specific case when $n = 3$, ref. [4] proved that the critical exponent can be determined as the positive root of the quadratic equation $(n-1)p^2 - (n+1)p - 2 = 0$. The exponent obtained from the quadratic equation is known as the Strauss exponent, denoted as p_S. Based on the Strauss exponent p_S, we can conclude that there is the global (in time) existence of small data weak solutions when $p \geq p_S$. However, for $p > 1$ and large data, we can only expect the local (in time) existence of solutions. The optimality of the Strauss exponent p_S in $\mathbb{R}^2$ was demonstrated in [5,6]. After that, the global existence of solutions for $n = 2,3$ was treated in [7], while for $n \geq 4$, it was addressed in [8,9]. The nonexistence of solutions with compactly supported data was studied in [10] for the range $1 < p < \frac{n+1}{n-1}$. For the specific case of $n = 3$, optimal results were proven in [11] for $p = 1 + \sqrt{2}$. Moreover, in [12], it was proved that for $n > 3$ and $1 < p < p_S$, there is a nonexistence result for small data.

In 2017, D'Abbicco et al. [13] studied the semi-linear fractional wave equation, which can be expressed as follows:

$$\partial_t^{1+\lambda} u - \Delta u = |u|^p, \qquad u(0,x) = u_0(x), u_t(0,x) = u_1(x), \tag{3}$$

where $\lambda \in (0,1)$, which represents the fractional Riemann–Liouville derivative. The authors successfully proved the critical power for the existence of solutions with small initial data in spatial dimensions that are relatively low. The case of non-null Cauchy data and the use of the Caputo fractional order were studied in [13].

In [14], they proved the global (in time) existence of small data solutions for semi-linear fractional σ-evolution equations. These equations incorporated either mass or power nonlinearity. Furthermore, a related problem was addressed in [15], where instead of the power nonlinearity, a memory term was considered.

For the weakly coupled system consisting of semi-linear heat equations, we have the following equations:

$$\begin{aligned} u_t - \Delta u &= |v|^p, \ u(0,x) = u_0(x), \ u_t(0,x) = u_1(x), \\ v_t - \Delta v &= |u|^q, \ v(0,x) = v_0(x), \ v_t(0,x) = v_1(x), \end{aligned}$$

where $t \in [0,\infty), x \in \mathbb{R}^d$, and $p, q > 1$ with $pq > 1$. In [16], it was shown that the exponents p and q satisfying

$$\frac{d}{2} = \frac{\max\{p,q\}+1}{pq-1}$$

are critical. This means that solutions exist globally if $\frac{d}{2} > \frac{\max\{p,q\}+1}{pq-1}$, while blow-up occurs for the opposite case. For more details on the system of semi-linear heat equations, please refer to [17–20].

Considerations are made in several papers regarding weakly coupled systems of semi-linear classical damped wave equations with power nonlinearities. The specific problem of interest is:

$$\begin{aligned} u_{tt} - \Delta u + u_t &= |v|^p, \; u(0,x) = u_0(x), \; u_t(0,x) = u_1(x), \\ v_{tt} - \Delta v + v_t &= |u|^q, \; v(0,x) = v_0(x), \; v_t(0,x) = v_1(x), \end{aligned} \tag{4}$$

where $t \in [0,\infty), x \in \mathbb{R}^d$. In 2007, Sun and Wang proved in [21] that

$$\lambda := \frac{\max\{p;q\}+1}{pq-1} < \frac{d}{2}, \tag{5}$$

For the case of $d = 1$ or $d = 3$, it has been proven that the solution exists globally in time for small initial data in weakly coupled systems of semi-linear classical damped wave equations with power nonlinearities. However, if $\lambda \geq \frac{d}{2}$, it has been shown that every solution with a positive average value does not exist globally.

In the paper [22], these results were generalized to the case where $d = 1,2,3$. Additionally, improved time-decay estimates have been provided specifically for the case of $d = 2$. In 2014, Nishihara and Wakasugi used the weighted energy method to prove the critical exponent for any space dimension in [23]. Furthermore, considering time-dependent dissipation terms, the authors in [24–26] demonstrated the global (in time) existence of small data solutions under certain conditions that illustrate the interplay between the exponents of the power nonlinearities.

During the last years, many authors have studied the Cauchy problem for weakly coupled systems, see, e.g., [24,27,28], where the derivative introduced in their work is the classical derivative. In [29], the authors studied a weakly coupled system where the fractional derivative involves in the equations with special Cauchy data.

The paper is organized into several sections. First, we provide an overview of the study and present the main results (Section 2). Following that, Section 3 introduces the necessary background information and definitions for the foundation used to prove the results. Then, the proofs of the theorems are presented, utilizing previous estimates of linear equations (Section 5). Finally, Section 6 summarizes the study, highlights its contributions, and suggests potential directions for future research.

In a recent paper [30], the author investigated the following Cauchy problem for weakly coupled systems of semi-linear fractional σ-evolution equations. The system involves mass terms and different power nonlinearities.

$$\begin{cases} \partial_t^{1+\alpha_1} u + (-\Delta)^{\sigma_1} u + M_1^2 u = |v|^{p_1}, \\ \partial_t^{1+\alpha_2} v + (-\Delta)^{\sigma_2} v + M_2^2 v = |u|^{p_2}, \\ u(0,x) = u_0(x), v(0,x) = v_0(x), \; u_t(0,x) = v_t(0,x) = 0, \end{cases} \tag{6}$$

where $\alpha_k \in (0,1), \sigma_k \geq 1$, $M_k > 0$ for $k = 1,2$, $(t,x) \in [0,\infty) \times \mathbb{R}^d$, $\partial_t^{1+\alpha_k} u = D_t^{\alpha_k}(u_t)$ with

$$D_t^{\alpha_k}(f) = \partial_t(I_t^{1-\alpha_k} f) \quad \text{and} \quad I_t^\beta f = \frac{1}{\Gamma(\beta)} \int_0^t (t-s)^{\beta-1} f(s)\, ds \;\text{ for }\; \beta > 0.$$

$D_t^\alpha(f)$ and $I_t^\beta f$ are defined as above.

The author proved the following results.

Proposition 1. *Let us assume* $0 < \alpha_1, \alpha_2 < 1$, $\sigma_1, \sigma_2 \geq 1$, $M_1, M_2 > 0$ *and* $m_1, m_2 \geq 1$. *Assume that for all* $\delta > 0$

$$p_1 > \max\Big\{\frac{m_2}{m_1} - \delta, \frac{1}{1-\alpha_2}\Big\},$$

and

$$p_2 > \max\Big\{\frac{m_1}{m_2} - \delta, \frac{1}{1-\alpha_1}\Big\}.$$

Then, there exists a positive constant ε, *such that for any data*

$$(u_0, v_0) \in \mathcal{A}_{m_1}^{m_2} := \big(L^{m_1}(\mathbb{R}^d) \cap L^\infty(\mathbb{R}^d)\big) \times \big(L^{m_2}(\mathbb{R}^d) \cap L^\infty(\mathbb{R}^d)\big),$$

with $\|(u_0, v_0)\|_{\mathcal{A}_{m_1}^{m_2}} \leq \varepsilon$, *we have a uniquely determined global (in time) Sobolev solution*

$$(u, v) \in \mathcal{C}\big([0, \infty), L^{m_1}(\mathbb{R}^d) \cap L^\infty(\mathbb{R}^d)\big) \times \mathcal{C}\big([0, \infty), L^{m_2}(\mathbb{R}^d) \cap L^\infty(\mathbb{R}^d)\big)$$

to the Cauchy problem (6). *Moreover, for all* $s \geq 0$, *the solution satisfies the following decay estimates:*

$$\|u(s, \cdot)\|_{L^r} \lesssim (1+s)^{\alpha_1 - 1}\|u_0\|_{L^{m_1} \cap L^\infty} \quad \textit{for all} \quad r \in [m_1, \infty],$$
$$\|v(s, \cdot)\|_{L^r} \lesssim (1+s)^{\alpha_2 - 1}\|v_0\|_{L^{m_2} \cap L^\infty} \quad \textit{for all} \quad r \in [m_2, \infty].$$

Proposition 2 (Loss of decay). *Let us assume* $0 < \alpha_1, \alpha_2 < 1$, $\sigma_1, \sigma_2 \geq 1$,$M_1, M_2 > 0$ *and* $m_1, m_2 \geq 1$. *Assume that for all* $\delta > 0$

$$\max\Big\{1, \frac{\alpha_1}{1-\alpha_2}, \frac{m_2}{m_1} - \delta\Big\} < p_1 < \frac{1}{1-\alpha_2},$$

$$p_2 > \max\Big\{\frac{m_1}{m_2} - \delta, \frac{1}{p_1(1-\alpha_2) - \alpha_1}\Big\}.$$

Then, there exists a positive constant ε, *such that for any data*

$$(u_0, v_0) \in \mathcal{A}_{m_1}^{m_2} \quad \textit{with} \quad \|(u_0, v_0)\|_{\mathcal{A}_{m_1}^{m_2}} \leq \varepsilon$$

we have a uniquely determined global (in time) Sobolev solution

$$(u, v) \in \mathcal{C}\big([0, \infty), L^{m_1}(\mathbb{R}^d) \cap L^\infty(\mathbb{R}^d)\big) \times \mathcal{C}\big([0, \infty), L^{m_2}(\mathbb{R}^d) \cap L^\infty(\mathbb{R}^d)\big)$$

to the Cauchy problem (6). *Moreover, for all* $s \geq 0$, *the solution satisfies the following decay estimates:*

$$\|u(s, \cdot)\|_{L^r} \lesssim (1+t)^{\alpha_1 - p_1(1-\alpha_2)}\|u_0\|_{L^{m_1} \cap L^\infty} \quad \textit{for all} \quad r \in [m_1, \infty],$$
$$\|v(s, \cdot)\|_{L^r} \lesssim (1+s)^{\alpha_2 - 1}\|v_0\|_{L^{m_2} \cap L^\infty} \quad \textit{for all} \quad r \in [m_2, \infty]$$

Proposition 3 (Loss of decay). *Let us assume* $0 < \alpha_1, \alpha_2 < 1$, $\sigma_1, \sigma_2 \geq 1$ *and* $M_1, M_2 > 0$. *Assume that* $\delta > 0$ *is small enough for all*

$$p_1 = \frac{1}{1-\alpha_2} \textit{ and } p_2 > \frac{1}{1-\alpha_1-\delta}.$$

Then, there exists a positive constant ε, *such that for any data*

$$(u_0, v_0) \in \mathcal{A}_1^1 \quad \textit{with} \quad \|(u_0, v_0)\|_{\mathcal{A}_1^1} \leq \varepsilon$$

we have a uniquely determined global (in time) Sobolev solution

$$(u,v) \in \mathcal{C}\big([0,\infty), L^1(\mathbb{R}^d) \cap L^\infty(\mathbb{R}^d)\big) \times \mathcal{C}\big([0,\infty), L^1(\mathbb{R}^d) \cap L^\infty(\mathbb{R}^d)\big)$$

to the Cauchy problem (6). *Moreover, for all* $s \geq 0$, *the solution satisfies the following decay estimates:*

$$\|u(s,\cdot)\|_{L^r} \lesssim \ln(2+s)(1+s)^{\alpha_1-1}\|u_0\|_{L^1\cap L^\infty} \quad \text{for all} \quad r \in [1,\infty],$$
$$\|v(s,\cdot)\|_{L^r} \lesssim (1+s)^{\alpha_2-1}\|v_0\|_{L^1\cap L^\infty} \quad \text{for all} \quad r \in [1,\infty].$$

In the subsequent sections, we will utilize the notation $f \lesssim g$, indicating the existence of a non-negative constant C, such that $f \leq Cg$. Our main findings concerning the global (in time) existence of small data Sobolev solutions will be presented in the following section.

2. Main Results

Theorem 1. *Let us assume* $0 < \alpha_\ell < 1$, $\alpha_\ell < \mu_\ell < 1$, $\sigma_\ell \geq 1$, $m_l \geq 1$, *and* $M_\ell > 0$ *for all* $\ell = 1, ..., k$. *Assume that for all* $\delta > 0$

$$p_1 > \max\Big\{\frac{m_k}{m_1} - \delta, \frac{1}{\mu_k - \alpha_k}\Big\},$$
$$p_\ell > \max\Big\{\frac{m_{l-1}}{m_l} - \delta, \frac{1}{\mu_{\ell-1} - \alpha_{\ell-1}}\Big\}, \quad \text{for all} \quad \ell = 2, ..., k.$$

Then, there exists a positive constant ε, *such that for any data* $(u_{01}, .., u_{0k}) \in \mathcal{A}_k := \prod_{\ell=1}^k \big(L^{m_l}(\mathbb{R}^d) \cap L^\infty(\mathbb{R}^d)\big)$ *with* $\|(u_{01}, .., u_{0k})\|_{\mathcal{A}_k} \leq \varepsilon$, *we have a uniquely determined global (in time) Sobolev solution*

$$u \in \prod_{\ell=1}^{k} \mathcal{C}\big([0,\infty), L^{m_l}(\mathbb{R}^d) \cap L^\infty(\mathbb{R}^d)\big)$$

to the Cauchy problem (1). *Moreover, for all* $s \geq 0$ *and* $l = 1, ..., k$, *the solution satisfies the following decay estimates:*

$$\|u_\ell(s,\cdot)\|_{L^q} \lesssim (1+s)^{\alpha_\ell - \mu_\ell}\|u_{0l}\|_{L^{m_l}\cap L^\infty} \quad \text{for all} \quad q \in [m_l, \infty].$$

Theorem 2 (Loss of decay). *Let us assume* $0 < \alpha_\ell < 1$, $\alpha_\ell < \mu_\ell < 1$, $\sigma_\ell \geq 1$, $m_l \geq 1$, *and* $M_\ell > 0$ *for all* $\ell = 1, ..., k$. *Assume that for all* $\delta > 0$

$$\max\Big\{1, \frac{\alpha_1 - \mu_1 + 1}{\mu_k - \alpha_k}, \frac{m_k}{m_1} - \delta\Big\} < p_1 < \frac{1}{\mu_k - \alpha_k},$$

$$\max\Big\{1, \frac{\alpha_2 - \mu_2 + 1}{\mu_1 - \alpha_1 - \gamma_{(\alpha_k)}^{(\mu_k)}(p_1)}, \frac{m_1}{m_2} - \delta\Big\} < p_2 < \frac{1}{\mu_1 - \alpha_1 - \gamma_{(\alpha_k)}^{(\mu_k)}(p_1)}$$

and for $l = 3, \cdots, k-1$

$$p_\ell < \frac{1}{\mu_{\ell-1} - \alpha_{\ell-1} - \gamma_{(\alpha_k,...,\alpha_{\ell-2})}^{(\mu_k,...,\mu_{\ell-2})}(p_1, ..., p_{\ell-1})},$$
$$p_l > \max\Big\{1, \frac{\alpha_\ell - \mu_\ell + 1}{\mu_{\ell-1} - \alpha_{\ell-1} - \gamma_{(\alpha_k,...,\alpha_{\ell-2})}^{(\mu_k,...,\mu_{\ell-2})}(p_1, ..., p_{\ell-1})}, \frac{m_{l-1}}{m_l} - \delta\Big\}$$

and

$$p_k > \max\Big\{\frac{m_k}{m_{k-1}} - \delta, \frac{1}{\mu_{k-1} - \alpha_{k-1} - \gamma_{(\alpha_k,...,\alpha_{k-2})}^{(\mu_k,...,\mu_{k-2})}(p_1, ..., p_{k-1})}\Big\},$$

where, for $l = 3, \cdots, k-1$

$$\begin{cases} \gamma^{(\mu_k)}_{(\alpha_k)}(p_1) = 1 - p_1(\mu_k - \alpha_k) \\ \gamma^{(\mu_k,\mu_1)}_{(\alpha_k,\alpha_1)}(p_1, p_2) = 1 - p_2(\mu_1 - \alpha_1) + p_2\gamma^{(\mu_k)}_{(\alpha_k)}(p_1) \\ \gamma^{(\mu_k,\dots,\mu_{\ell-1})}_{(\alpha_k,\dots,\alpha_{\ell-1})}(p_1, \dots, p_\ell) = 1 - p_\ell(\mu_\ell - \alpha_\ell) + p_\ell\gamma^{(\mu_k,\dots,\mu_{\ell-2})}_{(\alpha_k,\dots,\alpha_{\ell-2})}(p_1, \dots, p_{\ell-1}). \end{cases} \tag{7}$$

Then, there exists a positive constant ε*, such that for any data*

$$(u_{01}, .., u_{0k}) \in \mathcal{A}_k := \prod_{\ell=1}^{k} \left(L^{m_l}(\mathbb{R}^d) \cap L^\infty(\mathbb{R}^d)\right) \text{ with } \|(u_{01}, .., u_{0k})\|_{\mathcal{A}_k} \le \varepsilon,$$

we have a uniquely determined global (in time) Sobolev solution

$$u \in \prod_{\ell=1}^{k} C\left([0,\infty), L^{m_l}(\mathbb{R}^d) \cap L^\infty(\mathbb{R}^d)\right)$$

to the Cauchy problem (1)*. Moreover, for all* $s \ge 0$ *and* $l = 2, \cdots, k-1$*, the solution satisfies the decay estimate*

$$\begin{aligned} &\|u_1(s,\cdot)\|_{L^q} \lesssim (1+s)^{\alpha_1-\mu_1+\gamma^{\mu_k}_{\alpha_k}(p_1)}\|u_{01}\|_{L^{m_1}\cap L^\infty} \quad \text{for all} \quad q \in [m_1, \infty], \\ &\|u_\ell(s,\cdot)\|_{L^q} \lesssim (1+s)^{\alpha_\ell-\mu_\ell+\gamma^{(\mu_k,\dots,\mu_{\ell-1})}_{(\alpha_k,\dots,\alpha_{\ell-1})}(p_1,\dots,p_\ell)}\|u_{0l}\|_{L^{m_l}\cap L^\infty} \quad \text{for all} \quad q \in [m_l, \infty], \\ &\|u_k(s,\cdot)\|_{L^q} \lesssim (1+s)^{\alpha_k-\mu_k}\|u_{0k}\|_{L^{m_k}\cap L^\infty} \quad \text{for all} \quad q \in [m_k, \infty]. \end{aligned}$$

We suppose $m_1 = m_2 = 1$ in the following result.

Theorem 3 (Loss of decay). *Let us assume* $0 < \alpha_\ell < 1$, $\alpha_\ell < \mu_\ell < 1$, $\sigma_\ell \ge 1$, $M_\ell > 0$ *for all* $\ell = 1, \dots, k$*. Assume that for all* $\delta > 0$

$$p_1 = \frac{1}{\mu_k - \alpha_k}.$$

$$p_\ell = \frac{1}{\mu_{\ell-1} - \alpha_{\ell-1}}. \quad \ell = 2, \dots, k-1$$

$$p_k > \frac{1}{\mu_{k-1} - \alpha_{k-1} - \delta\gamma(p_{k-1})},$$

where

$$\begin{cases} \gamma(p_1) = 1 \\ \gamma(p_l) = 1 + p_l\gamma(p_{l-1}), \text{ for } l = 2, \cdots, k-1. \end{cases} \tag{8}$$

Then, there exists a positive constant ε*, such that for any data*

$$(u_{01}, .., u_{0k}) \in \mathcal{A}_k = \prod_{\ell=1}^{k} \left(L^1(\mathbb{R}^d) \cap L^\infty(\mathbb{R}^d)\right) \quad \text{with} \quad \|(u_{01}, .., u_{0k})\|_{\mathcal{A}_k} \le \varepsilon$$

we have a uniquely determined global (in time) Sobolev solution

$$u \in \prod_{\ell=1}^{k} C\left([0,\infty), L^1(\mathbb{R}^d) \cap L^\infty(\mathbb{R}^d)\right)$$

to the Cauchy problem (1). Moreover, for $l = 1, \cdots, k-1$ and for all $s \geq 0$, the solution satisfies the following decay estimate:

$$\|u_\ell(s,\cdot)\|_{L^q} \lesssim (1+s)^{\alpha_\ell - \mu_\ell} \big(\ln(2+s)\big)^{\gamma(p_l)} \|u_{0l}\|_{L^1 \cap L^\infty} \quad \text{for all} \quad q \in [1,\infty],$$
$$\|u_k(s,\cdot)\|_{L^q} \lesssim (1+s)^{\alpha_k - \mu_k} \|u_{0k}\|_{L^1 \cap L^\infty} \quad \text{for all} \quad q \in [1,\infty].$$

Remark 1. *The nonlinear term $F_{\mu,p}(t,w)$ in (2) may be written as*

$$F_{\mu,p}(t,w) = \Gamma(1-\mu) I_t^{1-\mu}(|w|^p)$$

where Γ is the Euler Gamma function, and $I_t^{1-\mu}(|w|^p)$ is the fractional Riemann–Liouville integral of $|w|^p$ in $[0,t]$. Therefore, it is reasonable to expect that the relations with the power nonlinearities introduced in Proposition 1, Proposition 2, and Proposition 3 as μ_l tend to 1, for all $l = 1, \cdots, k$ and $k = 2$.

3. Preliminaries

Let us consider the Cauchy problem

$$\begin{aligned} &\partial_t^{1+\alpha} v + (-\Delta)^\sigma v + m^2 v = F(t,x) \\ &v(x,0) = v_0(x), \quad v_t(0,x) = 0, \end{aligned} \tag{9}$$

With parameters $\alpha \in (0,1)$, $\sigma \geq 1$, and $m > 0$, and under the data condition $v_t(0,x) = 0$, the problem can be formally transformed into an integral equation. The solution of the problem is then given by:

$$u(t,x) = G^m_{\sigma,\alpha}(t,x) \star v_0(x) + N^m_{\alpha,\sigma}(v)(t,x) \tag{10}$$

with

$$G^m_{\sigma,\alpha}(t,x) = \int_{\mathbb{R}^d} e^{ix\cdot\xi} E_{\alpha+1}\big(-t^{\alpha+1}\langle\xi\rangle^2_{m,\sigma}\big)\, d\xi, \tag{11}$$

$$N^m_{\sigma,\alpha}(v)(t,x) = \int_0^t G^M_{\alpha,\sigma}(t-s) \star_{(x)} I^\alpha_s(F)(t,s)\, ds, \tag{12}$$

where the semigroup of operators $G^m_{\sigma,\alpha}(t,\cdot)_{t\geq 0}$ is defined through the Fourier transform as follows:

$$\widehat{(G^m_{\sigma,\alpha}(t,\cdot)f)}(t,\xi) = E_{\alpha+1}\big(-t^{\alpha+1}\langle\xi\rangle^2_{m,\sigma}\big)\hat{f}(\xi) \quad \text{with} \quad \langle\xi\rangle^2_{\sigma,m} = |\xi|^{2\sigma} + m^2.$$

Here, $E_\beta(z) = \sum\limits_{k=0}^{\infty} \frac{z^k}{\Gamma(\beta k+1)}$ denotes the Mittag-Leffler function (see [31]).

According to [14], a representation of solutions to the linear problem associated with Equation (9) (without the term $F(t,x)$) can be given as $v(t,x) = G^m_{\sigma,\alpha}(t,x) \star v_0(t,x)$. This representation involves convolving the initial data $v_0(t,x)$ with the semigroup of operators $G^m_{\sigma,\alpha}(t,x)$.

In [14], the authors proved the following result.

Proposition 4 (see [14]). *Let us assume that $\alpha \in (0,1)$, $r \geq 1$, $\sigma \geq 1$, and $v_0 \in L^r \cap L^\infty$. Then, the solution of the linear Cauchy problem*

$$\begin{aligned} &\partial_t^{1+\alpha} v + (-\Delta)^\sigma v + m^2 v = 0, \\ &v(x,0) = v_0(x), \quad v_t(0,x) = 0, \end{aligned} \tag{13}$$

for all $t \geq 0$ and $1 \leq r \leq q \leq \infty$, satisfies the following $L^r - L^q$ estimates:

$$\|v(t,\cdot)\|_{L^q} \lesssim (1+t)^{-(1+\alpha)} \|v_0\|_{L^r \cap L^\infty}. \tag{14}$$

4. Analysis of Weakly Coupled Linear Systems

We will use the decay estimates for solutions to:

$$\begin{cases} \partial_t^{1+\alpha_1} u_1 + (-\Delta)^{\sigma_1} u_\ell + M_1^2 u_1 = 0, \\ \partial_t^{1+\alpha_2} u_2 + (-\Delta)^{\sigma_2} u_2 + M_2^2 u_2 = 0, \\ \cdot \\ \cdot \\ \partial_t^{1+\alpha_k} u_k + (-\Delta)^{\sigma_k} u_k + M_k^2 u_k = 0, \\ u_\ell(0,x) = u_{0l}(x),\ \partial_t u_\ell(0,x) = 0, \quad \ell = 1,2,...,k. \end{cases} \tag{15}$$

In order to establish the global existence (over time) of Sobolev solutions with small initial data for the weakly coupled systems of semi-linear models (1), we express their solutions in the following form:

$$u_l^{ln}(t,x) := G_{\sigma_l,\alpha_l}^{M_l}(t,x) *_{(x)} u_{0l}(x), \text{ for all } l = 1,\cdots,k. \tag{16}$$

Proposition 5. *Let $u_{0l} \in L^{m_l} \cap L^\infty$ with $m_l \geq 1$ for all $l = 1,\cdots,k$. Then, the solution of the linear Cauchy problem* (15) *satisfies the following $L^{m_l} - L^q$ estimates:*

$$\left\| u_l^{ln}(t,\cdot) \right\|_{L^q} \lesssim (1+t)^{-(1+\alpha_l)} \|u_{0l}\|_{L^{m_l}\cap L^\infty} \textit{for all } q \in [m_l, \infty].$$

By applying Duhamel's principle and some fixed-point argument, we can derive the formal integral representation of solutions to (1) as follows:

$$\begin{aligned} u_1(t,x) &:= u_1^{ln}(t,x) + \textstyle\int_0^t G_{\sigma_1,\alpha_1}^{M_1}(t-\varrho,\cdot) *_{(x)} F_{\mu_1,p_1}(u_k) d\varrho = (u_1^{ln} + u_1^{nl})(t,x), \\ u_l(t,x) &:= u_l^{ln}(t,x) + \textstyle\int_0^t G_{\sigma_l,\alpha_l}^{M_l}(t-\varrho,\cdot) *_{(x)} F_{\mu_l,p_l}(u_{l-1}) d\varrho = (u_l^{ln} + u_l^{nl})(t,x). \end{aligned} \tag{17}$$

for all $l = 2,\cdots,k$.

Here, $u_1^{nl} = \int_0^t G_{\sigma_1,\alpha_1}^{M_1}(t-\varrho,\cdot) *_{(x)} F_{\mu_1,p_1}(u_k) d\varrho$ is the solution to

$$\begin{cases} \partial_t^{1+\alpha_1} u_1 + (-\Delta)^{\sigma_1} u_1 + M_1^2 u_l = F_{\mu_1,p_1}(u_k), \\ u_1(0,x) = 0,\ \partial_t u_1(0,x) = 0. \end{cases}$$

and $u_l^{nl} = \int_0^t G_{\sigma_l,\alpha_l}^{M_l}(t-\varrho,\cdot) *_{(x)} F_{\mu_l,p_l}(u_{l-1}) d\varrho$ is the solution to

$$\begin{cases} \partial_t^{1+\alpha_l} u_l + (-\Delta)^{\sigma_l} u_\ell + M_l^2 u_l = F_{\mu_l,p_l}(u_{l-1}), \\ u_l(0,x) = 0,\ \partial_t u_l(0,x) = 0, \quad \ell = 2,...,k. \end{cases}.$$

5. Proof of Main Results

Before showing our results, we recall the following lemma from [32].

Lemma 1. *Let us consider $\theta \in [0,1)$, $a \geq 0$, and $b \geq 0$. There exists a constant $C = C(a,b,\theta) > 0$, such that the following estimate holds for all $t > 0$:*

$$\begin{aligned} &\int_0^t (t-\varrho)^{-\theta}(1+t-\varrho)^{-a}(1+\varrho)^{-b}\, d\varrho \\ &\leq \begin{cases} C(1+t)^{-\min\{a+\theta,b\}} & \text{if} \quad \max\{a+\theta,b\} > 1, \\ C(1+t)^{-\min\{a+\theta,b\}} \ln(2+t) & \text{if} \quad \max\{a+\theta,b\} = 1, \\ C(1+t)^{1-a-\theta-b} & \text{if} \quad \max\{a+\theta,b\} < 1. \end{cases} \end{aligned} \tag{18}$$

5.1. Proof of Theorem 1

Let $T > 0$. We introduce the space $X^k(T)$ as follows:

$$X^k(T) := \prod_{\ell=1}^{k} C\big([0,T], L^{m_l}(\mathbb{R}^d) \cap L^\infty(\mathbb{R}^d)\big)$$

with the norm

$$\|u\|_{X^k(T)} := \|(u_1,u_2,...,u_k)\|_{X^k(T)} := \sup_{0\leqslant t\leqslant T} \Big\{ \sum_{\ell=1}^{k} R_\ell(t,u_l), \Big\},$$

where

$$R_\ell(t,u_l) = (1+t)^{\mu_\ell-\alpha_\ell}(\|u_\ell(t,\cdot)\|_{L^{m_l}} + \|u_\ell(t,\cdot)\|_{L^\infty}),$$

and the operator P by

$$P \,:\, u = (u_1,u_2,...,u_k) \in X^k(T) \to P(u) = P(u)(t,x) := u^{ln}(t,x) + u^{nl}(t,x).$$

In order to prove the global (in time) existence and uniqueness of Sobolev solutions in $X^k(T)$, we will demonstrate that the operator P satisfies the following two inequalities:

$$\|P(u)\|_{X^k(T)} \lesssim \|(u_{01},u_{02},...u_{0k})\|_{\mathcal{A}_k} + \sum_{\ell=1}^{\ell=k} \|u\|^{p_\ell}_{X^k(T)}, \tag{19}$$

$$\|P(u)-P(\tilde{u})\|_{X^k(T)} \lesssim \|u-\tilde{u}\|_{X^k(T)} \sum_{\ell=1}^{\ell=k} \Big(\|u\|^{p_\ell-1}_{X^k(T)} + \|\tilde{u}\|^{p_l-1}_{X^k(T)} \Big). \tag{20}$$

Using the definition of the norm in $X^k(T)$ and Proposition 5, we may conclude:

$$\|u^{ln}\|_{X^k(T)} \lesssim \|(u_{01},u_{02},...,u_{0k})\|_{\mathcal{A}_k}.$$

Hence, in order to complete the proof of (19), it is reasonable to show the following inequality:

$$\|u^{nl}\|_{X^k(T)} \lesssim \sum_{\ell=1}^{\ell=k} \|u\|^{p_\ell}_{X^k(T)}.$$

If $u := (u_1,u_2,\cdots,u_k) \in X^k(T)$, then by interpolation we derive for $l = 1,\cdots,k$

$$\|u_\ell(t,\cdot)\|_{L^q} \lesssim (1+t)^{(\alpha_\ell-\mu_\ell)}\|u\|_{X^k(T)} \quad \text{for all} \quad q \in [m_l,\infty].$$

On the other hand, we also have

$$\begin{aligned}
\|u_1^{nl}(t,\cdot)\|_{L^q} &\lesssim \Big\| \int_0^t G^{M_1}_{\sigma_1,\alpha_1}(t-\varrho,\cdot) *_{(x)} I_s^{\alpha_1}(F_{\mu_1,p_1}(u_k))d\varrho \Big\|_{L^q} \\
&\lesssim \int_0^t (1+t-\varrho)^{-(1+\alpha_1)} \int_0^\varrho (\varrho-s)^{\alpha_1-1} \int_0^s (s-\eta)^{-\mu_1} \|u_k(\eta,\cdot)\|^{p_1}_{L^{p_1q}}\, d\eta\, ds\, d\varrho \\
&\lesssim \|u\|^{p_1}_{X^k(T)} J_1(t) \quad \text{for all} \quad t \in [0,T] \quad \text{and} \quad p_1q \in [m_k,\infty],
\end{aligned}$$

where

$$J_1(t) = \int_0^t (1+t-\varrho)^{-(1+\alpha_1)} \int_0^\varrho (\varrho-s)^{\alpha_1-1} \int_0^s (s-\eta)^{-\mu_1}(1+\eta)^{-p_1(\mu_k-\alpha_k)}\, d\eta\, ds\, d\varrho. \tag{21}$$

We are interested in estimating the right-hand side of (21). For this we need Lemma 1. We put

$$\omega(s) = \int_0^s (s-\eta)^{-\mu_1}(1+\eta)^{-p_1(\mu_k-\alpha_k)}\,d\eta.$$

By using Lemma 1, we obtain $\omega(s) \lesssim (1+s)^{-\mu_1}$, if we assume that $p_1 > \frac{1}{\mu_k-\alpha_k}$. On the other hand, the conditions $q \in [m_1,\infty]$ and $p_1 q \in [m_k,\infty]$ imply that $p_1 \geq \frac{m_k}{m_1}$.

Once more, we apply Lemma 1 to obtain

$$\begin{aligned} J_1(t) &\lesssim \int_0^t (1+t-\varrho)^{-(1+\alpha_1)} \int_0^\varrho (\varrho-s)^{\alpha_1-1}(1+s)^{-\mu_1}\,ds\,d\varrho \\ &\lesssim \int_0^t (1+t-\varrho)^{-(1+\alpha_1)}(1+\varrho)^{\alpha_1-\mu_1}\,d\varrho \\ &\lesssim (1+t)^{\alpha_1-\mu_1}. \end{aligned}$$

For $l = 2,\cdots,k$ and $q \in [m_l,\infty]$, we have

$$\|u_\ell^{nl}(t,\cdot)\|_{L^q} \lesssim \|u\|^{p_\ell}_{X^k(T)} J_l(t) \quad \text{for all} \quad t \in [0,T] \quad \text{and} \quad p_\ell q \in [m_{l-1},\infty],$$

where

$$J_l(t) = \int_0^t (1+t-\varrho)^{-(1+\alpha_\ell)} \int_0^\varrho (\varrho-s)^{\alpha_\ell-1} \int_0^s (s-\eta)^{-\mu_\ell}(1+\eta)^{-p_\ell(\mu_{\ell-1}-\alpha_{\ell-1})}\,d\eta\,ds\,d\varrho. \quad (22)$$

To estimate the right-hand side of (22), we require the use of Lemma 1. Let

$$\omega(s) = \int_0^s (s-\eta)^{-\mu_\ell}(1+\eta)^{-p_\ell(\mu_{\ell-1}-\alpha_{\ell-1})}\,d\eta.$$

By using Lemma 1, we obtain $\omega(s) \lesssim (1+s)^{-\mu_\ell}$, if we assume that $p_\ell > \frac{1}{\mu_{\ell-1}-\alpha_{\ell-1}}$. On the other hand, the conditions $q \in [m_l,\infty]$ and $p_\ell q \in [m_{l-1},\infty]$ imply that $p_\ell \geq \frac{m_{l-1}}{m_l}$.

Once more, we apply Lemma 1 to obtain

$$\begin{aligned} J_l(t) &\lesssim \int_0^t (1+t-\varrho)^{-(1+\alpha_\ell)} \int_0^\varrho (\varrho-s)^{\alpha_\ell-1}(1+s)^{-\mu_\ell}\,ds\,d\varrho \\ &\lesssim \int_0^t (1+t-\varrho)^{-(1+\alpha_\ell)}(1+s)^{\alpha_\ell-\mu_\ell}\,d\varrho \\ &\lesssim (1+t)^{\alpha_\ell-\mu_\ell}. \end{aligned}$$

In order to prove (24), let us consider two vector-functions u and $\tilde{u}$ belonging to $X^k(T)$. Then, we have

$$\begin{aligned} &P(u) - P(\tilde{u}) \\ &= \Big(\int_0^t G^{M_1}_{\sigma_1,\alpha_1}(t-s) \star I^{\alpha_1}_s \Big(\int_0^s (s-\eta)^{-\mu_1} \Big(|u_k(\eta,\cdot)|^{p_1} - |\tilde{u}_k(\eta,\cdot)|^{p_1} \Big)\,d\eta \Big)(t,s,x)\,ds, \cdots, \\ &\int_0^t G^{M_k}_{\sigma_k,\alpha_k}(t-s) \star I^{\alpha_k}_s \Big(\int_0^s (s-\eta)^{-\mu_k} \Big(|u_{k-1}(\eta,\cdot)|^{p_k} - |\tilde{u}_{k-1}(\eta,\cdot)|^{p_k} \Big)\,d\eta \Big)(t,s,x)\,ds \Big). \end{aligned}$$

We estimate, for $q \in [m_1,\infty]$,

$$\begin{aligned} &\Big\| \int_0^t G^{M_1}_{\sigma_1,\alpha_1}(t-s) \star I^{\alpha_1}_s \Big(\int_0^s (s-\eta)^{-\mu_1} \Big(|u_k(\eta,\cdot)|^{p_1} - |\tilde{u}_k(\eta,\cdot)|^{p_1} \Big)\,d\eta \Big)(t,s,\cdot)\,ds \Big\|_{L^q} \\ &\lesssim \int_0^t (1+t-\varrho)^{-(1+\alpha_1)} \int_0^\varrho (\varrho-s)^{\alpha_1-1} \int_0^s (s-\eta)^{-\mu_1} \big\| |u_k(\eta,\cdot)|^{p_1} - |\tilde{u}_k(\eta,\cdot)|^{p_1} \big\|_{L^q} d\eta\,ds d\varrho. \end{aligned}$$

Using Hölder's inequality implies the inequality

$$\big\||u_k(s,\cdot)|^{p_1} - |\tilde{u}_k(s,\cdot)|^{p_1}\big\|_{L^q} \lesssim \big\|u_k(s,\cdot) - \tilde{u}_k(s,\cdot)\big\|_{L^{qp_1}} \big(\|u_k(s,\cdot)\|_{L^{qp_1}}^{p_1-1} + \|\tilde{u}_k(s,\cdot)\|_{L^{qp_1}}^{p_1-1}\big).$$

By using the definition of the norm of the solution space $X^k(T)$, for $p_1 \geq \frac{m_k}{m_1}$ and $0 \leqslant s \leqslant t$, we obtain the following estimates:

$$\begin{aligned}
&\big\|u_k(s,\cdot) - \tilde{u}_k(s,\cdot)\big\|_{L^{qp_1}} \lesssim (1+s)^{\alpha_k-\mu_k} R_k(s, u_k - \tilde{u}_k),\\
&\big\|u_k(s,\cdot)\big\|_{L^{qp_1}}^{p_1-1} \lesssim (1+s)^{(p_1-1)(\alpha_k-\mu_k)} \big\|u\big\|_{X^k(T)}^{p_1-1},\\
&\big\|\tilde{u}_k(s,\cdot)\big\|_{L^{qp_1}}^{p_1-1} \lesssim (1+s)^{(p_1-1)(\alpha_k-\mu_k)} \big\|u\big\|_{X^k(T)}^{p_1-1}.
\end{aligned}$$

Hence, we obtain

$$\begin{aligned}
\big\||u_k(s,\cdot)|^{p_1} - |\tilde{u}_k(s,\cdot)|^{p_1}\big\|_{L^q} &\lesssim (1+s)^{-p_1(\mu_k-\alpha_k)} R_k(s, u_k - \tilde{u}_k)\Big(\|u\|_{X^k(T)}^{p_1-1} + \|\tilde{u}\|_{X^k(T)}^{p_1-1}\Big)\\
&\lesssim (1+s)^{-p_1(\mu_k-\alpha_k)} \|u-\tilde{u}\|_{X^k(T)}\Big(\|u\|_{X^k(T)}^{p_1-1} + \|\tilde{u}\|_{X^k(T)}^{p_1-1}\Big).
\end{aligned}$$

By the same argument, for $l = 2, ..., k$ and $0 \leqslant s \leqslant t$, we obtain the following estimate:

$$\begin{aligned}
\big\||u_\ell(s,\cdot)|^{p_\ell} - |\tilde{u}_\ell(s,\cdot)|^{p_\ell}\big\|_{L^q} &\lesssim (1+s)^{p_\ell(\alpha_\ell-\mu_\ell)} R_l(s, u_{\ell-1} - \tilde{u}_{\ell-1})\Big(\|u\|_{X^k(T)}^{p_\ell-1} + \|\tilde{u}\|_{X^k(T)}^{p_\ell-1}\Big)\\
&\lesssim (1+s)^{p_\ell(\alpha_\ell-\mu_\ell)} \|u-\tilde{u}\|_{X^k(T)}\Big(\|u\|_{X^k(T)}^{p_\ell-1} + \|\tilde{u}\|_{X^k(T)}^{p_\ell-1}\Big).
\end{aligned}$$

So, for $p_1 > \frac{1}{\mu_k-\alpha_k}$ and $p_l > \frac{1}{\mu_{l-1}-\alpha_{l-1}}$ for all $l = 2, \cdots, k$, we obtain the desired estimate (20).

Remark 2. *All estimates (19) and (20) are uniform with respect to $T \in (0, \infty)$.*

From (19), we can see that P maps $X^k(T)$ into itself for all T and for small data. By using standard contraction arguments, the estimates (19) and (20) lead to the existence of a unique solution to $u = P(u)$ and, consequently, to (1). This implies that the solution of (1) satisfies the desired decay estimate. Since all constants are independent of T, we can let T tend to ∞, which yields a global (in time) existence result for small data solutions to (1). This concludes the proof.

5.2. Proof of Theorem 2

Let $T > 0$. We introduce the space $X^k(T)$ as follows:

$$X^k(T) := \prod_{\ell=1}^{k} C([0,T], L^{m_l}(\mathbb{R}^d) \cap L^\infty(\mathbb{R}^d))$$

with the norm

$$\|u\|_{X^k(T)} := \sup_{0\leqslant t\leqslant T} \Big\{(1+t)^{-\gamma^{(\mu_k)}_{(\alpha_k)}(p_1)} R_1(t,u_1) + \sum_{l=2}^{k-1}(1+t)^{-\gamma^{(\mu_k,\ldots,\mu_{\ell-1})}_{(\alpha_k,\ldots,\alpha_{\ell-1})}(p_1,\ldots,p_\ell)} R_\ell(t,u_l) + M_k(t,u_k)\Big\},$$

where, for $l = 1, \cdots, k$,

$$R_\ell(t, u_l) = (1+t)^{\mu_\ell - \alpha_\ell}\big(\|u_\ell(t,\cdot)\|_{L^{m_l}} + \|u_\ell(t,\cdot)\|_{L^\infty}\big), \text{ and}$$

$$\begin{cases} \gamma_{(\alpha_k)}^{(\mu_k)}(p_1) = 1 - p_1(\mu_k - \alpha_k) \\ \gamma_{(\alpha_k,\alpha_1)}^{(\mu_k,\mu_1)}(p_1, p_2) = 1 - p_2(\mu_1 - \alpha_1) + p_2\gamma_{(\alpha_k)}^{(\mu_k)}(p_1) \\ \gamma_{(\alpha_k,\alpha_1,\alpha_2)}^{(\mu_k,\mu_1,\mu_2)}(p_1, p_2, p_3) = 1 - p_3(\mu_2 - \alpha_2) + p_3\gamma_{(\alpha_k,\alpha_1)}^{(\mu_k,\mu_1)}(p_1, p_2) \\ \cdot \\ \cdot \\ \cdot \\ \gamma_{(\alpha_k,\dots,\alpha_{\ell-1})}^{(\mu_k,\dots,\mu_{\ell-1})}(p_1, \dots, p_\ell) = 1 - p_\ell(\mu_{l-1} - \alpha_{l-1}) + p_\ell\gamma_{(\alpha_k,\dots,\alpha_{\ell-2})}^{(\mu_k,\dots,\mu_{\ell-2})}(p_1, \dots, p_{\ell-1}), \end{cases}$$

for $l = 3, \cdots, k-1$. and the operator P by

$$P \; : \; u = (u_1, u_2, \dots, u_k) \in X^k(T) \to P(u) = P(u)(t,x) := u^{ln}(t,x) + u^{nl}(t,x).$$

We will prove that, for $u = (u_1, u_2, \dots, u_k)$; $\tilde{u} = (\tilde{u}_1, \tilde{u}_2, \dots, \tilde{u}_k)$ in $X^k(T)$, the operator P satisfies the following two inequalities:

$$\|P(u)\|_{X^k(T)} \lesssim \|(u_{01}, u_{02}, \dots u_{0k})\|_{\mathcal{A}_k} + \sum_{\ell=1}^{\ell=k} \|u\|_{X^k(T)}^{p_\ell}, \tag{23}$$

$$\|P(u) - P(\tilde{u})\|_{X^k(T)} \lesssim \|u - \tilde{u}\|_{X^k(T)} \sum_{\ell=1}^{\ell=k} \Big(\|u\|_{X^k(T)}^{p_\ell - 1} + \|\tilde{u}\|_{X^k(T)}^{p_l - 1}\Big). \tag{24}$$

Using the definition of the norm in $X^k(T)$ and Proposition 5, we may conclude:

$$\|u^{ln}\|_{X^k(T)} \lesssim \|(u_{01}, u_{02}, \dots, u_{0k})\|_{\mathcal{A}_k}.$$

Hence, in order to complete the proof of (19), it is reasonable to show the following inequality:

$$\|u^{nl}\|_{X^k(T)} \lesssim \sum_{\ell=1}^{\ell=k} \|u\|_{X^k(T)}^{p_\ell}.$$

If $u := (u_1, u_2, \cdots, u_k) \in X^k(T)$, then, for $l = 2, \cdots, k-1$, by interpolation, we derive

$$\begin{aligned} &\|u_1(t,\cdot)\|_{L^q} \lesssim (1+t)^{(\alpha_1 - \mu_1) + \gamma_{(\alpha_k)}^{(\mu_k)}(p_1)} \|u\|_{X^k(T)} \quad \text{for all} \quad q \in [m_1, \infty] \\ &\|u_\ell(t,\cdot)\|_{L^q} \lesssim (1+t)^{(\alpha_\ell - \mu_\ell) + \gamma_{(\alpha_k,\dots,\alpha_{\ell-1})}^{(\mu_k,\dots,\mu_{\ell-1})}(p_1,\dots,p_\ell)} \|u\|_{X^k(T)} \quad \text{for all} \quad q \in [m_l, \infty], \\ &\|u_k(t,\cdot)\|_{L^q} \lesssim \; (1+t)^{\alpha_k - \mu_k} \|u\|_{X^k(T)} \quad \text{for all} \quad q \in [m_k, \infty]. \end{aligned}$$

On the other hand, for $q \in [m_1, \infty]$, we have

$$\|u_1^{nl}(t,\cdot)\|_{L^q} \lesssim \|u\|_{X(T)}^{p_1} J_1(t) \quad \text{for all} \quad t \in [0,T] \quad \text{and} \quad p_1 q \in [m_k, \infty],$$

where

$$J_1(t) = \int_0^t (1+t-\varrho)^{-(1+\alpha_1)} \int_0^\varrho (\varrho - s)^{\alpha_1 - 1} \int_0^s (s-\eta)^{-\mu_1}(1+\eta)^{-p_1(\mu_k - \alpha_k)} \, d\eta \, ds \, d\varrho. \tag{25}$$

We are interested in estimating the right-hand side of (25). For this we need Lemma 1. We put

$$\omega(s) = \int_0^s (s-\eta)^{-\mu_1}(1+\eta)^{-p_1(\mu_k-\alpha_k)}\,d\eta.$$

Thanks to Lemma 1, we obtain $\omega(s) \lesssim (1+s)^{1-\mu_1-p_1(\mu_k-\alpha_k)}$, if we assume that $p_1 < \frac{1}{\mu_k-\alpha_k}$.

Once more, we apply Lemma 1 to obtain

$$\begin{aligned}
J_1(t) &\lesssim \int_0^t (1+t-\varrho)^{-(1+\alpha_1)} \int_0^\varrho (\varrho-s)^{\alpha_1-1}(1+s)^{1-\mu_1-p_1(\mu_k-\alpha_k)}\,ds\,d\varrho \\
&\lesssim \int_0^t (1+t-\varrho)^{-(1+\alpha_1)}(1+\varrho)^{1+\alpha_1-\mu_1-p_1(\mu_k-\alpha_k)}\,d\varrho \\
&\lesssim (1+t)^{1+\alpha_1-\mu_1-p_1(\mu_k-\alpha_k)} \\
&\lesssim (1+t)^{\alpha_1-\mu_1+\gamma_{\alpha_k}^{\mu_k}(p_1)}.
\end{aligned}$$

On the other hand, the conditions $q \in [m_1,\infty]$ and $p_1 q \in [m_k,\infty]$ imply that $p_1 \geq \frac{m_k}{m_1}$.

For $l = 2$ and $q \in [m_2,\infty]$, we have

$$\begin{aligned}
\|u_2^{nl}(t,\cdot)\|_{L^q} &\lesssim \int_0^t (1+t-\varrho)^{-(1+\alpha_2)} \int_0^\varrho (\varrho-s)^{\alpha_2-1} \| |u_1(s,\cdot)|^{p_2}\|_{L^q}\,ds\,d\varrho \\
&\lesssim \int_0^t (1+t-\varrho)^{-(1+\alpha_2)} \int_0^\varrho (\varrho-s)^{\alpha_2-1} \int_0^s (s-\eta)^{-\mu_2}\|u_1(\eta,\cdot)\|_{L^{p_2 q}}^{p_2}\,d\eta\,ds\,d\varrho \\
&\lesssim \|u\|_{X(T)}^{p_2} J_2(t) \quad \text{for all} \quad t\in[0,T] \quad \text{and} \quad p_2 q \in [m_1,\infty],
\end{aligned}$$

where

$$J_2(t) = \int_0^t (1+t-\varrho)^{-(1+\alpha_2)} \int_0^\varrho (\varrho-s)^{\alpha_2-1} \int_0^s (s-\eta)^{-\mu_2}(1+\eta)^{-p_2(\mu_1-\alpha_1)+p_2\gamma_{(\alpha_k)}^{(\mu_k)}(p_1)}\,d\eta\,ds\,d\varrho. \tag{26}$$

We are interested in estimating the right-hand side of (26). For this, we need Lemma 1. We put

$$\omega(s) = \int_0^s (s-\eta)^{-\mu_2}(1+\eta)^{-p_2(\mu_1-\alpha_1)+p_2\gamma_{(\alpha_k)}^{(\mu_k)}(p_1)}\,d\eta.$$

Thanks to Lemma 1, we obtain

$$\omega(s) \lesssim (1+s)^{1-\mu_2-p_2(\mu_1-\alpha_1)+p_2\gamma_{(\alpha_k)}^{(\mu_k)}(p_1)},$$

if we assume that $p_2 < \frac{1}{\mu_1-\alpha_1-\gamma_{(\alpha_k)}^{(\mu_k)}(p_1)}$ and $\mu_1-\alpha_1-\gamma_{(\alpha_k)}^{(\mu_k)}(p_1) > 0$.

The condition $\mu_1-\alpha_1-\gamma_{(\alpha_k)}^{(\mu_k)}(p_1) > 0$ is equivalent to $p_1 > \frac{1+\alpha_1-\mu_1}{\mu_k-\alpha_k}$.

Once more, we apply Lemma 1 to obtain

$$\begin{aligned}
J_2(t) &\lesssim \int_0^t (1+t-\varrho)^{-(1+\alpha_2)} \int_0^\varrho (\varrho-s)^{\alpha_2-1}(1+s)^{1-\mu_2-p_2(\mu_1-\alpha_1)+p_2\gamma_{(\alpha_k)}^{(\mu_k)}(p_1)}\,ds\,d\varrho \\
&\lesssim \int_0^t (1+t-\varrho)^{-(1+\alpha_2)}(1+\varrho)^{1+\alpha_2-\mu_2-p_2(\mu_1-\alpha_1)+p_2\gamma_{(\alpha_k)}^{(\mu_k)}(p_1)}\,d\varrho \\
&\lesssim (1+t)^{1+\alpha_2-\mu_2-p_2(\mu_1-\alpha_1)+p_2\gamma_{(\alpha_k)}^{(\mu_k)}(p_1)} \\
&\lesssim (1+t)^{1+\alpha_2-\mu_2-p_2(\mu_1-\alpha_1)+p_2\gamma_{(\alpha_k)}^{(\mu_k)}(p_1)} \\
&\lesssim (1+t)^{\alpha_2-\mu_2+\gamma_{(\alpha_k,\alpha_1)}^{(\mu_k,\mu_1)}(p_1,p_2)}.
\end{aligned}$$

On the other hand, the conditions $q \in [m_2, \infty]$ and $p_2 q \in [m_1, \infty]$ imply that $p_2 \geq \frac{m_1}{m_2}$.
For $l = 3, \cdots, k-1$ and $q \in [m_l, \infty]$, we have

$$\begin{aligned}
\|u_\ell^{nl}(t,\cdot)\|_{L^q} &\lesssim \int_0^t (1+t-\varrho)^{-(1+\alpha_\ell)} \int_0^\varrho (\varrho - s)^{\alpha_\ell - 1} \| |u_{\ell-1}(s,\cdot)|^{p_\ell} \|_{L^q} \, ds \, d\varrho \\
&\lesssim \int_0^t (1+t-\varrho)^{-(1+\alpha_\ell)} \int_0^\varrho (\varrho - s)^{\alpha_\ell - 1} \int_0^s (s-\eta)^{-\mu_\ell} \|u_{\ell-1}(\eta,\cdot)\|_{L^{p_\ell q}}^{p_\ell} \, d\eta \, ds \, d\varrho \\
&\lesssim \|u\|_{X(T)}^{p_\ell} J_l(t) \quad \text{for all} \quad t \in [0,T] \quad \text{and} \quad p_\ell q \in [m_{l-1}, \infty],
\end{aligned}$$

where

$$\begin{aligned}
J_l(t) = \int_0^t (1+t-\varrho)^{-(1+\alpha_\ell)} \int_0^\varrho (\varrho - s)^{\alpha_\ell - 1} \\
\times \int_0^s (s-\eta)^{-\mu_\ell} (1+\eta)^{-p_\ell(\mu_{\ell-1} - \alpha_{\ell-1}) + p_\ell \gamma_{(\alpha_k,\ldots,\alpha_{\ell-2})}^{(\mu_k,\ldots,\mu_{\ell-2})}(p_1,\ldots,p_{\ell-1})} \, d\eta \, ds \, d\varrho. \qquad (27)
\end{aligned}$$

On the other hand, we are interested in estimating the right-hand side of (27). For this, we need Lemma 1. We put

$$\omega(s) = \int_0^s (s-\eta)^{-\mu_\ell} (1+\eta)^{-p_\ell(\mu_{\ell-1} - \alpha_{\ell-1}) + p_\ell \gamma_{(\alpha_k,\ldots,\alpha_{\ell-2})}^{(\mu_k,\ldots,\mu_{\ell-2})}(p_1,\ldots,p_{\ell-1})} \, d\eta.$$

Thanks to Lemma 1, we obtain

$$\omega(s) \lesssim (1+s)^{1-\mu_\ell - p_\ell(\mu_{\ell-1} - \alpha_{\ell-1}) + p_\ell \gamma_{(\alpha_k,\ldots,\alpha_{\ell-2})}^{(\mu_k,\ldots,\mu_{\ell-2})}(p_1,\ldots,p_{\ell-1})},$$

if we assume that

$$p_\ell < \frac{1}{\mu_{\ell-1} - \alpha_{\ell-1} - \gamma_{(\alpha_k,\ldots,\alpha_{\ell-2})}^{(\mu_k,\ldots,\mu_{\ell-2})}(p_1,\ldots,p_{\ell-1})}$$

and

$$\mu_{\ell-1} - \alpha_{\ell-1} - \gamma_{(\alpha_k,\ldots,\alpha_{\ell-2})}^{(\mu_k,\ldots,\mu_{\ell-2})}(p_1,\ldots,p_{\ell-1}) > 0.$$

The last condition is equivalent to

$$p_{l-1} > \frac{1 + \alpha_{l-1} - \mu_{l-1}}{\mu_{\ell-2} - \alpha_{\ell-2} - \gamma_{(\alpha_k,\ldots,\alpha_{\ell-3})}^{(\mu_k,\ldots,\mu_{\ell-3})}(p_1,\ldots,p_{\ell-2})}$$

On the other hand, the conditions $q \in [m_l, \infty]$ and $p_\ell q \in [m_{l-1}, \infty]$ imply that $p_\ell \geq \frac{m_l - 1}{m_l}$.
Once more, we apply Lemma 1 to obtain

$$\begin{aligned}
J_l(t) &\lesssim \int_0^t (1+t-\varrho)^{-(1+\alpha_\ell)} \int_0^\varrho (\varrho - s)^{\alpha_\ell - 1} (1+s)^{1-\mu_\ell - p_\ell(\mu_{\ell-1} - \alpha_{\ell-1}) + p_\ell \gamma_{(\alpha_k,\ldots,\alpha_{\ell-2})}^{(\mu_k,\ldots,\mu_{\ell-2})}(p_1,\ldots,p_{\ell-1})} \, ds \, d\varrho \\
&\lesssim \int_0^t (1+t-\varrho)^{-(1+\alpha_\ell)} (1+s)^{\alpha_\ell - \mu_\ell + 1 - p_\ell(\mu_{\ell-1} - \alpha_{\ell-1}) + p_\ell \gamma_{(\alpha_k,\ldots,\alpha_{\ell-2})}^{(\mu_k,\ldots,\mu_{\ell-2})}(p_1,\ldots,p_{\ell-1})} \, d\varrho \\
&\lesssim (1+t)^{\alpha_\ell - \mu_\ell + 1 - p_\ell(\mu_{\ell-1} - \alpha_{\ell-1}) + p_\ell \gamma_{(\alpha_k,\ldots,\alpha_{\ell-2})}^{(\mu_k,\ldots,\mu_{\ell-2})}(p_1,\ldots,p_{\ell-1})} \\
&\lesssim (1+t)^{\alpha_\ell - \mu_\ell + \gamma_{(\alpha_k,\ldots,\alpha_{\ell-1})}^{(\mu_k,\ldots,\mu_{\ell-1})}(p_1,\ldots,p_\ell)}.
\end{aligned}$$

Finally, for $q \in [m_k, \infty]$, we have

$$\begin{aligned}\|u_k^{nl}(t,\cdot)\|_{L^q} &\lesssim \int_0^t (1+t-\varrho)^{-(1+\alpha_k)} \int_0^\varrho (\varrho - s)^{\alpha_k - 1} \| |u_{k-1}(s,\cdot)|^{p_k} \|_{L^q}\, ds\, d\varrho \\ &\lesssim \int_0^t (1+t-\varrho)^{-(1+\alpha_k)} \int_0^\varrho (\varrho - s)^{\alpha_k - 1} \int_0^s (s-\eta)^{-\mu_k} \|u_{k-1}(\eta,\cdot)\|_{L^{p_k q}}^{p_k}\, d\eta\, ds\, d\varrho \\ &\lesssim \|u\|_{X(T)}^{p_k} J_k(t) \quad \text{for all} \quad t \in [0,T] \quad \text{and} \quad p_k q \in [m_{k-1}, \infty],\end{aligned}$$

where

$$\begin{aligned}J_k(t) = &\int_0^t (1+t-\varrho)^{-(1+\alpha_k)} \int_0^\varrho (\varrho - s)^{\alpha_k - 1} \\ &\times \int_0^s (s-\eta)^{-\mu_k} (1+\eta)^{-p_k\left(\mu_{k-1} - \alpha_{k-1} - \gamma_{(\alpha_1,\dots,\alpha_{k-2})}^{(\mu_1,\dots,\mu_{k-2})}(p_1,\dots,p_{k-1})\right)}\, d\eta\, ds\, d\varrho. \qquad (28)\end{aligned}$$

We are interested in estimating the right-hand side of (28). For this we need Lemma 1. We put

$$\omega(s) = \int_0^s (s-\eta)^{-\mu_k} (1+\eta)^{-p_k\left(\mu_{k-1} - \alpha_{k-1} - \gamma_{(\alpha_1,\dots,\alpha_{k-1})}^{(\mu_1,\dots,\mu_{k-2})}(p_1,\dots,p_{k-1})\right)}\, d\eta.$$

Thanks to Lemma 1 we obtain $\omega(s) \lesssim (1+s)^{-\mu_k}$, if we assume that

$$p_k > \frac{1}{\mu_{k-1} - \alpha_{k-1} - \gamma_{(\alpha_k,\dots,\alpha_{k-2})}^{(\mu_k,\dots,\mu_{k-2})}(p_1,\dots,p_{k-1})}$$

and

$$\mu_{k-1} - \alpha_{k-1} - \gamma_{(\alpha_k,\dots,\alpha_{k-2})}^{(\mu_k,\dots,\mu_{k-2})}(p_1,\dots,p_{k-1}) > 0$$

which equivalent to

$$p_{k-1} > \frac{\alpha_{k-1} - \mu_{k-1} + 1}{\mu_{k-2} - \alpha_{k-2} - \gamma_{\alpha_k,\dots,\alpha_{k-3}}^{(\mu_k,\dots,\mu_{k-3})}(p_1,\dots,p_{k-2})}.$$

Once more, we apply Lemma 1 to obtain

$$\begin{aligned}J_k(t) &\lesssim \int_0^t (1+t-\varrho)^{-(1+\alpha_k)} \int_0^\varrho (\varrho - s)^{\alpha_k - 1} (1+s)^{-\mu_k}\, d\eta\, ds\, d\varrho \\ &\lesssim \int_0^t (1+t-\varrho)^{-(1+\alpha_k)} (1+\varrho)^{\alpha_k - \mu_k}\, d\varrho \\ &\lesssim (1+t)^{\alpha_k - \mu_k}.\end{aligned}$$

The proof of (24) is similar to the proof of (20) of Theorem 1. This completes the proof.

5.3. Proof of Theorem 3

Let $T > 0$. We introduce the space $X^k(T)$ as follows:

$$X^k(T) := \prod_{\ell=1}^{k} C\big([0,T], L^{m_l}(\mathbb{R}^d) \cap L^\infty(\mathbb{R}^d)\big)$$

with the norm

$$\|u\|_{X^k(T)} := \sup_{0 \leqslant t \leqslant T} \Big\{ \sum_{l=1}^{k-1} (1+t)^{-\gamma(p_l)} R_l(t,u_l) + R_k(t,u_k) \Big\},$$

where, for $l = 1, \cdots, k$,

$$R_\ell(t, u_l) = (1+t)^{\mu_\ell - \alpha_\ell}\big(\|u_\ell(t,\cdot)\|_{L^{m_l}} + \|u_\ell(t,\cdot)\|_{L^\infty}\big),$$
$$\begin{cases} \gamma(p_1) = 1 \\ \gamma(p_l) = 1 + p_l\gamma(p_{\ell-1}), \text{ for } l = 2, \cdots, k-1. \end{cases}$$

The operator P is defined by

$$P \;:\; u = (u_1, u_2, ..., u_k) \in X^k(T) \to P(u) = P(u)(t,x) := u^{ln}(t,x) + u^{nl}(t,x).$$

We will prove that, for $u = (u_1, u_2, ..., u_k)$; $\tilde{u} = (\tilde{u}_1, \tilde{u}_2, ..., \tilde{u}_k)$ in $X^k(T)$, the operator P satisfies the following two inequalities:

$$\|P(u)\|_{X^k(T)} \lesssim \|(u_{01}, u_{02}, ...u_{0k})\|_{\mathcal{A}_k} + \sum_{\ell=1}^{\ell=k} \|u\|^{p_\ell}_{X^k(T)}, \tag{29}$$

$$\|P(u) - P(\tilde{u})\|_{X^k(T)} \lesssim \|u - \tilde{u}\|_{X^k(T)} \sum_{\ell=1}^{\ell=k} \Big(\|u\|^{p_\ell - 1}_{X^k(T)} + \|\tilde{u}\|^{p_l - 1}_{X^k(T)}\Big). \tag{30}$$

Using the definition of the norm in $X^k(T)$ and Proposition 5, we may conclude:

$$\|u^{ln}\|_{X^k(T)} \lesssim \|(u_{01}, u_{02}, ..., u_{0k})\|_{\mathcal{A}_k}.$$

Hence, in order to complete the proof of (29), it is reasonable to show the following inequality:

$$\|u^{nl}\|_{X^k(T)} \lesssim \sum_{\ell=1}^{\ell=k} \|u\|^{p_\ell}_{X^k(T)}.$$

If $u := (u_1, u_2, \cdots, u_k) \in X^k(T)$, then by interpolation, we derive, for $l = 1, \cdots, k-1$,

$$\|u_\ell(t,\cdot)\|_{L^q} \lesssim (1+t)^{(\alpha_\ell - \mu_\ell) + \gamma(p_\ell)} \|u\|_{X^k(T)} \quad \text{for all} \quad q \in [1, \infty],$$
$$\|u_k(t,\cdot)\|_{L^q} \lesssim \; (1+t)^{\alpha_k - \mu_k} \|u\|_{X^k(T)} \quad \text{for all} \quad q \in [1, \infty].$$

On the other hand, for $q \in [1, \infty]$, we have

$$\|u_1^{nl}(t,\cdot)\|_{L^q} \lesssim \|u\|^{p_1}_{X(T)} J_1(t) \quad \text{for all} \quad t \in [0, T],$$

where

$$J_1(t) = \int_0^t (1+t-\varrho)^{-(1+\alpha_1)} \int_0^\varrho (\varrho - s)^{\alpha_1 - 1} \int_0^s (s-\eta)^{-\mu_1}(1+\eta)^{-p_1(\mu_k - \alpha_k)}\, d\eta\, ds\, d\varrho. \tag{31}$$

We are interested in estimating the right-hand side of (31). For this, we need Lemma 1. We put

$$\omega(s) = \int_0^s (s-\eta)^{-\mu_1}(1+\eta)^{-p_1(\mu_k - \alpha_k)}\, d\eta.$$

Thanks to Lemma 1, we obtain $\omega(s) \lesssim (1+s)^{-\mu_1}\ln(1+s)$, if we assume that $p_1 = \frac{1}{\mu_k - \alpha_k}$.

Once more, we apply Lemma 1 to obtain

$$\begin{aligned} J_1(t) &\lesssim \ln(2+t)\int_0^t (1+t-\varrho)^{-(1+\alpha_1)}\int_0^\varrho (\varrho-s)^{\alpha_1-1}(1+s)^{-\mu_1}\,ds\,d\varrho \\ &\lesssim \int_0^t (1+t-\varrho)^{-(1+\alpha_1)}(1+\varrho)^{\alpha_1-\mu_1}\,d\varrho \\ &\lesssim (1+t)^{\alpha_1-\mu_1}\ln(2+t) \\ &\lesssim (1+t)^{\alpha_1-\mu_1}\big(\ln(2+t)\big)^{\gamma(p_1)}. \end{aligned}$$

For $l=2,\cdots,k-1$ and $q\in[1,\infty]$, we have

$$\begin{aligned} \|u_\ell^{nl}(t,\cdot)\|_{L^q} &\lesssim \int_0^t (1+t-\varrho)^{-(1+\alpha_\ell)}\int_0^\varrho (\varrho-s)^{\alpha_\ell-1}\||u_{\ell-1}(s,\cdot)|^{p_\ell}\|_{L^q}\,ds\,d\varrho \\ &\lesssim \int_0^t (1+t-\varrho)^{-(1+\alpha_\ell)}\int_0^\varrho (\varrho-s)^{\alpha_\ell-1}\int_0^s (s-\eta)^{-\mu_\ell}\|u_{\ell-1}(\eta,\cdot)\|^{p_\ell}_{L^{p_\ell q}}\,d\eta\,ds\,d\varrho \\ &\lesssim \|u\|^{p_\ell}_{X(T)}J_l(t) \quad \text{for all} \quad t\in[0,T] \quad \text{and} \quad p_\ell q\in[m_{l-1},\infty], \end{aligned}$$

where

$$\begin{aligned} J_l(t) = &\int_0^t (1+t-\varrho)^{-(1+\alpha_\ell)}\int_0^\varrho (\varrho-s)^{\alpha_\ell-1} \\ &\times\int_0^s (s-\eta)^{-\mu_\ell}(1+\eta)^{-p_\ell(\mu_{\ell-1}-\alpha_{\ell-1})}\big(\ln(1+\eta)\big)^{p_\ell\gamma(p_{\ell-1})}\,d\eta\,ds\,d\varrho. \end{aligned}$$

We remark that

$$\begin{aligned} J_l(t) \lesssim \big(\ln(2+t)\big)^{p_\ell\gamma(p_{\ell-1})} &\int_0^t (1+t-\varrho)^{-(1+\alpha_\ell)}\int_0^\varrho (\varrho-s)^{\alpha_\ell-1} \\ &\times\int_0^s (s-\eta)^{-\mu_\ell}(1+\eta)^{-p_\ell(\mu_{\ell-1}-\alpha_{\ell-1})}\,d\eta\,ds\,d\varrho. \end{aligned} \tag{32}$$

On the other hand, we are interested in estimating the right-hand side of (32). For this, we need Lemma 1. We put

$$\omega(s) = \int_0^s (s-\eta)^{-\mu_\ell}(1+\eta)^{-p_\ell(\mu_{\ell-1}-\alpha_{\ell-1})}\,d\eta.$$

Thanks to Lemma 1, we obtain

$$\omega(s) \lesssim (1+s)^{-\mu_\ell},$$

if we assume that

$$p_\ell = \frac{1}{\mu_{\ell-1}-\alpha_{\ell-1}}.$$

Once more, we apply Lemma 1 to obtain

$$\begin{aligned} J_l(t) &\lesssim \big(\ln(2+t)\big)^{p_\ell\gamma(p_{\ell-1})}\int_0^t (1+t-\varrho)^{-(1+\alpha_\ell)}\int_0^\varrho (\varrho-s)^{\alpha_\ell-1}(1+s)^{-\mu_\ell}\,ds\,d\varrho \\ &\lesssim \big(\ln(2+t)\big)^{p_\ell\gamma(p_{\ell-1})}\int_0^t (1+t-\varrho)^{-(1+\alpha_\ell)}(1+\varrho)^{\alpha_\ell-\mu_\ell}\,d\varrho \\ &\lesssim (1+t)^{\alpha_\ell-\mu_\ell}\big(\ln(2+t)\big)^{p_\ell\gamma(p_{\ell-1})} \end{aligned}$$

Finally, for $q \in [1, \infty]$, we have

$$\begin{aligned} \|u_k^{nl}(t,\cdot)\|_{L^q} &\lesssim \int_0^t (1+t-\varrho)^{-(1+\alpha_k)} \int_0^\varrho (\varrho-s)^{\alpha_k-1} \| |u_{k-1}(s,\cdot)|^{p_k} \|_{L^q}\, ds\, d\varrho \\ &\lesssim \int_0^t (1+t-\varrho)^{-(1+\alpha_k)} \int_0^\varrho (\varrho-s)^{\alpha_k-1} \int_0^s (s-\eta)^{-\mu_k} \|u_{k-1}(\eta,\cdot)\|_{L^{p_k q}}^{p_k}\, d\eta\, ds\, d\varrho \\ &\lesssim \|u\|_{X(T)}^{p_k} J_k(t) \quad \text{for all} \quad t \in [0,T] \end{aligned}$$

where

$$J_k(t) = \int_0^t (1+t-\varrho)^{-(1+\alpha_k)} \int_0^\varrho (\varrho-s)^{\alpha_k-1} \times \int_0^s (s-\eta)^{-\mu_k} (1+\eta)^{-p_k(\mu_{k-1}-\alpha_{k-1})} \big(\ln(1+\eta)\big)^{p_k \gamma(p_{k-1})}\, d\eta\, ds\, d\varrho. \quad (33)$$

We are interested in estimating the right-hand side of (33). Let $\delta > 0$ be small enough and we use the fact that $\ln(2+t) \lesssim (1+t)^\delta$ to obtain

$$J_k(t) \lesssim \int_0^t (1+t-\varrho)^{-(1+\alpha_k)} \int_0^\varrho (\varrho-s)^{\alpha_k-1} \times \int_0^s (s-\eta)^{-\mu_k} (1+\eta)^{-p_k(\mu_{k-1}-\alpha_{k-1}-\delta\gamma(p_{k-1}))}\, d\eta\, ds\, d\varrho. \quad (34)$$

For this, we need Lemma 1. We put

$$\omega(s) = \int_0^s (s-\eta)^{-\mu_k} (1+\eta)^{-p_k(\mu_{k-1}-\alpha_{k-1}-\delta\gamma(p_{k-1}))}\, d\eta.$$

Thanks to Lemma 1, we obtain $\omega(s) \lesssim (1+s)^{-\mu_k}$, if we assume that

$$p_k > \frac{1}{\mu_{k-1}-\alpha_{k-1}-\delta\gamma(p_{k-1})}.$$

Once more, we apply Lemma 1 to obtain

$$\begin{aligned} J_k(t) &\lesssim \int_0^t (1+t-\varrho)^{-(1+\alpha_k)} \int_0^\varrho (\varrho-s)^{\alpha_k-1} (1+s)^{-\mu_k}\, d\eta\, ds\, d\varrho \\ &\lesssim \int_0^t (1+t-\varrho)^{-(1+\alpha_k)} (1+\varrho)^{\alpha_k-\mu_k}\, d\varrho \\ &\lesssim (1+t)^{\alpha_k-\mu_k}. \end{aligned}$$

The proof of (30) is similar to the proof of (20) of Theorem 1. This completes the proof.

6. Conclusions

In the present paper, we proved the global (in time) existence of small data Sobolev solutions to the weakly coupled system of k semi-linear fractional σ-evolution equations with mass and different memory terms. We studied the relationship between the regularity assumptions for the data, the memory terms, and the admissible range of exponents $(p_1, p_2, \ldots, p_k)$ in Equation (1). In a forthcoming paper, we will study the blow-up of solutions to (1).

Author Contributions: Methodology, A.M.D.; validation, A.A.-Q.; investigation, A.M.D.; writing—original draft, S.A.S., A.K.M., M.K.M. and A.M.D.; writing—review and editing, A.M.A.B.A. All authors have read and agreed to the published version of the manuscript.

Funding: This work was supported by the Deanship of Scientific Research, Vice Presidency for Graduate Studies and Scientific Research, King Faisal University, Saudi Arabia [Project No. GrantA532].

Data Availability Statement: Data are contained within the article.

Acknowledgments: The authors would like to thank the Deanship of Scientific Research, Vice Presidency for Graduate Studies and Scientific Research, King Faisal University, Saudi Arabia for supporting this work.

Conflicts of Interest: The authors declare no conflicts of interest.

References

1. Fujita, H.T. On the blowing-up of solutions of the Cauchy problem for $\partial_t u = \Delta u + u^{1+\lambda}$. *J. Fac. Sci. Univ. Tokyo Sect.* **1966**, *13*, 109–124.
2. Hayakawa, K. On the growing up problem for semi-linear heat equations. *Proc. Jpn. Acad.* **1973**, *49*, 503–505.
3. Kobayashi, K.; Sirao, T.; Tanaka, H. The Critical Exponent(s) for the Semilinear Fractional Diffusive Equation. *J. Math. Soc. Jpn.* **1977**, *29*, 407–424.
4. Strauss, W.A. Nonlinear scattering theory at low energy. *J. Funct. Anal.* **1981**, *41*, 110–133. [CrossRef]
5. Glassey, R.T. Existence in the large for $\Box u = F(u)$ in two space dimensions. *Math. Z.* **1981**, *178*, 233–261. [CrossRef]
6. Glassey, R.T. Finite-time blow-up for solutions of nonlinear wave equations. *Math. Z.* **1981**, *177*, 323–340. [CrossRef]
7. Schaeffer, J. The equation $\partial_{tt}u + -\Delta u = |u|^p$ for the critical value of p. *Proc. R. Soc. Edinb. Sect. A* **1985**, *101*, 31–44. [CrossRef]
8. Yordanov, B.T.; Zhang, Q.S. Finite time blow up for critical wave equations in high dimensions. *J. Funct. Anal.* **2006**, *231*, 361–374. [CrossRef]
9. Zhou, Y. Blow up of solutions to semilinear wave equations with critical exponent in high dimensions. *Chin. Ann. Math. Ser. B* **2007**, *28*, 205–212. [CrossRef]
10. Kato, T. Blow-up of solutions of some nonlinear hyperbolic equations. *Commun. Pure Appl. Math.* **1980**, *33*, 501–505. [CrossRef]
11. John, F. Blow-up of solutions of nonlinear wave equations in three space dimensions. *Manuscr. Math.* **1979**, *28*, 235–268. [CrossRef]
12. Sideris, T.C. Nonexistence of global solutions to semilinear wave equations in high dimensions. *J. Differ. Equ.* **1984**, *52*, 378–406. [CrossRef]
13. D'Abbicco, M.; Ebert, M.R.; Picon, T.H. The Critical Exponent(s) for the Semilinear Fractional Diffusive Equation. *J. Fourier Anal. Appl.* **2019**, *25*, 696–731. [CrossRef]
14. Kainane Mezadek, A.; Reissig, M. Semi-linear fractional σ–evolution equations with mass or power non-linearity. *Nonlinear Differ. Equ. Appl.* **2018**, *25*, 1–43. [CrossRef]
15. Kainane Mezadek, A. Global existence of small data solutions to Semi-Linear Fractional σ–Evolution Equations with mass and Nonlinear Memory. *Mediterr. J. Math.* **2020**, *17*, 159. [CrossRef]
16. Escobedo, M.; Herrero, A. Boundedness and blow up for a semilinear reaction-diffusion system. *J. Differ. Equ.* **1991**, *89*, 176–202. [CrossRef]
17. Andreucci, D.; Herrero, M.A.; Velázquez, J.L. Liouville theorems and blow up behaviour in semilinear reaction diffusion systems. *Ann. Inst. H. Poincaré Anal. Non Linéaire* **1997**, *14*, 1–53. [CrossRef]
18. Escobedo, M.; Levine, H.A. Critical blow up and global existence numbers for a weakly coupled system of reaction-diffusion equations. *Arch. Rational Mech. Anal.* **1995**, *129*, 47–100. [CrossRef]
19. Renclawowicz, J. Blow up, global existence and growth rate estimates in nonlinear parabolic systems. *Colloq. Math.* **2000**, *86*, 43–66. [CrossRef]
20. Snoussi, S.; Tayachi, S. Global existence, asymptotic behavior and self-similar solutions for a class of semilinear parabolic systems. *Nonlinear Anal.* **2002**, *48*, 13–35. [CrossRef]
21. Sun, F.; Wang, M. Existence and nonexistence of global solutions for a non-linear hyperbolic system with damping. *Nonlinear Anal.* **2007**, *66*, 2889–2910. [CrossRef]
22. Narazaki, T. Global solutions to the Cauchy problem for the weakly coupled of damped wave equations. *Conf. Publ.* **2009**, 592–601. [CrossRef]
23. Nishihara, K.; Wakasugi, Y. Critical exponant for the Cauchy problem to the weakly coupled wave system. *Nonlinear Anal.* **2014**, *108*, 249–259. [CrossRef]
24. Mohammed Djaouti, A.; Reissig, M. Weakly Coupled Systems of Semilinear Effectively Damped Waves with Different Time-Dependent Coefficients in the Dissipation Terms and Different Power Nonlinearities. In *New Tools for Nonlinear PDEs and Application. Trends in Mathematics*; D'Abbicco, E.M., Georgiev, M., Ozawa, T., Eds.; Birkhäuser: Basel, Switzerland, 2019; pp. 209–409.
25. Mohammed Djaouti, A. Semilinear Systems of Weakly Coupled Damped Waves. Ph.D. Thesis, TU Bergakademie Freiberg, Freiberg, Germany, 2018.
26. Mohammed Djaouti, A. Modified different nonlinearities for weakly coupled systems of semilinear effectively damped waves with different time-dependent coefficients in the dissipation terms. *Adv. Differ. Equ.* **2021**, *2021*, 66. [CrossRef]
27. Dao, T.A. Global existence of solutions for weakly coupled systems of semi-linear structurally damped σ–evolution models. *Appl. Anal.* **2022**, *101*, 1396–1429.
28. Qiao, Y.; Dao, T.A. On the Cauchy problem for a weakly coupled system of semi-linear σ–evolution equations with double dissipation. *arXiv* **2023**, arXiv:2311.06663.

29. Mohammed Djaouti, A. Weakly Coupled System of Semi-Linear Fractional $\theta-$Evolution Equations with Special Cauchy Conditions. *Symmetry* **2023**, *15*, 1341. [CrossRef]
30. Kainane Mezadek, A. Weakly Coupled Systems of Semi-Linear Fractional σ–Evolution Equations with Mass and Different Power Nonlinearities. *Mediterr. J. Math.* **2024**, *21*, 1–15.
31. Kilbas, A.A.; Srivastava, H.M.; Trujillo, J.J. *Theory and Applications of Fractional Differential Equations*; North-Holland Mathematics Studies; Elsevier Science B.V.: Amsterdam, The Netherlands, 2006; Volume 204.
32. Cui, S. Local and global existence of solutions to semilinear parabolic initial value problems. *Nonlinear Anal.* **2001**, *43*, 293–323.

mathematics MDPI

Article

Minimum Principles for Sturm–Liouville Inequalities and Applications

Phuc Ngo † and Kunquan Lan *

Department of Mathematics, Toronto Metropolitan University, 350 Victoria Street, Toronto, ON M5B 2K3, Canada; pngo@uoguelph.ca
* Correspondence: klan@torontomu.ca
† Current address: Department of Mathematics & Statistics, University of Guelph, 50 Stone Road East, Guelph, ON N1G 2W1, Canada.

Abstract: A minimum principle for a Sturm–Liouville (S-L) inequality is obtained, which shows that the minimum value of a nonconstant solution of a S-L inequality never occurs in the interior of the domain (a closed interval) of the solution. The minimum principle is then applied to prove that any nonconstant solutions of S-L inequalities subject to separated inequality boundary conditions (IBCs) must be strictly positive in the interiors of their domains and are increasing or decreasing for some of these IBCs. These positivity results are used to prove the uniqueness of the solutions of linear S-L equations with separated BCs. All of these results hold for the corresponding second-order differential inequalities (or equations), which are special cases of S-L inequalities (or equations). These results are applied to two models arising from the source distribution of the human head and chemical reactor theory. The first model is governed by a nonlinear S-L equation, while the second one is governed by a nonlinear second-order differential equation. For the first model, the explicit solutions are not available, and there are no results on the existence of solutions of the first model. Our results show that all the nonconstant solutions are increasing and are strictly positive solutions. For the second model, many results on the uniqueness of the solutions and the existence of multiple solutions have been obtained before. Our results are applied to prove that all the nonconstant solutions are decreasing and strictly positive.

Keywords: Sturm–Liouville inequalities; minimum principles; second-order differential inequalities; boundary value problems; strictly positive solutions

MSC: 34B24; 26D10; 34A12; 34A30; 34A34; 34B05

Citation: Ngo, P.; Lan, K. Minimum Principles for Sturm–Liouville Inequalities and Applications. *Mathematics* **2024**, *12*, 2088. https://doi.org/10.3390/math12132088

Academic Editors: Lingju Kong, Min Wang and David Carfì

Received: 11 May 2024
Revised: 27 June 2024
Accepted: 2 July 2024
Published: 3 July 2024

1. Introduction

We study the properties of solutions of a Sturm–Liouville (S-L) inequality of the form

$$-(p(x)u'(x))' \geq 0 \quad \text{for each } x \in [a,b], \tag{1}$$

where $p : [a,b] \to \mathbb{R}_+$ is a function satisfying $p(x) > 0$ for each $x \in (a,b)$, and u' denotes the first-order derivative of a function u.

A function $u : [a,b] \to \mathbb{R}$ is said to be a solution of (1) if $u \in C[a,b]$, $u'(x)$ and $(p(x)u'(x))'$ exist for each $x \in [a,b]$ and u satisfies (1). A solution of (1) is said to be strictly positive if $u(x) > 0$ for each $x \in (a,b)$.

Note that p may be zero at either a or b, and p is not required to be continuous or differentiable on $[a,b]$. We do not require pu' to be in $L^1[a,b]$, so pu' may not be an absolutely continuous function on $[a,b]$. Hence, if u is a solution of (1), then the following assertion may not be true:

$$\int_a^x (p(x)u'(x))'\,dx = p(x)u'(x) - p(a)u'(a) \quad \text{for each } x \in [a,b].$$

This shows that we cannot obtain any results by taking the integral from a to x on both sides of (1).

However, in this paper, we use monotonicity of the function pu' to derive a new minimum principle for nonconstant solutions of (1). More precisely, we prove that, if u is a nonconstant solution of (1), then u cannot reach its minimum in (a,b), that is,

$$\min\{u(x) : x \in [a,b]\} = \min\{u(a), u(b)\} < u(x) \quad \text{for each } x \in (a,b). \tag{2}$$

It is well known that, if a function $u : [a,b] \to \mathbb{R}$ is twice differentiable on $[a,b]$ and satisfies that $u''(x) \le 0$ for each $x \in [a,b]$, then u is concave down on $[a,b]$, that is, u satisfies

$$u(ta + (1-t)b) \ge tu(a) + (1-t)u(b) \quad \text{for each } t \in [0,1].$$

This implies that

$$u(x) \ge \min\{u(a), u(b)\} \quad \text{for each } x \in [a,b]. \tag{3}$$

Hence, the new minimum principle (2) with $p \equiv 1$ enhances (3) by replacing the inequality sign with the strict inequality on (a,b).

The minimum principle (2) holds for (1) without any boundary conditions (BCs). However, if we consider suitable BCs, then new properties of solutions for the boundary value problems can be obtained. Here, we apply the minimum principle to obtain new results on the positivity of the solutions of the S-L inequality (2) subject to the separated inequality boundary conditions (IBCs):

$$\alpha u(a) - \beta u'(a) \ge 0 \text{ and } \gamma u(b) + \delta u'(b) \ge 0, \tag{4}$$

where $\alpha, \beta, \gamma, \delta \in \mathbb{R}_+$ satisfy $(\alpha+\beta)(\gamma+\delta) > 0$. We refer to [1,2] for the study on a minimum principle (or strong minimum principle) and Hopf's boundary minimum principle for S-L inequality (1), which holds a.e on (a,b) with the IBCs $u(a) \ge 0$ and $u(b) \ge 0$.

The separated IBCs contain Dirichlet ($\beta = \delta = 0$), Robin ($\alpha = \gamma$ and $\beta = \delta$) and Neumann ($\alpha = \gamma = 0$) IBCs. We show that (1) with the Neumann IBCs $u'(a) \le 0$ and $u'(b) \ge 0$ only has constant solutions. By the minimum principle, we prove that all the nonconstant solutions of (1) with the other IBCs of (4) are strictly positive in (a,b) and are increasing if $\alpha > 0$ and $\gamma = 0$ or decreasing if $\alpha = 0$ and $\gamma > 0$. We apply these positivity results to obtain the uniqueness of the solutions of linear S-L equations with separated BCs

$$\alpha u(a) - \beta u'(a) = 0 \text{ and } \gamma u(b) + \delta u'(b) = 0 \tag{5}$$

with $\alpha > 0$ or $\gamma > 0$.

An important special case of S-L inequality (1) is the following second-order differential inequalities:

$$-u''(x) - r(x)u'(x) \ge 0 \quad \text{for each } x \in [a,b], \tag{6}$$

where $r : [a,b] \to \mathbb{R}$ is a continuous function. We prove that, if u is a solution of (6), then u is a solution of (1). Hence, the minimum principle, positivity result and uniqueness for (6) without or with the separated IBCs can be obtained via the results on S-L inequalities or equations.

The minimum principle and positivity results can be used to study solutions of nonlinear S-L equations such as

$$-(p(x)u'(x))' = f(x, u(x)) \quad \text{for each } x \in [a,b] \tag{7}$$

when $f(x,u(x)) \ge 0$ for each $x \in [a,b]$. There are many results on the existence of nonnegative solutions of (7) with suitable boundary conditions, for example, in [3–7], and on the eigenvalues of the following S-L equations (see [8–10]).

$$-(p(x)u'(x))' = \lambda u(x) \quad \text{for each } x \in [a,b], \tag{8}$$

The minimum principle and positivity results can be used to obtain the minimum principle and positivity on nonconstant solutions of (7) and eigenfunctions of the eigenvalue problem (8).

As illustrations, we consider two models arising in the heat conduction of the human head and chemical reactor theory. The first model is governed by a nonlinear S-L equation (see [8,11–16] for computations of solutions). The second one is governed by a nonlinear second-order differential equation (see [17,18] for the existence of solutions). For the first model, the explicit solutions are not available, and there are no results on the existence of solutions of the first model. There is little study on the existence of solutions, possibly because of the lack of Green's functions. Our results show that, if the solutions exist, then all the solutions are increasing and are strictly positive. For the second models from the chemical reactor theory, there have been many results on the uniqueness of the solutions and the existence of multiple solutions (see [17,18] and the references therein). We prove that all the solutions are decreasing and are strictly positive.

The structure of this paper is as follows: In Section 2 of this paper, we study the minimum principle, positivity and uniqueness of solutions for the S-L inequalities and linear S-L equations. In Section 3, we apply these results on the S-L inequalities or linear S-L equations to deal with some second-order differential equations. In Section 4, we consider the two models governed by a nonlinear S-L equation and a nonlinear second-order differential equation, respectively, and obtain the minimum principles and monotonicity of their solutions.

2. Sturm–Liouville Inequalities

We study the properties of solutions for the Sturm–Liouville (S-L) inequality of the form

$$-(p(x)u'(x))' \geq 0 \quad \text{for each } x \in [a,b], \tag{9}$$

where $p : [a,b] \to \mathbb{R}_+$ is a function satisfying $p(x) > 0$ for each $x \in (a,b)$, and u' denotes the first-order derivative of a function u. We allow p to be zero at a or b.

We denote by $C[a,b]$, $C^1[a,b]$ and $AC[a,b]$ the Banach space of continuous functions on $[a,b]$ with the maximum norm, the space of continuously differentiable functions on $[a,b]$ and the space of absolutely continuous functions on $[a,b]$, respectively. It is well known that

$$C^1[a,b] \subset AC[a,b] \subset C[a,b].$$

Definition 1. *A function $u : [a,b] \to \mathbb{R}$ is said to be a solution of (9) if $u \in C[a,b]$, $u'(x)$ and $(p(x)u'(x))'$ exist for each $x \in [a,b]$ and u satisfies (9). A solution u of (9) is said to be nonnegative if $u(x) \geq 0$ for each $x \in [a,b]$ and to be strictly positive on (a,b) if $u(x) > 0$ for each $x \in (a,b)$.*

In Definition 1, we only require a solution u to satisfy that $(p(x)u'(x))'$ exists for each $x \in [a,b]$. We do not require $(pu')' \in L^1[a,b]$, so pu' may not be in $AC[a,b]$.

Notation: For $c \in \mathbb{R}$, we define a constant function $\hat{c} : [a,b] \to \mathbb{R}$ by

$$\hat{c}(x) = c \quad \text{for each } x \in [a,b]. \tag{10}$$

It is trivial that the constant function $\hat{c}$ is a solution of (9) for each $c \in \mathbb{R}$. Hence, we concentrate on the nonconstant solutions of (9), that is, the solution u satisfies that there exist two different points $x_1, x_2 \in [a,b]$ such that $u(x_1) \neq u(x_2)$.

We first prove the following minimum principle for nonconstant solutions of (9), which shows that the minimum values of nonconstant solutions of (9) never occur at the interior points of $[a,b]$.

Theorem 1. *If u is a nonconstant solution of (9), then*

$$\min\{u(a), u(b)\} < u(x) \quad \textit{for each } x \in (a,b). \tag{11}$$

Proof. Let u be a nonconstant solution of (9). By Definition 1, u is a continuous function on $[a, b]$. Let m be the minimum value of u on $[a, b]$, that is,

$$m = \min\{u(x) : x \in [a, b]\}.$$

We prove that

$$m < u(x) \quad \text{for each } x \in (a, b). \tag{12}$$

If (12) is false, then there exists $x^* \in (a, b)$ such that

$$u(x^*) = \min\{u(x) : x \in [a, b]\}. \tag{13}$$

Since $u'(x)$ exists for each $x \in (a, b)$, it follows from Fermat's Theorem that $u'(x^*) = 0$. By (9), pu' is decreasing on $[a, b]$. Hence,

$$p(x)u'(x) \geq p(x^*)u'(x^*) = 0 \quad \text{for each } x \in [a, x^*] \tag{14}$$

and

$$0 = p(x^*)u'(x^*) \geq p(x)u'(x) \quad \text{for each } x \in [x^*, b]. \tag{15}$$

Since $p(x) > 0$ for each $x \in (a, b)$, by (14) and (15), we obtain $u'(x) \geq 0$ for each $x \in (a, x^*]$ and $u'(x) \leq 0$ for each $x \in [x^*, b)$. Hence, u is increasing on $(a, x^*]$ and decreasing on $[x^*, b)$. It follows that

$$u(x) \leq u(x^*) \quad \text{for each } x \in (a, b).$$

This with (13) implies that

$$u(x) = u(x^*) = \min\{u(x) : x \in [a, b]\} \quad \text{for each } x \in (a, b). \tag{16}$$

Since $u \in C[a, b]$, taking limits on (16) as $x \to a^+$ and $x \to b^-$ implies that $u(a) = u(x^*)$ and $u(b) = u(x^*)$. This with (16) shows that u is a constant function, which contradicts the hypothesis that u is a nonconstant function. Hence, (12) holds. Since $u \in C[a, b]$, there exists $x_0 \in [a, b]$ such that $u(x_0) = m$. It follows from (12) that $x_0 = a$ or $x_0 = b$, and the result holds. □

As an illustration of Theorem 1, we consider the S-L inequality

$$-(x^2u'(x))' \geq 0 \quad \text{for each } x \in [0, 1]. \tag{17}$$

Example 1. *Let*

$$u(x) = \cos\frac{\pi}{2}x \quad \textit{for } x \in [0, 1]. \tag{18}$$

Then, the following assertions hold:
(1) *u is a solution of* (17);
(2) $\min\{u(0), u(1)\} < u(x)$ *for each* $x \in (0, 1)$.

Proof. (1) Differentiating both sides of (18), we have

$$u'(x) = -\frac{\pi}{2}\sin\frac{\pi}{2}x \quad \text{for each } x \in [0, 1]. \tag{19}$$

By (19), we have

$$x^2u'(x) = -\frac{\pi}{2}x^2\sin\frac{\pi}{2}x \quad \text{for each } x \in [0, 1]. \tag{20}$$

Taking derivatives on both sides of the above equation implies that

$$-\left(x^2u'(x)\right)' = \frac{\pi}{2}\left[2x\sin\frac{\pi}{2}x + \frac{\pi}{2}x^2\cos\frac{\pi}{2}x\right] \geq 0 \quad \text{for each } x \in [0, 1]. \tag{21}$$

By (19), (20), (21) and Definition 1, u is a solution of (17).

(2) By (18) and the result (1), u is a nonconstant solution of (17). The result follows from Theorem 1. □

As an application of Theorem 1, we provide another new result which provides sufficient boundary value conditions ensuring that the first-order derivative of the nonconstant solutions of (9) at a (or at b) is greater than 0 (or less than 0). The new result will be used to derive a Hopf's boundary minimum principle for the S-L inequalities with a Dirichlet-type inequality BC (see Theorem 6).

To do this, we first prove the following lemma, which shows that the signs of the first-order derivative of solutions of (9) at a (or at b) determine the monotonicity that is decreasing or increasing on $[a,b]$ of solutions of (9).

Lemma 1. *Assume that $u:[a,b]\to\mathbb{R}$ is a solution of* (9). *Then, the following assertions hold:*
(i) If $u'(a)\le 0$, then u is decreasing on $[a,b]$;
(ii) If $u'(b)\ge 0$, then u is increasing on $[a,b]$.

Proof. (i) By (9), pu' is decreasing on $[a,b]$. This with $u'(a)\le 0$ implies that

$$p(x)u'(x)\le p(a)u'(a)\le 0 \quad \text{for each } x\in[a,b].$$

Since $p(x)>0$ for each $x\in(a,b)$, we have $u'(x)\le 0$ for each $x\in(a,b)$, and u is decreasing on (a,b). Since $u\in C[a,b]$, we have

$$u(b)\le u(x)\le u(a) \quad \text{for each } x\in[a,b]$$

and u is decreasing on $[a,b]$.

(ii) By (9), pu' is decreasing on $[a,b]$. This with $u'(b)\ge 0$ implies that

$$0\le p(b)u'(b)\le p(x)u'(x) \quad \text{for each } x\in[a,b].$$

Since $p(x)>0$ for each $x\in(a,b)$, we have $u'(x)\ge 0$ for each $x\in(a,b)$, and u is increasing on (a,b). Since $u\in C[a,b]$, u is increasing on $[a,b]$. □

By Theorem 1 and Lemma 1, we prove the new result, which is a key for obtaining the Hopf's boundary minimum principle (Theorem 6) for the S-L inequalities.

Theorem 2. *Assume that $u:[a,b]\to\mathbb{R}$ is a nonconstant solution of* (9). *Then, the following assertions hold:*
(1) If $u(a)\le u(b)$, then $u'(a)>0$;
(2) If $u(a)\ge u(b)$, then $u'(b)<0$.

Proof. (1) If the result (1) is false, then $u'(a)\le 0$. By Lemma 1 (1), u is decreasing on $[a,b]$, and $u(x)\le u(a)$ for each $x\in[a,b]$. This with Theorem 1 implies that

$$u(b)<u(x)\le u(a) \quad \text{for each } x\in(a,b),$$

which contradicts the hypothesis that $u(a)\le u(b)$.

(2) If the result (2) is false, then $u'(b)\ge 0$. By Lemma 1 (2), u is increasing on $[a,b]$, and $u(x)\le u(b)$ for each $x\in[a,b]$. This with Theorem 1 implies that

$$u(a)<u(x)\le u(b) \quad \text{for each } x\in(a,b),$$

which contradicts the hypothesis that $u(a)\ge u(b)$. □

Theorem 1 applies to any nonconstant solutions of (9) in $C[a,b]$ and does not involve any inequality boundary conditions (IBCs) at a or at b.

Below, we consider nonconstant solutions of (9) subject to the separated IBCs of the form

$$\alpha u(a)-\beta u'(a)\ge 0 \text{ and } \gamma u(b)+\delta u'(b)\ge 0. \tag{22}$$

where $\alpha, \beta, \gamma, \delta \in \mathbb{R}_+$ satisfy
$$(\alpha + \beta)(\gamma + \delta) > 0. \tag{23}$$

The separated IBCs (22) contain Dirichlet ($\beta = \delta = 0$), Robin ($\alpha = \gamma$ and $\beta = \delta$) and Neumann ($\alpha = \gamma = 0$) IBCs.

Under the assumption (23), it is easy to verify that (22) is equivalent to the following four IBCs:

(B_1) $u(a) - \beta u'(a) \geq 0$ and $u(b) + \delta u'(b) \geq 0$ for $\beta, \delta \in \mathbb{R}_+$. ($\alpha > 0, \beta \geq 0, \gamma > 0, \delta \geq 0$);
(B_2) $u(a) - \beta u'(a) \geq 0$ and $u'(b) \geq 0$ for $\beta \in \mathbb{R}_+$. ($\alpha > 0, \beta \geq 0, \gamma = 0, \delta > 0$);
(B_3) $u'(a) \leq 0$ and $u(b) + \delta u'(b) \geq 0$ for $\delta \in \mathbb{R}_+$. ($\alpha = 0, \beta > 0, \gamma > 0, \delta \geq 0$);
(B_4) $u'(a) \leq 0$ and $u'(b) \geq 0$. ($\alpha = 0, \beta > 0, \gamma = 0, \delta > 0$).

It is clear that if $\alpha > 0$ or $\gamma > 0$, then the BC (22) is equivalent to the three BCs (B_1), (B_2) and (B_3), and, if $\alpha = \gamma = 0$, then the BC (22) is (B_4).

Definition 2. *A function $u : [a, b] \to \mathbb{R}$ is said to be a solution (nonnegative solution or strictly positive solution) of* (9) *with* (22) *if $u \in C[a, b]$ is a solution (nonnegative solution or strictly positive solution) of* (9) *and satisfies* (22).

We state the following simple result of constant solutions of (9) with (22).

Theorem 3. *Let $c \in \mathbb{R}$. Then, the following assertions hold:*
(i) $\hat{c}$ is a solution of (9) *with (B_i) if and only if $c \geq 0$ for each $i \in \{1, 2, 3\}$;*
(ii) $\hat{c}$ is a solution of (9) *with (B_4).*

Theorem 4. *Assume that $u : [a, b] \to \mathbb{R}$ is a solution of* (9) *with (B_4). Then, u is a constant solution.*

Proof. By (B_4) and Lemma 1, u is decreasing and increasing on $[a, b]$. It follows that
$$u(b) \leq u(x) \leq u(a) \leq u(x) \leq u(b) \quad \text{for each } x \in [a, b].$$

This implies that $u(x) = u(b)$ for each $x \in [a, b]$, and the result holds. □

By Theorem 3 (ii) and Theorem 4, (9) with (B_4) has no nonconstant solutions. Therefore, we only discuss nonconstant solutions of (9) with (B_i) for each $i \in \{1, 2, 3\}$. Hence, from now on, we always assume that $\alpha, \beta, \gamma, \delta \in \mathbb{R}_+$ satisfy
$$(\alpha + \beta)(\gamma + \delta) > 0 \quad \text{and either } \alpha > 0 \text{ or } \gamma > 0, \tag{24}$$
which excludes the BC (B_4).

Lemma 2. *Assume that $u : [a, b] \to \mathbb{R}$ is a nonconstant solution of* (9). *Then, the following assertions hold:*
(i) If $u(a) \leq u(b)$ and $u(a) - \beta u'(a) \geq 0$, then $u(a) \geq 0$;
(ii) If $u(a) \geq u(b)$ and $u(b) + \delta u'(b) \geq 0$, then $u(b) \geq 0$.

Proof. Let $u : [a, b] \to \mathbb{R}$ be a nonconstant solution of (9) with (22). By Theorem 1, we have
$$\min\{u(a), u(b)\} < u(x) \quad \text{for each } x \in (a, b). \tag{25}$$

(i) Since $u(a) \leq u(b)$, by (25), we have
$$u(a) = \min\{u(a), u(b)\} < u(x) \quad \text{for each } x \in (a, b). \tag{26}$$

If the result were false, then $u(a) < 0$. Since $u(a) - \beta u'(a) \geq 0$, we have
$$0 > u(a) \geq \beta u'(a).$$

This implies that $\beta > 0$, and $u'(a) < 0$. Hence, there exists $\varepsilon_0 \in (0, b-a)$ such that

$$u(x) \leq u(a) \quad \text{for each } x \in [a, a+\varepsilon_0).$$

This with (26) implies that

$$u(a) < u(x) \leq u(a) \quad \text{for each } x \in [a, a+\varepsilon_0),$$

which is a contradiction.

(ii) Since $u(a) \geq u(b)$, by (25), we have

$$u(b) = \min\{u(a), u(b)\} < u(x) \quad \text{for each } x \in (a,b). \tag{27}$$

If the result is false, then $u(b) < 0$. Since $u(b) + \delta u'(b) \geq 0$, we have

$$0 > u(b) \geq -\delta u'(b).$$

This implies that $\delta > 0$, and $u'(b) > 0$. Hence, there exists $\varepsilon_0 \in (0, b-a)$ such that

$$u(x) \leq u(b) \quad \text{for each } x \in (b-\varepsilon_0, b].$$

This with (27) implies that

$$u(b) < u(x) \leq u(b) \quad \text{for each } x \in (b-\varepsilon_0, b],$$

which is a contradiction. □

Now we prove the positivity result on (9) subject to the BCs (B_1)–(B_3).

Theorem 5. *(i) If $u : [a,b] \to \mathbb{R}$ is a nonconstant solution of (9) with (B_1), then*

$$0 \leq \min\{u(a), u(b)\} < u(x) \quad \textit{for each } x \in (a,b). \tag{28}$$

(ii) If $u : [a,b] \to \mathbb{R}$ is a nonconstant solution of (9) with (B_2), then u is increasing on $[a,b]$, and

$$0 \leq u(a) < u(x) \leq u(b) \quad \textit{for each } x \in (a,b). \tag{29}$$

(iii) If $u : [a,b] \to \mathbb{R}$ is a nonconstant solution of (9) with (B_3), then u is decreasing on $[a,b]$, and

$$0 \leq u(b) < u(x) \leq u(a) \quad \textit{for each } x \in (a,b). \tag{30}$$

Proof. Let $u : [a,b] \to \mathbb{R}$ be a nonconstant solution of (9). By Theorem 1, we have

$$\min\{u(a), u(b)\} < u(x) \quad \text{for each } x \in (a,b). \tag{31}$$

(i) Since (B_1) holds, if $u(a) \leq u(b)$, then it follows from $u(a) - \beta u'(a) \geq 0$ and Lemma 2 (i) that $u(a) \geq 0$. If $u(a) \geq u(b)$, then by $u(b) - \beta u'(b) \geq 0$ and Lemma 2 (ii), we have $u(b) \geq 0$. This with (31) implies (28).

(ii) By (B_2), we have $u'(b) \geq 0$. By Lemma 1 (ii), u is increasing on $[a,b]$, and

$$u(a) \leq u(x) \leq u(b) \quad \text{for each } x \in [a,b].$$

This with (31) implies (29).

(iii) By (B_3), we have $u'(a) \leq 0$. By Lemma 1 (i), u is decreasing on $[a,b]$, and

$$u(b) \leq u(x) \leq u(a) \quad \text{for each } x \in [a,b].$$

This with (31) implies (30). □

As an application of Theorem 5, we consider the S-L inequality (17), that is,

$$-(x^2 u'(x))' \geq 0 \quad \text{for each } x \in [0,1] \tag{32}$$

subject to the IBC

$$u(0) - \beta u'(0) \geq 0 \quad \text{and } u(1) + \delta u'(1) \geq 0, \tag{33}$$

where $\beta, \delta \geq 0$ are given.

We first provide an example of a nonconstant solution u of (32), which is not a solution of (32)–(33).

Example 2. *Let u be the same as in* (18). *Then, u is a solution of* (32) *but is not a solution of* (32)–(33).

Proof. The first result follows from Example 1. By (18) and (19), we have

$$u(1) - \delta u'(1) = 0 - \delta \frac{\pi}{2} < 0.$$

Hence, u does not satisfy (33). □

Next, we provide an example of a nonconstant solution of (32)–(33).

Example 3. *Let $A \geq \frac{\pi}{2}\delta$, and*

$$u(x) = A + \cos \frac{\pi}{2} x \quad \textit{for } x \in [0,1]. \tag{34}$$

Then, the following assertions hold:
(1) u is a solution of (32)–(33);
(2) $0 \leq \min\{u(0), u(1)\} < u(x)$ for each $x \in (0,1)$.

Proof. (1) Differentiating both sides of (34), we have

$$u'(x) = -\frac{\pi}{2} \sin \frac{\pi}{2} x \quad \text{for } x \in [0,1]. \tag{35}$$

By (35), we have

$$x^2 u'(x) = -x^2 \frac{\pi}{2} \sin \frac{\pi}{2} x \quad \text{for } x \in [0,1].$$

Taking derivatives on both sides of the above equation implies that

$$-\left(x^2 u'(x)\right)' = \frac{\pi}{2}\left[2x \sin \frac{\pi}{2} x + x^2 \frac{\pi}{2} \cos \frac{\pi}{2} x\right] \geq 0 \quad \text{for } x \in [0,1]$$

and u satisfies (32). By (34) and (35), we have

$$u(0) - \beta u'(0) = (1 + A) - \beta[-\frac{\pi}{2} \sin \frac{\pi}{2}(0)] = 1 + A \geq 0.$$

and, since $A \geq \frac{\pi}{2}\delta$, we have

$$u(1) + \delta u'(1) = A - \delta \frac{\pi}{2} \geq 0.$$

Hence, u is a solution of (32)–(33).

(2) By the result (1), u is a nonconstant solution of (32)–(33). The result follows from Theorem 5 (i). □

Now, by applying Theorems 2 and 5, we give the Hopf's boundary minimum principle.

Theorem 6. *(i) If $u : [a,b] \to \mathbb{R}$ is a nonconstant solution of* (9) *with (B_1), then the following assertions hold:*
(1) If $u(a) = 0$, then $u'(a) > 0$;
(2) If $u(b) = 0$, then $u'(b) < 0$.

(ii) If $u : [a,b] \to \mathbb{R}$ *is a nonconstant solution of* (9) *with* (B_2)*, then* $u'(a) > 0$*;*
(iii) If $u : [a,b] \to \mathbb{R}$ *is a nonconstant solution of* (9) *with* (B_3)*, then* $u'(b) < 0$*.*

Proof. (1) Since $u(a) = 0$, it follows from Theorem 5 (i) that $u(a) = 0 \le u(b)$. By Theorem 2 (1), $u'(a) > 0$.

(2) Since $u(b) = 0$, it follows from Theorem 5 (i) that $u(b) = 0 \le u(a)$. By Theorem 2 (2), $u'(b) < 0$.
(ii) By Theorem 5 (ii), we have $u(a) < u(b)$. By Theorem 2 (1), $u'(a) > 0$.
(iii) By Theorem 5 (iii), we have $u(b) < u(a)$. By Theorem 2 (2), $u'(b) < 0$. □

Remark 1. *The Hopf's boundary minimum principle for some S-L inequalities with the BCs* $u(a) \ge 0$ *and* $u(b) \ge 0$ *was studied in [1] (p. 1072). Hence, Theorem 6* (i) *with* $\beta > 0$ *or* $\delta > 0$ *and* (ii) *and* (iii) *are new. Our method is different from that used in [1] (p. 1072).*

Applying Theorem 5, we study the uniqueness of the solutions of the boundary value problem (BVP) of the S-L equation

$$-(p(x)u'(x))' = 0 \quad \text{for each } x \in [a,b] \tag{36}$$

subject to the separated BC

$$\alpha u(a) - \beta u'(a) = 0 \quad \text{and } \gamma u(b) + \delta u'(b) = 0, \tag{37}$$

where $\alpha, \beta, \gamma, \delta \in \mathbb{R}_+$ satisfy (24).

Theorem 7. *Equation* (36) *with Equation* (37) *has only a zero solution.*

Proof. It is obvious that $\hat{0}$ is a solution of (36) with (37). Let u be a nonconstant solution of (36) with (37). Then it is easy to see that $-u$ is a solution of (36) with (37). By Theorem 5, we obtain $u = 0$. Hence, (36) with (37) has no nonconstant solutions. By Theorem 3 (i), (36) with (37) has no nonzero constant solutions. The result follows. □

We study the uniqueness of the solutions of the BVP of the S-L equation

$$-(p(x)u'(x))' = v(x) \quad \text{for each } x \in [a,b] \tag{38}$$

subject to the separated BC

$$\alpha u(a) - \beta u'(a) = c_0 \quad \text{and } \gamma u(b) + \delta u'(b) = c_1, \tag{39}$$

where $v : [a,b] \to \mathbb{R}$ is a function, $\alpha, \beta, \gamma, \delta \in \mathbb{R}_+$ satisfy (24) and $c_0, c_1 \in \mathbb{R}$.

Definition 3. *A function* $u : [a,b] \to \mathbb{R}$ *is said to be a solution of* (38) *if* $u \in C[a,b]$*,* $u'(x)$ *and* $(p(x)u'(x))'$ *exist for each* $x \in [a,b]$ *and* u *satisfies* (38).

Theorem 8. *Equation* (38) *with Equation* (39) *has at most one solution.*

Proof. Assume that (38) and (39) have a solution u_j for each $j \in \{1,2\}$. Let

$$u(x) = u_1(x) - u_2(x) \quad \text{for each } x \in [a,b].$$

It is easy to see that u is a solution of (36) with (37). By Theorem 7, (36) with (37) has only a zero solution. Hence, $u = 0$ and $u_1 = u_2$. □

3. Second-Order Linear Differential Inequalities

Closely related to the S-L inequality is the second-order differential inequality

$$-u''(x) - r(x)u'(x) \ge 0 \quad \text{for each } x \in [a,b], \tag{40}$$

where $r : [a,b] \to \mathbb{R}$ is assumed to be a continuous function. Note that r is not necessarily nonnegative. We can apply the results obtained in Section 2 to derive results on (40).

Definition 4. *A function* $u : [a,b] \to \mathbb{R}$ *is said to be a solution of* (40) *if* $u \in C^1[a,b]$, $u''(x)$ *exists for each* $x \in [a,b]$ *and* u *satisfies* (40).

In Definition 4, u is required to satisfy that $u''(x)$ exists for each $x \in [a,b]$, but u'' is not required to be continuous on (a,b). This is different from the the classical solutions, that is, $u \in C^2(a,b) \cap C^1[a,b]$ studied in (p. 634, [19]), where the one-dimensional strongly uniformly elliptic equations were considered.

The inequality (40) can be studied via the following S-L inequality:

$$-(p(x)u'(x))' \geq 0 \quad \text{for each } x \in [a,b], \tag{41}$$

where $p : [a,b] \to (0,\infty)$ is a function defined by

$$p(x) = e^{\int_a^x r(s)\,ds}. \tag{42}$$

We note that the function p satisfies $p(x) > 0$ for each $x \in [a,b]$ and is continuous on $[a,b]$. By (42) and continuity of r, we obtain

$$p'(x) = p(x)r(x) \quad \text{for each } x \in [a,b]. \tag{43}$$

Lemma 3. *If* u *is a solution of* (40)*, then* u *is a solution of* (41).

Proof. Let u be a solution of (40). By Definition 4, $u \in C^1[a,b]$ and $u''(x)$ exist for each $x \in [a,b]$. By (43), we have

$$\begin{aligned}(p(x)u'(x))' &= p(x)u''(x) + p'(x)u'(x) = p(x)u''(x) + p(x)r(x)u'(x) \\ &= p(x)[u''(x) + r(x)u'(x)] \leq 0 \quad \text{for each } x \in [a,b]\end{aligned} \tag{44}$$

and $(p(x)u'(x))'$ exist for each $x \in [a,b]$. It follows from Definition 1 that u is a solution of (41). □

Similar to (9), we have the following minimum principle for nonconstant solutions of (40).

Theorem 9. *If* u *is a nonconstant solution of* (40)*, then*

$$\min\{u(a), u(b)\} < u(x) \quad \textit{for each } x \in (a,b).$$

Proof. Let u be a nonconstant solution of (40). By Lemma 3, u is a nonconstant solution of (41). The results follow from Theorem 1. □

Definition 5. *A function* $u : [a,b] \to \mathbb{R}$ *is said to be a solution of* (40) *with* (22) *if* $u \in C^1[a,b]$ *is a solution of* (40) *and satisfies* (22).

Similar to (9), we have the following positivity result on (40) subject to the BCs (B_1)–(B_3).

Theorem 10. *(i) If* $u : [a,b] \to \mathbb{R}$ *is a nonconstant solution of* (40) *with* (B_1)*, then*

$$0 \leq \min\{u(a), u(b)\} < u(x) \quad \textit{for each } x \in (a,b). \tag{45}$$

(ii) If $u : [a,b] \to \mathbb{R}$ *is a nonconstant solution of* (40) *with* (B_2)*, then* u *is increasing on* $[a,b]$*, and*

$$0 \leq u(a) < u(x) \leq u(b) \quad \textit{for each } x \in (a,b). \tag{46}$$

(*iii*) *If* $u : [a,b] \to \mathbb{R}$ *is a nonconstant solution of* (40) *with* (B_3), *then* u *is decreasing on* $[a,b]$, *and*

$$0 \le u(b) < u(x) \le u(a) \quad \textit{for each } x \in (a,b). \tag{47}$$

Proof. Let u be a nonconstant solution of (40). By Lemma 3, u is a nonconstant solution of (41). The result follows from Theorem 5. □

Similar to S-L equations, we obtain the following uniqueness results.

Theorem 11. *The BVP of the second-order differential equation*

$$-u''(x) - r(x)u'(x) = 0 \quad \textit{for each } x \in [a,b] \tag{48}$$

subject to the separated BC (37) *has only a zero solution.*

Theorem 12. *The BVP of the second-order differential equation*

$$-u''(x) - r(x)u'(x) = v(x) \quad \textit{for each } x \in [a,b] \tag{49}$$

subject to the BC (39) *has at most one solution, where* $v : [a,b] \to \mathbb{R}$ *is a function.*

4. Applications

We consider the model arising from the source distribution of the human head governed by the following nonlinear S-L equation:

$$-(x^2u'(x))' = \lambda x^2 e^{-qu(x)} \quad \text{for each } x \in [0,1] \tag{50}$$

subject to the BC

$$u(0) = 0 \quad \text{and } \gamma u(1) + u'(1) = 0, \tag{51}$$

where $\lambda, q > 0$ (see [11]). Some related models can be found in [13,14]. The exact solutions of the BVP (50)–(51) are not available, and there are no results on the existence of solutions of (50)–(51); therefore, there are extensive studies on computation of solutions of (50)–(51) (see [12,14–16] and the reference therein). There are generalizations on the computation of solutions to fractional differential equations [8]. Since $p : [0,1] \to \mathbb{R}_+$ defined by $p(x) = x^2$ for $x \in [0,1]$ does not satisfy $1/p \in L^1[0,1]$, the Green's function does not exist. Hence, the previous results on the existence of solutions of the BVP for the S-L equations obtained, for example, in [3–5,7,20–22], via Green's functions cannot be used to deal with (50)–(51).

Here, we use Theorem 1 to obtain the following new result.

Theorem 13. (1) *If* u *is a solution of* (50), *then*

$$\min\{u(0), u(1)\} < u(x) \quad \textit{for each } x \in (0,1). \tag{52}$$

(2) *If* u *is a solution of the BVP* (50)–(51), *then* u *is decreasing on* $[0,1]$, *and*

$$0 \le u(1) < u(x) \le u(0) \quad \textit{for each } x \in (0,1). \tag{53}$$

Proof. Let $u \in C[0,1]$ be a solution of (50). By (50), it is easy to see that

$$-(x^2u'(x))' = \lambda x^2 e^{-qu(x)} \ge 0 \quad \text{for each } x \in [0,1] \tag{54}$$

and u is a nonconstant solution of (54).

(1) The result (1) follows from (54) and Theorem 1.

(2) Let $u \in C[0,1]$ be a solution of (50)–(51). Note that the BC (51) is a special case of (B_3). It follows from (54) and Theorem 10 (iii) that u is decreasing on $[0,1]$, and (53) holds. □

The second model we consider is the following BVP of the second-order differential equation

$$-\beta u''(x) + u'(x) = f(u(x)) \quad \text{for each } x \in [0,1] \tag{55}$$

subject to the BC

$$\alpha u(0) - \beta u'(0) = 0 \quad \text{and } u'(1) = 0, \tag{56}$$

where $f : \mathbb{R}_+ \to \mathbb{R}$ is defined by

$$f(u) = \lambda(q-u)e^{\frac{-k}{1+u}}. \tag{57}$$

The BVP (55)–(56) arises in chemical reactor theory. The function u represents the dimensionless temperature in the reactor, and $\lambda, q, k > 0$ are known constants. The function $f(u)$ in (57) is the Arrhenius reaction rate, which essentially represents the rates of chemical production of the species (or the rate of heat generation) in the reactor (see [17,18] and the references therein).

It is proved in Theorem 3.5 of [17] that, if $\left(\frac{f(u)}{u}\right)' < 0$ for $u \in [0,q]$, then (55)–(56) have a unique solution. When $k > 4(1+1/q)$, it is proved in [18] that, under suitable conditions on λ, (55)–(56) have at least two or three nonnegative solutions. However, these results do not show that these solutions are strictly positive solutions.

By Theorems 9 and 10, we prove the following result which shows that all the solutions of (55)–(56) are strictly positive.

Theorem 14. (1) *If $u \in C[0,1]$ is a solution of* (55), *then*

$$\min\{u(0), u(1)\} < u(x) \quad \text{for each } x \in (0,1). \tag{58}$$

(2) *If $u \in C[0,1]$ is a solution of the BVP* (55)–(56), *then u is increasing on $[0,1]$, u is a strictly positive solution and*

$$0 \le u(0) < u(x) \le u(1) \quad \text{for each } x \in (0,1). \tag{59}$$

Proof. Let u be a solution of (55). By (55) and (57), u is a nonconstant solution. By Theorem 3.1 of [17], $u(x) \le q$ for $x \in [0,1]$. By (57), we obtain

$$f(u(x)) \ge 0 \quad \text{for each } x \in [0,1].$$

This with (55) implies that

$$-\beta u''(x) + u'(x) = f(u(x)) \ge 0 \quad \text{for } x \in [0,1]. \tag{60}$$

(1) The result (1) follows from Theorem 9.

(2) Let u be a solution of (55)–(56). Note that the BC (51) is a special case of (B_2). The result (2) follows from Theorem 10 (ii). □

Author Contributions: Conceptualization, P.N. and K.L.; methodology, P.N. and K.L.; validation, P.N. and K.L.; formal analysis, P.N. and K.L.; investigation, P.N. and K.L.; resources, P.N. and K.L.; writing—original draft preparation, P.N. and K.L.; writing—review and editing, P.N. and K.L.; visualization, P.N. and K.L.; supervision, K.L.; project administration, K.L.; funding acquisition, K.L. All authors have read and agreed to the published version of the manuscript.

Funding: This research was supported in part by the Natural Sciences and Engineering Research Council of Canada, grant/award number RGPIN-2023-04024.

Data Availability Statement: There are no data to be used in this paper.

Conflicts of Interest: The authors declare no conflicts of interest.

References

1. Walter, W. A new approach to minimum and comparison principles for nonlinear ordinary differential operators of second order. *Nolinear Anal.* **1995**, *25*, 1071–1078. [CrossRef]
2. Walter, W. Differential inequalities and maximum principles:theory, new methods and applications. *Nonlinear Anal.* **1997**, *30*, 4695–4711. [CrossRef]
3. Anuradha, V.; Hai, D.D.; Shivaji, R. Existence results for superlinear semipositone BVP's. *Proc. Am. Math. Soc.* **1996**, *124*, 757–763. [CrossRef]
4. He, J.; Yang, L. Existence of positive solutions for systems of nonlinear Sturm-Liouville differential equations with weight functions. *Electr. J. Differ. Equ.* **2019**, *111*, 1–24.
5. Lan, K.Q. Multiple positive solutions of semi-positone Sturm-Liouville boundary value problems. *Bull. London Math. Soc.* **2006**, *38*, 283–293. [CrossRef]
6. Yang, G.C.; Feng, H.B. New results of positive solutions for the Sturm-Liouville problem. *Bound. Value Probl.* **2016**, *2016*, 64. [CrossRef]
7. Yang, G.C.; Lan, K.Q. A fixed point index theory for nowhere normal-outward compact maps and applications. *J. Appl. Anal. Comput.* **2016**, *6*, 665–683.
8. Amara, J.B.; Jihed, H. Lower bound for the ratio of eigenvalues of Schrödinger with nonpositive single-barrier potentials. *Math. Meth. Appl. Sci.* **2019**, *42*, 4409–4636.
9. Gu, M.; Sun, H. The eigenvalue ratio of the vibrating strings with mixed boundary condition. *Math. Meth. Appl. Sci.* **2024**, *47*, 409–418. [CrossRef]
10. Hedhly, J. Eigenvalue ratios for vibrating string equations with single-well densities. *J. Differ. Equ.* **2022**, *307*, 476–485. [CrossRef]
11. Anderson, N.; Arthurs, A.M. Complementary extremum principles for a nonlinear model of heat conduction in the human head. *Bull. Math. Biol.* **1981**, *43*, 341–346. [CrossRef] [PubMed]
12. Celik, E.; Tunc, H.; Sari, M. An efficient multi-derivative numerical method for chemical boundary value problems. *J. Math. Chem.* **2024**, *62*, 634–653. [CrossRef]
13. Flesch, U. The Distribution of heat sources in the human head: A theoretical consideration. *J. Theor. Biol.* **1975**, *54*, 285–287. [CrossRef]
14. Gray, B.F. The distribution of heat sources in the human head-theoretical consideration. *J. Theor. Biol.* **1980**, *82*, 473–476. [CrossRef] [PubMed]
15. Izadi, M.; Atangana, A. Computational analysis of a class of singular nonlinear fractional multi-order heat conduction model of the human head. *Sci. Rep.* **2024**, *14*, 3466. [CrossRef]
16. Roul, P.; Kumari, T. A quartic trigonometric *b*-spline collocation method for a general class of nonlinear singular boundary value problems. *J. Math. Chem.* **2022**, *60*, 128–144. [CrossRef]
17. Cohen, D.S. Multiple stable solutions of nonlinear boundary value problems arising in chemical reactor theory. *SIAM J. Appl. Math.* **1971**, *20*, 1–13. [CrossRef]
18. Williams, L.R.; Leggett, R.W. Multiple fixed point theorems for problems in chemical reactor theory. *J. Math. Anal. Appl.* **1979**, *69*, 180–193. [CrossRef]
19. Amann, H. Fixed point equations and nonlinear eigenvalue problems in ordered Banach spaces. *SIAM. Rev.* **1976**, *18*, 620–709. [CrossRef]
20. Li, H.Y.; Sun, J.X. Positive solutions of sublinear Sturm-Liouville problems with changing sign nonlinearity. *Comput. Math. Appl.* **2009**, *58*, 1808–1815. [CrossRef]
21. Sun, J.X.; Zhang, G.W. Nontrivial solutions of singular superlinear Sturm-Liouville problems. *J. Math. Anal. Appl.* **2006**, *313*, 518–536. [CrossRef]
22. Sun, J.X.; Zhang, G.W. Nontrivial solutions of singular suberlinear Sturm-Liouville problems. *J. Math. Anal. Appl.* **2007**, *326*, 242–251. [CrossRef]

mathematics

MDPI

Article

Radially Symmetric Positive Solutions of the Dirichlet Problem for the p-Laplace Equation

Bo Yang

Department of Mathematics, Kennesaw State University, Kennesaw, GA 30144, USA; byang@kennesaw.edu

Abstract: We consider the p-Laplace boundary value problem with the Dirichlet boundary condition. A new lower estimate for positive solutions of the problem is obtained. As an application of this new lower estimate, some sufficient conditions for the existence and nonexistence of positive solutions for the p-Laplace problem are obtained.

Keywords: boundary value problem; p-Laplacian; positive solution; existence and nonexistence

MSC: 35J91; 34B18

1. Introduction

Differential equations involving p-Laplace operators have wide applications in physics, and they have received quite some attention recently. For example, in 2007, by using the theory of lower and upper solutions, Jin, Yin, and Wang [1] studied the existence of positive radial solutions for the p-Laplacian boundary value problem

$$-\operatorname{div}(|\nabla u|^{p-2}\nabla u) = f(|x|, u), \quad x \in \Omega,$$
$$u(x) = 0, \quad x \in \partial\Omega,$$

where $p > 1$ and $\Omega \subset \mathbb{R}^n$ is the unit open ball centered at the origin. We refer the reader to [2] for a historical account of the origin of the p-Laplace operator. For a very short list of some recent papers on p-Laplace boundary value problems, we refer the reader to the papers [3–11].

In this paper, we consider the boundary value problem

$$\Delta_p w(x) + g(|x|)f(w(x)) = 0, \quad x \in \Omega, \tag{1}$$

$$w = 0, \quad x \in \partial\Omega. \tag{2}$$

Here, $\Omega \subset \mathbb{R}^n$ is the unit open ball centered at the origin, $|x|$ denotes the Euclidean norm of $x \in \mathbb{R}^n$, and

$$\Delta_p w = \operatorname{div}\Big(|\nabla w|^{p-2}\nabla w\Big).$$

Throughout the paper, we assume that

(H) $n \geq 1$ is a positive integer, $p \in (n, +\infty)$ is a positive real number, $g : [0,1] \to [0,+\infty)$ and $f : [0,+\infty) \to [0,+\infty)$ are continuous functions, and $g(t) \not\equiv 0$ on the interval $[0,1]$.

For convenience, we define the function $\Phi_p : \mathbb{R} \to \mathbb{R}$ by

$$\Phi_p(x) = \begin{cases} |x|^{p-2}x, & x \neq 0, \\ 0, & x = 0. \end{cases}$$

It is clear that $\Phi_p(x)$ is an increasing and continuous function, and $x\Phi_p(x) \geq 0$ for all real x. The inverse function of $\Phi_p(x)$ is denoted by $\Phi_p^{-1}(x)$ in this paper.

Citation: Yang, B. Radially Symmetric Positive Solutions of the Dirichlet Problem for the p-Laplace Equation. *Mathematics* **2024**, *12*, 2351. https://doi.org/10.3390/math12152351

Academic Editor: David Carfì

Received: 1 July 2024
Revised: 19 July 2024
Accepted: 25 July 2024
Published: 27 July 2024

It is well known (see [1], for example) that if we consider only radially symmetric positive solutions of problem (1),(2), then problem (1),(2) reduces to the following boundary value problem for a second-order ordinary differential equation:

$$t^{1-n}(t^{n-1}\Phi_p(u'(t)))' + g(t)f(u(t)) = 0, \quad 0 < t < 1, \tag{3}$$

$$u'(0) = 0, \quad u(1) = 0. \tag{4}$$

That is, if $u(t)$ is a solution to problem (3),(4), then $w(x) = u(|x|)$ solves the boundary value problem (1),(2), and vice versa.

Our main focus in this paper is on positive solutions to problem (3),(4). By a positive solution to problem (3),(4), we mean a solution $u(t)$ such that $u(t) > 0$ on $(0,1)$. As has been repeatedly pointed out in the literature (see [6,12], for example), in the study of positive solutions to boundary value problems, *a priori* upper and lower estimates for positive solutions play a crucial role. In particular, once we obtain some *a priori* upper and lower estimates, we can use these estimates to approximate the first eigenvalue of the corresponding eigenvalue problem (see [13], for example). Also, by using these upper and lower estimates, we can establish some nice existence results for multiple positive solutions (see [12,14], for example). The main purpose of this paper is to present a new lower estimate for positive solutions to problem (3),(4).

Throughout this paper, we let $X = C[0,1]$ be equipped with the supremum norm

$$\|v\| = \max_{t\in[0,1]} |v(t)| \quad \text{for all } v \in X.$$

Clearly, X is a Banach space. We define

$$Y = \{v \in X \mid v(t) \geq 0 \text{ for } 0 \leq t \leq 1\}.$$

It is clear that Y is a positive cone in X. It is also clear that the boundary value problem (3),(4) is equivalent to the integral equation

$$u(t) = \int_t^1 \Phi_p^{-1}\left(r^{1-n}\int_0^r s^{n-1}g(s)f(u(s))ds\right)dr, \quad 0 \leq t \leq 1.$$

Define the operator $T : Y \to X$ by

$$(Tu)(t) = \int_t^1 \Phi_p^{-1}\left(r^{1-n}\int_0^r s^{n-1}g(s)f(u(s))ds\right)dr, \quad 0 \leq t \leq 1, \ \forall u \in Y.$$

It is clear that if (H) holds, then $T(Y) \subset Y$. By some standard arguments, we can show that T is a completely continuous operator. Also, it is now clear that $u \in Y$ is a fixed point of T if and only if u is a non-negative solution to problem (3),(4).

This paper is organized as follows. In Section 2, we prove a new type of lower estimate for positive solutions of problem (3),(4). In Sections 3 and 4, we prove some existence and nonexistence results for positive solutions for problem (3),(4). An example is included at the end of the paper to illustrate our existence and non-existence results.

2. A New Lower Estimate

In this section, we present a new lower estimate for positive solutions to problem (3),(4). This lower estimate (see (7) below) is called by some authors the norm-type, for the simple reason that its expression is the norm $\|u\|$ times a function of t. To the best of our knowledge, there is no lower estimate of this type for problem (3),(4) in the literature.

For this purpose, we define the function $a : [0,1] \to [0,1]$ by

$$a(t) = 1 - t^{(p-n)/(p-1)}, \quad 0 \leq t \leq 1. \tag{5}$$

The function $a(t)$ is used to give the lower estimate for positive solutions of problem (3),(4). Since $p > n$, $a(t)$ is continuous on $[0,1]$, it is clear that $a(0) = 1$ and $a(1) = 0$. We leave it to the reader to verify that $a(t)$ is decreasing on $[0,1]$. We begin with some technical lemmas.

Lemma 1. *If $u \in C^2(0,1] \cap C^1[0,1]$ satisfies the boundary conditions* (4) *and u is such that*

$$(t^{n-1}\Phi_p(u'(t)))' \leq 0, \quad 0 < t < 1, \tag{6}$$

then,

$$u(t) \geq 0 \ \ \text{and} \ \ u'(t) \leq 0$$

on the interval $[0,1]$, and $u(0) = \|u\|$.

The proof of the lemma is quite straightforward and is, therefore, left to the reader. The next lemma gives a lower estimate for positive solutions of problem (3),(4).

Lemma 2. *Suppose that* (H) *holds. If $u \in C^2(0,1] \cap C^1[0,1]$ satisfies the boundary conditions* (4) *and the inequality* (6) *holds, then*

$$u(t) \geq \|u\|a(t), \quad 0 \leq t \leq 1. \tag{7}$$

Proof. By Lemma 1, we have $u(t) \geq 0$ on $[0,1]$ and $u(0) = \|u\|$. We define an auxiliary function $h(t)$ as follows:

$$h(t) = u(t) - \|u\|a(t), \quad 0 \leq t \leq 1.$$

It is easy to see that

$$h(0) = h(1) = 0.$$

To prove the lemma, it suffices to show that $h(t) \geq 0$ for $0 \leq t \leq 1$. We use the method of contradiction to prove the lemma. For this purpose, we assume, to the contrary, that $h(t_0) < 0$ for some $t_0 \in (0,1)$.

Since $h(0) = 0 > h(t_0)$, by the mean value theorem, there exists $t_1 \in (0, t_0)$ such that $h'(t_1) < 0$. Since $h(t_0) < 0 = h(1)$, there exists $s_1 \in (t_0, 1)$ such that $h'(s_1) > 0$.

Note that $h'(t_1) < 0$ and $h'(s_1) > 0$ imply that

$$u'(t_1) - \|u\|a'(t_1) < 0, \quad u'(s_1) - \|u\|a'(s_1) > 0.$$

Since Φ_p is strictly increasing, we have

$$\Phi_p(u'(t_1)) - \Phi_p(\|u\|a'(t_1)) < 0, \quad \Phi_p(u'(s_1)) - \Phi_p(\|u\|a'(s_1)) > 0.$$

We now define another auxiliary function $v(t)$ as follows:

$$v(t) = t^{n-1}\big(\Phi_p(u'(t)) - \Phi_p(\|u\|a'(t))\big), \quad 0 \leq t \leq 1. \tag{8}$$

It is clear that $v(t_1) < 0$ and $v(s_1) > 0$. Since $v(t_1) < 0 < v(s_1)$, there exists $t_2 \in (t_1, s_1) \subset (0,1)$ such that

$$v'(t_2) > 0. \tag{9}$$

On the other hand, by Equations (5), (6), and (8), we have

$$v'(t) = (t^{n-1}\Phi_p(u'(t)))' \leq 0, \quad 0 < t < 1,$$

which contradicts (9). The proof of the lemma is now complete. □

We now summarize our findings in the following theorems.

Theorem 1. *Suppose that* (H) *holds. If* $u \in C^2(0,1] \cap C^1[0,1]$ *satisfies the boundary conditions* (4)*, and the inequality* (6) *holds, then* $u(t) \geq 0$ *on* $[0,1]$*, and*

$$a(t)u(0) \leq u(t) \leq u(0), \quad 0 \leq t \leq 1. \tag{10}$$

In particular, if $u \in C^2(0,1] \cap C^1[0,1]$ *is a nonnegative solution to the boundary value problem* (3),(4)*, then* $u(t)$ *satisfies the estimates* (10).

The next theorem follows immediately.

Theorem 2. *Suppose that* (H) *holds. If* $w(x)$ *is a radially symmetric positive solution to the p-Laplace boundary value problem* (1),(2)*, then*

$$w(\mathbf{0}) \geq w(x) \geq w(\mathbf{0})a(|x|), \quad |x| < 1.$$

Here, $\mathbf{0} = (0,0,\cdots,0)$ *is the origin of the* $\mathbb{R}^n$ *space.*

Now, we define a subset P of Y as follows:

$$P = \{v \in Y : a(t)v(0) \leq v(t) \leq v(0) \ \text{ on } \ [0,1]\}.$$

Clearly, P is a positive cone of the Banach space X. From now on, we restrict the operator T on the cone P. Again, $T : P \to Y$ is a completely continuous operator. And, by the same arguments as those used to prove Theorem 1, we can show that $T(P) \subset P$ provided (H) holds. We also note that if $v \in P$, then

$$\|v\| = v(0).$$

Now, it is clear that, in order to solve problem (3),(4) for a positive solution, we only need to find a fixed point u of T in P such that $\|u\| > 0$.

3. Existence of Positive Solutions

As an application of the lower estimate obtained in the last section, we now establish some existence and nonexistence results for positive solutions to problem (3),(4). We use the following fixed point theorem, which is due to Krasnosel'skii [15], to prove our existence results.

Theorem 3. *Let* X *be a Banach space over the reals, and let* $P \subset X$ *be a cone in* X*. Let* $\leq$ *be the partial order on* X *determined by* P*. Assume that* Ω_1 *and* Ω_2 *are bounded open subsets of* X *with* $0 \in \Omega_1$ *and* $\overline{\Omega}_1 \subset \Omega_2$*. Let*

$$L : P \cap (\overline{\Omega}_2 - \Omega_1) \to P$$

be a completely continuous operator such that, either

(K1) $Lu \not\geq u$ *if* $u \in P \cap \partial\Omega_1$*, and* $Lu \not\leq u$ *if* $u \in P \cap \partial\Omega_2$*; or*
(K2) $Lu \not\leq u$ *if* $u \in P \cap \partial\Omega_1$*, and* $Lu \not\geq u$ *if* $u \in P \cap \partial\Omega_2$*.*

Then, L *has a fixed point in* $P \cap (\overline{\Omega}_2 - \Omega_1)$*.*

Remark 1. *In Theorem 3,* $\leq$ *is the partial order on* X *determined by* P*. That is, if* $f, g \in X$*, then*

$$f \leq g \iff (g - f) \in P.$$

Hence, the inequality $Lu \not\geq u$ *means that* $(Lu - u) \notin P$*, and the inequality* $Lu \not\leq u$ *means that* $(u - Lu) \notin P$*.*

We begin by defining constants A and B by

$$A = \int_0^1 \Phi_p^{-1}\left(r^{1-n}\int_0^r s^{n-1}g(s)(a(s))^{p-1}ds\right)dr$$

and

$$B = \int_0^1 \Phi_p^{-1}\left(r^{1-n}\int_0^r s^{n-1}g(s)ds\right)dr.$$

Also, we define the following constants that are related to the function f:

$$F_0 = \limsup_{x\to 0^+}\frac{f(x)}{x^{p-1}}, \quad f_0 = \liminf_{x\to 0^+}\frac{f(x)}{x^{p-1}},$$
$$F_\infty = \limsup_{x\to +\infty}\frac{f(x)}{x^{p-1}}, \quad f_\infty = \liminf_{x\to +\infty}\frac{f(x)}{x^{p-1}}.$$

These constants are used in the statements of our existence and nonexistence theorems. Our first existence result is given below. Though Krasnosel'skii's fixed point theorem has become quite a standard tool for finding positive solutions; the proof of the next theorem is included here for completeness and reference purposes.

Theorem 4. *If*

$$BF_0^{1/(p-1)} < 1 < Af_\infty^{1/(p-1)},$$

then problem (3),(4) *has at least one positive solution.*

Proof. Choose $\epsilon > 0$ such that $B(F_0+\epsilon)^{1/(p-1)} < 1$. Then, there exists $H_1 > 0$ such that

$$f(x) \le (F_0+\epsilon)x^{p-1} \text{ for } 0 < x \le H_1.$$

For each $u \in P$ with $\|u\| = H_1$, we have

$$\begin{aligned}(Tu)(0) &= \int_0^1 \Phi_p^{-1}\left(r^{1-n}\int_0^r s^{n-1}g(s)f(u(s))ds\right)dr\\
&\le \int_0^1 \Phi_p^{-1}\left(r^{1-n}\int_0^r s^{n-1}g(s)(F_0+\epsilon)(u(s))^{p-1}ds\right)dr\\
&= (F_0+\epsilon)^{1/(p-1)}\int_0^1 \Phi_p^{-1}\left(r^{1-n}\int_0^r s^{n-1}g(s)(u(s))^{p-1}ds\right)dr\\
&\le (F_0+\epsilon)^{1/(p-1)}\int_0^1 \Phi_p^{-1}\left(r^{1-n}\int_0^r s^{n-1}g(s)(u(0))^{p-1}ds\right)dr\\
&= (F_0+\epsilon)^{1/(p-1)}u(0)\int_0^1 \Phi_p^{-1}\left(r^{1-n}\int_0^r s^{n-1}g(s)ds\right)dr\\
&= (F_0+\epsilon)^{1/(p-1)}u(0)B\\
&< u(0) = \|u\|,\end{aligned}$$

that is, $(Tu-u)(0) < 0$, which implies that $(Tu-u) \notin P$. So, if we let

$$\Omega_1 = \{u \in X \mid \|u\| < H_1\},$$

then,

$$Tu \ngeq u, \quad \text{for any } u \in P\cap\partial\Omega_1.$$

To construct Ω_2, we first choose a positive real number $\hat{f}$ such that $\hat{f} < f_\infty$ and

$$1 < A\hat{f}^{1/(p-1)}.$$

Then, we choose $c \in (3/4, 1)$ and $\delta > 0$ such that

$$(\hat{f} - \delta)^{1/(p-1)} \int_0^c \Phi_p^{-1}\left(r^{1-n} \int_0^r s^{n-1} g(s)(a(s))^{p-1} ds\right) dr > 1.$$

Now, there exists $H_3 > 0$ such that $f(x) \geq (\hat{f} - \delta)x^{p-1}$ for $x \geq H_3$. Let $H_2 = H_1 + H_3/a(c)$. If $u \in P$ with $\|u\| = H_2$, then, for $0 \leq t \leq c$, we have

$$u(t) \geq a(t)\|u\| \geq a(c)H_2 > H_3.$$

So, if $u \in P$ with $\|u\| = H_2$, then

$$\begin{aligned}
(Tu)(0) &= \int_0^1 \Phi_p^{-1}\left(r^{1-n} \int_0^r s^{n-1} g(s) f(u(s)) ds\right) dr \\
&\geq \int_0^c \Phi_p^{-1}\left(r^{1-n} \int_0^r s^{n-1} g(s) f(u(s)) ds\right) dr \\
&\geq \int_0^c \Phi_p^{-1}\left(r^{1-n} \int_0^r s^{n-1} g(s)(\hat{f} - \delta)(u(s))^{p-1} ds\right) dr \\
&= (\hat{f} - \delta)^{1/(p-1)} \int_0^c \Phi_p^{-1}\left(r^{1-n} \int_0^r s^{n-1} g(s)(u(s))^{p-1} ds\right) dr \\
&\geq (\hat{f} - \delta)^{1/(p-1)} \int_0^c \Phi_p^{-1}\left(r^{1-n} \int_0^r s^{n-1} g(s)(u(0)a(s))^{p-1} ds\right) dr \\
&= (\hat{f} - \delta)^{1/(p-1)} u(0) \int_0^c \Phi_p^{-1}\left(r^{1-n} \int_0^r s^{n-1} g(s)(a(s))^{p-1} ds\right) dr \\
&> 1 \cdot u(0) = u(0) = \|u\|,
\end{aligned}$$

which means $Tu \not\leq u$. So, if we let $\Omega_2 = \{u \in X : \|u\| < H_2\}$, then $\overline{\Omega_1} \subset \Omega_2$, and

$$Tu \not\leq u, \quad \text{for any } u \in P \cap \partial\Omega_2.$$

Therefore, condition (K1) of Theorem 3 is satisfied, and so there exists a fixed point of T in P. This completes the proof of the theorem. □

Our next theorem is a companion result to the one above.

Theorem 5. *If*

$$BF_\infty^{1/(p-1)} < 1 < Af_0^{1/(p-1)},$$

then the boundary value problem (3),(4) *has at least one positive solution.*

The proof of Theorem 5 is similar to that of Theorem 4 and is, therefore, left to the reader.

4. Nonexistence Results and Example

In this section, we give some sufficient conditions for the nonexistence of positive solutions.

Theorem 6. *Suppose that* (H) *holds. If $f(x) < (x/B)^{p-1}$ for all $x \in (0, +\infty)$, then problem* (3),(4) *has no positive solutions.*

Proof. Assume, on contrary, that $u(t)$ is a positive solution of problem (3),(4). Then, $u \in P$, $u(t) > 0$ for $0 < t < 1$, and

$$u(0) = \int_0^1 \Phi_p^{-1}\left(r^{1-n} \int_0^r s^{n-1} g(s) f(u(s)) ds\right) dr$$

$$
\begin{aligned}
&< \int_0^1 \Phi_p^{-1}\left(r^{1-n}\int_0^r s^{n-1}g(s)(u(s)/B)^{p-1}ds\right)dr \\
&= B^{-1}\int_0^1 \Phi_p^{-1}\left(r^{1-n}\int_0^r s^{n-1}g(s)(u(s))^{p-1}ds\right)dr \\
&\le B^{-1}\int_0^1 \Phi_p^{-1}\left(r^{1-n}\int_0^r s^{n-1}g(s)(u(0))^{p-1}ds\right)dr \\
&= u(0)B^{-1}\int_0^1 \Phi_p^{-1}\left(r^{1-n}\int_0^r s^{n-1}g(s)ds\right)dr \\
&= u(0)B^{-1}B = u(0),
\end{aligned}
$$

which is a contradiction. The proof of the theorem is now complete. □

In a similar fashion, we can prove the next theorem.

Theorem 7. *Suppose that* (H) *holds. If* $f(x) > (x/A)^{p-1}$ *for all* $x \in (0, +\infty)$*, then problem* (3),(4) *has no positive solutions.*

We conclude this section with an example.

Example 1. *Consider the following p-Laplace boundary value problem:*

$$\Delta_p w(x) + \lambda g(|x|)f(w(x)) = 0, \quad x \in \Omega, \tag{11}$$

$$w = 0, \quad x \in \partial\Omega, \tag{12}$$

where $\lambda > 0$ *is a parameter,* $p = 4$, $\Omega \subset \mathbb{R}^2$ *is the unit open ball centered at the origin, and*

$$
\begin{aligned}
g(t) &= 1 - t^2, \quad 0 \le t \le 1, \\
f(u) &= \lambda u^3 \cdot \frac{1+8u}{1+u}, \quad u \ge 0.
\end{aligned}
$$

It is clear that, if we seek a radially symmetric solution only, then problem (11),(12) *reduces to the following problem:*

$$t^{-1}(t\Phi_4(u'(t)))' + g(t)f(u(t)) = 0, \quad 0 < t < 1, \tag{13}$$

$$u'(0) = 0, \quad u(1) = 0. \tag{14}$$

Here, $\Phi_4(x) = x^3$.

We easily see that problem (13),(14) *is a special case of problem* (3),(4) *in which* $n = 2$ *and* $p = 4$. *In this case, we have* $a(t) = 1 - t^{2/3}$. *Also, we have* $F_0 = f_0 = \lambda$ *and* $F_\infty = f_\infty = 8\lambda$. *It is clear that*

$$\lambda x^3 < f(x) < 8\lambda x^3, \quad x > 0.$$

Calculations by using a standard Computer Algebra System (CAS) indicate that

$$A \approx 0.317485, \quad B \approx 0.550302.$$

From Theorem 4, we see that if

$$3.906 \approx \frac{1}{8A^3} < \lambda < \frac{1}{B^3} \approx 6.0006, \tag{15}$$

then problem (13),(14) *has at least one positive solution. From Theorems 6 and 7, we see that if*

$$\text{either} \;\; \lambda < \frac{1}{8B^3} \approx 0.7501 \quad \text{or} \quad \lambda > \frac{1}{A^3} \approx 31.2487 \tag{16}$$

then problem (13),(14) *has no positive solutions.*

It follows that, if (15) *holds, then problem* (11),(12) *has at least one radially symmetric positive solution. And if* (16) *holds, then problem* (11),(12) *has no radially symmetric positive solutions.*

5. Conclusions

In summary, we present a new lower estimate for radially symmetric positive solutions to the Dirichlet boundary value problem for the p-Laplace equation. The proof of this new lower estimate is elementary, making it accessible to undergraduate students. As an application, some sufficient conditions for the existence and nonexistence of positive solutions are obtained. In proving the existence results, we apply Krasnosel'skii's fixed point theorem on cones.

Some future developments we would like to see include

- Using the lower estimate in conjunction with other fixed-point theorems to establish new existence results;
- Using the lower estimate to solve the corresponding singular boundary value problem.

Funding: This research received no external funding.

Data Availability Statement: No data sets were generated during this research.

Acknowledgments: The author is grateful to the anonymous referee for their valuable comments and suggestions.

Conflicts of Interest: The author declares no conflicts of interest.

References

1. Jin, C.; Yin, J.; Wang, Z. Positive radial solutions of p-Laplacian equation with sign changing nonlinear sources. *Math. Methods Appl. Sci.* **2007**, *30*, 1–14. [CrossRef]
2. Benedikt, J.; Girg, P.; Kotrla, L.; Takáč, P. Origin of the p-Laplacian and A. Missbach. *Electron. J. Differ. Equ.* **2018**, *2018*, 1–17.
3. Bae, S. A priori bounds for positive radial solutions of quasilinear equations of Lane-Emden type. *Arch. Math.* **2023**, *59*, 155–162. [CrossRef]
4. Graef, J.R.; Kong, L. Necessary and sufficient conditions for the existence of symmetric positive solutions of singular boundary value problems. *J. Math. Anal. Appl.* **2007**, *331*, 1467–1484. [CrossRef]
5. Graef, J.R.; Kong, L.; Wang, M. Existence of homoclinic solutions for second order difference equations with p-Laplacian. In Proceedings of the 10th AIMS Conference, Dynamical Systems, Differential Equations and Applications, Madrid, Spain, 7–11 July 2014; pp. 533–539.
6. Graef, J.R.; Yang, B. Positive solutions for a fourth-order p-Laplacian boundary value problem. *Georgian Math. J.* **2023**, *30*, 703–711. [CrossRef]
7. Hai, D.D.; Shivaji, R. An existence result on positive solutions for a class of p-Laplacian systems. *Nonlinear Anal.* **2004**, *56*, 1007–1010. [CrossRef]
8. Li, Y.; Wei, M. Positive radial solutions of p-Laplace equations on exterior domains. *AIMS Math.* **2021**, *6*, 8949–8958. [CrossRef]
9. Mi, L. Existence and boundary behavior of solutions to p-Laplacian elliptic equations. *Bound. Value Probl.* **2016**, *2016*, 119. [CrossRef]
10. Pašić, M. Nonexistence of spherically symmetric solutions for p-Laplacian in the ball. *C. R. Math. Acad. Sci. Soc. R. Can.* **1999**, *21*, 16–22.
11. Pašić, M. Minkowski-Bouligand dimension of solutions of the one-dimensional p-Laplacian. *J. Differ. Equations* **2003**, *190*, 268–305. [CrossRef]
12. Wang, L.; Yang, B. New upper estimate for positive solutions to a second order boundary value problem with a parameter. *Cubo* **2023**, *25*, 121–137. [CrossRef]
13. Webb, J.R.L. Nonlocal conjugate type boundary value problems of higher order. *Nonlinear Anal.* **2009**, *71*, 1933–1940. [CrossRef]
14. Yao, Q. Positive solutions of nonlinear beam equations with time and space singularities. *J. Math. Anal. Appl.* **2011**, *374*, 681–692. [CrossRef]
15. Krasnosel'skiĭ, M.A. *Positive Solutions of Operator Equations*; Boron, L.F., Ed.; Translated from the Russian by Richard E. Flaherty; P. Noordhoff Ltd.: Groningen, The Netherlands, 1964.

MDPI AG
Grosspeteranlage 5
4052 Basel
Switzerland
Tel.: +41 61 683 77 34

Mathematics Editorial Office
E-mail: mathematics@mdpi.com
www.mdpi.com/journal/mathematics

www.ingramcontent.com/pod-product-compliance
Lightning Source LLC
LaVergne TN
LVHW072321090526
838202LV00019B/2325